# Genealogical Gleanings from Early Newspapers for Residents In and Near Crawford County, Wisconsin, 1897–1902

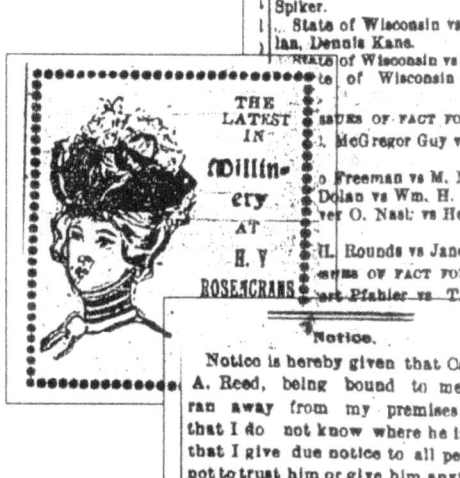

Compiled by
*Vernon D. Erickson*

HERITAGE BOOKS
2009

## HERITAGE BOOKS
*AN IMPRINT OF HERITAGE BOOKS, INC.*

### Books, CDs, and more—Worldwide

For our listing of thousands of titles see our website
at
www.HeritageBooks.com

Published 2009 by
HERITAGE BOOKS, INC.
Publishing Division
100 Railroad Ave. #104
Westminster, Maryland 21157

Copyright © 1999 Vernon D. Erickson

Other books by the author:

*Births, Deaths, Marriages and Other Genealogical Gleanings from Newspapers for Crawford, Vernon and Richland Counties, Wisconsin, 1873–1910*

*Genealogical Events from Newspapers for Crawford, Vernon and Grant Counties, Wisconsin, 1870–1901*

All rights reserved. No part of this book may be reproduced or transmitted in any form or by any means, electronic or mechanical, including photocopying, recording or by any information storage and retrieval system without written permission from the author, except for the inclusion of brief quotations in a review.

International Standard Book Numbers
Paperbound: 978-0-7884-1404-6
Clothbound: 978-0-7884-8278-6

*Dedicated to my parents,*

*Vernon ("Eric") Delbert Erickson*

*and*

*Margie Marie Ellis Erickson*

# Table of Contents

| | |
|---|---|
| Dedication | iii |
| Introduction | vii |
| Genealogical and Historical Data Abstracts from Newspapers | 1 |
| Appendix 1 – Maps | 341 |
| Appendix 2 – Gazetteer | 343 |
| Appendix 3 – Newspapers Researched for this Project | 347 |
| Appendix 4 – Crawford County Census | 349 |
| Index | 351 |

Genealogical Gleanings From Early Newspapers for Residents In and Near
Crawford County, Wisconsin, 1897-1902

# Introduction

*Purpose of Book* -- This book has been developed for three reasons. First, it is meant to fill a void for genealogists researching their ancestral roots in and near Crawford County, Wisconsin. Outside of a few local history books, little of genealogical significance has been published for people investigating their ties to the early settlers of this region. Second, the information is meant to tell us about our ancestor's interests and activities and give us a sense for the personalities of these people. Family history is more than names and dates on a series of charts. And last, the book is meant to help family historians get past "dead ends" in their research by uncovering clues for new avenues to investigate.

*Overview of Book* -- This volume is the second in a series of books on genealogical data abstracted from early newspapers published in southwestern Wisconsin. Over 6,200 citations have been culled from issues of the *Kickapoo Chief* that were published between 1897-1900. These newspapers were especially rich in local news. Over 12,000 people are mentioned in these entries. Of course, some people are mentioned several times in the book. The citations give information on people throughout Crawford County and parts of nearby counties; however, this book is especially useful to people researching ancestors in southern and central Crawford County. My first volume of newspaper abstracts (*Births, Deaths, Marriages and Other Genealogical Gleanings From Newspapers for Crawford, Vernon and Richland Counties, Wisconsin, 1873-1910*) had extensive coverage of northern parts of Crawford County.

*Background on Wauzeka, WI* -- The *Kickapoo Chief* was published in Wauzeka, Crawford County. The village was founded in 1855, about the time most of Crawford County was being settled, and in 1900 had a population of 471. Despite the villages' size, it was not isolated. Wauzeka is located at the junction of the Wisconsin River and Kickapoo River and it was a transportation center for river and rail traffic. The Chicago, Milwaukee and St. Paul Railway ran along the north bank of the Wisconsin River and the Kickapoo Valley & Northern Railway ran north along the Kickapoo River. As a crossroads for commerce and transportation, Wauzeka had ready access to the local and regional news. The editors capitalized on this situation by building a large cadre of correspondents who submitted news columns of happenings in their communities. They also encouraged visitors from out-of-town to make social calls at the newspaper office (and pay for their subscriptions to the newspaper). These were news gathering opportunities, too.

*Book Content, Organization and Structure* -- A wide variety of data has been included in this book. As expected, I have abstracted birth, death and marriage announcements. Since vital records were not consistently recorded in Wisconsin until 1907, these citations supplement the official records. A great deal of the local news items in early, small-town newspapers recorded who was sick and who visited whom. This can be useful information, as it may help establish family ties between people. Some of this data has been included in this book. I have also culled out data on:

- pensions
- teachers
- orphans
- family reunions
- immigrants/emigrants
- crime

Genealogical Gleanings From Early Newspapers for Residents In and Near
Crawford County, Wisconsin, 1897-1902

- military service
- probate hearings
- auctions
- real estate sales
- election results
- schools
- churches
- desertions by spouses
- recipients of county aid
- quarantines
- sanity hearings
- anniversaries
- civic organizations
- divorces
- fires
- accidents
- patents
- settlement history
- occupations
- business ownership

The data items are organized by surname, given name, source code (KC for Kickapoo Chief, followed by page number, column number and date of publication) and the event. The surnames are alphabetized according to the primary individual mentioned in each citation. Spouses for marriage announcements are cross-indexed. Many citations reference additional people, so an everyname surname index has been prepared. Please take the time to use this index as many citations include lists of people and it was not practical to give each person a separate entry in the book. Also, please notice that information surrounded by parentheses in the event column are notes provided by the author. The abbreviation, Supp., has been used to indicate that information was abstracted from a newspapers' supplement. The appendix contains maps, a gazetteer, population data and a list of the newspapers used in this book.

*Research Tips* -- Let me offer you a few words of advice. Researchers should be creative when trying to find a surname in the book. The newspaper editors did not use a standard spelling for many surnames. The French surnames in the Prairie du Chien area and the Bohemian surnames found in other parts of southern Crawford County take extra effort to research. I have attempted to abstract data I thought would be of genealogical significance, but I am sure I missed many items that would be useful. It may be worthwhile for others to review the newspapers, too. Also, be aware that the newspaper may have printed inaccurate or misleading news (and I may have made an error when compiling or typing the information). For example, there are numerous entries in the book that tell the readers about people who went west. "Going west" could have meant an individual: 1) relocated for seasonal or temporary work (harvesting crops in the Dakotas or laying track for the railroad); 2) went on vacation; 3) searched for cheap, fertile farm land; or 4) sold his possessions in Wisconsin and emigrated to another state or one of the territories. Finally, we all have a few sinners amongst the saints in our family trees. Nonetheless, keep in mind that not all people who were charged with a crime were guilty, nor were all individuals found insane by the courts mentally disturbed.

*Additional Help* -- Researchers may want to contact the Lower Wisconsin River Genealogical and Historical Research Center at P.O. Box 202, Wauzeka, Wisconsin 53826. Their website can be found at www.mwt.net/~bcobe/genealogy.html. The group (usually called the LWR) has a growing collection of genealogy reference materials. Many items are one-of-a-kind or are difficult to access. The LWR started a newspaper

Genealogical Gleanings From Early Newspapers for Residents In and Near
Crawford County, Wisconsin, 1897-1902

abstraction program several years ago that focuses on vital records from early newspapers published in Prairie du Chien, Wauzeka and Boscobel. They also have microfilmed copies of old *Kickapoo Chief*, *Kickapoo Papoose*, *Wauzeka Chief* and *Wauzeka Kickapoo Chief* newspapers. As a service to the genealogy public, the LWR will make copies of newspaper articles for a $3.00 fee. The LWR also has several publications for sale, including *Index to Crawford County Marriages, 1816-1866*, compiled by Carol Higgins.

*Concluding Remarks* -- I have been encouraged by many fellow genealogists who used my first book of newspaper abstracts. It is my hope that this book will be a useful supplement to the meager number of reference materials available to family history researchers interested in this part of Wisconsin.

Vern Erickson<br>Bellbrook, Ohio

Genealogical Gleanings From Early Newspapers for Residents In and Near
Crawford County, Wisconsin, 1897-1902

| LAST NAME | FIRST NAME | NEWSPAPER PAGE/COLUMN MONTH/DAY/YEAR | GENEALOGICAL DATA |
|---|---|---|---|
| Aaland | Martha | KC, Supp., 12/18/1902 | Crawford County Board of Supervisors allowed expenses in the Matter of Martha Aaland, Insane. |
| Abbey | Ernest | KC, p4c3, 4/21/1898 | Married Nora Gilder of Bell Center on April 17, 1898. Groom from Gays Mills. J. L. Stowell, J.P. officiated. |
| Abbey | R. W. | KC, p5c3, 5/8/1902 | R. W. Abbey of Gays Mills and Mr. Smith of Bell Center, veterans, returned home from the Soldiers Home at Milwaukee where they spent the last year. They will probably spend the summer in Crawford Co. |
| Abbey | Rollin W. | KC, p4c3, 3/9/1899 | Rollin W. Abbey, Jr.; Herb McDonnell; William Bauer; Frank Lagaman; Clarence Bryant and Henry Reeter returned last week. They were soldiers from Co. C, 4th WI Regt. Vol. Inf. Abbey from Gays Mills. All others were from Wauzeka. Reception given by townspeople on their return. Sgt. T. W. Swinson and John Rau of Gays Mills were detained by an attack of measles. |
| Abbey | Rolling | KC, p1c6, 5/12/1898 | Planned to volunteer for Spanish American War. From Gays Mills area. |
| Abbey | Samuel | KC, p1c6, 5/12/1898 | Planned to volunteer for Spanish American War. From Gays Mills area. |
| Abby | Earn | KC, p5c4, 3/8/1900 | Rented out his farm in Gays Mills. Planned to move to North Dakota. |
| Abby | R. W. | KC, p4c3, 6/30/1898 | R. W. Abby, Sam Abby, Tom Swinson and John Rau, all of Gays Mills, enlisted in the army at Boscobel. |
| Abby | R. W., Mrs. | KC, Supp., 12/29/1898 | Received aid from the Crawford County Soldiers Relief Commission. Resided in Clayton. |
| Abby | R. W., Mrs. | KC, Supp., 12/20/1900 | Crawford Co. Soldiers Relief Comm. approved aid to Mrs. R. W. Abby of Clayton. |
| Abraham | William | KC, p5c3, 5/20/1897 | Issues of fact for jury to be heard in the May term of the Crawford County Court. William Abraham vs. Milhiem Shabshab. |
| Ackerly | Mamie | KC, p8c3, 3/27/1902 | Recently married Edward Martner. Bride daughter of James Ackerly. Bride and groom from Prairie du Chien |
| Adams | Art | KC, p8c2, 12/9/1897 | Art Adams and Matt Shields were involved in a shooting scrape. Adams and Shields were from Town of Marietta. Mr. Adams, who did the shooting, was discharged from the trial. He acted in self-defense after being hit by a rock. |
| Adams | Eliza | KC, p1c3, 10/6/1898 | Died Sept. 27, 1898 at home in Marietta. Aged 37 years. Funeral held at St. Patrick's Church in Scott. |
| Adams | George | KC, p1c3, 2/10/1898 | Blind broom maker in Prairie du Chien. Called on customers in Wauzeka. |
| Adams | Joe | KC, p4c5, 1/24/1901 | Suffered with small pox in Ferryville. Entire town was quarantined. |
| Adams | John | KC, p5c3, 2/15/1900 | Returned from Dakota to his home in Mt. Sterling. Taught school in Dakota. |
| Adams | Josie | KC, p1c4, 7/15/1897 | Married James Young on July 3, 1897. Bride and groom from Town of Marietta. |
| Adams | Martin | KC, p1c5, 11/25/1897 | Stabbed Matt Shields at a party held at the Chauncey Steele home in Marietta Hollow. Shields lies in a precarious condition. Adams skipped the country. |

Genealogical Gleanings From Early Newspapers for Residents In and Near
Crawford County, Wisconsin, 1897-1902

| LAST NAME | FIRST NAME | NEWSPAPER PAGE/COLUMN MONTH/DAY/YEAR | GENEALOGICAL DATA |
|---|---|---|---|
| Adams | Martin | KC, Supp., 12/29/1898 | Crawford Co. Board of Supervisors approved Justices and Constables' expenses related to the case, State vs. Martin Adams. The witnesses were Edmond Fay, John Clark, Andrea Byer, Grant Williams, Matt Shields, George Shields, Jennie Riley, Chancy Steele, James Bain, Roy Hobble, William Smith, L. G. Armstrong, August (Shcor?), Emmy Steele, Eliza Adams and William Curtis. |
| Adams | Minnie | KC, p5c3, 5/20/1897 | Criminal case to be heard in the May term of the Crawford County Court, State of Wisconsin vs. Minnie Adams. |
| Adams | Mrs. | KC, p4c2, 5/19/1898 | Died May 16, 1898 at home of sister, Mrs. L. A. Bonney of Eastman. Resided in Iowa. Buried in Crandall Cemetery. |
| Adams | N., Mrs. | KC, p8c4, 9/30/1897 | Traveled from Ohio to visit sister, Mrs. L. A. Bonney of Eastman. |
| Adams | Thomas | KC, p8c4, 5/6/1897 | Recently died in Ferrisburg, SD. He was the son of T. Adams and brother of John. John lived in Mt. Sterling. |
| Adams | W. C. T. | KC, p4c1, 10/14/1897 | Married Miss Aikens on Oct. 10, 1897. Bride and groom were from Readstown. |
| Adlington | Mr. | KC, p5c3, 11/28/1901 | Resided in Viroqua. Opened a photographic gallery in Mt. Sterling. |
| Adney | C. | KC, p5c3, 4/4/1901 | Sold his farm in Knapp's Creek area. Planned to leave the area. |
| Adney | C., Mrs. | KC, p1c3, 5/29/1902 | Departed Soldiers Grove to visit 2 sisters and other relatives in Chicago. |
| Adney | Danny | KC, p5c3, 4/10/1902 | Arrived from St. Paul to visit parents on Knapps Creek. |
| Ady | C. E., Mrs. | KC, p5c1, 7/14/1898 | Traveled to Gays Mills from Omaha to visit parents, Mr. and Mrs. J. A. Robb. |
| Aikens | Miss | KC, p4c1, 10/14/1897 | Married W. C. T. Adams on Oct. 10, 1897. Bride and groom were from Readstown. |
| Aikins | Vern | KC, p5c2, 7/71898 | Vern Aikins, C. D. Carter, Guy Fish, Lester Hale, Fayette Johnstone, Bird Rosson, Isaac Ewers, Millard Dearman, Henry Sutherland, LaFayette Sutherland and Elmer H. Sime of Readstown enlisted in the army at Viroqua. |
| Akerman | Charles | KC, Supp., 12/18/1902 | Crawford County Board of Supervisors examined bills in the Justices and Constables' Account for State vs. Charles Akerman. |
| Aland | Mrs. | KC, p5c3, 9/25/1902 | Resided in Ferryville. Judged insane and sent to the asylum. |
| Aland | Mrs. | KC, p5c3, 9/25/1902 | Resided in Ferryville. Judged insane at court in Prairie du Chien. |
| Alder | Alf, Mrs. | KC, p5c3, 8/17/1899 | Mrs. Alf Alder and sons, Herbert and Charley, visited Mrs. Alder's parents, Mr. and Mrs. George Finney, Sr. Included in Eastman news items. Mrs. Alder has been a resident of South Dakota for the last 22 years (KC, p5c3, 8/24/1899). |
| Alder | Alfred | KC, p5c4, 6/8/1899 | Worked in milling business in Yankton, SD, where he has resided for last 20 years. Former resident of Eastman. Visited brother, C. E. Alder of Eastman. |

Genealogical Gleanings From Early Newspapers for Residents In and Near
Crawford County, Wisconsin, 1897-1902

| LAST NAME | FIRST NAME | NEWSPAPER PAGE/COLUMN MONTH/DAY/YEAR | GENEALOGICAL DATA |
|---|---|---|---|
| Alder | C. E. | KC, p4c2, 7/3/1902 | C. E. Alder and John Roach planned to open a mercantile business in Eastman. "John is a popular young man and Gene a special favorite of the ladies." |
| Alder | C. E. | KC, p4c1, 10/28/1897 | Traveled from Eastman to Dakota and Nebraska to visit relatives. |
| Alder | Louise | KC, p1c5, 12/1/1898 | Married James A. Dickson of Yankton, SD on Nov. 23, 1898. Bride was the sister of C. E. Alder and Mrs. Charles Campbell. |
| Alderman | Al. | KC, p1c3, 3/25/1897 | Died last week in the Kickapoo Valley. Former resident of Prairie du Chien. |
| Alderman | Album | KC, p1c6, 10/20/1898 | Wedding to Mattie Hamilton scheduled for Oct. 20, 1898. |
| Alderman | Allen | KC, p8c3, 4/1/1897 | Funeral held in Town of Haney last Sunday. Resided in Barnum. |
| Alderman | Allen D. | KC, p5c3, 4/22/1897 | Died Mar. 19, 1897. Aged 48 years, 4 months and 28 days. Born in LaFayette Co., WI. Moved to Crawford Co. as a child. Survived by 4 children, 2 brothers and 1 sister. |
| Alderman | George | KC, p5c3, 10/19/1899 | Resided in Steuben. Aged about 40 years. Died 6 weeks ago in a Milwaukee hospital. He injured himself with a knife while cutting corn. The wound did not heal. |
| Alderman | Minnie | KC, p1c2, 5/23/1901 | Married W. A. Stantorf on May 20, 1901. Bride and groom from Barnum. |
| Alderman | Mintie | KC, p5c4, 5/29/1902 | Mintie Alderman of Petersburg and Bessie Holden of Petersburg attended a teacher's institute in Crawford County. |
| Alderman | Mintie | KC, Supp., 12/12/1901 | Attended a Teacher's Institute in Crawford County in 1901. Resided in Petersburg. |
| Alex | Antony | KC, Supp., 12/20/1900 | Crawford Co. Board of Supervisors approved payment of expenses in the matter of State vs. Antony Alex. The witnesses were John Bitterly and B. Lechher. |
| Alex | Tony | KC, Supp., 12/18/1902 | Crawford County Board of Supervisors examined bills in the Justices and Constables' Account for State vs. Tony Alex. Frank Fuka, Thomas Dohse and Thomas Smrcina were witnesses. |
| Alex | Tony | KC, Supp., 12/18/1902 | Crawford County Board of Supervisors examined bills in the Justices and Constables' Account for State vs. Tony Alex, George Bower and Henry Dohse. |
| Alexander | Felecia | KC, p1c5, 2/9/1899 | Taught school in the Town of Clayton in 1899. E. E. Brindley, Crawford County Superintendent of Schools published a comprehensive list of all teachers in the county. |
| Alexander | Kittie | KC, p1c5, 2/9/1899 | Taught school in the Town of Clayton in 1899. E. E. Brindley, Crawford County Superintendent of Schools published a comprehensive list of all teachers in the county. |
| Alexander | Susie, Mrs. | KC, p5c5, 10/18/1900 | Arrived from Dubuque, IA to visit mother, Mrs. Richmond of Bell Center. |
| Alien | Goldie | KC, p8c3, 6/19/1902 | Married Cyrus Dietrich on June 18, 1902 at Prairie du Chien. |
| Alland | Hilda | KC, p5c4, 5/29/1902 | Hilda Alland of Reed attended a teacher institute in Crawford County. |

Genealogical Gleanings From Early Newspapers for Residents In and Near
Crawford County, Wisconsin, 1897-1902

| LAST NAME | FIRST NAME | NEWSPAPER PAGE/COLUMN MONTH/DAY/YEAR | GENEALOGICAL DATA |
|---|---|---|---|
| Allen | Alonzo, Mrs. | KC, p5c4, 2/8/1900 | Mrs. Allen and her brother, William Brady departed for La Crosse to visit their mother and brother. |
| Allen | Charles | KC, p4c2, 3/24/1898 | Charles Allen and George Pease of Lynxville were in Seattle on their way to the Klondike. Mrs. Pease visited her mother-in-law in Chicago. |
| Allen | Claud | KC, p5c3, 9/5/1901 | Left Lynxville for school in Milwaukee. |
| Allen | Claudine | KC, p5c3, 5/31/1900 | Graduated from school in Lynxville. |
| Allen | Emma | KC, p5c3, 9/28/1899 | Resided in Eastman. Visited sister, Mrs. Moore of Dodgeville. Mrs. Moore returned to Eastman to visit her parents. |
| Allen | Frank | KC, p5c?, 12/1/1898 | Worked as a coal dealer in Cleveland, OH for the last 13 years. Returned "home" (per Eastman items) for Thanksgiving dinner. |
| Allen | Frank, Mrs. | KC, p5c3, 7/24/1902 | Lived in Cleveland, OH. Visited her parents in Eastman. |
| Allen | George | KC, p5c5, 3/1/1900 | Resided in Lynxville. Found a pearl while clam fishing. Offered $165 for it. |
| Allen | George | KC, Supp., 12/29/1898 | Received aid from the Crawford County Soldiers Relief Commission. |
| Allen | girl | KC, p5c3, 8/14/1923 | Daughter recently born to Seymour Allen of the Town of Eastman. |
| Allen | Hartwell | KC, p5c5, 5/17/1900 | Died from suicide on May 14, 1900. He was one of the oldest settlers in Vernon County. |
| Allen | Jamie | KC, p1c5, 10/5/1899 | Died Sept. 28, 1899. She was the daughter of George and Lucinda Allen. Buried in Dixon Cemetery. |
| Allen | Seymour | KC, p1c4, 8/29/1901 | Planned to marry Tressie Haddock on Sept. 4, 1901 at the German Church in Town of Eastman. Bride was daughter of Frank Haddock of Town of Eastman. |
| Allen | Seymour | KC, p5c1, 8/11/1898 | Owned a feed mill in Eastman. |
| Allen | Seymour D. | KC, p1c4, 9/5/1901 | Married Theressa Haddock at German Church of Eastman on Sept. 4, 1901. Bride and groom from Town of Eastman. |
| Allen | Seymour D. | KC, p1c3, 6/6/1901 | Barber in Eastman. |
| Allen | W. | KC, p5c3, 5/3/1900 | Found the largest pearl ever uncovered in the waters around Lynxville. |
| Allen | W. A. | KC, p1c5, 4/13/1899 | Fire destroyed the John Vanderbilt & Co. Building, Davidson's livery barn and T. C. Bright's home and store in Lynxville. The fire later reached the A. E. Wolcott and W. A. Allen home, the William Huard home, the R. E. Hazen home and saloon, the T. C. Bright warehouse and the Schumann & Menges ice house. |
| Allen | W. S. | KC, p4c4, 11/15/1900 | Purchased a hotel in Lynxville, WI from James Maney. |
| Allen | W. S. | KC, p5c5, 4/5/1900 | Elected supervisor in Lynxville. |

Genealogical Gleanings From Early Newspapers for Residents In and Near
Crawford County, Wisconsin, 1897-1902

| LAST NAME | FIRST NAME | NEWSPAPER PAGE/COLUMN MONTH/DAY/YEAR | GENEALOGICAL DATA |
|---|---|---|---|
| Allen | W. S. | KC, Supp., 12/20/1900 | Represented Lynxville on the Crawford Co. Board of Supervisors in 1900. |
| Allen | Wallace | KC, p1c2, 3/4/1897 | Left for the south after a lengthy visit with his father, J. F. Allen of Prairie du Chien. |
| Allington | William | KC, p1c3, 7/29/1897 | Resided in Eastman. Arrested for assault and battery on Mrs. Matthews. Acquitted of charges. |
| Altenberg | H., Mrs. | KC, p1c4, 3/18/1897 | Died Mar. 16, 1897 at Dutch Ridge. Funeral held at the Evangelical Church. Buried in Lowertown Cemetery. |
| Amann | Charles | KC, p8c4, 8/9/1900 | Died Aug. 3, 1900 in Prairie du Chien. Born April 3, 1849 in Wurtenburg, Germany. Arrived in Troy, NY in 1872 where he met and married Katherine Christ. Moved to Lansing, IA in 1876 and to Prairie du Chien in 1887. Survived by wife and a son, Eugene. |
| Amann | Eugene | KC, p8c3, 5/15/1902 | Planned to marry Helen Emma Menges on May 14, 1902. Bride from Prairie du Chien. Groom from La Crosse. |
| Amann | Eugene Charles | KC, Supp., 5/15/1902 | Married Helen Emma Menges on May 14, 1902. Bride daughter of Hon. and Mrs. M. Menges of Prairie du Chien. Groom son of Mrs. Charles Amann of La Crosse. Married at St. Gabriel's Catholic Church in Prairie du Chien. Many relatives and guests listed. |
| Ambler | C. E., Mrs. | KC, p1c4, 5/30/1901 | Entertained mother, Mrs. James Jacobs, and sister-in-law, Carrie Jacobs, of Wyalusing at her home in Wauzeka. |
| Ames | D. N. | KC, p1c5, 6/16/1898 | D. N. Ames, Erastus Ames, Martin Hill, George Rutter and James Davenport, all of Ferryville area, attended a GAR encampment in Madison. |
| Ames | C. | KC, p5c5, 4/5/1900 | Elected supervisor in Town of Freeman. |
| Anderson | A., Mr. and Mrs. | KC, p1c3, 1/18/1900 | Visited by nephew and niece, George Bjornsen and wife of Chicago. Bjornson works for C.M. and St. Paul Rail Road. |
| Anderson | Albert | KC, Supp., 12/29/1898 | Crawford Co. Board of Supervisors approved Justices and Constables' expenses related to the case, State vs. Albert Anderson. |
| Anderson | Aleck | KC, p5c1, 6/2/1898 | Escaped while under arrest last January for selling intoxicants. Recently caught in La Crosse and returned to Prairie du Chien. |
| Anderson | Allick | KC, Supp., 12/29/1898 | Crawford Co. Board of Supervisors approved Justices and Constables' expenses related to the case, State vs. Allick Anderson |
| Anderson | Andrew | KC, p8c2, 4/20/1899 | Died Monday (April 17, 1899?) in Prairie du Chien. Remains sent to Milwaukee. |
| Anderson | August | KC, p1c2, 1/14/1897 | Married Mary Forde on Jan. 6, 1897 in Prairie du Chien. Bride and groom were from Clayton Co., IA. Wm. H. Evans officiated. |
| Anderson | August | KC, p1c2, 1/14/1897 | Married Mary Forde on Jan. 6, 1897 in Prairie du Chien. The bride and groom were from Clayton Co., IA. |
| Anderson | B. | KC, p1c6, 5/19/1898 | Issue of Fact for Jury to be heard in the May term of the Crawford County Circuit Court. Max Spero vs. B. Anderson. |

Genealogical Gleanings From Early Newspapers for Residents In and Near
Crawford County, Wisconsin, 1897-1902

| LAST NAME | FIRST NAME | NEWSPAPER PAGE/COLUMN MONTH/DAY/YEAR | GENEALOGICAL DATA |
|---|---|---|---|
| Anderson | B. | KC, p1c6, 6/2/1898 | In Crawford County Circuit Court, Max Spero vs. B. Anderson verdict for plaintiff; $15 and cost (another $15), allowed. |
| Anderson | Frank | KC, Supp., 12/29/1898 | Crawford Co. Board of Supervisors approved Justices and Constables' expenses related to the case, State vs. Frank Anderson. The witnesses were Malonia Guilder, R. H. Palmer, W___ Pecor, Elizabeth Coleman, Santie Nutter, Charles Pecor, Charles Buckmaster, Amelia Buckmaster, Nora Guilder, Clarence Copas, Justin Anderson, Amos Coleman, S. Coleman, Rachel Coleman, Eliza Welch, Jennie Evans, Eliza Purrington, Laura Miller, Ann Brown, David Coleman, Mary Coleman, James Coleman and Miles McKillop. |
| Anderson | Harry A. | KC, p5c2, 8/18/1898 | Named chairman of the Crawford County People's Party. |
| Anderson | Harry A. | KC, p1c6, 4/7/1898 | Elected Chairman for the Town of Wauzeka. |
| Anderson | Harry A. | KC, p1c5, 2/1/1900 | Died Jan. 28, 1900. Born July 14, 1836 in Norway. Father died when he was very young. In 1861 became an American sailor. Moved to Chicago. Moved to Wauzeka in 1889. Survived by wife and a brother, Daniel, of Stoughton. |
| Anderson | James | KC, p5c2, 3/3/1898 | Relocated family from Wheatville to new home in Black River Falls. |
| Anderson | John | KC, p1c4, 3/4/1897 | Died Feb. 27, 1897 in Pine Knob area. Survived by wife and 2 children. |
| Anderson | Julia | KC, p5c4, 5/29/1902 | Julia Anderson of Readstown attended a teacher institute in Crawford County. |
| Anderson | Julia | KC, Supp., 12/12/1901 | Attended a Teacher's Institute in Crawford County in 1901. Resided in Readstown. |
| Anderson | Justin | KC, Supp., 12/12/1901 | State vs. Justine Anderson heard in Crawford Co. Court. |
| Anderson | L. F. | KC, p1c6, 5/19/1898 | Issue of Fact for Court to be heard in the May term of the Crawford County Circuit Court. L. F. Anderson vs. Lizzie S. Drake and Peter L. Hanson et al. |
| Anderson | Mr. | KC, p5c2, 8/4/1898 | From Chicago. Visited sister, Mrs. Fred Smith of Mt. Sterling. |
| Anderson | Nettie | KC, p1c4, 1/28/1897 | Resided in Ferryville. Visited sister, Mrs. Lindstrom. |
| Anderson | Ole | KC, Supp., 12/20/1900 | Crawford Co. Board of Supervisors approved payment of expenses in the matter of State vs. Ole Anderson. |
| Anderson | R. | KC, Supp., 12/29/1898 | Crawford Co. Board of Supervisors approved Justices and Constables' expenses related to the case, State vs. R. Anderson and James _enkers. The witnesses were Mary Fox, Frank Fox, M. Henning, Jo Lable, Lizzie Steiner, and George Oben. |
| Anderson | S., Mr. | KC, p4c3, 2/4/1897 | Died last week at home near Pine Knob. Lived nearly 3 score and 10 years. |

Genealogical Gleanings From Early Newspapers for Residents In and Near
Crawford County, Wisconsin, 1897-1902

| LAST NAME | FIRST NAME | NEWSPAPER PAGE/COLUMN MONTH/DAY/YEAR | GENEALOGICAL DATA |
|---|---|---|---|
| Anderson | Joseph | KC, p1c4, 9/7/1899 | Pending marriage announced for Joseph Anderson of North McGregor, IA and Estella Hobbs of Prairie du Chien. Bride was daughter of Dan E. Hobbs and sister of Fred Hobbs. Fred lived in Soldiers Grove. Marriage took place Sept. 6, 1899 per p8c2. |
| Andrew | T. F. | KC, p1c6, 11/4/1897 | Issue of fact for court to be heard at the November term of the Circuit Court in Crawford County. T. F. Andrew vs. Lizzie S. Drake. |
| Andrews | Samuel, Mrs. | KC, p5c3, 3/9/1899 | Died Feb. 24, 1899 in Gays Mills. |
| Andrews | W. A. | KC, p1c5, 5/5/1898 | Station agent at Readstown. Made a device that amplifies volume when attached to a telephone receiver. It was sent to patent office in Washington, DC. |
| Appleby | James | KC, p1c2, 11/21/1901 | Resided in Boscobel. Worked as a surveyor. Died Nov. 18, 1901 at age 63. |
| Arden | Richard | KC, p8c3, 10/25/1900 | Heir to nephew's $80,000 estate in England. Resident of Prairie du Chien. |
| Arius | Mabel | KC, Supp., 12/12/1901 | Attended a Teacher's Institute in Crawford County in 1901. Resided in Hurlbut. |
| Arms | Clinton | KC, p1c4, 12/15/1898 | Married Bessie Oakes on Dec. 14, 1898 at the Methodist parsonage. Groom from Scott. Bride from Marietta. Rev. Webster officiated. |
| Arms | girl | KC, p5c4, 3/20/1902 | Daughter born Wednesday to C. D. Arms of West Wauzeka. |
| Arms | Jane, Mrs. | KC, p1c2, 11/11/1897 | From Haney. Visited parents, Mr. and Mrs. I. Johnson. |
| Arms | John | KC, p1c2, 11/6/1902 | Lived in Wauzeka. Returned from McHenry, ND where he had been threshing. |
| Arms | John | KC, p5c3, 3/2/1899 | Resided in Bell Center. Visited sister, Mrs. C. L. Lathrop of Wauzeka. |
| Arms | R., Mrs. | KC, p4c1, 9/2/1897 | Traveled from Missouri to visit friends in Town of Scott. |
| Arms | Wesley | KC, Supp., 12/20/1900 | Crawford Co. Board of Supervisors approved payment of expenses in the matter of State vs. Wesley Arms. |
| Armstrong | J. S. | KC, p4c1, 11/21/1901 | In the case J. S. Armstrong (plaintiff) vs. Fred Ahrens (defendant), the plaintiff was awarded $174. 36 in Crawford County Circuit Court. |
| Ashbacher | George, Mrs. | KC, p1c2, 7/29/1897 | Recently died in Froelich, IA. Husband was the brother of William Ashbacher of Prairie du Chien. |
| Aspenson | Aleck | KC, p1c4, 3/16/1899 | Died Mar. 12, 1899 in Mt. Sterling. Aged 25 years. Survived by wife and 2 children. |
| Aspenson | Thomas | KC, p5c3, 4/3/1902 | Married Betsey Severson last Wednesday at the Norwegian Church in Utica. Bride from Seneca. |
| Atchison | boy | KC, p1c2, 4/5/1900 | Son born April 3, 1900 to J. J. Atchison of Wauzeka area. |
| Atchison | Henry | KC, p1c5, 4/24/1902 | Arrived from La Crosse to visit relatives in Wauzeka. Planned to seek work in Green Bay, WI. |

Genealogical Gleanings From Early Newspapers for Residents In and Near
Crawford County, Wisconsin, 1897-1902

| LAST NAME | FIRST NAME | NEWSPAPER PAGE/COLUMN MONTH/DAY/YEAR | GENEALOGICAL DATA |
|---|---|---|---|
| Atchison | James | KC, p1c6, 5/19/1898 | Criminal case to be heard in the May term of the Crawford County Circuit Court. State of Wisconsin vs. James Atchison. |
| Atchison | James | KC, p1c6, 6/2/1898 | In Crawford County Circuit Court, State of Wisconsin vs. James Atchison, verdict for plaintiff. Atchison sentence to six months imprisonment in county jail. |
| Atchison | James | KC, Supp., 12/29/1898 | Crawford Co. Board of Supervisors approved Justices and Constables' expenses related to the case, State vs. James Atchison. The witnesses were William White, Robt. Fisher, James Roach, James Smrz, Sylvester Ellis, Peter Bachna, Anthony Peacha, Herb Finney, George Walker, Herman Walker, Anthony Wachuta, August Steinburg, Amy Atchison and Teressa Hadick. |
| Atchison | James, Jr. | KC, Supp., 12/29/1898 | Crawford Co. Board of Supervisors approved Justices and Constables' expenses related to the case, State vs. James Atchison Jr. |
| Atchison | Jennie | KC, p1c2, 3/31/1898 | Married J. H. Miller of Wauzeka on Mar. 23, 1898. Bride daughter of James Atchison of Eastman. |
| Atchison | John | KC, p1c2, 12/26/1901 | He was a son of Sam Atchison of Countney, ND. Visited relatives in Wauzeka. |
| Atchison | Sam | KC, p1c5, 11/11/1897 | Warrant issued against Sam Atchison for stabbing Vet Ellis at a wedding dance given by Messrs. Smith and Maxwell in Hazen's Hall Eastman. |
| Atchison | William | KC, p1c5, 11/27/1902 | Died Nov. 24, 1902 in Wauzeka. Born July 26, 1822 in County Antrim, Ireland. Migrated to Ontario, Canada in 1847 with his parents. Father soon died there. Married Jessie Harris in 1859. Fathered 4 children, William and James J. of Wauzeka, Mrs. Jane Lemere of Prairie du Chien and John Henry of Chicago. Wife died in 1869. Moved to Wauzeka in 1870. Brother of James Atchison Sr. of Wauzeka and Samuel of Dakota and 4 sisters in Canada. He was Presbyterian. Buried in Wauzeka Cemetery. |
| Atchison | William | KC, p1c4, 1/25/1900 | Proprietor of a store that sold agricultural implements in Wauzeka. |
| Atchison | William | KC, p1c4, 6/21/1900 | Census taker for Town and Village of Wauzeka. |
| Atchison | William | KC, p1c3, 9/6/1900 | Delegate to the Republican convention in Gays Mills. |
| Atchison | William | KC, p1c2, 6/16/1898 | Appointed deputy marshall under Marshall Kincannon. |
| Atchison | William | KC, p4c3, 4/27/1899 | Robert Harris and William Atchison of Wauzeka dissolved the firm Atchison & Harris. Atchison planned to continue the business. |
| Atchison | William | KC, p1c6, 4/7/1898 | Elected Clerk for the Village of Wauzeka. |
| Atchison | girl | KC, p1c3, 8/4/1898 | Daughter born Monday to William Atchison of Wauzeka. |
| Atherton | Joseph | KC, Supp., 12/12/1901 | Crawford Co. Board of Supervisors approved payments in the Matter of Joseph Atherton, Insane. |

Genealogical Gleanings From Early Newspapers for Residents In and Near
Crawford County, Wisconsin, 1897-1902

| LAST NAME | FIRST NAME | NEWSPAPER PAGE/COLUMN MONTH/DAY/YEAR | GENEALOGICAL DATA |
|---|---|---|---|
| Atherton | Joseph | KC, Supp., 12/18/1902 | The Crawford County Board of Supervisors allowed expenses in the Matter of Joseph Atherton, Insane. |
| Atherton | Lydia, Mrs. | KC, p4c4, 8/14/1902 | Died Aug. 3, 1902. Born Mar. 2, 1828 in Trumbell Co., OH. Nee Allen. Adopted at an early age by the late Rev. Elisha Warner. In 1838 left Wellsville, OH with adopted father and came to Bridgeport, Crawford Co., WI. Married Joseph Atherton on Dec. 8, 1844. Survived by 3 of her 7 children, Mrs. C. A. Mathew of Bridgeport, Mrs. Fred J. Barnum of Minneapolis and Joseph of Bridgeport. Her deceased children were Martha (wife of C. Blancher of Prairie du Chien, died 1870; George died in 1864 at age 15; and twins Charles H. and Joseph who died in 1864 at 10 months of age. Buried in Bridgeport Cemetery. |
| Atherton | Mrs. | KC, p8c4, 8/7/1902 | Died Aug. 3, 1902 at Bridgeport. |
| Athey | Alexander | KC, p1c2, 10/23/1902 | Democratic nominee for District Attorney in Crawford Co. Born in Johnson Co., IA on Oct. 28, 1859. Went to Cornell College in 1874. Studied law at Iowa College in 1878. Graduated in 1880. Spent a year surveying government land in New Mexico. Employed as law clerk in Marengo, IA for 3 years. Practiced law in Nebraska and West Superior, WI. Moved to Prairie du Chien 1 year ago. Portrait published. |
| Atkinson | L. E. | KC, p1c6, 11/4/1897 | Issue of fact for jury to be heard at the November term of the Circuit Court in Crawford County. L. E. Atkinson vs. Town of Clayton. |
| Atkinson | L. E. | KC, p1c6, 5/19/1898 | Issue of Fact for Jury to be heard in the May term of the Crawford County Circuit Court. L. E. Atkinson vs. Town of Clayton. |
| Atkinson | L. E. | KC, p1c6, 6/2/1898 | In Crawford County Circuit Court, L. E. Atkinson vs. Town of Clayton; verdict for defendant. |
| Atkinson | Mary, Mrs. | KC, p1c4, 7/19/1900 | Resided in Nora Springs, IA. Visited parents, M. C. Kincannon of Wauzeka. |
| Atkinson | Rebecca | KC, p5c3, 5/20/1897 | Issues of fact for jury to be heard in the May term of the Crawford County Court. Rebecca Atkinson vs. Town of Clayton. |
| Atkinson | William | KC, p8c4, 9/30/1897 | At a conference of the Methodist Church held in Platteville, William Atkinson was assigned to Dodgeville. |
| Atkinson | William | KC, p1c4, 9/29/1898 | At a conference of the Methodist Church held in Eau Claire, William Atkinson was assigned to Dodgeville. |
| Atwood | George T. | KC, p1c2, 9/29/1898 | Recently married Bessie Haggerty of Ferryville. Groom from Green Bay. |
| Atwood | George, Mrs. | KC, p1c2, 11/7/1901 | Resided in Gays Mills. Guest of parents, Mr. and Mrs. J. A. Haggerty of Ferryville. |
| Atwood | George, Mrs. | KC, p1c2, 11/7/1901 | Resided in Gays Mills. Visited parents, Mr. and Mrs. J. A. Haggerty of Ferryville. |
| Ault | Kate, Mrs. | KC, p8c3, 2/13/1902 | Died Feb. 10, 1902 in Prairie du Chien. Wife of Sylvester Ault. Buried in Cedar Rapids, IA. |

Genealogical Gleanings From Early Newspapers for Residents In and Near
Crawford County, Wisconsin, 1897-1902

| LAST NAME | FIRST NAME | NEWSPAPER PAGE/COLUMN MONTH/DAY/YEAR | GENEALOGICAL DATA |
|---|---|---|---|
| Ault | Stephen | KC, p14c4, 12/18/1902 | Recently died at Spooner, WI. Wife died less than a year ago. (Apparently he once lived in Lowertown area of Prairie du Chien.) |
| Austin | J., Mrs. | KC, p8c4, 7/24/1902 | Resided in Ferryville. Returned from trip to Dakota and brought back her daughter, Mrs. Caroline Williamson, for a short visit. |
| Austin | Jennie | KC, p4c3, 1/6/1898 | Married George Nelson on Dec. 23, 1897. (Bride and groom may be from Readstown area.) |
| Avery | Ralph | KC, p1c3, 6/16/1898 | Former resident of Crawford Co. Enlisted in the U.S. Army. On his way to Manila. Son of Rev. Avery. |
| Babcock | Warren | KC, p1c2, 10/20/1898 | Member of 2nd WI Inf. Served in Puerto Rico campaign. Formerly employed by Readstown Herald. Planned to return there. |
| Bacon | girl | KC, p5c4, 10/4/1900 | Daughter born Monday to F. Bacon of Gays Mills. |
| Bacon | James | KC, p5c4, 3/6/1902 | Peal Coleman and James Bacon of Bell Center departed for jobs in Iowa to get higher wages. |
| Bacon | John | KC, Supp., 12/18/1902 | Crawford County Board of Supervisors examined bills in the Justices and Constables' Account for State vs. John Bacon. Arthur Lathrop, Joseph Whiteaker, Thomas Spencer and Newton Bacon were witnesses. |
| Bacon | Julia | KC, p6c1, 3/18/1897 | Married James Wayne last week. Bride and groom may have been from Town of Marietta. |
| Bacon | Sylvester | KC, p1c6, 7/8/1897 | Died July 3, 1897 at home of son, Nute Bacon of Gays Mills. He was one of earliest settlers in county. Aged 87 years. Funeral service held in Bell Center. Buried in Gays Mills Cemetery. |
| Bailey | James | KC, p1c4, 5/31/1900 | Resided in Steuben. Daughter from Oregon came to visit him. |
| Bailey | H. G. | KC, p8c3, 1/9/1902 | Married Minnie Lang on Jan. 1, 1902. Bride and groom from Prairie du Chien area. |
| Bailey | Henry G. | KC, p1c4, 5/25/1899 | Prairie du Chien High School Class of 1899 consisted of Henry G. Bailey, Mamie M. Chase, Ralph G. Dietrich, Katheryn H. Heaton, Frank D. Hobbs, Lloyd P. Horsfall, Joseph D. McDonald, Anna C. Roth, Mabel C. Ryder and Bessie E. Ward. Also Adeline L. Hobbs (per KC, p1c3, 6/1/1899). |
| Bailey | W. G. | KC, p1c3, 2/6/1902 | Bailey and John Harkneimer of Prairie du Chien constructed a new 2 story blacksmith and wagon shop for O'Brien and Kriz in Steuben. |
| Bakeman | D. C. | KC, p1c2, 6/14/1900 | Resided near Barnum. Sold 232 acre farm to M. Pelton of Edgerton, WI. |
| Baker | Darius | KC, p5c3, 9/9/1897 | Died Sept. 4, 1897 in Gays Mills. |
| Baker | Ethel, Miss | KC, p5c4, 9/5/1901 | Lived in Seneca. Visited sister, Mrs. E. Thomson of Mt. Sterling. |
| Baker | G. C. | KC, p5c5, 4/5/1900 | Elected clerk in Soldiers Grove. |

Genealogical Gleanings From Early Newspapers for Residents In and Near
Crawford County, Wisconsin, 1897-1902

| LAST NAME | FIRST NAME | NEWSPAPER PAGE/COLUMN MONTH/DAY/YEAR | GENEALOGICAL DATA |
|---|---|---|---|
| Baker | George | KC, p1c5, 12/5/1901 | Died Nov. 29, 1901 in Soldiers Grove. Born in New York 61 years ago. Served in 89th NY Reg. In Civil War. After war moved to Wisconsin. Married Jennie Callaway of Town of Marietta in 1884. She survives. |
| Baker | J., Mrs. | KC, p8c4, 11/24/1898 | Recently died in Blanchardville. She was the mother of Mrs. Ira LoeBaron of Lowertown. (Prairie du Chien.) |
| Baker | Miss | KC, p1c3, 2/15/1900 | Married Neil Clemons on Feb. 6, 1900 at Platteville. |
| Baker | William | KC, p5c3, 3/27/1902 | Married Alverta Neidig on Mar. 19, 1902. Bride and groom from Town of Seneca. |
| Balch | M. B., Rev. | KC, p1c5, 4/7/1898 | Died Mar. 26, 1898 in Minneapolis. Aged 62 years. Survived by wife and 1 son. He was a former elder in an area Methodist Episcopal Church. |
| Balderston | Joseph, Mrs. | KC, p8c3, 6/12/1902 | Died June 8, 1902 in Prairie du Chien. |
| Bandler | Sara | KC, p4c4, 11/10/1898 | Criminal Issue to be heard in the November term of the Crawford County Circuit Court. State of Wisconsin vs. Sara Bandler. |
| Bandler (Bandier?) | Sarah | KC, Supp., 12/29/1898 | Crawford Co. Board of Supervisors approved Justices and Constables' expenses related to the case, State vs. Sarah Bandler (Bandier?). The witnesses were A. L. Lankford, Josephine Collins, Nettie Collins and L. C. Collins. |
| Bangs | girl | KC, p8c3, 1/7/1897 | Daughter born Dec. 22, 1896 to James Bangs of Rising Sun. |
| Bangs | infant | KC, p8c4, 3/25/1897 | Infant son of James Bangs of Rising Sun died last Friday. |
| Banks | Milo | KC, Supp., 12/29/1898 | Crawford Co. Board of Supervisors approved Justices and Constables' expenses related to the case, State vs. Milo Banks. The witnesses were J. R. Newman, Marion Guist, W. H. Forsythe, Ellen Forsythe, Jeff (Townsend?), Mrs. Clarinda Halton and Mrs. Clara Smith. |
| Bannen | Mary | KC, p1c5, 2/9/1899 | Taught school in Marietta in 1899. E. E. Brindley, Crawford County Superintendent of Schools published a comprehensive list of all teachers in the county. |
| Bannen | Mary | KC, Supp., 12/12/1901 | Attended a Teacher's Institute in Crawford County in 1901. Resided in Hurlbut. |
| Bannen | Richard | KC, p4c3, 5/30/1901 | Lived in Hurlbut. Found guilty of assault and attempt to commit rape of Ida Fosnow. |
| Bannen | Richard | KC, p4c2, 11/14/1901 | Sentenced in Circuit Court to 2 years in Green Bay Reformatory. An appeal to the Supreme Court was planned. |
| Bannen | Richard | KC, Supp., 12/20/1900 | Crawford Co. Board of Supervisors approved payment of expenses in the matter of State vs. Richard Bannen. The witnesses were Dr. S. Payman, Thomas Fosnow, Mary Fosnow, Ida Fosnow, John E. Coalburn and G. M. Dilley. |
| Bannen | Willie | KC, p1c2, 11/22/1900 | Resided in Hurlbut, Town of Scott. Represented the National Correspondence School. |
| Bannen | Willie | KC, Supp., 12/12/1901 | Attended a Teacher's Institute in Crawford County in 1901. Resided in Hurlbut. |

Genealogical Gleanings From Early Newspapers for Residents In and Near
Crawford County, Wisconsin, 1897-1902

| LAST NAME | FIRST NAME | NEWSPAPER PAGE/COLUMN MONTH/DAY/YEAR | GENEALOGICAL DATA |
|---|---|---|---|
| Bannon | E. R. | KC, p1c3, 3/25/1897 | Recently died in La Crosse. (May have been a former resident of Prairie du Chien.) |
| Banta | Delia, Mrs. | KC, p1c3, 3/10/1898 | Married James Mason of Steuben on Feb. 23, 1898. Bride from Scott. The Rev. N. C. Bradley of Excelsior officiated. |
| Barette | Charles | KC, p1c4, 3/27/1902 | Died Mar. 25, 1902 at Gays Mills. Father of Mrs. Charles Brandes. Aged 75 years. Buried in Prairie du Chien. |
| Barette | Charles | KC, p8c3, 4/3/1902 | Died Mar. 26, 1902. Aged 74 years. Lived in Bridgeport many years. Most recently lived in Gays Mills. Buried in Frenchtown Cemetery. |
| Barfell | Harvey | KC, p1c2, 10/13/1898 | Served in Co. C, 2nd WI Inf. Returned to Tampa, FL after visiting uncle, D. Whiteaker of Bell Center. Caught typhoid fever. Company C was known as the Whitewater Company. |
| Barham | M. | KC, p5c4, 5/29/1902 | The case Henry Henderson vs. M. Barham was heard at the May term of the Crawford County Circuit Court. Taken under advisement by the court. To be decided on briefs. |
| Barker | Eva | KC, p4c2, 2/11/1897 | Married Frank C. Brown on Feb. 7, 1897. Bride and groom may have been from Gays Mills. Justice Stowell officiated. |
| Barker | Francis M. | KC, p4c4, 11/10/1898 | Issues of Fact for Court heard in the November term of the Crawford County Circuit Court. Thomas A. La Vake vs. Francis M. Barker. |
| Barker | Vincent G. | KC, p5c3, 8/8/1901 | Died July 5, 1901 in Gays Mills. Suffered from cancer. |
| Barker | V. G. | KC, p4c4, 5/2/1901 | Left Gays Mills for Chicago to have a tumor removed from his face. |
| Barlow | Henry | KC, p1c5, 6/20/1901 | Married Mabel Briggs on June 15, 1901 at Gays Mills. The Rev. M. J. Cameron officiated. Bride was daughter of E. G. Briggs of Town of Utica. Groom from Town of Clayton. |
| Barlow | N. | KC, p5c5, 4/5/1900 | Elected assessor in Town of Clayton. |
| Barlow | Norman | KC, p1c6, 4/7/1898 | Elected Assessor for the Town of Clayton. |
| Barnes | Flora | KC, p8c1, 8/25/1898 | Recently married W. G. Caskey of Oberlin, OH. Bride daughter of Mrs. A. S. Barnes of Prairie du Chien. |
| Barnett | J. W. | KC, p8c4, 9/30/1897 | At a conference of the Methodist Church held in Platteville, J. W. Barnett was assigned to Benton. |
| Barnett | Mary L. | KC, p5c3, 5/12/1898 | Notice of a foreclosure sale published. Mary L Barnett (plaintiff) vs. Henry Evans and wife, Mary A. Evans. |
| Barney | Dr. | KC, p1c8, 2/11/1897 | Dentist. Advertised office hours in Ferryville, Seneca, Mt. Sterling, Gays Mills and Soldiers Grove. |
| Barney | F. A., Dr. | KC, p1c3, 10/30/1902 | Married Alvina Kasperek on Oct. 28, 1902. Groom from Soldiers Grove. |
| Barney | William | KC, p1c3, 5/22/1902 | Resided in Town of Clayton. Specialized in breeding good horses and good sheep. |
| Barney | William | KC, p5c3, 5/20/1897 | Issues of fact for court to be heard in the May term of the Crawford County Court. William Cater vs. M. B. Seward and William Barney. |
| Barney | William | KC, Supp., 12/18/1902 | Per Committee on County Poor, Crawford County received $35.95 from Wm. Barney, balance due Mrs. Julia Moses. |

Genealogical Gleanings From Early Newspapers for Residents In and Near
Crawford County, Wisconsin, 1897-1902

| LAST NAME | FIRST NAME | NEWSPAPER PAGE/COLUMN MONTH/DAY/YEAR | GENEALOGICAL DATA |
|---|---|---|---|
| Barnum | boy | KC, p1c2, 5/3/1900 | Son born April 18, 1900 to M. B. Barnum of Steuben area. |
| Barnum | Edward L. | KC, p5c4, 3/2/1899 | Died Feb. 24, 1899 in Barnum. Born Jan. 19, 1828 in Ontario Co., NY. When 2 years old moved to Marion, OH. To Jo Daviess Co., IL in 1849. Soon moved to northern Wisconsin pineries. To farm in Haney, Crawford Co., WI in 1856. To Barnum In 1893. Married Hannah R. Bennett of Boone Co., IL in 1857. Fathered 4 children: Mrs. A. N. Scoville of Seneca; Mrs. L. J. Haskins of Sioux City, IA; M. R. Barnum of Barnum and Frank G. Barnum who died in California in 1888. |
| Barnum | Ester May | KC, Supp., 2/23/1899 | Died Feb. 11, 1899. Born Nov. 16, 1898 to M. R. Barnum. |
| Barnum | Jerome, Mrs. | KC, p8c3, 2/15/1900 | Nee Mary Webster. She and husband to take charge of the insurance business formerly run by the late Maj. L. F. S. Viele. |
| Barnum | L. E. | KC, p5c4, 5/29/1902 | L. E. Barnum of Mt. Hope attended a teacher institute in Crawford County. |
| Barnum | M. R. | KC, p8c4, 11/13/1902 | In the November term of Crawford County Circuit Court, M. R. Barnum vs. Anna Mitchell, verdict for plaintiff and damages. |
| Barnum | M. R., Mr. and Mrs. | KC, p8c2, 2/16/1899 | Published a card of thanks after the death of "their little one". According to the KC, Supplement, 2/23/1899 the child was born Nov. 16, 1898 and died Feb. 11, 1899. |
| Barnum | M. W. | KC, p1c4, 11/14/1901 | M. W. Barnum of Emmettsburg, IA, formerly of Crawford Co. ordered the Kickapoo Chief. |
| Barnum | Mr. | KC, p5c4, 9/27/1900 | Visited sister at the county poor farm. |
| Barr | Cliff | KC, p8c3, 11/14/1901 | Married Cora Lindmer on Nov. 13, 1901. Bride may be from Prairie du Chien. The Rev. Arthur Pratt officiated. |
| Barrett | David | KC, p5c3, 9/25/1902 | Died Sept. 16, 1902 at the Headquarters Hotel in Soldiers Grove. Aged 76 years. Survived by 3 nephews, George, Michael and Thomas Barrett. Lived most of life in Town of Scott. Funeral held at St. Patrick's Catholic Church in Scott. |
| Barrett | Thomas | KC, p1c4, 1/12/1899 | Died Jan. 9, 1899 at Georgetown, Town of Scott at age of 83 years. Funeral held at St. Patrick's Catholic Church. |
| Barrette | Alpha | KC, p1c3, 2/18/1897 | Married Mina Lindig on Feb. 17, 1897. Bride and groom from Prairie du Chien. |
| Barrette | Alpha | KC, p1c2, 10/14/1897 | Went to Soldiers Grove to take charge of the Stauer & Daubenberger lumber yard. |
| Barrette | Arthur | KC, p1c2, 1/7/1897 | Died Jan. 1, 1897 in Wauzeka. Aged 22 years and 10 months. Youngest son of Mr. and Mrs. Paulette Barrette (newspaper says Paulette). Died in Wauzeka. Funeral held Jan. 3, 1897 at the Methodist Episcopal Church. |
| Barrette | Charles | KC, p5c3, 12/29/1898 | Resided in Bridgeport. Visited daughter, Mrs. Charles Brandes of Gays Mills. |
| Barton | J. J. | KC, p5c3, 10/12/1899 | From Independence, IA. Called home to attend the funeral of his father, per Seneca news items. |

Genealogical Gleanings From Early Newspapers for Residents In and Near
Crawford County, Wisconsin, 1897-1902

| LAST NAME | FIRST NAME | NEWSPAPER PAGE/COLUMN MONTH/DAY/YEAR | GENEALOGICAL DATA |
|---|---|---|---|
| Barton | Mrs. | KC, p8c4, 7/26/1900 | Married Patrick Burke on July 24, 1900. Bride from Richland County. |
| Barton | Thomas | KC, p1c4, 10/5/1899 | Died Sept. 30, 1899 at age 79 years in Town of Haney. Wife died about 8 years ago. He was father of J. J. Barton of Independence, IA and Patrick Barton of Haney. |
| Barton | Thomas | KC, p1c2, 4/17/1902 | Graduated from Haney Valley schools. |
| Bartos | boy | KC, p5c3, 4/5/1900 | Fourteen-month-old son of P. Bartos recently died at his home in Town of Seneca. Scalded after grabbing the rim of a bucket filled with boiling water. |
| Batchelder | Effie, Mrs. | KC, p1c2, 8/26/1897 | Traveled to Colon, MI from home in Wauzeka to visit sister. |
| Batchelder | F. | KC, p1c6, 4/7/1898 | Elected Councilman for the Village of Wauzeka. |
| Batchelder | Frank | KC, p1c2, 5/12/1898 | Newly elected officers of the Wauzeka Good Templars were Fred Batchelder, Herb McDonnell, Mrs. Hoisington, Alma Hoisington, Lulu Vaughan, T. A. Stamp, Mrs. Riley, William Schueler, E. Folbrecht, Winnie Hoisington, Edna Sanger and Frank Lagaman. |
| Batchelder | Fred | KC, p1c5, 11/18/1897 | Installed as an officer at the International Order of Good Templars (I.O.G.T.) Lodge in Wauzeka. |
| Batchelder | Fred | KC, p1c2, 11/3/1898 | Installed as an officer at the International Order of Good Templars (I.O.G.T.) Lodge in Wauzeka. |
| Batchelder | Hiram | KC, Supp., 12/29/1898 | Received aid from the Crawford County Soldiers Relief Commission. Resided in Prairie du Chien. |
| Batchelder | Ned | KC, p8c1, 2/10/1898 | Recently died in Minneapolis. Son of the late Frank Batchelder. Buried in Minneapolis. Mrs. P. Weisenberger of Prairie du Chien, his sister-in-law, attended the funeral. |
| Bates | Albert | KC, Supp., 12/29/1898 | Crawford Co. Board of Supervisors approved Justices and Constable's expenses related to the case, State vs. Albert Bates. |
| Bates | Edith Estella | KC, Supp., 12/29/1898 | Crawford Co. Board of Supervisors approved Justices and Constables' expenses related to the case, State vs. Edith Estella Bates. |
| Bates | Sally, Mrs. | KC, p5c3, 9/25/1902 | Recently buried at De Soto. She was over 80 years old and lived in Ferryville. |
| Bauer | Albert | KC, p8c2, 7/27/1899 | Died June or July of 1899 in Chillicothe, OH. Aged 58 years. Brother of John Bauer of Prairie du Chien. |
| Bauer | Barbara, Mrs. | KC, p8c1, 9/6/1900 | Married Albert Vondrak on Sept. 2, 1900. Bride from Chicago. Groom from Prairie du Chien. |
| Bauer | Frank | KC, p8c2, 7/27/1899 | Died July 22, 1899 in Chicago. Aged 41 years and 11 months. He was brother of John Bauer of Prairie du Chien. |
| Bauer | Will | KC, p1c2, 6/10/1897 | Son of John Bauer of Prairie du Chien. Injured in a train accident in Beulah, IA. Lost leg. Crushed left hand. Run over while working with train ties. |
| Bauer | William | KC, p1c2, 6/30/1898 | Enlisted in army. Left job as section boss at Viola. His position was taken over by H. F. Lawrence of Wauzeka. |
| Baugherty | Thomas, Mrs. | KC, p4c4, 12/13/1900 | Nee Bertha Gossel. Visited friends in Eastman. About to move from Minneapolis to a new home in Indianapolis. |

Genealogical Gleanings From Early Newspapers for Residents In and Near
Crawford County, Wisconsin, 1897-1902

| LAST NAME | FIRST NAME | NEWSPAPER PAGE/COLUMN MONTH/DAY/YEAR | GENEALOGICAL DATA |
|---|---|---|---|
| Beach | Artemus H. | KC, p8c4, 8/25/1898 | Recently died in Battle Creek, MI at age 93 years. Born 1805 in New York. Married when 19 years old. Survived by wife. He was oldest brother of Horace Beach, Sr. of Prairie du Chien. |
| Beach | Eliza, Mrs. A. | KC, p5c4, 11/24/1898 | Died Nov. 10, 1898 in Eastman. Born Nov. 22, 1819 in New York City. Wife of Zenas Beach. Survived by 6 children. |
| Beach | Ethel | KC, p5c3, 5/1/1902 | Married Bert Thompson on April 30, 1902. Married at Christian Church in Lynxville. |
| Beach | Horace, Sr. | KC, p1c4, 7/8/1897 | Horace aged 80 years. Biography published. Father, Elah Beach, was born in 1780. Grandfather, Joseph Beach, Jr. of Torrington, CT, settled in Peru, NY in 1796. |
| Beach | Zenas | KC, p5c1, 8/4/1898 | Died July 28, 1898 at home in Eastman. He was an "aged resident." Had a daughter, Mrs. Mary Zander of Omaha, NB. |
| Beach | Zenas, Mrs. | KC, p5c2, 11/17/1898 | Died Nov. 10, 1898 in Eastman. Aged 77 years. Survived by 2 sons and 4 daughters. |
| Bean | A. C. | KC, p1c6, 5/19/1898 | Leased Beesecker House at Bridgeport. |
| Bean | James | KC, p8c4 12/5/1901 | Recently died. Body found on bank of Mississippi River. Buried in Lowertown Cemetery. Served in 3rd WI Infantry in Civil War. |
| Bear | Miss | KC, p5c3, 11/2/1899 | Resided in Boscobel. Guest of her sister, Mrs. Scoffeld of Steuben. |
| Beaumaster | Carrie, Miss | KC, p1c2, 8/21/1902 | Lived in Boscobel. Visited sister, Mrs. Roy Vaughan of Wauzeka. |
| Beaumeister | May | KC, p8c2, 9/28/1899 | Married Ray Vaughan of Wauzeka on Sept. 28, 1899 in Boscobel. Bride was from Boscobel. Groom son of O. P. Vaughan (per 10/5/1899 issue, p1c3). |
| Beaumont | boy | KC, p4c2, 3/3/1898 | Son born Feb. 14, 1898 to Draydon Beaumont of Steuben. |
| Beaumont | D. | KC, p1c5, 6/20/1901 | Brought grist to Wauzeka to be milled. |
| Beaumont | D. | KC, Supp., 12/19/1901 | D. Beaumont came to Steuben from Grant Co. in 1898 and started a sawmill business. |
| Beaumont | Mary | KC, p5c3, 10/5/1899 | Married Fletcher Lock on Oct. 1, 1899. (Bride may be from Steuben.) |
| Beck | George, Mr. and Mrs. | KC, p1c4, 6/14/1900 | Arrived from Madison, SD to visit friends in Wauzeka. |
| Beckendorf | Elnora | KC, p1c4, 6/5/1902 | Married Elton E. Brandes on Jan. (June?) 5, 1902 in St. Paul, MN. Bride from St. Paul. Groom son of George Brandes of Wauzeka. |
| Beckwith | William | KC, Supp., 12/18/1902 | Crawford County Board of Supervisors examined bills in the Justices and Constables' Account for State vs. William Beckwith. |
| Becor | Charles | KC, Supp., 12/29/1898 | Crawford Co. Board of Supervisors approved Justices and Constables' expenses related to the case, State vs. Charles Becor. |

Genealogical Gleanings From Early Newspapers for Residents In and Near
Crawford County, Wisconsin, 1897-1902

| LAST NAME | FIRST NAME | NEWSPAPER PAGE/COLUMN MONTH/DAY/YEAR | GENEALOGICAL DATA |
|---|---|---|---|
| Becwar | Frank | KC, p1c3, 9/8/1898 | Resided in Ortonville, MN. Visited in Wauzeka. Led a brass band of students, aged 10-16. Mike Chapek also lived in Ortonville. |
| Becwar | George | KC, p5c3, 12/14/1899 | George Becwar and John Yumbara of Eastman left for the pineries. |
| Becwar | J. W. | KC, p1c6, 8/4/1898 | J. W. Becwar, Anton Bieloh and John P. Kazda provided bonds to the Wauzeka Village Board entitling them to sell liquor. |
| Becwar | J. W. | KC, p1c2, 4/3/1902 | Left Wauzeka for North Dakota. Considering a move there. |
| Becwar | J. W. | KC, p1c2, 5/1/1902 | Resided in Wauzeka. Purchased a mercantile business and 160 acre farm in North Dakota. Planned to move July 1st. |
| Becwar | Anthony | KC, p1c4, 4/12/1900 | Worked as a machine salesman. Visited brother, John of Wauzeka. |
| Becwith | William | KC, p1c3, 6/19/1902 | Arrested for repeatedly beating his wife. No bond given. |
| Beebe | Alexander | KC, Supp., 12/18/1902 | Crawford County Board of Supervisors allowed expenses in the Matter of Alexander Beebe, Insane. |
| Beebe | L. F. | KC, p5c5, 4/5/1900 | Elected supervisor in Town of Scott. |
| Beebe | Sylvia | KC, p8c4, 11/16/1899 | Received marriage license in Crawford Co. Bride from Town of Clayton. Groom J. W. Rinehart, from Clayton. |
| Beer | George | KC, p10c1, 10/13/1898 | Married Mamie Holden on Oct. 10, 1898 at St. Gabriel Church in Prairie du Chien. Bride and groom from Ossian, LA. Bride's sister married groom's brother at the same ceremony. |
| Beer | Joseph | KC, p10c1, 10/13/1898 | Married Carrie Holden on Oct. 10, 1898 at St. Gabriel Church in Prairie du Chien. Bride and groom from Ossian, LA. Bride's sister married groom's brother at the same ceremony. |
| Beers | Pluma, Miss | KC, p1c4, 9/7/1899 | Lived in Sioux City. Visited uncle, H. Evans of Wauzeka area. |
| Beesecker | L. | KC, p1c5, 10/20/1898 | L. Beesecker and Chester Burgess of Wauzeka brought before Justice Bock on charge of killing tame geese belonging to August Kessler. |
| Begley | M. J. | KC, p1c4, 12/26/1901 | Left home in Wheatville for Waubesha, MN to spend the holidays with parents and a sister. |
| Begley | Michael, Sr., Mr. and Mrs. | KC, p1c4, 10/31/1901 | Rented their farm in Scott for the winter and went to Waubena, MN to visit their daughter, Mrs. Frank Fox. Mr. Fox was County Auditor in Waubena. |
| Begley | Mrs. | KC, p1c3, 11/2/1899 | Resided in Scott. She and her daughters, Mrs. Mat Rowe and Mrs. James McCormick, visited relatives in Minneapolis. |
| Behnken | Mrs. | KC, p1c2, 10/13/1898 | Resided in Aota, MN. Visited brother, John Lewig of Wauzeka. |
| Beier | boy | KC, p1c3, 7/21/1898 | Son born July 17, 1898 to Max Beier of Wauzeka. |
| Beier | boy | KC, p1c6, 10/13/1898 | Infant son of Max Beier died Oct. 6, 1898 in Wauzeka. Aged 12 weeks. |

Genealogical Gleanings From Early Newspapers for Residents In and Near
Crawford County, Wisconsin, 1897-1902

| LAST NAME | FIRST NAME | NEWSPAPER PAGE/COLUMN MONTH/DAY/YEAR | GENEALOGICAL DATA |
|---|---|---|---|
| Beier | George | KC, p1c4, 3/27/1902 | Sent letter home from Warner, ID describing son's mining accident and injuries. Son, Willie, was unconscious for 4 days. Fell 150' down a mineshaft. |
| Beier | George | KC, p1c2, 1/20/1898 | Rented the J. J. Hurlbut store at Steuben. |
| Beier | George | KC, p1c3, 5/19/1898 | Discontinued his branch store in Steuben. |
| Beier | George | KC, p1c2, 9/8/1898 | George Beier, Mrs. F. Gink and Mrs. John Langaman went to Fernwood, WI to visit a sister. |
| Beier | George | KC, p1c3, 1/25/1900 | Featured in an article on Wauzeka's business concerns. Boot and shoe dealer. Sold jewelry, neckwear, and clothing. |
| Beier | George, Mrs. | KC, p4c4, 6/15/1899 | Resided in Wauzeka. Traveled to Racine to attend her father, enfeebled by age. She planned to bring him to Wauzeka to spend his remaining days with her. |
| Beier | George, Mrs. | KC, p1c3, 7/27/1899 | Called to Racine by a telegram announcing death of her father. |
| Beier | Max | KC, p1c3, 7/28/1898 | Purchased the Jetter property from Jacob Christ, administrator of the estate. |
| Beier | Walter | KC, p1c3, 6/14/1900 | Departed Wauzeka for a clerking position in Brooklyn, WI. |
| Beier | Walter | KC, p1c2, 11/1/1900 | Planned to depart Wauzeka to open a shoe store and repair shop in Brooklyn, WI. |
| Beier | Walter | KC, p1c2, 4/20/1899 | Visited his parents in Wauzeka. Employed in a Janesville shoe store. He was the son of George Beier. |
| Beier | Willie | KC, p1c4, 11/22/1900 | Beier and Adolph Sanger left Wauzeka for the West to find work as railroad brakemen. |
| Beier | Willie | KC, p1c5, 3/20/1902 | Seriously injured in a mine accident near Warner, ID. Dispatch sent to father, George Beier, by Adolph Sanger. Father departed for Idaho and got snowbound in Dawson, ND. Later word sent to Mrs. Beier said Willie was doing better. |
| Beier | Willie | KC, p1c3, 3/24/1898 | Adolph Sanger, Frank Lagaman and Willie Beier of Wauzeka departed for Grand Junction, CO to seek their fortune. |
| Beier | Willie | KC, p1c2, 9/22/1898 | Paid $5.75 and court costs to August Oesterich as compensation for death of a cow that took place at a picnic at Plum Creek. There was no direct evidence that Beier caused cow's death. Ordered by Justice Peacock and the Board of Arbitration. |
| Beier | Zelma | KC, p1c2, 4/12/1900 | Taught school in the Citron Valley. |
| Beier | Zelma | KC, p1c4, 5/2/1901 | Taught school in the Wayne District. |
| Beier | Zelma | KC, p1c5, 2/9/1899 | Taught school in Haney in 1899. E. E. Brindley, Crawford County Superintendent of Schools published a comprehensive list of all teachers in the county. |
| Beir | Willie A. | KC, p1c2, 8/16/1900 | Resided in Wauzeka. Listed as a victim of malaria. |

Genealogical Gleanings From Early Newspapers for Residents In and Near
Crawford County, Wisconsin, 1897-1902

| LAST NAME | FIRST NAME | NEWSPAPER PAGE/COLUMN MONTH/DAY/YEAR | GENEALOGICAL DATA |
|---|---|---|---|
| Bell | A. N., Mrs. | KC, p1c4, 6/22/1899 | Departed her home in Wauzeka to see her sister in Nebraska. |
| Bell | boy | KC, p1c2, 10/30/1902 | Son born last Saturday to David Bell of Excelsior. |
| Bell | D., Rev. | KC, p5c3, 7/6/1899 | Married Mrs. Anna Coalburn on June 27, 1899 in Prairie du Chien. Bride and groom from Mt. Sterling. Groom was pastor of M.E. Church in Mt. Sterling. |
| Bell | D., Rev. | KC, p5c4, 11/21/1901 | Left Excelsior and moved to a farm near Mt. Sterling. |
| Bell | Dennis | KC, p4c3, 12/19/1901 | Bell Center was named after Dennis Bell who in 1854 purchased the land upon which the village stands. The land was entered by Silas Anderson in 1853. W. W. Tate & Co. were pioneers in the mercantile business and conducted a general store here for many years. This firm was followed by Huffman & Onstine who did a thriving business for several years. In 1900 F. A. Onstine became the sole proprietor of the large merchandise and lumber business. He buys hundreds of thousands of feet of hardwood logs and manufactures them into lumber. |
| Bell | Dora | KC, p5c4, 5/29/1902 | Recently divorced. Spouse was Lee Bell. |
| Bell | Dora | KC, p5c4, 5/29/1902 | The case Dora Bell vs. Lee Bell was heard at the May term of the Crawford County Circuit Court. Decree of divorce and judgement signed. |
| Bell | F. F. | KC, p1c3, 10/16/1902 | Lived in Mt. Sterling. Exhibited a breed of chickens known as The Kickapoos at the Gays Mills Fair. Mr. Bell developed the breed. They resemble Buff Cochins. |
| Bell | Frank | KC, p8c4, 9/30/1897 | At a conference of the Methodist Church held in Platteville, Frank Bell was assigned to South Wayne, WI. |
| Bell | Frank | KC, Supp., 12/20/1900 | Crawford Co. Board of Supervisors approved payment of expenses in the matter of State vs. Frank Bell. The witnesses were Dell Ridgeman, Frank Campbell, Johh Pfahler, Rob Shultz, Frank Johnson, James Mustum and J. D. Merrill. |
| Bell | Frank, Rev. | KC, p5c4, 3/2/1899 | Resided in Soldiers Grove. Will hold services in the Mt. Sterling Methodist Episcopal Church while Rev. David Bell of Mt. Sterling holds services in Soldiers Grove. |
| Bell | J. | KC, p1c6, 4/7/1898 | Elected Trustee for the Village of Soldiers Grove. |
| Bell | Levi | KC, p4c3, 4/21/1898 | Hired to build a kitchen for J. Cummins of Wheatville. Lived on Knapps Creek. |
| Bell | Mr. | KC, p1c5, 1/17/1901 | Gave speech on small fruit at the Farmer's Institute held in Eastman. |
| Bell | Frank | KC, p1c4, 9/29/1898 | At a conference of the Methodist Church held in Eau Claire, Frank Bell was assigned to Soldiers Grove. |
| Bellows | A. D. | KC, p5c4, 12/7/1899 | Moved to Mt. Sterling. Hired to clerk in the Gays Mills post office, but unable to find a suitable dwelling. |
| Bellows | A. D. | KC, Supp., 12/15/1898 | Quit drug and candy business in Mt. Sterling and sold stock to Sherwood Bros. |

Genealogical Gleanings From Early Newspapers for Residents In and Near
Crawford County, Wisconsin, 1897-1902

| LAST NAME | FIRST NAME | NEWSPAPER PAGE/COLUMN MONTH/DAY/YEAR | GENEALOGICAL DATA |
|---|---|---|---|
| Bellows | A. D. | KC, p5c3, 10/5/1899 | From Gays Mills. Accepted position at the post office. |
| Bellows | A. D., Mr. | KC, p1c2, 3/16/1899 | Planned to open a law and collection office in Gays Mills. He was the father of Mrs. J. O'Neil of Wauzeka. |
| Bellows | A. D., Mrs. | KC, p1c3, 9/6/1900 | Resided in Mt. Sterling. Caring for her daughter, Mrs. J. O'Neil who was sick with malaria. |
| Bellows | A. D., Mrs. | KC, p5c4, 10/5/1899 | Called to Mt. Sterling. From Gays Mills. Grandson, Gerald, was seriously ill. |
| Bellows | boy | KC, p1c4, 10/5/1899 | Son of J. A. Bellows died Oct. 2, 1899 in Mt. Sterling. Aged 3 months and 3 days. |
| Bellows | Charles | KC, p5c3, 3/8/1900 | Teacher in Mt. Sterling. |
| Bellows | Charlie | KC, p5c3, 4/4/1901 | Lived in Mt. Sterling. Visited his sister, Mrs. J. O'Neil of Wauzeka. |
| Bellows | Edna | KC, p5c3, 1/26/1899 | Married Jeremiah O'Neil on Jan. 18, 1899. (Bride and groom may be from Mt. Sterling area.) |
| Bellows | Emma | KC, p5c3, 3/8/1900 | Teacher in Mt. Sterling. |
| Bellows | Emma | KC, p4c3, 12/20/1900 | Hired to teach in the Brockway District, near Mt. Sterling. |
| Bellows | Emma | KC, p1c5, 2/9/1899 | Taught school in Utica in 1899. E. E. Brindley, Crawford County Superintendent of Schools published a comprehensive list of all teachers in the county. |
| Bellows | Emma | KC, Supp., 12/12/1901 | Attended a Teacher's Institute in Crawford County in 1901. Resided in Mount Sterling. |
| Bellows | Emma, Miss | KC, p5c4, 4/5/1900 | Lived in Mt. Sterling. Visited sister, Mrs. J. A. Hayes of Gays Mills. |
| Bellows | J. A. | KC, p1c3, 4/21/1898 | Resided in Gays Mills. Purchased an interest in the *Kickapoo Chief*. |
| Bellows | J. R. | KC, p4c4, 1/7/1897 | Advertised sale of horse blankets and harnesses in Mt. Sterling. |
| Bellows | twin boys | KC, p1c2, 7/6/1899 | Twin boys born Saturday to J. A. Bellows of Mt. Sterling. |
| Bellrichard | boy | KC, p5c3, 8/14/1923 | Son born last Tuesday to Albert Bellrichard of Eastman. |
| Bellrichard | Henry | KC, p1c4, 6/26/1902 | Married Ivey Wagner on June 18, 1902 in La Crosse. Bride daughter of Frank Wagner of Wauzeka. Groom brother of Albert Bellrichard of Town of Eastman. |
| Belrichard | Albert | KC, p5c4, 11/7/1901 | Married (Bessie?) Speck on Oct. 28, 1901 at Methodist Episcopal Church in Hazen's Corners. Bride from (Town of Eastman?). Emma Cherrier was a cousin of bride. Henry Belrichard was a brother of groom. |
| Bender | John | KC, Supp., 12/29/1898 | Crawford Co. Board of Supervisors approved Justices and Constables' expenses related to the case, State vs. John Bender. The witnesses were William Gremore, John Gremore, Jane Gremore, Peter Gremore, Johny Bender, Annie Bender and Albert Kelana. |
| Benhart | Will | KC, p5c5, 1/30/1902 | Benhart and Carl Messling planned to move to Pocahontas, IA. |

Genealogical Gleanings From Early Newspapers for Residents In and Near
Crawford County, Wisconsin, 1897-1902

| LAST NAME | FIRST NAME | NEWSPAPER PAGE/COLUMN MONTH/DAY/YEAR | GENEALOGICAL DATA |
|---|---|---|---|
| Benhart | William | KC, p5c3, 3/21/1901 | Harness maker in Seneca. |
| Benhart | William | KC, p1c4, 9/26/1901 | Did harness work and horse shoeing in Seneca. |
| Benhart | William | KC, p5c3, 1/23/1902 | Visited relatives in Lynxville and Prairie du Chien before departing for new home in Somerset, IA. |
| Benhart | William | KC, p4c6, 8/24/1899 | Opened a new harness and shoe shop in Seneca. |
| Benish | Anton | KC, p8c2, 3/31/1898 | Died of suicide on Mar. 25, 1898. Kept a saloon. Funeral held at St. John Bohemian Church. |
| Benish | Frank, Mrs. | KC, p1c2, 10/27/1898 | Resided in Vlasaty, MN. Former resident of Wauzeka. Visited friends in hometown. |
| Bennart | Frank | KC, p5c3, 9/5/1901 | Lived in Lynxville. Pulled a purse out of the water while fishing. Contained $60 that was lost 3 months ago by Fritz Phaler. |
| Benner | Emma | KC, p5c1, 7/29/1897 | Married Louis Rider on June 30, 1897 in Madison. Bride and groom from Wauzeka. |
| Benner | George | KC, p1c3, 11/7/1901 | Resided east of Wauzeka across the river. Sold farm to Mr. Muns of Grant Co. for $5300, which equaled about $25 an acre. Planned to go west, probably to Washington. |
| Benner | George | KC, p4c3, 12/19/1901 | Resided in Wauzeka. Returned from Spokane, WA where he purchased land. |
| Benner | George | KC, p1c3, 2/27/1902 | The George Benner family and Lou Rider family departed area for new homes in Rockford, WA. |
| Benner | George | KC, p1c6, 4/7/1898 | Elected Supervisor for the Town of Wauzeka. |
| Benner | George | KC, p5c5, 4/5/1900 | Elected supervisor in Town of Wauzeka. |
| Benner | J. H. | KC, p1c2, 8/30/1900 | Served in Co. K, 34th US Vol. Inf. in the Philippines. He was son of George Benner of the Wauzeka area. |
| Benner | J. H. | KC, p1c2, 6/27/1901 | Married Miss Miller on Mar. 29, 1901. Groom brother of Mrs. Lou Rider of Wauzeka. Bride from Milpitas, CA. Planned to live in Milpitas. |
| Bennett | Blanche | KC, p5c4, 6/14/1900 | Graduated this week from Mt. Sterling schools. |
| Bennett | Blanche | KC, p6c2, 11/15/1900 | Left Mt. Sterling to visit her mother, Mrs. David Bell of Excelsior. |
| Bennett | Blanche | KC, p5c3, 8/3/1899 | Replaced Letha Vaughan in the telephone office and post office in Mt. Sterling. |
| Bennett | boy | KC, p1c4, 3/24/1898 | Son born Mar. 11, 1998 to H. E. Bennett of La Farge. |
| Bennett | Charles | KC, p5c3, 11/30/1899 | Resided in Gays Mills. He was one of the oldest pioneer settlers in the county. Visited Mr. and Mrs. George Chamberlain of Steuben. "Charley is still hale and hearty and able to hunt coons as well as of yore." |
| Bennett | J. V. | KC, p1c4, 9/29/1898 | At a conference of the Methodist Church held in Eau Claire, J. V. Bennett was assigned to South Wayne. |
| Bennett | Josiah V. | KC, p8c4, 9/30/1897 | At a conference of the Methodist Church held in Platteville, Josiah B. Bennett was assigned to Argyle. |

Genealogical Gleanings From Early Newspapers for Residents In and Near
Crawford County, Wisconsin, 1897-1902

| LAST NAME | FIRST NAME | NEWSPAPER PAGE/COLUMN MONTH/DAY/YEAR | GENEALOGICAL DATA |
|---|---|---|---|
| Bennett | W. W. | KC, p4c1, 12/2/1897 | From Soldiers Grove. Accepted a job in Madison with a farm implement company. His territory will be in eastern Wisconsin. |
| Bennett | W. W. | KC, p1c6, 6/2/1898 | Announced plans to run for Crawford County Sheriff. Resident of Clayton. |
| Berg | Betsey | KC, p1c5, 10/28/1897 | Married Edward Holverson of Ferryville on Oct. 14, 1897 in Viroqua. Bride from Viroqua. The Rev. G. W. Nuzum officiated. |
| Bernann | Emil | KC, p5c3, 1/14/1897 | Left Eastman for his home in northern Wisconsin. |
| Bernier | Agnes | KC, p5c4, 3/1/1900 | Married John Lynch on Feb. 22, 1900. Bride and groom from Seneca. Bride's brother, Joe Bernier, runs a creamery in Iowa. |
| Bernier | J. F. | KC, p1c3, 2/15/1900 | Arrived from Nansen, IA to visit his old home in Seneca, WI. |
| Bernier | Joe | KC, p5c3, 3/9/1899 | Left Seneca for Nansen, IA to work in the creamery business. |
| Bernier | Michael | KC, p1c5, 4/27/1899 | Recently married Josie Leary at St. Patrick's Catholic Church in Seneca. |
| Berry | Anna | KC, p1c5, 2/17/1898 | Married Thomas McWilliams of Boscobel on Feb. 7, 1898. Bride was the daughter of John Berry of McGregor IA. Planned to live in Soldiers Grove. |
| Berry | William | KC, p5c4, 8/29/1901 | Land office at Eau Claire, WI published a notice that William Berry of Seneca had filed a notice of intention to make final proof in support of his land claim. Several witnesses were named as people who could attest that he had continuous occupation of the land. They were John Lucy of Ferryville, Thomas Flaherty of Mt. Sterling, John Fitzgibbons of Seneca and Michael P. Berry of Seneca. |
| Berry | William | KC, Supp., 12/29/1898 | Crawford Co. Board of Supervisors approved Justices and Constables' expenses related to the case, State vs. William Berry. The witnesses were John Spencer, Mary Spencer, Walter Spencer, John Fitzgibbons and Albert Aspenson. |
| Bertbeck | Prof. | KC, p1c5, 2/9/1899 | Taught school in the Town of Clayton in 1899. E. E. Brindley, Crawford County Superintendent of Schools published a comprehensive list of all teachers in the county. |
| Besaw | Louis | KC, Supp., 12/12/1901 | State vs. Louis Besaw heard in Crawford Co. Court. Witnesses were Mrs. Rose St. Joque and Miss Verviginia Lapoint, Madi____ Lapoint and Frank Lapoint. |
| Biddy | Lawrence | KC, p5c4, 3/20/1902 | Died Mar. 6, 1902. |
| Biederman | Alice R. | KC, p1c4, 2/15/1900 | Resided in Bell Center. Authored many poems and articles. Published under the name Leigh Revelix. |
| Biederman | August | KC, p8c3, 1/26/1899 | Died Jan. 11, 1899 near Wells, Faribault Co. (Probably in Minnesota.) Wife was the former Mabel Goodwin. (Appears to be a former resident of Prairie du Chien.) |
| Biederman | Celeste | KC, p8c3, 4/1/1897 | Married John Curley of Mt. Sterling on Mar. 22, 1897. Bride from Halls Branch. |

Genealogical Gleanings From Early Newspapers for Residents In and Near
Crawford County, Wisconsin, 1897-1902

| LAST NAME | FIRST NAME | NEWSPAPER PAGE/COLUMN MONTH/DAY/YEAR | GENEALOGICAL DATA |
|---|---|---|---|
| Biehloh | O. | KC, p1c4, 3/7/1901 | In a recent court case, he was found "guilty but not proven" for selling alcohol on Sunday. |
| Biehloh | Oscar | KC, p5c2, 6/10/1897 | Lived in Wauzeka. Accepted a position with Clauder's Orchestra to play clarinet in Milwaukee for the summer. |
| Biehn | John | KC, p1c5, 3/3/1898 | Died by suicide in father's home in Highland. He was brother of Mrs. Henry E. Howe. |
| Bieloh | A. | KC, p1c5, 3/15/1900 | Returned to his home in Wauzeka after an operation at St. Francis Hospital, La Crosse, in which cancer was successfully removed from his face. |
| Bieloh | Frank, Mrs. | KC, p1c3, 8/28/1902 | Lived in Cudahy, WI. Came to Wauzeka to care for her very ill father, I. Johnson. |
| Bieloh | Frank, Mrs. | KC, p1c3, 6/16/1898 | Traveled from West Superior to Wauzeka to visit parents, Mr. and Mrs. I. Johnson. |
| Bieloh | J. A. | KC, p1c8, 2/15/1900 | Operated a grocery store in Babcock WI. He was the son of A. Bieloh of Wauzeka. |
| Bieloh | Jno., Mr. and Mrs. | KC, p5c4, 9/21/1899 | Resided in Bridgeport. Departed for a new home in Babcock WI. |
| Bieloh | Oscar | KC, p1c3, 7/24/1902 | Lived in Wauzeka. Bought 320 acres of land in Kilton Co., MN, about 4 1/2 miles from Kennedy in the Red River Valley. |
| Biely | Mike, Mrs. | KC, p8c4, 3/22/1900 | Died Mar. 20, 1900 in Prairie du Chien. |
| Bier | George | KC, p4c5, 1/18/1900 | Advertised sale at his shoe store in Wauzeka. |
| Bigelow | Florence | KC, p5c1, 8/18/1898 | From New Haven, CT. Spent summer with uncle, J. S. Bigelow of Seneca. |
| Bigley | J. F. | KC, p1c2, 3/15/1900 | Resided in Soldiers Grove. Ran a harness shop formerly run by William Brady. |
| Biitner (Bittner?) | boy | KC, p8c4, 5/1/1902 | Recently died from a gun accident. He was the 8-year-old son of Frank Biitner (Bittner? of Prairie du Chien.) |
| Biley | Barbara | KC, p8c3, 6/14/1900 | Married Harry Knott on June 12, 1900. Bride and groom from Prairie du Chien. Planned to live in Winona, MN. |
| Biller | O. A. | KC, p5c4, 1/17/1901 | Foreman of the Keogh excelsior factory in Petersburg. |
| Birch | Joseph | KC, p8c3, 11/9/1899 | Died Nov. 3, 1899 on farm 8 miles north of Prairie du Chien. Survived by wife, 3 sons and 5 daughters. Buried at the Catholic Cemetery in Prairie du Chien. |
| Birchard | Ervin | KC, p1c2, 11/21/1901 | Married Daisy Brookins on Nov. 17, 1901 at Gays Mills. Bride from Gays Mills. Groom from Boscobel. Planned to live in Boscobel. |
| Birchard | N. E. | KC, p1c2, 6/26/1902 | Operated a hotel in Bell Center. |
| Bitterlee | John | KC, p8c1, 8/3/1899 | The case, State vs. John Bitterlee, was settled. |
| Bitterlee | L. | KC, p8c3, 8/10/1899 | Died July 27, 1899 in Prairie du Chien. Aged 86 years. Moved to Crawford Co. from Columbus, OH in 1850. Survived by wife and 3 sons. Buried in Catholic Cemetery. |
| Bitterlee | L., Mrs. | KC, p8c3, 1/16/1902 | Died Jan. 14, 1902 in Prairie du Chien. |

Genealogical Gleanings From Early Newspapers for Residents In and Near
Crawford County, Wisconsin, 1897-1902

| LAST NAME | FIRST NAME | NEWSPAPER PAGE/COLUMN MONTH/DAY/YEAR | GENEALOGICAL DATA |
|---|---|---|---|
| Bitterly | John | KC, Supp., 12/20/1900 | Crawford Co. Board of Supervisors approved payment of expenses in the matter of State vs. John Bitterly. |
| Black | Elam | KC, p8c1, 8/26/1897 | Died last Thursday at home of son, W. W. Black of Prairie du Chien. Aged 84 years. Born in New York. Lived in the west for last 40 years. Survived by 4 sons and 3 daughters. Remains taken to Mazeppa, MN, his former home. |
| Black | Emogene, Mrs. | KC, p5c3, 10/19/1899 | Recently died. Wife of Fred Black of Lynxville. Survived by husband, 1 child, parents, and 2 sisters. |
| Black | Fred | KC, Supp., 6/5/1902 | Married Anna Randall on May 31, 1902. Included in section with news from Lynxville. |
| Black | Fred | KC, p5c3, 8/28/1902 | Fred Black, Fred Waddle and Arthur Hopkins left Lynxville for North Dakota to take up land. |
| Black | Reuben | KC, p1c2, 3/17/1898 | From Lancaster. Accidentally killed when a Winchester he was cleaning discharged into his heart. |
| Black | W. W. | KC, p8c5, 12/16/1897 | Died Dec. 12, 1897. Born Nov. 29, 1841 in Monroeville, Huron Co., OH. Enlisted in army in Galena, IL. Later lived in Mazeppa, MN and Zumbrota, MN. Married Dec. 22, 1864 to Dora Dudley at Galena. Father of 5 sons and 2 daughters. Lived in Prairie du Chien for the last 4 years. |
| Blackburn | Ida M. | KC, p8c3, 9/21/1899 | Died Sept. 8, 1899 at Beetown. Wife of Fred Blackburn. Born July 1, 1879 in Lancaster. Eldest daughter of Joshua Day. Married Oct. 16, 1898 in Lancaster. Interred in Lancaster Cem. |
| Blaha | J. H. | KC, p1c5, 2/17/1898 | Announced an auction to be held on his farm outside Wauzeka. Selling farm implements. Planned to move to North Dakota. Farm located in Town of Freeman per KC, p1c2, 2/21/1898. |
| Blahna | Frank | KC, p5c3, 3/8/1900 | Moved family from Town of Eastman to farm in Grant Co. |
| Blahna | J. H. | KC, p4c4, 12/19/1901 | Arrived in Wauzeka from Countney, ND to visit relatives. He was father of John (9 years old), Leonard (5 years old) and Gaylord (2 years old). Farmed 400 acres in North Dakota. Harvest activities were detailed. |
| Blahna | J. H. | KC, p1c3, 3/17/1898 | Left Crawford Co. for a new home in Kensal, ND. |
| Blakesly | Mrs. | KC, p1c3, 8/10/1899 | Recently died in Hurlburt (Town of Scott, WI). Grandmother of Mrs. H. B. Brown of Wauzeka. |
| Blanchard | C., Mrs. | KC, p1c2, 4/1/1897 | Sold household goods in Prairie du Chien and moved to Minneapolis to live with her daughter. |
| Blanchard | R. D., Lt. | KC, p1c4, 9/14/1899 | Resident of Boscobel. Spoke at the Soldiers Reunion in Gays Mills. Tried to recruit men for the Philippine army. |
| Blasek | Martin | KC, p8c3, 1/23/1902 | Married Miss Kahler on Jan. 22, 1902. Bride and groom from Prairie du Chien area. |
| Blazek | Johnnie | KC, p1c2, 3/23/1899 | Resided in Wauzeka. Under treatment for paralysis of the face. |
| Bliss | W. A. | KC, p1c5, 7/1/1897 | Died June 25, 1897 in Grant Junction, CO. Born and raised in Readstown. In 1895 went west for his health. Survived by wife, mother, and 2 sisters. |

Genealogical Gleanings From Early Newspapers for Residents In and Near
Crawford County, Wisconsin, 1897-1902

| LAST NAME | FIRST NAME | NEWSPAPER PAGE/COLUMN MONTH/DAY/YEAR | GENEALOGICAL DATA |
|---|---|---|---|
| Bliss | W. A., Mrs. | KC, p4c1, 10/14/1897 | Departed from Readstown for Grand Junction, CO to settle business affairs. Planned to travel to the Pacific Coast where her parents resided. |
| Bliss | Will | KC, p12c2, 7/8/1897 | Extensive obituary published for Will Bliss, who died at Grand Junction, CO. More than 40 years ago his grandfather, Hon. Albert Bliss, came to Readstown and built a large store and hotel. "And during the days of the old stage line, the Bliss House became noted throughout the state for its generous hospitality and cordial welcome extended to its patrons." Will Bliss was born in the hotel. Will's father, A. P. Bliss, died at a young age, leaving Will in charge of the business. He was later compelled to give up the business when his health started to fail. His sisters were Mrs. J. O. Davidson and Mrs. F. P. Briggs of Soldiers Grove. 4,000 people attended his funeral in Readstown. |
| Blojeck | Otto | KC, Supp., 12/29/1898 | Crawford Co. Board of Supervisors approved Justices and Constables' expenses related to the case, State vs. Otto Blojeck. The witnesses were Mike Serabda, Willie Cherrier, Leroy Taylor and Otto Schultz. |
| Blondell | E. B., Mr. and Mrs. | KC, p1c3, 3/4/1897 | Mr. and Mrs. E. B. Blondell (nee Herald), and child, of La Crosse, visited relatives in Prairie du Chien. |
| Bloom | Sadie, Mrs. | KC, p4c2, 2/10/1898 | Called from her home in St. Paul, MN to the bedside of her sick mother, Mrs. T. W. Sampson of Gays Mills. |
| Bloom | Sadie, Mrs. | KC, p8c3, 6/9/1898 | Traveled from St. Paul to Gays Mills to help her father, T. W. Sampson. |
| Blosser | B. F., Dr. | KC, p1c1, 1/18/1900 | Advertised dental services. Practice based in Boscobel. |
| Bluet | Charles | KC, p1c2, 9/2/1897 | Broke and dislocated his arm in an accident at the creamery. He was a boy who lived with Will Stuckey in Wauzeka. |
| Bock | Allie H. | KC, p1c4, 4/6/1899 | Died April 2, 1899 in Boscobel. Aged about 25 years. |
| Bock | G. R. | KC, p5c5, 4/5/1900 | Elected police justice in Wauzeka. |
| Bock | George | KC, p1c6, 4/7/1898 | Elected Police Justice for the Village of Wauzeka. |
| Bock | George R. | KC, p1c3, 9/21/1899 | Died Aug. 26, 1899 in Hamburg, Germany at 70 years of age. He was father of Mr. Bock who lived in Wauzeka. |
| Bock | George R. | KC, p1c4, 1/25/1900 | Lived in Wauzeka. Agent for the Michel Brewing Co. of La Crosse. |
| Bock | George R. | KC, p1c3, 1/25/1900 | Featured in an article on Wauzeka's businesses. Agent of the Michel Brewing Co. of La Crosse. Established in Wauzeka two years ago. |
| Bock | Gustav A. | KC, p8c4, 3/21/1901 | Died Mar. 12, 1901 at Johnson's Creek, Jefferson Co., WI. He was the brother of Fred E. Bock of Boscobel. Aged 43 years. |
| Boisvert | B. | KC, p1c4, 5/13/1897 | B. Boisvert and wife of Prairie du Chien were served warrant for keeping a "disreputable joint." |
| Boland | Anna | KC, p8c4, 12/5/1901 | Taught school at Copper Creek. |

Genealogical Gleanings From Early Newspapers for Residents In and Near
Crawford County, Wisconsin, 1897-1902

| LAST NAME | FIRST NAME | NEWSPAPER PAGE/COLUMN MONTH/DAY/YEAR | GENEALOGICAL DATA |
|---|---|---|---|
| Boland | Anna | KC, Supp., 12/12/1901 | Attended a Teacher's Institute in Crawford County in 1901. Resided in Seneca. |
| Boland | Patrick | KC, p5c3, 11/22/1900 | Died Nov. 17, 1900 in Town of Seneca. |
| Boland | Patrick | KC, p5c3, 11/29/1900 | Died Nov. 17, 1900 in Town of Seneca. Born Aug. 2, 1832 in King's Co., Ireland. Emigrated as a youth to Pennsylvania. Moved to Crawford Co. in 1867. Married Ellen Calahan on Oct. 26, 1869. Survived by wife, 9 (6 daughters and 3 sons) of his 11 children and 2 sisters (Mrs. Owen Clark and Mrs. John Carney of Pennsylvania). |
| Boland | Rose | KC, p1c5, 11/3/1898 | Rose Boland, teacher for the Seneca Primary School, reported the following pupils were not absent in October: Vincie Bowe; Leo Bowe; Leota Marston; May Halpin; Dannie Dagnon; Francis Halpin; Guy Porter; Ruby Collins; Eda Stuart; Willie Porter; Earl Bigelow; Aggie Garvey and Falie Bowe. |
| Boland | Rose | KC, p1c5, 2/9/1899 | Taught school in Seneca in 1899. E. E. Brindley, Crawford County Superintendent of Schools published a comprehensive list of all teachers in the county. |
| Boland | Thomas | KC, Supp., 12/12/1901 | Inquest on the bodies of Thomas Boland and George Halvorson heard in Crawford Co. Court. No witnesses listed. |
| Bolstad | Hans P. | KC, Supp., 12/12/1901 | Crawford Co. Board of Supervisors approved payments in the case, State vs. Hans P. Bolstad. |
| Bolstad | Hans P. | KC, Supp., 12/20/1900 | Crawford Co. Board of Supervisors approved payment of expenses in the matter of State vs. Hans P. Bolstad. The witnesses were John Olson; Andrew Bringes; Albert Sandy; Thomas T. Sandy; George Peterson; Ole Oleson; Iver N. Dab; Darwin Lescke; John Hagie, Jr.; John Hagie, Sr.; Beatha Hagie; Martha Hagie; Louis Nash; John Tiffin and Asa Bringe. |
| Bolstead | Hans | KC, Supp., 12/12/1901 | State vs. Hans Bolstead heard in Crawford Co. Court. |
| Bolsted | Hans | KC, p1c5, 11/8/1900 | Resided in Sugar Grove. Assaulted Andrew Johnson of Folsom with an iron rod, crushing his skull. Result of an old feud. |
| Bolsted | Mr. | KC, p1c3, 6/6/1901 | Resided in Freeman. Sentence to 18 months in Waupon for assaulting a neighbor with an iron bar last fall. |
| Bomaster | L., Miss | KC, p5c5, 1/7/1897 | Ran a millinery shop in Boscobel. |
| Bond | Jennie | KC, p1c3, 4/14/1898 | Died Apr. 9, 1898 in Boscobel. Aged 19 years and 11 months. She was daughter of W. J. C. Bond, minister at the Congregational Church. |
| Bond | W. J. C., Rev. | KC, p1c4, 9/8/1898 | Resided in Boscobel. Delivered dedicatory sermon for the Congregational Church in Gays Mills. Rev. Cheney of Janesville, Rev. Cook of Maple Ridge, Rev. Flett of Eastman and Rev. Cameron of Gays Mills also attended the service. |

Genealogical Gleanings From Early Newspapers for Residents In and Near
Crawford County, Wisconsin, 1897-1902

| LAST NAME | FIRST NAME | NEWSPAPER PAGE/COLUMN MONTH/DAY/YEAR | GENEALOGICAL DATA |
|---|---|---|---|
| Bonney | Adelaide | KC, Supp., 12/18/1902 | Crawford County Soldiers Relief Committee provided funds to Adelaide Bonney of Soldiers Grove. |
| Bonney | girl | KC, p5c4, 6/19/1902 | Daughter born May 7, 1902 to Fred Bonney of Eastman. |
| Bonney | J. H. | KC, p1c4, 12/9/1897 | Arrived from New Rockford, ND to visit friends in Eastman, his former home. |
| Bonney | L. A., Mrs. | KC, p1c5, 1/12/1899 | Died Jan. 9, 1899 near Eastman in her 77th year. |
| Bonney | L. A., Mrs. | KC, p1c5, 1/26/1899 | Died Jan. 9, 1899 in Eastman. Nee Jane Fisher. Born Aug. 18, 1822 in Crawford Co., PA. Married L. A. Bonney on June 30, 1850. They moved to Eastman in 1856. Survived by the following children: Hugh Bonney of New Rockford, ND; Mrs. Emma Jones of O'Neil, NB; James Gear of British Columbia; Fred Bonney of Eastman; Mrs. Velma Campbell of Eastman and Mrs. Ella Larson of Eastman. Buried in Campbell Cemetery. |
| Booman | Hannah | KC, p8c2, 1/26/1899 | Recently married William Brertsprcher of Elkader, IA at the Commercial Hotel. Bride from Boardman, IA. |
| Borgendine | Laura | KC, Supp., 12/29/1898 | Crawford Co. Board of Supervisors approved payment of expenses in the matter of Laura Borgendine, feeble minded. |
| Borgendine | Lena | KC, p8c2, 2/23/1899 | Married Will Grapp on Feb. 21, 1899. (Bride and groom may be from Prairie du Chien area.) Rev. Gruber, pastor of the German Lutheran Church, officiated. Rev. Gruber planned to move to Nebraska after spending the last four years in Prairie du Chien. |
| Bosch | Josephine | KC, Supp., 12/12/1901 | Crawford County filed suit against Andrew Bosch father of Josephine Bosch, to recover costs for care provided his daughter at the State Hospital for the Insane. |
| Boucher | Dan, Mrs. | KC, p5c3 12/4/1902 | Nee Ellen Bellrichard. Came from Butler, MN to visit her father in Eastman. Gone for 6 years. |
| Boucher | Joseph P. | KC, p8c2, 8/31/1899 | Married Margaret A. Doran on Aug. 29, 1899 at Spring Green. Planned to live in Lone Rock, WI. |
| Boucher | Robert | KC, Supp., 12/18/1902 | The Crawford County Board of Supervisors allowed expenses in the Matter of Robert Boucher, Insane. |
| Boucher | Samuel | KC, p1c6, 4/7/1898 | Elected Supervisor for the Town of Eastman. |
| Boucher | Louise | KC, p8c4, 6/27/1901 | Married Arthur Kloth on June 26, 1901 at St. Gabriel's Church in Prairie du Chien. |
| Bourne | Nathan | KC, p4c1, 9/29/1898 | Married Lotta Marsten of Gays Mills on Sept. 21, 1898. Groom from Freeman. Planned to live at West Prairie. |
| Bourne | Nathan | KC, p5c2, 12/16/1897 | From Freeman. Taught school in Victory. |
| Bourne | Nathan, Mr. and Mrs. | KC, p5c3, 12/29/1898 | Resided in West Prairie. Spent Christmas with Mrs. Bourne's parents, Mr. and Mrs. E. A. Marsten of Gays Mills. |
| Bowe | girl | KC, p5c3, 12/7/1899 | Daughter born Nov. 26, 1899 to H. Bowe of Seneca. |
| Bowe | J. F. | KC, p1c3, 8/16/1900 | Announced an auction of his personal property and livestock at his home in Seneca. |

Genealogical Gleanings From Early Newspapers for Residents In and Near
Crawford County, Wisconsin, 1897-1902

| LAST NAME | FIRST NAME | NEWSPAPER PAGE/COLUMN MONTH/DAY/YEAR | GENEALOGICAL DATA |
|---|---|---|---|
| Bowe | John | KC, p5c3, 12/26/1901 | Bowe and son, Leo, were guests of Joe Halpin of Seneca. Bowe sold a livery stable and hotel in Waucoma, IA and bought a farm in North Dakota. |
| Bowe | John | KC, p5c3, 1/2/1902 | Former resident of Seneca. Recently purchased a cattle ranch in Dakota. Wife was staying with her father, C. Rogers at Rising Sun. |
| Bower | Christian | KC, p5c3, 11/28/1901 | Died Nov. 6, 1901 at Shanghi Ridge. Aged resident. Survived by wife, 2 daughters and 6 grandchildren. Buried in German Cemetery. |
| Bowers | J. W., Mrs. | KC, p1c2, 7/3/1902 | Lived in Eastman. Entertained sister, Mrs. D. Hoover, of Beatrice, NB, and mother, of Onalaska. Mrs. Bowers had not seen her sister for 8 years. |
| Bowers | Mary, Mrs. | KC, p1c3, 2/22/1900 | Accepted a position at the Ray Hotel in Wauzeka. |
| Bowers | Perry | KC, p1c2, 10/31/1901 | Resided on Maple Ridge. Delivered cattle to A. W. Steisel in Wauzeka. Perry now learning how to make cheese. |
| Boyd | Arthur | KC, Supp., 12/19/1901 | Arthur Boyd was a pioneer merchant in the Village of Steuben. (Steuben was established in 1882.) He moved west years ago. |
| Boyd | girl | KC, p5c1, 2/10/1898 | Daughter born Feb. 4, 1898 to A. Boyd of Steuben. |
| Boyd | Robert, Mrs. | KC, p1c3, 6/19/1902 | Died June 15, 1902 at Steuben. Recent resident of McHenry, ND. Aged 46 years per KC, p5c3, June 26, 1902. |
| Bradley | N. C. | KC, p8c4, 9/30/1897 | At a conference of the Methodist Church held in Platteville, N. C. Bradley was assigned to Excelsior, WI. |
| Bradley | N. C. | KC, p1c4, 9/29/1898 | At a conference of the Methodist Church held in Eau Claire, N. C. Bradley was assigned to Excelsior. |
| Brady | Frank | KC, p5c4, 1/16/1902 | Married Clara Cummings on Jan. 13, 1902. Bride from Rolling Ground, Town of Clayton. Groom from Knapps Creek. Rev. H. F. Duffy officiated. |
| Brady | Frank | KC, p4c3, 5/4/1899 | Resident of Eastman. Duped by an agent of the St. Louis Wrought Iron Range Co. |
| Brady | Frank | KC, p5c5, 4/5/1900 | Elected supervisor in Eastman. |
| Brady | Frank | KC, p5c4, 4/12/1900 | Frank Brady, Chairman, reported the following men were appointed by the Town Board of Eastman to serve as Road Commissioners: Fred A. Bonney; Joseph Lechner, Jr.; G. L. Hazen; W. Granzow; Charles E. Campbell; Douglas Onstine; Jac Becwar; Dan Ducharme; Dominick Ducharme; Jake Vavruska; H. R. Finney; T. Sinko; Sam Ducharme; Henry Hoffman; Charles Granzow; John Seekatz; Anton Poupe; John Panka; Frank Mezera and William Alington. |
| Brady | Frank | KC, Supp., 12/20/1900 | Represented Eastman on the Crawford Co. Board of Supervisors in 1900. |
| Brady | girl | KC, p5c2, 2/11/1897 | Daughter born Sunday afternoon to William Brady of Wauzeka. |
| Brady | Hattie & Julia | KC, p5c4, 4/27/1899 | Left Eastman for positions in St. Joseph, MO. |

Genealogical Gleanings From Early Newspapers for Residents In and Near
Crawford County, Wisconsin, 1897-1902

| LAST NAME | FIRST NAME | NEWSPAPER PAGE/COLUMN MONTH/DAY/YEAR | GENEALOGICAL DATA |
|---|---|---|---|
| Brady | Julia | KC, p5c3, 12/7/1899 | Returned to Eastman from St. Joseph, MO where she had spent the summer. |
| Brady | Julia A. | KC, p5c4, 5/24/1900 | Married Henry M. Seekatz on May 21, 1900. Bride and groom from Town of Eastman. Bride daughter of Frank Brady. |
| Brady | Rosa | KC, p1c5, 2/9/1899 | Taught school in the Town of Clayton in 1899. E. E. Brindley Crawford County Superintendent of Schools published a comprehensive list of all teachers in the county. |
| Brainard | E. C. | KC, p8c3, 9/5/1901 | Recently died at Richland Center Hospital. From Prairie du Chien. Buried in Elmwood Cemetery, Mason City. |
| Brainard | Eugene | KC, Supp., 12/29/1898 | Crawford Co. Board of Supervisors approved payment of expenses in the matter of Eugene Brainard, Insane. |
| Brainerd | Josephine | KC, p8c3, 11/21/1901 | Married William Campbell on Nov. 16, 1901. Bride from Prairie du Chien. Groom from Milwaukee. Bride daughter of Conductor E. C. Brainerd. Planned to live in Fond du Lac. |
| Brandes | Bernie | KC, p1c2, 11/3/1898 | Installed as an officer at the International Order of Good Templars (I.O.G.T.) Lodge in Wauzeka. |
| Brandes | Bernie, Miss | KC, p9c3, 7/1/1897 | Taught at the Scott school. |
| Brandes | Bernie, Miss | KC, p1c2, 3/31/1898 | Resided in Haney. Taught school in Wauzeka. |
| Brandes | Carrie | KC, Supp., 12/12/1901 | Attended a Teacher's Institute in Crawford County in 1901. Resided in West Prairie. |
| Brandes | Charles | KC, p5c2, 3/15/1900 | Operated a general store in Gays Mills. |
| Brandes | Charles | KC, p8c3, 11/4/1897 | Took family to Minneapolis to visit daughter who has spent the last 6 months visiting relatives in Minnesota. From Gays Mills. |
| Brandes | Charles | KC, p5c3, 2/9/1899 | Left Gays Mills for Michigan to attend sister-in-law's funeral. |
| Brandes | Charles, Mrs. | KC, p1c2, 1/9/1902 | Resided in Gays Mills. Called to Bridgeport to see her ill father, Mr. Barrette. Father was 76 years old. |
| Brandes | Elton E. | KC, p1c4, 6/5/1902 | Married Elnora Beckendorf on Jan. (June?) 5, 1902 in St. Paul, MN. Bride from St. Paul. Groom son of George Brandes of Wauzeka. |
| Brandes | Eva | KC, p1c2, 11/3/1898 | Installed as an officer at the International Order of Good Templars (I.O.G.T.) Lodge in Wauzeka. |
| Brandes | Fred | KC, p1c2, 12/19/1901 | Served as a postmaster in Wauzeka. Received a pension increase. |
| Brandes | George | KC, p1c3, 5/29/1902 | Resided in Wauzeka. "Uncle Sam" gave him a pension increase. Now gets $10 per month. |
| Brandes | George | KC, p1c3, 11/13/1902 | Moved harness shop from Wauzeka to Lynxville. |
| Brandes | George | KC, p1c2, 5/5/1898 | From Gays Mills. Organized a company of volunteers for the war. |
| Brandes | Gertie | KC, p1c3, 8/22/1901 | Daughter of Charles Brandes of Gays Mills. Left for new home in Minneapolis. |

Genealogical Gleanings From Early Newspapers for Residents In and Near
Crawford County, Wisconsin, 1897-1902

| LAST NAME | FIRST NAME | NEWSPAPER PAGE/COLUMN MONTH/DAY/YEAR | GENEALOGICAL DATA |
|---|---|---|---|
| Brandes | Gertie | KC, p1c3, 11/13/1902 | Lived in Gays Mills. Went to South Carolina to spend the winter with her aunt, Mrs. St. Germain. |
| Brandes | Mrs. | KC, p1c3, 6/28/1900 | Resided in Wauzeka. Sisters came for a visit. They were Mrs. Simons of Meade Co., SD; Mrs. J. Hartnet of Ellenboro, WI and Mrs. Baker of Ellenboro, WI. |
| Brandes | Sarah Jane Moore | KC, p8c4, 5/12/1898 | Died April 27, 1898 in Prairie du Chien. Born Jan. 6, 1843 in Columbiana Co., OH. Moved to Millville, WI when 4 years old. Married Henry Brandes of Bridgeport, WI in 1860. Mother of George, Will, and Mrs. Mattie Bogar of Boscobel. Sister of Mrs. William White. (Lengthy obituary.) |
| Brandes | William, Mrs. | KC, p1c5, 1/16/1902 | Resided in Mt. Hope. Visited father, Carl Oswald of near Wauzeka. |
| Brandt | Leo | KC, Supp., 12/18/1902 | Crawford County Board of Supervisors allowed expenses in the Matter of Leo Brandt Dependent Child. |
| Breinard | Frank | KC, p5c4, 8/31/1899 | Married Adelia Hart, daughter of F. T. Hart of Haney Ridge, on Aug. 23, 1899. Groom from Boscobel. |
| Brennan | Mike | KC, Supp., 12/29/1898 | Crawford Co. Board of Supervisors approved Justices and Constables' expenses related to the case, State vs. Mike Brennan |
| Brennan | Mrs. | KC, p5c3, 2/23/1899 | Buried Feb. 22, 1899 in Steuben Catholic Cemetery. |
| Brenner | George | KC, p5c4, 5/22/1902 | Prairie du Chien High School class of 1902. |
| Brenner | Levi A. | KC, p8c4, 9/30/1897 | At a conference of the Methodist Church held in Platteville, Levi A. Brenner was assigned to Belmont. |
| Brenner | Mr. | KC, p1c3, 4/1/1897 | Died last Tuesday of suicide in Prairie du Chien. |
| Brenner | Mr. | KC, p1c3, 4/1/1897 | Committed suicide last Tuesday. Shot himself. He was an old man who lived with his wife in the New York store building on Main St. in Prairie du Chien. Very poor. Supported himself by fishing and raising "garden truck". |
| Brenner | L. A. | KC, p1c4, 9/29/1898 | At a conference of the Methodist Church held in Eau Claire, L. A. Brenner was assigned to Belmont. |
| Brertsprcher | William | KC, p8c2, 1/26/1899 | Recently married Hannah Booman of Boardman, IA at the Commercial Hotel. Groom was from Elkader, IA. |
| Brew | William, Mrs. | KC, p8c3, 7/31/1902 | Died July 25, 1902 in Prairie du Chien. Survived by husband, 2 sons and 2 daughters. Husband was an alderman. |
| Bricker | Henry | KC, p1c6, 11/4/1897 | Issue of fact for court to be heard at the November term of the Circuit Court in Crawford County. Lydia Brickner vs. Henry Brickner. |
| Brickner | Lydia | KC, p1c6, 11/4/1897 | Issue of fact for court to be heard at the November term of the Circuit Court in Crawford County. Lydia Brickner vs. Henry Brickner. |
| Briggs | Bessie | KC, p5c4, 6/14/1900 | Graduated this week from Mt. Sterling schools. |
| Briggs | boy | KC, p5c3, 4/6/1899 | Son recently born to Charles Briggs of Bridgeport. |

Genealogical Gleanings From Early Newspapers for Residents In and Near
Crawford County, Wisconsin, 1897-1902

| LAST NAME | FIRST NAME | NEWSPAPER PAGE/COLUMN MONTH/DAY/YEAR | GENEALOGICAL DATA |
|---|---|---|---|
| Briggs | E. G. | KC, p1c4, 3/15/1900 | Elected secretary of the newly formed Crawford County Farmers Mutual Insurance Co. Other officers were J. W. McCullock, T. T. Sime, and J. A. Hays. |
| Briggs | Fay P. | KC, p1c6, 4/7/1898 | Elected President for the Village of Soldiers Grove. |
| Briggs | Gardner | KC, p8c3, 6/27/1901 | Married Ada Whaley at Tomahawk, WI last Monday evening. Bride and groom from Prairie du Chien. |
| Briggs | Mabel | KC, p1c5, 6/20/1901 | Married Henry Barlow on June 15, 1901 at Gays Mills by Rev. M. J. Cameron. Bride was daughter of E. G. Briggs of Town of Utica. Groom from Town of Clayton. |
| Briggs | Mable | KC, p5c3, 1/24/1901 | Lived in Mt. Sterling. Taught school in Pine Knob. |
| Briggs | Mae | KC, Supp., 12/12/1901 | Attended a Teacher's Institute in Crawford County in 1901. Resided in Mount Sterling. |
| Briggs | Mary | KC, p5c3, 6/13/1901 | Graduated from school in Mt. Sterling. |
| Bright | Allie | KC, p5c5, 1/10/1901 | Taught school in Lynxville. |
| Bright | Allie | KC, p5c4, 3/13/1902 | Resident of Lynxville. Finished her term of school and will now work in the post office. |
| Bright | Allie | KC, p5c4, 5/15/1902 | Married Albert Rice on Sunday. Bride from Lynxville. Groom from Boscobel. |
| Bright | Allie | KC, Supp., 12/12/1901 | Attended a Teacher's Institute in Crawford County in 1901. Resided in Lynxville. |
| Bright | T. C. | KC, p1c5, 4/13/1899 | Fire destroyed the John Vanderbilt & Co. Building, Davidson's livery barn and T. C. Bright's home and store in Lynxville. The fire later reached the A. E. Wolcott and W. A. Allen home, the William Huard home, the R. E. Hazen home and saloon, the T. C. Bright warehouse and the Schumann & Menges ice house. |
| Bright | Alice | KC, p5c3, 5/31/1900 | Graduated from school in Lynxville. |
| Brightman | F. C. | KC, p1c2, 4/19/1900 | Departed Bell Center for Chippewa Co., WI to explore opportunities to invest in land. |
| Brightman | F. C. | KC, p1c3, 7/20/1899 | Left his home in Bell Center to attend his ill son, Joseph, in Boscobel. |
| Brightman | Frank C. | KC, p1c4, 4/28/1898 | Sold farm near Petersburg. Will probably move to Minnesota. |
| Brightman | Frank, Mrs. | KC, p8c4, 11/21/1901 | Departed with 3 sons and 1 daughter for Madera, CA to join her husband. Folks in Bell Center and Petersburg bid adieu at the train station. |
| Brightman | Joe | KC, p5c5, 4/12/1900 | Recently departed Bell Center for the west. |
| Brightman | Mae | KC, Supp., 12/12/1901 | Attended a Teacher's Institute in Crawford County in 1901. Resided in Bell Center. |

Genealogical Gleanings From Early Newspapers for Residents In and Near
Crawford County, Wisconsin, 1897-1902

| LAST NAME | FIRST NAME | NEWSPAPER PAGE/COLUMN MONTH/DAY/YEAR | GENEALOGICAL DATA |
|---|---|---|---|
| Brightman | Mary Herrick, Mrs. | KC, p1c6, 12/9/1897 | Died Dec. 1, 1897 in Bell Center. Born Aug. 25, 1822 in Essex Co., NY. Parents were English and strict Baptists. She was one of 9 children. Parents died at ages of 80 and 82 many years ago. Married Joseph H. Brightman on Nov. 19, 1837 when she was 16 years old. He was 5 years older than she was. Moved to Wisconsin in 1840. Husband died in 1888. Lived in Crawford Co. for 40 years. Had many children. Only one mentioned by name was Mrs. M. R. Tate of Bell Center. |
| Brightman | May | KC, p5c3, 5/9/1901 | Hired to teach in Bell Center. |
| Brimer | George | KC, Supp., 12/29/1898 | Crawford Co. Board of Supervisors approved Justices and Constables' expenses related to the case, State vs. George Brimer. |
| Brindley | Albert | KC, p1c3, 8/30/1900 | Son of Joe Brindley of Town of Haney. Departed for college in Sioux City, IA. |
| Brindley | Arthur | KC, p1c3, 8/29/1901 | Hired to teach school at Bell Center. |
| Brindley | E. E. | KC, Supp. 10/27/1898 | Nominated by the Crawford County Republican Party for the office of Superintendent of Schools. Asking for re-election after 4 years of service in position. Resident of Soldiers Grove. (Picture, short bio. and character sketch provided.) |
| Brindley | Joe | KC, p5c4, 3/15/1900 | Brindley Thomas Cleary, Pat Cleary, Thomas Cox, Thomas P. Garvey, L. S. Haskins, B. J. Kneeland, William H. Langdon, M. A. Lowe, William H. Lowe, N. J. Stantorf and Gilbert Stuart met in Seneca to form the Crawford County Horse Breeders Association. |
| Brindley | John, Sr. | KC, p1c2, 6/8/1899 | Recently died in Hickory Grove, Grant Co. Aged 80 years. Lived in Grant Co. for nearly 50 years. He was father of Joseph and Edward E. of Crawford Co. |
| Brindley | Joshua | KC, p1c2, 4/17/1902 | Graduated from Haney Valley schools. |
| Brindley | William | KC, p1c2, 11/2/1899 | Recently died. Funeral held in Boscobel. |
| Brisbois | H. | KC, p8c3, 11/28/1901 | Recently died in a hospital for the insane. Remains were brought to Prairie du Chien. |
| Brittner | Henry | KC, p8c3, 4/1/1897 | Recently married. Bride's name not given. Groom from Town of Haney. |
| Brock | Cora | KC, p1c5, 2/9/1899 | Taught school in Haney in 1899. E. E. Brindley, Crawford County Superintendent of Schools published a comprehensive list of all teachers in the county. |
| Brock | J. | KC, p5c3, 5/20/1897 | Issues of fact for jury to be heard in the May term of the Crawford County Court. Henry Green vs. J. Brock. |
| Brock | Joe, Mrs. | KC, p8c4, 2/4/1897 | Resided in Town of Scott. Went to Nebraska where her father recently died. |
| Brock | Mrs. | KC, p8c4, 2/22/1900 | Funeral held Feb. 16, 1900. She was from McGregor. Nee Cole. She was sister-in-law of Mrs. Charles Cole of Lowertown. |

Genealogical Gleanings From Early Newspapers for Residents In and Near
Crawford County, Wisconsin, 1897-1902

| LAST NAME | FIRST NAME | NEWSPAPER PAGE/COLUMN MONTH/DAY/YEAR | GENEALOGICAL DATA |
|---|---|---|---|
| Brock | Mattie | KC, p1c2, 3/16/1899 | Married Dennis Posey on Mar. 13, 1899 at the Boscobel Congregational Church. Bride from Haney. |
| Brockway | boy | KC, p5c3, 5/3/1900 | Son recently born to Ed Brockway of Mt. Sterling. |
| Brockway | Ed | KC, p5c3, 3/16/1899 | Married Susie George of Mar. 15, 1899. (Bride may be from Mt. Sterling area.) |
| Brockway | | KC, p5c3, 8/9/1900 | The infant child of Ed Brockway recently died in Mt. Sterling. |
| Brodt | Taylor | KC, p8c4, 8/21/1902 | Organized a Yeoman Lodge in Prairie du Chien. From Bagley, WI (per KC, p5c4, 9/11/1902). |
| Bronson | Art | KC, Supp., 12/18/1902 | Crawford County Soldiers Relief Committee provided funds to Art Bronson of Prairie du Chien. |
| Bronson | Art | KC, Supp., 12/20/1900 | Crawford Co. Soldiers Relief Comm. approved aid to Art Bronson of Prairie du Chien. |
| Bronson | Arthur | KC, Supp., 12/12/1901 | Received funds from the Crawford Co. Soldiers Relief Commission. Resided in Prairie du Chien. |
| Brookins | Daisy | KC, p1c2, 11/21/1901 | Married Ervin Birchard on Nov. 17, 1901 at Gays Mills. Bride from Gays Mills. Groom from Boscobel. Planned to live in Boscobel. |
| Brookins | E. | KC, p1c3, 6/20/1901 | Operated a furniture store in Gays Mills. |
| Brookins | Ralph | KC, Supp., 12/18/1902 | Crawford County Board of Supervisors examined bills in the Justices and Constables' Account for State vs. Ralph Brookins. Ray Lange, J. Milluce and J. L. Stowell were witnesses. |
| Brooks | Mrs. | KC, p5c4, 6/19/1902 | She and son, George, left home in Eastman for a visit in Janesville, their former home. |
| Brooks | Prof. | KC, p5c4, 11/30/1899 | Profs. Brooks and Wilson ("the blind boys") have opened up a carpet-weaving establishment in Eastman. |
| Brose | William | KC, p1c4, 3/9/1899 | Auction sale to be held at home of William Brose of Shanghai Ridge. |
| Brown | (E.?) L. | KC, p1c6, 6/2/1898 | Announced plans to run for Crawford County Register of Deeds. Resided in Town of Clayton. |
| Brown | Andrew | KC, p1c5, 7/10/1902 | Lived in Boydtown. Badly injured in a fight with a neighbor, T. Young. Young hit Brown with a hammer. In critical condition. |
| Brown | Andrew | KC, p1c3, 12/11/1902 | Sold his farm in Steuben. Purchased a quarter section in North Dakota. Received $2000 for his 80 acres in Crawford Co. Paid $4000 for 160 acres in North Dakota. He did not plan to go west to farm the land. |
| Brown | Ann, Mrs. | KC, Supp., 12/29/1898 | Received aid from the Crawford County Soldiers Relief Commission. Resided in Haney. |
| Brown | Ann, Mrs. | KC, Supp., 12/20/1900 | Crawford Co. Soldiers Relief Comm. approved aid to Mrs. Ann Brown of Haney. |
| Brown | boy | KC, p5c4, 5/16/1901 | Son born May 9, 1901 to Frank Brown of Gays Mills. |
| Brown | boy | KC, p1c2, 10/30/1902 | Son born Oct. 30, 1902 to Dell Brown of Wauzeka. Later died, per KC, p1c2, 11/13/1902. |

Genealogical Gleanings From Early Newspapers for Residents In and Near
Crawford County, Wisconsin, 1897-1902

| LAST NAME | FIRST NAME | NEWSPAPER PAGE/COLUMN MONTH/DAY/YEAR | GENEALOGICAL DATA |
|---|---|---|---|
| Brown | boy | KC, p4c2, 12/16/1897 | The infant son of Frank Brown died Dec. 13, 1897 in Gays Mills. |
| Brown | boy | KC, p1c3, 2/16/1899 | Son born Feb. 13, 1899 to Dell Brown of Wauzeka. Died Wednesday when 3 days old, per KC, p4c3, 2/16/1899. |
| Brown | Charles | KC, Supp., 12/18/1902 | Crawford County Board of Supervisors allowed expenses in the Matter of Charles Brown, Insane. |
| Brown | Dell | KC, p1c3, 4/5/1900 | Sold his butcher shop in Wauzeka to W. A. Steisel of Hawkeye, IA. |
| Brown | Dell | KC, p1c2, 6/7/1900 | Resided in Wauzeka. Visited by uncle, John Hammond, who has lived in Utah for many years. |
| Brown | Dell | KC, p1c5, 6/21/1900 | Brown and Ben Pittzenberger raked a Revolutionary War musket from the Mississippi River while clam fishing near the mouth of the Wisconsin River. |
| Brown | Dell | KC, p4c2, 9/5/1901 | Received a liquor license in Wauzeka. |
| Brown | Dr. | KC, p1c6, 4/7/1898 | Elected Trustee for the Village of Soldiers Grove. |
| Brown | Fannie | KC, p5c2, 4/8/1897 | Teacher. Fannie Brown of Bell Center and her brother, George emigrated to Countney, ND. |
| Brown | Fannie | KC, p5c3, 7/71898 | Returned to Bell Center after spending the last year teaching in North Dakota. |
| Brown | Frank C. | KC, p4c2, 2/11/1897 | Married Eva Barker on Feb. 7, 1897. Bride and groom may have been from Gays Mills. Justice Stowell officiated. |
| Brown | girl | KC, p1c3, 5/3/1900 | Daughter born Saturday to Dell Brown of Wauzeka area. |
| Brown | H. B. | KC, p1c5, 11/30/1899 | H. B. Brown and G. F. Dennis dissolved their partnership in a farm machinery and twine business. |
| Brown | Henry | KC, p5c2, 7/7/1898 | Married Lydia Hall on July 3, 1898. (Bride and groom may be from Readstown. Bride's surname may be Hail.) |
| Brown | Henry | KC, p5c2, 7/71898 | Married Lydia Hall last Sunday per Readstown news column. Rev. George W. Nuzum officiated. |
| Brown | Ina | KC, p8c3, 5/20/1897 | Died May 1, 1897 at home in Bell Center. Born in Town of Clayton, Crawford Co. WI on March 26, 1863. Married April 14, 1883 to Ernest D. Stevens. Had 2 daughters, one already deceased. Survived by daughter, mother, father, 2 sisters and 2 brothers. |
| Brown | J. F., Dr. | KC, p5c3, 6/17/1897 | Resided in Soldiers Grove. Father, also a physician, arrived from Maine to visit for the summer. |
| Brown | Jim | KC, p8c6, 6/5/1902 | Placed in jail. He was a Sioux Indian who lived with his squaw in a wigwam below De Soto in the Winnebago settlement. While intoxicated he stabbed and clubbed his wife and then through her into Mississippi River. An Indian boy saved her. Brown was given a 20 day sentence. The wife died on Wednesday. Brown held for murder. He was 65 years old. |
| Brown | Jim | KC, Supp., 12/18/1902 | Crawford County Board of Supervisors examined bills in the Justices and Constables' Account for State vs. Jim Brown, Matt. Littlejohn, Albert Henry and George Brown were witnesses. Frank Whitewater was an interpreter. |

Genealogical Gleanings From Early Newspapers for Residents In and Near
Crawford County, Wisconsin, 1897-1902

| LAST NAME | FIRST NAME | NEWSPAPER PAGE/COLUMN MONTH/DAY/YEAR | GENEALOGICAL DATA |
|---|---|---|---|
| Brown | Jim, Mrs. | KC, p8c6, 6/5/1903 | Died from a beating given her by husband. She and husband were Winnebago Indians and lived at an Indian settlement near De Soto. Died June 5, 1902. |
| Brown | L. | KC, p1c4, 5/3/1900 | Visited by daughter, Mrs. Charles Keyes of Hartford, CT; grandson, Clarence Keyes; daughter, Mrs. W. R. Dowling of Norcacor, KS; and daughter, Mrs. G. F. Dennis of Wauzeka. |
| Brown | Lebbeus | KC, p1c3, 12/18/1902 | Died Nov. 21, 1902 at home in Town of Scott. Born June 17, 1825 at Avon, Lorain Co., OH. Married Sarah A. Moore on Aug. 30, 1846 at Harbor Creek, Erie Co., PA. In 1851 moved family to Ohio. Moved to Geneva, IL for a short time. Moved April 1855 to Georgetown, WI, where he ran a store. Went to Boscobel when Georgetown moved to Boscobel. Survived by wife and 4 children: Mrs. W. R. Dowling of Norcatur, KS; Charles E. Brown of Scott; Mrs. C. R. Keyes of Hartford CT and Mrs. G. F. Dennis of Wauzeka. One child died earlier. Funeral conducted by the Rev. William Shepherd of Boscobel Methodist Episcopal Church. |
| Brown | M. E. | KC, p4c2, 12/30/1897 | Merchant in Town of Scott. Carried a "fine display of Christmas goods." |
| Brown | Marve | KC, Supp., 12/18/1902 | Crawford County Soldiers Relief Committee provided funds to Marve Brown of Bell Center. |
| Brown | Mrs. | KC, p5c4, 3/20/1902 | Resided in North Clayton. Visited daughter, Mrs. Ernie Shaw of Barnum. |
| Brown | Mrs. | KC, p5c2, 8/11/1898 | From Bell Center. Took daughter, Anna, to Chicago to get care for lameness from Dr. Dowie, a faith healer. |
| Brown | Ninn | KC, p4c3, 6/2/1898 | Traveled to Bell Center from Iowa to pay a surprise visit to parents. |
| Brown | Otto | KC, p1c5, 3/31/1898 | Joined Fisk & Weldon Orchestra. Played cornet. Resided in Viroqua. |
| Brown | Robert, Mr. and Mrs. | KC, p1c3, 7/19/1900 | Arrived from Janesville to visit Mr. Brown's brother, Dell Brown of Wauzeka, and Mrs. Brown's father, John Lagamann. |
| Brown | S. L. | KC, p5c1, 2/18/1897 | Elected an officer in Utica Farmers' Mutual Insurance Co. Resided in Town of Clayton. |
| Brown | S. L. | KC, Supp. 10/27/1898 | Nominated by the Crawford County Republican Party for the office of Representative. Resident of Town of Clayton for 40 years. Moved here in 1858 with his parents. Served on County Board and in town affairs in many positions. (Picture, short bio. and character sketch provided.) |
| Brown | S. L. | KC, Supp., 12/19/1901 | In 1898 an Agricultural and Driving Park Assoc. was organized in Gays Mills by S. L. Brown J. A Hays, G. L. Miller, A. Peterson, and W. H. Thomson. |
| Brudes | Carrie | KC, Supp., 12/12/1901 | Carrie Brudes of West Prairie attended the summer Teacher's Institute in Soldiers Grove. |
| Brudos | Ellen | KC, p5c4, 5/29/1902 | Ellen Brudos of West Prairie attended a teacher institute in Crawford County. |

Genealogical Gleanings From Early Newspapers for Residents In and Near
Crawford County, Wisconsin, 1897-1902

| LAST NAME | FIRST NAME | NEWSPAPER PAGE/COLUMN MONTH/DAY/YEAR | GENEALOGICAL DATA |
|---|---|---|---|
| Brumfield | Mr. | KC, p5c5, 2/14/1901 | Arrived from Ohio to visit a brother in Barnum. |
| Brunson | Arthur | KC, Supp., 12/29/1898 | Received aid from the Crawford County Soldiers Relief Commission. Resided in Prairie du Chien. |
| Bryan | E. C. | KC, p1c2, 9/16/1897 | His home in Marietta was burglarized. Two suits of clothing, revolver and a razor taken. Burglars caught in Riverview, Richland Co. |
| Bryant | Clarence | KC, p5c2, 7/14/1898 | Letter written by Bryant on life at Camp Douglas published. Member of Co. C, 4th Reg. WI Vol. |
| Bryant | Charles | KC, p8c4, 11/13/1902 | In the November term of Crawford County Circuit Court, State vs. Charles Bryant and M. Monahan, case was continued. |
| Bryant | Charles | KC, Supp., 12/18/1902 | Crawford County Board of Supervisors allowed expenses in the Criminal Case, State vs. Charles Bryant and Mike Monahan. |
| Bryant | Charles | KC, Supp., 12/18/1902 | Crawford County Board of Supervisors allowed expenses in the Criminal Case, State vs. Charles Bryant and Ray Wells on Requisition. |
| Bryant | Charles | KC, Supp., 12/18/1902 | Crawford County Board of Supervisors examined bills in the Justices and Constables' Account for State vs. Charles Bryant and Ray Wells. James W. Quinn, Frank Portcamp and Charles Flucke were witnesses. |
| Buchanan | Josie | KC, p4c4, 11/10/1898 | Issues of Default heard in the November term of the Crawford County Circuit Court. Levi Bros. & Co. vs. Josie Buchanan. |
| Buckmaster | | KC, p1c6, 5/19/1898 | Issue of Law for Court to be heard in the May term of the Crawford County Circuit Court. D. R. Lawrence vs. E. Stickler and Buckmaster et al. |
| Buckmaster | Charles | KC, p1c4, 3/13/1902 | Returned to Bell Center after visiting his farm in South Dakota. |
| Buckmaster | George | KC, p1c4, 3/8/1900 | Son of O. P. Peck of Boydtown. (notes not clear) |
| Buckmaster | George | KC, p1c2, 8/21/1902 | George Buckmaster and Lee Dunbar went to North Dakota to help with the harvest. |
| Buckmaster | H. | KC, Supp., 12/12/1901 | State vs. H. Buckmaster and Scott Vanderport heard in Crawford Co. Court. |
| Buckmaster | H. | KC, Supp., 12/12/1901 | State vs. H. Buckmaster and S. Vanderpost heard in Crawford Co. Court. Witnesses were Elisha Hubanks, Albert Hubanks, Walter Porter, Silas Garner, Elmer Garner, Chauncey Steele, George Stantorf, Dave Coleman and Charles Welch. |
| Buckmaster | Henry | KC, p1c3, 5/22/1902 | Returned from Des Moines with his mother where they had gone to consult medical specialists for cancer. Physicians spoke encouragingly and they hope to cure it without the knife. |
| Buckmaster | Henry | KC, p8c3, 11/16/1899 | Plaintiff did not appear in the case Andrew LaGeune vs. Henry Buckmaster and P. W. Redfield. Plaintiff will have to pay costs to continue the same. Case heard at the November term of the Crawford County Circuit Court. |

Genealogical Gleanings From Early Newspapers for Residents In and Near
Crawford County, Wisconsin, 1897-1902

| LAST NAME | FIRST NAME | NEWSPAPER PAGE/COLUMN MONTH/DAY/YEAR | GENEALOGICAL DATA |
|---|---|---|---|
| Buckmaster | Henry | KC, Supp., 12/12/1901 | State vs. Henry Buckmaster and Scott Vanderport heard in Crawford County Court. Witnesses were Albert McDowell, Wilbert McDowell, John Mullikin, Dave Mullikin, Elmer Ellis and Alanson Taft, Jr. |
| Buckmaster | J. | KC, p5c4, 3/1/1900 | Buckmaster and Maud Lathrop won a prize for "most prettily dressed" at a masquerade ball given by C. Haggerty and J. Rhinehart in Gays Mills. Fred Rhinehart and Clara Wheeler won a prize for comical dress. |
| Buckmaster | J., Mrs. | KC, p4c4, 5/15/1902 | Had a foreign growth on her face. Her son, Henry, of Petersburg and Dr. William Smith of Mt. Sterling took her to Des Moines to see specialists. It was probably cancer. |
| Buckmaster | Jesse | KC, p1c3, 9/22/1898 | Died Sept. 16, 1898 at residence in Crow Hollow, near Petersburg. Aged over 80 years. He was an early settler in the area. Survived by wife and children: Dawson, Charles, Henry, Mrs. Henry Hamilton, Mrs. Elliot and Mrs. P. M. Peck. These children lived nearby. Other children live out of state. |
| Buckmaster | Jessie | KC, p5c3, 5/20/1897 | Default case to be heard in the May term of the Crawford County Court. Jessie Buckmaster and Catherine Buckmaster his wife, Charles Buckmaster and Amelia Buckmaster his wife and Henry Buckmaster. |
| Buckmaster | Maud | KC, p5c3, 2/8/1900 | Employed at the hotel in Gays Mills. |
| Buckmaster | William | KC, p1c3, 8/8/1901 | William Buckmaster, Norm Newcomb, Walt Newcomb, Ernest Ward, James Ward, Alonzo Ward and Ben Jones left Boydtown to help with the harvest in southern Minnesota. |
| Buckmaster | William | KC, Supp., 12/29/1898 | Crawford Co. Board of Supervisors approved Justices and Constables' expenses related to the case, State vs. William Buckmaster. |
| Bull | boy | KC, p5c3, 7/7/1898 | Son born July 3, 1898 to Frank Bull of Lynxville. |
| Bull | John | KC, p7c2, 10/13/1898 | Died last Wednesday of suicide in Prairie du Chien. Brother of Norman Bull. Born Oct. 2, 1822 in Xenia, OH. Buried in Lowertown Cem. |
| Bull | John | KC, Supp., 12/29/1898 | Crawford Co. Board of Supervisors approved Justices and Constables' expenses related to the Inquest of John Bull. Mrs. R. Rittenhouse and Dr. Rowley were witnesses. |
| Bump | Flora | KC, p8c3, 6/14/1900 | Married Charles Patalaff on June 5, 1900. Bride from Cripple Creek, CO. Groom was mayor of Prairie du Chien. |
| Bunnel | Ben | KC, p5c3, 2/15/1900 | Arrived from North Dakota to visit relatives in Steuben area. |
| Bunnell | Benjamin H. | KC, p5c1, 4/15/1897 | Married Mrs. Edith Logan on Feb. 27. 1897. Bride and groom from Marietta. |
| Bunnell | Benjamin H. | KC, p5c1, 4/8/1897 | Married Edith Logan on Mar. 27, 1897 at home of the groom. Bride and groom were from Marietta. J. P. McKinney, J. P. officiated. |
| Burdick | W. E. | KC, p8c3, 7/3/1902 | Recently married Mattie Loveland. Bride was the daughter of A. B. Loveland of Prairie du Chien. The groom was from La Crosse. Planned to live in La Crosse. |

Genealogical Gleanings From Early Newspapers for Residents In and Near
Crawford County, Wisconsin, 1897-1902

| LAST NAME | FIRST NAME | NEWSPAPER PAGE/COLUMN MONTH/DAY/YEAR | GENEALOGICAL DATA |
|---|---|---|---|
| Burgess | Amelia | KC, p4c2, 1/21/1897 | Married Bert Hiers several weeks ago. Bride and groom may be from Town of Eastman. |
| Burgess | Jo. Fred | KC, p5c4, 11/28/1901 | Recently died in Sergeant Bluff, IA. Aged 28 years, 2 months and 26 days. He was the son of Prof. And Mrs. J. F. Burgess. Married Mary Charlotte Dick on Aug. 9, 1900. They lived in California Junction. |
| Burk | A. J. | KC, p4c1, 12/2/1897 | From Soldiers Grove. Suffered a partial paralytic stroke. |
| Burk | P., Mrs. | KC, p1c4, 12/26/1901 | Funeral held on Dec. 25, 1901 at Cross Plains. She was the aunt of Thomas Murphy of Knapps Creek. |
| Burk | | KC, Supp., 12/29/1898 | Crawford Co. Board of Supervisors approved Justices and Constables' expenses related to the case, State vs. Burk. The witnesses were Joseph Burk, L. Burk, J. M. Burk, Thomas Burk and M. Robinson. |
| Burke | Patrick | KC, p8c4, 7/26/1900 | Married Mrs. Barton on July 24, 1900. Bride from Richland County. |
| Burke | Patrick | KC, p1c2, 6/8/1899 | Sold farm located 7 m. north of Prairie du Chien. Planned to sell his stock, implements and household goods at auction. |
| Burkhard | Caroline | KC, p8c3, 7/11/1901 | Married Edward Ziel on July 8, 1901. |
| Burns | Christopher | KC, Supp., 12/29/1898 | Crawford Co. Board of Supervisors approved Justices and Constables' expenses related to the case, State vs. Christopher Burns. |
| Burns | Clara, Miss | KC, p5c3, 11/13/1902 | Guest of honor at a party held by Mrs. J. A. Haggerty of Ferryville. Miss Burns planned to leave area to go to her father's home in North Carolina. |
| Burns | Edward | KC, Supp., 12/18/1902 | Crawford County Board of Supervisors examined bills in the Justices and Constables' Account for State vs. Edward Burns. |
| Burns | Fay | KC, p5c3, 7/17/1902 | Lived in Chadbourn, NC. Visited his mother, Mrs. Mark Ames of Ferryville. Continued his travels in Minnesota. |
| Burns | Frank, Mrs. | KC, p1c2, 12/7/1899 | Died Dec. 5, 1899 at Elsie, NB. Born in Crawford Co. She was sister of W. R. Graves of Prairie du Chien and Joe Graves of Haney. Daughter of Mrs. H. Graves of Haney (per Dec. 21, 1899 issue, p1c2.) |
| Burns | James | KC, Supp., 12/12/1901 | State vs. James Burns heard in Crawford Co. Court. Witnesses were Mary Rathburn, Frank Rathburn, John Rathburn, Albert Kalinn, John Stackland, Thomas Welch, Herman Rhein, Dan Higgins, Charles Lindner, T. Klucka, George Fairfield, J. C. Rowley, George Ingles, Ed Ziel, Jerry Higgins, Charles Flueke, (Pat?) McGaughey, James Venish and Emily Venish. |
| Burns | James | KC, Supp., 12/18/1902 | Crawford County Board of Supervisors examined bills in the Justices and Constables' Account for State vs. James Burns 1901. William Smith, Mary Lessard, Edna Loovis, Nettie Loovis and Fred Richards were witnesses. |

Genealogical Gleanings From Early Newspapers for Residents In and Near
Crawford County, Wisconsin, 1897-1902

| LAST NAME | FIRST NAME | NEWSPAPER PAGE/COLUMN MONTH/DAY/YEAR | GENEALOGICAL DATA |
|---|---|---|---|
| Burns | L. H. | KC, Supp., 12/18/1902 | Crawford County Board of Supervisors examined bills in the Justices and Constables' Account for State vs. L. H. Burns and D. R. Mullikin. Elden Haggerty, Samuel Noble, Delos Bateman, John Abrams, Oscar Burns, Peter Reynolds and David Mullikin were witnesses. |
| Burns | Mary | KC, p8c3, 3/4/1897 | Married William McManus on Mar. 1, 1897. Bride and groom were from Rising Sun. |
| Burns | Mary | KC, p1c3, 5/9/1901 | Married William Mahan on May 6, 1901. Bride daughter of Mrs. M. A. Burns of Rising Sun and sister of Rose Burns of Wauzeka. Groom son of William Mahan, deceased. |
| Burns | Rose | KC, p1c2, 5/24/1900 | Employed at the Kickapoo Chief. On vacation at her home in Rising Sun. |
| Burns | William | KC, Supp., 12/12/1901 | State vs. William Burns heard in Crawford County Court. Witnesses were J. M. Stulka and George Fogel. |
| Burrel | Agnes | KC, p8c4, 2/14/1901 | Married James Norris on Feb. 6, 1901 at St. Gabriel's Church. Bride and groom from Bridgeport. Planned to live at Wright's Ferry. |
| Burrell | Joseph | KC, p1c4, 1/16/1902 | Farmer from Bridgeport. Son of John Burrell. Took a claim in Dakota. Left his farm in Wisconsin in the hands of his younger brother. |
| Burris | Hattie | KC, p1c4, 9/7/1899 | Resident of Boscobel. Hired to teach at the Woodman School. |
| Burrows | George W. | KC, p5c3, 3/11/1897 | Died Tuesday at home of his aunt, Mrs. Racey of Wauzeka. Resided in Richland Co. Aged 42 years. Survived by wife, 4 children and brother, Charles W. Burrows. |
| Burt | H. F. | KC, p1c4, 10/14/1897 | From Bloomington. His 8-year-old son accidentally shot little sister in right temple. Wound is not dangerous. |
| Burton | C. C. | KC, p1c3, 12/27/1900 | Former resident of Seneca. Now lives in Sheridan, WY. |
| Burton | C. C. | KC, p1c4, 5/10/1900 | Recently departed Town of Seneca for new home in Sheridan, WY. |
| Burton | Charles C. | KC, p5c3, 3/21/1901 | Arrived from Sheridan, WY to visit relatives in Seneca. |
| Burton | Charles, Mrs. | KC, p1c6, 10/28/1897 | Died Oct. 19, 1897 in Seneca. Nee Kate Joy. Married Charles Burton 2 years ago. Mother of 1 child, 7 months old. |
| Burton | Jim | KC, p5c3, 3/13/1902 | Departed Seneca for North Dakota. |
| Burton | Jim | KC, p4c2, 4/7/1898 | Jim Burton and D. Scoville left Seneca for Dakota. |
| Burton | John | KC, p5c3, 4/19/1900 | Planned to leave Town of Seneca for new home in Dakota. |
| Burton | Wilfred Clarence | KC, p8c4, 3/11/1897 | Born Tuesday in Seneca to C. C. Burton. |
| Busch | Rosie | KC, p8c3, 12/6/1900 | Married John Pitzer on Dec. 4, 1900. Bride from Prairie du Chien. Groom from Grant Co. |

Genealogical Gleanings From Early Newspapers for Residents In and Near
Crawford County, Wisconsin, 1897-1902

| LAST NAME | FIRST NAME | NEWSPAPER PAGE/COLUMN MONTH/DAY/YEAR | GENEALOGICAL DATA |
|---|---|---|---|
| Busche | Max E. | KC, p8c2, 5/18/1899 | Married Carrie Grelle on May 16, 1899 at the Catholic parsonage in Prairie du Chien. Bride was daughter of ex-Mayor, Charles Grelle, of Prairie du Chien and sister of Emma and M. Grelle. Groom from St. Paul. He was the brother of Alex and Walter Busche. |
| Bush | Caroline, Mrs. | KC, p1c5, 8/22/1901 | Died August 19, 1901 in Wauzeka area. Born December 13, 1864 in Wauzeka as Caroline Kuchenbecker. Married William Herold on February 2, 1884. Three of 4 children from marriage survive. First husband died about 12 years ago. Married William Bush on December 13, 1893. This union produced 2 more children. |
| Bush | Peter W. | KC, p5c4, 7/12/1900 | Died June 16, 1900 at Town of Marietta. Aged 66 years. Husband of S. L. Bush. Buried in Boydtown Cemetery. |
| Bushey | | KC, p5c1, 2/10/1898 | Infant child of S. Bushey of Eastman was recently buried. |
| Butler | George | KC, p1c4, 7/29/1897 | Married Susan Cotton on July 27, 1897 in Prairie du Chien. Bride from Prairie du Chien. Groom from North McGregor, IA. |
| Butler | William Allen | KC, p1c6, 11/4/1897 | Issue of fact for court to be heard at the Nov. term of the Circuit Court in Crawford County. Lowell Lathrop vs. William Allen Butler. |
| Butt | W. E., Dr. | KC, p1c3, 2/10/1898 | Recently moved to La Farge to practice medicine. Lived in Fox Lake for last 3 years. "'Tom' is well known to many of our readers, having served a year as principal of the Mt. Sterling school." He was the son of Col. C. M. Butt of Viroqua. |
| Butt | W. E., Dr. | KC, p8c4, 5/31/1901 | Married Nellie M. Wagner on May 28, 1900 at the W. H. Thompson residence. Bride from Hillsboro. Groom from La Farge. He was son of Col. C. M. Butt of Viroqua. |
| Byers | Jack | KC, Supp., 12/18/1902 | Crawford County Soldiers Relief Committee provided funds to Jack Byers of Scott. |
| Cahill | Chas., Mrs. | KC, p1c3, 4/1/1897 | Remains brought to Prairie du Chien from New Ashton, ND last Wednesday. Buried at St. Gabriel's Catholic Church. She was a former resident of Dutch Ridge. |
| Calahan | John | KC, p8c3, 9/5/1901 | Died Aug. 30, 1901. Formerly from Prairie du Chien. Buried in Catholic Cemetery, Prairie du Chien. |
| Calkins | A. D. | KC, p1c3, 6/20/1901 | Opened a new jewelry shop in Wauzeka. |
| Calkins | A. D. | KC, p1c4, 7/11/1901 | Married on July 1, 1901 in Viola. |
| Callaway | J. M. | KC, p5c3, 4/29/1897 | Died Thursday. Resided in Marietta. Aged 87. Funeral held in Boscobel. |

Genealogical Gleanings From Early Newspapers for Residents In and Near
Crawford County, Wisconsin, 1897-1902

| LAST NAME | FIRST NAME | NEWSPAPER PAGE/COLUMN MONTH/DAY/YEAR | GENEALOGICAL DATA |
|---|---|---|---|
| Callaway | J. M. | KC, p1c4, 5/6/1897 | Died April 22, 1897 in Marietta. Born Nov. 25, 1809 in Franklin Co., VA. Lived in Missouri from 1830 to 1846. Moved to Iowa Co, WI in 1846. Married Margaret Daily on July 23, 1847. In 1856 moved to Henrietta, Richland Co. In 1866 moved to Marietta, Crawford Co. Survived by wife and 9 children: Joel of Ravenna, NB; Millard of Boscobel; J. Victor of Prairie du Chien; Frank C and Douglas of Marietta; Mrs. Jennie Baker of Soldiers Grove; Mrs. Ruth Putnam of Madison, WI; Mrs. Dolly Frame of La Crosse and Mrs. May Lambrecht of Meta, WA. |
| Callaway | J. V. | KC, p5c4, 11/2/1899 | Operated a lumber yard in Petersburg. |
| Callaway | J. V. | KC, p1c6, 6/2/1898 | Expected to run for re-election as Crawford County Register of Deeds. |
| Callinan | John | KC, p8c4, 3/30/1899 | Died Mar. 20, 1899 in Madison, SD. Interred in Prairie du Chien Catholic Cemetery. Born near Montreal, Canada in June 22, 1842. Moved to Prairie du Chien in 1860. Moved to South Dakota in 1884. Married Ellen Gilmartin of Prairie du Chien in 1864. Survived by 4 of 5 children: Francis of Minneapolis and Edward, Margaret and John of Madison, SD. Mrs. Callinan died in 1892. In 1894 he remarried to Mrs. Catharine Hines of Madison, SD. He was brother-in-law of Capt. P. and Dennis Gilmartin of Prairie du Chien. |
| Calloway | Grace | KC, Supp., 12/12/1901 | Attended a Teacher's Institute in Crawford County in 1901. Resided in Millett. |
| Cameron | Mr. | KC, p5c5, 1/25/1900 | Died Jan. 15, 1900. He was father of M. J. Cameron of Gays Mills. Buried in Chicago. |
| Campbell | | KC, p5c4, 1/10/1901 | One of the twin babies recently born to N. Campbell of Gays Mills died. |
| Campbell | C. E., Mrs. | KC, p4c2, 5/19/1898 | Departed home in Eastman for Yankton, SD to visit sister, Miss Louise Alder. |
| Campbell | Charles | KC, Supp., 12/29/1898 | Crawford Co. Board of Supervisors approved Justices and Constables' expenses related to the case, State vs. (Charles Campbell?). |
| Campbell | Fred | KC, p5c3, 8/24/1899 | Resided in Courtland, MN. Visited mother, Mrs. Nettie Campbell of Poplar Ridge area. |
| Campbell | girl | KC, p1c3, 8/18/1898 | The daughter of Wallace Campbell of Marietta died last Wednesday at age 2 years. Died of cholera. Funeral held at Maple Ridge Church by Rev. Cook. |
| Campbell | Harriet A. | KC, p8c2, 1/19/1899 | Died Jan. 13, 1899 at Prairie du Chien. Born Mar. 7, 1855 in Arena, Iowa Co., WI. Nee Coulson. Married William M. Campbell on Jan. 15, 1878 and moved to Prairie du Chien. Member of the Congregational Church. Survived by 5 sons, 1 daughter, mother, 4 sisters and 2 brothers. Husband and 1 son deceased. Many names given in the obituary. |
| Campbell | Herbert | KC, Supp., 12/12/1901 | Attended a Teacher's Institute in Crawford County in 1901. Resided in Steuben. |

Genealogical Gleanings From Early Newspapers for Residents In and Near
Crawford County, Wisconsin, 1897-1902

| LAST NAME | FIRST NAME | NEWSPAPER PAGE/COLUMN MONTH/DAY/YEAR | GENEALOGICAL DATA |
|---|---|---|---|
| Campbell | Isabella | KC, p5c1, 2/3/1898 | Died Jan. 27, 1898 in Eastman. Born Mar. 29, 1826 in Ireland. Emigrated to New Brunswick when 3 with parents, Mr. and Mrs. Nelson. Married James Campbell who died 6 years ago. Moved to Wisconsin 40 years ago. Survived by 10 of 11 children: Edward, James, Charles, Mrs. Maggie Banmeister of Boscobel, Mrs. Belle Bonney of N.D., Mrs. Letitia Thompson, Mrs. Ellen Wallin, Mrs. Ida Finney, Mrs. Julia Bonney and Mrs. Sarah Thomas of Washington. |
| Campbell | Leila | KC, p5c3, 6/20/1901 | Graduated from Steuben schools. |
| Campbell | Robert | KC, p8c4, 4/4/1901 | Campbell and family returned to Steuben after vacationing in California, Colorado and Mexico. Children stayed with their uncle, James Smethurst in Odell, NB. |
| Campbell | Robert | KC, p5c3, 12/6/1900 | Family reunion held on Thanksgiving Day at Robert Campbell residence in Steuben. Those present were W. G. Campbell and family of Soldiers Grove, Lee Wannemaker, Jim Campbell, Robert Guthrie and families of Steuben, Charles Smethurst and family of Eastman, Thomas Campbell of Darlington and Wallace Campbell of Maple Ridge. All the Campbell brothers and sisters were present except a half-sister who lived in Scotland. |
| Campbell | Robert | KC, Supp., 12/19/1901 | Robert Campbell was a large live stock dealer in Steuben. Established the business about 1890. |
| Campbell | W. G., Atty. | KC, p1c3, 10/19/1899 | Resided in Soldiers Grove. Went to Kansas to sell Kansas farmland for J. W. Fritz of Warner, WI. Campbell planned to visit Oklahoma, Alabama (where he has a sister), Mississippi and Texas. |
| Campbell | Wallace | KC, p5c3, 8/21/1902 | Proprietor of Steuben's hotel. |
| Campbell | Wallace | KC, p1c6, 4/7/1898 | Elected Assessor for the Town of Marietta. |
| Campbell | Wallace | KC, p5c5, 4/5/1900 | Elected assessor in Marietta. |
| Campbell | Wallace, Mrs. | KC, p1c2, 6/2/1898 | Traveled from Marietta to Rock Island, IL to visit her sister. |
| Campbell | William | KC, p8c3, 11/21/1901 | Married Josephine Brainerd on Nov. 16, 1901. Bride from Prairie du Chien. Groom from Milwaukee. Bride daughter of Conductor E. C. Brainerd. Planned to live in Fond du Lac. |
| Campbell | William, Mrs. | KC, p1c2, 6/5/1902 | Lived in Prairie du Chien. Visited her parents, Mr. and Mrs. J. P. Kazda of Wauzeka. |
| Cane (Kane?) | Cornelius | KC, p1c5, 6/1/1899 | The May term of the Crawford County Circuit Court closed. In the case, Cornelius Cane vs. Ed Wallin and J. N. Kast, judgement against Wallin for $1. |
| Canfield | Francis, Mrs. | KC, p4c3, 12/13/1900 | Departed Mt. Sterling to rejoin her husband in Shrieveport, IA. |
| Canfield | N. F. | KC, Supp., 12/12/1901 | Received funds from the Crawford Co. Soldiers Relief Commission. Resided in Lynxville. |

Genealogical Gleanings From Early Newspapers for Residents In and Near
Crawford County, Wisconsin, 1897-1902

| LAST NAME | FIRST NAME | NEWSPAPER PAGE/COLUMN MONTH/DAY/YEAR | GENEALOGICAL DATA |
|---|---|---|---|
| Canfield | N. F. | KC, Supp., 12/18/1902 | Crawford County Soldiers Relief Committee provided funds to N. F. Canfield of Lynxville. |
| Canfield | Nate | KC, p5c3, 2/8/1900 | Found a valuable pearl in the river. Resided in Lynxville. |
| Cannon | Eliza, Miss | KC, p8c4, 12/14/1899 | Returned to Chicago after attending the funeral of the Hon. James Lawler. Miss Mamie Lawler, who will resume her studies in the Chicago Conservatory of Music, accompanied her. |
| Cantwell | Maggie | KC, p1c4 and p4c2, 9/15/1898 | Married Peter Farris on Sept. 7, 1898 in Boscobel. Bride and groom from Steuben. P. B. Richardson, J.P. officiated. |
| Cantwell | Minnie | KC, p1c2, 11/7/1901 | Married Thomas Farris (probably on Oct. 29, 1901) at Steuben, WI. |
| Cantwell | Minnie | KC, p1c3, 8/10/1899 | Mrs. Maggie Farris, Minnie Cantwell Nellie Cantwell, Earl Kielley and G. W. Farris left Steuben for Countney, ND. "Courtney and vicinity now has a large number of Crawford County people among its inhabitants." |
| Card | Nels, Mrs. | KC, p8c3, 12/14/1899 | Died Dec. 8, 1899 in Prairie du Chien. Buried in Catholic Cemetery. (Surname spelling is questionable.) |
| Cardin | Albert | KC, p8c3, 10/26/1899 | Sold a pearl he found in a clam for $105. Resided in Prairie du Chien area. |
| Cardin | Dan | KC, p8c3, 12/7/1899 | Resided in Prairie du Chien. Found a pearl while clam fishing. Valued at $150. |
| Cardin | Godfray | KC, Supp., 12/29/1898 | Crawford Co. Board of Supervisors approved Justices and Constables' expenses related to the case, State vs. Godfray Cardin and Justice Drummel. The witnesses were G. L. Miller, Joe LaRocke and George Miller. |
| Cardin | Godfrey | KC, Supp., 12/12/1901 | State vs. Godfrey Cardin heard in Crawford Co. Court. |
| Cardin | Louis | KC, p8c3, 9/27/1900 | Died Sept. 25, 1900 in Prairie du Chien. |
| Cardin | Mrs. | KC, p1c4, 9/16/1897 | Died Sept. 10, 1897 at County Poor Farm. Aged nearly 80 years old. Former resident of Prairie du Chien. |
| Cardine | Godfrey | KC, p8c6, 6/5/1902 | Resided in Prairie du Chien. Sold a pearl he found while clam fishing to P. O. Heide for $2000. |
| Carey | George E. | KC, p1c2, 6/17/1897 | Married Olive I. DeLap of Prairie du Chien on June 3, 1897. Groom from McGregor, IA. |
| Carl | Fritz | KC, p8c3, 2/2/1899 | Resided in Bridgeport. Suffered from cancer. |
| Carmack | Frank, Mrs. | KC, p8c2, 7/29/1897 | Died this morning in Lynxville. Son lived in Updegraph, IA. |
| Carmack | Julia | KC, p4c1, 5/20/1897 | Died May 10, 1897 in Lynxville. Aged 65 years. |
| Carpenter | Nora | KC, p4c4, 8/3/1899 | Married W. A. Mills of Wauzeka on Aug. 1, 1899 in Soldiers Grove. Bride from Viola. |
| Carrell | Charles | KC, Supp., 12/18/1902 | Crawford County Soldiers Relief Committee provided funds to Charles Carrell of Soldiers Grove. |

Genealogical Gleanings From Early Newspapers for Residents In and Near
Crawford County, Wisconsin, 1897-1902

| LAST NAME | FIRST NAME | NEWSPAPER PAGE/COLUMN MONTH/DAY/YEAR | GENEALOGICAL DATA |
|---|---|---|---|
| Carrol | John | KC, p5c3, 5/20/1897 | Issues of fact for jury to be heard in the May term of the Crawford County Court. John Carrol vs. Chicago, Burlington & Northern Ry. Co. |
| Carron | L. E., Miss | KC, p7c4, 1/25/1900 | Received marriage license in Crawford Co. L. M. Phillips was the prospective spouse. Bride and groom-to-be from Howard Co., IA. |
| Carson | H. A. | KC, p1c3, 10/14/1897 | Dentist from Boscobel. Kicked to unconsciousness by Marshall Tom Abel at the Richland Center Fair. Carson was ordered to sit down when there was no place to sit on the grand stand. Abel was arrested and paid a fine. |
| Carter | George R., Judge | KC, p1c5, 3/17/1898 | Resided in Lancaster. Determined to be insane and sent to Mendota. |
| Carter | Helen | KC, Supp., 12/12/1901 | Attended a Teacher's Institute in Crawford County in 1901. Resided in Readstown. |
| Case | Edward L. | KC, p7c1, 12/12/1901 | Agreed to pay for the support of his son, Lawrence Case, at the State Hospital for the Insane. |
| Case | Edward L. | KC, Supp., 12/20/1900 | Crawford Co. Board of Supervisors approved bills related to expenses of Edward L. Case, insane. |
| Case | Ella | KC, p1c3, 6/10/1897 | Daughter of Charles Case. Taught piano and guitar in Prairie du Chien. |
| Case | Laura | KC, p8c3, 1/23/1902 | Married Edward P. Sherry on Jan. 22, 1902. Bride daughter of Lawrence Case of Prairie du Chien and sister of Mrs. Carrie Gilchrist. Groom from Milwaukee. Planned to live in Milwaukee. |
| Case | Laura | KC, p1c1, 2/4/1897 | Daughter of L. Case of Prairie du Chien. Starred in the play, "Under the Red Robe" at the Empire Theater in New York City. |
| Case | Lawrence | KC, Supp., 12/12/1901 | Crawford County subpoenaed Lawrence Case regarding financial liability for his son, Edward L. Case at the State Hospital for the Insane. |
| Caskey | W. G. | KC, p8c1, 8/25/1898 | Recently married Flora Barnes, daughter of Mrs. A. S. Barnes of Prairie du Chien. Groom from Oberlin, OH. |
| Casper | Christina | KC, p8c2, 9/2/1897 | Married G. E. Gratton of Prairie du Chien on Aug. 31, 1897. Bride from Cassville. |
| Caswell | E. A. | KC, p1c6, 6/2/1898 | Announced plans to run for Crawford County Register of Deeds. Resided in Town of Utica. |
| Caswell | E. A., Mrs. | KC, p1c4, 1/13/1898 | From Mt. Sterling. Had 2 tumors removed from her breast at a Milwaukee hospital. |
| Caswell | Grace | KC, p5c3, 10/24/1901 | Hired to teach in district 12 near Taft Ridge. |
| Caswell | Grace | KC, Supp., 12/12/1901 | Attended a Teacher's Institute in Crawford County in 1901. Resided in Mount Sterling |
| Cater | William | KC, p5c3, 5/20/1897 | Issues of fact for court to be heard in the May term of the Crawford County Court. William Cater vs. M. B. Seward and William Barney. |
| Cavanaugh | H. P. | KC, p1c2, 11/28/1901 | Chief train dispatcher in Channing, MI. Visited his brother, D. L., in Wauzeka and parents in Muscoda. |

Genealogical Gleanings From Early Newspapers for Residents In and Near
Crawford County, Wisconsin, 1897-1902

| LAST NAME | FIRST NAME | NEWSPAPER PAGE/COLUMN MONTH/DAY/YEAR | GENEALOGICAL DATA |
|---|---|---|---|
| Cavanaugh | W. E. | KC, Supp., 12/29/1898 | Crawford Co. Board of Supervisors approved Justices and Constables' expenses related to the case, State vs. W. E. Cavanaugh. |
| Caya | A. | KC, p6c1, 7/15/1897 | Died July 8, 1897 at home in Lynxville. Survived by wife, 2 sons, 1 sister and several brothers. Funeral held in Seneca. |
| Caya | Antone, Mrs. | KC, p8c3, 11/22/1900 | Died Nov. 17, 1900 at the Surgical Institute. Resident of Lynxville. (This may be Alice Caya mentioned in KC, p8c4, 1/10/1901.) |
| Caya | Antone, Mrs. | KC, p5c3, 11/29/1900 | Resided in Lynxville. Buried Tuesday. |
| Caya | boy | KC, p8c3, 1/5/1899 | Son born last week to Fritz Caya of Lynxville. |
| Caya | Fred | KC, p5c5, 4/5/1900 | Elected clerk in Lynxville. |
| Caya | Fred | KC, Supp., 12/29/1898 | Crawford Co. Board of Supervisors approved Justices and Constables' expenses related to the case, State vs. Fred Caya, Matt Underburger was the witness. |
| Caya | Fritzy | KC, p5c1, 10/20/1898 | Recently married Mable Day. Now live in the Menges building in Lynxville. |
| Caya | infant | KC, p5c3, 9/5/1901 | The infant son of Frank Caya died Saturday in Lynxville. |
| Caya | Louis, Mrs. | KC, p8c4, 8/28/1902 | Died from suicide in Prairie du Chien. Born Virginia Durocher on Sept. 7, 1879 in Town of Eastman. Died Aug. 22, 1902. Married Louis Caya of Prairie du Chien on Nov. 26, 1900 at Cloquet, MN. |
| Caya | Morris | KC, p5c3, 7/24/1902 | Morris Caya, Frank Porter, Frank Vanderbilt, Will Otman, A. M. Laird and Fred Waddle, all of Lynxville, found "good pearls" while clam fishing. |
| Caya | R., Mrs. | KC, p4c1, 9/22/1898 | Traveled to Postville, IA from Lynxville to visit her grandmother. |
| Caya | | KC, p5c4, 11/13/1902 | Infant child of Morris Caya died in Lynxville last week. |
| Cecka | Albert | KC, Supp., 12/12/1901 | State vs. Albert Cecka heard in Crawford Co. Court. Witnesses were Frank Smircina, Frank Uher, Theo. Schreader, W. W. Evans, J. Lechnir, Joe Mara, Frank Fox, C. Grelle, Sr., Fred Shultz, James Garvey, Otto Kieser and Carl Patzlaff. |
| Cecka | Albert | KC, Supp., 12/18/1902 | Crawford County Board of Supervisors examined bills in the Justices and Constables' Account for State vs. Albert Cecka. Martin, Mary and Eva Nolan were witnesses. |
| Cecka | Albert | KC, Supp., 12/18/1902 | Crawford County Board of Supervisors examined bills in the Justices and Constables' Account for State vs. Albert Cecka. John Ziel, Chas. Honzell and Louis Spiker were witnesses. |
| Chabela | Jacob | KC, p5c5, 1/18/1900 | Advertised his shoe and clothing store in Prairie du Chien. |
| Chabela | Stasia | KC, p8c4, 9/12/1901 | Married Joe Valacity at St. Johns Church on Monday (Sept. 7, 1901?) and left for Chicago. |

Genealogical Gleanings From Early Newspapers for Residents In and Near
Crawford County, Wisconsin, 1897-1902

| LAST NAME | FIRST NAME | NEWSPAPER PAGE/COLUMN MONTH/DAY/YEAR | GENEALOGICAL DATA |
|---|---|---|---|
| Chadwick | boy | KC, p5c1, 6/2/1898 | Son born May 25, 1898 to John Chadwick of Barnum. |
| Chadwick | | KC, p5c3, 3/20/1902 | Chadwick family quarantined with small pox at their home on Knapps Creek. |
| Chadwick | John L. | KC, Supp., 4/20/1899 | Died April 13, 1899 in North Clayton. Aged 52 years, 1 month and 2 days. Born in Illinois in 1847. Moved to Wisconsin when a child. Married Adella Brown in 1876. Lived in Barnum until Mar. 4, 1899 when he moved to North Clayton. Survived by 6 of 12 children. Also survived by wife, 1 brother and 5 sisters. |
| Chadwick | Melvin | KC, Supp., 4/20/1899 | Died Mar. 16, 1899 at Soldiers Grove. Aged 9 months and 19 days. Son of John Chadwick. |
| Chadwick | Silas | KC, p5c3, 4/6/1899 | Recently married his former wife in Steuben. |
| Chamberlain | George | KC, p5c2, 12/2/1897 | George Chamberlain, Tom Farris and Earl Kielley of Steuben joined the International Order of Good Templars. |
| Chamberlain | Mertie | KC, p5c3, 2/15/1900 | Employed at the Syverson House (hotel) in Steuben. |
| Chamberlain | Sam | KC, p4c1, 3/18/1897 | Lost a finger while chopping wood. Resided in Steuben. |
| Chamberlain | W. M. | KC, p1c3, 7/29/1897 | Married Estella Chandler on July 26, 1897 in Prairie du Chien. Bride and groom were from Bailey IA. |
| Chambers | Dwight | KC, p8c4, 1/16/1902 | Married Stacia Garvey on Jan. 15, 1902. Bride and groom from Prairie du Chien. Groom son of John Mortimer Chambers. Bride daughter of Mrs. (C?) Garvey and niece of Very Rev. Dean Trant of Racine, WI. |
| Chandler | Estella | KC, p1c3, 7/29/1897 | Married W. M. Chamberlain on July 26, 1897 in Prairie du Chien. Bride and groom were from Bailey IA. |
| Chandler | R., Mrs. | KC, p8c3, 1/7/1897 | Resided in Richland Center. Visited sister, Mrs. J. F. Pier of Eastman. |
| Chandler | W. F. | KC, p5c4, 11/10/1898 | Fire destroyed buildings at the Wisconsin River railroad bridge. Lost all household items. Fire caused by spark from a passing train. |
| Chapek | Emma | KC, p1c3, 10/31/1901 | Took out a claim on 160 acres adjoining her brother in Anamoose, ND. |
| Chapek | Emma | KC, p1c2, 11/3/1898 | Installed as an officer at the International Order of Good Templars (I.O.G.T.) Lodge in Wauzeka. |
| Chapek | F. | KC, p1c2, 12/12/1901 | Sold saloon, house, opera house and barns in Wauzeka to James Tesar. |
| Chapek | Frank | KC, p1c5, 5/2/1901 | Killed 7 wolves in a den near his sheep pasture. |
| Chapek | Frank | KC, p1c2, 7/18/1901 | Traveled from Wauzeka to Ortonville, MN to visit friends and relatives. Saw his brother, Mat, and the Becwar brothers. |

Genealogical Gleanings From Early Newspapers for Residents In and Near
Crawford County, Wisconsin, 1897-1902

| LAST NAME | FIRST NAME | NEWSPAPER PAGE/COLUMN MONTH/DAY/YEAR | GENEALOGICAL DATA |
|---|---|---|---|
| Chapek | Frank, Mr. and Mrs. | KC, p1c4, 11/9/1899 | Resided in Wauzeka. Went out west to visit relatives. Letter they wrote about their experiences was published in newspaper. They visited: brother, Matt, in Ortonville, MN; youngest sister, Mrs. Slama, in Milton, ND (close to Canadian border); 2 sisters at Pisek, Walsh Co., ND ("a thoroughly Bohemian town"). Disliked the alkali water. Noted that though North Dakota was a prohibition state, the people had no trouble getting whatever they wanted. |
| Chapek | John | KC, p1c3, 3/27/1902 | John Chapek and Henry Leefeldt left Wauzeka for their claims in Anamoose, ND. Took 2 carloads of goods, 10 horses, 3 cows, etc. |
| Chapek | John, Sr. | KC, p1c4, 2/23/1899 | Died Feb. 22, 1899 in Eastman. Aged 88 years. Moved to Crawford Co. in 1869. Survived by children: Mrs. Blazek of Eastman; Frank of Wauzeka; Mathias of Ortonville, MN; and Mrs. Solboda, Mrs. Bazal and Mrs. Slama of North Dakota. |
| Chapek | Louisa | KC, p1c5, 5/10/1900 | Married William Stukey of Solon Springs on May 6, 1900. |
| Chapek | Will | KC, p1c3, 2/21/1898 | Played in Chapek's orchestra at area balls. |
| Chapman | Elisha | KC, p1c3, 4/28/1898 | Died April 24, 1898 at home in Boydtown. Survived by wife and 2 sons. Buried in Wauzeka Cemetery. |
| Chapman | G. L. | KC, p8c3, 4/17/1902 | Died April 16, 1902 in Prairie du Chien. Proprietor of the Hub Saloon. |
| Chapman | G. L. | KC, p5c3, 7/12/1900 | New landlord of the Hazen Hotel in Eastman. |
| Chapman | George | KC, p5c4, 4/24/1902 | Resided in Steuben. Daughter, Mrs. Charles _restler of St. Paul, came for a visit. |
| Chapman | George L. | KC, p5c4, 5/29/1902 | The case Wisconsin vs. George L. Chapman for keeping a house of ill fame, was heard at the May term of the Crawford County Circuit Court. Convicted. Nolle prosequi entered by Dist. Atty. |
| Chapman | Leonard | KC, p5c3, 1/25/1900 | Resided in Steuben. Visited sister, Mrs. Davey, near Seneca. |
| Chapman | O. | KC, Supp., 12/19/1901 | O. Chapman operated a livery in Steuben. |
| Chapman | O. D. | KC, p1c3, 12/13/1900 | The O. D. Chapman Post No. 80 of the G. A. R. at Gays Mills elected the following officers: Alex Turk, George Cooper, Loyd Kelley, N. A. Tallman, G. R. Rounds, G. R. Twining, Henry Moon, John Lowe and Charles Rhinehart. |
| Chapman | O. W. | KC, Supp., 12/18/1902 | Crawford County Board of Supervisors examined bills in the Justices and Constables' Account for State vs. O. W. Chapman and Zeph Foust. |
| Chase | Clark | KC, p1c6, 5/19/1898 | Criminal case to be heard in the May term of the Crawford County Circuit Court. State of Wisconsin vs. Clark Chase burglary. |
| Chase | Clark | KC, p4c4, 11/10/1898 | Criminal Issue to be heard in the November term of the Crawford County Circuit Court. State of Wisconsin vs. Clark Chase |

Genealogical Gleanings From Early Newspapers for Residents In and Near
Crawford County, Wisconsin, 1897-1902

| LAST NAME | FIRST NAME | NEWSPAPER PAGE/COLUMN MONTH/DAY/YEAR | GENEALOGICAL DATA |
|---|---|---|---|
| Chase | Clark | KC, Supp., 12/29/1898 | Crawford Co. Board of Supervisors approved Justices and Constables' expenses related to the case, State vs. Clark Chase. The witnesses were Mr. Barnum, Paul Walker, Thomas Murphy, O. J. Day, Frank Webb, Philip Helwig, Frank Smrcina, Sherman Bisbee and others whose names could not be read. |
| Chase | D. S. | KC, p1c4, 7/28/1898 | Bought Chauncey Duncan farm in Town of Scott. As partial payment, traded his property in Prairie du Chien. |
| Chase | Eva | KC, p1c3, 3/4/1897 | Eva Chase of Prairie du Chien started teaching her fifth term in the Cherrier district. |
| Chase | Eva Lyn | KC, p1c5, 2/9/1899 | Taught school in Prairie du Chien in 1899. E. E. Brindley, Crawford County Superintendent of Schools published a comprehensive list of all teachers in the county. |
| Chase | J. W. | KC, p1c5, 6/22/1899 | Planned to move from Wauzeka to La Crosse where he will work in the Burlington shops. |
| Chase | Lulu M. | KC, p8c4, 10/11/1900 | Died Sept. 28, 1900 in Prairie du Chien. Born in Patch Grove on Sept. 2, 1884 to Clark and Laura Chase. Funeral held in the M. E. Church. Buried in Lowertown Cemetery. |
| Chase | Lulu M. | KC, p8c4, 6/21/1900 | Graduated at Wauzeka High School. Class of 1900. |
| Chase | Lulu, Miss | KC, p8c3, 9/27/1900 | Died Sept. 25, 1900 in Prairie du Chien. Aged about 18 years. |
| Chase | Nellie | KC, p8c2, 9/2/1897 | Married Michael Rhyne of St. Paul Park on Sept. 1, 1897 at St. Gabriel's Catholic Church. Bride daughter of C. C. Chase of Prairie du Chien. |
| Chase | | KC, p8c2, 8/24/1899 | Held a family reunion at their home in Prairie du Chien. John Chase of Boston attended. He had moved away 10 years ago. Others that attended were Mr. and Mrs. Neable of Mason City and Mr. and Mrs. Ryan of St. Paul. |
| Chatman | Mr. | KC, p4c2, 4/28/1898 | Recently died. (May have been from Steuben.) |
| Chatterton | W. A. | KC, p1c2, 3/1/1900 | Departed Wauzeka for a new home in Spring Green. |
| Chatterton | W. A. | KC, p5c2, 3/15/1900 | Agent for the C. M. and St. Paul Railroad. |
| Chatterton | W. A. | KC, p4c5, 1/7/1897 | Advertised that he was a Wauzeka dealer in wood ties, agricultural implements and livestock. |
| Chatterton | W. A. | KC, p5c1, 6/10/1897 | Ran a wood and railroad tie business in Crawford County. |
| Chatterton | W. A., Mrs. | KC, p5c1, 6/24/1897 | Entertained her mother, Mrs. P. A. Parsons of Spring Green at her home in Wauzeka. |
| Cheaka | Mary | KC, p8c2, 11/13/1902 | Married Joe Kozelka on Nov. 11, 1902 at the Bohemian Catholic Church. |
| Check | John | KC, p1c6, 4/7/1898 | Elected Supervisor for the Town of Eastman. |
| Cherrier | boy | KC, p8c1, 2/9/1899 | Son born Feb. 2, 1899 to Flavin Cherrier of Prairie du Chien. |
| Cherrier | Comb | KC, p8c2, 10/5/1899 | Came to America over 60 years ago. Near death in Prairie du Chien. |

Genealogical Gleanings From Early Newspapers for Residents In and Near
Crawford County, Wisconsin, 1897-1902

| LAST NAME | FIRST NAME | NEWSPAPER PAGE/COLUMN MONTH/DAY/YEAR | GENEALOGICAL DATA |
|---|---|---|---|
| Cherrier | Cora | KC, p5c3, 3/30/1899 | From Prairie du Chien. Employed in the home of Charles MaGee of Bridgeport. |
| Cherrier | Cora, Miss | KC, p8c3, 5/1/1902 | Died April 28, 1902 in Waterloo, IA. She was the daughter of Adolph Cherrier of Prairie du Chien. |
| Cherrier | Emma | KC, Supp., 12/12/1901 | Attended a Teacher's Institute in Crawford County in 1901. Resided in Prairie du Chien. |
| Cherrier | Laura | KC, Supp., 12/12/1901 | Attended a Teacher's Institute in Crawford County in 1901. Resided in Prairie du Chien. |
| Cherrier | Louis | KC, p7c3, 1/25/1900 | Married Emma Ziel on Jan. 20, 1900 at the Catholic Parsonage. Bride and groom from Prairie du Chien. |
| Cherrier | Will | KC, p8c2, 5/4/1899 | Worked as a baker in Prairie du Chien. Accepted a job on the railroad in Montana. |
| Cherwak | John, Mrs. | KC, p1c2, 2/4/1897 | Died last Thursday in Prairie du Chien. She was Bohemian. |
| Cherwak | Myrtle | KC, p8c2, 12/23/1897 | Died Dec. 13, 1897. Aged 6 months and 2 days. She was daughter of John Cherwak of Prairie du Chien. |
| Chierrier | William O. | KC, p8c4, 4/17/1902 | Funeral held April 14, 1902. Died in a railroad accident in Kalispell, MT. Native of Prairie du Chien. |
| Childs | Harry | KC, Supp., 12/12/1901 | Attended a Teacher's Institute in Crawford County in 1901. Resided in Millett. |
| Childs | Lottie | KC, p5c3, 9/14/1899 | Hired to teach school in Crow Hollow. |
| Childs | Lottie | KC, Supp., 12/12/1901 | Attended a Teacher's Institute in Crawford County in 1901. Resided in Millett. |
| Chilson | Ida M. | KC, p1c2, 9/7/1899 | Married Daniel M. Withee on Aug. 20, 1899 at residence of A. B. Withee. Bride and groom from Seneca. |
| Chitik | Anastacia | KC, p5c4, 10/10/1901 | Married Peter Pivot at the Catholic Church in Wauzeka on Oct. 7, 1901. Bride from Ft. Atkinson, IA. Groom had a brother, Frank, and a sister, Kate. Planned to live in Marietta. |
| Christ | Charles, Mrs. | KC, p1c2, 12/4/1902 | Lived on Maple Ridge. Spent Thanksgiving with sister, Mrs. H. L. Reichmann. |
| Christianson | Andrew | KC, Supp., 12/18/1902 | Per Report on the Committee on Public Property, Crawford Co., Andrew Christianson paid taxes in 1863 on a portion of a larger tract for which no taxes were paid in 1862. The Register of Deeds was authorized to cancel that portion of a deed issued for N.E. 1/4 of the S.E. 1/4 of Sec. 31, Town 11, range 3 for the reason that the taxes were duly paid. |
| Christianson | Martin | KC, Supp., 12/29/1898 | Crawford Co. Board of Supervisors approved payment of expenses in the matter of Martin Christianson, insane. |
| Christie | Lillian, Mrs. | KC, p8c3, 1/2/1902 | Married Patrick W. Connell on Dec. 25, 1901. Bride and groom from Prairie du Chien. |
| Chunot | Anthony | KC, p1c4, 4/5/1900 | Lost a finger from a circle saw on the farm of A. Lemire near Eastman. |
| Churchhill | G. W., Mrs. | KC, p4c2, 8/5/1897 | Died July 20, 1897 at Clay Center, NB. Former resident of Crawford County. |
| Churchhill | Peter | KC, p6c1, 7/1/1897 | Recently died. (Much data lost. Microfilmed page was torn.) Buried in Dickson Cemetery. Services held in Congregational Church. Survived by wife and 2 children. |

Genealogical Gleanings From Early Newspapers for Residents In and Near
Crawford County, Wisconsin, 1897-1902

| LAST NAME | FIRST NAME | NEWSPAPER PAGE/COLUMN MONTH/DAY/YEAR | GENEALOGICAL DATA |
|---|---|---|---|
| Churchill | boy | KC, p4c2, 8/19/1897 | A young son of Mrs. Peter Churchill died Sunday in Lynxville. |
| Churchill | F. B., Mrs. | KC, p1c3, 6/6/1901 | Resided in Clarks, NB. Visited parents, Mr. and Mrs. Smith Haines of Mt. Sterling. |
| Churchill | Frank | KC, p1c3, 2/3/1898 | Recently married Hattie Haines. Bride from Mt. Sterling. Groom from Clay City, NB. |
| Churchill | Frank, Mrs. | KC, p1c3, 10/5/1899 | Resided in Clay Center, NB. Visited with parents, Mr. and Mrs. Smith Haynes of Mt. Sterling. |
| Churchill | Frank, Mrs. | KC, p4c1, 2/10/1898 | Entertained 25 friends before leaving for new home in Nebraska. Husband was a lawyer. |
| Churchill | Hattie, Mrs. | KC, p5c3, 6/20/1901 | Nee Haynes. Arrived from Nebraska to visit her father in Mt. Sterling. Three weeks ago attended the funeral of her sister, Mrs. Bloss, in Janesville, WI. Mother died 2 months ago. |
| Churchill | Isabel | KC, p5c4, 1/24/1901 | Called home from Eastman to help care for her sister, Mrs. Mansfield of (Lynxville?). |
| Churchill | Peter | KC, p8c2, 6/17/1897 | An old resident. Very ill and not expected to last much longer. Mrs. Lawrence went to Stoddard upon hearing the news, per Lynxville news. |
| Churchill | Rebecca, Mrs. | KC, p5c4, 1/9/1902 | Died Dec. 31, 1901 in Steuben. Survived by husband and 5 children. |
| Chynoweth | H. H. | KC, p1c4, 9/29/1898 | At a conference of the Methodist Church held in Eau Claire, H. H. Chynoweth was assigned to Prairie du Chien. |
| Chynoweth | W. H. | KC, p8c4, 9/30/1897 | At a conference of the Methodist Church held in Platteville, W. H. Chynoweth was assigned to Prairie du Chien. |
| Clack | William, Rev. | KC, p8c4, 3/7/1901 | Recently died. Baptist minister. Lived in Milwaukee. Former resident of Prairie du Chien. Buried near his children in Lowertown Cemetery. |
| Clancy | Frank | KC, p4c3, 7/1/1897 | Married Mamie Kane on June 23, 1897 at St. Patrick's Church in Seneca. Planned to live in Soldiers Grove. |
| Clancy | girl | KC, p1c4, 10/24/1901 | Daughter born Oct. 11, 1901 to T. F. Clancy of Soldiers Grove. |
| Clancy | Frank | KC, p1c6, 4/7/1898 | Elected Trustee for the Village of Soldiers Grove. |
| Clark | Auntie | KC, p4c1, 8/19/1897 | Died June 30, 1897 at home of son in Winfield, IA. Aged 95 years. Resident of Town of Eastman where she lived with a niece, Mrs. I. McLusky. |
| Clark | Billy | KC, p5c1, 6/16/1898 | Died in Crawford Co. in 1866. |
| Clark | Etta | KC, p8c4, 2/11/1897 | Resided in De Soto. Sewed for Mrs. King of Ferryville this week. |
| Clark | George, Mrs. | KC, p8c4, 11/23/1899 | Arrived from Chicago to visit her parents, Mr. and Mrs. T. Savage of Prairie du Chien. |
| Clark | H. | KC, p5c4, 1/17/1901 | Resided in Petersburg. Expects to get a patent for a device that carries a lantern on the end of a (wagon) tongue. |
| Clark | H. | KC, p1c2, 4/19/1900 | Departed Petersburg for Chippewa Co., WI to explore opportunities to invest in land. |
| Clark | J. J. | KC, Supp., 12/18/1902 | Crawford County Soldiers Relief Committee provided funds to J. J. Clark of Marietta. |

Genealogical Gleanings From Early Newspapers for Residents In and Near
Crawford County, Wisconsin, 1897-1902

| LAST NAME | FIRST NAME | NEWSPAPER PAGE/COLUMN MONTH/DAY/YEAR | GENEALOGICAL DATA |
|---|---|---|---|
| Clark | James | KC, p5c3, 5/20/1897 | Criminal case to be heard in the May term of the Crawford County Court, State of Wisconsin vs. James Clark and James Garrity. |
| Clark | John | KC, p5c3, 4/12/1900 | Arrived from Harpers Ferry, IA to visit cousin, Mrs. C. H. Speck of Eastman. |
| Clark | Lewis | KC, p1c4, 9/29/1898 | Recently married Sarah Pitsenberger. Bride and groom were former residents of Wauzeka area. Bride 66 years old. Groom 77 years old. |
| Clark | Lewis, Mrs. | KC, p1c3, 10/6/1898 | Nee Pitsenburger. Returned to Wauzeka to settle affairs. Recently married in Primghar, IA. |
| Clark | M., Mrs. | KC, p8c4, 2/20/1902 | Funeral held Feb. 18, 1902 at Harper's Ferry, IA. |
| Clark | Mrs. | KC, p4c3, 4/8/1897 | Arrived from De Soto to visit daughter, Mrs. Kloak of Ferryville area. |
| Clark | Mrs. | KC, p1c5, 4/21/1898 | Resided in Victory. Visited daughter, Mrs. D. Sappington of Lynxville. |
| Clark | W. H. | KC, p5c3, 7/22/1897 | Served as Grand Chief Templar. Scheduled to give a temperance address at the Evangelical Church in Wauzeka. |
| Clark | | KC, p1c4, 2/7/1901 | N. L. James and his son-in-law, Mr. Clark of Big Timber, MT visited Clark's brother in La Farge. |
| Clarke | John | KC, p1c2, 5/12/1898 | Committed suicide by hanging last Wednesday in Richland Center. |
| Cleary | Ellen, Mrs. | KC, p5c3, 5/16/1901 | Died May 12, 1901 in Town of Seneca. Survived by 7 children. |
| Cleary | Thomas | KC, p5c4, 5/29/1902 | The case Thomas Cleary vs. Edward Garvey, et al was heard at the May term of the Crawford County Circuit Court. Judgement for plaintiff for specific performance of land contract and costs. |
| Cleary | Tom | KC, p5c3, 6/28/1900 | Killed a large rattlesnake in the summer kitchen of his home on Pine Creek. |
| Clement | Bessie | KC, p5c4, 6/14/1900 | Graduated this week from Mt. Sterling schools. |
| Clement | girl | KC, p8c3, 4/1/1897 | Daughter born Mar. 19, 1897 to Clarence Clement of Mt. Sterling. |
| Clement | Oscar S. | KC, p8c4, 1/10/1901 | Recently died. Member of Seneca Lodge, No. 324, I.O.O.F. |
| Clement | Oscar, Mrs. | KC, p4c3, 12/20/1900 | Died last Saturday at her home in Mt. Sterling. |
| Clemons | Neil | KC, p1c3, 2/15/1900 | Married Miss Baker on Feb. 6, 1900 at Platteville. |
| Clinton | boy | KC, p1c2, 4/8/1897 | Son born April 3, 1897 to Fred S. Clinton of Prairie du Chien. |
| Clumfor | Mary | KC, p4c2, 4/29/1897 | Married John Linder on April 26, 1897. Bride and groom were from the Town of Eastman. |
| Coalburn | Anna, Mrs. | KC, p5c3, 7/6/1899 | Married Rev. D. Bell on June 27, 1899 in Prairie du Chien. Bride and groom from Mt. Sterling. Groom was pastor of M.E. Church in Mt. Sterling. |
| Coalburn | Charles, Mr. and Mrs. | KC, p4c3, 5/9/1901 | Resided in Town of Scott. Celebrated their golden wedding anniversary on April 27, 1901. |

Genealogical Gleanings From Early Newspapers for Residents In and Near
Crawford County, Wisconsin, 1897-1902

| LAST NAME | FIRST NAME | NEWSPAPER PAGE/COLUMN MONTH/DAY/YEAR | GENEALOGICAL DATA |
|---|---|---|---|
| Coalburn | Henry | KC, Supp., 12/20/1900 | Crawford Co. Soldiers Relief Comm. approved aid to Henry Coalburn of Gays Mills. |
| Coats | Charles | KC, p1c5, 1/27/1898 | Resided in Petersburg. Accidentally shot himself in the chest. Bullet exited through the shoulder. |
| Coats | James | KC, p5c3, 3/2/1899 | Arrived from North Dakota to visit his mother in Eastman. |
| Coats | N. | KC, p1c4, 11/4/1897 | Resident of Town of Eastman. Bought a newspaper subscription for his brother, O. P. Coats of Bowers, WI, and T. W. Williams of Montrose, SD. |
| Coats | Napoloen | KC, p8c4, 9/20/1900 | Recently married Bertha Finney. Groom from Town of Eastman. Mrs. William Hunter of Prairie du Chien was a sister of the groom. |
| Cobb | girl | KC, p5c3, 3/23/1899 | Daughter recently born to John R. Cobb of Steuben. |
| Coburn | Lafe | KC, p8c3, 10/9/1902 | Died Oct. 4, 1902 at Omaha, NB. Former resident of Prairie du Chien. Buried in Lowertown Cemetery. |
| Colburn | C. F. | KC, p1c6, 5/19/1898 | Issue of Fact for Jury to be heard in the May term of the Crawford County Circuit Court. C. F. Colburn vs. Crawford County. |
| Colburn | H. C. | KC, p5c2, 10/27/1898 | Resided in Gays Mills. Went to Kansas to spend winter with son, Fred. |
| Cole | Bell, Mrs. | KC, p5c3, 7/31/1902 | Mrs. Bell Cole, her son Frank, and niece Rachael Smith visited her parents, Dr. and Mrs. William Smith. Per Mt. Sterling news items. |
| Cole | Belle, Mrs. | KC, p5c3, 8/3/1899 | Arrived in Mt. Sterling from home in Chicago. Visited parents, Dr. and Mrs. Smith. |
| Cole | C. E., Dr. | KC, p1c1, 1/18/1900 | Advertised medical services. Practice based in Prairie du Chien. |
| Cole | C. E., Dr. | KC, p1c2, 8/3/1899 | Supervised the new sanitarium in Prairie du Chien. Planned to attract rheumatism patients with dry, hot air baths. |
| Cole | C. E., Mrs. | KC, p1c3, 7/18/1901 | Lived in Prairie du Chien. Visited sister, Mrs. H. F. Lawrence, and father, Mr. C. Rice, in Wauzeka. |
| Cole | Harvey | KC, p1c2, 3/13/1902 | Hired by Mr. Sanger to work as a blacksmith in Wauzeka. |
| Coleman | Clarence | KC, p1c2, 5/2/1901 | Shipped load of livestock from Petersburg to Milwaukee. |
| Coleman | Clarence, Esq. | KC, p5c2, 11/8/1900 | Moved from Bell Center to Petersburg for health reasons. |
| Coleman | Dave | KC, Supp., 4/24/1902 | Resided in Lynxville. Visited daughter, Mrs. Williams. |
| Coleman | Emett | KC, p5c3, 1/31/1901 | Lived in Barnum. Suffered with rheumatism. |
| Coleman | Emmet | KC, p1c4, 9/18/1902 | Lived in Barnum. Operated the "large Joe Brindley farm." |
| Coleman | Emmet | KC, Supp., 12/15/1898 | Married Addie McDaniel on Dec. 8, 1898 in La Crosse. Bride and groom from Barnum. |
| Coleman | Emmett | KC, p5c4, 1/23/1902 | Coleman and Miss Eva Peck won the most valued prizes when the medicine troop from La Crosse showed up in Barnum. |

Genealogical Gleanings From Early Newspapers for Residents In and Near
Crawford County, Wisconsin, 1897-1902

| LAST NAME | FIRST NAME | NEWSPAPER PAGE/COLUMN MONTH/DAY/YEAR | GENEALOGICAL DATA |
|---|---|---|---|
| Coleman | Emmett | KC, p5c1, 4/1/1897 | Resided in Barnum. "Started for the Dakota." |
| Coleman | H. | KC, p5c5, 4/5/1900 | Elected treasurer in Town of Haney. |
| Coleman | H. C., Mrs. | KC, p5c4, 7/17/1902 | Lived in Bell Center. Visited daughter, Mrs. Pearl Shockey in North Dakota. |
| Coleman | H., Mrs. | KC, p4c3, 4/21/1898 | Lived in Bell Center. Visited sick father, Alanson Taft. |
| Coleman | Harrison | KC, p1c2, 1/13/1898 | Appointed postmaster at Bell Center. Replaced M. D. Masten. |
| Coleman | Harrison | KC, p1c5, 2/10/1898 | Served as tax collector in Town of Haney. |
| Coleman | Harrison | KC, p1c6, 4/7/1898 | Elected Treasurer for the Town of Haney. |
| Coleman | Harrison and wife | KC, p1c3, 6/7/1900 | Resided in Bell Center area. Mr. Coleman went to a Grand Lodge meeting of the I.O.O.F. in Green Bay. Mrs. Coleman visited a cousin, Mrs. J. Dietzman of Wauzeka. |
| Coleman | James | KC, p8c3, 10/16/1902 | Lived in Prairie du Chien. Transferred to Madison to take a position as city ticket agent. |
| Coleman | Jane | KC, p5c3, 3/18/1897 | Widow of William Coleman. Advertised the sale of family farm. Judge James Curran wrote Louis McCullick, Esq. of Bell Center that an application should be made to the court to administer estate in the interest of the heirs. Judge Curran believed Mrs. Coleman was not of sound mind. Judge Curran advised Mrs. Coleman's daughter, Mrs. Rebecca Winden of Bell Center, to see an attorney regarding the estate. |
| Coleman | John | KC, p1c4, 6/7/1900 | Resided in Bell Center area. Examined by the pension board in Prairie du Chien. He served 3 years in Civil War. |
| Coleman | Levi | KC, p3c4, 5/20/1897 | Died Mar. 22, 1897 at home near Gays Mills. Born in 1846 in Allen Co., IN. Served in Co. G, 152 Infantry (Indiana). |
| Coleman | M. | KC, p4c3, 4/21/1898 | Resided in Bell Center. Rented his farm to John Shockley. Planned to "try his luck" in northern Wisconsin. |
| Coleman | M. L. | KC, p1c5, 5/8/1902 | M. H. Kelly and M. L. Coleman of Bell Center returned from a trip to Madera, CA. Planned to move families there. |
| Coleman | Otto | KC, p8c4, 3/7/1901 | Died Feb. 24, 1901. Aged 9 months and 10 days. Son of Scott Coleman. Buried in Readstown Cemetery. |
| Coleman | Peal (Pearl?) | KC, p5c4, 3/6/1902 | Peal Coleman and James Bacon of Bell Center departed for jobs in Iowa to get higher wages. |
| Coleman | R. P. | KC, Supp., 12/29/1898 | Received aid from the Crawford County Soldiers Relief Commission. Resided in Haney. Orphan. |
| Coleman | R. V. | KC, Supp., 12/20/1900 | Crawford Co. Soldiers Relief Comm. approved aid to R. V. Coleman of Scott. |
| Coleman | Rachael | KC, p5c1, 2/10/1898 | Died Feb. 2, 1898 when 67 years old. Wife of Salathial Coleman of near Bell Center. Born in Indiana and married there. Came to Crawford Co. 43 years ago. Five of 8 children survive: Mrs. Anna Brown, Mrs. Lizzie Anderson, Mrs. Hattie M. Whiteaker, D. V. Coleman and M. L. Coleman. |

Genealogical Gleanings From Early Newspapers for Residents In and Near
Crawford County, Wisconsin, 1897-1902

| LAST NAME | FIRST NAME | NEWSPAPER PAGE/COLUMN MONTH/DAY/YEAR | GENEALOGICAL DATA |
|---|---|---|---|
| Coleman | Rose | KC, p1c2, 9/1/1898 | Married Oliver R. Taft of Petersburg on Aug. 22, 1898 at the Congregational Church in Boscobel. Bride from Bell Center. |
| Coleman | Salathial | KC, p5c1, 8/11/1898 | From Bell Center. Very ill with enlarged heart. Staying at home of daughter, Mrs. H. Whitaker. |
| Coleman | Will | KC, p8c4, 2/4/1897 | "…talking of renting the old house on the Coleman place, owned by M. A. and Will Lowe." Haney news item. |
| Collins | Albert | KC, p8c3, 1/3/1901 | Died Dec. 29, 1900 in Waukon, IA. He was the son of J. M. Collins |
| Collins | Albert | KC, p5c3, 3/20/1902 | Sold his Knapps Creek farm. Planned to have an auction sale of other property and then move. |
| Collins | Bessie | KC, p4c3, 4/21/1898 | Baptized by Rev. Casper of the Methodist Church according to Bell Center news. |
| Collins | Fannie, Miss | KC, p5c3, 4/20/1899 | Ran a millinery business in Seneca. |
| Collins | Joe | KC, p4c5, 12/20/1900 | Married Marguerite Sherman on Wednesday in Cassville, at the home of the bride's parents. Planned to live in Minneapolis. |
| Collins | Joe | KC, p4c1, 3/17/1898 | Served as assistant postmaster in Seneca. |
| Collins | John | KC, p5c3, 10/12/1899 | Bought the old parsonage in Seneca. Intended to move the building and remodel it. |
| Collins | John, Mrs. | KC, p5c3, 4/3/1902 | Left home in Seneca to visit her sons in Montana. |
| Collins | Rob | KC, p5c3, 7/31/1902 | Departed for Montana per Gays Mills news items. |
| Collins | Will | KC, p5c3, 2/21/1901 | Departed Seneca for Montana. |
| Collins | Winnifred | KC, p8c4, 10/14/1897 | Died Oct. 2, 1897. Born July 11, 1897 to Frank Collins of Lowertown. |
| Coltard | Joseph | KC, p1c3, 10/21/1897 | From Elk Grove, WI. Visited uncle, Joseph Peacock, Sr. of Wauzeka. |
| Comb | Clarence | KC, Supp., 12/18/1902 | Crawford County Board of Supervisors examined bills in the Justices and Constables' Account for State vs. Clarence Comb. |
| Comerine | Edith | KC, p6c1, 3/18/1897 | Married Ben Schockley last week. Bride and groom may have been from the Town of Marietta. |
| Compa | Leo | KC, p5c5, 3/1/1900 | Died Feb. 22, 1900. Aged about 3 years. Only child of Mike Compa of Town of Eastman. |
| Comstock | Henry | KC, p5c4, 1/30/1902 | Former resident of Lynxville. Planned to make Manchester, MN his new home. |
| Comstock | Kate | KC, p1c5, 2/9/1899 | Taught school in Freeman in 1899. E. E. Brindley, Crawford County Superintendent of Schools published a comprehensive list of all teachers in the county. |
| Comstock | Velina | KC, p5c3, 7/3/1902 | Married Henry Hand on Sunday in Lynxville. |
| Coney | Carrie | KC, p4c3, 12/15/1898 | Recently married George Smith. Bride and groom from Scott. |

Genealogical Gleanings From Early Newspapers for Residents In and Near
Crawford County, Wisconsin, 1897-1902

| LAST NAME | FIRST NAME | NEWSPAPER PAGE/COLUMN MONTH/DAY/YEAR | GENEALOGICAL DATA |
|---|---|---|---|
| Coney | Henry | KC, p5c2, 10/14/1897 | Building an addition to his blacksmith shop in Town of Scott. |
| Conklin | George E. | KC, p1c6, 11/4/1897 | Issue of fact for jury to be heard at the November term of the Circuit Court in Crawford County. George E. Conklin et al vs. Peter O. Yetter. |
| Conley | John J. | KC, p8c3, 7/3/1902 | Returned to Prairie du Chien from Reedsburg to resume his position as salesman at the T & M Nurphy (Murphy?) dry goods store. |
| Conley | John J., Mrs. | KC, p8c3, 12/5/1901 | Died Dec. 3, 1901 in Reedstown. Buried in Prairie du Chien. |
| Conley | William | KC, p5c3, 2/20/1902 | Resided in Wheatville. Died Feb. 11, 1902 at age 90 years. |
| Connell | Dennis | KC, p1c5, 7/31/1902 | Recently died in a train wreck. Aged 49 years. Father of a daughter in Madison and a son, James, of Prairie du Chien. |
| Connell | Patrick | KC, p8c3, 3/27/1902 | Died Mar. 22, 1902. Operated a saloon in Prairie du Chien. Buried in Elkader, IA. |
| Connell | Patrick W. | KC, p8c3, 1/2/1902 | Married Mrs. Lillian Christie on Dec. 25, 1901. Bride and groom from Prairie du Chien. |
| Connelly | Maria | KC, p1c5, 10/26/1899 | Married Dan O'Neil on Oct. 23, 1899 at the Catholic Church in Rising Sun. Bride was daughter of Jeremiah Connelly of Bray Ridge. Groom from Gays Mills. |
| Connelly | Thomas | KC, Supp., 12/18/1902 | Crawford County Board of Supervisors examined bills in the Justices and Constables' Account for State vs. Thomas Connelly and John Brown. Thomas Stackland, John DuCharme, G. L. Miller, Carl Deidrick, P.O. Heide, Charles Flucke, William Zeil, Mrs. Saul Swingle, Mrs. H. Keifer, Wallace Martner and Fritz Grelle were witnesses. |
| Connely | Peter | KC, p8c3, 6/28/1900 | Married Mamie McCloskey on June 27, 1900. Groom from Milwaukee. (Bride may be from Prairie du Chien.) |
| Conopa | M. | KC, p1c5, 6/20/1901 | Brought grist to Wauzeka to be milled. |
| Conopa | Vince | KC, p10c3, 12/12/1901 | Bought a lot from M. Donahue, Jr. Planned to erect a shoestore and house in Eastman. |
| Conopy | Sophia | KC, p8c1, 5/11/1899 | Married Frank Fox of Prairie du Chien on May 10, 1899 at the Bohemian Catholic Church. |
| Contel | | KC, p8c1, 8/24/1899 | Died Aug. 15, 1899 in Prairie du Chien. Aged 6 years. Son of Charles Contel. |
| Cook | Anson, Mrs. | KC, p1c3, 12/1/1898 | Recently died at home of son, Jerome Kinder of Marietta. She was a former resident of Crawford Co., but recently lived in Devall's Bluff, AR. |
| Cook | C. | KC, p8c4, 9/30/1897 | At a conference of the Methodist Church held in Platteville, C. Cook was assigned to Linden, WI. |
| Cook | Christopher | KC, p1c4, 9/29/1898 | At a conference of the Methodist Church held in Eau Claire, Christopher Cook was assigned to Linden. |
| Cook | Mr. | KC, p4c1, 10/7/1897 | Lived on an island opposite Ferryville. Supported his family by catching fish. Game wardens cut up his nets. |

Genealogical Gleanings From Early Newspapers for Residents In and Near
Crawford County, Wisconsin, 1897-1902

| LAST NAME | FIRST NAME | NEWSPAPER PAGE/COLUMN MONTH/DAY/YEAR | GENEALOGICAL DATA |
|---|---|---|---|
| Cook | Pizarro | KC, p8c5, 5/15/1902 | Served in Co. A, 31st Regt. WI Vol. Interviewed by Dr. Porter who wrote a story on Cook's recollections of the Battle of Bentonville, NC of Mar. 19, 1865. (Part of a series in newspaper.) |
| Cooley | Almond | KC, p1c5, 11/18/1897 | Installed as an officer at the International Order of Good Templars (I.O.G.T.) Lodge in Wauzeka. |
| Cooley | Bertha | KC, p1c2, 2/28/1901 | Worked out of the Ray Hotel in Wauzeka as a dressmaker. |
| Cooley | Edgar | KC, p1c3, 3/2/1899 | Left Wauzeka for a job as a stenographer at the A. A. Cooper Vehicle Co. in Dubuque. |
| Cooley | Edith | KC, p1c5, 10/26/1899 | Married Frank Schwartz of Wauzeka on Oct. 25, 1899. Bride was daughter of John Cooley of Marietta. |
| Cooley | Elmer | KC, p1c2, 3/20/1902 | Son of John Cooley of Wauzeka. Returned home from work in the pineries of northern Wisconsin. |
| Cooley | John | KC, p1c5, 8/14/1902 | Found a 15 grain pearl in the Kickapoo River. |
| Cooley | John | KC, p1c3, 11/13/1902 | Found a bee tree with over 100 pounds of good honey. Largest seen for over 35 years. Lived near Wauzeka. |
| Cooley | Robert | KC, p5c3, 4/8/1897 | Died Tuesday, Mar. 6, 1897 in Wauzeka. Aged 70 years. Interred in Village Cemetery. |
| Cooley | Robert | KC, p1c5, 4/15/1897 | Died April 6, 1897 in Marietta. Born July 21, 1828 in Washington Co., KY. Lived in Missouri from 1829 to 1845 when he moved to Wisconsin to work in the lead mines. Married Dec. 14, 1845 to Margaret McGuiness. Moved to Marietta in 1851. Survived by 8 of his 8 children. Extensive detail in obituary. |
| Coope (Cooper?) | Bert | KC, p4c1, 1/26/1899 | Served in Co. C, 4th WI Vol. Letter he wrote on camp conditions in Anniston, AL published. |
| Coorough | Gus, Mrs. | KC, p1c1, 8/12/1897 | Died last week Tuesday in Prairie du Chien. Aged 36 years. Survived by husband, 3 sons and 1 daughter. Funeral held at St. Gabriel's Catholic Church. |
| Coorough | William, Sr. | KC, p1c3, 3/25/1897 | Died Tuesday in Prairie du Chien. Worked as a blacksmith. Survived by wife and grown sons and daughters. Funeral held at St. Gabriel's Catholic Church. |
| Coorough | William, Sr. | KC, p1c3, 2/18/1897 | Retiring from his blacksmith position in Prairie du Chien. Ill health. |
| Copas | Dan | KC, Supp., 12/18/1902 | Crawford County Board of Supervisors allowed expenses in the case, State vs. Dan Copas, Abandonment of Wife and Family. Witnesses for State were Amos Beebe, Matte Rowe, Rosetta Stowell, Mrs. St. John, Mrs. N. Jurgensen, C. M. Toney and Sam Copas. Witnesses for defendant were Robert Copas and Margaret S. Copas. |
| Copas | Dan | KC, Supp., 12/18/1902 | Crawford County Board of Supervisors examined bills in the Justices and Constables' Account for State vs. Dan Copas. Mrs. N. Jurgensen, Rosella Stowell, A. L. Stowell, Frank Pierce and F. W. Lewis were witnesses. |

Genealogical Gleanings From Early Newspapers for Residents In and Near
Crawford County, Wisconsin, 1897-1902

| LAST NAME | FIRST NAME | NEWSPAPER PAGE/COLUMN MONTH/DAY/YEAR | GENEALOGICAL DATA |
|---|---|---|---|
| Copas | Daniel | KC, Supp., 12/20/1900 | Crawford Co. Board of Supervisors approved payment of expenses in the matter of State vs. Daniel Copas. William Copas, (Mae Glena?) Copas and Margaret Copas were witnesses. |
| Copas | George | KC, p9c1, 7/8/1897 | Fourteen-year-old daughter and 16-year-old son of George Copas killed by lightning at home 5 miles east of Soldiers Grove. |
| Copas | Glena and Smith, Nancy | KC, Supp., 12/18/1902 | Crawford County Board of Supervisors allowed expenses in the Matter of Glena Copas and Nancy Smith, Dependent Children. |
| Copas | James, Mr. and Mrs. | KC, p5c4, 7/17/1902 | Lived in Bell Center. Visited daughter, Mrs. John Turk. |
| Copas | John | KC, p5c3, 7/3/1902 | Entertained Mr. and Mrs. J. H. McCullick of Mapleville at his home near Bell Center. |
| Copas | John | KC, p5c2, 10/20/1898 | Resided in Wheatville. Hired Lynn and Co. to drill a well. |
| Copas | May | KC, p5c4, 7/31/1902 | Visited sister, Mrs. John Turk, in Bell Center. |
| Copas | Roy | KC, p10c4, 12/12/1901 | Roy Copas and George Abrams were callers in Bell Center. |
| Copas | S. and wife | KC, p1c2, 3/29/1900 | Returned to Gays Mills after visiting with friends in Green Co., WI. |
| Copas | Susan A. | KC, Supp., 12/18/1902 | Crawford County Board of Supervisors allowed expenses in the Matter of Susan A. Copas, Incorrigible. |
| Copas | Susan A. | KC, Supp., 12/18/1902 | Crawford County Board of Supervisors allowed expenses for the return of Susan A. Copas from Milwaukee Industrial School by Court Order. |
| Copper | D. W., Mrs. | KC, p1c2, 3/1/1900 | Died Feb. 21, 1900 at the Bigelow House in the Town of Seneca. Aged 47 years and 6 months. Funeral was held at Gays Mills Congregational Church. |
| Copper | Ed | KC, p5c3, 8/21/1902 | Painted the post office in Ferryville. Oscar Torgerson was his apprentice. |
| Copper | Mollie | KC, p1c4, 7/3/1902 | Married F. J. Perrin on June 26, 1902 in Prairie du Chien at the City Hotel. Bride, the youngest daughter of O. B. Copper Sr., was from Ferryville. Groom youngest brother of Dr. Perrin, was from Wauzeka. |
| Copper | O. B. | KC, p1c3, 4/24/1902 | Former foreman in the Chief office. Now working in Chicago in a job printing office. |
| Copper | O. B., Jr. | KC, p1c3, 11/13/1902 | Hired to manage the *De Soto Argus*. |
| Copper | O. B., Sr. | KC, p1c3, 3/23/1899 | O. B. Copper Sr. of Freeman and his daughter, Molly, moved to Wauzeka. |
| Copper | O. Bryon | KC, p1c5, 11/20/1902 | Married Bernice Rosencrans on Nov. 20, 1902. Bride, daughter of A. Rosencrans, from Wauzeka and sister of Mrs. Henry Farris of Steuben (KC, p1c2, 11/27/1902). Groom from De Soto. |
| Copper | Ockey | KC, p1c5, 11/18/1897 | Installed as an officer at the International Order of Good Templars (I.O.G.T.) Lodge in Wauzeka. |

Genealogical Gleanings From Early Newspapers for Residents In and Near
Crawford County, Wisconsin, 1897-1902

| LAST NAME | FIRST NAME | NEWSPAPER PAGE/COLUMN MONTH/DAY/YEAR | GENEALOGICAL DATA |
|---|---|---|---|
| Copper | Oscar Byron | KC, Supp., 4/24/1902 | Arrived from Chicago to visit in Prairie du Chien. Oscar was editor of *Copper's Critique*, a periodical issued monthly in Chicago. |
| Copper | R. | KC, Supp., 12/18/1902 | Per Committee on County Poor, Crawford County paid Dr. E. J. Gable of De Soto $49 for services to R. Copper while sick with typhoid fever. |
| Copper | Ralph | KC, p5c4, 3/14/1901 | Foreclosure Sale Notice was published. John Lewis, plaintiff vs. Heirs at Law of Ralph Copper, children -- Diana Ames, Hareus N. Ames, Dana Valentine, O. B. Copper, Amanda Lee, Emma Rounds, Alice Torgeson, Ralph Copper and Stella Purrington. |
| Copper | Ralph | KC, p5c4, 6/22/1899 | Notice of Hearing published for Probate Court, Crawford County. Ralph W. Copper applied to administer the estate of Ralph Copper. |
| Copper | Ralph | KC, p1c6, 11/4/1897 | Issue of fact for court to be heard at the November term of the Circuit Court in Crawford County. Martin Host vs. Ralph Copper |
| Copper | Ralph | KC, p1c2, 5/25/1899 | Died about May 23, 1899 in Ferryville. He was father of O. B. Copper St. and grandfather of O. B. Copper, Jr. and Millie Copper of Wauzeka. |
| Copper | Ralph | KC, p5c4, 6/1/1899 | Died May 21, 1899 in Town of Freeman. Born Oct. 28, 1814 in Beaver Co., PA. He was the fourth son of 12 children. Lived in Licking and Van Wert Counties, OH for awhile. Moved to Crawford Co, WI in 1857. Married Dec. 25, 1840 to the late Mary Anne Williams. He was the father of Marcus (died in Civil War); Mary E. (Mrs. Horace Lewis, who died in Bell Center); Mrs. D. N. Ames of Retreat; Oscar B of Wauzeka; Mrs.J. Valentine of Newburg, OR; Mrs. E. G. Lees of Marshfield; Mrs. E. F. Rounds of Denver, CO; Mrs. P. H. Torgerson of Ferryville and Ralph W. of De Soto. His second wife, the former Mrs. Nancy Wilder, is also dead. Buried in Retreat Cemetery. Rev. Nuzum of Viroqua conducted the funeral. |
| Copper | Ralph | KC, p1c6, 11/4/1897 | Issue of fact for court to be heard at the November term of the Circuit Court in Crawford County. John Lewis vs. Ralph Copper. |
| Copper | Walter | KC, p5c3, 4/10/1902 | Moved family from Seneca to Lindsey, WI. |
| Copper | Walter | KC, p5c3, 1/3/1901 | Married Essie P. Cron on Dec. 25, 1900. Bride was daughter of Hiram Cron of Town of Seneca. |
| Copper | Walter | KC, p4c2, 5/12/1898 | From Seneca. Called to the bedside of his ill mother in Ohio. |
| Copper | Willis, Mrs. | KC, p5c3, 10/26/1899 | Mrs. Willis Copper and 2 children traveled from Fostoria, OH to Seneca to spend the winter. Mrs. Copper reported to be in very poor health. |
| Copsey | Albert | KC, p5c3, 11/20/1902 | Albert Copsey and Samuel George constructed a building for Henry Mills in Mt. Sterling to use as a barber shop. |
| Copsey | Alonzo | KC, p5c3, 10/25/1900 | Arrived from Custer Co., NB to visit parents in Mt. Sterling. |

Genealogical Gleanings From Early Newspapers for Residents In and Near
Crawford County, Wisconsin, 1897-1902

| LAST NAME | FIRST NAME | NEWSPAPER PAGE/COLUMN MONTH/DAY/YEAR | GENEALOGICAL DATA |
|---|---|---|---|
| Copsey | boy | KC, p5c4, 1/30/1902 | Son recently born to Perry Copsey of Lynxville area. |
| Copsey | boy | KC, p5c3, 10/2/1902 | Son born Friday to Ray Copsey of Lynxville. Weighed 12 pounds. |
| Copsey | Cora | KC, p5c3, 5/31/1900 | Graduated from school in Lynxville. |
| Copsey | Fred | KC, p1c6, 4/7/1898 | Elected Supervisor for the Town of Freeman. |
| Copsey | girl | KC, p4c3, 9/16/1897 | Daughter born Thursday to F. Copsey of Ferryville. |
| Copsey | John William | KC, p5c4, 2/20/1902 | Died Feb. 12, 1902 in Mt. Sterling. Born June 4, 1821 in Suffolk, England. He was second of 17 children born to John and Mary Copsey. When 17 moved with parents to Utica, NY. Lived there for 7 years. Married Susan Green in Utica on Sept. 25, 1847. Fathered 10 children. Moved to Crawford Co. in 1859. Served in Co. A, 41st WI Vol. Inf. during Civil War. Service ruined his health. Funeral held in Methodist Episcopal Church. Buried in Willitts Cemetery. |
| Copsey | L. F. | KC, p1c6, 8/12/1897 | Appointed administrator for the McDowell children. "We have been told that they returned to Updegraph, IA, where they intend to remain." per Lynxville news items. |
| Copsey | L. F. | KC, p5c5, 4/5/1900 | Elected treasurer in Lynxville. |
| Copsey | L. F., Mrs. | KC, p4c1, 9/22/1898 | Mrs. L. F. Copsey, Mrs. A. Randall, Mrs. Shipley and Mrs. Frank Lewis were officers in the Ladies Aid Society at the Congregational Church in Lynxville. |
| Copsey | Perry H. | KC, Supp., 12/18/1902 | Crawford County Board of Supervisors allowed expenses in the Matter of Perry H. Copsey, Abandonment of Wife. |
| Copsey | Ray | KC, p5c2, 8/4/1898 | Ray Copsey and Densmore Randall of Lynxville left for South Dakota. |
| Copus | Anna, Miss | KC, p5c3, 4/4/1901 | Hired to do housework for Mrs. Brady in Knapp's Creek neighborhood. |
| Corbett | Helen, Mrs. | KC, p1c3, 2/3/1898 | Traveled from Wayne NB to visit parents, Mr. and Mrs. Drake of Soldier Grove. Has been absent from area for 6 years. |
| Corcoran | Jennie | KC, p5c3, 4/4/1901 | Lived in Mt. Sterling. Taught school in Prairie du Chien. |
| Corcoran | Jennie | KC, p1c3, 2/27/1902 | Native of Crawford Co., WI. Teaching school in Sioux City, IA. |
| Corcoran | Jennie | KC, p1c5, 2/9/1899 | Taught school in Utica in 1899. E. E. Brindley, Crawford County Superintendent of Schools published a comprehensive list of all teachers in the county. |
| Corcoran | Louis | KC, p1c4, 11/1/1900 | Democratic candidate for Superintendent of Schools in Crawford County. Born in Prairie du Chien in 1876. Graduated from Prairie du Chien High School in 1893. Taught school for awhile. Graduated from Platteville Normal School in 1898. |

Genealogical Gleanings From Early Newspapers for Residents In and Near
Crawford County, Wisconsin, 1897-1902

| LAST NAME | FIRST NAME | NEWSPAPER PAGE/COLUMN MONTH/DAY/YEAR | GENEALOGICAL DATA |
|---|---|---|---|
| Corcoran | Louis | KC, p1c6, 7/14/1898 | From Prairie du Chien. Hired to be principal in Wauzeka schools. He was a June graduate of Platteville Normal School. Miss Mattie O'Kief hired as the primary teacher. |
| Corcoran | Louis | KC, p1c5, 2/9/1899 | Taught school in Wauzeka in 1899. E. E. Brindley, Crawford County Superintendent of Schools published a comprehensive list of all teachers in the county. |
| Cornell | William, Mrs. | KC, p5c3, 8/3/1899 | Mrs. William Cornell, her son (William) and Miss Anna Shultz returned to Sioux Falls, SD after visiting the Folbrecht family of Harris Ridge. |
| Cornford | Alfred | KC, p8c1, 10/14/1897 | Pending wedding announced to Julia Schaufenbuhl. Bride and groom from Prairie du Chien. |
| Cornford | Alfred | KC, p8c3, 10/28/1897 | Married Julia Schaufenbuhl on Oct. 26, 1897. Bride and groom were from Prairie du Chien. |
| Cornford | Laura | KC, p8c4, 10/17/1901 | Married Ben Edlebach on Oct. 16, 1901. Bride from Prairie du Chien. Groom from Postville, IA. |
| Cotter | James | KC, Supp., 12/18/1902 | Crawford County Board of Supervisors examined bills in the Justices and Constables' Account for State vs. James Cotter. |
| Cotton | Susan | KC, p1c4, 7/29/1897 | Married George Butler on July 27, 1897 in Prairie du Chien. Bride from Prairie du Chien. Groom from North McGregor, IA. |
| Couey | E. A. | KC, p1c2, 3/8/1900 | Barber in Wauzeka. |
| Couey | Henry | KC, p5c3, 12/11/1902 | Moved his family from Barnum to Mt. Sterling. Purchased a house from Mrs. Lindstrom, who moved to West Prairie. |
| Couey | Henry | KC, p5c3, 12/18/1902 | Blacksmith for Town of Scott. Started selling hardware in Mt. Sterling. |
| Couey | R. A. | KC, p1c3, 6/14/1900 | Lived in Wauzeka. Began a new job as agent for the McCormick Harvesting Co. |
| Couey | R. A. | KC, p1c4, 12/14/1899 | Recently moved from Prairie du Chien to Wauzeka where he opened a barber shop. |
| Couey | R. A., Mrs. | KC, p4c5, 2/21/1901 | Shipped household goods from Wauzeka to Tomah. |
| Couey | Royal | KC, p4c3, 4/21/1898 | Traveled from Scott to Brownsville to visit father, H. Couey. |
| Coughlin | John | KC, p8c2, 4/27/1899 | Died April 25, 1899 in Prairie du Chien. Aged about 87 years. Funeral held at Catholic Church. |
| Coughlin | John | KC, p5c4, 5/4/1899 | Died April 25, 1899 in Prairie du Chien. Born in 1821 in County Cork, Ireland. When 17, came to America. Served in Mexican-American War. At war's close, moved to Wisconsin. Married Margaret Murrane in 1865. Survived by 2 children: John Coughlin, Jr. of Mitchell, SD and Mrs. James Quinn of Chicago. Wife died in Wauzeka while he served in the Civil War. Married 2 more times. |
| Coughlin | Mrs. | KC, p1c3, 5/4/1899 | Resident of Soldiers Grove. Found insane by Judge Curran of Prairie du Chien. Taken to Mendota by Sheriff Hunter. |
| Coulson | E., Mrs. | KC, p8c4, 8/1/1901 | Recently died in Corwith, IA. Buried in Arena, WI. Grandmother of Frank A. Campbell of Prairie du Chien. |

Genealogical Gleanings From Early Newspapers for Residents In and Near
Crawford County, Wisconsin, 1897-1902

| LAST NAME | FIRST NAME | NEWSPAPER PAGE/COLUMN MONTH/DAY/YEAR | GENEALOGICAL DATA |
|---|---|---|---|
| Coulson | Mary, Mrs. | KC, p5c3, 6/20/1901 | Nee Sherwood. Departed Mt. Sterling for her new home in Colorado. |
| Coulson | Norman | KC, p1c4, 2/28/1901 | Married Mary Sherwood on Feb. 14, 1901 in Boulder, CO. Bride was daughter of Mr. and Mrs. Sherwood of Mt. Sterling. Groom was from Boulder, CO. |
| Courtney | J. L. | KC, p1c6, 5/19/1898 | Issue of Fact for Court to be heard in the May term of the Crawford County Circuit Court. J. M. Dowling vs. J. L. Courtney and J. H. Thompson. |
| Coville | Mrs. | KC, p1c4, 7/31/1902 | Lived in Milwaukee. Visited brother, Mr. Popper of Wauzeka. |
| Cowder | Mrs. | KC, p8c3, 11/24/1898 | Died Nov. 18, 1898 in Prairie du Chien. She was the sister of Jacob Walker. |
| Cowdery | Edith, Miss | KC, p8c3, 4/14/1898 | Died Apr. 4, 1898 in Elkhorn. Born July 15, 1872 in Elkhorn. She was a teacher and assistant principal at Prairie du Chien High School. |
| Cowdrey | Edith, Miss | KC, p1c3, 5/6/1897 | Assistant Principal in Prairie du Chien High School. Resigned due to a typhoid-like sickness. |
| Cox | Lulu | KC, p8c4, 3/25/1897 | Married George Harris on Mar. 4, 1897 at the home of the bride's parents. Bride was from Rising Sun. Groom was from Viroqua. W. C. Warren officiated. |
| Cox | Thomas | KC, p5c4, 5/29/1902 | The case, Thomas Cox vs. estate of Martin Duffy, was heard at the May term of the Crawford County Circuit Court. Judgement for plaintiff. |
| Coyer | Mrs. | KC, p8c3, 6/27/1901 | Died June 23, 1901 in Prairie du Chien. Aged over 80 years. |
| Coyne | Joseph | KC, p4c4, 6/1/1899 | Died May 29, 1899 in Town of Scott. About 40 years old. Survived by wife and family. |
| Cradwell | Postmaster | KC, p5c1, 2/18/1897 | Died Feb. 11, 1897 in Boscobel. |
| Craig | William | KC, p5c1, 2/17/1898 | Recently married Ella Cummins of Wheatville at St. Phillips Church. Groom from Knapp's Creek. |
| Craigo | Grant | KC, p4c1, 6/17/1898 | Married Laura Johnson (of Readstown?) on June 10, 1897. Bride was daughter of William Johnson. Groom from Readstown. |
| Crandall | Charles | KC, p5c3, 8/8/1901 | Lived in Lynxville. Found a pearl while clam fishing. Valued at $300. |
| Crasper | W. E. | KC, p5c3, 1/12/1899 | Resided in Fond du Lac. Planned to move to North Gays Mills where he had an interest in a sawmill business. W. E. Rounds was his head sawyer. |
| Crawford | Mary, Mrs. | KC, Supp., 12/12/1901 | Received funds from the Crawford Co. Soldiers Relief Commission. Resided in De Soto. |
| Crawford | Nancy, Mrs. | KC, Supp., 12/18/1902 | Crawford County Soldiers Relief Committee provided funds to Mrs. Nancy Crawford of De Soto. |
| Crawford | P. H. | KC, Supp., 12/20/1900 | Crawford Co. Board of Supervisors approved bills related to expenses of P. H. Crawford, insane. |

Genealogical Gleanings From Early Newspapers for Residents In and Near
Crawford County, Wisconsin, 1897-1902

| LAST NAME | FIRST NAME | NEWSPAPER PAGE/COLUMN MONTH/DAY/YEAR | GENEALOGICAL DATA |
|---|---|---|---|
| Crawford | P. H., Mr. | KC, p1c2, 2/8/1900 | Aged man from Gays Mills. Brought to Prairie du Chien by Matt Rowe, Town Chairman of Town of Clayton, and W. W. Bennett, Deputy Sheriff of Soldiers Grove. Had an impaired mind. Judged insane and sent to the hospital for insane at Mendota. |
| Crawford | T. J. | KC, p1c5, 4/10/1902 | Married Mamie Lagan on April 9, 1902 at the Seneca Catholic Church. Bride daughter of John Lagan, a former teacher and resident of Mt. Sterling. Groom was proprietor of a general merchandise store in Petersburg. |
| Crawford | T. J. | KC, p1c3, 8/16/1900 | Purchased a stock of goods from W. A. Vaughan and Son at Petersburg. Planned to go into the mercantile business. Had prior experience in mercantile business in Chicago. |
| Crawford | T. J. | KC, p1c3, 3/27/1902 | T. J. Crawford of Petersburg and Mamie A. Lagan of Mt. Sterling planned to host a grand ball on April 9, 1902 at King's Hall in Mt. Sterling to celebrate their marriage (planned for April 9, 1902). |
| Crawford Co. Board | | KC, p4c3, 11/15/1900 | Crawford County Board was composed of: W. S. Allen, Lynxville; Frank Brady, Eastman; James Dinsdale, Soldiers Grove; Joseph Doll, Wauzeka Twp.; Fred Evert, Prairie du Chien; Bernard Foran, Town of Prairie du Chien; Fred Hammerly, Haney; James Harris, Marietta; J. D. Hudson, Scott; A. F. Jones, Bridgeport; Martin Loftus, De Soto; R. M. McAuley, Gays Mills; John McCullick, Utica; M. Menges, Prairie du Chien; Chris. Nugent, Prairie du Chien; Mat Rowe, Clayton; T. T. Sime, Freeman; E. H. Standorf, Prairie du Chien; Robert Stuart, Seneca; O. P. Vaughan, Wauzeka and Lee Wannemaker, Steuben. |
| Crehan | James | KC, Supp., 12/20/1900 | Crawford Co. Board of Supervisors approved payment of expenses in the matter of State vs. James Crehan. |
| Croft | Carry, Mrs. | KC, p1c3, 10/5/1899 | Sent 4 boxes of grapes from her home in Grand Junction, CO to her friend, Mrs. Henry Reichmann of Wauzeka. |
| Cron | Essie P. | KC, p5c3, 1/3/1901 | Married Walter Copper on Dec. 25, 1900. Bride was daughter of Hiram Cron of Town of Seneca. |
| Cron | Frank | KC, p1c3, 1/10/1901 | Former resident of Seneca. Now employed at the Great Northern Express Co. in Minneapolis. His father, Bow Cron, works at a feed business in Minneapolis. |
| Cron | H., Mrs. | KC, p10c3, 12/12/1901 | Arrived from Prairie du Chien to visit daughter, Mrs. W. Copper of Seneca. |
| Cron | Hiram | KC, p5c3, 4/18/1901 | Planned to sell his personal property in Seneca and travel to Washington. If the family liked the area, they planned to stay. |
| Cron | N. | KC, Supp., 11/24/1898 | Died last Saturday. Oldest man in Town of Seneca. Funeral held at the Methodist Episcopal Church. |
| Cronsage | George | KC, p1c5, 7/13/1899 | Resided in Boscobel. Drowned Tuesday in the Wisconsin River. Aged about 18 years. His companion, Will Cradwell, unable to assist him. |
| Croome | J. F. | KC, Supp., 12/18/1902 | Per Committee on County Poor, Crawford County received $12 from J. F. Croome for boarding man and horse. |

Genealogical Gleanings From Early Newspapers for Residents In and Near
Crawford County, Wisconsin, 1897-1902

| LAST NAME | FIRST NAME | NEWSPAPER PAGE/COLUMN MONTH/DAY/YEAR | GENEALOGICAL DATA |
|---|---|---|---|
| Crow | A. L. | KC, p1c3, 10/25/1900 | Advertised an auction sale to be held at his home near Petersburg. |
| Crow | A. L. | KC, p1c4, 11/15/1900 | A. L. Crow and his brother, Leslie departed Petersburg for a new home in Berendo, CA. (spelling error?) |
| Crow | A. L. | KC, p8c4, 12/20/1900 | Recent resident of Petersburg. Has decided to move to Madera, CA. |
| Crow | A. L. | KC, p1c4, 1/24/1901 | Wrote letter from Madera, CA that was published in the newspaper. |
| Crow | A. L. | KC, p8c4, 5/30/1901 | Native of Gays Mills. In a letter published in the newspaper he mentioned that he was working in a lumber yard in Madera, CA. |
| Crow | A. L. | KC, p1c4, 5/8/1902 | A. L. Crow and his brother, "Dep," now live in Madera, Ca where they have sowed 1100 acres of wheat and 500 acres of barley. They own 26 mules and 5 horses on a ranch of 2400 acres. Former residents of Petersburg. |
| Crow | Catherine, Mrs. | KC, p1c4, 9/5/1901 | Died Aug. 25, 1901 at home of her son, O. E. Miller, of Madera, CA. Born Nov. 29, 1829 in Ohio. At age 16 came with parents, James H. and Louisa Kast, to Darlington, WI. Married John H. Miller on July 22, 1848. One of 7 children survives. Mr. Miller died in 1864 (or 1854). She and parents moved to Petersburg. In 1865 (or 1855) she married Henry Crow. He died Aug. 22, 1883. Five of 11 children survive this marriage: Lois C. Riley of Scott; Rozella Buckmaster of Bell Center; and Albert, Benjamin and Leslie Crow of Madera, CA. Also survived by Ira F. Kast of Petersburg, brother; Mrs. Mary Haskins of Town of Marietta, sister; and Mrs. Ellen Burton of Steuben, sister. Mrs. Crow moved to Boscobel in 1892 to live with son, Leslie. Last November she and 3 sons moved to California. |
| Crow | D. | KC, p8c2, 1/12/1899 | Resided in Petersburg. Called to Boscobel to see her ill mother. |
| Crowley | A. L. | KC, p1c6, 4/7/1898 | Elected Supervisor for the Town of Haney. |
| Crowley | Alice | KC, Supp., 11/8/1900 | Married Edward Fogarty on Oct. 30, 1900. Bride from Town of Seneca. Groom from Bridgeport. |
| Crowley | Ed | KC, p1c6, 4/7/1898 | Elected Clerk for the Town of Marietta. |
| Crowley | Edward | KC, Supp., 11/24/1898 | Married Miss Morse of Steuben on Nov. 24, 1898. |
| Crowley | Edward | KC, p1c2, 9/25/1902 | Died Sept. 22, 1902. Father of James E. Crowley of Steuben and Mrs. Ed Fogarty of Madison. |
| Crowley | Elizabeth, Mrs. | KC, p1c4, 12/18/1902 | Died Dec. 10, 1902 at home in Citron Valley. Aged 28 years and 1 month. Daughter of Michael Leary of Town of Seneca. Married P. C. Crowley on Oct. 6, 1902. Died after giving birth to a boy that died on Dec. 8, 1902. |
| Crowley | girl | KC, p5c3, 5/9/1901 | Daughter born May 4, 1901 to Ed Crowley of Steuben. |

Genealogical Gleanings From Early Newspapers for Residents In and Near
Crawford County, Wisconsin, 1897-1902

| LAST NAME | FIRST NAME | NEWSPAPER PAGE/COLUMN MONTH/DAY/YEAR | GENEALOGICAL DATA |
|---|---|---|---|
| Crowley | James | KC, p4c2, 10/21/1897 | Married Laura Garvey on Oct. 18, 1897 at Seneca Catholic Church. (Bride and groom may have been from Steuben area.) |
| Crowley | John | KC, p8c4, 6/2/1898 | Probate Hearing notice published. Late of Eastman. Margaret M. Crowley, wife, petitioned to administer estate. |
| Crowley | John | KC, p5c5, 1/18/1900 | Taught school in Crawford Co. |
| Crowley | John | KC, p5c2, 12/2/1897 | Taught school on Donahue Ridge. |
| Crowley | John | KC, p4c2, 5/12/1898 | From Steuben. Taught at Swatek school in Eastman. |
| Crowley | John | KC, p8c4, 6/16/1898 | Crawford County Probate Court published a Notice of Hearing. Margaret Crowley petitioned the court to administer the estate of John Crowley, late of the Town of Eastman. |
| Crowley | John E. | KC, p1c5, 2/9/1899 | Taught school in Eastman in 1899. E. E. Brindley, Crawford County Superintendent of Schools published a comprehensive list of all teachers in the county. |
| Crowley | John E., Mr. and Mrs. | KC, p5c3, 9/20/1900 | Arrived from Duluth, MN to visit parents in Eastman. Arrived from Cloquet, MN per KC, p8c1, 9/20/1900. |
| Crowley | John P. | KC, p1c5, 2/9/1899 | Taught school in Seneca in 1899. E. E. Brindley, Crawford County Superintendent of Schools published a comprehensive list of all teachers in the county. |
| Crowley | John, Sr. | KC, p4c2, 5/26/1898 | Died at home on Pine Creek (Seneca?). Buried May 15, 1898 at Catholic Cemetery. He was one of the area's oldest settlers. Survived by wife and 9 children. |
| Crowley | Patrick C. | KC, p1c5, 10/10/1901 | Married Lizzie Leary on Oct. 7, 1901 at St. Patrick's in Seneca. Bride and groom from Seneca. Groom brother of Thomas Crowley. Bride sister of Maggie Leary. An extensive list of presents and guests printed in a supplement to the Oct. 31, 1901 issue of this newspaper. |
| Crowley | Patrick, Jr., Mrs. | KC, p1c4, 7/3/1902 | Recently died in Mason City, IA. Husband has relatives in Steuben area. Husband is brother of Mrs. F. Fogarty of Madison. |
| Crowley | | KC, Supp., 12/19/1901 | Crowley Bros. established a mercantile business in Steuben in 1895. |
| Crowley | E. W. | KC, p1c3, 12/1/1898 | E. W. Crowley married Julia Morse at Seneca on Nov. 24, 1898. The Rev. J. M. Kelley officiated. Groom was a junior partner in the firm of Crowley Bros., a general merchandise store in Steuben. Bride was daughter of Mrs. Henry Hamilton. |
| Crowley | J. J. | KC, p5c3, 5/20/1897 | Issues of fact for jury to be heard in the May term of the Crawford County Court. A. N. Searle vs. J. J. Crowley, Dan Garvey and Frank White. |
| Crume | boy | KC, p5c3, 3/14/1901 | Son recently born to Will Crume of Mt. Sterling. Weighed 9 pounds. |
| Crume | Erma | KC, p4c2, 2/2/1899 | Died Jan. 25, 1899 in Wonowoc. Aged 12 years. Former resident of Mt. Sterling. |

Genealogical Gleanings From Early Newspapers for Residents In and Near
Crawford County, Wisconsin, 1897-1902

| LAST NAME | FIRST NAME | NEWSPAPER PAGE/COLUMN MONTH/DAY/YEAR | GENEALOGICAL DATA |
|---|---|---|---|
| Crume | J. F. | KC, p8c2, 1/16/1902 | Purchased the furniture and undertakers stock from A. E. Mills & Son in Mt. Sterling. |
| Crume | John | KC, p5c3, 2/15/1900 | New owner of the Mt. Sterling Hotel. |
| Crume | John | KC, p5c3, 8/28/1902 | Sold furniture business in Mt. Sterling to Julius Anderson of Viroqua. |
| Crume | John | KC, p4c1, 3/24/1898 | Moved family from Mt. Sterling to Wonowoc, Juneau Co. |
| Crume | Sadie | KC, p8c3, 1/6/1898 | Married Tom Larson on Dec. 29, 1897. Bride and groom from Towerville. |
| Crume | Will | KC, p1c3, 4/18/1901 | Worked as a phone line repairman. Lived in Mt. Sterling. |
| Crume | William | KC, p1c6, 7/21/1898 | From Towerville. Promoted to corporal by Capt. Silbaugh of the Viroqua company at Camp Douglas. |
| Crume | William | KC, p1c5, 8/4/1898 | Served in Co. M, 4th Regt. WI Vol. Sent letter from Camp Douglas. Printed in newspaper. |
| Crume | William | KC, p1c3, 1/5/1899 | Married Melvina Hankins on Dec. 27, 1898 at residence of the Rev. W. H. Fauke. Groom formerly from Towerville. He was on a 15-day furlough. Served in Co. M., 4th Regt. WI Vol. Bride from Chicago. |
| Crusan | J. | KC, p5c5, 4/5/1900 | Elected supervisor in Eastman. |
| Cuban | William | KC, Supp., 12/20/1900 | Crawford Co. Board of Supervisors approved payment of expenses in the matter of State vs. William Cuban. |
| Cullen | James | KC, p1c2, 11/13/1902 | Lived in Boydtown. Moved here from Iowa Co. a year ago. |
| Cullen | John, Mrs. | KC, p5c4, 2/27/1902 | Resided in Boydtown. Thomas P. Cody of Ellensburg, WA, an engineer of the Northern Pacific for the last 12 years, paid a surprise visit to his sister, Mrs. John Cullen. His last visit to Wisconsin was 5 years ago. |
| Cullen | Marguerite | KC, p5c4, 5/29/1902 | Marguerite Cullen of Boydtown attended a teacher institute in Crawford County. |
| Culver | Alva | KC, p1c2, 9/16/1897 | Called to his home in Barnum. Spent summer with Henry Phillips of Wauzeka. Sister died. |
| Cumerine | Frank | KC, p1c6, 4/7/1898 | Elected Supervisor for the Town of Marietta. |
| Cummings | Bryant | KC, p1c6, 7/14/1898 | Bryant Cummings and Bert Cooper of Lynxville enlisted in army. |
| Cummings | Clara | KC, p5c4, 1/16/1902 | Married Frank Brady on Jan. 13, 1902. Bride from Rolling Ground, Town of Clayton. Groom from Knapps Creek. Rev. H. F. Duffy officiated. |
| Cummings | Clara | KC, p1c5, 2/9/1899 | Taught school in the Town of Clayton in 1899. E. E. Brindley, Crawford County Superintendent of Schools published a comprehensive list of all teachers in the county. |
| Cummings | Mable | KC, p1c5, 4/21/1898 | Hired to teach in Gronert District per Lynxville news items. |
| Cummins | Ed | KC, p5c4, 12/22/1898 | Resided 3 miles east of Eastman. Gave lodging to a man named Miller traveling to Dubuque. Miller robbed $100 from Albert Young, who was staying with Cummins. |

Genealogical Gleanings From Early Newspapers for Residents In and Near
Crawford County, Wisconsin, 1897-1902

| LAST NAME | FIRST NAME | NEWSPAPER PAGE/COLUMN MONTH/DAY/YEAR | GENEALOGICAL DATA |
|---|---|---|---|
| Cummins | Ella | KC, p5c1, 2/17/1898 | Recently married William Craig of Knapp's Creek at St. Phillips Church. Bride from Wheatville. |
| Cummins | girl | KC, p5c4, 2/23/1899 | Daughter recently born to John Cummins of Wheatville. |
| Cummins | John | KC, p1c6, 4/7/1898 | Elected Supervisor for the Town of Clayton. |
| Cupps | George | KC, p1c5, 12/5/1901 | Reported to *Boscobel Sentinel* that he did $4100 worth of threshing in McHenry, ND for George Cupps, A. Posey, S. Hamilton, M. Simmons, J. T. McDaniel, Pat Foley, George Sloan and E. Posey. |
| Cupps | George | KC, p5c3, 4/6/1899 | He was an "old timer." Left Steuben for North Dakota. |
| Cupps | Samuel | KC, p1c5, 2/17/1898 | Died Feb. 11, 1898 in Boydtown. Aged 28 years. Only son of John Cupps. Unmarried. |
| Curley | boy | KC, p1c2, 10/12/1899 | Son born Oct. 7, 1899 to James Curley of Ferryville. |
| Curley | girl | KC, p5c3, 11/9/1899 | Daughter born Nov. 4, 1899 to Will Curley of Gays Mills. |
| Curley | John | KC, p8c3, 4/1/1897 | Married Celeste Biederman of Halls Branch on Mar. 22, 1897. Groom from Mt. Sterling. |
| Curley | John | KC, p1c6, 4/1/1897 | New resident of Gays Mills. Planned to drive stage between Gays Mills and Lynxville. |
| Curley | Thomas | KC, p5c3, 8/4/1898 | Died Sunday (July 31, 1898?) at age 30. Buried in Seneca at Catholic Cemetery. He was brother of John of Gays Mills and Thomas of Prairie du Chien. (p8c4). |
| Curley | Will | KC, p5c4, 4/10/1902 | Bought Heal's meat market in Gays Mills. |
| Curley | Will | KC, p4c1, 12/9/1897 | Stage driver between Mt. Sterling and Gays Mills. Had a runaway accident. |
| Curley | William | KC, p8c1, 1/5/1899 | Married Netta Phillips on Jan. 1, 1899 at the Congregational Church. (Bride and groom may be from Gays Mills.) |
| Curley | | KC, p5c2, 2/3/1898 | Infant child of J. Curley died Monday in Seneca. Buried in the Catholic Cemetery. |
| Curran | Edna | KC, p5c5, 1/18/1900 | Taught school in Crawford Co. |
| Curran | James A. | KC, p8c3, 8/18/1898 | A group of Prairie du Chien residents took the steamer, Pauline, to Dubuque to attend Buffalo Bill's Wild West Show. They arrived there at 1:00 p.m. and returned at 6:00 a.m. the next day. The attendees were Mr. and Mrs. James A. Curran, Mr. and Mrs. John Svatos, Henry Otto and son, Dr. Huwatscheck, Dr. F. A. Barney, Mrs. Charles Lindner and daughter, Mrs. W. H. Evans and daughter, W. Roach, Thomas Kelly, T. DeLap, C. Kelina, Will Merrill, Otto Wendt, Virginia and Lizzie DuCharme and Minnie Johnson. |
| Curran | Rose | KC, Supp., 12/12/1901 | Attended a Teacher's Institute in Crawford County in 1901. Resided in Prairie du Chien. |

Genealogical Gleanings From Early Newspapers for Residents In and Near
Crawford County, Wisconsin, 1897-1902

| LAST NAME | FIRST NAME | NEWSPAPER PAGE/COLUMN MONTH/DAY/YEAR | GENEALOGICAL DATA |
|---|---|---|---|
| Currie | Bertha, Mrs. | KC, p1c2, 9/5/1901 | Departed home in Viola for De Soto to attend the wedding of her sister, Lizzie, to a professor at an Indiana college. Nee French. |
| Currie | R. | KC, p5c3, 9/4/1902 | Miller in Gays Mills. Planned to move to Viola where he rented a mill. |
| Currie | R. L. | KC, p5c3, 1/12/1899 | Elected to be an officer for the Modern Woodman Association (MWA) in Gays Mills. |
| Currie | Robert | KC, p1c3, 6/5/1902 | Attended the Masonic Lodge in Boscobel. From Gays Mills. |
| Curry | girl | KC, p5c4, 8/24/1899 | Daughter born August 16, 1899 to Robert Curry of Gays Mills. |
| Curry | Robert, Mrs. | KC, p5c3, 10/12/1899 | Resided in Gays Mills. Visited parents in La Crosse. |
| Curtis | Bertha | KC, p4c1, 11/25/1897 | Married Thomas Seymour of Marietta on Nov. 17, 1897. Bride from Town of Scott. Many relatives mentioned. |
| Curtis | D. B. | KC, Supp., 12/18/1902 | Crawford County Soldiers Relief Committee provided funds to D. B. Curtis of Scott. |
| Curtis | D. B. | KC, Supp., 12/12/1901 | Received funds from the Crawford Co. Soldiers Relief Commission. Resided in Scott. |
| Curtis | D. B. | KC, Supp., 12/12/1901 | Received funds from the Crawford Co. Soldiers Relief Commission. Resided in Scott. |
| Curtis | D. B. | KC, Supp., 12/29/1898 | Received aid from the Crawford County Soldiers Relief Commission. Resided in Scott. |
| Curtis | D. B. | KC, Supp., 12/20/1900 | Crawford Co. Soldiers Relief Comm. approved aid to D. B. Curtis of Scott. |
| Curtis | Fred | KC, p5c2, 7/21/1898 | Married Edna Jenkins on July 9, 1898 at Mt. Sterling. (Bride and groom may be from Barnum.) |
| Curtis | Mabel | KC, p5c2, 3/3/1898 | Married Herbert Ward of Boscobel (per KC, 3/10/1898) last Wednesday (Feb. 23, 1898?). (Bride may be from Steuben.) |
| Curtis | Mabel | KC, p1c4, 3/10/1898 | Married Herbert Ward on Feb. 223, 1898. Bride from Steuben. Groom from Boscobel. The Rev. Thomas Crouch officiated. |
| Curtis | Ray | KC, p1c6, 6/9/1898 | Died from poisoning on June 3, 1898 at Steuben at age of 18. Son of Ed Curtis. He and Samuel Welch mistook hemlock root for artichoke. |
| Curtiss | Mr. | KC, p5c3, 3/2/1899 | He should get a share of the soldier's relief fund. Served as an artilleryman during the Civil War and only receives a small pension. Shortly after the war he lost his right hand to a threshing machine. He now has a broken hip and a large family of little children. Father of Willie Curtiss. Part of the Town of Scott news items. |
| Cushing | Mary | KC, p1c4, 5/12/1898 | Returned to Wauzeka to teach school. Went to De Soto to care for father who recently died. |
| Cushing | Mary | KC, p5c1, 6/17/1897 | Taught school in Wauzeka. Native of De Soto. |
| Custer | J. W. | KC, p8c4, 9/30/1897 | At a conference of the Methodist Church held in Platteville, J. W. Custer (sub) was assigned to Mt. Sterling. |

Genealogical Gleanings From Early Newspapers for Residents In and Near
Crawford County, Wisconsin, 1897-1902

| LAST NAME | FIRST NAME | NEWSPAPER PAGE/COLUMN MONTH/DAY/YEAR | GENEALOGICAL DATA |
|---|---|---|---|
| Custer | J. W., Rev. | KC, p5c1, 10/7/1897 | New Methodist Episcopal minister on the circuit for Gays Mills and Mt. Sterling. |
| Custer | Rev. | KC, p1c4, 9/29/1898 | At a conference of the Methodist Church held in Eau Claire, Rev. Custer, who was in charge of Mt. Sterling last year, was selected as pastor of a new charge consisting of Homer, Heberline, Blue River, Wayne Marietta and Barnum. |
| Daggert | Jud | KC, p1c3, 1/18/1900 | Worked as a livery driver in Gays Mills. |
| Daggett | Judd | KC, p5c3, 11/30/1899 | Worked as a liveryman in Seneca. |
| Dagnon | Thomas | KC, p5c3, 1/23/1902 | Died Jan. 15, 1902 of Seneca. Survived by wife and 7 children -- Mary, Francis, Margaret, Agnes, Gabriel, Joseph and Robert. |
| Dagnon | Will | KC, p10c3, 12/12/1901 | Resided in Seneca. "...owner of a fine black team. Will has always been popular with the ladies, but since he drives the blacks he is the only boy in town." |
| Dahlmer | John | KC, p5c2, 1/18/1900 | Published an estray notice. Found a black bull in Town of Eastman. |
| Damm | George, Mr. and Mrs. | KC, p1c5, 9/14/1899 | Resided in Lancaster. Died a week ago Thursday from burns caused by gasoline explosion. |
| Damm | John | KC, p1c4, 3/24/1898 | From Richland Co. Recently married. Received telegram from parents. It read, "Accept congratulations from the whole Damm family." |
| Daniels | Charles Henry | KC, p1c5, 1/30/1902 | Died Aug. 14, 1901 (is this a newspaper typo?). Drowned in the White River. Aged 10 years. James Crowley of Steuben was a brother of the boy's mother. |
| Daniels | L(onie?), Mrs. | KC, p8c3, 3/3/1898 | Visited parents, Mr. and Mrs. W. H. Moon, per Soldiers Grove news items. |
| Darrow | Frances | KC, p1c3, 7/31/1902 | Lived in Yellowstone, La Fayette Co. She was the niece of Mr. and Mrs. D. Lyons. |
| Dase | H. | KC, Supp., 12/29/1898 | Crawford Co. Board of Supervisors approved Justices and Constables' expenses related to the case, State vs. H. Dase. The witnesses were George Asbacker, W. Garrity, Fred Caya, W. Finke, Del Ridgman and A. Lamson. |
| Daugherty | George S. | KC, p5c3, 7/11/1901 | Married Kate Stevenson on July 6, 1901 in Boydtown. Bride from Barnum. Groom from Boydtown. |
| Davenport | Arthur | KC, Supp., 12/20/1900 | Crawford Co. Board of Supervisors approved payment of expenses in the matter of State vs. Arthur Davenport. The witnesses were Slathial Coleman, Mary Coleman, J. J. Briggs, Sarah Briggs, Frank Daw, Abraham Mook, Bige Pinkham, Martha Mook and Aaron Copas. |
| Davenport | B. | KC, Supp., 12/12/1901 | Received funds from the Crawford County Soldiers Relief Commission. Resided in Haney. |
| Davenport | Benona | KC, Supp., 12/18/1902 | Crawford County Soldiers Relief Committee provided funds to Benona Davenport of Bell Center. |
| Davenport | Bill | KC, p1c6, 1/7/1897 | Lived in Ferryville. Traveled to Chicago on business. |
| Davenport | David | KC, p8c4, 11/16/1899 | Received marriage license in Crawford Co. to marry Eve Martin. Bride and groom from Town of Clayton |

Genealogical Gleanings From Early Newspapers for Residents In and Near
Crawford County, Wisconsin, 1897-1902

| LAST NAME | FIRST NAME | NEWSPAPER PAGE/COLUMN MONTH/DAY/YEAR | GENEALOGICAL DATA |
|---|---|---|---|
| Davenport | Mr. | KC, p5c3, 8/28/1902 | "Mr. Davenport of Viola has been receiving apples here this week." (per Gays Mills news) |
| Davenport | Mrs. | KC, Supp., 12/29/1898 | Received aid from the Crawford County Soldiers Relief Commission. Resided in Soldiers Grove. |
| Davenport | Rachel | KC, Supp., 12/18/1902 | Crawford County Board of Supervisors allowed expenses in the Matter of Rachel Davenport, Insane. |
| Davenport | W. H. | KC, p1c5, 6/1/1899 | The May term of the Crawford County Circuit Court closed. In the case, A. Dolan vs. W. H. Davenport, the plaintiffs settled. |
| Davenport | Walter, Mrs. | KC, p8c3, 8/28/1902 | Died Aug. 23, 1902 in Prairie du Chien. Funeral held at St. Gabriel's Catholic Church. |
| Davenport | William | KC, p1c6, 6/16/1898 | Celebrated 30th wedding anniversary on June 1, 1898 at home in Ferryville. Davenport was 45 years old. |
| Davenport | William | KC, Supp., 12/8/1898 | Tried to get his feeble minded child enrolled in a special school. A. W. Wilwarth, Superintendent, said their was no room. |
| Davenport | William H. | KC, p4c4, 11/10/1898 | Issues of Fact for Jury heard in the November term of the Crawford County Circuit Court. A. Dolan vs. William H. Davenport. |
| Davenport | William H. | KC, Supp., 12/29/1898 | At a meeting of the Crawford County Board of Supervisors, the matter of the feeble minded child of William Davenport was brought up and a communication was read from A. W. Wilwarth, Superintendent of the home for the feeble minded, stating that the institution was full and could not admit more patients at present. |
| Davey | Alice | KC, p4c4, 11/2/1899 | Died Oct. 15, 1899 in De Soto. Born April 13, 1893 to Patrick Davey. Buried in Brownsville, MN. |
| Davey | M. T. | KC, p1c4, 6/1/1899 | Arrived from family home in Jackson, MI to visit relatives in Wauzeka. Mrs. Davey planned to visit other relatives in Courtney, ND. |
| David | J. H. | KC, p5c5, 4/5/1900 | Elected supervisor in Town of Haney. |
| Davidson | George | KC, p5c5, 4/5/1900 | Elected treasurer in Soldiers Grove. |
| Davidson | J. | KC, p8c4, 4/8/1897 | Worked as a liveryman in Lynxville. |
| Davidson | James | KC, p1c2, 2/25/1897 | Lived in New Rockford, ND. Former resident of Crawford Co. Visited friends in Prairie du Chien. |
| Davidson | John | KC, p5c3, 8/28/1902 | Sold home in Lynxville to Orin White. Planned to move to Soldiers Grove and go into the livery business. |
| Davidson | John | KC, p5c3, 10/19/1899 | Sold his livery barn and rigs in Lynxville to Brockway & McPherson. Rumor has it that Davidson and Gene White will start up a button factory. |
| Davidson | John, Mrs. | KC, p5c1, 12/2/1897 | From Bridgeport. Visited sister, Mrs. Gene Waite of Seneca. |
| Davidson | Mary | KC, p5c3, 5/31/1900 | Graduated from school in Lynxville. |
| Davidson | Mary | KC, p5c5, 1/10/1901 | Taught school in Lynxville. |

Genealogical Gleanings From Early Newspapers for Residents In and Near
Crawford County, Wisconsin, 1897-1902

| LAST NAME | FIRST NAME | NEWSPAPER PAGE/COLUMN MONTH/DAY/YEAR | GENEALOGICAL DATA |
|---|---|---|---|
| Davidson | Mary | KC, Supp., 12/12/1901 | Attended a Teacher's Institute in Crawford County in 1901. Resided in Lynxville. |
| Davidson | J. O. | KC, p1c6, 4/7/1898 | Elected Treasurer for the Village of Soldiers Grove. |
| Davig | Albert | KC, Supp., 12/12/1901 | Attended a Teacher's Institute in Crawford County in 1901. Resided in Soldiers Grove. |
| Davis | Agnes | KC, p8c3, 4/8/1897 | From Excelsior. Employed at Gays Mills House. |
| Davis | Chris | KC, p1c2, 2/17/1898 | Resided in Petersburg. Operated on for kidney disease. |
| Davis | George | KC, p1c4, 2/11/1897 | Married Mary Simek on Feb. 3, 1897 in Prairie du Chien. Bride and groom from Clayton Co., IA. |
| Davis | Goldie | KC, Supp., 12/12/1901 | Attended a Teacher's Institute in Crawford County in 1901. Resided in Towerville. |
| Davis | Goldie | KC, Supp., 12/12/1901 | Goldie Davis and Vernie McCormick of Towerville attended the summer Teacher's Institute in Soldiers Grove. |
| Davis | Idabel | KC, Supp., 12/12/1901 | Idabel Davis of Viroqua attended the summer Teacher's Institute in Soldiers Grove. |
| Davis | Idabell | KC, p5c4, 5/29/1902 | Idabell Davis of Viroqua attended a teacher institute in Crawford County. |
| Davis | Isabel | KC, Supp., 12/12/1901 | Attended a Teacher's Institute in Crawford County in 1901. Resided in Viroqua. |
| Davis | J. C. | KC, p1c4, 1/17/1901 | Advertised the sale of 3 lots, new saloon and house in Petersburg. |
| Davis | J. H. | KC, p1c3, 1/13/1898 | From Petersburg. Gored by the tusk of a hog he was driving. |
| Davis | James | KC, Supp., 12/29/1898 | Received aid from the Crawford County Soldiers Relief Commission. Resided in Scott. |
| Davis | James, Mrs. | KC, Supp., 12/29/1898 | Received aid from the Crawford County Soldiers Relief Commission. Resided in Scott. |
| Davis | Mrs. | KC, p4c1, 10/21/1897 | Funeral held. Attended by cousin, Miss Helena Christianson of La Crosse. |
| Davis | Mrs. | KC, p1c2, 7/26/1900 | Departed from Steuben for Chicago to undergo a surgical operation. She was an aged lady. |
| Davis | N. | KC, p5c3, 11/13/1902 | Lived in Ferryville. Bought land in the west. |
| Davis | Nancy | KC, Supp., 12/12/1901 | Received funds from the Crawford County Soldiers Relief Commission. Resided in Scott. |
| Davis | Nancy | KC, Supp., 12/29/1898 | Received aid from the Crawford County Soldiers Relief Commission. Resided in Scott. |
| Davis | Nancy | KC, Supp., 12/20/1900 | Crawford Co. Soldiers Relief Comm. approved aid to Nancy Davis of Scott. |
| Davit | boy | KC, p1c6, 10/13/1898 | Infant son of Frank Davit died Thursday (Oct. 6, 1898?). |
| Davit | | KC, p1c3, 10/7/1897 | Infant child of Frank Davit died Wednesday in Wauzeka. |
| Davitt | boy | KC, p1c4, 2/13/1902 | Son born Feb. 4, 1902 to Frank Davitt of the Wauzeka area. |

Genealogical Gleanings From Early Newspapers for Residents In and Near
Crawford County, Wisconsin, 1897-1902

| LAST NAME | FIRST NAME | NEWSPAPER PAGE/COLUMN MONTH/DAY/YEAR | GENEALOGICAL DATA |
|---|---|---|---|
| Davitt | child | KC, p1c2, 3/6/1902 | The one-month-old child of Frank Davitt died Tuesday in Wauzeka. |
| Davitt | Frank, Mrs. | KC, p1c3, 9/29/1898 | Resided in Wauzeka. She and mother, Mrs. Semrad of Muscoda, took infant to a physician in Muscoda. |
| Davy | W. | KC, Supp., 12/12/1901 | Inquest on Body of W. Davy heard in Crawford Co. Court. Guy Montgomery was the witness. |
| Dawse | A. L. | KC, Supp., 12/19/1901 | Operated a saloon in Steuben. |
| Dawson | Celia | KC, p1c6, 11/4/1897 | Issue of default to be heard at the November term of the Circuit Court in Crawford County. Celia Dawson vs. Martin A. Robinson. |
| Dawson | John | KC, p1c4, 10/26/1899 | Old resident and miner. He was rumored to have discovered gold ore east of La Farge in Vernon County. |
| Dawson | Rob, Mrs. | KC, p1c4, 4/15/1897 | Lived in Newport, MN. Visited grandmother, Mrs. A. Coburn of Prairie du Chien. |
| Day | Alphonso | KC, p4c3, 12/30/1897 | Traveled from Mason City, IA to visit Mabel Day, daughter and postmistress in Lynxville. He also visited his sisters, Mrs. Eugene White of Seneca and Mrs. J. Davidson of Lynxville. |
| Day | Alphonso | KC, p1c5, 4/21/1898 | Returned to Lynxville from Mason City, IA. Expected to go into the livery business with his brother-in-law, John Davidson. |
| Day | Elphonso | KC, p5c3, 7/25/1901 | Elphonso Day and his bride arrived from Victory, WI to visit his daughter, Mrs. F. Caya in Lynxville. |
| Day | Jeheil | KC, Supp., 12/20/1900 | Crawford Co. Soldiers Relief Comm. approved aid to Jeheil Day of Scott. |
| Day | Mabel | KC, p1c6, 7/14/1898 | Planned to leave Lynxville for a visit in Ellensburg, WA. |
| Day | Mable | KC, p5c1, 10/20/1898 | Recently married Fritzy Caya. Now live in the Menges building in Lynxville. |
| Day | Mrs. | KC, p4c2, 9/30/1897 | Died Sept. 21, 1897 in Lynxville at home of son-in-law, E. M. White. Born in New York nearly 65 years ago. Married Mr. Day in Dane Co., WI. Husband died 4 years ago. Survived by three children -- Mrs. John Davidson of Lynxville, Mrs. E. M. White of Seneca and a son in the far west. Buried in Dickson Cemetery. |
| Day | Rev. | KC, p5c5, 4/12/1900 | Preached in Bell Center. |
| Day | W. F. | KC, p1c2, 1/27/1898 | Native of Crawford Co. Recently returned to area from Nebraska. New resident of Lynxville. |
| Day | Maggie | KC, p1c5, 1/10/1901 | Married William Mercer on Jan. 3, 1901. Bride and groom from Wauzeka. |
| De Lacy | James | KC, Supp., 12/29/1898 | Crawford Co. Board of Supervisors approved payment of expenses in the matter of James De Lacy |
| De Lacy | Thomas | KC, p5c1, 2/18/1897 | Elected an officer in Utica Farmers' Mutual Insurance Co. Resided in Freeman. |
| De Lacy | Thomas | KC, p4c1, 12/9/1897 | Resided in Freeman. Government approved his pension request. |

Genealogical Gleanings From Early Newspapers for Residents In and Near
Crawford County, Wisconsin, 1897-1902

| LAST NAME | FIRST NAME | NEWSPAPER PAGE/COLUMN MONTH/DAY/YEAR | GENEALOGICAL DATA |
|---|---|---|---|
| De Lamater | Lillian | KC, Supp., 12/12/1901 | Attended a Teacher's Institute in Crawford County in 1901. Resided in Gays Mill. |
| De Larimier | Charles | KC, Supp., 12/18/1902 | Crawford County Board of Supervisors allowed expenses in the Matter of Charles De Larimier (also spelled Delarimere), Insane. |
| Dean | Eliza J. | KC, p1c4, 7/19/1900 | Died July 6, 1900 at Hoquiam, WA. Wife of J. D. Dean of Crawford Co, WI. Aged 27 years. Mother of 2 children. A. N. Searls of Lynxville was J. D. Dean's uncle. |
| Dearman | John | KC, p4c2, 6/23/1898 | In Vernon Co. court case, Wisconsin vs. John Dearman, defendant found guilty. |
| Deary | Mrs. | KC, p8c3, 8/3/1899 | Mrs. Deary received a visit from her brother, William Dunn, last week. He departed Tuesday for his home in South America. |
| DeChamp | Louisa | KC, p8c3, 2/27/1902 | Died Feb. 23, 1902 in Prairie du Chien. Born April 1798 in Prairie du Chien. She was the "oldest native born woman in Wisconsin." She was the daughter of Charles LaPointe of Montreal who was born in 1775. He moved to Wisconsin in 1796. Her mother was Susan Ataya. She was born in 1775 in St. Louis. Mrs. DeChamp was the mother of Mrs. Moses Duquette. |
| Deering | William | KC, p5c4, 5/29/1902 | The case Wm. Deering, et al vs. Bank of Prairie du Chien was heard at the May term of the Crawford County Circuit Court. Case to be decided on Attys. Briefs. |
| Deerman | William | KC, 12/27/1900 | Resided in Readstown. This issue reported that Deerman was shot and killed on Wednesday by his son-in-law, Mr. McCoey or McCouey. The next issue of the paper, dated 1/3/1901, said that Deerman was expected to recover. Deerman was an old man and an ex-soldier. |
| Deggon | John, Mrs. | KC, p1c4, 1/19/1899 | Died Jan. 15, 1899 in Marietta. Survived by husband. |
| Degnan | Allie | KC, p1c6, 1/23/1902 | Planned to marry Charles Feldmann. Bride and groom from Wauzeka. |
| Degnan | Allie | KC, p1c6, 1/30/1902 | Married Charles G. Feldmann on Jan. 27, 1902 at the parsonage in Town of Eastman. Bride daughter of James Degnan. Groom son of Mrs. J. N. Feldmann. Bride and groom from Wauzeka. |
| Degnan | Allie | KC, p1c4, 10/18/1900 | Learning to set type at the *Kickapoo Chief*. |
| Degnan | Felix | KC, p1c5, 1/9/1902 | Resided in Wauzeka. Expected to open copper mines on his farm. |
| Degnan | Henrietta | KC, p5c1, 3/31/1898 | "Hattie" died Sunday (Mar. 27, 1898?) at home of father, James Degnan of near Wauzeka. Aged 19 years. Funeral held at Sacred Heart. |
| Degnan | James | KC, p1c3, 10/4/1900 | Died Oct. 3, 1900 of typhoid fever in Wauzeka. He was the 12-year-old son of Felix of Degnan. |
| Degnan | James | KC, p1c5, 9/2/1897 | Resided in Wauzeka area. His log barn was struck by lightning and burned to the ground. A good team of horses died in the fire. |

Genealogical Gleanings From Early Newspapers for Residents In and Near
Crawford County, Wisconsin, 1897-1902

| LAST NAME | FIRST NAME | NEWSPAPER PAGE/COLUMN MONTH/DAY/YEAR | GENEALOGICAL DATA |
|---|---|---|---|
| Degnan | Julia | KC, p1c5, 11/28/1901 | Died Nov. 21, 1901. Born Oct. 10, 1876. She was the daughter of Mr. and Mrs. James Degnan of Wauzeka. |
| Degnan | Mary | KC, p4c2, 5/19/1898 | Died May 16, 1898 at home near Wauzeka. Born Sept. 23, 1860 in Eastman. Father died 9 years ago at which time she and mother moved to Prairie du Chien. Mother died 3 years ago. Sister of Felix of Wauzeka and James of Eastman. |
| Deidlehof | Joe | KC, p5c4, 11/23/1899 | New blacksmith in Tavera. |
| Delamater | R. | KC, p1c2, 4/25/1901 | Drove to Wauzeka from Johnstown with his granddaughter, Blanche Mitchell. She was a teacher in the Onstine District. |
| DeLameter | Mina | KC, p1c5, 6/1/1899 | The May term of the Crawford County Circuit Court closed. The case, A. H. Rounds, Rose B. Young and Mina DeLameter vs. Jane Reynolds, was referred to court. |
| Delano | John and Delano, Delia | KC, Supp., 12/20/1900 | Crawford Co. Board of Supervisors approved payment of expenses in the matter of State vs. John Delano and Delia Delano. The witnesses were Thomas Kelley, William Boun, Martin Loftus and Cora Delano. |
| Delano | | KC, p1c4, 5/31/1900 | Mr. Delano of De Soto was sentenced to one year at Waupon for illicit relations with an unmarried woman. |
| DeLap | Olive I. | KC, p1c2, 6/17/1897 | Married George E. Carey of McGregor, IA on June 3, 1897. Bride from Prairie du Chien. |
| Delap | Rufus | KC, p8c2, 2/2/1899 | Married Ida Gokey on Tuesday (Jan. 31, 1899?). (Bride and groom may be from Prairie du Chien area.) |
| Delury | James, Mrs. | KC, p8c1, 2/16/1899 | Died Tuesday (Feb. 14, 1899?) in Prairie du Chien at 75 years of age. |
| Delury | Mary | KC, Supp., 12/29/1898 | Received aid from the Crawford County Soldiers Relief Commission. Resided in Eastman. |
| Denio | Aaron | KC, p4c2, 8/25/1898 | Left home in Prairie du Chien for St. Paul to visit relatives. Has a brother in Minnesota. |
| Denio | Aaron | KC, p8c2, 6/1/1899 | Resided in St. Paul. Arrived in Prairie du Chien to attend court. |
| Denio | Aaron | KC, Supp., 12/29/1898 | Received aid from the Crawford County Soldiers Relief Commission. Resided in Prairie du Chien. |
| Denio | Aaron, Mrs. | KC, p8c2, 6/23/1898 | Found unconscious at her Prairie du Chien home by a neighbor. Suffered a stroke. |
| Denio | Delena A., Mrs. | KC, p8c4, 8/18/1898 | Died Aug. 10, 1898 in Prairie du Chien. She was wife of Aaron Denio. Born Sept. 2, 1831 in Brasher, St. Lawrence Co., NY. Married in New York in 1879. (Marriage date may be a newspaper typo.) Buried in Lowertown Cemetery. |
| Denneman | Mark | KC, Supp., 12/20/1900 | A Committee of the Crawford Co. Board of Supervisors reported that Mark Denneman, insane, was not a resident of Crawford Co. and should not be supported by said county. |
| Denneman | Mark E. | KC, Supp., 12/12/1901 | Listed as an insane person whose support was charged to Crawford Co. |
| Denning | Henry | KC, p8c4, 1/14/1897 | Resided in Sergeant, Dakota. Visited relatives on Bragg Ridge. Ferryville news item. |
| Denning | Mary | KC, p1c4, 4/14/1898 | Married Arnie Favor of Vernon Co. on Mar. 30, 1898. The Rev. Geo. W. Nuzum officiated. |

Genealogical Gleanings From Early Newspapers for Residents In and Near
Crawford County, Wisconsin, 1897-1902

| LAST NAME | FIRST NAME | NEWSPAPER PAGE/COLUMN MONTH/DAY/YEAR | GENEALOGICAL DATA |
|---|---|---|---|
| Dennis | A. L. and G. F. | KC, p5c5, 2/4/1897 | A. L. and G. F. Dennis published a notice of dissolution of their partnership, Dennis Brothers, in Wauzeka. |
| Dennis | G. F. | KC, p4c1, 1/18/1900 | Proprietor of the Wauzeka Roller Mills. |
| Dennis | G. F. | KC, p1c3, 8/16/1900 | Miller in Wauzeka. Visited sister in northern Minnesota. |
| Dennis | G. F. | KC, p1c2, 12/11/1902 | Placed notice in newspaper requesting payment from customers for milling services. |
| Dennis | G. F. | KC, p1c5, 11/30/1899 | H. B. Brown and G. F. Dennis dissolved their partnership in a farm machinery and twine business. |
| Dennis | G. F. | KC, p5c5, 4/5/1900 | Elected village trustee in Wauzeka. |
| Dennis | G. F. | KC, p1c2, 9/8/1898 | Resided in Wauzeka. Traveled to Madison to celebrate parent's 50th wedding anniversary. |
| Dennis | G. F., Mr. and Mrs. | KC, p1c2, 12/8/1898 | Mr. And Mrs. G. F. Dennis and their daughter, Sarah, all of Wauzeka, were baptized by the Rev. F. A. Mundt on Dec. 5, 1898. |
| Dennis | G. F., Mrs. | KC, p1c2, 11/27/1902 | Mrs. Dennis of ? and her sister, Mrs. Charles Keys of Hartford CT, visited their mother, Mrs. Brown of the Town of Scott. |
| Dennis | G. F., Mrs. | KC, p1c2, 3/17/1898 | Resided in Wauzeka. She "showed her bravery by driving through bad roads to the town of Scott. Sunday to her sick mother." |
| Dennis | G. F., Mrs. | KC, p1c3, 3/2/1899 | Resided in Wauzeka. Cared for her father, Libbeus Brown of Scott. He was dangerously ill. |
| Dennis | George | KC, Supp., 11/10/1898 | Died Nov. 3, 1898. Son of G. F. Dennis. Grandchild of Mr. and Mrs. Brown of Marietta. Born Sept. 10, 1895. Buried in Boscobel. |
| Dennis | girl | KC, p1c4, 8/24/1899 | Daughter born Tuesday to G. F. Dennis of Wauzeka. |
| Dennis | Mr. | KC, p1c3, 1/25/1900 | Featured in an article on Wauzeka's business concerns. Operated the Wauzeka Roller Mills. Made flour. Sold farm machinery, lime, construction materials. |
| Derouche | Louisa | KC, p8c4, 11/20/1902 | In the November term of Crawford County Circuit Court, Louisa Derouche vs. William Zable, plaintiff was awarded $100 damages and costs. |
| Derry | Walter | KC, p1c4, 6/20/1901 | Died in the Kickapoo River near Soldiers Grove on June 15, 1901. Aged 17 years. Resided in Sugar Grove. |
| Desch | Louis | KC, Supp., 12/12/1901 | State vs. Louis Desch heard in Crawford Co. Court. |
| DesChamps | A., Mr. | KC, p8c1, 9/6/1900 | Died Sept. 3, 1900 in Chippewa Falls. Born and buried in Prairie du Chien. Survived by a 100-year-old mother and a sister, Mrs. M. Duquette. |
| Desmond | boy | KC, p5c3, 5/11/1899 | Son born April 23, 1899 to Dan Desmond of Mt. Sterling. |
| Desmond | D., Mrs. | KC, p1c3, 7/19/1900 | Miss Anderson of Viroqua arrived in Marietta to visit her sister, Mrs. D. Desmond. |
| Desmond | girl | KC, p1c3, 7/19/1900 | Daughter born June 27, 1900 to Dan Desmond of Marietta. |

Genealogical Gleanings From Early Newspapers for Residents In and Near
Crawford County, Wisconsin, 1897-1902

| LAST NAME | FIRST NAME | NEWSPAPER PAGE/COLUMN MONTH/DAY/YEAR | GENEALOGICAL DATA |
|---|---|---|---|
| Devenport | William | KC, p5c1, 7/71898 | From Ferryville. Enlisted in army at Viroqua. |
| Devine | Dan | KC, p1c5, 6/16/1898 | Dan Devine and Roy Warne of Ferryville went to La Crosse to enlist in the army. |
| Devine | James | KC, p4c3, 3/28/1901 | Hauled logs to a sawmill to build a new home for himself in Knapp's Creek neighborhood. |
| Devine | James | KC, p5c3, 4/24/1902 | Resided in Richland Center. Visited parents on Knapps Creek. |
| Devine | James | KC, Supp., 12/12/1901 | Attended a Teacher's Institute in Crawford County in 1901. Resided in Ferryville. |
| Dewane | Sarah E. | KC, Supp., 12/20/1900 | Crawford Co. Board of Supervisors approved bills related to expenses of Sarah E. Dewane, dependent child. |
| Dewey | Charles | KC, p5c2, 4/1/1897 | Employed as a horse trainer. |
| Dexter | Almon | KC, p5c4, 5/29/1902 | The case Almon Dexter vs. Newton Bacon was heard at the May term of the Crawford County Circuit Court. Judgement for plaintiff. |
| Dicks | Fred | KC, Supp., 12/12/1901 | State vs. Fred Dicks heard in Crawford Co. Court. |
| Dicks | Fred | KC, Supp., 12/20/1900 | Crawford Co. Board of Supervisors approved payment of expenses in the matter of State vs. Fred Dicks. |
| Dickson | boy | KC, p4c2, 5/27/1897 | Son recently born to James Dickson of Lynxville. |
| Dickson | James | KC, p4c1, 5/19/1898 | A tramp burglarized his home in Lynxville. He was tracked and apprehended. |
| Dickson | James A. | KC, p1c5, 12/1/1898 | Married Louise Alder on Nov. 23, 1898. Bride was the sister of C. E. Alder and Mrs. Charles Campbell. Groom from Yankton, SD. |
| Dickson | Will | KC, p5c4, 6/12/1902 | Returned to Lindsey, WI after a visit in Lynxville. |
| Dieter | Ella | KC, p1c5, 2/7/1901 | Married Dr. E. E. Haggerty last Friday in Minnesota. Bride and groom from Excelsior. Groom was the son of David Haggerty of the Town of Scott. |
| Dietrich | Cyrus | KC, p8c3, 6/19/1902 | Married Goldie Alien (Allen?) on June 18, 1902 at Prairie du Chien. |
| Dietrich | John | KC, p8c3, 10/25/1900 | Married Mary Drew on Oct. 23, 1900. Bride from Prairie du Chien. Groom from Milwaukee. |
| Dietrich | Pearl | KC, p4c4, 8/17/1899 | Married A. H. Long on Aug. 17, 1899. Bride and groom from Prairie du Chien. |
| Dietzman | J. | KC, p1c2, 4/12/1900 | Sold 4 acres of land to Village of Wauzeka for a city park. |
| Dietzman | Jacob | KC, p1c5, 3/6/1902 | Advertised the sale of personal property at public auction in Wauzeka. |
| Dietzman | Jacob, Mr. and Mrs. | KC, p4c1, 8/8/1901 | Divorced at Lancaster at a court for Crawford Co. Parents of two children. From Wauzeka. Wife moved to Platteville. |
| Dikeman | J. D., Mrs. | KC, p5c3, 3/1/1900 | Arrived from Lansing, IA to visit relatives in Lynxville. |

Genealogical Gleanings From Early Newspapers for Residents In and Near
Crawford County, Wisconsin, 1897-1902

| LAST NAME | FIRST NAME | NEWSPAPER PAGE/COLUMN MONTH/DAY/YEAR | GENEALOGICAL DATA |
|---|---|---|---|
| Dilley | Coosa | KC, p5c4, 5/29/1902 | Coosa Dilley of Bell Center and Margie C. Rounds of Bell Center attended a teacher's institute in Crawford County. |
| Dilley | Coosa | KC, Supp., 12/12/1901 | Attended a Teacher's Institute in Crawford County in 1901. Resided in Excelsior. |
| Dilley | G. M. | KC, p1c3, 8/15/1901 | Lived in Town of Scott. Popularly known as "Mac" Dilley. He was son-in-law of Mr. And Mrs. O. P. Peck of the Boydtown area. |
| Dilley | I. F. | KC, Supp., 12/12/1901 | Received funds from the Crawford Co. Soldiers Relief Commission. Resided in Scott. |
| Dilley | Ira F. | KC, Supp., 12/12/1901 | Received funds from the Crawford County Soldiers Relief Commission. Resided in Scott. |
| Dilley | Ira T. | KC, Supp., 12/18/1902 | Crawford County Soldiers Relief Committee provided funds to Ira T. Dilley of Scott. |
| Dilley | Ira T. | KC, Supp., 12/20/1900 | Crawford Co. Soldiers Relief Comm. approved aid to Ira T. Dilley of Scott. |
| Dilley | M. R. | KC, Supp., 12/12/1901 | Attended a Teacher's Institute in Crawford County in 1901. Resided in Hurlbut. |
| Dilley | Manuel | KC, p1c4, 7/26/1900 | Badly injured in a runaway accident on the G. M. Dilley farm in Scott. He was the grandson of Ira T. Dilley of Excelsior. |
| Dilley | Millard | KC, p1c5, 2/9/1899 | Taught school in Scott in 1899. E. E. Brindley, Crawford County Superintendent of Schools published a comprehensive list of all teachers in the county. |
| Dillman | A. B., Dr. | KC, p1c6, 1/18/1900 | Advertised medical services. Practice based in Steuben. |
| Dillman | A. E., MD | KC, p5c1, 1/7/1897 | Advertised medical services. Office based in Barnum. |
| Dillman | boy | KC, p5c4, 8/9/1900 | Son born August 3, 1900 to A. E. Dillman of Steuben. |
| Dillman | Dr. | KC, Supp., 12/19/1901 | Steuben was the base for his large medical practice. |
| Dillman | Golda Mae | KC, p8c4, 4/1/1897 | Died Mar. 22, 1897. Born Mar. 6, 1897 to Mr. and Mrs. A. E. Dillman. Buried in Haney Cemetery. |
| Dilly | Ira T. | KC, Supp., 12/29/1898 | Received aid from the Crawford County Soldiers Relief Commission. Resided in Scott. |
| Dilly | Millard | KC, p1c6, 1/28/1897 | Attended a teacher meeting in Haney. |
| Dimock | R. C. | KC, p8c2, 5/5/1898 | Died recently in Milwaukee. Formerly from Prairie du Chien. |
| Dinsdale | James | KC, p5c5, 4/5/1900 | Elected supervisor in Soldiers Grove. |
| Dinsdale | James | KC, Supp., 12/20/1900 | Represented Soldiers Grove on the Crawford Co. Board of Supervisors in 1900. |
| Dittman | William | KC, p1c3, 4/17/1902 | Resided in Wauzeka. Dittman's barns and other outbuildings were burned to the ground last Friday. Detailed story. |
| Divers | Floyd E. | KC, p1c2, 2/18/1897 | Married Emma M. Evert, daughter of Fred Evert of Prairie du Chien, on Feb. 10, 1897. Groom from New York. The Rev. G. W. Reichert officiated. |

Genealogical Gleanings From Early Newspapers for Residents In and Near
Crawford County, Wisconsin, 1897-1902

| LAST NAME | FIRST NAME | NEWSPAPER PAGE/COLUMN MONTH/DAY/YEAR | GENEALOGICAL DATA |
|---|---|---|---|
| Dixon | A. J. | KC, p1c4, 9/29/1898 | At a conference of the Methodist Church held in Eau Claire, A. J. Dixon was assigned to Rewey. |
| Dixon | J. A. | KC, p8c4, 9/30/1897 | At a conference of the Methodist Church held in Platteville, J. A. Dixon was assigned to Cassville. |
| Dobson | David | KC, Supp., 12/18/1902 | Crawford County Board of Supervisors examined bills in the Justices and Constables' Account for State vs. David Dobson. Carl Childs, Arbie Childs, James Childs, Sidney Childs, Lowell Lathrop, Alvin Gibbs, Fred Dobson, Bert Dobson, Thomas Dobson and George Sampson were witnesses. |
| Dodd | L. A. | KC, p5c1, 1/18/1900 | Advertised painting services in Mt. Sterling. |
| Dodd | L. A. | KC, Supp., 12/18/1902 | Crawford County Board of Supervisors allowed expenses in the Criminal Case, State vs. L. A. Dodd. |
| Dodd | L. A. | KC, p5c4, 5/29/1902 | The case Wisconsin vs. L. A. Dodd, for incest, was heard at the May term of the Crawford County Circuit Court. Convicted. Sentenced to Waupon for two years. |
| Doge | Jessie | KC, p1c5, 2/9/1899 | Taught school in Eastman in 1899. E. E. Brindley, Crawford County Superintendent of Schools published a comprehensive list of all teachers in the county. |
| Dohse | L. | KC, p8c3, 4/14/1898 | Married Mamie Mazera on Apr. 12, 1898 at St. John Bohemian Catholic Church. Bride and groom from Prairie du Chien. |
| Dolan | A. | KC, p4c4, 11/10/1898 | Issues of Fact for Jury heard in the November term of the Crawford County Circuit Court. A. Dolan vs. William H. Davenport. |
| Dolan | A. | KC, p1c5, 6/1/1899 | The May term of the Crawford County Circuit Court closed. In the case, A. Dolan vs. W. H. Davenport, the plaintiffs settled. |
| Dolan | Anna F., Miss | KC, p1c5, 3/24/1898 | Traveled from Ferryville to Chama, NM to visit her brother. |
| Dolan | M. J. and Kane, D. | KC, Supp., 12/20/1900 | Crawford Co. Board of Supervisors approved payment of expenses in the matter of State vs. M. J. Dolan and D. Kane. Expenses to C. Crady, Antony Karahan, Henry Shulko and Dick West were disallowed. |
| Dolan | M. J. and Kane, Denis | KC, Supp., 12/29/1898 | Crawford Co. Board of Supervisors approved Justices and Constables' expenses related to the case, State vs. M. J. Dolan and Dennis Kane. Isaac Latimore and W. H. Davenport were witnesses. |
| Dolan | Michael | KC, p4c4, 11/10/1898 | Criminal Issue to be heard in the November term of the Crawford County Circuit Court. State of Wisconsin vs. Michael Dolan and Dennis Kane. |
| Dolan | Michael | KC, p1c5, 6/1/1899 | The May term of the Crawford County Circuit Court closed. In the case, State of Wisconsin vs. Dennis Kane, guilty. |
| Dolan | Michael | KC, Supp., 12/29/1898 | Crawford Co. Board of Supervisors approved Justices and Constables' expenses related to the case, State vs. Michael Dolan. |

Genealogical Gleanings From Early Newspapers for Residents In and Near
Crawford County, Wisconsin, 1897-1902

| LAST NAME | FIRST NAME | NEWSPAPER PAGE/COLUMN MONTH/DAY/YEAR | GENEALOGICAL DATA |
|---|---|---|---|
| Dolan | Michael and Kane, Denis | KC, Supp., 12/29/1898 | County Board of Supervisors approved Justices and Constables' expenses related to the case, State vs. Michael Dolan and Denis Kane. The witnesses were J. A. Haggerty, (Ed?) Anderson, Carl Knudson, _. J. Robertson, Isaac Lattimore, W. (H.?) Davenport, _at Lucy, J. Sterling, A. C. Newton, John Hitchcock, James Rogers, W. Johnson, John Lucy and James H_ren. |
| Dolan | Winnie | KC, p1c5, 2/9/1899 | Taught school in Utica in 1899. E. E. Brindley, Crawford County Superintendent of Schools published a comprehensive list of all teachers in the county. |
| Dolan | Winnie | KC, Supp., 12/12/1901 | Attended a Teacher's Institute in Crawford County in 1901. Resided in Rising Sun. |
| Dolejs | boy | KC, p5c3, 7/27/1899 | Son recently born to Frank Dolejs of Eastman. |
| Doll | Anna | KC, p1c2, 10/21/1897 | Married George Schoeffer on Oct. 18, 1897. Bride daughter of Joseph Doll. Bride and groom from Wauzeka. |
| Doll | Joe, Jr. | KC, p1c2, 3/8/1900 | Hauled many loads of railroad ties to Wauzeka during the winter. |
| Doll | Joe, Sr. | KC, p5c5, 4/5/1900 | Elected supervisor in Town of Wauzeka. |
| Doll | John | KC, Supp., 12/20/1900 | Represented Wauzeka on the Crawford Co. Board of Supervisors in 1900. |
| Doll | Joseph, Jr. | KC, p1c4, 1/20/1898 | Married Lena Schoeffer, daughter of E. Schoeffer of Prairie du Chien on Monday (Jan. 17, 1898?) at Prairie du Chien. Bride and groom were from Wauzeka. |
| Dolphin | George | KC, p5c4, 7/6/1899 | Crawford County Circuit Court. Summons published in the case of George Dolphin, plaintiff vs. Mary E. Dolphin, defendant. |
| Donahue | Anna Isabel | KC, p8c3, 9/12/1901 | Married John Smrcina on Sept. 10, 1901 at St. Raphaels Catholic Church in Madison. Bride daughter of J. J. Donahue of Madison. Groom second son of F. Smrcina of Prairie du Chien. |
| Donahue | boy | KC, p5c4, 2/27/1902 | Son recently born to Mike Donahue of Eastman. |
| Donahue | boy | KC, p5c3, 12/1/1898 | Son born Nov. 13, 1898 to M. Donahue, Jr. of (Eastman?). |
| Donahue | John | KC, p5c4, 10/3/1901 | Married Kate Gleason on Sept. 25, 1901 at Chamberlain, SD. Groom formerly of Town of Eastman. |
| Donahue | John | KC, p1c2, 1/25/1900 | Operated a cattle ranch in Dirkstown, SD. Visited relatives in Eastman, his former home. |
| Donahue | Johnnie | KC, p5c4, 1/18/1900 | Arrived from South Dakota to visit parents in Town of Eastman. |
| Donahue | Timothy, Mrs. | KC, p4c1, 1/28/1897 | Resided in South Dakota. Visited sister-in-law, Mrs. John Joy of Lynxville. |
| Doner | Hugh | KC, p8c3, 8/29/1901 | Died Aug. 22, 1901 in Prairie du Chien. |
| Donner | Hugh | KC, p1c4, 5/13/1897 | Married Maggie Foley of Seneca on May 10, 1897 at St. Patricks Church in Seneca. Groom from Prairie du Chien. |

Genealogical Gleanings From Early Newspapers for Residents In and Near
Crawford County, Wisconsin, 1897-1902

| LAST NAME | FIRST NAME | NEWSPAPER PAGE/COLUMN MONTH/DAY/YEAR | GENEALOGICAL DATA |
|---|---|---|---|
| Donovan | Jerry | KC, Supp., 12/12/1901 | State vs. Jerry Donovan heard in Crawford Co. Court. |
| Doran | Margaret A. | KC, p8c2, 8/31/1899 | Married Joseph P. Boucher on Aug. 29, 1899 at Spring Green. Planned to live in Lone Rock, WI. |
| Dougherty | George | KC, p5c4, 1/17/1901 | Blacksmith in Petersburg. Called to the sick bed of his father in Boydtown. |
| Dougherty | Roda, Miss | KC, p5c4, 12/14/1899 | Miss Roda Dougherty was expected to return to Boydtown after visiting her sister in Joplin, MO. According to KC, p5c4, 12/21/1899, she came back with her niece, Miss Bessie Carr. |
| Dowling | Amasa | KC, p5c3, 9/27/1900 | Recently married Grace Fransburg. (Bride and groom may be from Town of Scott.) |
| Dowling | Frank | KC, p1c5, 7/31/1902 | Age 18. Critically ill with appendicitis. Son of "Okey" Dowling of Haney. |
| Dowling | girl | KC, p1c5, 11/17/1898 | Daughter born Nov. 14, 1898 to John Dowling of Town of Scott. |
| Dowling | Roswell | KC, p5c4, 10/25/1900 | Democratic candidate for Crawford County Clerk. Born April 2, 1855 in Mercer Co., PA. Moved to Grant Co., WI in 1857. Moved to Town of Haney, Crawford Co. in 1859. Portrait printed in newspaper. |
| Dowling | J. M. | KC, p1c6, 5/19/1898 | Issue of Fact for Court to be heard in the May term of the Crawford County Circuit Court. J. M. Dowling vs. J. L. Courtney and J. H. Thompson. |
| Dowling | O. R. | KC, p1c6, 4/7/1898 | Elected Assessor for the Town of Haney. |
| Dowse | A. | KC, p5c3, 6/15/1899 | J. T. Farris, A. Dowse, T. Kast and Seth Reynolds went to Iowa to do railway work. Resided in Steuben area. |
| Doyle | girl | KC, p5c3, 8/10/1899 | Daughter recently born to Frank Doyle of Eastman. Weighed 11 pounds. |
| Doyle | James | KC, Supp., 12/12/1901 | State vs. James Doyle heard in Crawford Co. Court. Witnesses were Eliza Heaman, James Heaman, Joseph Heaman, Dennis Nolan, James Nolan, Pat Dunne, Thomas McGrath, Thomas McGrath, Jr. and James Dunne. |
| Doyle | Katie | KC, p1c5, 2/9/1899 | Taught school in Eastman in 1899. E. E. Brindley, Crawford County Superintendent of Schools published a comprehensive list of all teachers in the county. |
| Doyle | Mayme | KC, Supp., 12/12/1901 | Attended a Teacher's Institute in Crawford County in 1901. Resided in Prairie du Chien. |
| Drake | Lizzie S. | KC, p1c6, 11/4/1897 | Issue of fact for court to be heard at the November term of the Circuit Court in Crawford County. T. F. Andrew vs. Lizzie S. Drake. |
| Drake | Lizzie S. | KC, p1c6, 5/19/1898 | Issue of Fact for Court to be heard in the May term of the Crawford County Circuit Court. L. F. Anderson vs. Lizzie S. Drake and Peter L. Hanson et al. |
| Drake | J. C., Mr. and Mrs. | KC, p5c3, 7/20/1899 | Resided in Soldiers Grove. Entertained daughter, Mrs. Hattie Van Clees, and granddaughter, Louisa, of Chicago. |
| Drew | Joseph | KC, p8c4, 9/12/1901 | Funeral held Sept. 8, 1901 at St. Gabriel's Catholic Church in Prairie du Chien. He was nearly 90 years old. |

Genealogical Gleanings From Early Newspapers for Residents In and Near
Crawford County, Wisconsin, 1897-1902

| LAST NAME | FIRST NAME | NEWSPAPER PAGE/COLUMN MONTH/DAY/YEAR | GENEALOGICAL DATA |
|---|---|---|---|
| Drew | Mary | KC, p8c3, 10/25/1900 | Married John Dietrich on Oct. 23, 1900. Bride from Prairie du Chien. Groom from Milwaukee. |
| Drew | Mrs. | KC, p8c3, 8/8/1901 | Died August 4, 1901 at home near Prairie du Chien. Funeral held at St. Gabriel's Church. |
| Drexel | Otto | KC, p5c4, 2/22/1900 | Arrived from Decorah, IA to visit his father-in-law, John Sekatz of the Town of Eastman. |
| Drexel | Otto | KC, p1c3, 11/28/1901 | Arrived from Decorah, IA to visit his father-in-law, John Seekatz, Sr. of Eastman, who had his 83rd birthday on Nov. 20, 1901. |
| Drexel | Otto, Mrs. | KC, p4c5, 1/10/1901 | Arrived from Decorah, IA to visit relatives in Eastman and Steuben. She was the sister of John, Henry and Fred Seekatz. |
| Drudik | J. W., Mrs. | KC, p5c4, 11/13/1902 | Lived in Eastman. Went to grandmother's funeral in Yuba City. |
| du Chien | Annie | KC, p4c1, 1/13/1898 | Married Paul LaBonne on Jan. 10, 1898 at St. Gabriel Catholic Church. Bride and groom from Prairie du Chien. |
| Ducharme | Archie | KC, p8c3, 11/16/1899 | Found a pearl valued at $100 in a clam. Resided in Prairie du Chien area. |
| DuCharme | Johanna, Miss | KC, p5c1, 9/29/1898 | Died Monday (Sept. 26, 1898?) at home 9 miles north of Prairie du Chien. Daughter of Dominie DuCharme. |
| Ducharme | John | KC, p8c3, 9/11/1902 | Married Emma Martell on Sept. 8, 1902 at St. Gabriel's Catholic Church in Prairie du Chien. Bride from Harper's Ferry, IA. Groom from Prairie du Chien.. |
| Ducharme | John, Mrs. | KC, p4c4, 4/26/1900 | Died April 24, 1900 in Prairie du Chien from childbirth complications. |
| DuCharme | Louisa | KC, Supp., 12/29/1898 | Received aid from the Crawford County Soldiers Relief Commission. Resided in Prairie du Chien. |
| Ducharme | T. | KC, p8c3, 11/16/1899 | Refused $175 offer for a pearl he found in a clam. Resided in Prairie du Chien area. |
| Ducharme | Virginia | KC, p8c4, 5/10/1900 | Pending wedding to Otto Wendt announced. Bride and groom from Prairie du Chien. |
| DuCharme | Virginia | KC, p8c4, 5/24/1900 | Married Otto Wendt on May 23, 1900. Bride and groom from Prairie du Chien. |
| Dudley | Cynthia | KC, p5c1, 9/15/1898 | Recently died. Notice for Probate Hearing published. |
| Dudley | Cynthia | KC, p5c1, 9/22/1898 | Notice of Final Hearing published by Crawford County Courts. W. A. Wayne petitioned to be executor. |
| Dudley | Cynthia Wayne | KC, p4c1, 12/23/1897 | Died Dec. 16, 1897 in Boydtown. Born Dec. 7, 1830 in Erie, PA. As a child moved to Fennimore, Grant Co., WI. She was daughter of Dr. Pratt. Married James Wayne in Fennimore. Moved to Boydtown in 1850. First husband died in 1882. Survived by 6 of 9 children: Jasper of Platteville, WI; Frank of Waslena (sp.?), IA; Eugene of Sioux City, IA; William of Boydtown; Mrs. Mary Coleman of Petersburg and Mrs. Jennie Harrison of Monroe, SD. Buried in Wauzeka Cemetery. |
| Dudley | Harvey | KC, p5c2, 3/10/1898 | Four years old. Brought from the State School in Sparta and taken to Arthur Bell where he will make his new home. |

Genealogical Gleanings From Early Newspapers for Residents In and Near
Crawford County, Wisconsin, 1897-1902

| LAST NAME | FIRST NAME | NEWSPAPER PAGE/COLUMN MONTH/DAY/YEAR | GENEALOGICAL DATA |
|---|---|---|---|
| Dudley | J. S. | KC, p5c3, 4/22/1897 | An old veteran from Gays Mills. Left for a new home in Beaver Dam. |
| Dudley | J. S. | KC, p1c5, 10/14/1897 | Traveled from Beaver Dam to visit old friends in Gays Mills, his hometown. |
| Dudley | Jennie | KC, p5c3, 4/4/1901 | Lived in Mt. Sterling. Taught school in De Soto. |
| Dudley | Lizzie | KC, p8c3, 4/1/1897 | Married Will Sterling on Mar. 23, 1897 at Gays Mills. Bride and groom from Mt. Sterling. |
| Dudley | Sumner | KC, p4c1, 5/6/1897 | Married Mrs. Mary Farr in Beaver Dam, WI in April 1897. Groom from Gays Mills. |
| Duffy | Agnes | KC, p1c4, 10/14/1897 | From Prairie du Chien. Taught school in Mt. Sterling. |
| Duffy | James | KC, Supp., 12/18/1902 | Crawford County Soldiers Relief Committee provided funds to James Duffy of Prairie du Chien. |
| Duffy | James | KC, Supp., 12/20/1900 | Crawford Co. Soldiers Relief Comm. approved aid to James Duffy of Prairie du Chien. |
| Duffy | Kate | KC, p1c5, 2/9/1899 | Taught school in Prairie du Chien in 1899. E. E. Brindley, Crawford County Superintendent of Schools published a comprehensive list of all teachers in the county. |
| Duffy | Margaret Norris | KC, p8c4, 1/9/1902 | Died Jan. 4, 1902 in Prairie du Chien. She was the mother of Mrs. J. L. Phelan; Josie I. and Agnes Dana Duffy of Chicago; the late Mrs. F. J. Rowley of Oconomowoc; Com. Sergt. J. Duffy, U.S. Artillery; Michael A. of Havre, MT; Martin, Mary and James of Prairie du Chien. Born Dec. 28, 1845 in Cashel, Tipperary Co., Ireland. Came to America as a child. Married James S. Duffy at Milwaukee on Aug. 8, 1862. |
| Duffy | Martin | KC, p1c4, 3/28/1901 | Died Mar. 22, 1901 in the Town of Seneca. Born Jan. 1828 in County Mayo, Ireland. Aged 73 years. He was the nephew of P. Barton of Town of Seneca. Never married. Survived by nieces and nephews: J. J. Barton of Independence, IA; P. Barton of Town of Seneca; P Burke and James Duffy of Prairie du Chien and Mrs. Sweeney of McGregor, IA. Buried in the Seneca Catholic Cemetery. |
| Duffy | Mike, Corp. | KC, p8c1, 10/19/1899 | Member of Co. K, South Dakota Regulars. Recently discharged and returned from Manila. Family lived in Prairie du Chien. |
| Duha | John | KC, p5c4, 4/26/1900 | Resident of Eastman. Diagnosed with cancer of the face. |
| Duha | John | KC, p5c4, 4/11/1901 | Returned to Eastman after receiving treatment in Milwaukee for cancer on his face. |
| Duha | Mr. | KC, p4c2, 5/5/1898 | Died last Saturday (Apr. 30, 1898?). He was an aged resident who lived near Eastman. Buried in Horal Cemetery. |
| Dull | Ed. and John | KC, p1c5, 6/1/1899 | The May term of the Crawford County Circuit Court closed. In the case, W. F. Kepler vs. Ed and John Dull, judgement for plaintiff. |
| Dunbar | Edwin Harley | KC, p1c5, 7/31/1902 | Died July 27, 1902. Drowned in Wisconsin River. Aged 18 years. Brother of Herb Dunbar. |

Genealogical Gleanings From Early Newspapers for Residents In and Near
Crawford County, Wisconsin, 1897-1902

| LAST NAME | FIRST NAME | NEWSPAPER PAGE/COLUMN MONTH/DAY/YEAR | GENEALOGICAL DATA |
|---|---|---|---|
| Dunbar | Edwin Harley | KC, p4c4, 7/31/1902 | Died July 27, 1902. Born April 19, 1884 in Town of Marietta. Third son of William Dunbar. Had 5 brothers and 2 sisters. Nephew of Edwin Lawrence. Brother of Lee Dunbar of McHenry, ND, per KC, p1c2, Aug. 7, 1902. |
| Dunbar | Emily | KC, p1c6, 5/19/1898 | Issue of Fact for Jury to be heard in the May term of the Crawford County Circuit Court. Emily Dunbar vs. Daniel Vollmer. |
| Dunbar | Emily | KC, p1c6, 6/2/1898 | In Crawford County Circuit Court, Sarah Ann Lawrence vs. D. Vollmer and Emily Dunbar vs. D. Vollmer. Both cases were decided by one trial as "practically the same testimony was to decide both cases". Verdict for defendant. |
| Dunbar | Lee | KC, p1c4, 10/10/1901 | Recently returned from North Dakota where he contracted cholera. Under care of Dr. Perrin. |
| Dunbar | William | KC, p1c2, 8/29/1901 | The case John Schmidt vs. William Dunbar was settled out of court in Wauzeka. It was a trespass and damages suit. |
| Duncan | Otilla M. | KC, p5c1, 4/15/1897 | Married Munroe Hughbanks of Barnum on April 5, 1897 in Haney. Bride from Town of Scott. Justice James Dowling officiated. |
| Dunham | girl | KC, p1c4, 9/9/1897 | Daughter born Thursday to William Dunham of Boydtown. |
| Dunn | Ella | KC, p1c3, 9/27/1900 | Resided in Henrietta, Richland Co. Engaged to teach in Dutch Ridge school. |
| Dunn | Ella | KC, Supp., 12/12/1901 | Attended a Teacher's Institute in Crawford County in 1901. Resided in Wauzeka. |
| Dunn | Hugh | KC, p4c4, 9/5/1901 | Crawford County Probate Court published Notice of Hearing. Hugh Dunn, Jr. applicant for estate of Hugh Dunn, deceased. |
| Dunne | Arthur | KC, p1c3, 7/25/1901 | Mr. Dunne was superintendent of the pontoon bridge at Wabasha on the Mississippi River. He was the brother of Mrs. James Degnan of Wauzeka and B. Dunne of Eastman. |
| Dunne | Barney | KC, p1c6, 10/7/1897 | Swindled by a lightning rod salesman. Lived 8 miles outside Wauzeka. |
| Dunne | Bridget | KC, p5c3, 3/4/1897 | Married Fred Noe on Mar. 1, 1897 at Wabasha, MN. Bride and groom may have been from Wauzeka. |
| Dunne | Charles | KC, p8c4, 11/17/1898 | Recently died at Minneapolis. Former resident of Prairie du Chien. |
| Dunne | P. J. | KC, p1c2, 10/23/1902 | Democratic candidate for Crawford County Clerk. Born 37 years ago last March in Town of Prairie du Chien. Elected Town Clerk in 1894. Resident of Prairie du Chien for last 4 years. Elected to office of assessor last spring. Portrait published. |
| Dunne | P. J., Mrs. | KC, p8c3, 12/5/1901 | Died Dec. 3, 1901 in Prairie du Chien. Mother of James Dunne of La Crosse. |
| Durham | Mary | KC, p1c6, 9/23/1897 | Died Sept. 13, 1897. Wife of John William Durham. Born Dec. 6, 1877 to Mike Pivot of Town of Marietta. Married Sept. 21, 1896. Mother deceased. |
| Durham | William, Mrs. | KC, p1c4, 9/16/1897 | Died Sept. 13, 1897 during childbirth at her home near Boydstown. Aged 19 years. Daughter of Michael Pivot. Remains interred in Wauzeka Cemetery. |

Genealogical Gleanings From Early Newspapers for Residents In and Near
Crawford County, Wisconsin, 1897-1902

| LAST NAME | FIRST NAME | NEWSPAPER PAGE/COLUMN MONTH/DAY/YEAR | GENEALOGICAL DATA |
|---|---|---|---|
| Durham |  | KC, p1c2, 10/7/1897 | A 4 week old child of William Durham of Wauzeka died Sept. 30, 1897 at home of Mr. and Mrs. Loyd Ray in Steuben. Buried in Wauzeka Cem. (Some data from p5c2.) |
| Duselaf | J. | KC, Supp., 12/20/1900 | Crawford Co. Board of Supervisors approved payment of expenses in the matter of State vs. J. Duselaf. |
| Dvorak | J. A. | KC, p5c3, 3/27/1902 | Father came from Sillville, IA to visit him in Eastman. |
| Dworak | Barbara | KC, p5c3, 5/20/1897 | Issues of fact for court to be heard in the May term of the Crawford County Court. Barbara Dworak et. al. vs. Thomas McCann. |
| Dworak | boy | KC, p1c4, 7/19/1900 | Son born July 9, 1900 to John Dworak of Wauzeka area. |
| Dworak | boy | KC, p1c4, 10/7/1897 | Son recently born to John Dworak in Wauzeka. Weighed 10 lbs. |
| Dworak | John | KC, p1c2, 2/27/1902 | Auction scheduled on his farm. Selling personal property, farm animals and equipment. Located 4 miles north of Wauzeka. O. P. Vaughan hired as auctioneer. |
| Dworak | John | KC, p8c4, 6/26/1902 | While clam fishing found a pearl valued at $1000. |
| Dworak | John A. | KC, p1c2, 5/29/1902 | Dworak and his son, George found 7 pearls while clamming near Prairie du Chien. The most valuable pearl was worth $1200 to $1500. |
| Dwork | John | KC, p1c3, 2/28/1901 | His old house near Wauzeka was destroyed by fire. Unoccupied. His family lived in a new home close by. House used for storage. Lost summer clothing, many provisions and $600 in cash. There was no insurance. |
| Dyer | Albert | KC, p1c4, 6/9/1898 | Married Lottie Smith of on May 26, 1898. Groom from Marietta. M. A. Robinson, Justice of the Peace, officiated. |
| Dyer | Dell, Mrs. | KC, p1c5, 4/21/1898 | Lived in De Soto. Visited her parents, Mr. and Mrs. William Huard of Lynxville. |
| Dyer | E., Mrs. | KC, p5c3, 4/19/1900 | Arrived from Dakota to visit parents in Lynxville. Mrs. Dyer and a sister, Minnie Huard, planned to move to Minneapolis. |
| Dyer | Henry | KC, p5c2, 7/28/1898 | Married Ella Jones last Sunday, per Hurlbut news. |
| Dyer | Thomas | KC, p5c2, 7/21/1898 | Married Ella Jones of Scott on July 10, 1898 at the Christian Church. Groom from Sand Prairie. |
| Easton | W. A. | KC, p1c2, 1/3/1901 | Arrived from Fairmont, SD to visit his brother, W. S. Easton of Viola. |
| Easton | W., Mr. and Mrs. | KC, p1c4, 1/7/1897 | Resided in Fairmount, ND. They visited relatives in Mt. Sterling. According to KC, 1/14/1897, p5c2, Mr. and Mrs. Warren Easton were from Fairmount, SD. |
| Easton | Warren | KC, p5c3, 3/15/1900 | Arrived from Fairmont, SD to visit father-in-law, A. E. Mills of Mt. Sterling area. |
| Easton | Warren | KC, p5c4, 2/20/1902 | From Viola. Sold his farm in Dakota. Planned to move there and open a store. |
| Easton | Warren, Mrs. | KC, p6c2, 11/15/1900 | Lived in Viola. Visited her parents in Mt. Sterling. |

Genealogical Gleanings From Early Newspapers for Residents In and Near
Crawford County, Wisconsin, 1897-1902

| LAST NAME | FIRST NAME | NEWSPAPER PAGE/COLUMN MONTH/DAY/YEAR | GENEALOGICAL DATA |
|---|---|---|---|
| Easton | Warren, Mrs. | KC, p1c3, 1/20/1898 | Traveled from Fairmount, SD to Wauzeka. Brought her adopted son with her. Visited sister, Mrs. W. H. Thompson. Also visited parents, Mr. and Mrs. A. E. Mills of Mt. Sterling. |
| Eckenberger | Tobias | KC, p1c5, 8/21/1902 | Died August 14, 1902. He was a homeless Scandinavian who was well-known in Grant and Richland Counties. Aged 50 years. Charles McMillan and Sherm Streeter, painters from Boscobel, were charged with his murder. They were later acquitted. |
| Edlebach | Ben | KC, p8c4, 10/17/1901 | Married Laura Cornford on Oct. 16, 1901. Bride from Prairie du Chien. Groom from Postville, IA. |
| Edwards | Thomas and Carr, Charles | KC, Supp., 12/20/1900 | Crawford Co. Board of Supervisors approved payment of expenses in the matter of State vs. Thomas Edwards and Charles Carr. The witnesses were Amanda Atherton, Fred Evans, William Haupt, Katie Haupt and Elizabeth Beeseckee. |
| Egan | Rosana | KC, p8c4, 6/21/1900 | Marriage license issued to Rosanna Egan and Francisco Gutherie of Bell Plains, IA. |
| Ehorn | Bridget, Mrs. | KC, p4c3, 12/15/1898 | Arrived from Washington (state) to visit relatives in Wheatville area. |
| Eitsert | Henry | KC, p5c2, 2/4/1897 | Eitsert named a post office. Given the name Boma. It was located between Mt. Sterling and Ferryville. |
| Eldridge | Fred R. | KC, p8c3, 8/15/1901 | Died Aug. 12, 1901 in Prairie du Chien. |
| Election Returns | | KC, p1c4, 4/4/1901 | Village of Wauzeka -- President, J. O'Neil; Trustees, W. A. Vaughan, George Sanger, G. H. Perrin, John Gossell, G. F Dennis, H. M. Wagner; Clerk, F. J. Perrin; Treasurer, J. G. Widmann; Supervisor, O. P. Vaughan; Marshal, D. Lyons; Justice of the Peace, Myron Hoover; Constable, Lou Rider; Assessor. H. Reeter, Sr. |
| Election Returns | | KC, p1c4, 4/4/1901 | Town of Wauzeka -- Supervisors, Joe Doll, Sr., Lou Marfelius and Jerome Rose (per 4/11/1901); Clerk, E. E. Trautsch; Treasurer, J. Scwartz; Assessor, John Schwert; Justice of the Peace, F. Geitz, I. P. Lawrence; Constables', Fred Weniger, James Tesar and Ed. H. Porter. |
| Election Returns | | KC, p1c4, 4/4/1901 | Town of Utica -- Supervisors, J. W. McCullick, Samuel Iverson, Peter J. O'Neil; Clerk, Erdman Strecker; Treasurer, Orin A. Lester; Assessor, George B. Mitchell; Justices of the Peace, Thomas Finnegan, A. D. Bellows, P. M. Peck; Constables, M. J. Phalin, Jr., A. E. Spencer, Asa J. Tainter, John H. Lester. |
| Election Returns | | KC, p1c4, 4/4/1901 | Village of Steuben -- President, Peter Ferris; Trustees, Joseph Kritz, Robert Jones, James Kelley, Charles Young, H. C. Musselman, A. E. Dillman; Clerk, E. W. Crowley; Treasurer, H. M. Pond; Assessor, J. E. Foley; Supervisor, Lee Wannemaker; Justice of the Peace, W. W. Kelley; Constable, Zeph Foust. |

Genealogical Gleanings From Early Newspapers for Residents In and Near
Crawford County, Wisconsin, 1897-1902

| LAST NAME | FIRST NAME | NEWSPAPER PAGE/COLUMN MONTH/DAY/YEAR | GENEALOGICAL DATA |
|---|---|---|---|
| Election Results | | KC, p1c4, 4/4/1901 | Village of Gays Mills -- President, J. A. Hayes; Trustees, N. Jurgensen, J. B. Gilligan, F. F. Twining, D. E. Gander, L. G. Lester, Charles Thomson; Clerk, H. W. Stuckey; Treasurer, F. J. Lewis; Assessor, V. G. Barker; Justices of the Peace, J. L. Stowell, 2 years, William Rhienhart, 1 year; Police Justice, A. L. Stowell; Constables, A. E. Moon, J. E. Curley; Supervisor, J. A. Hays |
| Election Results | | KC, p1c4, 4/4/1901 | Town of Eastman -- Supervisors, Charles Iverson, Steve Allen, Jacob Becwar; Clerk, J. F. Sprosty; Treasurer, Anthony Prochaska; Assessor, B. Dunne; Justices of the Peace, J. Morris, Full Term, Chris Garvey, Full Term, E. J. Crowley, Vacancy, John Seekatz Vacancy; Constables, H. Bourque (Burk), J. Roach, Jr. W. Honslik. |
| Election Returns | | KC, p1c4, 4/4/1901 | Town of Seneca -- Supervisors, Robert Stuart, Ole Alland, John Lynch, Sr.; Clerk, Thomas Taylor; Treasurer, John Fitzgibbon; Assessor, B. J. Kneeland; Justices of the Peace, C. Bennett, F. H. Young, Edward McNamara; Constables, A. C. Withee, J. E. Olson, Joseph Kettle * Village of Soldiers Grove, President, A. Peterson; Trustees, J. K. Sorenson, R. L. Smith. E. E. Rogers. O. K. Himley, H. Natwick, J. Mitchell; Supervisor, Dr. J. Dinsdale; Police Justice, W. G. Campbell * City of Prairie du Chien;, Mayor, Charles Greele, Sr.; Treasurer, Frank Smrcina; Clerk, Fred J. Evans; Marshal, Charles Lindner; Assessor, George Oswald; Police Justice, George Harrington; Supervisors, L. Quinn, M. Menges, H. Otto C. Nugent; Aldermen, Ed McCluskey, _ Tesar, _ Kiezer and James Duffy. |
| Election Returns | | KC, p1c4, 4/4/1901 | Town of Marietta -- Supervisors, J. B. Kinder, Will Scott, James Trumbull; Clerk, Will Ferrell; Treasurer, David Patten; Assessor, Martin Robinson * Town of Haney -- Supervisors, F. Hammerly, William Lowe, James Campbell; Clerk, Alanson Taft; Treasurer, Elmer Garner; Assessor, T. A. McDowell * Town of Freeman -- Supervisors, T. T. Sime, A. Runice, C. Bishop; Clerk, C. T. Tower; Treasurer, John Sterling; Assessor, Peter Lysne; Justices, T. T. Sime, J. Sterling. |
| Election Returns | | KC, p1c4, 4/4/1901 | Town of Prairie du Chien; -- Supervisors, B. Foran, Herman Zable, Thomas Lechnir; Clerk, Ernest Hoffman; Assessor, Louis Cherrier; Treasurer, Louis Kaizer; Justices, Louis Nickerson, Charles Eukey. |
| Election Returns | | KC, p1c4, 4/4/1901 | Bell Center -- President, George Divall; Trustees, J. M. Campbell; Willis Rounds, William Young, David Kimmel, C J. Miller, H. C. Whiteaker; Clerk, George Wood; Treasurer, H. Coleman; Supervisor, J. N. Kast; Assessor, R. C. Rounds; Justice of the Peace, M. L. Brown; Constable, D. W. Whiteaker * Town of Scott -- Chairman, James Turk; Clerk, J. D. Hudson; Treasurer, Ervin Pittsley; Assessor, William Wilt. |

Genealogical Gleanings From Early Newspapers for Residents In and Near
Crawford County, Wisconsin, 1897-1902

| LAST NAME | FIRST NAME | NEWSPAPER PAGE/COLUMN MONTH/DAY/YEAR | GENEALOGICAL DATA |
|---|---|---|---|
| Election Returns | | KC, p1c4, 4/4/1901 | Lynxville -- President, W. M. Huard; Supervisor, William Allen; Treasurer, L. F. Copsey; Assessor, Phil. Soucy; Clerk, Stacy Wolcott. |
| Election Returns | | KC, p1c4, 4/4/1901 | Town of Clayton -- Supervisors, Thomas Barlow, William Briggs, John Hounsell; Clerk, E. D. Mullikin; Treasurer, M. Malone; Assessor, J. Dull; Justices, S. Copas, Warren Haskins; Constables', Tim Murphy, Dan Hill. |
| Election Returns | | KC, p1c4, 4/4/1901 | Bridgeport -- Supervisors, A. F. Jones, John F. Herold, Sol Laraviere (per 4/11/1901); Clerk, E. G. Ward; Treasurer, John Lawless; Assessor, C. W. Kuckenbecker; Justices, William Bieloh, C. E. McGree, F. E. Dull. |
| Election Returns | | KC, p1c5, 4/3/1902 | The Crawford County Board will be composed of O. P. Vaughan of Wauzeka, Joe Schwartz of the Town of Wauzeka, D. Lenehan of Prairie du Chien, T. J. Murphy of Prairie du Chien, Henry Otto of Prairie du Chien, William Brew of Prairie du Chien, B. F. Foran of the Town of Prairie du Chien, J. E. Ostrander of Eastman, Enos Gay of Seneca, P. N. Peterson of Utica, Thomas De Lacy of Freeman, Norman Barlow of Clayton, J. H. Turk of Scott, Fred Hammerly of Haney, Jerome Kinder of Marietta, Herman Stukey of Bridgeport, C. A. Cryderman of Soldiers Grove, F. W. Lewis of Gays Mills, J. N. Kast of Bell Center, John Cobb of Steuben, W. S. Allen of Lynxville and Martin Loftus of De Soto. |
| Eley | Arrilla | KC, p1c5, 10/28/1897 | Married Frank E. Gay on Oct. 24, 1897 at home of Joseph Peacock, Sr. Bride and groom from La Farge. |
| Elgar | John | KC, p8c3, 10/24/1901 | Funeral held October 20, 1901. Resided in Prairie du Chien. Father of Mrs. Christie. |
| Ellefson | C. | KC, p5c1, 2/18/1897 | Elected an officer in Utica Farmers' Mutual Insurance Co. Resided in Franklin. |
| Elliot | boy | KC, p5c1, 8/11/1898 | Son recently born to Mr. and Mrs. Elliot of Bell Center. |
| Elliot | Celia | KC, p4c3, 4/25/1901 | Died April 12, 1901. Born Feb. 1, 1829 at Franklin, Kentucky. (Maiden surname may be Breedlove.) Moved to Grant Co., WI when she was 15. Married William Elliot in 1846 and shortly thereafter moved to Crawford Co. Husband died in 1879. Survived by 7 of her 10 children. Three children live in Wisconsin, 1 lives in Iowa, 2 live in Nebraska and 1 lives in California. Moved to Nebraska 2 years ago to live with son, D. C. Elliot. Buried in Belwood Cemetery in Fullerton, NB. |
| Elliot | Celia, Mrs. | KC, p1c3, 4/25/1901 | Her funeral was held April 15, 1901 in Fullerton, NB. Attended by son, D. C. Elliot of Hurlbut, WI. |
| Elliot | Will | KC, p5c4, 3/1/1900 | Departed Town of Scott for a job in Fennimore. |
| Ellis | H. | KC, p4c2, 1/13/1898 | Traveled from South Dakota to visit in Gays Mills after an absence of many years in the west. |
| Ellis | LeRoy | KC, p8c4, 9/30/1897 | At a conference of the Methodist Church held in Platteville, LeRoy Ellis (sub) was assigned to Patch Grove. |

Genealogical Gleanings From Early Newspapers for Residents In and Near
Crawford County, Wisconsin, 1897-1902

| LAST NAME | FIRST NAME | NEWSPAPER PAGE/COLUMN MONTH/DAY/YEAR | GENEALOGICAL DATA |
|---|---|---|---|
| Ellis | Sylvester "Vet" | KC, p1c6, 8/18/1898 | Returned from his travels in the South and West to visit his father in Eastman. |
| Ellis | W. H. | KC, p8c3, 9/12/1901 | Married Belle Harris on Sept. 2 or Sept 9, 1901. Bride was from Prairie du Chien. Groom was from Platteville. |
| Ellis | Willis | KC, p8c3, 2/18/1897 | Married Jennie Hazen on Feb. 15, 1897 in Prairie du Chien. Bride and groom were from Town of Eastman. |
| Ellithorpe | Winnie | KC, p1c3, 8/22/1901 | Departed Wauzeka to teach in Savannah, IL. |
| Ellithorpe | Winnie | KC, p1c5, 2/9/1899 | Taught school in Wauzeka in 1899. E. E. Brindley, Crawford County Superintendent of Schools published a comprehensive list of all teachers in the county. |
| Ellithorpe | Winnifred | KC, p1c2, 1/20/1898 | Winnifred Ellithorpe, Katie Meyer and Walter Newcomb joined the Good Templar Lodge in Wauzeka. |
| Ellithrope | Winifred | KC, p4c1, 1/28/1897 | Wrote a letter condemning drunken behavior of men in Wauzeka. Published in paper. |
| Ellston | Henry | KC, p1c4, 5/29/1902 | Resided in Muscoda. He made telephones and worked as an electrician. |
| Ellsworth | Fannie, Miss | KC, p5c3, 11/23/1899 | Returned to Tavera. Went to Montana last spring. |
| Elton | Violet | KC, Supp., 4/24/1902 | Died April 22, 1902. Daughter of Sam Elton of Bloomington. |
| Elton | Sam | KC, p8c3, 5/1/1902 | Died April 27, 1902 in Bloomington. |
| Elvin | Hilda | KC, p1c5, 2/9/1899 | Taught school in Freeman in 1899. E. E. Brindley, Crawford County Superintendent of Schools published a comprehensive list of all teachers in the county. |
| Emerson | Mary | KC, p8c4, 4/1/1897 | Visited friends and relatives in Seneca and departed for her former home in Nebraska. |
| Emery | A. B., Mrs. | KC, p5c3, 4/15/1897 | Arrived from Beulah, IA to visit parents, Mr. and Mrs. John Newton of Wauzeka. |
| Emigrant train | | KC, p1c4, 3/27/1902 | An emigrant train left for North Dakota on Tuesday with the following: Charles Buckmaster, A. H. Rounds, P. L. Purrington, E. M. Kast, Lou Courtney -- all of Bell Center; Orrin Gay and John Spencer of Seneca; Will Purrington, Steve Rotan, Asa Miller, Dick Ellis, John Bacon, Elmer Turk, Minnie Turk -- all of Bell Center; Henry Buckmaster of Petersburg; Will Stowell of Gays Mills; William Meyers, Norm. Onstine and wife, Lee Dunbar, Will and George McDaniel and Robert Cooley -- all of Wauzeka. |
| Emigrant train | | KC, p5c4, 4/3/1902 | Emigrant train left for North Dakota. Peter Farris of Steuben went to Hope, ND. F. M. Haines of Steuben went west. Walter Posey went west. Fred Davey went west. Other Crawford County citizens on the train were Childs Chadwick, Charles Wayne, Tom Sloane, Art Young, James Mason, D. G. Lawrence and William Bunnell. H. Peterson of Steuben was the emigrant agent. |
| Emshoff | John | KC, p8c3, 3/3/1898 | Called from his home in Soldiers Grove to father's bedside in Sextonville, Richland Co. |

Genealogical Gleanings From Early Newspapers for Residents In and Near
Crawford County, Wisconsin, 1897-1902

| LAST NAME | FIRST NAME | NEWSPAPER PAGE/COLUMN MONTH/DAY/YEAR | GENEALOGICAL DATA |
|---|---|---|---|
| Enerson | Carrie | KC, p1c5, 1/13/1898 | Married Edward Johnson on Dec. 30, 1897. Groom was son of T. Johnson of Towerville. |
| England | Frank, Sr. | KC, p8c1, 4/21/1898 | Feared dead from an avalanche in Alaska. Former resident of Patch Grove. |
| English | Catherine | KC, Supp., 12/29/1898 | Crawford Co. Board of Supervisors approved payment of expenses in the matter of Catherine English, Insane. |
| Enke | Charles | KC, p1c4, 8/9/1900 | Died Aug. 2, 1900 at Dutch Ridge. Aged 77 years. |
| Enright | J. C., Mrs. | KC, p4c4, 11/16/1899 | Granted a pension increase to $8 per month. Each of the 3 minor children get $2 per month until they reach 16 years of age. |
| Enright | John | KC, p1c4, 7/28/1898 | Died July 16, 1898 in Seneca. Survived by wife and 3 small children. |
| Erickson | Anna | KC, p5c3, 4/26/1900 | Married Charles Johnson on April 23, 1900. Groom was from Gays Mills. He was brother of Mrs. Sam Halverson. |
| Erickson | Anna | KC, p1c2, 2/15/1900 | Employed at City Hotel in Wauzeka. Called home to help with sick mother. |
| Erickson | Hans | KC, Supp., 12/29/1898 | Crawford Co. Board of Supervisors approved Justices and Constables' expenses related to the case, State vs. Hans Erickson. |
| Erickson | Martin | KC, p4c4, 3/17/1898 | Traveled from Cashton to visit brother, Albert Erickson of Soldiers Grove. |
| Erickson | Albert H. | KC, p1c2, 3/3/1898 | Married Mary Oleson in Excelsior on Feb. 21, 1898. Bride and groom from Soldiers Grove. |
| Ertel | F. E. | KC, p5c4, 2/22/1900 | Arrived from Haddam, KS to visit sister, Mrs. C. E. Thompson of Gays Mills. Departed Crawford Co. 18 years ago. |
| Ertel | Albert | KC, p4c2, 7/22/1897 | Married Mary Garrity of La Crosse on July 15, 1897. Groom from Lynxville. C. H. Speck, Justice of the Peace, officiated. |
| Ertel | J. C. | KC, Supp., 12/12/1901 | Attended a Teacher's Institute in Crawford County in 1901. Resided in Eastman. |
| Ertel | James | KC, p5c4, 2/15/1900 | Former school principal in Eastman. |
| Ertel | James C. | KC, p1c2, 4/19/1900 | Native of Lynxville. Recently graduated from Valparaiso. Took a temporary job teaching in Richland Center. |
| Ertel | V. | KC, p5c3 12/4/1902 | Lived in Seneca. Entertained his daughter, Mrs. Mary Thomson of Gays Mills and Mrs. Grant Nickerson. |
| Ertel | V. | KC, p5c1, 2/21/1898 | Lived in Seneca. Visited brother in Quincy, IL. |
| Ertel | Valentine | KC, p1c2, 2/17/1898 | Married Mary Welsh of Glen Haven on Feb. 7, 1898. Groom from Lynxville. Andrew Welsh was a cousin of bride. Maggie Welsh was bride's sister. |
| Ertel | Valentine | KC, p5c3, 2/27/1902 | Resided in Seneca. Attended brother's funeral in Quincy, IL. Brother owned an orange grove in California. |
| Evans | Fred | KC, p8c2, 3/31/1898 | Married Mabel Rienow, daughter of Henry Rienow of Prairie du Chien on Mar. 28, 1898. Groom from McGregor, IA. Many relatives and guests mentioned. |

Genealogical Gleanings From Early Newspapers for Residents In and Near
Crawford County, Wisconsin, 1897-1902

| LAST NAME | FIRST NAME | NEWSPAPER PAGE/COLUMN MONTH/DAY/YEAR | GENEALOGICAL DATA |
|---|---|---|---|
| Evans | Fred J. | KC, p5c5, 4/5/1900 | Elected clerk in City of Prairie du Chien. |
| Evans | Henry | KC, p5c2, 1/14/1897 | Resided in Wauzeka. Went to Winona to supervise production of his motors. |
| Evans | Henry | KC, p1c4, 8/26/1897 | E. W. Newton and Henry Evans of Wauzeka were inventors of an egg case. Patent received. |
| Evans | Henry | KC, p1c2, 3/10/1898 | Caught what was "probably the last otter in country" in the Wisconsin bottom. Measured 5 foot 5 inches. |
| Evans | J. P. | KC, p1c1, 1/18/1900 | Advertised legal services. Attorney based in Prairie du Chien. |
| Evans | Joseph P. | KC, p8c4, 6/7/1901 | Married Constance Marie Garvey on June 4, 1900. Bride was daughter of James Garvey of Prairie du Chien. Groom was son of William H. Evans of Prairie du Chien. |
| Evans | Joseph P. | KC, p1c4, 11/1/1900 | Democratic candidate for District Attorney in Crawford County. Born Mar. 4, 1868 in Town of Clayton. Oldest son of W. H. Evans of Prairie du Chien. Father was elected District Attorney in 1877. Graduated from Sacred Heart College in 1888. Fluent in German, Bohemian and French |
| Evans | Sarah A. | KC, Supp., 12/20/1900 | Crawford Co. Soldiers Relief Comm. approved aid to Sarah A. Evans of Clayton. |
| Evans | Walter, Mrs. | KC, p8c1, 8/31/1899 | Nee Ida Morrison. Visited parents in Prairie du Chien and then returned to her home in St. Louis |
| Evans | William H. | KC, p1c5, 3/28/1901 | Candidate for Crawford County Judge. Born at Pittsburg, VA on Nov. 3, 1842 to Joseph Evans and Mary (Hall) Evans. His father was a gunsmith and moved family to several large cities in the East, South and West. William moved to Clayton, Crawford Co. in 1860, following his father who moved here in 1856. Enlisted in Co. D, 31st WI Infantry in 1862. Wounded in the head in Atlanta, GA in 1864. Engaged in farming and general merchandise in Yankeetown after the war. Cleared land in sections 11, 10 and 4. Married Mary J. Flanagan in 1867. Studied law and was admitted to the bar in 1873. Served as member of Assembly and district attorney. Practiced law in the courts of WI, IL, IA, MN and SD. (More detail in his biography.) |
| Evert | Emma M. | KC, p1c2, 2/18/1897 | Married Floyd E. Divers of New York on Feb. 10, 1897. Bride was the daughter of Fred Evert of Prairie du Chien. The Rev. G. W. Reichert officiated. |
| Evert | Fred | KC, Supp., 12/20/1900 | Represented 3rd Ward of Prairie du Chien on the Crawford Co. Board of Supervisors in 1900. |
| Everts | Charles | KC, p5c1, 2/21/1898 | Traveled from Iowa to visit friends in Haney. |
| Ewell | Elizabeth I. | KC, p8c2, 5/18/1899 | Married John Wetzel on May 17, 1899 in Prairie du Chien. Bride and groom from Charles City, IA. |
| Ewers | D. O. | KC, p1c2, 4/19/1900 | Departed Readstown for Chippewa Co., WI to explore opportunities to invest in land. |
| Eyers | Samuel | KC, p5c4, 1/30/1902 | Died Jan. 26, 1902 in Town of Scott at 37 years of age. |

Genealogical Gleanings From Early Newspapers for Residents In and Near
Crawford County, Wisconsin, 1897-1902

| LAST NAME | FIRST NAME | NEWSPAPER PAGE/COLUMN MONTH/DAY/YEAR | GENEALOGICAL DATA |
|---|---|---|---|
| Faber | Ernest | KC, p1c6, 5/19/1898 | Issue of Fact for Jury to be heard in the May term of the Crawford County Circuit Court. I. C. McGregor vs. Ernest Faber. |
| Faber | Ernest | KC, p4c4, 11/10/1898 | Issues of Fact for Jury heard in the November term of the Crawford County Circuit Court. I. C. McGregor Guy vs. Ernest Faber. |
| Fach | John | KC, p1c3, 6/3/1897 | Lived in Prairie du Chien. Lost 2 fingers while working with a wood saw for Frank Wetzel. |
| Fagan | John M. | KC, p5c5, 1/25/1900 | Marble dealer in Bridgeport. |
| Fagen | John M. | KC, p1c3, 12/26/1901 | Monument dealer in Prairie du Chien. |
| Fagen | Mrs. | KC, p1c5, 6/19/1902 | Died June 12, 1902. Aunt of Thomas Couglin of Town of Seneca. |
| Fairbank | Harry D. | KC, 1/21/1898 | Married Stasia Krall of Calmar, IA on Jan. 12, 1897 at the Dousman House. Groom from Cresco, IA. The Rev. G. W. Reichert officiated. |
| Fairfield | Anna, Mrs. | KC, p8c1, 2/16/1899 | Married Thomas Nugent on Feb. 14, 1899. Bride and groom from Prairie du Chien. |
| Falkner | Zena | KC, p4c3, 2/11/1897 | Moved to the Hiram Whiteaker farm near Bell Center. |
| Fannon | | KC, p8c2, 8/10/1899 | The Fannons were . . . "noted crooks from Dubuque (who) worked the shell game at Battle Island." |
| Farley | Tom | KC, Supp., 12/18/1902 | Crawford County Board of Supervisors examined bills in the Justices and Constables' Account for State vs. Tom Farley. |
| Farmer | Mr. | KC, p8c3, 11/16/1899 | Died Nov. 11, 1899. (May have been from North McGregor.) |
| Farr | Mary, Mrs. | KC, p4c1, 5/6/1897 | Married Sumner Dudley of Gays Mills in Beaver Dam, WI in April 1897. |
| Farrington | John, Mrs. | KC, p1c3, 8/8/1901 | Arrived from home in Minneapolis to visit parents and brother, Robert Hines, in Wheatville. |
| Farris | boy | KC, p5c3, 9/5/1901 | Son born Aug. 28, 1901 to John Farris of Steuben. |
| Farris | Clara, Mrs. | KC, p4c2, 8/26/1897 | Resided in Steuben. Visited parents in Wauzeka. |
| Farris | Cora | KC, p5c4, 6/6/1901 | Opened a restaurant in Steuben. |
| Farris | G. W., Jr. | KC, p5c3, 6/15/1899 | Resided in Hope, ND. Visited friends in Steuben. |
| Farris | girl | KC, p4c2, 1/14/1897 | Daughter recently born to J. T. Farris of Steuben. |
| Farris | girl | KC, p8c3, 4/8/1897 | Three-month-old daughter of J. T. Farris died Mar. 29, 1897 in Steuben. |
| Farris | girl | KC, p5c2, 10/7/1897 | Daughter born Sept. 24, 1897 to Henry Farris of Steuben. |
| Farris | Gladys | KC, p8c3, 5/12/1898 | Died May 5, 1898 at Steuben. Aged 5 years, 2 months and 3 days. Daughter of Henry and Clara Farris. |

Genealogical Gleanings From Early Newspapers for Residents In and Near
Crawford County, Wisconsin, 1897-1902

| LAST NAME | FIRST NAME | NEWSPAPER PAGE/COLUMN MONTH/DAY/YEAR | GENEALOGICAL DATA |
|---|---|---|---|
| Farris | H. C. | KC, p5c3, 11/2/1899 | Purchased the Schweiger hotel in Steuben. |
| Farris | Henry | KC, p5c3, 9/5/1901 | Henry Farris, Peter Farris and James Kelly, all of Steuben, took jobs on railroad at Grant Springs. |
| Farris | Henry | KC, p8c3, 6/24/1897 | Served as pathmaster in Steuben. |
| Farris | J. T. | KC, p5c3, 6/15/1899 | J. T. Farris, A. Dowse, T. Kast and Seth Reynolds went to Iowa to do railway work. Resided in Steuben area. |
| Farris | J., Mrs. | KC, p5c4, 8/29/1901 | Lived in Steuben. Party given Saturday evening to celebrate her 69th birthday. |
| Farris | Jane | KC, p4c2, 8/26/1897 | Traveled to North Dakota from home in Steuben to visit her sons. |
| Farris | John | KC, p5c3, 3/16/1899 | Recently died in (Steuben area?). Resident of area over 40 years. Father of G. W. Farris and W. H. Farris of Hope, ND. |
| Farris | John, Sr. | KC, Supp., 12/19/1901 | John Farris, Sr. built the first house in what became the Village of Steuben. |
| Farris | Lincoln | KC, p1c5, 5/19/1898 | Killed 18 rattlesnakes in a den near Steuben. |
| Farris | Maggie, Mrs. | KC, p1c3, 8/10/1899 | Mrs. Maggie Farris, Minnie Cantwell, Nellie Cantwell, Earl Kielley and G. W. Farris left Steuben for Courtney, ND. "Courtney and vicinity now has a large number of Crawford County people among its inhabitants." |
| Farris | Pete | KC, p5c4, 7/29/1897 | Peter Farris, his mother and James Kielley planned to leave Steuben for a new start in North Dakota. |
| Farris | Pete | KC, p5c4, 7/27/1899 | Pete Farris, Ed Posey, Tom Jones, Ben Kielley and little Henry Farris left Steuben for Dakota. |
| Farris | Peter | KC, p1c4 and p4c2, 9/15/1898 | Married Maggie Cantwell on Sept. 7, 1898 in Boscobel. Bride and groom from Steuben. P. B. Richardson, J.P. officiated. |
| Farris | Rosa | KC, p1c3, 9/22/1898 | Married Marcus D. Smith of (Seneca?) on Sept. 11, 1898 in Seneca. Bride from Steuben. This was a double wedding with Lillie May Updyke and Charles E. Smith. |
| Farris | Thomas | KC, p1c2, 11/7/1901 | Married Minnie Cantwell (probably on Oct. 29, 1901) at Steuben, WI. |
| Farris | W. | KC, p5c4, 6/8/1899 | Resided in Hope, ND. Visited friends in Steuben. |
| Faulkner | Z. | KC, p4c1, 3/24/1898 | Resided in Wheatville. Moved to the Barney Hines place. |
| Faust | H. J. | KC, p1c2, 7/24/1902 | Married Maggie Spiker on July 19, 1902. Groom from Steuben. J. O. Hanks, J.P. officiated. |
| Faust | Mart | KC, p4c2, 12/9/1897 | Hosted a wood bee and dance in Steuben. |
| Favor | Arnie | KC, p1c4, 4/14/1898 | Married Mary Denning on Mar. 30, 1898. The Rev. Geo. W. Nuzum officiated. Groom from Vernon County. |
| Favre | Theodore | KC, p8c3, 6/13/1901 | Married Rose Fox on June 9, 1901 at St. Gabriel's Church. Bride and groom were from Prairie du Chien. |
| Felde | Alma | KC, Supp., 12/12/1901 | Alma Felde of Reed attended the summer Teacher's Institute in Soldiers Grove. |

Genealogical Gleanings From Early Newspapers for Residents In and Near
Crawford County, Wisconsin, 1897-1902

| LAST NAME | FIRST NAME | NEWSPAPER PAGE/COLUMN MONTH/DAY/YEAR | GENEALOGICAL DATA |
|---|---|---|---|
| Felde | Alma | KC, Supp., 12/12/1901 | Attended a Teacher's Institute in Crawford County in 1901. Resided in Reed. |
| Feldman | Alex | KC, p1c2, 9/2/1897 | Left Wauzeka for a 3-year apprenticeship in a Milwaukee jewelry store. |
| Feldman | Charles | KC, p1c2, 11/3/1898 | Installed as an officer at the International Order of Good Templars (I.O.G.T.) Lodge in Wauzeka. |
| Feldman | Mary M. | KC, p1c6, 11/4/1897 | Issue of default to be heard at the November term of the Circuit Court in Crawford County. Mary M. Feldman vs. Herman Gregerson et. al. |
| Feldmann | Alex | KC, p1c4, 6/5/1902 | Severely burned hand. Threw a leaking can of gasoline out the window of D. Brown's saloon in Wauzeka. Some gasoline spilled on floor and caught on fire. Prevented a great deal of damage. |
| Feldmann | Alex | KC, p1c3, 7/24/1902 | Purchased J. G. Widmann's hardware store in Wauzeka. |
| Feldmann | Charles | KC, p1c6, 1/23/1902 | Planned to marry Allie Degnan. Bride and groom from Wauzeka. |
| Feldmann | Charles G. | KC, p1c6, 1/30/1902 | Married Allie Degnan on Jan. 27, 1902 at the parsonage in Town of Eastman. Bride daughter of James Degnan. Groom son of Mrs. J. N. Feldmann. Bride and groom from Wauzeka. |
| Feldmann | J. N., Mrs. | KC, p1c5, 1/25/1900 | Operated a general store in Wauzeka. |
| Feldmann | J. N., Mrs. | KC, p1c3, 1/25/1900 | Featured in an article on Wauzeka's business concerns. Mrs. Feldman and her son, Charles, operated a general store. |
| Ferguson | S. C. | KC, Supp., 12/12/1901 | Received funds from the Crawford Co. Soldiers Relief Commission. Resided in Prairie du Chien. |
| Fernett | Mrs. | KC, p8c4, 2/20/1902 | Recently died in St. Paul while visiting her children. Resident of Prairie du Chien. |
| Fernette | Paul | KC, Supp., 12/12/1901 | Received funds from the Crawford Co. Soldiers Relief Commission. Resided in Prairie du Chien. |
| Fernette | Paul, Jr. | KC, p8c3, 4/3/1902 | Died April 2, 1902 in Prairie du Chien. |
| Ferrel | Dollie | KC, p1c5, 2/9/1899 | Taught school in Marietta in 1899. E. E. Brindley, Crawford County Superintendent of Schools published a comprehensive list of all teachers in the county. |
| Ferrell | William | KC, p5c5, 4/5/1900 | Elected clerk in Marietta. |
| Ferrick | John | KC, p5c5, 4/5/1900 | Elected supervisor in Town of Scott. |
| Ferrick | Thomas | KC, p1c2, 11/10/1898 | Married Anna O'Kane on Nov. 9, 1898 at St. Patrick's Catholic Church in Town of Scott. |
| Ferrick | Thomas H. | KC, p1c3, 2/20/1902 | Managed a mattress factor at Petersburg. |
| Figum | P. | KC, p1c5, 11/30/1899 | Resided in Decorah, IA. Purchased the City Hotel in Wauzeka. Former hardware dealer in Soldiers Grove and proprietor of the National Hotel in Decorah. |

Genealogical Gleanings From Early Newspapers for Residents In and Near
Crawford County, Wisconsin, 1897-1902

| LAST NAME | FIRST NAME | NEWSPAPER PAGE/COLUMN MONTH/DAY/YEAR | GENEALOGICAL DATA |
|---|---|---|---|
| Figum | P. | KC, p1c3, 1/25/1900 | Featured in an article on Wauzeka's business concerns. Operated the City Hotel. |
| Figum | Peter | KC, p1c3, 9/5/1901 | Departed home in Soldiers Grove for northern Wisconsin to engage in timber business. Wife and kids stayed behind. |
| Fillmore | Peter | KC, p8c3, 5/20/1897 | Died May 7, 1897 at home in Bell Center. |
| Filmore | Helena | KC, Supp., 12/29/1898 | Crawford Co. Board of Supervisors approved payment of expenses in the matter of Helena Filmore, insane. |
| Filmore | Riley | KC, Supp., 12/29/1898 | Crawford Co. Board of Supervisors approved payment of expenses in the matter of Riley Filmore, dependent child. |
| Finley | Arthur | KC, Supp., 12/12/1901 | State vs. Arthur Finley heard in Crawford Co. Court. |
| Finley | Bridget | KC, p8c3, 1/14/1897 | Taught school on Bragg Ridge. Ferryville news item. |
| Finley | Catherine | KC, p8c4, 8/29/1901 | Married Fred Smethurst on Aug. 26, 1901 at Catholic Church in Town of Seneca. Bride and groom were from Town of Seneca. |
| Finley | J. H., Mrs. | KC, p5c3, 4/11/1901 | Returned to Seneca after caring for her ill mother, Mrs. T. Joy of Copper Creek. |
| Finley | James F. | KC, p5c3, 2/21/1901 | Married Catherine Lynch on Feb. 18, 1901. Bride was from Town of Seneca. Groom was from Boma. Bride was daughter of John Lynch and sister of Hannah Lynch. |
| Finley | John and Nellie, Miss | KC, p8c3, 1/14/1897 | Resided on Bragg Ridge. Went to Denver, CO for Nellie's health. Ferryville news item. |
| Finley | John H. | KC, Supp., 11/8/1900 | Married Bridget Joy on Oct. 30, 1900 at St. Patrick's Church. Bride was daughter of Thomas Joy (of Town of Seneca?). |
| Finley | Johnnie | KC, p5c1, 12/2/1897 | John Roach and daughter, Nellie, of Eastman recently attended the Johnnie Finley funeral in Rising Sun. |
| Finley | Laura | KC, Supp., 12/12/1901 | Attended a Teacher's Institute in Crawford County in 1901. Resided in Boma. |
| Finley | Laura and Rose | KC, Supp., 12/12/1901 | Laura and Rose Finley of Boma attended the summer Teacher's Institute in Soldiers Grove. |
| Finley | Patrick | KC, p8c3, 11/15/1900 | Died Nov. 13, 1900 in Prairie du Chien at age 83. Served in Co. D., 31st Regiment of WI Volunteers in Civil War. |
| Finley | Rosa | KC, p1c5, 2/9/1899 | Taught school in Utica in 1899. E. E. Brindley, Crawford County Superintendent of Schools published a comprehensive list of all teachers in the county. |
| Finley | Rose | KC, p8c6, 3/8/1900 | Taught school in Boma. |
| Finley | Rose | KC, Supp., 12/12/1901 | Attended a Teacher's Institute in Crawford County in 1901. Resided in Boma. |
| Finley | T. | KC, p5c3, 2/6/1902 | Resided in Seneca. Putting up his season's ice. |
| Finley | T., Mrs. | KC, p5c3, 11/2/1899 | Hosted a quilting bee in Seneca. Made 3 quilts. The boys came for a dance later in the evening. |
| Finley | Tim | KC, p1c2, 12/16/1897 | Advertised that he was giving a New Year's ball in Seneca. Music to be provided by Oppreicht's orchestra. |

Genealogical Gleanings From Early Newspapers for Residents In and Near
Crawford County, Wisconsin, 1897-1902

| LAST NAME | FIRST NAME | NEWSPAPER PAGE/COLUMN MONTH/DAY/YEAR | GENEALOGICAL DATA |
|---|---|---|---|
| Finley | Tressa | KC, p1c5, 2/9/1899 | Taught school in Utica in 1899. E. E. Brindley, Crawford County Superintendent of Schools published a comprehensive list of all teachers in the county. |
| Finn | John | KC, p1c5, 10/28/1897 | Died Monday from injuries suffered from falling out of a buggy last Saturday evening. He worked for John Mulhiem of Bridgeport. Thrown out while he and Mulheim returned from trading in Bridgeport. Remains sent to a sister in Iowa. |
| Finnette | Rudolph, Mrs. | KC, p1c4, 2/15/1900 | Recently moved to the Wauzeka area from Garner, IA. |
| Finney | Albert | KC, p5c5, 4/5/1900 | Elected supervisor in Eastman. |
| Finney | Bertha | KC, p8c4, 9/20/1900 | Recently married Napoloen Coats of Town of Eastman. Mrs. William Hunter of Prairie du Chien was a sister of the groom. |
| Finney | Bertha | KC, p1c5, 2/9/1899 | Taught school in Eastman in 1899. E. E. Brindley, Crawford County Superintendent of Schools published a comprehensive list of all teachers in the county. |
| Finney | boy | KC, p5c4, 2/27/1902 | Son born last Monday to Alfred Finney of Eastman. |
| Finney | George | KC, p1c5, 12/26/1901 | Resided in Eastman. Found a large snake in his well. Very unusual because of the winter weather. |
| Finney | William | KC, p1c4, 1/19/1899 | Resided in Steuben. Attended school for blind in Janesville. |
| Fischeretal | James | KC, p5c3, 5/20/1897 | Issues of fact for jury to be heard in the May term of the Crawford County Court. Mary Velt vs. James Fischeretal. |
| Fish | E. N. | KC, p8c4, 1/14/1897 | Rented the Prochaska saloon in Eastman. |
| Fish | John, Sr. | KC, p5c3, 8/17/1899 | Died Aug. 12, 1899 near Eastman. Survived by wife and 3 sons (2 live here and 1 in Chicago). Buried in Catholic Cemetery. |
| Fish | Mayme | KC, p1c4, 5/8/1902 | Former ward of William Stuckey of Wauzeka. Hired a horse and rig in Prairie du Chien. Didn't return. Found at the Dennis Syverson residence near the Kickapoo River and brought back to Wauzeka. Had no money. Later took a new pair of shoes from an employer, Mrs. Art O'Neil. Aged 19 years. |
| Fish | Nonce and Ernest | KC, p5c3, 6/29/1899 | Nonce Fish of Chicago and Ernest Fish of Eastman attended the sick bed of their father who was dangerously ill in Eastman. |
| Fisher | Berdie | KC, p1c5, 2/9/1899 | Taught school in Wauzeka in 1899. E. E. Brindley, Crawford County Superintendent of Schools published a comprehensive list of all teachers in the county. |
| Fisher | Birdie | KC, Supp., 3/30/1899 | Hired to teach school in West Wauzeka. |
| Fisher | Charles | KC, p1c6, 4/1/1897 | Departed Gays Mills area for new home in Iowa. |

Genealogical Gleanings From Early Newspapers for Residents In and Near
Crawford County, Wisconsin, 1897-1902

| LAST NAME | FIRST NAME | NEWSPAPER PAGE/COLUMN MONTH/DAY/YEAR | GENEALOGICAL DATA |
|---|---|---|---|
| Fisher | James | KC, p8c3, 1/3/1901 | Funeral held on Jan. 2, 1901 in Town of Eastman. He was an old settler. Father of Mrs. Robert Stuart of Town of Seneca (per KC, p5c3, 1/10/1901). |
| Fisher | James | KC, p1c6, 11/4/1897 | Issue of fact for court to be heard at the November term of the Circuit Court in Crawford County. Mary Viet vs. James Fisher. |
| Fisher | James Jr. | KC, p1c4, 4/14/1898 | Resided in Eastman. His picture and biography were printed in the last issue of the *Wisconsin Farmer*. |
| Fisher | James, Sr. | KC, p5c5, 1/17/1901 | Died Jan. 1, 1901 at his home in the Town of Eastman. Born Feb. 5, 1816 in Crawford Co., PA. Moved to Wisconsin in 1836. Married Margaret Gordon in 1861. She died in 1871 leaving 4 children -- James Jr.; Mrs. Robert Stuart; Mrs. Sam Boucher and Mrs. William Kussmaul. He was twice elected a senator to the territorial legislature and seven times elected to the state legislature. He was buried in Campbell Cemetery. |
| Fisher | Lucinda, Mrs. | KC, p7c2, 3/18/1897 | Died Mar. 8, 1897 at home near Gays Mills. Aged 73 years. She was the mother of Charles Fisher, Mrs. Elmer E. Stephenson and Edward Jackson of Gays Mills; Mrs. _ W. Schafer of Bryantsburg, IA and 1 son in Texas. (See citation for Mrs. Jackson.) |
| Fisher | twin girls | KC, p5c1, 11/3/1898 | Twin daughters born last week to James Fisher, Jr. of Eastman. |
| Fisher | William | KC, p5c4, 5/25/1899 | Married Georgie E. Whitemore on May 17, 1899. Groom from Fennimore. (Bride may have been from Gays Mills area.) |
| Fisher | Alexander P. | KC, p8c3, 2/8/1900 | Died Jan. 17, 1900 in Manitoba. Born and brought up in Prairie du Chien. He has been in the northwest for about 48 years. Mrs. Fenton of Kaukanna was his sister. |
| Fisher | James | KC, p4c2, 8/29/1901 | Lived in Eastman. Known as an "aristocrat in the production of full blood Chester White wine" in Wisconsin and several other states. |
| Fitch | C., Mrs. | KC, p1c3, 8/21/1902 | Lived in Minneapolis. Visited relatives in Wauzeka. Cousin of Dr. and F. J. Perrin and Mrs. O. P. Vaughan. |
| Fitzgibbon | J. | KC, p1c6, 4/7/1898 | Elected Treasurer for the Town of Seneca. |
| Fitzgibbons | boy | KC, p5c3, 4/19/1900 | Son recently born to J. Fitzsimmons of Town of Seneca. |
| Fitzgibbons | John | KC, p4c2, 11/3/1898 | John Fitzgibbons and Charles Burton published a notice of dissolution of their partnership, Fitzgibbons and Burton, in Seneca. |
| Fitzgibbons | John | KC, p5c5, 4/5/1900 | Elected treasurer in Seneca. |
| Fitzgibbons | M., Mr. | KC, p5c3, 8/24/1899 | Mr. M. Fitzgibbons of Seneca entertained his daughter, Mary of Chicago. |
| Fitzsimmons | Jane, Mrs. | KC, p1c2, 10/3/1901 | Lived in Bridgeport. Visited her brother, Henry King of Mt. Sterling. |
| Fiuke | Charles | KC, p8c2, 2/9/1899 | Celebrated 25th wedding anniversary on Feb. 3, 1899 in Prairie du Chien. |

Genealogical Gleanings From Early Newspapers for Residents In and Near
Crawford County, Wisconsin, 1897-1902

| LAST NAME | FIRST NAME | NEWSPAPER PAGE/COLUMN MONTH/DAY/YEAR | GENEALOGICAL DATA |
|---|---|---|---|
| Flaherty | Francis | KC, p1c2, 12/18/1902 | Returned to Mt. Sterling for a visit. Working in Gypsum, IA. |
| Flanagan | Hannah, Miss | KC, p5c4, 2/28/1901 | Resided in Prairie du Chien. Advertised the sale of hair goods in Lynxville. |
| Flannagan | Delia | KC, p1c6, 3/4/1897 | Married James Maney on Mar. 1, 1897. Bride and groom may be from Town of Seneca. |
| Fleeman | girl | KC, p5c3, 4/19/1900 | Daughter recently born to John Fleeman of Town of Seneca. |
| Fleeman | J., Mrs. | KC, p5c3, 3/9/1899 | Visited her parents, Mr. and Mrs. J. Riley, according to Seneca news items. |
| Fleeman | John | KC, p1c3, 12/1/1898 | Married Julia Riley on Nov. 22, 1898. Bride and groom were from Seneca. Bride daughter of John Riley. |
| Fleming | Maggie | KC, p1c5, 2/9/1899 | Taught school in the Town of Clayton in 1899. E. E. Brindley, Crawford County Superintendent of Schools published a comprehensive list of all teachers in the county. |
| Fluke | Frank | KC, p8c1, 4/7/1898 | Died April 4, 1898 at age 23. Born Dec. 26, 1875. Son of Charles Fluke of Prairie du Chien. Survived by wife and a child. Married for 2 years. Funeral held at St. Gabriel Church. |
| Flynn | Pat | KC, p1c3, 6/6/1901 | Departed Petersburg for a new job in Emmettsburg, IA. |
| Fogarty | boy | KC, p5c4, 2/23/1899 | A 12-pound son was recently born to Joe Fogarty of Bridgeport. |
| Fogarty | Edward | KC, Supp., 11/8/1900 | Married Alice Crowley on Oct. 30, 1900. Bride from Town of Seneca. Groom from Bridgeport. |
| Fogarty | Edward, Mrs. | KC, p1c3, 12/26/1901 | Arrived from Madison to visit parents who lived in the Steuben area. |
| Fogarty | Thomas | KC, p1c3, 2/16/1899 | Died Feb. 13, 1899 at Wright's Ferry. Aged 22 years. Youngest son of Thomas Fogarty, Sr., of Wright's Ferry. Funeral held at Catholic Church in Wauzeka. |
| Fogarty | Thomas | KC, p4c4, 3/9/1899 | Died Feb. 13, 1899 at home in Wright's Ferry. Aged 22 years. Member of Prairie du Chien. High School Class of 1894. Youngest son of T. J. Fogarty. Suffered with consumption for the last 5 years. Buried in family cemetery where his mother and brother were laid to rest. Survived by father, 2 brothers and 1 sister. |
| Fogh | girl | KC, p1c2, 5/3/1900 | Daughter born April 8, 1900 to Dietrick Fogh of Steuben area. |
| Folbrecht | Edith | KC, Supp., 12/12/1901 | Attended a Teacher's Institute in Crawford County in 1901. Resided in Wauzeka. |
| Folbrecht | Edwin | KC, p5c5, 1/18/1900 | Taught school in Crawford Co. |
| Foley | girl | KC, p4c2, 12/9/1897 | Daughter born Nov. 29, 1897 to Tom Foley of Steuben. |
| Foley | J. E. | KC, p4c1, 1/7/1897 | Resided in Steuben. Advertised sale of farm machinery and services as a blacksmith. |
| Foley | J. E. | KC, Supp., 12/19/1901 | Ran a lumber yard in Steuben. Recently sold business to John Faust. |

Genealogical Gleanings From Early Newspapers for Residents In and Near
Crawford County, Wisconsin, 1897-1902

| LAST NAME | FIRST NAME | NEWSPAPER PAGE/COLUMN MONTH/DAY/YEAR | GENEALOGICAL DATA |
|---|---|---|---|
| Foley | James A. | KC, p1c2, 4/24/1902 | Resided in Boscobel. Purchased a half interest in a thoroughbred running stallion. Planned to race the horse in Grant and Crawford Counties this season. |
| Foley | Maggie | KC, p1c4, 5/13/1897 | Married Hugh Donner of Prairie du Chien on May 10, 1897 at St. Patricks Church in Seneca. Bride from Seneca. |
| Foley | Martin F. | KC, p1c3, 9/14/1899 | Married Mary Hamilton on Sept. 1, 1899 at Eastman. Bride and groom from Steuben. Bride daughter of Henry Hamilton. Rev. Kiefner officiated at the ceremony. |
| Foley | Mike | KC, p8c4, 4/4/1901 | Part of a group that left Steuben and Wauzeka for the West. Most of the group went to McHenry, North Dakota. |
| Foley | Pat | KC, p5c3, 3/30/1899 | Pat Foley sold his saloon in Steuben to Greg Posey. Foley planned to go to North Dakota in April. |
| Foley | T. | KC, Supp., 12/19/1901 | Operated a saloon in Steuben. |
| Foley | Thomas W. | KC, p1c3, 8/28/1902 | Sold his interest in a saloon and left for Courtney, ND. Planned to do threshing work and then file a land claim. Before leaving, Mrs. Foley will visit her sister, Mrs. O'Brien of Currie, MN. |
| Foley | Tom | KC, p4c3, 2/25/1897 | Married Nellie Niland on Feb. 22, 1897. Bride and groom were from Wauzeka. |
| Foley | Tom | KC, p5c4, 2/7/1901 | Lived in Steuben. Bought a saloon in Petersburg. |
| Foley | Tom | KC, p1c2, 6/5/1902 | Lived in Steuben. Visited brother-in-law, George Schweiger at Prairie du Chien. |
| Foran | Bernard | KC, Supp., 12/20/1900 | Represented Prairie du Chien on the Crawford Co. Board of Supervisors in 1900. |
| Foran | Thomas | KC, Supp., 12/18/1902 | County Board of Supervisors examined bills in the Justices and Constables' Account for State vs. Thomas Foran and James Chamberlain. Grover Faust, Jack Kelley, Felch Zack, George H. Green, Sam Chamberlain, Oria Chamberlain and Ben Kelly were witnesses. |
| Foran | W. | KC, Supp., 12/29/1898 | Crawford Co. Board of Supervisors approved Justices and Constables' expenses related to the case, State vs. W. Foran. Ed O'Dea and A Bickof were witnesses in the case. |
| Foran | William | KC, Supp., 12/12/1901 | State vs. William Foran heard in Crawford Co. Court. Witnesses were Richard Foran, William Harding and Frank Kramer. |
| Forde | Mary | KC, p1c2 1/14/1897 | Married August Anderson on Jan. 6, 1897 in Prairie du Chien. Bride and groom were from Clayton Co., IA. Wm. H. Evans officiated. |
| Forde | Mary | KC, p1c2, 1/14/1897 | Married August Anderson on Jan. 6, 1897 in Prairie du Chien. Bride and groom were from Clayton Co., IA. |
| Forst | | KC, p1c4, 9/15/1898 | Infant son of Joseph Forst (Forest, Frost, Faust?) died Sept. 11, 1898 at age 7 weeks old in Prairie du Chien. Funeral held at St. John Bohemian Catholic Church. |
| Fortney | Carl | KC, p1c4, 7/3/1902 | Married Rhoda Gander of Liberty Pole on June 29, 1902. Bride daughter of George J. Gander of Soldiers Grove. |

Genealogical Gleanings From Early Newspapers for Residents In and Near
Crawford County, Wisconsin, 1897-1902

| LAST NAME | FIRST NAME | NEWSPAPER PAGE/COLUMN MONTH/DAY/YEAR | GENEALOGICAL DATA |
|---|---|---|---|
| Fortney | Nels | KC, p1c4, 9/4/1902 | Died Aug. 28, 1902 at Soldiers Grove. Aged 84 years. Survived by wife, 6 sons and 2 daughters. All children live in Soldiers Grove area, except 1 son who lives in Texas. Father of Atley, Peter N. and Nels Peterson. Came to Crawford Co. over 50 years ago. |
| Fortney | Ole | KC, p1c3, 12/19/1901 | Married Julia Mitchell on Dec. 18, 1901 at Johnstown, WI. |
| Fortun | Joseph | KC, p1c4, 5/19/1898 | Lived in West Prairie. His 12-year-old daughter was assaulted by a tramp named Scrivens. Scrivens was captured near Rising Sun, plead guilty and given 20 years in the penitentiary. |
| Foss | Ole | KC, p4c1, 6/3/1897 | Died May 29, 1897 in Soldiers Grove at the home of N. O. Peterson. Aged 36 years. Funeral held at the Lutheran Church. |
| Fountain | Mary | KC, Supp., 12/12/1901 | Crawford Co. Board of Supervisors approved payments in the Matter of Mary Fountain, Insane. Taken to Mendota. |
| Foust | D., Mrs. | KC, p4c1, 7/29/1897 | Traveled from Woodman to Boydtown to visit parents, Mr. and Mrs. Jacob Daughtery. |
| Foust | Daniel L. | KC, p4c4, 12/15/1898 | Notice of Final Proof published. Needed to establish continued residence on property in Town of Marietta to finalize his land claim. Witnesses: W. W. Kielley, Ralph Foust, William Ward and John T. Francis, Jr., all of Marietta. |
| Foust | Daniel, Mrs. | KC, p5c3, 7/13/1899 | Planned to leave Steuben for a new home in Countney, ND. Three sons and 2 daughters reside there. |
| Foust | David | KC, p5c2, 11/3/1898 | Severely ill. Daughter, Mrs. William Kielley of Steuben, cared for him. |
| Foust | David L. | KC, p5c4, 2/23/1899 | Died Feb. 18, 1899 at home of daughter, Mrs. W. W. Kielley. Born Dec. 30, 1836 in Randolph Co., IN. Survived by 2 sons and 2 daughters. Funeral held at Congregational Church. Buried in Boydtown Cemetery. Member of U.B.. Church. |
| Foust | girl | KC, p8c3, 6/24/1897 | Daughter born June 15, 1897 to Joseph Foust of Steuben. |
| Foust | girl | KC, p5c1, 9/1/1898 | Daughter born Aug. 20, 1898 to Zeph Foust of Steuben. |
| Foust | Pearlie | KC, p5c3, 4/11/1901 | Died April 6, 1901 in Steuben. Daughter of Christ and Dora Foust. |
| Foust | Pearlie | KC, p5c3, 4/11/1901 | Died April 6, 1901. He/she was child of Christ and Dora Foust of Steuben. |
| Foust | William | KC, p5c4, 5/29/1902 | The case Wisconsin vs. William Foust, for assault and battery, was heard at the May term of the Crawford County Circuit Court. Not in court. Incomplete returns. |
| Foust | | KC, p4c2, 6/9/1898 | Infant daughter of Zeph Foust died May 25, 1898 at Steuben. Aged 11 months and 13 days. |
| Foust | | KC, p5c3, 5/18/1899 | The 14-year-old son of John Foust was kicked in the bowels by a horse. He died Saturday. |

Genealogical Gleanings From Early Newspapers for Residents In and Near
Crawford County, Wisconsin, 1897-1902

| LAST NAME | FIRST NAME | NEWSPAPER PAGE/COLUMN MONTH/DAY/YEAR | GENEALOGICAL DATA |
|---|---|---|---|
| Fox | Albert | KC, Supp., 12/29/1898 | Crawford Co. Board of Supervisors approved Justices and Constables' expenses related to the case, State vs. Albert Fox et al. |
| Fox | Anna, Mrs. | KC, p12c2, 12/29/1898 | Died Dec. 25, 1898. Born July 25, 1838 in Vegden, Bohemia. Married Thomas Fox. Moved to Prairie du Chien in 1871. She was the mother of John, Joseph, Frank, Gus and Anna. Three other daughters deceased. |
| Fox | Frank | KC, p8c1, 5/11/1899 | Married Sophia Conopy on May 10, 1899 at the Bohemian Catholic Church. Groom from Prairie du Chien. |
| Fox | John L. | KC, p8c3, 9/11/1902 | Married Lulu McElroy on Aug. 21, 1902 at Joliet, IL. Bride from Sabula, IA. Groom from Prairie du Chien. |
| Fox | Frank | KC, p5c4, 5/29/1902 | The case Wisconsin vs. Frank Fox, for selling liquor on Sunday, was heard at the May term of the Crawford County Circuit Court. Nolle prosequi entered by Dist. Atty. |
| Fox | Rose | KC, p8c3, 6/13/1901 | Married Theodore Favre on June 9, 1901 at St. Gabriel's Church. Bride and groom were from Prairie du Chien. |
| Foye | A. E. | KC, p4c3, 5/2/1901 | Purchased the creamery at Petersburg. |
| Foye | A. E. | KC, p1c2, 6/27/1901 | Cheesemaker in Petersburg. Departed for Lime Springs, IA to see sick sister, Mrs. Dr. Simons. |
| Foye | A. E., Mrs. | KC, p1c3, 7/17/1902 | Returned to Soldiers Grove after a visit with parents in Black Earth. |
| Fralick | Ed | KC, p1c2, 12/5/1901 | "Hotel man of Steuben." At request of wife, brought before county judge for a sanity hearing. Found to be sane. |
| Fralick | Ed | KC, Supp., 12/19/1901 | Operated a hotel in Steuben. |
| Fralick | Edward | KC, Supp., 12/18/1902 | Crawford County Board of Supervisors allowed expenses in the Matter of Edward Fralick, Insane. |
| France | girl | KC, p5c3, 9/21/1901 | John France's 3 year old daughter recently died in Gays Mills. Buried in Boscobel. |
| France | J. F. | KC, Supp., 12/19/1901 | Operated a jewelry store in Gays Mills. |
| Fransburg | Grace | KC, p5c3, 9/27/1900 | Recently married Amasa Dowling. (Bride and groom may be from Town of Scott.) |
| Fransche | Victor | KC, p5c3, 5/4/1899 | Married Mary J. Malone on April 25, 1899 at St. Phillip's Catholic Church. Bride and groom from Town of Scott. |
| Frasher | Mr. | KC, p4c3, 7/22/1897 | Married Minnie Kimble on July 18, 1897. (Bride may be from Barnum.) |
| Frasier | J. H. | KC, p1c3, 5/17/1900 | Editor of the *Viola Intelligencer*. Attended the burial of his father-in-law in Indianapolis, IN. |
| Frazier | Vernier | KC, p1c5, 4/7/1898 | Admitted to the Academy at West Point. |
| Fredenberg | Miss | KC, Supp., 12/5/1901 | Married William Young on Nov. 28, 1901. Groom former resident of Eastman. Now from Moose Lake, MN. Bride from Moose Lake, MN. |
| Freeman | Fred | KC, p5c4, 3/27/1902 | Planned to leave Mt. Sterling for a livery job in Viroqua. |
| Freeman | George W. | KC, Supp., 12/29/1898 | Received aid from the Crawford County Soldiers Relief Commission. Resided in De Soto. |

Genealogical Gleanings From Early Newspapers for Residents In and Near
Crawford County, Wisconsin, 1897-1902

| LAST NAME | FIRST NAME | NEWSPAPER PAGE/COLUMN MONTH/DAY/YEAR | GENEALOGICAL DATA |
|---|---|---|---|
| Freeman | Milo | KC, p4c4, 11/10/1898 | Issues of Fact for Jury heard in the November term of the Crawford County Circuit Court. Milo Freeman vs. M. N. Talcott. |
| Freeman | Olive | KC, p8c4, 11/16/1899 | Received marriage license in Crawford Co. to marry David Jenkins. Bride and groom from Town of Clayton |
| French | Bertha | KC, p8c3, 4/15/1897 | Taught school in Eastman. Spent vacation with parents in De Soto. |
| French | C. D. | KC, p5c4, 12/21/1899 | Resided in Boydtown. Planned to travel to Buffalo, NY in April 1900 where he would vacation for 3 months. |
| French | Charles E. | KC, p5c4, 9/20/1900 | Court Summons published for Crawford County Court. Charles E. French, plaintiff, vs. Lucinda French, defendant. |
| French | Charles E. | KC, Supp., 12/20/1900 | Crawford Co. Board of Supervisors approved payment of expenses in the matter of State vs. Charles E. French. The witnesses were Henry Brown, E. L. Brown, Lottie Brown, Edward Buske, Hiram Comstock, John Mayo, Ada Buske, Jane Brown and Edith Buske. |
| French | Charles, Mrs. | KC, p5c1, 2/4/1897 | Left Boydtown to visit a son in Keystone, IA. |
| French | James | KC, p8c1, 10/14/1897 | James French and William Gray recently tried to escape from jail in Prairie du Chien. Tried and sentenced to 1 year at Waupon. |
| French | Lizzie | KC, p1c2, 9/5/1901 | Planned to wed a professor at an Indiana college. She was the sister of Mrs. Bertha Currie of Viola. |
| French | Mrs. | KC, p1c3, 11/1/1900 | Departed Wauzeka to attend funeral of sister, Mrs. Calahan, in Dubuque. |
| French | Osee, Mrs. | KC, p8c3, 1/12/1899 | Died Jan. 6, 1899 in Wauzeka. Born in 1824 in Allegheny Co., NY. Married G. W. French in Oct. 1841 in Turnersville, PA. Moved to Dodgeville, WI in 1854 and later to Wauzeka. Mr. French died Mar. 15, 1890. Buried in village cemetery. |
| Fresche | Eugene | KC, p1c3, 8/24/1899 | He was a defendant in a criminal case before Justice Peacock. Represented by W. G. Campbell of Soldiers Grove and Wm. H. Evans and J. P. Evans of Prairie du Chien. Case was adjourned. No witnesses were present. |
| Friar | John | KC, p5c4, 11/9/1899 | Recently died. Probate hearing published. |
| Fritche | John | KC, Supp., 12/20/1900 | Crawford Co. Board of Supervisors approved payment of expenses in the matter of State vs. John Fritche. |
| Fritsche | boy | KC, p1c2, 5/31/1900 | Son born May 27, 1900 to Charles Fritsche of Wright's Ferry. |
| Fritsche | Charles | KC, p4c2, 12/2/1897 | Hosted a husking bee and dance at home in Bridgeport. |
| Fritsche | Susan, Mrs. | KC, p1c4, 3/15/1900 | Died Mar. 11, 1900 in Prairie du Chien. Born Mar. 28, 1845 in Kentucky. Survived by 9 of 9 children. Her first husband, Charles Kuchenbecker, died many years ago. Her second husband, Mr. Fritsche, died in 1872. She was the sister of Mrs. Whalley of Prairie du Chien. Buried in Lowertown Cemetery. |

Genealogical Gleanings From Early Newspapers for Residents In and Near
Crawford County, Wisconsin, 1897-1902

| LAST NAME | FIRST NAME | NEWSPAPER PAGE/COLUMN MONTH/DAY/YEAR | GENEALOGICAL DATA |
|---|---|---|---|
| Fry | Riley | KC, p5c4, 2/13/1902 | Son of Dock Fry of Knapps Creek. Dangerously ill with lung fever. Mrs. A. Taft was helping to care for the boy. |
| Fry | S., Mrs. | KC, p8c3, 11/2/1899 | Died Wednesday (Nov. 1, 1899?) in Prairie du Chien when she was 72 years old. |
| Fryseth | Andrew | KC, Supp., 12/20/1900 | Crawford Co. Board of Supervisors approved bills related to expenses of Andrew Fryseth, insane. |
| Fuka | Anna | KC, p6c3, 1/17/1901 | Married Charles Reik on Jan. 9, 1901. Bride from Prairie du Chien. Groom from Chicago. They plan to live in Chicago. |
| Fuka | John | KC, p8c3, 11/7/1901 | Married Mary Wher on Nov. 4, 1901. Bride and groom from Prairie du Chien. |
| Fuka | Joseph | KC, p5c3, 6/29/1899 | Resided in Chicago. Visited brother, Frank, in Eastman. |
| Fuke | Mary | KC, p8c4, 11/16/1899 | Received marriage license in Crawford Co. to marry Emanuel Prechaska. The bride was from Bridgeport. |
| Fuller | H. C., Judge | KC, p1c4, 2/25/1897 | Died Feb. 18, 1897 in Prairie du Chien. Born June 30, 1849 in PA. Settled in Dane Co., WI in 1853. Married Clara Espenet in Windsor, Dane Co. on June 19, 1877. Survived by 6 children. |
| Funk | Albert | KC, p5c5, 4/12/1900 | Recently departed Bell Center for the west. |
| Funk | Grandma | KC, p5c3, 4/7/1898 | Traveled from Canton, MN to visit friends in Bell Center. Former Sunday school teacher. |
| Furgurson | S. C. | KC, Supp., 12/20/1900 | Crawford Co. Soldiers Relief Comm. approved aid to S. C. Furgurson of Prairie du Chien. |
| Furman | G. W. | KC, Supp., 12/12/1901 | Received funds from the Crawford County Soldiers Relief Commission. Resided in De Soto. |
| Furman | George | KC, Supp., 12/20/1900 | Crawford Co. Soldiers Relief Comm. approved aid to George Furman of De Soto. |
| Furman | George, Mrs. | KC, Supp., 12/18/1902 | Crawford County Soldiers Relief Committee provided funds to Mrs. George Furman of De Soto. |
| Fusbi | Charles | KC, Supp., 12/12/1901 | State vs. Charles Fusbi heard in Crawford Co. Court. |
| Gaffney | boy | KC, p1c5, 12/22/1898 | Son recently born to William Gaffney of Bell Center |
| Gaffney | | KC, Supp., 12/19/1901 | Gaffney & Murphy operated a saloon in Gays Mills. |
| Gage | Eva, Mrs. | KC, p5c3, 9/11/1902 | Arrived from California to care for her grandmother, Mrs. A. N. Hazen of Eastman, who was very ill. |
| Gald | Sophia | KC, p1c4, 3/24/1898 | Married Chris Halverson on Mar. 14, 1898 in Rochester, MN. Bride and groom from Soldiers Grove. Planned to live in Geneva, MN. |
| Gambel | R. T., MD | KC, p5c1, 1/7/1897 | Advertised homeopathic medical services. Office based in Boscobel. |
| Gamble | R. T., MD | KC, p5c2, 3/1/1900 | Homeopathist. Practice based in Boscobel. |
| Gander | Bertha | KC, p1c4, 1/5/1899 | Married Earl Truesdale of Viola on Jan. 1, 1899. Bride daughter of G. J. Gander of near Soldiers Grove. |

Genealogical Gleanings From Early Newspapers for Residents In and Near
Crawford County, Wisconsin, 1897-1902

| LAST NAME | FIRST NAME | NEWSPAPER PAGE/COLUMN MONTH/DAY/YEAR | GENEALOGICAL DATA |
|---|---|---|---|
| Gander | boy | KC, p5c3, 10/5/1899 | Son born Sept. 26, 1899 to D. E. Gander of Gays Mills. |
| Gander | boy | KC, p8c3, 4/22/1897 | Son born April 13, 1897 to D. E. Gander of Gays Mills area. |
| Gander | D. E. | KC, p5c3, 1/12/1899 | Elected to be an officer for the Modern Woodman Association (MWA) in Gays Mills. |
| Gander | Dave and Nate | KC, p5c3, 11/27/1902 | Built a new home for N. A. Tallman of Gays Mills. |
| Gander | George J. | KC, p1c2, 4/5/1900 | Lived in Soldiers Grove. Employed as a traveling salesman for Monmouth Pottery Co. |
| Gander | Laura | KC, p1c8, 11/22/1900 | Married Clarence Green on Nov. 18, 1900. Bride daughter of George J. Gander of North Clayton. Groom formerly of De Soto, now Garrison, MT. |
| Gander | Rhoda | KC, p1c4, 7/3/1902 | Married Carl Fortney of Liberty Pole on June 29, 1902. Bride daughter of George J. Gander of Soldiers Grove. |
| Gander | Rhoda | KC, p1c5, 11/3/1898 | Rhoda Gander, teacher for the upper department at the Bell Center School, reported the following pupils were not absent in October: Hallie Huffman; Clyde Copas; Henry Rounds; Lora Stevens; Ray Rounds; Goldie Rotan; Dora Shockley; Robbie Duke; Louis Masten; Latie Whiteaker; Bunnie Brightman; Viola Whiteaker and Edith Whiteaker. |
| Gander | Rhoda | KC, p1c5, 2/9/1899 | Taught school in the Town of Clayton in 1899. E. E. Brindley, Crawford County Superintendent of Schools published a comprehensive list of all teachers in the county. |
| Gander | T. | KC, p5c3, 7/19/1900 | Hired to teach school in Gays Mills. From North Clayton. |
| Gander | Thomas | KC, p1c3, 7/24/1902 | Lived in Soldiers Grove. Went to Janesville to business courses. |
| Gander | Thomas | KC, p1c4, 10/31/1901 | Taught school in Mt. Sterling. |
| Gander | Tom | KC, Supp., 12/12/1901 | Attended a Teacher's Institute in Crawford County in 1901. Resided in Soldiers Grove. |
| Ganyer | boy | KC, p5c3, 2/15/1900 | Son born Feb. 3, 1900 to Buss Ganyer of Lynxville. |
| Gardipe | Harriet, Mrs. | KC, p8c3, 7/19/1900 | Recently died in La Crosse. Buried in Prairie du Chien. |
| Gardner | Lottie | KC, p5c3, 10/16/1902 | Married John Scofield on Oct. 13, 1902. Bride from Lynxville. Groom from Boscobel. |
| Garner | Elmer | KC, p5c3, 8/30/1900 | Opened a grocery store in Petersburg. |
| Garner | Elmer | KC, p1c3, 3/20/1902 | Resided in Petersburg. Served as Haney Township treasurer. |
| Garner | Elmer | KC, p1c3, 6/5/1902 | Attended the Masonic Lodge in Boscobel. From Petersburg. |
| Garner | Elmer | KC, p1c4, 7/17/1902 | Lived in Petersburg. Picked up his wife in Prairie du Chien who had returned from a visit with parents in southern Canada. |
| Garner | Elmer | KC, p1c3, 8/31/1899 | Appointed postmaster at Petersburg after the resignation of D. R. Lawrence. |

Genealogical Gleanings From Early Newspapers for Residents In and Near
Crawford County, Wisconsin, 1897-1902

| LAST NAME | FIRST NAME | NEWSPAPER PAGE/COLUMN MONTH/DAY/YEAR | GENEALOGICAL DATA |
|---|---|---|---|
| Garner | Elmer, Mrs. | KC, p1c2, 5/1/1902 | Resided in Petersburg. Went to Sault St. Marie, Canada to visit her parents. |
| Garner | M. | KC, Supp., 12/20/1900 | Crawford Co. Board of Supervisors approved payment of expenses in the matter of State vs. M. Garner. |
| Garner | Melvin | KC, Supp., 12/12/1901 | State vs. Melvin Garner heard in Crawford Co. Court. |
| Garner Bros. | | KC, p5c5, 12/11/1902 | Proprietors of a general store in Petersburg. |
| Garrett | Nathan | KC, p5c3, 7/12/1900 | Married Mrs. Maud Karr at the City Hotel in Prairie du Chien on July 4, 1900. The groom was the former creamery operator in Eastman. He now has same position in Steuben. The bride was from Pennsylvania. |
| Garrison | John | KC, Supp., 12/18/1902 | Crawford County Board of Supervisors examined bills in the Justices and Constables' Account for State vs. John Garrison. |
| Garrity | James | KC, p5c3, 5/20/1897 | Criminal case to be heard in the May term of the Crawford County Court, State of Wisconsin vs. James Clark and James Garrity. |
| Garrity | John | KC, p5c1, 1/18/1900 | Justice of the Peace and insurance salesman in Prairie du Chien. |
| Garrity | Mary | KC, p4c2, 7/22/1897 | Married Albert Ertel of Lynxville on July 15, 1897. Bride from La Crosse. C. H. Speck, Justice of the Peace, officiated. |
| Garrity | Mary | KC, p5c6, 2/8/1900 | Taught school in district 4, Town of Seneca. |
| Garrity | Mary | KC, p4c1, 9/22/1898 | From Prairie du Chien. Taught school in East Gays Mills. |
| Garrity | Mary | KC, p1c5, 11/3/1898 | Mary Garrity, teacher in school district number 16, Town of Clayton, reported the following pupils were not absent in October: Francis Howe; Annie Rowe; Clarence Dupee; Katie Rowe; Maud Flemming; Gertrude Flemming; Ella Rowe; Grace Fisher. Those not tardy were: Charles Dupee; Grace Fisher; Ella Rowe; Katie Rowe; Mary Kelly; George Rowe; Cooke Fisher; Clyde Harry; Lillie and Sylvan DeLaMater; and Anna and Frances Howe. |
| Garrity | Mary | KC, p1c5, 2/9/1899 | Taught school in the Town of Clayton in 1899. E. E. Brindley, Crawford County Superintendent of Schools published a comprehensive list of all teachers in the county. |
| Garrity | William | KC, p8c4, 5/9/1901 | Married Mary Steinwand on May 6, 1901. Bride and groom from Prairie du Chien. |
| Garrow | Leona | KC, p1c3, 6/28/1900 | She was the daughter of F. Garrow of Bridgeport. Visited her grandparents, Mr. and Mrs. A. Bieloh of Wauzeka. |
| Garrow | Leona and Cleora | KC, p1c2, 11/30/1899 | Daughters of William Garrow of Bridgeport. Visited their grandparents, Mr. and Mrs. A. Biehloh of Wauzeka. |
| Garvey | Clara | KC, p1c4, 9/7/1899 | Married P. Mullaney on Sept. 6, 1899. Bride was daughter of T. Garvey. |

Genealogical Gleanings From Early Newspapers for Residents In and Near
Crawford County, Wisconsin, 1897-1902

| LAST NAME | FIRST NAME | NEWSPAPER PAGE/COLUMN MONTH/DAY/YEAR | GENEALOGICAL DATA |
|---|---|---|---|
| Garvey | E. | KC, p4c3, 1/23/1902 | Store he owned in Seneca robbed. Money in cash drawer and a new suit of clothes were taken. Pat Casey, a 6' 2" farm hand was suspected of the crime but was not arrested. Robber took "leg bail for security and departed for parts unknown". Casey believed to be on his way to Chicago where he had relatives. |
| Garvey | Clara | KC, p5c4, 9/14/1899 | Married Pat Mullaney on Sept. 6, 1899. Bride from Seneca. Extensive guest and gift list published. |
| Garvey | Clara | KC, p1c5, 11/18/1897 | Taught school in Stoney Point District. |
| Garvey | Constance Marie | KC, p8c4, 6/7/1900 | Married Joseph P. Evans on June 4, 1900. Bride was daughter of James Garvey of Prairie du Chien. Groom was son of William H. Evans of Prairie du Chien. |
| Garvey | Dan | KC, p5c3, 5/20/1897 | Issues of fact for jury to be heard in the May term of the Crawford County Court. A. N. Searle vs. J. J. Crowley, Dan Garvey and Frank White. |
| Garvey | E. | KC, p5c3, 12/11/1902 | Proprietor of a general store in Seneca. |
| Garvey | Edward | KC, p11c4, 12/18/1902 | Died Dec. 12, 1902 at Town of Seneca. Born Mar. 4, 1839 in County Down, Ireland. To Wisconsin in 1854. Joined brother, Thomas in a mercantile business in 1869. Married Miss Mahoney of Seneca in Sept. 1875. Fathered 4 boys and 2 girls. All surviving. Wife died August 1893. Buried in Catholic Cemetery in Seneca. |
| Garvey | Edward | KC, p5c4, 5/29/1902 | The case Thomas Cleary vs. Edward Garvey, et al was heard at the May term of the Crawford County Circuit Court. Judgement for plaintiff for specific performance of land contract and costs. |
| Garvey | Edward and Thomas | KC, p1c2, 10/6/1898 | Dissolved their partnership of 29 years. Thomas retired and planned to farm. Edward planned to continue the business in Seneca, extend the store 30 feet, spend the winter in the south and travel to Europe. Thomas Crawford will manage the business. |
| Garvey | James | KC, p5c4, 2/8/1900 | Departed Seneca for Fort Dodge, IA. |
| Garvey | Laura | KC, p4c2, 10/21/1897 | Married James Crowley on Oct. 18, 1897 at Seneca Catholic Church. (Bride and groom may have been from Steuben area.) |
| Garvey | Maria | KC, p4c4, 11/10/1898 | Issues of Default heard in the November term of the Crawford County Circuit Court. Maria Garvey vs. Mary Quinn. |
| Garvey | Mayme | KC, p4c2, 3/17/1898 | Taught school in Garvey District, Town of Seneca. |
| Garvey | Mayme | KC, p1c5, 2/9/1899 | Taught school in Seneca in 1899. E. E. Brindley, Crawford County Superintendent of Schools published a comprehensive list of all teachers in the county. |
| Garvey | Monica Leona | KC, p8c4, 3/11/1897 | Born last Tuesday in Seneca to T. Garvey. |

Genealogical Gleanings From Early Newspapers for Residents In and Near
Crawford County, Wisconsin, 1897-1902

| LAST NAME | FIRST NAME | NEWSPAPER PAGE/COLUMN MONTH/DAY/YEAR | GENEALOGICAL DATA |
|---|---|---|---|
| Garvey | Stacia | KC, p8c4, 1/16/1902 | Married Dwight Chambers on Jan. 15, 1902. Bride and groom from Prairie du Chien. Groom son of John Mortimer Chambers. Bride daughter of Mrs. (C?) Garvey and niece of Very Rev. Dean Trant of Racine, WI. |
| Garvey | Susan | KC, p1c3, 9/28/1899 | Married John L. McLaughlin on Sept. 19, 1899 at St. Patrick's Catholic Church in Seneca. Bride sister of Julia V. Garvey. |
| Garvey | Susanna E. | KC, p1c2, 11/1/1900 | Married Earl Brooks Rees at Dubuque, IA on Oct. 24, 1900. Bride daughter of Edward Garvey of Town of Seneca. Groom was a lawyer from Galena, IL. (also p5c3) |
| Garvey | Susie E. | KC, p8c3, 10/25/1900 | Recently married Earl B. Reese in Dubuque. Bride was from Town of Seneca. Groom was from Galena, IL. |
| Garvey | Vernie | KC, p5c4, 9/27/1900 | Died Sept. 23, 1900 in Seneca. Aged 14 years. Daughter of Peter Garvey. |
| Garvey | Willie A. | KC, p5c3, 6/14/1900 | Graduated from the graded school in Seneca. |
| Gasligh | James | KC, Supp., 12/18/1902 | Crawford County Board of Supervisors examined bills in the Justices and Constables' Account for State vs. James Gasligh. |
| Gauche | Mr. | KC, p4c3, 3/20/1902 | Arrived from Cloquet, MN to visit brother-in-law, Sam Boucher of Eastman. |
| Gaulke | Herman | KC, p8c3, 8/13/1897 | Married Olga Qualiman on Aug. 17, 1897 at bride's home. Bride daughter of the late John Quallman of Grand Grey. Husband lived in La Crosse (formerly from Crawford Co.). |
| Gaulke | Mrs. | KC, p1c4, 3/18/1897 | Remains brought to Prairie du Chien from Milwaukee on Mar. 13, 1897 for burial in Lowertown Cemetery. Related to Henry Kurtz of Milwaukee; Mrs. and Mrs. H. Wasco of Volney, IA; Charles Gaulke and wife of North McGregor; and Mrs. C J. Oehring and sons (William, Charles, Fred) of Postville, IA. |
| Gaunsor | Miss | KC, Supp., 4/24/1902 | Worked as a housekeeper at the Catholic parsonage in Eastman. Shot a revolver at a tramp who attempted to enter building. |
| Gay | Enice | KC, p1c6, 4/7/1898 | Elected Supervisor for the Town of Seneca. |
| Gay | Frank E. | KC, p1c5, 10/28/1897 | Married Arrilla Eley on Oct. 24, 1897 at home of Joseph Peacock, Sr. Bride and groom from La Farge. |
| Gay | James | KC, Supp., 12/19/1901 | James Gay erected the first bridge across the Kickapoo River in 1857 in what became Gays Mills. Mr. Tallman who still resides near the village did the work. Mr. Gay built a sawmill at this place in 1848. |
| Gay | Nora | KC, p1c5, 12/2/1897 | Married Adam J. Taylor on Nov. 17, 1897. Bride daughter of Lot Gay of Seneca. |
| Gay | T. W. | KC, Supp., 12/19/1901 | T. W. Gay, a son of J. Gay, and G. M. Wilbur erected a gristmill at Gays Mills in 1865. J. G. Robb and S. H. Robb, brother-in-law of T. W. Gay, became part owners of the gristmill under the name Gay, Robb & Co. It became one of the leading flouring mills of the country under the management of Lewis & Haggerty. |

Genealogical Gleanings From Early Newspapers for Residents In and Near
Crawford County, Wisconsin, 1897-1902

| LAST NAME | FIRST NAME | NEWSPAPER PAGE/COLUMN MONTH/DAY/YEAR | GENEALOGICAL DATA |
|---|---|---|---|
| Gaylor | Frank | KC, p8c2, 12/30/1897 | Married Nina Miller of Prairie du Chien on Dec. 26, 1897. Groom from South Dakota. |
| Gaylord | Olive C. | KC, p8c2, 4/20/1899 | Married John Lester of Red Wing, MN on Tuesday (April 18, 1899?) in Prairie du Chien. Bride from Rochelle, IL. |
| Geider | Kate | KC, p8c4, 6/20/1901 | Married John Tulley on June 19, 1901 in Lansing, Iowa. |
| Geisler | Ed | KC, p5c3, 4/13/1899 | Lost a team of mules while crossing the Pine Creek bridge near the Gleason farm in Eastman. Ed was nearly drowned. Area was flooded. |
| Geisler | Ed | KC, p5c3, 4/20/1899 | The Town of Eastman settled a suit with Ed Geisler for the loss of a team of mules that drowned at a defective bridge across Pine Creek. |
| Geisler | L. | KC, p1c3, 7/24/1902 | New postmaster in Steuben. |
| Geisler | Lizzie | KC, p8c1, 1/27/1898 | Married George Moeller on Jan. 20, 1898 at Evangelical Lutheran Church in Prairie du Chien. Bride and groom were from Wauzeka. |
| Geitz | boy | KC, p1c2, 12/4/1902 | Son born Nov. 16, 1902 to Louis Geitz of Wauzeka. |
| Geitz | Henry | KC, p1c4, 3/31/1898 | Government granted him a pension of $6 a month. Lived in Wauzeka. |
| Geitz | John | KC, p7c1, 12/12/1901 | Crawford Co. District Attorney instructed to file suit against John Geitz to get financial support for his daughter, Lillie Geitz. |
| Geitz | John | KC, p1c4, 1/26/1899 | Resided in Wauzeka. Thief took a purse from home with $1000. It was later found in the yard where the thief dropped it. |
| Geitz | Lillie | KC, Supp., 12/12/1901 | Crawford County filed suit against John Geitz, father of Lillie Geitz, to recover costs for care provided his daughter at the State Hospital for the Insane. |
| Geitz | Louis | KC, p1c5, 10/26/1899 | Married Clara Schwartz of Wauzeka on Oct. 25, 1899. Groom of Grand Grae, was brother of Mrs. H. J. Wagner, whose residence the wedding was held. Bride was daughter of Anthony Swartz. |
| Geitz | Louisa M. | KC, p1c4, 6/6/1901 | Married Albert H. Wagner on June 4, 1901. Bride was daughter of Henry Geitz of Wauzeka. Groom from Steuben. |
| Geld (Gald?) | Ole | KC, p1c4, 1/26/1899 | Died Tuesday (Jan. 17, 1899?) in Soldiers Grove. |
| Gentil | Thurman | KC, p8c3, 9/8/1898 | Recently died in British Columbia. Former resident of Prairie du Chien. |
| George | Adaline | KC, p8c3, 11/4/1897 | Died Oct. 26, 1897 near Gays Mills. Nee Connard or Coanard. Born April 10, 1847 in Germany. Immigrated to Green Co., WI in 1856. Father died during voyage from Germany. Mother, 4 brothers and 2 sisters came to Crawford Co. when she was still a child. Married David George here. Survived by husband, 3 sons and 3 daughters. |
| George | David Mrs. | KC, p1c6, 10/28/1897 | Died Oct. 25, 1897 at her home in Mt. Sterling. |

Genealogical Gleanings From Early Newspapers for Residents In and Near
Crawford County, Wisconsin, 1897-1902

| LAST NAME | FIRST NAME | NEWSPAPER PAGE/COLUMN MONTH/DAY/YEAR | GENEALOGICAL DATA |
|---|---|---|---|
| George | David, Mrs. | KC, p5c2, 1/28/1897 | Resided in Gays Mills. Returned from Milwaukee where her right eye was removed. Had a cancerous tumor behind the eye. Cancer on her breast was also removed. She was in the hospital for 6 weeks. |
| George | Henry, Jr. | KC, p1c2, 1/2/1902 | Resided in Gays Mills. Returned from the Wisconsin pineries with small pox or Cuban Itch. Home quarantined. |
| George | Sperry | KC, p4c2, 1/28/1897 | Married Golda Maynard on Jan 22, 1897. Bride and groom from Gays Mills. Justice Stowell officiated. |
| George | Susie | KC, p5c3, 3/16/1899 | Married Ed Brockway of Mar. 15, 1899. (Bride may be from Mt. Sterling area.) |
| George | Bessie | KC, p1c4, 9/14/1899 | Recently married Park Morse of Steuben. Bride from Mt. Sterling. |
| George | Bessie | KC, p4c1, 7/8/1897 | Taught at Coates District School per Eastman news items. |
| George | Bessie | KC, p1c5, 2/9/1899 | Taught school in Haney in 1899. E. E. Brindley, Crawford County Superintendent of Schools published a comprehensive list of all teachers in the county. |
| George | Dave, Mrs. | KC, p8c3, 4/22/1897 | Lived in Gays Mills. Very ill. Little hope for recovery. |
| George | Sam | KC, p1c5, 7/1/1897 | Served as pathmaster in Mt. Sterling. |
| George | Sperry, Mr. and Mrs. | KC, p8c3, 4/8/1897 | Left Gays Mills to spend summer in Countney, ND. |
| Gerhardt | John | KC, p1c2, 10/13/1898 | Resided in Soldiers Grove. Wants to sell his saloon in Stitzer. |
| Gerhardt | John | KC, p1c6, 5/19/1898 | Issue of Fact for Court to be heard in the May term of the Crawford County Circuit Court. John Gerhardt vs. Betsey F. Peterson, Atley Peterson and others. |
| Gerhart | girl | KC, p1c2, 10/3/1901 | Daughter born Sept. 28, 1901 to John Gerhart of Steuben. Weighted 12 lbs. |
| Gibbs | Albert | KC, p8c3, 6/3/1897 | Died May 18, 1897 at home near Boscobel. Aged 10 years, 2 months and 6 days. Survived by parents (Thomas and Dellie Gibbs), 1 brother and 4 sisters. |
| Giddings | H. | KC, Supp., 12/18/1902 | Crawford County Soldiers Relief Committee provided funds to H. Giddings of Scott. |
| Giddings | Henry | KC, Supp., 12/29/1898 | Received aid from the Crawford County Soldiers Relief Commission. Resided in Scott. |
| Giegel | Mat | KC, p1c2, 4/25/1901 | Planned to erect a cheese factory on his farm in Wauzeka. |
| Gierhart | H. S. | KC, p1c2, 2/6/1902 | Successor of Alpha Barrette at the Prairie du Chien Insurance Agency. |
| Gifford | H. | KC, p5c4, 1/24/1901 | Lived in Lynxville. Sold a pearl he found while clam fishing to George Hurad for $140. |
| Gifford | Harvey | KC, p5c4, 3/20/1902 | Resided in Lynxville. Called an expert boat builder. |
| Gifford | M. H. | KC, p4c1, 1/7/1897 | Resided in Lynxville. Advertised his services as a contractor, builder and mover. |
| Gilder | Carl | KC, p5c3, 2/8/1900 | He has "taken up" the (Christian) Crusader work in Gays Mills. |

Genealogical Gleanings From Early Newspapers for Residents In and Near
Crawford County, Wisconsin, 1897-1902

| LAST NAME | FIRST NAME | NEWSPAPER PAGE/COLUMN MONTH/DAY/YEAR | GENEALOGICAL DATA |
|---|---|---|---|
| Gilder | Carl | KC, p5c3, 1/30/1902 | Gilder and Sam Halverson hired to cut wood on Louis Lee's farm per Gays Mills correspondent. |
| Gilder | Malvina Rounds | KC, p5c1, 3/31/1898 | Died Mar. XX, 1898 at Bell Center. Born Jan. 10, 1851 in Palmyra, Jefferson Co., WI. Married Oscar Gilder on Aug. 25, 1872 in Gays Mills. Went West and returned to Gays Mills/Bell Center area in 1884. Survived by 4 of her 10 children. Funeral held at Methodist Episcopal Church. Buried in Gays Mills Cemetery. |
| Gilder | Nora | KC, p4c3, 4/21/1898 | Married Ernest Abbey of Gays Mills on April 17, 1898. Bride from Bell Center. J. L. Stowell, J.P. officiated. |
| Gilder | O. C. | KC, Supp., 12/18/1902 | Crawford County Board of Supervisors examined bills in the Justices and Constables' Account for O. C. Gilder. C. P. Bennett, Walter Hays, Clara Hays, Maston Hays, William Beckwith, Earn Abbey, Joe Bacon, Albert St. John, Ora Delamater, John Rhinehart, Bob Twining, Fraun (sp.?) Bacon, Lola Guilder and Bertha Guilder. |
| Gilder | O. C. | KC, Supp., 12/18/1902 | Crawford County Board of Supervisors examined bills in the Justices and Constables' Account for State vs. O. C. Gilder. C. P. Bennett, Walter Hays, Clara Hays, Maston Hays, William Beckwith, Earn Abbey, Joe Bacon, Albert St. John, Ora Delamater, John Rhinehart, Bob Twining, Fraun Bacon, Lola Gilder, Bertha Gilder and M. A. Robinson, J. P. were witnesses. |
| Gilder | O. C., Mrs. | KC, p4c3, 3/24/1898 | Died Tuesday in Bell Center/Gays Mills of pneumonia. She was daughter of Mrs. Orin Rounds of Belle Center. (See also p1c3.) |
| Gilder | Oscar | KC, p5c3, 7/24/1902 | Arrested for shooting at Walter Hays. Taken to Prairie du Chien for trial. Per Gays Mills news items. |
| Gilder | O. C. | KC, p8c4, 11/20/1902 | In the November term of Crawford County Circuit Court, State vs. O. C. Gilder for shooting with intent to kill, jury disagreed, prisoner discharged on his own recognizance to appear at next term of court for trial. |
| Gill | Abby | KC, p4c3, 9/16/1897 | Petitioned Crawford County Probate Court to admit the will of James N. Gill of Marietta, lately deceased. |
| Gill | Enos | KC, p1c3, 6/14/1900 | Married Martha Taylor on June 15, 1900 in Dubuque, IA. Bride and groom were from Town of Seneca. |
| Gill | Enos | KC, p4c3, 1/5/1899 | Resided in Steuben. Published notice that Calvin A. Reed, who was bound to him, has run away. Gill warned the public that he would not accept financial responsibility for Reed's debts. |
| Gill | James | KC, p4c2, 8/26/1897 | Recently died at his home in the Steuben area. Left area this spring to visit his mother and improve his health. Survived by wife, daughter and several brothers in Steuben area. |
| Gill | James M. | KC, p4c3, 9/30/1897 | Notice for Probate Hearing published. Late of Town of Marietta. Abby Gill petitioned to administer the estate. |

Genealogical Gleanings From Early Newspapers for Residents In and Near
Crawford County, Wisconsin, 1897-1902

| LAST NAME | FIRST NAME | NEWSPAPER PAGE/COLUMN MONTH/DAY/YEAR | GENEALOGICAL DATA |
|---|---|---|---|
| Gilligan | J. B. | KC, p1c2, 2/8/1900 | His hardware store burglarized in Gays Mills. Posse pursued burglars. Posse composed of John Posey, John Farris, Sam Farris, Clint Arms, Marion Reynolds, Enos Gill and Charles Gill. |
| Gilligan | J. B. | KC, p4c5, 1/7/1897 | Ran a hardware store in Gays Mills. |
| Gilligan | J., Mrs. | KC, p5c4, 4/5/1900 | Resided in Gays Mills. Visited parents, Mr. and Mrs. F. Haynes of Mt. Sterling area. |
| Gilligan | James | KC, p8c4, 2/4/1897 | Married Alberta Haynes on Jan. 25, 1897 in Seneca. Bride from Seneca. Groom from Gays Mills. The Rev. J. M. Keely officiated. |
| Gilligan | James | KC, p5c3, 2/20/1902 | Erecting a hardware store in Gays Mills. |
| Gilligan | Mrs. | KC, p1c4, 7/26/1900 | Died July 22, 1900 at Northfield, MN. Mother of J. R. Gilligan of Gays Mills. |
| Gilligan | | KC, p5c3, 1/17/1901 | Son recently born to J. Gilligan of Gays Mills. Mrs. Gilligan is being cared for by her mother, Mrs. T. Haynes of near Mt. Sterling. |
| Gillis | Art, Mr. and Mrs. | KC, p1c3, 10/14/1897 | Traveled by bicycle from Prairie du Chien to parent's home in Boydtown. |
| Gilman | W. W. | KC, p5c6, 7/4/1901 | Advertised his legal services. Office was in Boscobel. |
| Gimmel | I., Mrs. | KC, p1c3, 3/20/1902 | Lived in West Boxford, MA. Purchased a subscription to newspaper. |
| Gink | Albert, Mr. and Mrs. | KC, p1c4, 7/5/1900 | Arrived from Fergus Falls, MN to visit parents, Mr. and Mrs. F. Gink of Wauzeka. |
| Gink | Frank | KC, p1c2, 4/28/1898 | Left Wauzeka to visit relatives in California. |
| Gink | Fred | KC, p4c5, 3/6/1902 | Ordered by Wauzeka Village Board to move his hay shed from the street. |
| Gink | George, Mrs.. | KC, p1c2, 8/2/1900 | Mrs. George Gink, Eva Brandes, Jessie Harris, Alma Millspaugh, Fred Gink, Sr., Lilly Gink and Rose Burns were suffering with malaria. (Probably from Wauzeka.) |
| Gink | girl | KC, p9c1, 7/8/1897 | Daughter born June 18, 1897 to George Gink of Wauzeka. |
| Gink | Katherine | KC, p1c5, 9/13/1900 | Died Sept. 9, 1900 of malaria. Born June 15, 1861 at Pellisville, OH. Moved to Wauzeka in 1865. Married Theodore Gink on Mar. 8, 1885. Nee Funk. Survived by husband and 2 children. Buried in Wauzeka Cemetery. Funeral held at Evangelical Church. She was sister of Mrs. Kruckenberg of Los Angeles per KC, p1c2, 9/20/1900. |
| Gink | Theodore | KC, p1c2, 8/15/1901 | Appointed an agent for Michel Brewing Co. in Wauzeka. |
| Girdler | G. D. | KC, p4c5, 1/18/1900 | Sold farm implements and buggies in Gays Mills. |
| Girdler | G. D. | KC, p1c3, 11/10/1898 | Sold 1/2 interest in Gays Mills. Livery and his threshing outfit to James Kane of Seneca. |
| Gleason | Kate | KC, p5c4, 10/3/1901 | Married John Donahue on Sept. 25, 1901 at Chamberlain, SD. Groom formerly of Town of Eastman. |

Genealogical Gleanings From Early Newspapers for Residents In and Near
Crawford County, Wisconsin, 1897-1902

| LAST NAME | FIRST NAME | NEWSPAPER PAGE/COLUMN MONTH/DAY/YEAR | GENEALOGICAL DATA |
|---|---|---|---|
| Gleason | Tony | KC, p1c5, 8/8/1901 | Lived in Steuben. His brother, William, lived in Mason City, IA. William is president of a new "Iowa Life Insurance Co." and gets a salary of $3000 a year. |
| Glenn | Bessie | KC, Supp., 12/12/1901 | Bessie Glenn of Wyalusing attended the summer Teacher's Institute in Soldiers Grove. |
| Glenn | Bessie | KC, Supp., 12/12/1901 | Attended a Teacher's Institute in Crawford County in 1901. Resided in Wyalusing. |
| Glover | A. O. | KC, Supp., 12/18/1902 | Crawford County Board of Supervisors examined bills in the Justices and Constables' Account for State vs. A. O. Glover and Michael Monohan. |
| Glovke | A. O. | KC, Supp., 12/18/1902 | Crawford County Board of Supervisors examined bills in the Justices and Constables' Account for State vs. A. O. Glovke and Michael Monahan. |
| Gluss | Minnie | KC, p5c1, 9/30/1897 | Married Grant Williams on Sept. 16, 1897. Bride and groom from Readstown. The Rev. Nuzum of Viroqua officiated. |
| Glynn | Will | KC, p1c5, 8/28/1902 | Age 25. Single. From Woodman Township. Stabbed by Thomas Mulrooney, aged 18 or 19, in Woodman at a party near the slough. |
| Going | Adeline | KC, p1c6, 5/19/1898 | Issue of Default to be heard in the May term of the Crawford County Circuit Court. Adeline Going vs. John T. Going. |
| Going | John T. | KC, p1c6, 5/19/1898 | Issue of Default to be heard in the May term of the Crawford County Circuit Court. Adeline Going vs. John T. Going. |
| Gokey | Alpha | KC, Supp., 12/12/1901 | Inquest on Alpha Gokey heard in Crawford Co. Court. Thomas Caya and L. Gokey were witnesses. |
| Gokey | Ida | KC, p8c2, 2/2/1899 | Married Rufus Delap on Tuesday (Jan. 31, 1899?). (Bride and groom may be from Prairie du Chien area.) |
| Gokey | Louis | KC, p1c3, 10/11/1900 | Died Oct. 3, 1900 at Duluth, MN. Buried in Prairie du Chien. |
| Goldfinger | Antone | KC, Supp., 12/29/1898 | Crawford Co. Board of Supervisors approved Justices and Constables' expenses related to the case, State vs. Antone Goldfinger. |
| Goldsmith | George | KC, p1c2, 4/25/1901 | General Editor of the *Boscobel Sentinel*. |
| Gommell | Lena, Mrs. | KC, p8c4, 4/29/1897 | Lived in North Andover. Visited relatives in Boma. |
| Gonier | Lizzie | KC, Supp., 12/29/1898 | Crawford Co. Board of Supervisors approved payment of expenses in the matter of Lizzie Gonier, incorrigible. |
| Goodwin | Ada | KC, p4c3, 12/1/1898 | Married Thomas Lawrence of De Soto on Nov. 22, 1898. Planned to live in Tucson, AZ. Bride was daughter of A. D. Goodwin of Mazomanie. |
| Goodwin | Blanche | KC, p8c2, 10/7/1897 | Died Oct. 1, 1897 in Milwaukee. She was the niece of Mr. and Mrs. H. Batchelder. |
| Goodwin | Charles | KC, p8c2, 7/20/1899 | Died Friday in Mazomanie. Buried in Lowertown Cemetery. |

Genealogical Gleanings From Early Newspapers for Residents In and Near Crawford County, Wisconsin, 1897-1902

| LAST NAME | FIRST NAME | NEWSPAPER PAGE/COLUMN MONTH/DAY/YEAR | GENEALOGICAL DATA |
|---|---|---|---|
| Goodwin | Hannah | KC, p8c3, 4/17/1902 | Funeral held April 12, 1902. Mother of Conductor Dan Goodwin. Aged 73 years. Funeral held at First Methodist Episcopal Church in Prairie du Chien. Buried in Lowertown Cemetery. |
| Gordon | J. C. | KC, p1c4, 9/29/1898 | At a conference of the Methodist Church held in Eau Claire, J. C. Gordon was assigned to Montfort. |
| Gorman | James | KC, p5c4, 5/1/1902 | Died April 26, 1902. Aged 70 years. Survived by 1 son and 8 daughters. Resided in Knapp's Creek neighborhood. Funeral held at St. Phillip's Catholic Church. |
| Gorman | James | KC, p5c3, 4/10/1902 | Resided at Knapps Creek. Visited daughter, Mrs. William Malone. |
| Gorman | Kieran | KC, p1c2, 5/30/1901 | Recently died in Cross Plains. Aged 79 years and 6 months. He was the father of Mrs. D. Ryan and Mrs. M. Ryan of Soldiers Grove. He was the first section foreman of the C. M. and S. P. Railroad at Middleton, WI. |
| Gorman | Michael | KC, p1c6, 4/20/1899 | Probate Court Notice published. Deceased from Town of Clayton. Margaret Gorman applied to administer estate. |
| Gorman | | KC, p1c3, 11/11/1897 | Gorman sisters married last week in Wheatville. |
| Gossel | Albert | KC, p1c3, 6/19/1902 | Age 16. Taken to reform school in Waukesha for disobedience and waywardness. Son of Fred Gossell of Eastman. |
| Gossel | Albert | KC, Supp., 12/18/1902 | Crawford County Board of Supervisors examined bills in the Justices and Constables' Account for State vs. Albert Gossel. Aug. Gossel and C. H. Speck were witnesses. |
| Gossel | Aug | KC, p1c5, 12/19/1901 | Received medical care for his hands that were frozen while driving from Prairie du Chien to his home in Eastman. |
| Gossel | Aug. | KC, p1c5, 8/8/1901 | Lived in Eastman. While hauling grain, wagon landed in Kickapoo River after the drawbar broke. Lost all his grain. |
| Gossel | girl | KC, p5c3, 11/28/1901 | Daughter born Nov. 16, 1901 to Wallace Gossel of Eastman. |
| Gossel | girl | KC, p1c2, 11/3/1898 | Daughter born Oct. 29, 1898 to John Gossel of Wauzeka. |
| Gossel | John | KC, p1c2, 10/20/1898 | Caught malaria while working on the pontoon bridge in Prairie du Chien. |
| Gossel | Sadie Sarah Elizabeth | KC, p1c3, 5/11/1899 | Baptized by Rev. Mundt last Sunday in Wauzeka. She was the daughter of John Gossel. |
| Gossel | Wallace | KC, p5c3, 10/5/1899 | Married Rosa Otchenosock last Monday (Oct. 2, 1899?). |
| Gossell | John | KC, p5c3, 3/22/1900 | Recently died in Town of Eastman. Moved from Columbus, WI in 1860. Served in 6th Reg., WI Vol. in Civil War. Aged 66 years. Survived by wife and 6 children: Mrs. H. Huffman, William August, Wallace of Eastman, John and Mrs. R. Hutt of Wauzeka. |

Genealogical Gleanings From Early Newspapers for Residents In and Near
Crawford County, Wisconsin, 1897-1902

| LAST NAME | FIRST NAME | NEWSPAPER PAGE/COLUMN MONTH/DAY/YEAR | GENEALOGICAL DATA |
|---|---|---|---|
| Granzow | Charles | KC, p5c3, 11/28/1901 | Died Nov. 20, 1901 at his home on Shanghi Ridge. Aged 67 years. He came to America in 1862, first to Pennsylvania and then to Shanghi Ridge, where he lived for the last 33 years. Survived by wife, 5 daughters, 3 sons and 21 grandchildren. His daughters were Mrs. Meisenbek, Mrs. Anna Kries, Mrs. Tillie Leefeldt and Mrs. (Tarry?) Kries (all of Mendota, IL) and Mrs. Amelia Keiser of Prairie du Chien. His sons were Fred of Mason City, IA and George and Robert of the homestead. One brother and sister-in-law came to the funeral from Pennsylvania. He was buried in the German Cemetery. |
| Granzow | Charles | KC, p1c5, 11/28/1901 | Died Nov. 20, 1901 at home on Shanghi Ridge. Aged about 67 years. |
| Granzow | Emanuel, Mrs. | KC, p8c2, 2/10/1898 | Died Feb. 7, 1898 in Eastman. Aunt of Fred Granzow of Prairie du Chien. |
| Granzow | Emanuel, Mrs. | KC, p5c2, 2/21/1898 | Died Feb. 7, 1898 at Shanghai Ridge in Town of Eastman at an advanced age. Buried in German Cemetery. |
| Granzow | Fred | KC, p4c1, 11/4/1897 | Traveled from Duluth to visit relatives and friends in Eastman and Prairie du Chien. |
| Granzow | girl | KC, p5c4, 5/16/1901 | Daughter born Sunday to George Granzow of Eastman. |
| Granzow | Henry | KC, p5c3, 7/24/1902 | Died July 10, 1902. Son of Manuel Granzow, Jr. of the Town of Eastman. |
| Granzow | Robert | KC, p5c2, 2/21/1898 | Resided in Town of Eastman. Visited sister in Mendota, IL. |
| Grap | Isaac | KC, p8c1, 1/27/1898 | Resided in Prairie du Chien. Turned himself in to authorities and admitted his role in stealing wheat from the elevators last month. Claimed Clark Chase was the ring leader. |
| Grapp | August | KC, p1c6, 5/19/1898 | Criminal case to be heard in the May term of the Crawford County Circuit Court. State of Wisconsin vs. George Quinn, Thomas McClusky and August Grapp, burglary. |
| Grapp | August | KC, Supp., 12/29/1898 | Crawford Co. Board of Supervisors approved Justices and Constables' expenses related to the case, State vs. August Grapp. |
| Grapp | Will | KC, p8c2, 2/23/1899 | Married Lena Borgendine on Feb. 21, 1899. (Bride and groom may be from Prairie du Chien area.) |
| Grate | Enos | KC, p8c2, 10/12/1899 | Marriage license issued in Crawford Co. to him and Susie Mills. Both parties from Seneca. |
| Grate | Enos, Mrs. | KC, p1c3, 7/31/1902 | Lived in Petersburg. Visited her sister, Mrs. J. Graves of Wauzeka. |
| Gratton | G. E. | KC, p8c2, 9/2/1897 | Married Christina Casper of Cassville on Aug. 31, 1897. Groom from Prairie du Chien. |
| Graul | Henry | KC, p1c5, 8/7/1902 | Died Aug. 1, 1902 in Wauzeka. Aged 79 years and 8 months. Born in Germany. Survived by son, William and daughter, Emma (Mrs. Aaron Larson of St. Paul). Buried in the Dutch Ridge Cemetery. |
| Graul | William | KC, p5c2, 8/18/1898 | Named secretary of the Crawford County People's Party. |

Genealogical Gleanings From Early Newspapers for Residents In and Near
Crawford County, Wisconsin, 1897-1902

| LAST NAME | FIRST NAME | NEWSPAPER PAGE/COLUMN MONTH/DAY/YEAR | GENEALOGICAL DATA |
|---|---|---|---|
| Graves | Benjamin, Mrs. | KC, p1c3, 10/19/1899 | Traveled from Platteville to visit brother, Mr. W. Ray of Wauzeka. Mr. Ray was uncle of W.R. and Joe Graves of Crawford Co. |
| Graves | George | KC, p1c4, 8/18/1898 | Architect. From Fennimore. Prepared plans for a Congregational Church at Steuben. D. Syverson hired him to design a hotel for Steuben. |
| Graves | girl | KC, p1c3, 7/31/1902 | Daughter born July 25, 1902 to Joe Graves of Wauzeka. |
| Graves | Joe | KC, p1c5, 12/6/1900 | Married Emma Mills on Nov. 28, 1900 in Mt. Sterling. Bride was daughter of Mr. and Mrs. F. Mills of Town of Seneca. Groom from Town of Haney. |
| Graves | John W. | KC, p1c4, 3/4/1897 | Died Feb. 23, 1897 in Prairie du Chien. Born Aug. 13, 1815 in Blaremont, NH. Moved to Grant Co., WI in 1845 and married Marie B. Watrous on Jan. 27, 1845. Fathered 7 children. Moved to Prairie du Chien in 1877. Buried in Lowertown Cemetery. |
| Graves | Maria R., Mrs. | KC, p8c2, 4/7/1898 | Died April 2, 1898 in Prairie du Chien. Born Mar. 22, 1820 in Claremont, NH. Married John A. Graves on Jan. 27, 1845 at Windsor NH. Moved to Cassville, WI in 1847 and Prairie du Chien in 1877. Husband died 2 years ago. Survived by children: Dell and Norman of Minneapolis; John of Latcher, SD; Clarence and Alice of Prairie du Chien. Buried in Lowertown Cemetery. |
| Graves | Mrs. | KC, p1c2, 7/12/1900 | Arrived from Baraboo to visit mother, Mrs. M. C. Kincannon of Wauzeka. |
| Graves | Will R. | KC, Supp. 10/27/1898 | Nominated by the Crawford County Republican Party for the office of Clerk of Court. He was a self-made man. Father died of wounds during Civil War. Attended Boscobel High School and the State University, where he graduated at the head of his class. Worked as a teacher. (Short bio. and character sketch provided.) |
| Graves | Joe | KC, p1c4, 7/31/1902 | Began a new job as a carpenter at Hutt & Gossel. |
| Gray | Edward | KC, p4c2, 9/9/1897 | Died Aug. 28, 1897 in Gays Mills. Born in England in 1834. Moved to Canada in 1839 with his mother and 2 brothers. Moved to Connecticut in 1842. Married Elizabeth Brown on July 3, 1859. Settled near Gays Mills in 1861. Enlisted in Army in 1862, Company A, 31st Wis. Reg. Later transferred to Company K. |
| Greeley | A. L. | KC, p8c3, 11/24/1898 | Married Mastia H. Phillips on Nov. 20, 1898. Bride and groom from Arlington, IA. |
| Greemore | John | KC, p8c3, 5/1/1902 | Drowned in the Mississippi River near Waukon Junction on April 29, 1902. He was a member of the 48th WI Vol. Inf. |
| Green | Asa | KC, Supp., 12/20/1900 | Crawford Co. Board of Supervisors approved bills related to expenses of Asa Green, insane. |
| Green | C. L. | KC, Supp., 12/18/1902 | Crawford County Soldiers Relief Committee provided funds to C. L. Green of Clayton. |
| Green | C. L. | KC, Supp., 12/20/1900 | Crawford Co. Soldiers Relief Comm. approved aid to C. L. Green of Clayton. |

Genealogical Gleanings From Early Newspapers for Residents In and Near
Crawford County, Wisconsin, 1897-1902

| LAST NAME | FIRST NAME | NEWSPAPER PAGE/COLUMN MONTH/DAY/YEAR | GENEALOGICAL DATA |
|---|---|---|---|
| Green | Charles | KC, Supp., 12/12/1901 | Received money from the Crawford Co. Soldiers Relief Commission. Resided in Soldiers Grove. |
| Green | Clarence | KC, p1c8, 11/22/1900 | Married Laura Gander on Nov. 18, 1900. Bride daughter of George J. Gander of North Clayton. Groom formerly of De Soto, now Garrison, MT. |
| Green | Clarence | KC, p1c4, 2/13/1902 | Returned to home in Garrison, ND following funeral of his mother, Mrs. Green (nee Laura Gander, daughter of G. J. Gander of Soldiers Grove). Mother lived in De Soto. |
| Green | George | KC, p5c4, 3/1/1900 | Arrived from Iowa to visit his uncle, J. Pittsley of the Town of Scott. |
| Green | Henry | KC, p5c3, 5/20/1897 | Issues of fact for jury to be heard in the May term of the Crawford County Court. Henry Green vs. J. Brock. |
| Green | Mrs. | KC, p4c2, 3/24/1898 | Moved to Mt. Sterling from Iowa to be near her sister, Mrs. John Copsey. |
| Green | Thomas | KC, Supp., 12/20/1900 | Crawford Co. Board of Supervisors approved payment of expenses in the matter of State vs. Thomas Green. |
| Green |  | KC, Supp., 12/19/1901 | Mr. Green operated a saloon in Gays Mills. |
| Greene | Marie | KC, Supp., 12/12/1901 | Attended a Teacher's Institute in Crawford County in 1901. Resided in Boscobel. |
| Greene | Merle | KC, Supp., 12/12/1901 | Merle Greene, Grace Wannamaker and Martin Robinson of Boscobel attended the summer Teacher's Institute in Soldiers Grove. |
| Gregerson | Charles | KC, p1c2, 11/3/1898 | Installed as an officer at the International Order of Good Templars (I.O.G.T.) Lodge in Wauzeka. |
| Gregerson | Henry | KC, p1c5, 10/20/1898 | Resided in Wauzeka. Taken to Prairie du Chien on a charge of assault and battery. Called part of a "school boys" altercation. Found not guilty, per KC, p1c2, 11/3/1898. |
| Gregerson | Herman | KC, p1c6, 11/4/1897 | Issue of default to be heard at the November term of the Circuit Court in Crawford County. Mary M. Feldman vs. Herman Gregerson et. al. |
| Gregerson | Mrs. | KC, p8c3, 12/26/1901 | Funeral held Dec. 20, 1901 at Wauzeka. Mother of Willie Gregerson of Prairie du Chien. |
| Gregerson | Peter | KC, p1c5, 4/15/1897 | Died April 11, 1897 in Wauzeka. Born Feb. 11, 1825 in Egensend, Denmark. Married Johanna C. Feldman (sister of J. N. Feldman, deceased, of Wauzeka). She died Dec. 24, 1871 in Marietta. Married Mrs. Hermina Schueler on April 1, 1880. Survived by 6 of 8 children: Christian, Edward, Maria and Peter of Wauzeka; Mrs. Emma Overton of Channel Lake IL and Mrs. Elv. Stuart of Eldgin, IL. |
| Gregerson | Peter, Mrs. | KC, p1c2, 12/11/1902 | Arrived from Dubuque to visit son, Will Schueler, and other relatives in Wauzeka. |

Genealogical Gleanings From Early Newspapers for Residents In and Near
Crawford County, Wisconsin, 1897-1902

| LAST NAME | FIRST NAME | NEWSPAPER PAGE/COLUMN MONTH/DAY/YEAR | GENEALOGICAL DATA |
|---|---|---|---|
| Gregeson (Gregorson?) | Henry | KC, Supp., 12/29/1898 | Crawford Co. Board of Supervisors approved Justices and Constables' expenses related to the case, State vs. Henry Gregeson. The witnesses were Leroy William, Emil Bier, Fred Batchelder, Henry Savage, Charles Felderman, L. C. Halsted, M. C. Kincannon, Clara Logerman, Fred Williams, Harley Brown, G. H. Perrin, Henry Pleuard, Joseph Peacock, Charles Reeder, Anna Gregerson, Phillip Pleuard and Dr. Perrin. |
| Gregorsen | Chris | KC, p1c4, 3/27/1902 | Moved to Petersburg from Wauzeka. |
| Gregorson | C., Mrs. | KC, p1c4, 12/19/1901 | Died Dec. 18, 1901 in Wauzeka. Aged 36 years. Survived by husband and 6 children. |
| Gregorson | Ed | KC, p1c3, 9/20/1900 | Resided in Wauzeka. Attacked by malaria. |
| Gregorson | Peter, Sr. | KC, p4c3, 9/30/1897 | Court Summons for Heirs of Peter Gregorson published: Hermine Gregorson, widow; Peter Gregorson, Jr.; Christian Gregorson and Mary A., his wife; Edward Gregorson and Annie, his wife; Maria Wiedner and William her husband; Emma Overton and William, her husband; Emelia Stewart and Edward, her husband; Mabel, Harry and Nettie Fuhrman (infant heirs). |
| Greisbach | Caroline C. | KC, p8c4, 6/21/1900 | Salutatorian at Wauzeka High School Class of 1900. |
| Greisbach | Mamie | KC, p5c4, 5/22/1902 | Prairie du Chien High School class of 1902. |
| Greisback | Carrie | KC, Supp., 10/3/1901 | Married Casper Wachter on Sept. 25, 1901. Bride from Prairie du Chien. |
| Grell | John | KC, p1c2, 12/27/1900 | Arrived from Hawkeye, IA to visit relatives in Wauzeka for the holidays. |
| Grelle | Carrie | KC, p8c2, 5/18/1899 | Married Max E. Busche of St. Paul on May 16, 1899 at the Catholic parsonage in Prairie du Chien. Bride was daughter of ex-Mayor, Charles Grelle, of Prairie du Chien and sister of Emma and M. Grelle. Groom was brother of Alex and Walter Busche. |
| Grelle | Charles, Sr. | KC, p14c4, 12/18/1902 | Died Dec. 11, 1902 in Prairie du Chien. Mayor of Prairie du Chien. He was the son of Christopher Grelle. Born Jan. 21, 1845 in Millhausen, Alsache on the Rhine, Germany. Moved directly to Prairie du Chien from Germany in 1849. Father died Dec. 28, 1880. Married Caroline Stuckey, daughter of Henry Stuckey of Wauzeka, on Dec. 29, 1864. Survived by 6 or 7 children. Operated a furniture and undertaking business. Buried in Frenchtown Cemetery. |
| Grelle | Charles, Sr. | KC, p1c2, 12/18/1902 | Died Friday in Prairie du Chien. Mr. and Mrs. Frank Chapek of Wauzeka attended funeral. Mr. Grelle was a brother-in-law. |

Genealogical Gleanings From Early Newspapers for Residents In and Near
Crawford County, Wisconsin, 1897-1902

| LAST NAME | FIRST NAME | NEWSPAPER PAGE/COLUMN MONTH/DAY/YEAR | GENEALOGICAL DATA |
|---|---|---|---|
| Gremore | Charles | KC, Supp., 12/12/1901 | State vs. Charles Gremore heard in Crawford Co. Court. Witnesses were Mrs. Gus Coorough, Mary LaBon, G. E. Harrington, Viola Gremore, Edwish Gremore, Charles, Gremore, Emma LaBon, Olive Gremore and Frank Gremore. |
| Gremore | Charles | KC, Supp., 12/12/1901 | Crawford Co. Board of Supervisors approved payments in the Matter of Charles Gremore, Insane. |
| Gremore | Charles | KC, Supp., 12/20/1900 | Crawford Co. Board of Supervisors approved payment of expenses in the matter of State vs. Charles Gremore. |
| Gremore | Edvish | KC, p5c3, 7/18/1901 | Summons published for the Circuit Court of Crawford County. Edvish Gremore, plaintiff, vs. Charles Gremore, defendant. |
| Gremore | J., Mrs. | KC, Supp., 12/18/1902 | Crawford County Soldiers Relief Committee provided funds to Mrs. J. Gremore of Prairie du Chien. |
| Gremore | John | KC, Supp., 12/29/1898 | Received aid from the Crawford County Soldiers Relief Commission. Resided in Prairie du Chien. |
| Gremore | Peter | KC, Supp., 12/12/1901 | State vs. Peter Gremore heard in Crawford Co. Court. Witnesses were Joe Marvin, Carl Dietrick, John Cornford and John Steiner. |
| Gremore | Will | KC, p8c1, 8/17/1899 | Married Mamie Richards last week at Waukon, IA. |
| Gremore | William | KC, Supp., 12/20/1900 | Crawford Co. Board of Supervisors approved payment of expenses in the matter of State vs. William Gremore. |
| Gremore | Willie | KC, Supp., 12/29/1898 | Crawford Co. Board of Supervisors approved Justices and Constables' expenses related to the case, State vs. Willie Gremore. The witnesses were G. L. Miller, Louis Gokey, Henry Prew and Pat Nolan. |
| Gremore | | KC, Supp., 12/18/1902 | Crawford County Board of Supervisors allowed expenses in the Matter of Six Gremore Children, Dependent. |
| Grenmore | Joseph | KC, Supp., 12/12/1901 | Received funds from the Crawford Co. Soldiers Relief Commission. Resided in Prairie du Chien. |
| Grenmore | Peter | KC, p8c1, 10/14/1897 | Married Lizzie Richard on Oct. 11, 1897 at St. Gabriel's Catholic Church. Bride and groom were from Prairie du Chien. |
| Grey | Edwin | KC, p4c2, 9/30/1897 | Died August 28, 1897 in Gays Mills. Settled there in 1860. |
| Grey | Elizabeth, Mrs. | KC, Supp., 12/20/1900 | Crawford Co. Soldiers Relief Comm. approved aid to Mrs. Elizabeth Grey of Gays Mill. |
| Gribble | Bert | KC, P5c2, 1/6/1898 | Jeweler in Seneca. Spent his holidays at home in Viola. |
| Gribble | L. R. | KC, p4c2, 12/30/1897 | Fire destroyed his home in Kickapoo. |
| Griesbach | Minnie | KC, p1c5, 2/9/1899 | Taught school in Wauzeka in 1899. E. E. Brindley, Crawford County Superintendent of Schools published a comprehensive list of all teachers in the county. |
| Griesbach | Minnie | KC, Supp., 12/12/1901 | Attended a Teacher's Institute in Crawford County in 1901. Resided in Prairie du Chien. |

Genealogical Gleanings From Early Newspapers for Residents In and Near
Crawford County, Wisconsin, 1897-1902

| LAST NAME | FIRST NAME | NEWSPAPER PAGE/COLUMN MONTH/DAY/YEAR | GENEALOGICAL DATA |
|---|---|---|---|
| Griffin | Frank | KC, p1c6, 5/19/1898 | Criminal case to be heard in the May term of the Crawford County Circuit Court. State of Wisconsin vs. Frank Griffin, rape. |
| Griffin | Mrs. | KC, p1c3, 8/24/1899 | Mrs. Griffin returned to Chicago after visiting parents, Mr. and Mrs. John McCormick of Wheatville. Reunion was held with all children, 8 daughters and 3 sons. |
| Griffith | Frank | KC, p1c6, 11/4/1897 | Criminal issue to be heard at the November term of the Circuit Court in Crawford County. State of Wisconsin vs. Frank Griffith, rape. |
| Griffith | Samuel | KC, p1c4, 10/19/1899 | Recently died at age 17 years, 6 months and 12 days. Lived with Jap Davis of near Petersburg for the last 7 years. Funeral held at Haney Valley Church. |
| Gronert | M. | KC, Supp., 12/12/1901 | Inquest, Body of M. Gronert heard in Crawford Co. Court. |
| Gronert | Michael | KC, p8c4, 8/29/1901 | Died Aug. 19, 1901. Born Mar. 28, 1829 in Gauhern, Bavaria, Germany. Emigrated in 1846. Married Magdaline Knapp in 1852. She died in 1865. Married Mrs. Anna Antony, a sister of Michael Menges (of Prairie du Chien in 1866. She died Feb. 22, 1890. Fathered 5 children by first marriage and 3 children by second. One son's name was George. Served in Co. C, 43rd WI Vol. in Civil War. |
| Gronert | Mr. | KC, p8c3, 8/22/1901 | Died Aug. 20, 1901 in Prairie du Chien. Father of George Gronert. |
| Groom | boy | KC, p5c2, 11/3/1898 | Son born Oct. 18, 1898 to Enoch Groom of Steuben. |
| Groom | boys | KC, p5c3, 8/22/1901 | Twin sons born Aug. 17, 1901 to R. Groom of Steuben. |
| Grow | James | KC, Supp., 11/24/1898 | Resided in Wheatville. Died last week. Returned sick after spending summer in Dakota. (Crow?) |
| Guernsey | Stella | KC, p1c3, 3/14/1901 | Married Bert Shipley on Mar. 12, 1901. Groom from Boscobel. Planned to live in Wauzeka. |
| Guernsey | Stella | KC, p8c4, 3/21/1901 | Married Bert Shipley on Mar. 12, 1901 at the residence of A. J. Guernsey of Boscobel. The Rev. Thomas Crouch officiated. |
| Gugler | Robert P. | KC, p1c2, 1/5/1899 | Married Bertha Kruscheke Jan. 1, 1899 at Lutheran Church in Wauzeka. Bride from Wauzeka. Groom previously from Milwaukee, but now from Prairie du Chien. |
| Guist | (Cleason?) | KC, p1c6, 11/4/1897 | Issue of default to be heard at the November term of the Circuit Court in Crawford County. Mary Guist vs. (Cleason?) Guist. |
| Guist | May | KC, p1c6, 11/4/1897 | Issue of default to be heard at the November term of the Circuit Court in Crawford County. Mary Guist vs. (Cleason?) Guist. |
| Gunderson | Bessie | KC, p5c4, 12/29/1898 | Married Claude Rounds on Dec. 25, 1898. Bride and groom from Gays Mills. |
| Gunderson | Ole | KC, p1c2, 3/10/1898 | Married Mrs. Betsy Rogers on Feb. 23, 1898 in La Crosse. Bride and groom from Towerville. |

Genealogical Gleanings From Early Newspapers for Residents In and Near
Crawford County, Wisconsin, 1897-1902

| LAST NAME | FIRST NAME | NEWSPAPER PAGE/COLUMN MONTH/DAY/YEAR | GENEALOGICAL DATA |
|---|---|---|---|
| Gunderson | Ole A. | KC, p5c4, 5/29/1902 | The case A. E. Rogers, et al vs. Ole A. Gunderson, et al was heard at the May term of the Crawford County Circuit Court. Continued. |
| Gunderson | Olena | KC, p5c1, 5/20/1897 | Died May 15, 1897 at home near Mt. Sterling. She was the second daughter of Benedict Gunderson. |
| Gurman | Martin | KC, Supp., 12/18/1902 | Crawford County Board of Supervisors examined bills in the Justices and Constables' Account for State vs. Martin Gurman (Gorman?). |
| Gurnsey | boy | KC, p5c3, 6/7/1900 | Son born last Sunday to George Gurnsey of Lynxville. |
| Gurtson | Peter | KC, p1c3, 7/28/1898 | Died July 26, 1898 at parent's home in Westby. Resided in Soldiers Grove. |
| Gutherie | Francisco | KC, p8c4, 6/21/1900 | Marriage license issued to Rosanna Egan and Francisco Gutherie of Bell Plains, IA. |
| Gutknecht | girl | KC, p1c4, 6/16/1898 | Daughter born May 31, 1898 to Mrs. Henry Gutknecht of Milwaukee (daughter of John Schmidt of Wauzeka). |
| Guy | I. C. McGregor | KC, p1c6, 11/4/1897 | Issue of fact for jury to be heard at the November term of the Circuit Court in Crawford County. I. C. McGregor Guy vs. John W. Nelson. |
| Guy | I. C. McGregor | KC, p4c4, 11/10/1898 | Issues of Fact for Jury heard in the November term of the Crawford County Circuit Court. I. C. McGregor Guy vs. Ernest Faber. |
| Gwindle | J. | KC, Supp., 12/18/1902 | Crawford County Board of Supervisors examined bills in the Justices and Constables' Account for State vs. J. Gwindle. |
| Haas | Ida, Miss | KC, p8c1, 1/12/1899 | Died Jan. 6, 1899 in Prairie du Chien. Buried in Lowertown Cemetery. |
| Hackheimer | William | KC, p1c5, 1/12/1899 | Recently married Mrs. Slama of Prairie du Chien. Groom from Eastman. |
| Hadden | George | KC, p8c3, 4/15/1897 | Married last Thursday. Bride's name not given. Groom from Steuben. |
| Hadden | J. W., Rev. | KC, p4c2, 1/14/1897 | Pastor in Steuben. |
| Hadden | J. W., Rev. and Mrs. | KC, p1c4, 6/23/1898 | Departed for Riverton, NB to visit Mrs. Hadden's son, Arniz, who has enlisted and will go to the Philippines, per *Spring Green Home News*. |
| Haddock | Emma | KC, p1c6, 2/25/1897 | Married Frank Walker on Feb. 17, 1897. Rev. Reichert officiated. Bride and groom were from the Town of Eastman. |
| Haddock | Theressa | KC, p1c4, 9/5/1901 | Married Seymour D. Allen at German Church of Eastman on Sept. 4, 1901. Bride and groom from Town of Eastman. |
| Haddock | Tressie | KC, p1c4, 8/29/1901 | Planned to marry Seymour Allen on Sept. 4, 1901 at the German Church in Town of Eastman. Bride was daughter of Frank Haddock of Town of Eastman. |
| Haddock | Tressie | KC, p1c4, 8/29/1901 | The parents of Tressie Haddock, Mr. and Mrs. Frank Haddock of Eastman, sent out invitations for wedding to Seymour Allen of Eastman. Wedding to take place September 4, 1901 at the German Church in Eastman. |

Genealogical Gleanings From Early Newspapers for Residents In and Near
Crawford County, Wisconsin, 1897-1902

| LAST NAME | FIRST NAME | NEWSPAPER PAGE/COLUMN MONTH/DAY/YEAR | GENEALOGICAL DATA |
|---|---|---|---|
| Haffa | J. E. | KC, p1c6, 4/7/1898 | Elected Constable for the Village of Soldiers Grove. |
| Haggarty | J. A. | KC, p5c3, 11/30/1899 | J. A. Haggarty of Ferryville (KC p1c2, 12/7/1899) and M. W. Twining took 4 car loads of hogs to Chicago by train. |
| Haggerty | Bessie | KC, p1c2, 9/29/1898 | Recently married George T. Atwood of Green Bay. Bride from Ferryville. |
| Haggerty | Bessie | KC, p5c1, 9/9/1897 | Hired to teach in Ferryville. |
| Haggerty | C. R. | KC, p1c2, 5/16/1901 | Returned to Gays Mills from Montana with Sheriff Bennett. Arraigned under a charge of seduction under promise of marriage. Pleaded not guilty. |
| Haggerty | C. R. | KC, p4c3, 7/18/1901 | The court case, State vs. C. R. Haggerty, "faded away". The complaining witness decided not to testify. |
| Haggerty | Clarence | KC, Supp., 12/12/1901 | State vs. Clarence Haggerty heard in Crawford Co. Court. |
| Haggerty | Clarence | KC, Supp., 12/12/1901 | State vs. Clarence Haggerty heard in Crawford Co. Court. Witnesses were Addie Ray, W. H. Smith and Fred Reinhart. |
| Haggerty | E. E., Dr. | KC, p1c5, 2/7/1901 | Married Ella Dieter last Friday in Minnesota. Bride and groom from Excelsior. Groom was the son of David Haggerty of the Town of Scott. |
| Haggerty | Emmet | KC, p5c4, 11/24/1898 | Married Nellie Pickett on Nov. 20, 1898 in Boscobel. Bride and groom from Scott. |
| Haggerty | Emmett | KC, p1c6, 1/28/1897 | Attended a teacher meeting in Haney. |
| Haggerty | Emmett | KC, p1c5, 2/9/1899 | Taught school in Scott in 1899. E. E. Brindley, Crawford County Superintendent of Schools published a comprehensive list of all teachers in the county. |
| Haggerty | J. A. | KC, p1c2, 1/24/1901 | Resided in Ferryville. Served in the State Assembly. |
| Haggerty | J. A. | KC, p4c1, 8/29/1901 | Operated a general merchandise store in Gays Mills. |
| Haggerty | J. A. | KC, p8c1, 1/7/1897 | Operated a general store in Gays Mills. J. A. Hayes was the store manager. |
| Haggerty | John A. | KC, p4c4, 11/10/1898 | Issues of Default heard in the November term of the Crawford County Circuit Court. John A. Haggerty vs. Andrew M Larson. |
| Haggerty | Patrick D. | KC, p5c3, 1/9/1902 | Died Dec. 30, 1901 at home of son in Seneca. Born in County Wess, Meath, Ireland on Oct. 3, 1815. Moved to New York when 24. Married Maria Teresa Quinn in 1841. She died 26 years ago. Survived by 3 of 6 children: Martha, Bridget (Mrs. John Enright) and James. |
| Hagne | John | KC, p4c3, 5/29/1902 | Died May 22, 1902. Born Nov. 1836 in Germany. Moved to Prairie du Chien from Germany when he was 21. Survived by wife, 7 daughters, an adopted son and 2 sisters (Mrs. Sebastian of Prairie du Chien and another sister in Kansas City). His daughters were Mrs. E. Rogers, Mrs. A. Schaer, Mrs. J. J. Dahigg, Mrs. John Nelson, Kate, Susie and Martha. Buried in St. Gabriel's Cemetery. |

Genealogical Gleanings From Early Newspapers for Residents In and Near
Crawford County, Wisconsin, 1897-1902

| LAST NAME | FIRST NAME | NEWSPAPER PAGE/COLUMN MONTH/DAY/YEAR | GENEALOGICAL DATA |
|---|---|---|---|
| Hahn | Joe | KC, p1c2, 3/14/1901 | Auction of livestock and farm machinery was held at his home at Wright's Ferry. A. F. Jones of Bridgeport was the auctioneer. F. E. Garrow was the clerk. |
| Haines | boy | KC, p5c3, 2/22/1900 | Son born Feb. 14, 1900 to Harry Haines in Mt. Sterling. |
| Haines | Elbert S. | KC, p4c4, 9/5/1901 | Summons published by Crawford County Circuit Court. Elbert S. Haines (plaintiff) vs. Adeline Haines (defendant) |
| Haines | Hattie L. | KC, p1c3, 2/3/1898 | Recently married Frank B. Churchill. Bride from Mt. Sterling. Taught school. Groom from Clay City, NB. |
| Haines | J. S. | KC, p4c4, 12/6/1900 | J. S. Haines, Mrs. J. L. Bloss, Willis Haines and Pearl Haines published a card of thanks for assistance given them during the death of their wife and mother. (See Haynes) |
| Haines | Will | KC, p1c2, 11/20/1902 | Resided in Mt. Sterling. Returned from the asylum in Mendota where he visited his wife. She is improving and doctors are hopeful that she will recover. |
| Haines | Willis, Mrs. | KC, p1c4, 6/19/1902 | From Mt. Sterling. Adjudged insane and taken to Mendota for treatment. |
| Hains | Pearl | KC, Supp., 12/18/1902 | Crawford County Board of Supervisors allowed expenses in the Matter of Pearl Hains, Insane. |
| Hall | C. G., Mrs. | KC, p4c1, 12/30/1897 | Traveled from Nebraska to visit with Mr. and Mrs. John Emshoff of Soldiers Grove. |
| Hall | Delia, Mrs. | KC, p1c3, 12/9/1897 | Traveled from McGregor, IA to visit parents, Mr. and Mrs. Fred Stuckey of Wauzeka, and sister, Lena. |
| Hall | Lydia | KC, p5c2, 7/7/1898 | Married Henry Brown on July 3, 1898. (Bride and groom may be from Readstown. Bride's surname may be Hail.) |
| Hall | Lydia | KC, p5c2, 7/71898 | Married Henry Brown last Sunday per Readstown news column. Rev. George W. Nuzum officiated. |
| Hall | Mrs. | KC, p1c5, 1/23/1902 | Returned to Dubuque after visiting her sister, Miss Lena Stuckey in Wauzeka. |
| Halsey | A. C. | KC, p8c4, 9/30/1897 | At a conference of the Methodist Church held in Platteville, A. C. Halsey was assigned to Cuba City, WI. |
| Halsey | A. C. | KC, p1c4, 9/29/1898 | At a conference of the Methodist Church held in Eau Claire, A. C. Halsey was assigned to Cuba City. |
| Halsey | R. M., Mrs. | KC, p1c5, 10/6/1898 | Resided in Everly, IA. Visited sister, Mrs. E. M. Wright of Prairie du Chien. |
| Halsted | L. C. | KC, p1c2, 1/5/1899 | Planned to move. Auction scheduled to sell residence, household goods, tobacco shed, etc. Called one of Crawford Counties' oldest residents. |
| Halsted | Levi, Dr. | KC, p1c4, 12/18/1902 | Died Dec. 12, 1902 at Soldiers Home Hospital in Milwaukee. Former resident of Wauzeka. Aged 84 years. Served as an Army Surgeon in Civil War. Native of New York. Moved to Wawautosa, WI. Wife died there. |
| Halverson | Chris | KC, p1c4, 3/24/1898 | Married Sophia Gald on Mar. 14, 1898 in Rochester, MN. Bride and groom from Soldiers Grove. Planned to live in Geneva, MN. |
| Halverson | George | KC, p1c5, 9/21/1901 | Died Sept. 8, 1901. He and George Knutson drowned. From Rush Creek. |
| Halverson | Girl | KC, p1c3, 7/5/1900 | Daughter born June 24, 1900 to S. A. Halverson of Gays Mills. |

Genealogical Gleanings From Early Newspapers for Residents In and Near
Crawford County, Wisconsin, 1897-1902

| LAST NAME | FIRST NAME | NEWSPAPER PAGE/COLUMN MONTH/DAY/YEAR | GENEALOGICAL DATA |
|---|---|---|---|
| Halverson | Ole | KC, p1c5, 12/2/1897 | Died Nov. 29, 1897 in North Dakota. Formerly of Towerville, Crawford Co. |
| Halverson | Ole | KC, p1c6, 4/7/1898 | Elected Trustee for the Village of Soldiers Grove. |
| Halverson | Sam | KC, p5c1, 12/30/1897 | Married Maggie Johnson on Dec. 22, 1897 at Utica Lutheran Church. |
| Halverson | Sam | KC, p5c3, 2/6/1902 | Resided in Gays Mills. Worked as a painter. |
| Halverson | Sam | KC, p5c4, 2/13/1902 | Resided in Gays Mills. Held a wood bee. |
| Halverson Bros. | | KC, p5c3, 9/4/1902 | Opened a saloon in Gays Mills. |
| Hamilton | H. | KC, p5c3, 9/27/1900 | Departed Steuben to visit sons, Lot and Hugh of Webster, ND. |
| Hamilton | Henry | KC, p1c3, 4/19/1900 | Sold farm in Steuben and went to South Dakota to visit sons. |
| Hamilton | Henry | KC, p4c2, 8/15/1901 | Wrote a letter from Webster, SD that was published in the newspaper. His sons, Hugh and Lot, bought 1200 acres of land there 2 years ago. Hugh sold out and bought a livery in town. |
| Hamilton | Henry | KC, p1c6, 5/19/1898 | Issue of Fact for Jury to be heard in the May term of the Crawford County Circuit Court. Kickapoo Valley Creamery vs. Henry Hamilton. |
| Hamilton | Henry | KC, p1c6, 6/2/1898 | In Crawford County Circuit Court, Kickapoo Valley Creamery Co. vs. Henry Hamilton; verdict for plaintiff; $71 claimed by Creamery Co. allowed. |
| Hamilton | James | KC, p1c2, 8/19/1897 | Traveled from Dirkstown, SD to Chicago to Steuben to visit father. Delivered 3 carloads of sheep in Chicago. |
| Hamilton | John | KC, Supp., 12/18/1902 | Crawford County Board of Supervisors allowed expenses in the Matter of John Hamilton, Insane. |
| Hamilton | Lot | KC, p4c4, 8/3/1899 | Married Rosa A. Young of Town of Scott last Wednesday (July 26, 1899?). Groom from Steuben. |
| Hamilton | Mattie | KC, p1c6, 10/20/1898 | Wedding to Album Alderman scheduled for Oct. 20, 1898. |
| Hamilton | Henry | KC, p1c4, 2/7/1901 | Lived in Steuben. He and F. C. Brightman of Bell Center traveled to Oklahoma to investigate the purchase of land. |
| Hamilton | Lot | KC, p1c4, 3/31/1898 | Dr. Dillman took him to a Chicago hospital. Had a very bad ankle. Small chance of saving the foot. Resided in Steuben. |
| Hamilton | Lot | KC, p1c5, 4/7/1898 | Foot amputated above ankle in Chicago according to brother, Hugh Hamilton of Steuben. Bone was diseased. |
| Hamilton | Mary | KC, p1c3, 9/14/1899 | Married Martin F. Foley on Sept. 1, 1899 at Eastman. Bride and groom from Steuben. Bride daughter of Henry Hamilton. Rev. Kiefner officiated at the ceremony. |
| Hammerly | Fred | KC, p1c4, 4/5/1900 | Served as Town Chairman for Haney. |
| Hammerly | Fred | KC, p5c5, 4/5/1900 | Elected supervisor in Town of Haney. |

Genealogical Gleanings From Early Newspapers for Residents In and Near
Crawford County, Wisconsin, 1897-1902

| LAST NAME | FIRST NAME | NEWSPAPER PAGE/COLUMN MONTH/DAY/YEAR | GENEALOGICAL DATA |
|---|---|---|---|
| Hammerly | Fred | KC, Supp., 12/20/1900 | Represented Haney on the Crawford Co. Board of Supervisors in 1900. |
| Hammerly | Frederick | KC, p1c6, 4/7/1898 | Elected Chairman for the Town of Haney. |
| Hammerly | L., Sr. | KC, p4c4, 3/17/1898 | Lived in Mt. Sterling. Bought a meat market in Soldiers Grove from L. Heal. |
| Hammerly | Leonard | KC, p1c2, 3/10/1898 | Public auction will be held at his Mt. Sterling area farm. Selling machinery, livestock, hay and clover seed. |
| Hammerly | Leonard, Sr. | KC, p1c4, 5/23/1901 | Died May 16, 1901 in Soldiers Grove. Aged 73 years and 9 months. Born in Switzerland. Came here more than 40 years ago. Lived in Town of Utica on a farm until 4 years ago. Survived by wife and 7 children. |
| Hancock | Alma, Miss | KC, p8c3, 2/2/1899 | Resided in Iowa. Visited grandparents, Mr. and Mrs. Wilkins of Bridgeport. |
| Hancock | B. T. | KC, p1c6, 1/18/1900 | Advertised a general hardware store he operated in Steuben. |
| Hancock | B. T. | KC, p5c2, 7/6/1899 | Resided in Steuben. Advertised the sale of a line of paint. |
| Hancock | F., Mrs. | KC, p1c4, 8/12/1897 | Mrs. Hancock and children left Prairie du Chien for new home in Bozeman, MT. |
| Hand | Henry | KC, p5c3, 7/3/1902 | Married Velina Comstock on Sunday in Lynxville. |
| Haney | James | KC, Supp., 12/18/1902 | Crawford County Soldiers Relief Committee provided funds to James Haney of Prairie du Chien. |
| Hankins | Alice | KC, p4c1, 10/21/1897 | Recently married Charles Drinkhorn. Bride from Ferryville. Groom from Guttenberg. A charivari was carried out at the Hankins residence. |
| Hankins | Melvina | KC, p1c3, 1/5/1899 | Married William Crume on Dec. 27, 1898 at residence of the Rev. W. H. Fauke. Groom formerly from Towerville. He was on a 15-day furlough. Served in Co. M., 4th Regt. WI Vol. Bride from Chicago. |
| Hankins | Mrs. | KC, p4c3, 6/24/1897 | Received a pension. Given $300 back pay and $16 a month for herself and children. Family lived in Ferryville. |
| Hanks | Sarah, Mrs. | KC, p5c3, 4/10/1902 | Mrs. Sarah Hanks of Barnum and her sister, Frances Jenkins, departed for North Dakota. |
| Hanks | Sarah, Mrs. | KC, p4c2, 5/27/1898 | Nee Jenkins. She and daughter, Mamie, returned to Soldiers Grove after visiting in Barnum. |
| Hansen | Lizzie | KC, Supp., 12/12/1901 | Attended a Teacher's Institute in Crawford County in 1901. Resided in Soldiers Grove. |
| Hansen | Richard | KC, Supp., 12/12/1901 | Crawford Co. Board of Supervisors approved payments in the Matter of State of Wisconsin vs. Richard Hansen. |
| Hanson | babies | KC, p1c3, 2/22/1900 | Two girls and 1 boy born to Mrs. N. L. Hanson last Friday in Excelsior. |
| Hanson | Hannah | KC, p8c3, 8/16/1900 | Marriage license issued to Hannah Hanson and Ole R. Thomson. Both from Town of Utica. |
| Hanson | Peter L. | KC, p1c6, 5/19/1898 | Issue of Fact for Court to be heard in the May term of the Crawford County Circuit Court. L. F. Anderson vs. Lizzie S. Drake and Peter L. Hanson et al. |

Genealogical Gleanings From Early Newspapers for Residents In and Near
Crawford County, Wisconsin, 1897-1902

| LAST NAME | FIRST NAME | NEWSPAPER PAGE/COLUMN MONTH/DAY/YEAR | GENEALOGICAL DATA |
|---|---|---|---|
| Hanthack | Mary, Mrs. | KC, p1c2, 7/24/1902 | Came from Chicago to visit John Chunot and James Tesar and other relatives in Wauzeka. |
| Harding | William F. | KC, p1c2, 11/6/1902 | Former resident of Mt. Sterling. Now from Hynes, CA. Brother of Theodore Harding. |
| Harding | Will | KC, p5c3, 4/4/1901 | Departed Mt. Sterling. Took family to a new home in California. |
| Harding | Will | KC, p5c2, 12/2/1897 | Returned from Iowa to visit friends in Seneca, his former home. |
| Harford | Taylor | KC, p1c4, 5/31/1900 | Foreman of the Western Wisconsin Rail Road stone quarry. |
| Harford | Taylor | KC, p5c3, 9/21/1901 | Replaced Charles Moon as marshall in Gays Mills. |
| Harkheimer | William P., Mrs. | KC, p5c3, 9/9/1897 | Died Sept. 7, 1897 at home in Town of Eastman. Survived by husband and 6 children. |
| Harkneimer | John | KC, p1c3, 2/6/1902 | W. G. Bailey and John Harkneimer of Prairie du Chien constructed a new 2 story blacksmith and wagon shop for O'Brien and Kriz in Steuben. |
| Harriman | H. A. | KC, p1c5, 6/20/1901 | Died June 12, 1901. Resided in Hampton, IA. He was the brother-in-law of A. D. Smith of Soldiers Grove. |
| Harrington | Bert | KC, Supp., 12/29/1898 | Crawford Co. Board of Supervisors approved Justices and Constables' expenses related to the case, State vs. Bert Harrington. |
| Harrington | Charles | KC, p1c2, 1/7/1897 | Planned to consolidate his Bluff St. livery business with his father's liver on lower Bluff St. in Prairie du Chien. |
| Harrington | Eva | KC, p1c2, 8/30/1900 | Married Elsworth Trumbull in Prairie du Chien on August 26, 1900. Bride from Prairie du Chien. Groom from Boscobel. |
| Harrington | George | KC, p5c5, 4/5/1900 | Elected police justice in City of Prairie du Chien. |
| Harrington | Mrs. | KC, p1c4, 11/20/1902 | Married George Lathrop on Nov. 11, 1902 at Prairie du Chien. Bride from Muscoda. Groom from Gays Mills. Groom brother of C. L. and Fred Lathrop of Wauzeka. |
| Harrington | Bridget | KC, Supp., 12/20/1900 | Crawford Co. Board of Supervisors approved bills related to expenses of Bridget Harrington, insane. |
| Harrington | George E. | KC, p8c4, 2/13/1902 | Died Jan. 31, 1902 at Prairie du Chien. Born April 6, 1826 at Acton, MA. He was the son of Isaac and Relief Harrington. Reared on a farm. Moved to Madison, WI in Nov. 1854. Moved to Town of Scott, Crawford Co. in Sept. 1855. In 1869 moved to Prairie du Chien after election to sheriff. Held several political offices. Married Betsy Duncan of Richland Co. in Feb. 1858 (or 1868?). She was born in Bath, NH. Father of Charles; Arabella, who died at age 6; and Annie, an adopted child, now married to Geo. D. Cottrell. Served in Company G, 33rd WI Regiment and the 47th Regiment during Civil War. |
| Harrington | George E. | KC, p5c3, 5/20/1897 | Issues of fact for court to be heard in the May term of the Crawford County Court. John Maher, respondent vs. George E. Harrington, petitioner. |

Genealogical Gleanings From Early Newspapers for Residents In and Near Crawford County, Wisconsin, 1897-1902

| LAST NAME | FIRST NAME | NEWSPAPER PAGE/COLUMN MONTH/DAY/YEAR | GENEALOGICAL DATA |
|---|---|---|---|
| Harrington | George H. | KC, Supp., 12/29/1898 | Received aid from the Crawford County Soldiers Relief Commission. Resided in Prairie du Chien. |
| Harrington | R. | KC, Supp., 12/20/1900 | Crawford Co. Board of Supervisors approved payment of expenses in the matter of State vs. R. Harrington and Charles Bell. The witnesses were John Meyer and George Meyer. |
| Harris | Bell | KC, p1c5, 2/9/1899 | Taught school in Marietta in 1899. E. E. Brindley, Crawford County Superintendent of Schools published a comprehensive list of all teachers in the county. |
| Harris | Belle | KC, p5c2, 1/7/1897 | Native of Wauzeka. Attended Platteville Normal School. |
| Harris | Bertha | KC, p5c1, 11/18/1897 | From Lynxville. Found guilty of fourth degree murder for the death of her baby. |
| Harris | Bertha | KC, p1c6, 11/4/1897 | Criminal issue to be heard at the November term of the Circuit Court in Crawford County. State of Wisconsin vs. Bertha Harris, murder. |
| Harris | Bertha, Mrs. | KC, p1c3, 6/3/1897 | Suspected of killing a newborn baby found in the Mississippi River. Arrested. She was 23 and lived in Lynxville. Baby found by T. C. Bright. (KC, p5c3, 6/3/1897 -- more detail) |
| Harris | David | KC, p1c2, 12/29/1898 | Resided in Elgin, NB. Visited uncle, George Harris of Wauzeka. |
| Harris | George | KC, p1c2, 6/19/1902 | George Harris and Lou Folbrecht erected a barn for Frank Haddock in Wauzeka. They also built barns for Andrew Schwert and Isaac Larson this summer. |
| Harris | George | KC, p8c4, 3/25/1897 | Married Lulu Cox on Mar. 4, 1897 at the home of the bride's parents. Bride was from Rising Sun. Groom was from Viroqua. W. C. Warren officiated. |
| Harris | George | KC, p1c3, 11/30/1899 | Resided in Wauzeka. Injured while jumping off a freight train moving at full speed through Boscobel. Worked for the railroad. Ordered to Boscobel from Madison by the C. M. & St. P. |
| Harris | George | KC, Supp., 12/12/1901 | State vs. George Harris heard in Crawford Co. Court. Witnesses were Mrs. Jane Rathbun and _. Rathbun. |
| Harris | George | KC, Supp., 12/18/1902 | Crawford County Board of Supervisors allowed expenses in the Criminal Case, State vs. George Harris. |
| Harris | George, Mrs. | KC, p1c3, 8/30/1900 | Mrs. Kussmaul of Eastman arrived to visit her daughter in Wauzeka. |
| Harris | George, Mrs. | KC, Supp., 12/29/1898 | Crawford Co. Board of Supervisors approved Justices and Constables' expenses related to the case, State vs. Mrs. George Harris. |
| Harris | girl | KC, p5c3, 9/5/1901 | Daughter born Aug. 29, 1901 to Willie Harris of Steuben. |
| Harris | James | KC, p1c4, 4/5/1900 | Served as Town Chairman for Marietta. |
| Harris | James | KC, p1c6, 4/7/1898 | Elected Chairman for the Town of Marietta. |
| Harris | James | KC, p5c5, 4/5/1900 | Elected supervisor in Marietta. |

Genealogical Gleanings From Early Newspapers for Residents In and Near
Crawford County, Wisconsin, 1897-1902

| LAST NAME | FIRST NAME | NEWSPAPER PAGE/COLUMN MONTH/DAY/YEAR | GENEALOGICAL DATA |
|---|---|---|---|
| Harris | James | KC, Supp., 12/20/1900 | Represented Marietta on the Crawford Co. Board of Supervisors in 1900. |
| Harris | Jane, Mrs. | KC, p1c3, 11/25/1897 | Died Sunday, Nov. 21, 1897 at home of son, James Harris. Resided in Wauzeka. Aged 78 years. |
| Harris | Jane, Mrs. | KC, p1c6, 12/2/1897 | Died Nov. 21, 1897 in Marietta. Nee Turnbull. Born in Nov. 1819 at Springfield, Perth Shire, Scotland. Married William Harris in Dec. 1838. Moved to Canada in 1854. Husband died July 9, 1865. In. Nov. 1865 moved to Wauzeka. Gave birth to 6 sons and 5 daughters. Survived by Helen (Mrs. John Smith), Jessie (Mrs. Wm. Atchison), Belle (Mrs. Robt. York) and Peter. Other names given in obituary. |
| Harris | John | KC, p8c4, 9/30/1897 | At a conference of the Methodist Church held in Platteville, John Harris was assigned to Fayette. |
| Harris | John and Hays, John | KC, Supp., 12/29/1898 | Crawford Co. Board of Supervisors approved Justices and Constables' expenses related to the case, State vs. John Harris and John Hays. John Nugent was the witness. |
| Harris | Maggie | KC, p1c4, 4/5/1900 | Departed Harris Ridge for employment as a dressmaker in Leroy, MN. |
| Harris | Maggie | KC, p1c2, 11/3/1898 | Installed as an officer at the International Order of Good Templars (I.O.G.T.) Lodge in Wauzeka. |
| Harris | Robert | KC, p1c3, 12/11/1902 | Married Edna Williams on Nov. 28, 1902 at Madison, WI. Bride from Barnum. Groom from Maple Ridge, Crawford Co. |
| Harris | Robert | KC, p4c3, 4/27/1899 | Robert Harris and William Atchison of Wauzeka dissolved the firm Atchison & Harris. Atchison planned to continue the business. |
| Harris | William, Jr. | KC, p1c6, 8/25/1898 | Large barn owned by him in Wauzeka was destroyed by fire. |
| Harris | Belle | KC, p8c3, 9/12/1901 | Married W. H. Ellis on Sept. 2 or Sept 9, 1901. Bride was from Prairie du Chien. Groom was from Platteville. |
| Harrison | John | KC, p1c4, 9/29/1898 | At a conference of the Methodist Church held in Eau Claire, John Harrison was assigned to Fayette. |
| Harrison | Lillian, Miss | KC, p1c2, 12/18/1902 | Lived in Lisbon, ND. Came to Wauzeka to visit her uncle, C. E. Wagner. |
| Hart | Adelia | KC, p5c4, 8/31/1899 | Married Frank Breinard of Boscobel on Aug. 23, 1899. Bride daughter of F. T. Hart of Haney Ridge. |
| Hart | F. S. | KC, p1c4, 9/29/1898 | At a conference of the Methodist Church held in Eau Claire, F. S. Hart was assigned to be an agent of the Church Insurance company. |
| Hart | Frank | KC, p1c5, 5/26/1898 | Died May 4, 1898 in Omaha. Aged 25 years. Son of Mrs. Sarah Hart of Woodstock. |
| Hart | Fred E. | KC, p1c3, 12/9/1897 | From Viola. Worked at the *Kickapoo Chief* office. |
| Hart | girl | KC, p8c3, 6/24/1897 | Daughter born June 16, 1897 to John Hart of Steuben area. |
| Hart | girl | KC, p5c2, 7/14/1898 | Infant daughter of John Hart died July 3, 1898 in Steuben. |

Genealogical Gleanings From Early Newspapers for Residents In and Near
Crawford County, Wisconsin, 1897-1902

| LAST NAME | FIRST NAME | NEWSPAPER PAGE/COLUMN MONTH/DAY/YEAR | GENEALOGICAL DATA |
|---|---|---|---|
| Hart | Julia | KC, Supp., 12/18/1902 | Crawford County Board of Supervisors allowed expenses in the Matter of Julia Hart, Insane. |
| Hart | Stephen | KC, p1c2, 1/28/1897 | Buried Jan. 22, 1897 in Lowertown. Recently from Dubuque, IA. Former resident of Prairie du Chien. Survived by daughter, Mrs. George Hamilton of Dubuque. |
| Hartford | Taylor | KC, p5c4, 5/16/1901 | Hartford and Eugene Marston of Gays Mills killed 22 rattlesnakes. |
| Hartley | girl | KC, p5c1, 6/2/1898 | Daughter born May 26, 1898 to Abe Hartley of Barnum. |
| Harvat | F. H. | KC, p1c6, 4/7/1898 | Elected Treasurer for the Town of Eastman. |
| Harvat | Flora | KC, p1c6, 8/26/1897 | His house and feed mill burned to the ground in Eastman. |
| Harvat | John | KC, p5c3, 3/8/1900 | Resided in Town of Eastman. Sold his interest in a sawmill to his partners. Went into the clam fishing business. |
| Harvat | John | KC, p1c2, 4/10/1902 | Lived in Eastman. Advertised his violin repair service in newspaper. |
| Harvat | John | KC, p1c3, 10/13/1898 | Resided in Eastman. Bought Bruno Meyer building in Wauzeka to establish a blacksmith and wagon shop. |
| Harvat | S. | KC, p1c2, 11/6/1902 | Planned to hold an auction of stock and farm equipment at his farm in Eastman. C. H. Speck to cry the sale. |
| Harvat & Co. | | KC, p5c3, 9/9/1897 | Dissolved partnership. Flora Harvat bought interest in a blacksmith shop. Seymour Allen may rebuild the feed mill. |
| Harvey & Elsworth | | KC, p1c4, 11/4/1897 | Harvey & Elsworth Drug Store in Excelsior was destroyed by fire. Mr. Harvey lived upstairs. When fire started Harvey found his wife unconscious and wrapped her in a quilt to carry her out. Fell through a landing, but got out. Face, hands and feet badly burned. Mrs. Harvey's injuries were painful but not serious. |
| Hasart | Henry, Mrs. | KC, p5c2, 3/31/1898 | Died Mar. 16, 1898 in Town of Marietta. Aged 66 years. Survived by husband and 6 children: Mrs. David Patten and Mrs. Marion Reynolds of Marietta, Mary Hasart of Milwaukee, Mrs. George Squires of Iowa and William and Frank of Marietta. |
| Haskel | Frank, Mrs. | KC, Supp., 11/10/1898 | Resided in Nebraska. Visited mother, Mrs. H. I. Haskel, and sister, Mrs. Altie Watson, per Lynxville news items. |
| Haskell | Dexter M. | KC, p1c4, 5/1/1902 | Married Lita Linclemm on April 30, 1902. Bride from Wauzeka. Groom from (Fisktava?), IL. |
| Haskell | George, Mrs. | KC, p5c3, 8/17/1899 | "Mrs. George Haskell and Mrs. Kingsland of Lincoln, Neb. are visiting relatives and friends" in the Lynxville area. |
| Haskell | N. L., Mrs. | KC, p5c3, 2/15/1900 | Confined to home in Lynxville with neuralgia of the heart. |
| Haskins | Bert | KC, p4c2, 1/28/1897 | Died Jan. 24, 1897. Aged 24 years. From near Johnstown. |
| Haskins | Bert | KC, p5c3, 2/4/1897 | Died of lung fever at home near Johnstown. Aged 24 years. |
| Haskins | boy | KC, p5c3, 10/24/1901 | Son born Oct. 21, 1901 to Roy Haskins of Barnum. |

Genealogical Gleanings From Early Newspapers for Residents In and Near
Crawford County, Wisconsin, 1897-1902

| LAST NAME | FIRST NAME | NEWSPAPER PAGE/COLUMN MONTH/DAY/YEAR | GENEALOGICAL DATA |
|---|---|---|---|
| Haskins | Cora | KC, p1c6, 3/24/1898 | Died Mar. 15, 1898 at age of 23. She was daughter of Ed Haskins of Haney. |
| Haskins | Cordelia Ann, Mrs. | KC, p1c5, 11/11/1897 | Died Sept. 26, 1897 in Haney Valley. Born Aug. 20, 1825 in Massachusetts. Nee Powers. Married J. F. Haskins on Sept. 26, 1846. Gave birth to 8 children. Two daughters dead. Survived by husband; Loren and Lemy Haskins of Sioux City, IA; L. S. Haskins of Haney Valley; Mrs. Emma Bateman of Haney; Mrs. Eva Brindley of Blue River and Mrs. Minnie Brindley of Haney Valley. |
| Haskins | Dwella | KC, p5c3, 5/20/1897 | Issues of fact for jury to be heard in the May term of the Crawford County Court. Dwella Haskins vs. Henry C. Kast and Sarah E. Kast. |
| Haskins | Dwelly F. | KC, p5c3, 6/20/1901 | Married Sophia E. McDowell on June 12, 1901 at Harris Ridge. Rev. Harding Hogan officiated. Groom from Town of Haney. |
| Haskins | J. F. | KC, p1c2, 3/10/1898 | Returned to Barnum from New York "where he viewed scenes of his younger years. He was accompanied by his sister who will spend the summer here." |
| Haskins | J. F., Mrs. | KC, p4c3, 9/30/1897 | Died Sunday in the Haney Valley. |
| Haskins | J. F., Mrs. | KC, p1c3, 10/7/1897 | Died Sunday. Funeral held in Barnum. Son, L. A. Haskins, lived in Sioux City. |
| Haskins | Jacob, Mrs. | KC, p1c2, 2/21/1901 | Died of pneumonia Feb. 10, 1901 in Town of Clayton. Aged 67 years. Funeral held at St. Phillips Church. Survived by husband and 2 children -- Mrs. John Cummings of Rolling Ground and William Haskins of Washington state. |
| Haskins | Lanty | KC, p4c3, 1/14/1897 | Resided in Steuben. Recently buried 4-year-old son. Daughter not expected to live much longer. |
| Haskins | Leroy | KC, p5c4, 1/24/1901 | Haskins and family returned from Missouri to make their home in Crawford Co. |
| Haskins | Loren | KC, p1c2, 9/9/1897 | Traveled from Sioux City, IA to visit grandparents, Mr. and Mrs. J. F. Haskins of Haney Valley. |
| Haskins | Mary | KC, p8c3, 4/29/1897 | Taught school in Reynolds District, Town of Haney. |
| Haskins | R. F. | KC, p1c5, 4/17/1902 | Authored a letter published in newspaper that described his trip to Hood River, OR. Sent to Marion Reynolds of Steuben. |
| Haskins | Zora | KC, Supp., 12/12/1901 | Attended a Teacher's Institute in Crawford County in 1901. Resided in Sugar Grove. |
| Haskins Lathrop & Co | | KC, p1c6, 11/4/1897 | Issue of fact for court to be heard at the November term of the Circuit Court in Crawford County. In receivership of Haskins Lathrop & Co. |
| Hasselbach | Charles E. | KC, p8c2, 6/29/1899 | Resided in Prairie du Chien. Entertained a brother from Falls Creek, PA, whom he had not seen for 30 years. |
| Hauge | Ingbert J. | KC, p5c2, 2/11/1897 | Ingbert J. Hauge and his brother, Henry, of Mt. Sterling visited their uncle, A. I. Helgerson of Wauzeka. Later went to Madison to see other relatives. |

Genealogical Gleanings From Early Newspapers for Residents In and Near
Crawford County, Wisconsin, 1897-1902

| LAST NAME | FIRST NAME | NEWSPAPER PAGE/COLUMN MONTH/DAY/YEAR | GENEALOGICAL DATA |
|---|---|---|---|
| Haupt | Frank | KC, p8c6, 4/19/1900 | Married Julia Johnson on April 18, 1900. Bride was from Prairie du Chien. Groom was from Key Springs, IL. |
| Haupt | William | KC, Supp., 12/12/1901 | State vs. William Haupt heard in Crawford Co. Court. |
| Haupt | William | KC, Supp., 12/12/1901 | State vs. William Haupt heard in Crawford Co. Court. Witnesses were Mrs. Alena Raffauf, Mrs. Alena Haupt, James A. Curran, John Herold, A. R. Kloth and John Garrity. |
| Hawthorne | Ed | KC, p8c1, 8/17/1899 | Ed Hawthorne and George Turner were jailed for stealing from Morrison's store in Prairie du Chien. They picked the jail lock and escaped. It was believed they swam the river into Iowa. |
| Hayden | Frank | KC, p1c6, 7/1/1897 | Brought to Ferryville from his home in West Prairie by Dr. Lerche for an operation on his hand. He fell out of a wagon when a team ran away. |
| Hayes | Hammond V. | KC, p1c6, 5/19/1898 | Issue of Fact for Jury to be heard in the May term of the Crawford County Circuit Court. Hammond V. Hayes, et al vs. John S. Malone. |
| Hayes | Hammond V. | KC, p1c6, 5/19/1898 | Issue of Fact for Jury to be heard in the May term of the Crawford County Circuit Court. Hammond V. Hayes, et al vs. P. M. Randall. |
| Hayes | J. A. | KC, p1c2, 5/9/1901 | Left Gays Mills for Chicago to be with his stepfather who recently underwent an operation to remove cancer of the face. |
| Hayes | J. A. | KC, Supp., 12/19/1901 | Manager of the excelsior plants of the Keogh Mfg. Co. in Petersburg and Soldiers Grove. The Petersburg plant was opened in 1896. The course excelsior is used for mattresses, the fine for upholstering and packing goods. It pays its staff $1.25 to $2.00 a day. George Standorf is the foreman at Petersburg and John Mitchell at Soldiers Grove. |
| Hayes | John | KC, p5c3, 8/17/1899 | Resided in Gays Mills. Accepted a job as foreman at the Excelsior Mills in Petersburg. |
| Hayes | Laura, Mrs. | KC, p5c5, 4/5/1900 | Resided in Gays Mills. Visited brother, R. W. Abby, Jr. |
| Hayes | J. A. | KC, p8c1, 1/5/1899 | J. A. Hayes and wife and J. G. Robb, all of Gays Mills, attended the Masonic banquet at Boscobel. |
| Haynes | Alberta | KC, p8c4, 2/4/1897 | Married James Gilligan of Gays Mills on Jan. 25, 1897 in Seneca. Bride from Seneca. The Rev. J. M. Keely officiated. |
| Haynes | boy | KC, p5c3, 5/29/1902 | Son born Sunday to Leroy Haynes of Gays Mills. Weighed 12 pounds. |
| Haynes | boy | KC, p1c4, 11/3/1898 | Son recently born to Ernest Haynes of Gays Mills. |
| Haynes | boy | KC, p5c3, 4/27/1899 | The infant son of Ernest Haynes died April 19, 1899 in Gays Mills. It was buried Thursday. Mrs. Haynes of Barnum attended the funeral. |
| Haynes | Ernest | KC, p1c5, 1/20/1898 | Married Rose Turk of Bell Center last Sunday (Jan. 16, 1898?). Groom from Gays Mills. |

Genealogical Gleanings From Early Newspapers for Residents In and Near
Crawford County, Wisconsin, 1897-1902

| LAST NAME | FIRST NAME | NEWSPAPER PAGE/COLUMN MONTH/DAY/YEAR | GENEALOGICAL DATA |
|---|---|---|---|
| Haynes | F. M., Mrs. | KC, p5c3, 7/5/1900 | Resided in Steuben. Entertained her brother and sister, Noble and Dora Shockley of Bell Center. |
| Haynes | Forest | KC, p4c1, 10/14/1897 | Blacksmith in Steuben. A little boy working for him had a hand badly crushed while fooling with a well drill. |
| Haynes | Frank | KC, p4c3, 1/14/1897 | Took over as operator of a shop in Steuben. Previously owned by Nile Jennings. |
| Haynes | H. | KC, p5c4, 4/5/1900 | H. Haynes and S. Brown opened a new meat market in Gays Mills. |
| Haynes | Jennie, Miss | KC, p4c2, 8/11/1898 | From Seneca. Nursed sister, Mrs. J. B. Gilligan of Gays Mills, who was sick with malarial fever. |
| Haynes | Lottie | KC, p5c4, 9/4/1902 | Married William Brookins on Aug. 31, 1902. Bride from Gays Mills. Groom may have been from Boscobel. Son of Eugene Brookins. |
| Haynes | Paul | KC, p5c4, 5/4/1899 | Died April 19, 1899. Born Oct. 30, 1898 to Earnest Haynes. |
| Haynes | Smith, Mrs. | KC, p5c4, 11/29/1900 | Died Nov. 26, 1900 in Mt. Sterling. |
| Haynes | Smith, Mrs. | KC, p5c4, 12/6/1900 | Recently died. Forest Haynes of Steuben was her nephew and attended the funeral. |
| Haynes | | KC, Supp., 12/19/1901 | Haynes & Schweiger operated a blacksmithing and woodwork shop in Steuben. |
| Hays | girl | KC, p1c6, 4/1/1897 | Daughter born Mar. 25, 1897 to Roy Hayes of Gays Mills area. |
| Hays | J. A. | KC, p1c4, 3/15/1900 | Elected treasurer of the newly formed Crawford County Farmers Mutual Insurance Co. Other officers were J. W. McCullock, T. T. Sime and E. G. Briggs. |
| Hays | James | KC, p1c2, 4/7/1898 | Back of head crushed in a train accident. Not likely to survive. Resided in Belvidere, IL. Former resident of Wauzeka. |
| Hays | John | KC, p5c3, 7/24/1902 | Lived in Gays Mills. Purchased a new gasoline car from the Excelsior Co. "... the way it goes over the road isn't slow." |
| Hays | Alice | KC, p1c3, 6/28/1900 | Died June 24, 1900 in Prairie du Chien. Buried in Catholic Cemetery. She was the sister of Mrs. C. Gregorson. |
| Hayward | Elisha and Allen | KC, p1c4, 7/14/1898 | Returned to Scott from work in Grant Co. Prepared to start for Dakota. |
| Hazelbach | Charles | KC, p8c4, 2/28/1901 | Died Feb. 27, 1901 in (Prairie du Chien). |
| Hazelwood | Charles P. | KC, p1c3, 6/14/1900 | John E. Dyer of Fostoria, OH arrived to visit his cousin, Charles P. Hazelwood of Wauzeka. |
| Hazelwood | girl | KC, p1c3, 5/4/1899 | Daughter born May 2, 1899 to W. E. Hazelwood of Wauzeka. Baby weighed 12 pounds. |
| Hazelwood | Hattie | KC, p1c2, 6/16/1898 | Married William F. Schueler on June 7, 1898 at Boscobel. Bride and groom may be from Wauzeka. The Rev. Crouch officiated. |
| Hazelwood | W. E. | KC, p1c4, 3/24/1898 | Sold his pool table to the Foley Brothers, proprietors of a new saloon in Steuben. |
| Hazelwood | Walter | KC, p1c3, 4/11/1901 | Learning harness making trade in West Salem. Visited relatives in Wauzeka. |

Genealogical Gleanings From Early Newspapers for Residents In and Near
Crawford County, Wisconsin, 1897-1902

| LAST NAME | FIRST NAME | NEWSPAPER PAGE/COLUMN MONTH/DAY/YEAR | GENEALOGICAL DATA |
|---|---|---|---|
| Hazelwood | William E. | KC, p1c3, 10/20/1898 | William Hazelwood and Armie Meyer returned to Wauzeka from a hunting trip in northern Minnesota. Will "had the fun of killing a black bear, a young one, weighing about one hundred pounds." |
| Hazen | Addie, Miss | KC, p5c4, 8/9/1900 | Resided in Eastman. Spent summer with her aunt, Mrs. McGowen of Clear Lake, IA. |
| Hazen | Aron | KC, p4c2, 5/5/1898 | Returned to Eastman after working on a farm in Sanborn, IA. Injured an eye while shelling corn. |
| Hazen | boy | KC, p5c3, 12/6/1900 | Son born Nov. 25, 1900 to R. E. Hazen of Lynxville. |
| Hazen | G., Mrs. | KC, p5c2, 2/21/1898 | Resided in Town of Eastman. Last week, attended brother's funeral in La Crosse. |
| Hazen | George, Mrs. | KC, p1c4, 8/29/1901 | Arrived with her 2 little sons from Luverne, MN to visit her parents, Mr. and Mrs. James Degnan in Wauzeka. |
| Hazen | Jennie | KC, p8c3, 2/18/1897 | Married Willis Ellis on Feb. 15, 1897 in Prairie du Chien. Bride and groom were from Town of Eastman. |
| Hazen | Joe | KC, p5c3, 5/23/1901 | Returned to Eastman after spending the last 2 years in the military while serving in the Philippines. |
| Hazen | Leslie | KC, p1c2, 11/6/1902 | Son of George L. Hazen of Hazen Corners. Went to Madison to take the dairy course of study at the University of Wisconsin. |
| Hazen | Lottie May | KC, p5c3, 4/11/1901 | Married Benjamin F. Speck on April 8, 1901. Bride and groom from Town of Eastman. |
| Hazen | Louisa | KC, p5c3, 8/7/1902 | Lived in LaVerne, MN. Visited relatives in Town of Eastman. |
| Hazen | Nathan | KC, p5c3, 8/9/1900 | Funeral last Wednesday at Viroqua. He was nephew of P. Larsen of Eastman. |
| Hazen | Orphie, Mrs. | KC, p5c3, 9/25/1902 | Died Sept. 13, 1902 at home in Eastman. Born Feb. 12, 1822 in Vermont. Married first to William Larabee. Survived by 2 or 3 sons from this union, Hollis of Washington and Sylvester of Eastman. Husband died when children in infancy. Later married Abram Hazen. Buried in German Cemetery next to deceased daughter. |
| Hazen | R. E. | KC, p1c5, 4/13/1899 | Fire destroyed the John Vanderbilt & Co. Building, Davidson's livery barn and T. C. Bright's home and store in Lynxville. The fire later reached the A. E. Wolcott and W. A. Allen home, the William Huard home, the R. E. Hazen home and saloon, the T. C. Bright warehouse and the Schumann & Menges ice house. |
| Hazen | | KC, p4c4, 11/2/1899 | The home of Mr. Hazen, Sr. and his son, William of Hazen's Corner entirely consumed by fire. Arson suspected. |
| Heal | girl | KC, p1c5, 2/21/1898 | Daughter born Feb. 9, 1898 to James Heal of Mt. Sterling. |
| Heal | girl | KC, p5c3, 2/21/1898 | Daughter born Feb. 8, 1898 to Jim Heal of Mt. Sterling. |
| Heal | James | KC, p8c4, 4/8/1897 | Married Lillian Sutton of Seneca on April 4, 1897. |

Genealogical Gleanings From Early Newspapers for Residents In and Near
Crawford County, Wisconsin, 1897-1902

| LAST NAME | FIRST NAME | NEWSPAPER PAGE/COLUMN MONTH/DAY/YEAR | GENEALOGICAL DATA |
|---|---|---|---|
| Heal | Jim | KC, p1c6, 4/8/1897 | Married Lillian Sutton on Sunday. Bride from Lynxville. Groom from Mt. Sterling area. |
| Heal | L. | KC, p1c8, 3/11/1897 | Left home in Mt. Sterling to visit 3 brothers and a sister in New York. |
| Healy | James | KC, Supp., 12/20/1900 | Crawford Co. Board of Supervisors approved payment of expenses in the matter of State vs. James Healy. |
| Heaton | Webb, Mr. and Mrs. | KC, p1c5, 10/6/1898 | Resided in Prairie du Chien. Entertained their children, Mr. and Mrs. Will Keenan of Savanna. |
| Heaton | | KC, p1c2, 3/4/1897 | Infant child of Mr. and Mrs. Wilbur Heaton died last Tuesday in Prairie du Chien. It was buried in the Catholic Cemetery. |
| Heiden | Mary | KC, p7c4, 1/25/1900 | Received marriage license in Crawford Co. James Walters was the prospective spouse. Bride-to-be from Elkander and groom-to-be from Waukon Junction. |
| Heidenwald | boy | KC, p1c2, 11/16/1899 | The son of Mr. and Mrs. Heidenwald of Prairie du Chien ran away. He was held in Wauzeka. |
| Heilman | Minnie | KC, p8c3, 7/4/1901 | Married Charles E. Skinner on July 3, 1901 at Trinity Church. The Rev. Arthur Pratt officiated. |
| Hein | Lee | KC, p1c3, 11/17/1898 | Married Bertha Lawrence on Wednesday at Wm. Reeter residence. |
| Heise | William | KC, p1c3, 3/22/1900 | Former resident of Wauzeka. Died Mar. 14, 1900 in Milwaukee. |
| Heisz | boy | KC, p1c2, 5/3/1900 | Son born April 25, 1900 to Lincoln Heisz of Steuben area. |
| Heisz | Clara, Mrs. | KC, p5c4, 7/17/1902 | Visited her mother, Mrs. Wheeler, per Bell Center news items. |
| Heisz | Lincoln | KC, p5c4, 11/16/1899 | Married Tressa Staar on Nov. 13, 1899 at Seneca. Bride was daughter of Andrew Staar of Seneca. Groom was son of Michael Heisz of Steuben. The Rev. J. M. Keeley officiated. |
| Heisz | Michael | KC, p1c4, 3/14/1901 | Advertised the sale of 61 beehives in Steuben. |
| Helgerson | Albert | KC, Supp., 12/12/1901 | State vs. Albert Helgerson heard in Crawford Co. Court. Witnesses were Martha Fortney, Alex Sorena, and Knut Olson. |
| Helgerson | Henry | KC, p4c1, 4/15/1897 | Died April 8, 1897 at his home near Mt. Sterling. Funeral held at the Lutheran Church. |
| Helgerson | Henry | KC, p8c3, 4/22/1897 | Died April 19, 1897 in Town of Utica. Born 1832 in Norway. Immigrated in 1856. Moved to Madison, WI in 1857 and soon after came to Crawford Co. Survived by wife and 9 children: Elsie, Ole, Henry, Peter of Utica; Bertha and Sam of Oslo, MN; Lena of North Andover, MA; Christiana of Chicago and Ida of Gunnison, CO. |
| Helgerson | Henry, Mrs. | KC, p5c3, 7/11/1901 | Recently died in the Town of Freeman. P.P. Olson of Viola, a nephew, attended the funeral. |
| Helgerson | Lena, Miss | KC, p5c4, 5/27/1897 | Died last Saturday at home on Howe Ridge. |
| Heligas | Allie | KC, p4c4, 8/3/1899 | Married Frank Onstine of Bell Center on July 30, 1899. Bride from Lynxville. |

Genealogical Gleanings From Early Newspapers for Residents In and Near
Crawford County, Wisconsin, 1897-1902

| LAST NAME | FIRST NAME | NEWSPAPER PAGE/COLUMN MONTH/DAY/YEAR | GENEALOGICAL DATA |
|---|---|---|---|
| Heligas | Allie | KC, p1c5, 2/9/1899 | Taught school in Seneca in 1899. E. E. Brindley, Crawford County Superintendent of Schools published a comprehensive list of all teachers in the county. |
| Heligas | Elma | KC, Supp., 12/12/1901 | Attended a Teacher's Institute in Crawford County in 1901. Resided in Bell Center. |
| Heligas | Elma, Miss | KC, p1c5, 9/8/1898 | Left Lynxville for Sioux City, IA to attend school. |
| Heligas | J. | KC, p5c5, 4/5/1900 | Elected President of the board in Lynxville. |
| Heligas | John | KC, p4c1, 4/28/1898 | Volunteered to fight in Spanish American War. From Lynxville. |
| Helligas | Allie | KC, xxxx, 7/1/1897 | Taught school in Bell Center. On medical advice, planned to take a trip to South Dakota. |
| Helligas | David, Mrs. | KC, p5c1, 3/10/1898 | Recently died. Funeral held Jan. 19, 1898 at the Congregational Church in Lynxville. Buried in Dickson Cemetery. She was an old settler. |
| Helmont | A. C. | KC, p1c3, 11/15/1900 | Proprietor of the Readstown meat market. |
| Henderson | H. | KC, p5c5, 4/5/1900 | Elected treasurer in Town of Freeman. |
| Henderson | Henry | KC, p1c5, 6/1/1899 | The May term of the Crawford County Circuit Court closed. The case Oliver Nash vs. Henry Henderson was settled. |
| Henderson | Henry | KC, p5c4, 5/29/1902 | The case Henry Henderson vs. M. Barham was heard at the May term of the Crawford County Circuit Court. Taken under advisement by the court to be decided on briefs. |
| Henderson | Henry | KC, p4c4, 11/10/1898 | Issues of Fact for Jury heard in the November term of the Crawford County Circuit Court. Oliver O. Nash vs. Henry Henderson. |
| Hendrick | Mary | KC, p1c2, 11/25/1897 | Married Albert Straub on Nov. 17, 1897 at St. Vaclav Catholic Church. Of Eastman. |
| Hennesey | Joe | KC, Supp., 12/20/1900 | Crawford Co. Board of Supervisors approved payment of expenses in the matter of State vs. Joe Hennesey. |
| Hennessy | Bessie | KC, p1c5, 2/9/1899 | Taught school in the Town of Clayton in 1899. E. E. Brindley, Crawford County Superintendent of Schools published a comprehensive list of all teachers in the county. |
| Henning | Mrs. | KC, p1c2, 8/21/1902 | Lived in Cedar Rapids. Visited cousin, Mrs. A. Shipley of Wauzeka. |
| Henthorn | Clement A. | KC, p1c5, 11/1/1900 | Democratic candidate for State Senator, 20th District. Born April 27, 1864 in Monroe Co., OH. Moved to Sylvan, Richland Co., WI in 1865. Moved to Viola in 1896. Attended Commercial College in Keokuk, IA. Former postmaster. Sells general merchandise in Viola. Served as Town Treasurer in Sylvan. |
| Henthorn | Minnie | KC, p1c5, 2/9/1899 | Taught school in the Town of Clayton in 1899. E. E. Brindley, Crawford County Superintendent of Schools published a comprehensive list of all teachers in the county. |
| Henthorn | Stella | KC, Supp., 12/12/1901 | Attended a Teacher's Institute in Crawford County in 1901. Resided in Sugar Grove. |

Genealogical Gleanings From Early Newspapers for Residents In and Near
Crawford County, Wisconsin, 1897-1902

| LAST NAME | FIRST NAME | NEWSPAPER PAGE/COLUMN MONTH/DAY/YEAR | GENEALOGICAL DATA |
|---|---|---|---|
| Henthorne | Stella | KC, p5c4, 5/29/1902 | Stella Henthorne of Sylvan attended a teacher institute in Crawford County. |
| Herald | Edith | KC, p5c5, 1/18/1900 | Taught school in Crawford Co. |
| Herald | George | KC, p1c2, 6/2/1898 | He and wife celebrated their silver wedding anniversary on May 26, 1898 in (Wauzeka?). |
| Herold | Anna | KC, p8c3, 11/21/1901 | Married Leo Kesslea (Kessler?) on Nov. 20, 1901. Bride daughter of George Herald of Prairie du Chien. Groom son of George Kessler of West Wauzeka. |
| Herold | Anna | KC, p1c3, 6/5/1902 | Married Wallace Schurtz on June 9, 1902. Bride and groom from Wauzeka. |
| Herold | boy | KC, p1c3, 2/21/1901 | Son born Sunday evening to George Herold of Wauzeka. |
| Herold | Edith | KC, p1c3, 6/5/1902 | Married Louis Steinbach on June 4, 1902. Bride daughter of George Herold of Wauzeka. Groom son of Mrs. Phillip Steinbach. |
| Herold | Edith | KC, Supp., 12/12/1901 | Attended a Teacher's Institute in Crawford County in 1901. Resided in Wauzeka. |
| Herold | George | KC, p1c6, 4/7/1898 | Elected Councilman for the Village of Wauzeka. |
| Herold | Lillian | KC, p8c3, 3/8/1900 | Died Feb. 25, 1900. Born Feb. 18, 1877 at Bridgeport, WI. She was sister of Mrs. E. Blondell of Sioux City, IA; Mrs. Jules Vernon of New York City and Mrs. Hahn of Bridgeport. Buried in Lowertown Cemetery. She was daughter of John Herold, per KC, 3/1/1900. |
| Herold | Paul | KC, p8c4, 1/24/1901 | Married Anna Philomena Oswald on Jan. 22, 1901 at St. Gabriel Church. Bride daughter of George Oswald of Prairie du Chien. Groom son of John Herold of Prairie du Chien. |
| Herpel | August | KC, p8c3, 11/27/1902 | Married Jennie Standorf last week. Groom was brother of Julius Herpel of Richland Center and Mrs. Umpaugh. |
| Herrling | Alma | KC, p1c6, 8/7/1902 | Married Bernard (Ben) O'Neil on July 30, 1902 at Mazomanie. Bride from Cross Plains. Groom from Black Earth. |
| Hess | Frank | KC, Supp., 12/18/1902 | Per Report of Special Committee on Insane, Crawford County, Frank Hess was liberated from the asylum but became insane again and sent to the asylum. He had $250 in his possession. The money will go to the county for payment of his support. |
| Hess | Frank, Sr. | KC, p7c1, 12/12/1901 | Agreed to pay $50 toward care of his son, Frank Hess, Jr., at the State Hospital for the Insane. |
| Hess | Frank, Sr. | KC, Supp., 12/12/1901 | Crawford County subpoenaed Frank Hess, Sr. regarding financial liability for his son, Frank Hess, Jr., an insane person. Mr. Hess claimed he was old and not very well off and offered to pay $50 to satisfy the claim. |
| Hess | Simeon | KC, Supp., 12/18/1902 | Crawford County Board of Supervisors allowed expenses in the Criminal Case, State vs. Simeon Hess. |

Genealogical Gleanings From Early Newspapers for Residents In and Near
Crawford County, Wisconsin, 1897-1902

| LAST NAME | FIRST NAME | NEWSPAPER PAGE/COLUMN MONTH/DAY/YEAR | GENEALOGICAL DATA |
|---|---|---|---|
| Hess | Simeon | KC, Supp., 12/18/1902 | Crawford County Board of Supervisors examined bills in the Justices and Constables' Account for State vs. Simeon Hess. Louis Caya, Frank Gremore, Joseph Coryer, Lucien Gravel, Poney Konechek and Alvin Gremore were witnesses. |
| Hess | Simon | KC, p8c4, 11/2/1899 | Married Rose McMullen on Oct. 31, 1899 at the Catholic Church in Prairie du Chien. Bride from Eastman. Groom from Lowertown. |
| Hesse | Frank | KC, Supp., 12/20/1900 | Crawford Co. Board of Supervisors approved bills related to expenses of Frank Hesse, insane. |
| Hesse | Simeon | KC, Supp., 12/20/1900 | Crawford Co. Board of Supervisors approved payment of expenses in the matter of State vs. Simeon Hesse. The witnesses were John Sage, Peter Flannagan, Clark Chase, A. Reitemeyr, Mary Hesse, Rose Hesse and Sarah Denning. |
| Hickey | R. R. | KC, p1c4, 2/21/1901 | Arrived from Ossian, IA to visit aunt and uncle, Mr. and Mrs. M. C. Kincannon of Wauzeka. |
| Hicklin | Edna F. | KC, p1c3, 3/16/1899 | Married Ralph E. Patch on Mar. 4, 1899 at Prairie du Chien. Bride was niece of Henry Evans of Wauzeka. Plan to move to Poplar, MT. Bride from Patch Grove. |
| Hicklin | J. W., Mrs. | KC, p1c2, 9/1/1898 | Arrived from Chicago to visit relatives in Gays Mills. |
| Hiena | Hanna, Mrs. | KC, Supp., 12/18/1902 | Per Committee on County Poor, Crawford County received $180 from Mrs. Hanna Hiena to apply to her keeping in Poorhouse. |
| Hiers | Bert | KC, p4c2, 1/21/1897 | Married Amelia Burgess several weeks ago. Bride and groom may be from Town of Eastman. |
| Hiers | James | KC, Supp., 12/29/1898 | Crawford Co. Board of Supervisors approved Justices and Constables' expenses related to the case, State vs. James Hiers. The witnesses were Thomas Taylor, John Ingham, Michael O'Neil and Michael Snell, Jr. |
| Higgins | Dan | KC, p8c4, 8/1/1901 | Died July 28, 1901 in Prairie du Chien. Buried in Lowertown Cemetery. |
| Hilfritch | Martha, Mrs. | KC, p8c4, 3/15/1900 | Died Mar. 11, 1900 in Prairie du Chien from childbirth complications. Born Dec. 25, 1863 in Prairie du Chien. Married Oct. 5, 1897 to Henry C. Hilfritch. Child born Mar. 1, 1900. |
| Hill | Charlotte, Mrs. | KC, p5c1, 12/9/1897 | Nee Adams. Arrived from Dakota to visit relatives in Mt. Sterling. |
| Hill | Frances E. and (P?)ercy C. | KC, Supp., 12/29/1898 | Crawford Co. Board of Supervisors approved payment of expenses in the matter of Frances E. Hill and (P?)ercy C. Hill, dependent children. |
| Hilldritsch | Henry | KC, p8c1, 10/7/1898 | Married Caroline Kahler, daughter of Chas. Kahler of Bridgeport, on Oct. 6, 1897. Groom from Prairie du Chien. |
| Hillfritch | Henry | KC, p8c4, 4/3/1902 | Died Mar. 29, 1902 at a La Crosse hospital. Resided in Prairie du Chien. Buried in Lowertown Cemetery. Survived by a son and a sister in Madison. |
| Hilliman | Elvira | KC, p1c6, 11/4/1897 | Issue of default to be heard at the November term of the Circuit Court in Crawford County. Elvira Hilliman vs. Frederick Hilliman. |

Genealogical Gleanings From Early Newspapers for Residents In and Near
Crawford County, Wisconsin, 1897-1902

| LAST NAME | FIRST NAME | NEWSPAPER PAGE/COLUMN MONTH/DAY/YEAR | GENEALOGICAL DATA |
|---|---|---|---|
| Hilliman | Frederick | KC, p1c6, 11/4/1897 | Issue of default to be heard at the November term of the Circuit Court in Crawford County. Elvira Hilliman vs. Frederick Hilliman. |
| Hillman | Fred | KC, p4c2, 1/7/1897 | Visited his family in the Town of Scott for Christmas and returned to his job in a machine shop in Milwaukee. |
| Hillman | George | KC, p5c4, 12/11/1902 | Left Seneca to work in the pinery of northern Wisconsin. |
| Hillman | Mrs. | KC, p1c5, 3/21/1901 | Died Mar. 16, 1901 in Wauzeka from the complications of childbirth. Wife of Rev. Hillman and daughter of Mr. and Mrs. Reichert. Buried in Clinger, IA. |
| Hillman | W. J., Rev. | KC, p5c3, 12/6/1900 | Mrs. Lottie Rider, E. Rider and Mrs. E. Lathrop organized a bow sociable at the Rider schoolhouse for the benefit of Rev. W. J. Hillman. The girls were requested to come prepared with two bows and a basket with supper for two, one of the bows to be worn, the other was to be attached to the basket. |
| Hiltan | D., Mrs. | KC, p5c4, 1/2/1902 | Arrived from Weissert, NB to visit her parents, Mr. and Mrs. George Chapman of Steuben. (Hilton?) |
| Himley | O. K. | KC, p1c4, 12/14/1899 | Resided in Soldiers Grove. Changed surname from Knutson to Himley. |
| Hines | Jesie | KC, p1c3, 6/13/1901 | Returned to Minneapolis after a 2-month visit with parents in Wheatville. |
| Hines | Maggie | KC, p1c3, 6/26/1902 | Returned from Minneapolis to visit parents, Mr. and Mrs. Frank Hines of Wheatville. |
| Hines | Maggie | KC, p1c5, 2/9/1899 | Taught school in the Town of Clayton in 1899. E. E. Brindley, Crawford County Superintendent of Schools published a comprehensive list of all teachers in the county. |
| Hines | Sarah, Mrs. | KC, p1c3, 1/26/1899 | Died Jan. 20, 1899 in Scott at age of 87. She had sons Frank Hines of Scott, F. Hines and B. Hines and daughter Mrs. Peter O'Neil of Clayton. Buried in St. Phillips Catholic Cemetery. |
| Hired | Cora | KC, Supp., 12/18/1902 | Crawford County Board of Supervisors examined bills in the Justices and Constables' Account for State vs. Cora Hired |
| Hobbs | A. J. | KC, Supp., 12/20/1900 | Crawford Co. Soldiers Relief Comm. approved aid to A. J. Hobbs of Lynxville. |
| Hobbs | Addie | KC, p8c3, 5/16/1901 | Married Harry Sells May 13, 1901 at the Episcopal Church. Bride and groom from Prairie du Chien. |
| Hobbs | Andy | KC, p5c4, 11/2/1899 | Fire destroyed his residence in Lynxville. There was no insurance. |
| Hobbs | Estella | KC, p1c4, 9/7/1899 | Pending marriage announced for Joseph Anderson of North McGregor, IA and Estella Hobbs of Prairie du Chien. Bride was daughter of Dan E. Hobbs and sister of Fred Hobbs. Fred lived in Soldiers Grove. Marriage took place Sept. 6, 1899 per p8c2. |
| Hobbs | Minnie H. | KC, p8c4, 6/21/1900 | Married Albert B. Sperbach on June 20, 1900. Bride from Prairie du Chien. Groom from Marinette, WI. |

Genealogical Gleanings From Early Newspapers for Residents In and Near
Crawford County, Wisconsin, 1897-1902

| LAST NAME | FIRST NAME | NEWSPAPER PAGE/COLUMN MONTH/DAY/YEAR | GENEALOGICAL DATA |
|---|---|---|---|
| Hobbs | Queen Victoria | KC, p8c1, 6/29/1899 | Married Joe Kopan of Chicago on June 28, 1899 at Trinity Episcopal Church (per KC, p1c5, 7/1/1899). Bride was daughter of Capt. Hobbs. |
| Hodge | Celia | KC, Supp., 12/18/1902 | Crawford County Board of Supervisors allowed expenses in the Matter of Celia Hodge, Insane. |
| Hoffland | Dora | KC, Supp., 12/12/1901 | Attended a Teacher's Institute in Crawford County in 1901. Resided in Soldiers Grove. |
| Hoffland | John | KC, p1c2, 10/20/1898 | Resided in Towerville. Visited relatives in Stoughton. |
| Hoffland | Mattie | KC, p1c5, 2/9/1899 | Taught school in Utica in 1899. E. E. Brindley, Crawford County Superintendent of Schools published a comprehensive list of all teachers in the county. |
| Hoffman | Anna | KC, p4c1, 9/8/1898 | Daughter of Henry Hoffman of Eastman. Two of her fingers were badly crushed in the gears of a cider mill. |
| Hogan | girl | KC, p1c4, 3/7/1901 | Daughter born Mar. 1, 1901 to Rev. and Mrs. Hogan of Harris Ridge. |
| Hogan | Harding A. | KC, p5c3, 10/11/1900 | Admitted to the ministry by a council of Congregational Churches in Steuben. |
| Hogan | Rev., Mrs. | KC, p5c3, 4/11/1901 | Departed Steuben for Ashland, WI to visit father, Dr. Andrus. |
| Hogenfrost | Rev., Father | KC, p8c4, 7/25/1901 | Died July 21, 1901 at Wauzeka. Aged 63 years. |
| Hoisington | Alma | KC, p1c3, 11/4/1897 | Taught school in Boydtown. |
| Hoisington | Alma | KC, p1c5, 11/18/1897 | Installed as an officer at the International Order of Good Templars (I.O.G.T.) Lodge in Wauzeka. |
| Hoisington | Alma | KC, p1c2, 11/3/1898 | Installed as an officer at the International Order of Good Templars (I.O.G.T.) Lodge in Wauzeka. |
| Hoisington | Alma | KC, Supp., 12/12/1901 | Attended a Teacher's Institute in Crawford County in 1901. Resided in Wauzeka. |
| Hoisington | George R. | KC, p1c2, 1/19/1899 | Worked in a creamery last year in Wessington Springs, SD. Hired to work at the Wauzeka Butter Co. |
| Hoisington | M. L., Mrs. | KC, p1c5, 11/18/1897 | Installed as an officer at the International Order of Good Templars (I.O.G.T.) Lodge in Wauzeka. |
| Hoisington | M. L., Mrs. | KC, p1c2, 11/3/1898 | Installed as an officer at the International Order of Good Templars (I.O.G.T.) Lodge in Wauzeka. |
| Hoisington | Mrs. | KC, p1c5, 12/30/1897 | Taught a Bible class at the Wauzeka Evangelical Church (Evangelical Association). During the Christmas exercises, her class gave her a rocking chair. |
| Hoisington | Winnie | KC, p1c3, 5/2/1901 | Native of Wauzeka. Taught school near Boscobel. |
| Hoisington | Winnie | KC, p1c2, 3/13/1902 | Resided in Wauzeka. Attended teachers meeting in Steuben. |
| Hoisington | Winnie | KC, p1c5, 11/18/1897 | Installed as an officer at the International Order of Good Templars (I.O.G.T.) Lodge in Wauzeka. |
| Hoisington | Winnie | KC, p1c2, 8/31/1899 | Resident of Wauzeka. Taught at Haney Valley School. |
| Holden | Anna, Mrs. | KC, p1c2, 11/20/1902 | Lived in Petersburg. Attended Herpel-Standort wedding at Prairie du Chien last Tuesday. |

Genealogical Gleanings From Early Newspapers for Residents In and Near Crawford County, Wisconsin, 1897-1902

| LAST NAME | FIRST NAME | NEWSPAPER PAGE/COLUMN MONTH/DAY/YEAR | GENEALOGICAL DATA |
|---|---|---|---|
| Holden | Bessie | KC, Supp., 12/12/1901 | Bessie Holden and Mintie Alderman of Petersburg attended the summer Teacher's Institute in Soldiers Grove. |
| Holden | Bessie | KC, Supp., 12/12/1901 | Attended a Teacher's Institute in Crawford County in 1901. Resided in Petersburg. |
| Holden | Carrie | KC, p10c1, 10/13/1898 | Married Joseph Beer on Oct. 10, 1898 at St. Gabriel Church in Prairie du Chien. Bride and groom from Ossian, IA. Bride's sister married groom's brother at the same ceremony. |
| Holden | Mamie | KC, p10c1, 10/13/1898 | Married George Beer on Oct. 10, 1898 at St. Gabriel Church in Prairie du Chien. Bride and groom from Ossian, IA. Bride's sister married groom's brother at the same ceremony. |
| Holiday | J. H. | KC, Supp., 12/29/1898 | Crawford Co. Board of Supervisors approved Justices and Constables' expenses related to the case, State vs. J. H. (Holiday?) The witnesses were Mary Stantorf, A. Stantorf, D. I. Clark, Henry Rinter, Clara Rinter, Delia Stantorf, Charles Smith, Judd Smith, David (Holiday?), H. C. C. Kast, Absalom Taff, C. R. Kast. |
| Holister | John, Mrs. | KC, p5c1, 12/9/1897 | Lived in Woodman. Visited parents, Mr. and Mrs. Charles French of Boydtown. |
| Holliday (Halliday?) | David | KC, Supp., 12/20/1900 | Crawford Co. Board of Supervisors approved payment of expenses in the matter of State vs. David Halliday. The witnesses were William Stevenson, Mary J. Haskins, H. C. C. Kast, James Nicholson, Silas Thompson, Nellie Thompson, W. R. Vanhorn, George Porter, Mrs. George Porter, Robert McDaniel, Mrs. Annie Stiab and Mrs. G. Thomas. |
| Holliday | David | KC, p1c4, 5/8/1902 | Died May 4, 1902 at Barnum. Aged 51 years and 10 months. Survived by wife, 5 children, 3 brothers and 1 sister. Buried in Haney Cemetery. |
| Holliday | John | KC, p1c6, 11/4/1897 | Criminal issue to be heard at the November term of the Circuit Court in Crawford County. State of Wisconsin vs. John Holliday, rape. |
| Hollister | J. J. | KC, p1c5, 8/21/1902 | Recently died at Phillips, WI where he moved about 3 years ago. Former resident of Wauzeka. Born in Danville, NY in 1824 and came to Wisconsin 45 years ago. Survived by wife, 2 sons and 1 daughter. |
| Hollister | John | KC, Supp., 4/20/1899 | Died April 4, 1899. He was the second son of James Hollister. Born Mar. 27, 1840 in Dodgeville, WI. Married 19, 1896 to Miss Minnie French of Wauzeka. Survived by wife, parents, 4 sisters and 3 brothers. Buried in Shaw Hollow Cemetery in Barnum. |
| Hollister | John, Mrs. | KC, p5c3, 12/7/1899 | Returned to Boydtown from Fennimore to spend the winter. She had been giving music lessons in Fennimore. |
| Holly | Peter | KC, p8c4, 3/20/1902 | Resided in Eastman. Body pulled from Mississippi River. Missing since November when he disappeared from the Ahrens farm. Died by drowning. |

Genealogical Gleanings From Early Newspapers for Residents In and Near
Crawford County, Wisconsin, 1897-1902

| LAST NAME | FIRST NAME | NEWSPAPER PAGE/COLUMN MONTH/DAY/YEAR | GENEALOGICAL DATA |
|---|---|---|---|
| Holly | Peter | KC, Supp., 12/18/1902 | Crawford County Board of Supervisors examined bills in the Justices and Constables' Account for State vs. Peter Holly. Mat. Sage, Frank Rod, Joe Rubecheck, John Zeman and Frank Fox were witnesses. John D. Merrell was given funds for care of the corpse. |
| Holm | John | KC, Supp., 12/18/1902 | Crawford County Board of Supervisors examined bills in the Justices and Constables' Account for State vs. John Holm, Oscar Holm and Sam Cole. B. J. Kneeland, Byron Kneeland, Mat. Kneeland, Christ Leary, Michael Heirs, Michael Crowley, Mary Holm, Charles Holm, Steven Hart, John Holm, Andrew Holm, Oscar Holm and Samuel Cole were witnesses. |
| Holman | M. D. | KC, p1c3, 8/25/1898 | Mother arrived from Chicago to visit him in Wauzeka. |
| Holverson | Albert | KC, p1c6, 11/4/1897 | Issue of fact for jury to be heard at the November term of the Circuit Court in Crawford County. Albert Holverson vs. James H. Thompson. |
| Holverson | Albert | KC, p1c6, 5/19/1898 | Issue of Fact for Jury to be heard in the May term of the Crawford County Circuit Court. Albert Holverson vs. A. Thomson. |
| Holverson | Edward | KC, p1c5, 10/28/1897 | Married Betsey Berg of Viroqua on Oct. 14, 1897 in Viroqua. Groom from Ferryville. The Rev. G. W. Nuzum officiated. |
| Holverson | Albert | KC, p1c6, 6/2/1898 | In Crawford County Circuit Court, Albert Holverson vs. James H. Thompson; verdict for plaintiff; $35 allowed Holverson. |
| Home | Thomas | KC, Supp., 12/20/1900 | Crawford Co. Board of Supervisors approved payment of expenses in the matter of State vs. Thomas Home, William Home, John Johnson, et al. John Ferris was the witness. |
| Homewood | Charles | KC, p8c4, 12/8/1898 | Died last Thursday (Dec. 1, 1898?) in Boscobel. From Blue River, Grant Co. |
| Homuth | Chris | KC, p5c3, 12/21/1899 | Returned to home in Halls Valley after spending the summer in Germany. |
| Hon | boy | KC, p5c4, 1/26/1899 | Son born Jan. 16, 1899 to John Hon of Steuben. |
| Hon | John | KC, p5c4, 6/8/1899 | Missing. Worked as a laborer on the Hopkin's farm near Steuben. May have deserted his wife and 3 small children. Per KC, p5ac3, 6/15/1899, Hon had returned and moved to Barnum. |
| Honsel | Armedia | KC, p5c6, 1/16/1902 | Died Jan. 6, 1902 of typhoid fever. Aged 27 years. She was second death in the family in last 6 weeks. Three more family members are reported to be sick. |
| Honzel | John, Mrs. | KC, p1c2, 4/22/1897 | Lived in Prairie du Chien. Daughter's dress caught on fire while playing near a rubbish fire. Mother smothered flames on dress with her hands. She and daughter were severely burned. Both out of danger. |
| Hoopman | Cora | KC, p1c4, 8/23/1900 | Married David Syverson on Aug. 20, 1900 at Prairie du Chien. Bride and groom from Steuben. |

Genealogical Gleanings From Early Newspapers for Residents In and Near
Crawford County, Wisconsin, 1897-1902

| LAST NAME | FIRST NAME | NEWSPAPER PAGE/COLUMN MONTH/DAY/YEAR | GENEALOGICAL DATA |
|---|---|---|---|
| Hopkins | Arthur | KC, p5c3, 8/28/1902 | Fred Black, Fred Waddle and Arthur Hopkins left Lynxville for North Dakota to take up land. |
| Hopkins | Dr. | KC, p5c4, 9/21/1899 | Returned to Lynxville from the Indian Territory. In poor health. Planned to stay for the winter. |
| Hopwood | boy | KC, p5c2, 7/28/1898 | Son born July 19, 1898 to Sylvester Hopwood of Steuben. |
| Horal | Anna | KC, Supp., 12/12/1901 | Attended a Teacher's Institute in Crawford County in 1901. Resided in Lynxville. |
| Horal | Anna C. | KC, p1c4, 8/3/1899 | Wrote an essay titled, "Our Public Schools." It was published in the newspaper. |
| Horal | Frank | KC, p5c3, 11/16/1899 | Celebrated 10th wedding anniversary on Nov. 11, 1899 in Eastman. |
| Horal | Frank Bernard | KC, p8c4, 10/26/1899 | Died Oct. 10, 1899 in Eastman. Born Mar. 7, 1826 in Karlove, Bohemia. Served in Austrian army for 10 years. Married Marie Votruba on Feb. 3, 1857 in Bohemia. Immigrated to Chicago in 1864. Moved to Eastman in 1869. Survived by wife, 3 sons, 3 daughters, 2 brothers and 1 sister. Three children predeceased him. Buried in Horal's Cemetery in Eastman. |
| Horal | girl | KC, p8c3, 4/15/1897 | Daughter born April 1, 1897 to William Horal of Eastman. |
| Horal | Joe, Mrs. | KC, p5c4, 7/19/1900 | Arrived from Galena, IL to visit relatives and friends in Eastman. |
| Horal | Mary, Miss | KC, p5c3, 5/29/1902 | Came from Chicago to visit brother, Will, in Eastman. |
| Horal | | KC, p5c3, 11/28/1901 | An infant of Joe Horal of Galena, IL was brought to Eastman for burial. |
| Horan | Timothy, Mrs. | KC, p1c6, 2/3/1898 | Died Jan. 24, 1898 at age 61 in Waukon Junction, IA at home of Mr. and Mrs. James McCann. She was a native of Galway, Ireland. Survived by husband and 2 sisters. |
| Horrigan | Cornelius | KC, p8c3, 11/16/1899 | In the criminal case, State vs. Cornelius Horrigan, the defendant was convicted of assault and battery. The case was heard at the November term of the Crawford County Circuit Court. |
| Horsfall | James Henry | KC, p8c4, 8/30/1900 | Died Aug. 26, 1900. Aged 53 years, 4 months and 7 days. Born in Lisbon, OH to Henry and Martha Horsfall. His ancestors were English. Moved to Millville, WI in 1854 with parents and siblings. Moved to Clay Co., KS in 1859. Married Mary L. Winsworth in 1870. Survived by wife; 2 daughters, Mattie and Mable; 1 son, Alton; an adopted son, Willie; and several brothers. Died at home of brother, D. F. Horsfall of Prairie du Chien. Buried in Clay Center, KS. |
| Host | Martin | KC, p1c6, 11/4/1897 | Issue of fact for court to be heard at the November term of the Circuit Court in Crawford County. Martin Host vs. Ralph Copper. |
| Houga | Christina, Mrs. | KC, p1c5, 8/9/1900 | Resided in Town of Franklin, Vernon Co. Bitten by a rattlesnake while picking berries. Treated by Drs. McDowell and Lerche in Soldiers Grove. |

Genealogical Gleanings From Early Newspapers for Residents In and Near
Crawford County, Wisconsin, 1897-1902

| LAST NAME | FIRST NAME | NEWSPAPER PAGE/COLUMN MONTH/DAY/YEAR | GENEALOGICAL DATA |
|---|---|---|---|
| Hounsel | John | KC, 5/4/1899 | Left Soldiers Grove for Stanford, Montana. |
| Hounsel | John | KC, p5c5, 4/5/1900 | Elected supervisor in Town of Clayton. |
| Hounsel | Samuel | KC, p5c3, 12/26/1901 | Died Dec. 22, 1901 in (Knapps Creek?). Aged 25 years. Survived by aged father and mother, 7 sisters and 2 brothers. He was buried in the Mook Cemetery. |
| Hounsel | | KC, p5c3, 1/9/1902 | Three members of the Hounsel family of Knapps Creek dangerously ill with typhoid fever. |
| Houston | Walter | KC, p1c4, 2/15/1900 | Married Sara Husher on Feb. 13, 1900. Bride from Town of Marietta. Groom from (Wauzeka?) |
| Houston | Walter | KC, p8c4, 4/4/1901 | Part of a group that left Steuben and Wauzeka for the West. Most of the group went to McHenry, North Dakota. |
| Hover | M. E. | KC, p1c2, 11/3/1898 | Installed as an officer at the International Order of Good Templars (I.O.G.T.) Lodge in Wauzeka. |
| Hover | M. E. | KC, Supp., 12/12/1901 | State vs. M. E. Hover heard in Crawford Co. Court. Witnesses were Wayne Williams, William Pomeraning, William Leivig, G. W. Roach, Joe Demock, John Lageman, Charles Leivig, Henry Evans and Henry Williams. |
| Hovey | T. O. | KC, p5c3, 11/6/1902 | Married Clara Paulsen on Oct. 2, 1902 at Clear Lake IA. Bride from Mason City. Groom from Prairie du Chien. |
| Howard | John | KC, p8c3, 2/13/1902 | Died Feb. 10, 1902 in Grand Crossing. |
| Howe | Frances | KC, p5c1, 9/9/1897 | Hired to teach in Ferryville. |
| Howe | Frances | KC, Supp., 12/12/1901 | Attended a Teacher's Institute in Crawford County in 1901. Resided in Ferryville. |
| Howe | Francis | KC, p1c5, 2/9/1899 | Taught school in Seneca in 1899. E. E. Brindley, Crawford County Superintendent of Schools published a comprehensive list of all teachers in the county. |
| Howe | Frank, Mrs. | KC, p5c3, 7/18/1901 | Died July 16, 1901 at Mt. Sterling home. Survived by husband and children -- Elden, Ora, Mrs. L. F. Copsy of Lynxville and Mrs. Horace Miller of Mt. Sterling. |
| Howe | Lillian | KC, p4c1, 8/26/1897 | Married Fred McCormick of Towerville on Aug. 25, 1897 at Town of Freeman. Bride from Ferryville. |
| Howe | Mr. | KC, p5c3, 9/5/1901 | Mr. Howe and his son, Ora, of Mt. Sterling were the guest of L. F. Copsey in Lynxville. Mr. Howe planned to make his future home with Mrs. Copsey, his daughter. |
| Howe | W. E. | KC, p1c6, 1/18/1900 | Advertised legal services. Attorney based in Boscobel. |
| Howell | Frank, Mrs. | KC, p8c2, 5/11/1899 | Died May 8, 1899 in Elk Creek, SD. Nee Laura Raffauf. Born April 7, 1875 in Prairie du Chien. Married Frank Howell on Feb. 1, 1899. |
| Howell | Joseph | KC, Supp., 12/29/1898 | Crawford Co. Board of Supervisors approved Justices and Constables' expenses related to the case, State vs. Joseph Howell et al. |
| Huard | George A. | KC, p4c4, 11/15/1900 | He was a pearl buyer in Lynxville. Purchased a pearl for $125 from H. Gifford. |

Genealogical Gleanings From Early Newspapers for Residents In and Near
Crawford County, Wisconsin, 1897-1902

| LAST NAME | FIRST NAME | NEWSPAPER PAGE/COLUMN MONTH/DAY/YEAR | GENEALOGICAL DATA |
|---|---|---|---|
| Huard | girl | KC, p6c1, 7/15/1897 | Daughter born July 1, 1897 to D. A. (or P. A.) Huard of Lynxville. |
| Huard | James | KC, p5c3, 7/25/1901 | Resided in Lynxville. Sold a pearl he found while clam fishing in the river for $181. |
| Huard | William | KC, p1c5, 4/13/1899 | Fire destroyed the John Vanderbilt & Co. Building, Davidson's livery barn and T. C. Bright's home and store in Lynxville. The fire later reached the A. E. Wolcott and W. A. Allen home, the William Huard home, the R. E. Hazen home and saloon, the T. C. Bright warehouse and the Schumann & Menges ice house. |
| Hubbel | Dave | KC, p8c2, 1/12/1899 | Fire seriously damaged his home in Town of Scott. |
| Hubbel | T. N. | KC, p1c3, 3/14/1901 | Funeral held Mar. 12, 1901 in Boscobel. |
| Hubert | J. | KC, p5c1, 12/2/1897 | J. Hubert, Victor and Lawrence Kramer, John Lewison and Willie Roach returned to Eastman after working in the west. |
| Hudson | Ben | KC, p5c3, 2/27/1902 | Resided in Ferryville. Circulated a petition against a bill that would regulate the clam industry. |
| Hudson | Ed, Mr. and Mrs. | KC, p5c1, 10/6/1898 | Traveled from Portland, OR to visit brothers in Town of Scott. |
| Hudson | J. D. | KC, p5c4, 1/16/1902 | Assisted in meetings of the Christian Church on Knapps Creek. |
| Hudson | J. D. | KC, p5c5, 4/5/1900 | Elected supervisor in Town of Scott. |
| Hudson | J. D. | KC, Supp., 12/20/1900 | Represented Scott on the Crawford Co. Board of Supervisors in 1900. |
| Hudson | Nellie | KC, p1c5, 2/9/1899 | Taught school in Scott in 1899. E. E. Brindley, Crawford County Superintendent of Schools published a comprehensive list of all teachers in the county. |
| Hudson | Olive | KC, Supp., 12/12/1901 | Attended a Teacher's Institute in Crawford County in 1901. Resided in Ferryville. |
| Hudson | B. D. | KC, p4c1, 10/7/1897 | Celebrated China Wedding Anniversary on Oct. 7, 1897 in Ferryville. |
| Huffman | C. A. | KC, p1c2, 10/9/1902 | Former resident of Bell Center. Arrived from Ladysmith to attend the Gays Mills fair. |
| Huffman | C. A. | KC, p1c4, 6/8/1899 | C. A. Huffman, formerly of Bell Center, and F. W. Lewis, Crawford County Treasurer, purchased the general merchandise and furniture stock from H. M. Pond at Readstown. They planned to sell under the name Huffman & Lewis. |
| Huffman | C. A., Mrs. | KC, p1c2, 5/5/1898 | Lived in Bell Center. Visited brother, F. W. Lewis of Prairie du Chien. |
| Huffman | C. E. | KC, p1c3, 10/31/1901 | Left Readstown for a new home at Ladysmith, WI. |
| Huffman | Henry | KC, p5c5, 4/5/1900 | Elected treasurer in Eastman. |
| Huffman | Mrs. | KC, p5c5, 4/19/1900 | Departed home in Readstown to visit brother, Frank Lewis of Gays Mills. |

Genealogical Gleanings From Early Newspapers for Residents In and Near
Crawford County, Wisconsin, 1897-1902

| LAST NAME | FIRST NAME | NEWSPAPER PAGE/COLUMN MONTH/DAY/YEAR | GENEALOGICAL DATA |
|---|---|---|---|
| Huffman & Onstine | | KC, p4c1, 1/18/1900 | Advertised general store they operated in Bell Center. |
| Huffman & Onstine | | KC, p5c6, 3/8/1900 | Operated in Belle Center. Had a fine supply of logs on hand. |
| Huffsmidth | C. W. | KC, Supp., 12/29/1898 | Crawford Co. Board of Supervisors approved Justices and Constables' expenses related to the case, State vs. C. W. Huffsmidth. |
| Hughbank | Elisha | KC, p5c3, 5/20/1897 | Issues of fact for jury to be heard in the May term of the Crawford County Court. Elisha Hughbanks vs. John Varrell. |
| Hughbanks | Elijah | KC, p1c4, 8/25/1898 | Died Aug. 11, 1898 in Marietta. Born April 14, 1850 in Mineral Point. Settled in Crawford Co. in 1873. Married Belle Wayne in 1876. Survived by 6 or 6 children. Had 5 brothers and 4 sisters. Many names given in obituary. |
| Hughbanks | Elisha | KC, p5c4, 3/21/1901 | Moved from Millett to Petersburg to run the hotel and saloon. |
| Hughbanks | Etta | KC, Supp., 12/12/1901 | Attended a Teacher's Institute in Crawford County in 1901. Resided in Millett. |
| Hughbanks | Gertie M. | KC, p1c3, 10/6/1898 | Married Fred A. Meyers of Lancaster on Sept. 22, 1898. Bride from Marietta. Rev. Webster of Boscobel officiated. |
| Hughbanks | Munroe | KC, p5c1, 4/15/1897 | Married Otilla M. Duncan of the Town of Scott on April 5, 1897 in Haney. Groom from Barnum. Justice James Dowling officiated. |
| Hughes | girl | KC, p1c2, 6/6/1901 | Daughter born Wednesday evening to Mrs. Pat Hughes of Wauzeka. |
| Hughes | Joseph | KC, p8c4, 7/21/1898 | Died July 18, 1898 in Prairie du Chien at age 20. |
| Hughey | Mrs. | KC, p5c4, 7/31/1902 | Mrs. Hughey and her daughter came from Fremont, IN to visit her brothers, Lyman and Ed Noggle in Lynxville. She last saw Ed 21 years ago and last saw Lyman 34 years ago. "These people came from Rev. A. M. Laird's old home in the Hoosier state, being former neighbors of his parents." |
| Hughs | Joseph | KC, Supp., 12/29/1898 | Crawford Co. Board of Supervisors approved Justices and Constables' expenses related to the case, State vs. Joseph Hughs, Inquest. The witnesses were Joseph Laroque and Dan Hobbs. |
| Hunt | Walter | KC, p8c3, 9/11/1902 | Lived in Lexington, KY. Visited friends in Prairie du Chien his former home. Gone for 10 years. |
| Hunter | James | KC, p8c1, 3/23/1899 | Spent 3 months visiting in Prairie du Chien and then returned to his home in Devils Lake North Dakota. |
| Hunter | Louis | KC, p8c3, 11/22/1900 | Married Emma Quinn on Nov. 21, 1900. Bride from Prairie du Chien. Groom from Ion, IA. |
| Hunter | William | KC, p8c2, 4/20/1899 | Died Wednesday (April 19, 1899). Aged 82 years. Father of Mrs. John Stackland. Buried in Eastman. |
| Hunter | William | KC, p1c6, 6/2/1898 | Announced plans to run for Crawford County Sheriff. Resident of Wauzeka. |
| Hunter | William | KC, Supp. 10/27/1898 | Nominated by the Republican Party for the office of sheriff in Crawford County. Resident of Eastman. (Picture, short bio. and character sketch provided.) |

Genealogical Gleanings From Early Newspapers for Residents In and Near
Crawford County, Wisconsin, 1897-1902

| LAST NAME | FIRST NAME | NEWSPAPER PAGE/COLUMN MONTH/DAY/YEAR | GENEALOGICAL DATA |
|---|---|---|---|
| Huntington | S., Mrs. | KC, p4c2, 6/10/1897 | Traveled from Omaha, NB to visit brother, Mr. Kahlar of Ferryville. |
| Hurd | W. T. | KC, p5c1, 1/7/1897 | Advertised dental services. Office based in Boscobel. |
| Hurd | W. T., Dr | KC, p1c1, 1/18/1900 | Advertised dental services. Practice based in Boscobel. |
| Hurlburt | Mertle | KC, p1c5, 2/17/1898 | Married Holly M. Pond on Feb. 16, 1898. Bride from Readstown, formerly from Wauzeka and Steuben. Bride daughter of W. S. Hurlburt. |
| Hurlburt | J. J. | KC, p5c3, 7/6/1899 | Married Jennie Peterson on July 4, 1899. Bride and groom from Steuben. |
| Hurlbut | A. L. | KC, Supp., 12/18/1902 | Per Report on the Committee on Public Property, Crawford Co., A. L. Hurlbut, County Surveyor, would be paid $1.50 per day for his services. |
| Hurlbut | Albert | KC, p5c5, 4/5/1900 | Elected clerk in Town of Scott. |
| Hurlbut | Editor | KC, p1c5, 5/19/1898 | Ceased publication of the *Daily Union*. It was an unprofitable venture. |
| Hurlbut | girl | KC, p5c4, 8/15/1901 | Daughter born Aug. 10, 1901 to J. J. Hurlbut of Steuben. |
| Hurlbut | J. J. | KC, Supp., 12/19/1901 | J. J. Hurlbut was a business pioneer in the Village of Steuben. He established a sawmill and general store there in 1887. He continued the store until 1895. The sawmill was still active. |
| Hurlbut | John | KC, p5c3, 5/20/1897 | Issues of fact for jury to be heard in the May term of the Crawford County Court. W. S. Hurlbut vs. John Hurlbut. |
| Hurlbut | Mabel | KC, p1c5, 8/22/1901 | Married Dan Phillips on August 14, 1901. Bride from Readstown. Groom from Mt. Sterling. Planned to move to North Dakota. |
| Hurlbut | Scott | KC, p5c4, 8/29/1901 | Lived in Readstown. Visited daughter, Mrs. Pond of Steuben. |
| Hurlbut | Scott | KC, Supp., 12/19/1901 | Scott Hurlbut ran the Steuben's blacksmith shop as early as 1888. He later engaged in the mercantile business until 1896 when he left for Readstown. |
| Hurlbut | W. S. | KC, p9c3, 7/1/1897 | Plaintiff (from Readstown) in a trail against J. J. Hurlbut of Seneca. |
| Hurlbut | W. S. | KC, p5c3, 5/20/1897 | Issues of fact for jury to be heard in the May term of the Crawford County Court. W. S. Hurlbut vs. John Hurlbut. |
| Hurlbut | W. S. | KC, p1c6, 5/19/1898 | Issue of Fact for Court to be heard in the May term of the Crawford County Circuit Court. W. S. Hurlbut vs. John J. Hurlbut. |
| Hurlbut | W. S. | KC, p1c6, 11/4/1897 | Issue of fact for jury to be heard at the November term of the Circuit Court in Crawford County. W. S. Hurlbut vs. John Hurlbut. |
| Husher | Miss | KC, p5c4, 5/18/1899 | James Jones married Miss Husher last week. Groom son of Tom Jones. Groom and bride were not of legal age. |
| Husher | Sara | KC, p1c4, 2/15/1900 | Married Walter Houston on Feb. 13, 1900. Bride from Town of Marietta. Groom from (Wauzeka?) |

Genealogical Gleanings From Early Newspapers for Residents In and Near
Crawford County, Wisconsin, 1897-1902

| LAST NAME | FIRST NAME | NEWSPAPER PAGE/COLUMN MONTH/DAY/YEAR | GENEALOGICAL DATA |
|---|---|---|---|
| Hutchison | Anna | KC, p4c1, 6/17/1897 | Died June 11, 1897 at Readstown. She was the sister of Register of Deeds Hutchison. |
| Hutchison | Bernice | KC, p4c1, 1/20/1898 | Died Jan. 9, 1898. Aged 2 years, 2 month and 15 days. Daughter of Mr. and Mrs. Frank Hutchison of Readstown. |
| Hutchison | Elizabeth L. C, Mrs. | KC, p5c4, 12/6/1900 | Died Oct. 22, 1900 at Omaha, NB. She was the wife of William Hutchison. Former resident of Mt. Sterling. |
| Hutchison | May | KC, p5c2, 9/1/1898 | Died Aug. 18, 1898 in Readstown. She was niece of Wallace Morley of Waupun. |
| Hutson | B. D. | KC, p5c3, 7/21/1898 | The families of B. D. Hutson and E. E. Swan went to Copper Creek, dug into an Indian burial mount and unearthed a skull, pipe and a few darts. From Ferryville news items. |
| Hutson | Olive | KC, p5c4, 5/29/1902 | Olive Hutson and Eldora Lankford of Ferryville attended a teacher institute in Crawford County. |
| Hutson | William | KC, Supp., 12/29/1898 | Received aid from the Crawford County Soldiers Relief Commission. Resided in De Soto. |
| Hutt | Laura | KC, p1c2, 9/11/1902 | Eldest daughter of Rud Hutt of Wauzeka. Critically ill with diphtheria. Per 9/25/1902 issue, she recovered. |
| Hutt | Mrs. | KC, p1c3 12/4/1902 | Arrived from Detroit to visit her son, Rud, and daughter, Mrs. John Gossel. |
| Hutt | Rud | KC, p1c3, 12/9/1897 | Paid $352 at auction for the Stemmiller estate. |
| Hyde | Mr. | KC, p1c3, 8/25/1898 | From La Farge. Twenty-four years ago he was a minister in charge of the Wauzeka pastorate. Spoke at the Evangelical Church on Monday, before leaving for St. Paul. |
| Immigrants | | KC, p8c4, 4/4/1901 | "Gone West." Departed from Steuben and Wauzeka for the West. Most went to McHenry, ND. H. Peterson and family, Walter Houston and family, Lev. Reynolds, Walker McCord, Robert Standorf, Joseph Meyers and family, Walter Posey, Mike Foley, Fred Meyers, Norman Onstine, Mat Posey, Albert Jeffries. |
| Infield | Willie | KC, Supp., 12/12/1901 | Attended a Teacher's Institute in Crawford County in 1901. Resided in Millett. |
| Ingham | James | KC, p5c3, 12/26/1901 | Died Dec. 16, 1901. He was an aged resident of Town of Seneca. Father of John Ingham. |
| Ingham | John | KC, p1c6, 4/7/1898 | Elected Chairman for the Town of Seneca. |
| Ingham | John J. | KC, p1c6, 2/22/1900 | Married Nettie Lawler on Feb. 14, 1900. Bride and groom from Town of Seneca. |
| Ingham | Mr. | KC, p5c3, 12/26/1901 | Recently died. He was grandfather of Postmistress Miss Watson of Town of Seneca. |
| Ingles | Joseph | KC, p8c1, 7/6/1899 | Leased the corner saloon at Main and Bluff in Prairie du Chien. |
| Ingles | Mark | KC, p8c2, 12/8/1898 | Died Dec. 1, 1898 in Prairie du Chien. From Canada. Survived by wife, 3 sons and 2 daughters. Funeral held at St. Gabriel Catholic Church. |
| Ingles | Mr. | KC, p4c3, 12/8/1898 | Died last week in Prairie du Chien. Father of Mrs. Charles Speck of Eastman. |

Genealogical Gleanings From Early Newspapers for Residents In and Near
Crawford County, Wisconsin, 1897-1902

| LAST NAME | FIRST NAME | NEWSPAPER PAGE/COLUMN MONTH/DAY/YEAR | GENEALOGICAL DATA |
|---|---|---|---|
| Ingles | Will | KC, p4c2, 7/22/1897 | Traveled from Canada to visit the C. H. Speck family of Eastman. |
| Inter City Concert Co. | | KC, p1c3, 1/24/1901 | Belonged to the Inter City Concert Co. which gave concerts and played at dances -- O. Bieloh, F. Batchelder and F. Chapek of Wauzeka; Herb Beach, J. P. Zeman, Otto Wendt, Harmon Knops, Will Knops and Will Chapek of Prairie du Chien. Matt Bromley of McGregor and Fred Beimborn of Boscobel. They recently played in La Farge and Viola. |
| Ishmael | Melvin | KC, p1c3, 7/22/1897 | Melvin Ishmael and his mother moved to Denver, CO from Prairie du Chien. |
| Iverson | Bell | KC, p1c5, 2/9/1899 | Taught school in Eastman in 1899. E. E. Brindley, Crawford County Superintendent of Schools published a comprehensive list of all teachers in the county. |
| Iverson | Belle | KC, p5c4, 2/8/1900 | Taught school in Upper Shanghi Ridge District. |
| Iverson | Belle | KC, p4c3, 4/7/1898 | Hired to teach in Kramer District. |
| Iverson | Charles, Mrs. | KC, p5c4, 11/13/1902 | Lived in Eastman. Returned from a visit with a sick daughter in Rhodes, IA. |
| Iverson | Hattie | KC, p5c4, 6/20/1901 | Graduated from the Eastman graded schools. |
| Iverson | Hattie | KC, Supp., 12/12/1901 | Attended a Teacher's Institute in Crawford County in 1901. Resided in Eastman. |
| Iverson | Henry | KC, Supp., 12/29/1898 | Crawford Co. Board of Supervisors approved Justices and Constables' expenses related to the case, State vs. Henry Iverson. |
| Iverson | Henry | KC, Supp., 12/20/1900 | Crawford Co. Board of Supervisors approved payment of expenses in the matter of State vs. Henry Iverson. |
| Iverson | Iver | KC, Supp., 12/20/1900 | Crawford Co. Board of Supervisors approved payment of expenses in the matter of State vs. Iver Iverson. |
| Iverson | Nannie | KC, p5c4, 6/20/1901 | Graduated from the Eastman graded schools. |
| Iverson | Nellie | KC, p5c3, 4/11/1901 | Taught school in the Hazen District. |
| Iverson | Nellie | KC, Supp., 12/12/1901 | Attended a Teacher's Institute in Crawford County in 1901. Resided in Eastman. |
| Iverson | Sophia | KC, Supp., 12/12/1901 | Attended a Teacher's Institute in Crawford County in 1901. Resided in Rising Sun. |
| Iverson | Allie and Mattie | KC, p5c3, 9/21/1899 | Departed for Casselton, ND after spending the summer with parents in Eastman. |
| Iverson | Iver | KC, Supp., 12/12/1901 | Crawford Co. Board of Supervisors approved payments in the Matter of Iver Iverson, Insane. |
| Jackson | boy | KC, p1c3, 6/6/1901 | Son recently born to Theodore Jackson of Mt. Sterling. |
| Jackson | boys | KC, p1c4, 10/24/1901 | Twin sons born Oct. 11, 1901 to Ed Jackson of Gays Mills. |
| Jackson | girl | KC, p5c4, 2/20/1902 | A daughter of Jacob Jackson of Mt. Sterling area died last Saturday from diphtheria. Six other family members have the disease. |

Genealogical Gleanings From Early Newspapers for Residents In and Near
Crawford County, Wisconsin, 1897-1902

| LAST NAME | FIRST NAME | NEWSPAPER PAGE/COLUMN MONTH/DAY/YEAR | GENEALOGICAL DATA |
|---|---|---|---|
| Jackson | girl | KC, p1c6, 7/8/1897 | Daughter born July 1, 1897 to Edward Jackson of Gays Mills. |
| Jackson | Lewis | KC, p5c4, 5/22/1902 | Resided in Mt. Sterling. Granted an $8.00 per month pension. |
| Jackson | Matilda Josephine | KC, p1c4, 8/30/1900 | Died Aug. 20, 1900 at Minneapolis. Daughter of Jacob and Maria Jackson of the Town of Utica. Aged 22 years. Buried in Utica Cemetery. |
| Jackson | Mrs. | KC, p6c1, 3/18/1897 | Died Mar. 9, 1897 at home of daughter, Mrs. Elmer Stevenson, in Gays Mills. (See citation for Mrs. Lucinda Fisher.) |
| Jackson | Theo., Mr. and Mrs. | KC, p4c1, 6/17/1897 | Visited Mrs. Jackson's parents, Mr. and Mrs. Tosten Olsen of Johnstown. |
| Jackson | Theodore | KC, p5c4, 8/15/1901 | Lived in Mt. Sterling. Very ill with typhoid fever. |
| Jackson Bros. | | KC, p5c4, 4/12/1900 | Ran a blacksmith shop in Mt. Sterling. |
| Jacob | Ed | KC, p1c3, 7/15/1897 | Married Ella Johnson on July 12, 1897 in Prairie du Chien. Bride and groom from McGregor, IA. The Rev. Ira La Baron officiated. |
| Jacobs | Jane, Mrs. | KC, p1c4, 12/18/1902 | Died Dec. 13, 1902 at home of her daughter, Mrs. C. E. Ambler of Wauzeka. Aged 59 years and 3 months. Remains taken to Wyalusing for burial. |
| Jamboi | Rosella | KC, p1c4, 7/21/1898 | Married P. J. McManamy of Liberty Pole on July 13, 1898. Bride from Genoa. |
| James | David G. | KC, p8c4, 3/6/1902 | Resided in Richland Center. Sued by Mrs. Sarah Slatten of Sauk Co. for kissing her 3 times. |
| James | Henry | KC, p8c1, 9/28/1899 | Resided in De Soto. Attended the National Encampment at Philadelphia, PA. Veteran of the Civil War. |
| James | N. L. | KC, p4c3, 5/30/1901 | Manager of the Western Wisconsin Railroad in Wauzeka. Called to Richland Center where his mother had died at age 85. |
| James | Norman L. | KC, p1c5, 2/15/1900 | Worked as General Manager of the Kickapoo Valley Railway. |
| Jarvis | D. T. | KC, p1c4, 2/11/1897 | Married Miss Johnson in Soldiers Grove on Feb. 4, 1897. |
| Jarvis | D. T. | KC, p1c4, 8/10/1899 | Wrote a letter from Guthrie, OK describing Oklahoma for newspaper readers. |
| Jarvis | D. T. | KC, p1c6, 5/19/1898 | Issue of Fact for Jury to be heard in the May term of the Crawford County Circuit Court. D. T. Jarvis vs. Northwestern Mutual Relief Association. |
| Jeffries | Albert | KC, p8c4, 4/4/1901 | Part of a group that left Steuben and Wauzeka for the West. Most of the group went to McHenry, North Dakota. |
| Jenkins | David | KC, p8c4, 11/16/1899 | Received marriage license in Crawford Co. to marry Olive Freeman. Bride and groom from Town of Clayton. |
| Jenkins | Edna | KC, p5c2, 7/21/1898 | Married Fred Curtis on July 9, 1898 at Mt. Sterling. (Bride and groom may be from Barnum.) |
| Jenkins | Francis | KC, p5c4, 6/28/1900 | Recently graduated from the Barnum village school. |

Genealogical Gleanings From Early Newspapers for Residents In and Near
Crawford County, Wisconsin, 1897-1902

| LAST NAME | FIRST NAME | NEWSPAPER PAGE/COLUMN MONTH/DAY/YEAR | GENEALOGICAL DATA |
|---|---|---|---|
| Jenkins | Harvey | KC, p5c4, 6/28/1900 | Recently graduated from the Barnum village school. |
| Jenkins | Jennie | KC, p1c4, 3/2/1899 | Married Frank Stearns of Barnum on Feb. 15, 1899 in Gays Mills. Bride from Barnum. |
| Jenkins | John, Mrs. | KC, p1c5, 3/10/1898 | Returned to Barnum after getting medical treatment at a hospital in Chicago. She was a sister of Frank Mercer. |
| Jenkins | Rye, Mrs. | KC, p5c3, 7/28/1898 | Planned to travel from home in Barnum to visit with son working in Dakota. |
| Jennay | Victor | KC, p8c3, 12/25/1902 | Died Dec. 23, 1902 of consumption in Prairie du Chien. He was a barber. Funeral held at St. Gabriel's Catholic Church. |
| Jetter | Johanne | KC, p5c4, 1/7/1897 | Crawford County Probate Court Notice. Jacob Christ applied to administer the estate of Johanne Jetter, late of Marietta. |
| Jewett | Georgie | KC, p1c4, 6/8/1899 | Married Jack Stocum, of Avalanche, on June 4, 1899. |
| Jewett | H. E. and wife | KC, p8c2, 6/17/1897 | Traveled from Avalanche to Gays Mills to visit daughter, Mrs. R. Currie. |
| Jewett | H. E., Mr. and Mrs. | KC, p4c2, 6/2/1898 | Jewetts and their daughter, Georgia, of Avalanche visited another daughter, Mrs. R. L. Currie of Gays Mills. |
| Jewett | Mr. | KC, p5c3, 2/9/1899 | Former Gays Mills resident. Visited daughter, Mrs. R. L. Currie. |
| Johnson | Albert | KC, p5c3, 12/21/1899 | Mr. Albert Johnson married Miss Larson last Saturday in Buck Creek, per the Mt. Sterling news column. |
| Johnson | Bennie | KC, p8c3, 4/15/1897 | Recently married Christina Michelson. (Bride may have been from Boma area.) |
| Johnson | Bertha | KC, p4c2, 10/13/1898 | Married Rudolph Nash of Decorah, IA on Oct. 5, 1898 at the Utica Church. (Bride from Gays Mills area?) |
| Johnson | boy | KC, p1c2, 7/5/1900 | Son born June 23, 1900 to Ed Johnson of Johnstown. |
| Johnson | Charles | KC, p5c3, 4/26/1900 | Married Anna Erickson on April 23, 1900. Groom was from Gays Mills. He was brother of Mrs. Sam Halverson. |
| Johnson | Charles | KC, p1c2, 3/8/1900 | Barber in Gays Mills. Visited his sick sister at the City Hotel in Wauzeka. |
| Johnson | Charles | KC, p5c3, 7/13/1899 | His new dwelling and barbershop in Gays Mills nearly ready for occupancy. |
| Johnson | Christ B. | KC, p8c4, 11/13/1902 | In the November term of Crawford County Circuit Court, Christ B. Johnson vs. La Crosse Steel Roofing Co., case was continued. |
| Johnson | Ed, Mrs. | KC, p1c2, 7/5/1900 | Two sisters from Norway came to visit Mrs. Ed Johnson of Johnstown. |
| Johnson | Edward | KC, p1c5, 1/13/1898 | Married Carrie Enerson on Dec. 30, 1897. Groom was son of T. Johnson of Towerville. |
| Johnson | Elias | KC, p4c4, 5/2/1901 | Left Soldiers Grove for a trip to Norway, their native land. Andrew Lee, Peter Upholm, Elias Johnson and Christ Scoggen. |
| Johnson | Ella | KC, p1c3, 7/15/1897 | Married Ed Jacob on July 12, 1897 in Prairie du Chien. Bride and groom from McGregor, IA. The Rev. Ira La Baron officiated. |

Genealogical Gleanings From Early Newspapers for Residents In and Near
Crawford County, Wisconsin, 1897-1902

| LAST NAME | FIRST NAME | NEWSPAPER PAGE/COLUMN MONTH/DAY/YEAR | GENEALOGICAL DATA |
|---|---|---|---|
| Johnson | Emma | KC, p1c5, 2/9/1899 | Taught school in the Town of Clayton in 1899. E. E. Brindley, Crawford County Superintendent of Schools published a comprehensive list of all teachers in the county. |
| Johnson | Erick | KC, p1c2, 11/15/1900 | Departed home in the Town of Utica several years ago. Now a partner in Dunning and Johnson of Charles City and Greene, Iowa. Handles Aberdeen Angus cattle. |
| Johnson | Erik | KC, p1c3, 10/17/1901 | Former resident of Mt. Sterling area. Now living in Greene, IA. |
| Johnson | George | KC, p1c3, 6/6/1901 | Left Petersburg to visit his parents, Mr. and Mrs. George Johnson, Sr., and sister, Mrs. E. W. Newton of Wauzeka. |
| Johnson | George | KC, p1c2, 6/13/1901 | Sold his interest in a Petersburg saloon. Planned to move to Wauzeka to live with his parents. Father very ill. |
| Johnson | girl | KC, p4c4, 11/15/1900 | Daughter born last week to Charles Johnson of Gays Mills. |
| Johnson | girl | KC, p4c2, 9/15/1898 | Daughter born Aug. 26, 1898 to E. Johnson of Johnstown. |
| Johnson | girl | KC, p1c3, 12/29/1898 | Daughter born Dec. 28, 1898 to Sherman Johnson of Wauzeka. |
| Johnson | Harlan J. | KC, p1c3, 4/12/1900 | Harlan J. Johnson, lately connected with the *Dial-Enterprise*, of Boscobel, purchased the *Grant County Herald* for $5000. |
| Johnson | I., Mrs. | KC, p1c3, 9/30/1897 | Traveled to Durand, WI to visit a daughter. (This is probably Mrs. Isaac Johnson of Wauzeka, not Mrs. Israel Johnson of Town of Clayton.) |
| Johnson | Isaac | KC, p1c4, 10/21/1897 | Resided in Wauzeka. Bought 2 bottles of sarsaparilla from strangers for 60 cents. When given a $10 bill, strangers said they would leave change at W. A. Vaughan's store. They left town, but were later found in Boscobel and sentenced to 60 days in jail. |
| Johnson | Isaac, Mr. and Mrs. | KC, p1c2, 3/2/1899 | Mr. And Mrs. Isaac Johnson and their daughter-in-law, Mrs. Sherman Johnson, were ill with pneumonia. All lived in the same household in Wauzeka. |
| Johnson | John, Jr. | KC, p4c2, 12/9/1897 | Died Nov. 30, 1897 in Readstown. Norwegian descent. |
| Johnson | John N. | KC, p1c5, 6/16/1898 | Left Ferryville for a visit to Norway. |
| Johnson | Julia | KC, p8c6, 4/19/1900 | Married Frank Haupt on April 18, 1900. Bride was from Prairie du Chien. Groom was from Key Springs, IL. |
| Johnson | K. O. | KC, Supp., 12/12/1901 | Attended a Teacher's Institute in Crawford County in 1901. Resided in Mount Sterling |
| Johnson | Laura | KC, p4c1, 6/17/1897 | Married Grant Craigo of Readstown on June 10, 1897. Bride was daughter of William Johnson (of Readstown?). |
| Johnson | Maggie | KC, p5c1, 12/30/1897 | Married Sam Halverson on Dec. 22, 1897 at Utica Lutheran Church. |
| Johnson | Mary | KC, p5c3, 7/19/1900 | Hired to teach school in Granard District. From Lynxville. |
| Johnson | Mary | KC, p4c2, 4/28/1898 | Moved from Gays Mills to Viroqua to work in a hotel. |

Genealogical Gleanings From Early Newspapers for Residents In and Near
Crawford County, Wisconsin, 1897-1902

| LAST NAME | FIRST NAME | NEWSPAPER PAGE/COLUMN MONTH/DAY/YEAR | GENEALOGICAL DATA |
|---|---|---|---|
| Johnson | Miss | KC, p1c4, 2/11/1897 | Married D. R. Jarvis in Soldiers Grove on Feb. 4, 1897. |
| Johnson | Robert | KC, p8c3, 2/8/1900 | Died Feb. 6, 1900 in Prairie du Chien. |
| Johnson | Sherman | KC, p1c3, 6/13/1901 | Found a valuable pearl while claming at Prairie du Chien. Its estimated worth is several hundred dollars. |
| Johnson | Sherman | KC, Supp., 12/20/1900 | Crawford Co. Board of Supervisors approved payment of expenses in the matter of State vs. Sherman Johnson. The witnesses were George Reynolds, Andy Reynolds, Jackson Brownly, Wesley Arms, Justin Arms, Mary Arms, Clinton Arms, George Dyer and Charles Haskins. |
| Johnson | William | KC, p1c4, 7/21/1898 | Recently died at home near Viroqua. |
| Jones | A. F. | KC, Supp., 12/20/1900 | Represented Bridgeport on the Crawford Co. Board of Supervisors in 1900. |
| Jones | boy | KC, p1c2, 7/17/1902 | Son born July 16, 1902 to Ben Jones of Boydtown. |
| Jones | boy | KC, p4c3, 1/13/1898 | Son born Jan. 4, 1898 to Albert Jones of Bridgeport. |
| Jones | Edna | KC, p5c4, 5/29/1902 | Edna Jones attended a teacher institute in Crawford County. |
| Jones | Ella | KC, p5c2, 7/21/1898 | Married Thomas Dyer of Sand Prairie on July 10, 1898 at the Christian Church. Bride from Scott. |
| Jones | Ella | KC, p5c2, 7/28/1898 | Married Henry Dyer last Sunday, per Hurlbut news. |
| Jones | girl | KC, p8c4, 4/15/1897 | Daughter born April 3, 1897 to Jim Jones of Boydtown. |
| Jones | girl | KC, p8c3, 4/29/1897 | Daughter born April 21, 1897 to Rob Jones of Boydtown. |
| Jones | J. D., Dr. | KC, p8c5, 12/23/1897 | Died Dec. 22, 1897. Born Sept. 16, 1818 in Middleton, CT. Married Josephine S. Brisbois, daughter of Col. B. W. Brisbois, on June 15, 1854 (in Prairie du Chien?). Father of Mrs. Josephine M. Gillis (wife of J. A. Gillis) of Prairie du Chien; Dr. Bernard W. Jones of Vulcan, MI; Dr. Joe D. Jones of Iron Mountain, MI; J. Russell Jones of Calumet, MI. An extensive genealogy was printed that dated back to 1623. |
| Jones | James | KC, p5c4, 5/18/1899 | James Jones married Miss Husher last week. Groom son of Tom Jones. Groom and bride were not of legal age. |
| Jones | John | KC, Supp., 12/18/1902 | Crawford County Board of Supervisors examined bills in the Justices and Constables' Account for State vs. John Jones |
| Jones | Rosa | KC, p1c2, 2/16/1899 | Married Walter Lawrence on Feb. 12, 1899. Bride and groom from Boydtown. Joseph Peacock, J.P., officiated. |
| Jones | Ross | KC, p1c5, 4/11/1901 | Resided in Boydtown. Bought out the stock from J. M. Daugherty, his only merchant competitor in town. |
| Jones | Ross | KC, p1c3, 3/6/1902 | Left Boydtown for South Dakota. Considering a move to the area. |

Genealogical Gleanings From Early Newspapers for Residents In and Near
Crawford County, Wisconsin, 1897-1902

| LAST NAME | FIRST NAME | NEWSPAPER PAGE/COLUMN MONTH/DAY/YEAR | GENEALOGICAL DATA |
|---|---|---|---|
| Jones | William | KC, p5c4, 11/23/1899 | Died Nov. 19, 1899 from suicide in Eastman. Bachelor. Aged 85 years. Buried in Campbell Cemetery. |
| Joy | Abbie | KC, Supp., 12/12/1901 | Attended a Teacher's Institute in Crawford County in 1901. Resided in Seneca. |
| Joy | Abby | KC, p1c5, 2/9/1899 | Taught school in Eastman in 1899. E. E. Brindley, Crawford County Superintendent of Schools published a comprehensive list of all teachers in the county. |
| Joy | Bridget | KC, Supp., 11/8/1900 | Married John H. Finley on Oct. 30, 1900 at St. Patrick's Church. Bride was daughter of Thomas Joy (of Town of Seneca?). |
| Joy | girl | KC, p5c3, 1/16/1902 | Daughter born Jan. 10, 1902 to Rob Joy of Seneca. |
| Joy | girl | KC, p8c3, 6/17/1897 | Daughter born June 10, 1897 to R. Joy of Seneca. |
| Joy | Hannah | KC, Supp., 12/12/1901 | Attended a Teacher's Institute in Crawford County in 1901. Resided in Seneca. |
| Joy | John J. | KC, p1c4, 1/12/1899 | Died Jan. 8, 1899 near Ferryville. |
| Joy | Loretta | KC, p5c3, 3/13/1902 | Died Mar. 9, 1902. Born Jan. 10, 1902 to R. R. Joy of the Town of Seneca. |
| Joy | Mamie | KC, p5c2, 1/6/1898 | Died Dec. 24, 1897 near Mt. Sterling. Aged 28 years. Buried in Catholic Cemetery in Seneca. |
| Joy | Mamie | KC, p5c3, 5/30/1901 | Graduated from school in Lynxville. Read her essay on American poets. |
| Joy | Mrs. | KC, p5c4, 11/14/1901 | Died Nov. 10, 1901 in Town of (Seneca?). Survived by 7 children: Maurice, David Robert, Thomas James Richard and Bridget (Mrs. James Finley). Three other children, John, Mary and Catherine, predeceased her. Also survived by husband. Funeral was held at St. Patrick's Catholic Church. |
| Joy | R. J. | KC, p1c6, 4/7/1898 | Elected Supervisor for the Town of Seneca. |
| Joy | R. J. | KC, p5c5, 4/5/1900 | Elected supervisor in Seneca. |
| Joy | Robert R. | KC, p5c3, 4/17/1902 | Auctioned off all stock, machinery and household goods at his farm in Seneca. C. H. Speck of Eastman cried the sale. |
| Joy | Ruth | KC, p5c4, 11/14/1901 | Died Nov. 10, 1901 in Town of Seneca. Aged 9 years. Daughter of Maurice J. Joy. |
| Joy | Ruth | KC, p4c2, 11/21/1901 | Died Nov. 10, 1901. Aged 9 years and 26 days. Youngest child of Maurice Joy. Funeral held at St. Patrick's Church in Seneca. Survived by parents, 4 sisters and 2 brothers. |
| Joy | Thomas H. | KC, p1c6, 11/4/1897 | Issue of law for court to be heard at the November term of the Circuit Court in Crawford County. A. N. Searle vs. Thomas H. Joy et al. |
| Junker | L., Mrs. | KC, p8c3, 8/18/1898 | Died Aug. 10, 1898 in Prairie du Chien. Aged nearly 74 years. Buried in Burnett Junction. Wife of retired minister. |
| Jurgensen | girls | KC, p1c2, 6/28/1900 | Twin daughters born on June 27, 1900 to N. Jurgensen of Gays Mills. |

Genealogical Gleanings From Early Newspapers for Residents In and Near
Crawford County, Wisconsin, 1897-1902

| LAST NAME | FIRST NAME | NEWSPAPER PAGE/COLUMN MONTH/DAY/YEAR | GENEALOGICAL DATA |
|---|---|---|---|
| Jurgensen | Mable | KC, p4c3, 4/18/1901 | Died April 14, 1901 of pneumonia. Aged 9 months and 17 days. She was one of the twin daughters of N. Jurgensen of Gays Mills. |
| Jurgenson | Chris | KC, p1c3, 9/8/1898 | Resided in Trevor, WI. Visited friends and relatives in Wauzeka. |
| Jurgenson | Christ | KC, p1c4, 3/13/1902 | Resided in Wauzeka. Planned to go west to help construct railroad. |
| Jurgenson | Christ | KC, p1c3, 11/13/1902 | Moved to New Castle, PA from Wauzeka. Placed in charge of reconstructing the yards of the Baltimore and Ohio Railroad. Will be gone a few months. |
| Jurgenson | N. | KC, p4c1, 1/18/1900 | Advertised general store he operated in Gays Mills. |
| Kadoch | Charles | KC, p8c3, 11/10/1898 | Married Hannah Novak on Nov. 4, 1898 at St. John's Bohemian Church. (Bride and groom may have been from Prairie du Chien area.) |
| Kage | Christiana, Mrs. | KC, p1c2, 1/14/1897 | Died Dec. 31, 1896. Aged 75 years, 11 months and 22 days. Born in Frognitz, Prussia. Survived by husband, 2 sons and 2 sisters. Interred in German Ridge Cemetery. |
| Kage | John | KC, p5c4, 5/29/1902 | Recently divorced. Spouse was Catherine Kage. |
| Kage | John | KC, p5c4, 5/29/1902 | The case John Kage vs. Catherine Kage for divorce was heard at the May term of the Crawford County Circuit Court. Judgement for decree of divorce signed. |
| Kahler | Caroline | KC, p8c1, 10/7/1897 | Married Henry Hilldritsch of Prairie du Chien on Oct. 6, 1897. Bride, daughter of Chas. Kahler, was from Bridgeport. |
| Kahler | Miss | KC, p8c3, 1/23/1902 | Married Martin Blasek on Jan. 22, 1902. Bride and groom from Prairie du Chien area. |
| Kahler | Mr. | KC, p5c3, 4/27/1899 | Planned to move from Gays Mills to Minnesota. |
| Kahoun | Joseph | KC, p4c4, 6/12/1902 | Age 12. Gave the welcoming speech for the Veterans Day ceremony at Campbell Cemetery. Speech published in the newspaper. |
| Kaiser | Anna | KC, p8c1, 4/21/1898 | Married Louis Varo of Eastman on April 12, 1898. Bride was daughter of Louis Kaiser of Prairie du Chien. |
| Kaiser | Laura | KC, p8c1, 4/13/1899 | Recently married Ted Wilkins of Bridgeport. Bride from Prairie du Chien. |
| Kalina | Mary | KC, p8c3, 1/30/1902 | Married John Sturnot on Jan. 28, 1902 at St. John's Bohemian Catholic Church. Included in Prairie du Chien news items. |
| Kane | boy | KC, p5c3, 1/10/1901 | Son born Dec. 30, 1900 to J. Kane of Gays Mills. |
| Kane | boy | KC, p5c3, 3/9/1899 | Son recently born to Cornelius Kane in Seneca. |
| Kane | C. C., Mrs. | KC, p1c2, 10/5/1899 | Resided in Madison. Visited relatives and friends in Eastman and Seneca. While there, she sold her husband's 160-acre farm in Seneca to Fred Wall for $2500. |
| Kane | C., Mrs. | KC, p4c2, 7/22/1897 | Lived in Prairie du Chien. Visited parents, Mr. and Mrs. M. Lennehan of Eastman. |

Genealogical Gleanings From Early Newspapers for Residents In and Near
Crawford County, Wisconsin, 1897-1902

| LAST NAME | FIRST NAME | NEWSPAPER PAGE/COLUMN MONTH/DAY/YEAR | GENEALOGICAL DATA |
|---|---|---|---|
| Kane | Con | KC, p4c4, 11/16/1899 | Resided in Seneca. Granted a pension increase to $12 per month. |
| Kane | Cornelius | KC, p1c3, 9/26/1901 | Died Sept. 24, 1901 in Town of Seneca. Born Sept. 4, 1832 in County Cork, Ireland. Emigrated in 1852. Moved to Seneca in 1855. Married Margaret Connelly in 1859. Survived by 4 of 5 children: C. C. Kane of Madison, James, Dennis and Mrs. P. Maney of Seneca. After first wife's death, he married Mary Garvey who soon died. Married Eliza Nugent on Sept. 10, 1877. She and 8 children by this marriage survive him: Mrs. Frank Clancey of Soldiers Grove, William, Thomas, Mida, Elizabeth, Daniel, Laura and Bernard. John died in infancy. Served in Co. H., 50th WI Vol. in Civil War. Operated the Kane Hotel in Seneca. |
| Kane | D. | KC, p4c2, 4/8/1897 | Butcher in Ferryville. |
| Kane | Dan | KC, Supp, 12/29/1898 | Crawford Co. Board of Supervisors approved Justices and Constables' expenses related to the case, State vs. Dan Kane. The witnesses were Henry Hanson, Martin Christenson, (Manie?) Nash, Henry Turgenson, John Thythamer and Martin Munson. |
| Kane | Daniel | KC, p5c4, 2/21/1901 | Died Feb. 13, 1901 in Boulder, CO. Former resident of Town of Seneca. Brother of Dennis Kane. Buried in Catholic Cemetery in Seneca. Born Feb. 15, 1868. |
| Kane | Dennis | KC, p4c4, 11/10/1898 | Criminal Issue to be heard in the November term of the Crawford County Circuit Court. State of Wisconsin vs. Michael Dolan and Dennis Kane. |
| Kane | Dennis | KC, p1c5, 6/1/1899 | The May term of the Crawford County Circuit Court closed. In the case, State of Wisconsin vs. Dennis Kane guilty. |
| Kane | Dennis | KC, p1c4, 3/1/1900 | Chaired a meeting of farmers at Lee's Hall in Gays Mills to establish a mutual fire insurance company for the farmers of Crawford County. J. A. Hayes was secretary. Farmers were unhappy with delayed service and high prices of the Utica Mutual Farmers Company. The following signed articles of agreement to establish the company: J. A. Hays, Dennis Kane, J. W. McCormick, E. E. Thomson, A. N. Scoville, M. Barham (Barnum? Bonham?), Timothy Finley, Samuel Iverson, G. L. Miller, S. Kivgne, O. S. Clement, M. W. Twining, E. A. Marston, J. C. Gunderson, Erdmin Strecker, Ole P. Olson, J. N. Campbell, H. W. Stukey, Bannen Brothers., B. J. Donaldson and A. J. Kvigne. |
| Kane | Dennis, Jr. | KC, Supp, 12/29/1898 | Crawford Co. Board of Supervisors approved Justices and Constables' expenses related to the case, State vs. Dennis Kane Jr. |
| Kane | Dennis, Jr. | KC, p1c5, 6/5/1902 | Died at home of father, Dennis Kane on Copper Creek, near Mt. Sterling on June 2, 1902. Aged 32 years. Buried in Seneca Catholic Cemetery. |

Genealogical Gleanings From Early Newspapers for Residents In and Near
Crawford County, Wisconsin, 1897-1902

| LAST NAME | FIRST NAME | NEWSPAPER PAGE/COLUMN MONTH/DAY/YEAR | GENEALOGICAL DATA |
|---|---|---|---|
| Kane | Eliza, Mrs. | KC, p1c4, 12/11/1902 | Ran the Kane Hotel in Seneca. |
| Kane | James | KC, p1c3, 9/7/1899 | Married Ica (Ida?) Thompson on Sept. 5, 1899. Bride was a teacher. Groom from Gays Mills. |
| Kane | James | KC, p1c3, 6/6/1901 | Arrived from California to visit relatives in Seneca. |
| Kane | James | KC, p4c2, 3/2/1899 | Purchased G. D. Girdler's interest in the livery business in Gays Mills. |
| Kane | Mamie | KC, p4c3, 7/1/1897 | Married Frank Clancy on June 23, 1897 at St. Patrick's Church in Seneca. Planned to live in Soldiers Grove. |
| Kane | Mamie | KC, p5c3, 11/21/1901 | Mamie Kane and her sister, Hannah Joy, were diagnosed with diphtheria. They were the daughters of D. Kane. |
| Kane | Mary | KC, p5c3, 4/10/1902 | Died April 9, 1902. Aged 20 years. She was the second daughter of Dennis Kane, Sr. of Town of Seneca. |
| Kane | Michael | KC, p8c1, 11/4/1897 | Died Oct. 27, 1897. Aged 18 months. Son of Mr. and Mrs. Con Kane of Prairie du Chien. |
| Kane | Pat | KC, Supp., 12/12/1901 | State vs. Pat Kane heard in Crawford Co. Court. Case No. 36. |
| Kane | Pat | KC, Supp., 12/12/1901 | State vs. Pat Kane heard in Crawford Co. Court. Case No. 48. Witnesses were Chancey Steele, Mat Shields, Minnie Adams, Martin Adams, Mike Shields, Mrs. Mike Shields, Julia Schofield, Aleta Wayne, L. H. Loomis, Mathew Loomis, J. M. Trumbull, George E. Lance, Joseph Tierney, Mrs. Joseph Tierney, James Shockley, Mary Noon, Rose Carlin, M. A. Robinson, Mrs. M. A. Robinson, Mrs. Joseph Kane, Mrs. L. U. McGraw and Bridget Ferrick. |
| Kane | Pat | KC, Supp., 12/18/1902 | Crawford County Board of Supervisors allowed expenses in the Criminal Case, State vs. Pat Kane. |
| Kane | Pat, Mrs. | KC, Supp., 12/12/1901 | Inquest, body of wife of Pat Kane heard in Crawford Co. Court. Witnesses were Martin Adams, Minnie Adams, Mary Tierney, Mrs. Marshal Robinson and Dr. Hayman. |
| Kane | Patrick | KC, p1c5, 11/21/1901 | Acquitted for the Oct. 24, 1901 death of his wife. Insufficient evidence. Mrs. Kane's body was exhumed and examined. |
| Kane | Patrick, Mrs. | KC, p1c5, 10/10/1901 | Died Oct. 4, 1901 in Town of Scott. Shot by husband. Believed shooting to be an accident; however, husband was held in jail to wait for a hearing. Married in Boscobel in May 1900. Survived by an eight-month-old child. |
| Karnopp | Charles | KC, p8c4, 7/26/1900 | Died July 23, 1900 in Prairie du Chien. |
| Karnopp | Mrs. | KC, p1c4, 4/22/1897 | Funeral held last Thursday. Resided in Prairie du Chien. Buried in Lowertown Cemetery. |
| Karon | Martin | KC, p1c3, 1/27/1898 | Died Tuesday near Eastman. Aged about 40 years. Survived by wife and 7 children. Mrs. Dell Brown was a sister-in-law. |
| Karr | Maud, Mrs. | KC, p5c3, 7/12/1900 | Married Nathan Garrett at the City Hotel in Prairie du Chien on July 4, 1900. The groom was the former creamery operator in Eastman. He now has same position in Steuben. The bride was from Pennsylvania. |

Genealogical Gleanings From Early Newspapers for Residents In and Near
Crawford County, Wisconsin, 1897-1902

| LAST NAME | FIRST NAME | NEWSPAPER PAGE/COLUMN MONTH/DAY/YEAR | GENEALOGICAL DATA |
|---|---|---|---|
| Kasperek | Alvina | KC, p1c3, 10/30/1902 | Married Dr. F. A. Barney on Oct. 28, 1902. Groom from Soldiers Grove. |
| Kast | Ada | KC, p1c5, 2/9/1899 | Taught school in Haney in 1899. E. E. Brindley, Crawford County Superintendent of Schools published a comprehensive list of all teachers in the county. |
| Kast | Ada | KC, p5c2, 1/3/1901 | Married George E. Lance on Dec. 25, 1900. Bride was daughter of Ira Kast of Petersburg. Groom from Platteville. |
| Kast | Ada | KC, p5c2, 1/3/1901 | Married George E. Lance on Dec. 25, 1900 at home of bride's father in Petersburg. Bride, daughter of Ira Kast, taught school in Bell Center. Planned to continue the position until the school term ended in June. Groom from Platteville. Extensive guest list and gift list published. |
| Kast | Bird, Mrs. | KC, p8c3, 1/5/1899 | Left Petersburg with her children to visit relatives in Canada. |
| Kast | C. C. | KC, Supp., 12/19/1901 | The Village of Steuben started in the 1882 when a post office was established there. C. C. Kast was the first postmaster. |
| Kast | Clint S., Mrs. | KC, p5c4, 1/21/1897 | Died Tuesday in Belle Center at age of 31 years. Daughter of Simon Smith of Town of Haney. Survived by sisters, Mrs. D. Kimmel of Petersburg and Mrs. Wood of Boscobel. |
| Kast | Emmett | KC, p5c4, 2/6/1902 | Resided in Haney. Held a wood bee and later gave the boys an oyster supper. |
| Kast | George W. | KC, p1c5, 6/1/1899 | The May term of the Crawford County Circuit Court closed. In the case James H. Thompson vs. George W. Kast, judgement for plaintiffs. |
| Kast | George W. | KC, p5c4, 5/29/1902 | The case Wisconsin vs. George W. Kast, for larceny, was heard at the May term of the Crawford County Circuit Court. Continued. |
| Kast | George W. | KC, p8c4, 11/20/1902 | In the November term of Crawford County Circuit Court, State vs. George W. Kast, found guilty of stealing timber and discharged by judge on his own recognizance until May term. |
| Kast | girl | KC, p5c3, 6/19/1902 | Daughter born June 14, 1902 to J. N. Kast of Bell Center. |
| Kast | girl | KC, p1c5, 12/22/1898 | Daughter recently born to Lev Kast of Bell Center. |
| Kast | H. C. | KC, p1c4, 5/31/1900 | Proprietor of a general store in Barnum. |
| Kast | H. J. | KC, p5c3, 5/20/1897 | Issues of fact for jury to be heard in the May term of the Crawford County Court. Cream City Sash & Door Co. vs. P. A. Lathrop impleaded with H. J. Kast as co-partner, under name of P. A. Lathrop & Co. appellant. |
| Kast | Henry C. and Sarah E. | KC, p5c3, 5/20/1897 | Issues of fact for jury to be heard in the May term of the Crawford County Court. Dwella Haskins vs. Henry C. Kast and Sarah E. Kast. |
| Kast | J. N. | KC, p1c5, 6/1/1899 | The May term of the Crawford County Circuit Court closed. In the case, Cornelius Cane vs. Ed Wallin and J. N. Kast, judgement against Wallin for $1. |

Genealogical Gleanings From Early Newspapers for Residents In and Near
Crawford County, Wisconsin, 1897-1902

| LAST NAME | FIRST NAME | NEWSPAPER PAGE/COLUMN MONTH/DAY/YEAR | GENEALOGICAL DATA |
|---|---|---|---|
| Kast | Lev | KC, p4c2, 8/25/1898 | Moved back to Bell Center from northern, WI. His stock did not do well. |
| Kast | Lev | KC, p4c3, 4/21/1898 | Resided in Black River Falls, WI. Visited friends in Bell Center. |
| Kast | Lucy | KC, Supp., 12/12/1901 | Attended a Teacher's Institute in Crawford County in 1901. Resided in Bell Center. |
| Kast | T. | KC, p5c3, 6/15/1899 | J. T. Farris, A. Dowse, T. Kast and Seth Reynolds went to Iowa to do railway work. Resided in Steuben area. |
| Kavanda | Joseph | KC, p8c4, 11/16/1899 | Recently married Mary Stevens at the Bohemian Catholic Church in Prairie du Chien. |
| Kazda | Earl | KC, p1c4, 6/12/1902 | Died June 6, 1902 in Wauzeka. Born May 27, 1893. He was the son of John P. and Amelia M. Kazda, per KC, p1c3, July 24, 1902. |
| Kazda | J. P. | KC, p1c2, 11/30/1899 | Lived in Wauzeka. His mother, of Lowertown (Prairie du Chien), found a pearl in a clam. It was valued at $35. |
| Kazda | J. P. | KC, p1c6, 4/7/1898 | Elected Councilman for the Village of Wauzeka. |
| Kazda | J. P. | KC, p1c2, 12/21/1899 | J. P. Kazda sold his saloon in Wauzeka to John C. Lewig of Hawkeye, IA. |
| Kazda | Johnnie | KC, p1c3, 4/24/1902 | Left home in Wauzeka for a day clerk position at the Dousman House in Prairie du Chien. |
| Keago | John | KC, p8c1, 6/23/1898 | Married Catherine Reinhold on June 16, 1898. Bride and groom from Prairie du Chien. |
| Keeley | Regis | KC, Supp., 12/12/1901 | Attended a Teacher's Institute in Crawford County in 1901. Resided in Seneca. |
| Keenan | James, Mrs. | KC, p5c5, 2/7/1901 | Died Jan. 21, 1901 in Sioux City, IA. She was oldest daughter of Sam Hazen, Sr. of Town of Eastman. Survived by husband, 9 children, father, 3 sisters and 5 brothers. |
| Keifer | H., Mrs. | KC, Supp., 12/18/1902 | Crawford County Board of Supervisors examined bills in the Justices and Constables' Account for State vs. Mrs. H. Keifer. Jennie Chapman was a witness. |
| Keilley | Minnie | KC, p6c3, 11/15/1900 | Married Franklin Scott on Nov. 10, 1900. Included in Steuben news column. |
| Keizer | A., Mrs. | KC, p8c3, 7/13/1899 | Died July 8, 1899 in Prairie du Chien. |
| Kelley | Glady | KC, p5c4, 6/24/1897 | Infant daughter of Merit and Mary Kelley died June 20, 1897. Born May 30, 1897. Funeral held at Bell Center Church on June 21, 1897. Rev. Harris officiated. |
| Kelley | James | KC, Supp, 12/20/1900 | Crawford Co. Board of Supervisors approved payment of expenses in the matter of State vs. James Kelley. |
| Kelley | John | KC, p1c3, 2/6/1902 | Machine salesman from Minnesota. Attended funeral of mother in Gays Mills area. Brother of Patrick and James Kelley of Gays Mills. |
| Kelley | John | KC, p4c3, 6/15/1899 | Bound for trial for a burglary. Claimed he was in custody in Kansas City, MO at the time Mr. Vaughan's store was burglarized, but produced no evidence. |
| Kelley | Kettie (Kittie?) | KC, p7c4, 1/25/1900 | Received marriage license in Crawford Co. George E. Purrington was the prospective spouse. Bride and groom-to-be from Town of Clayton. |

Genealogical Gleanings From Early Newspapers for Residents In and Near
Crawford County, Wisconsin, 1897-1902

| LAST NAME | FIRST NAME | NEWSPAPER PAGE/COLUMN MONTH/DAY/YEAR | GENEALOGICAL DATA |
|---|---|---|---|
| Kelley | Mary J. | KC, p1c6, 2/16/1899 | Notice of Sale published in the case of Wisconsin vs. Guardianship of Mary J. Kelley, minor. The guardian, Patrick Kelley, wanted to sell property left to Mary J. Kelley. |
| Kelley | Thomas, Mrs. | KC, p5c3, 2/6/1902 | Died Tuesday at home 2 miles south of Gays Mills. She was an aged lady. |
| Kellogg | Hiram | KC, p4c1, 4/14/1898 | Resided in Readstown. Broke collar bone after falling from a horse while racing. |
| Kellogg | Milton | KC, p8c2, 3/2/1899 | Married Emma Leitner of Mason City, IA last Wednesday (Feb. 22, 1899?). Groom from Mason City, IA. Bride sister to Mrs. Fred Granzow and Otto Leitner. |
| Kelly | Ed | KC, p4c2, 10/13/1898 | Resided in Chicago where he worked for City Railway Co. Visited parents in East Gays Mills. Brother of James Kelly. |
| Kelly | Gladna | KC, p4c2, 9/30/1897 | Died Sept. 26, 1897. Born May 30, 1897 to Merit and Mary Kelly. |
| Kelly | H., Mr. and Mrs. | KC, p4c1, 9/22/1898 | From East Gays Mills. Hosted a farewell party for Miss Ellis of Scotland. |
| Kelly | Jim | KC, p5c4, 3/1/1900 | Recently married (Kate Tower?). Groom from East Clayton. |
| Kelly | M. H. | KC, p1c5, 5/8/1902 | M. H. Kelly and M. L. Coleman of Bell Center returned from a trip to Madera, CA. Planned to move families there. |
| Kelly | Patrick | KC, p1c6, 2/3/1898 | Died Jan. 25, 1898 near Mt. Sterling. Aged 74 years. Civil War veteran. Buried in St. Patrick Catholic Church Cemetery. |
| Kelts | Mrs. | KC, p4c4, 1/7/1897 | Ran a millinery shop in Prairie du Chien. |
| Kennedy | William J., Mr. and Mrs. | KC, p8c1, 8/31/1899 | Returned to their home in Denver, CO after a visit with Mrs. M. Garrity of Prairie du Chien. |
| Kenneson Bros. | | KC, p5c4, 4/12/1900 | Sold their farm in Mt. Sterling. Moved to Wood Co., WI. |
| Kenyon | Mrs. | KC, p1c3, 8/14/1902 | Lived in McGregor. An aged lady. Visited friends in Wauzeka. |
| Kenyon | O. A. | KC, p5c1, 6/17/1897 | Resident of McGregor, IA for 40 years. Visited his nephew. W. A. Vaughan of Wauzeka. |
| Keop | George | KC, p5c3, 8/31/1899 | Resided in Eastman. While riding a bicycle, he and a team collided. Both were driving on the same side of the road. Bicycle was demolished. |
| Kepler | W. F. | KC, p1c5, 6/1/1899 | The May term of the Crawford County Circuit Court closed. In the case, W. F. Kepler vs. Ed and John Dull, judgement for plaintiff. |
| Kern | Maggie | KC, p8c3, 7/11/1901 | Married George Wells on July 8, 1901. |
| Kerrigan | Bryan | KC, Supp, 12/20/1900 | Crawford Co. Board of Supervisors approved payment of expenses in the matter of State vs. Bryan Kerrigan. |
| Kerrigan | John | KC, Supp., 12/12/1901 | Crawford Co. Board of Supervisors approved payments in the Matter of John Kerrigan, Dependent Child. Witnesses were John Stagman, Joseph Beckwar, Mrs. M. Donahue, Maggie Donahue, William H. Evans and M. Lenehan. |

Genealogical Gleanings From Early Newspapers for Residents In and Near
Crawford County, Wisconsin, 1897-1902

| LAST NAME | FIRST NAME | NEWSPAPER PAGE/COLUMN MONTH/DAY/YEAR | GENEALOGICAL DATA |
|---|---|---|---|
| Kerrigan | Patrick, Mrs. | KC, p1c3, 9/22/1898 | Died Sept. 13, 1898 in Scott. Aged 60 years. Funeral held at St. Phillips Catholic Church. |
| Kessler | August and George | KC, p1c2, 6/9/1898 | August and George Kessler; Joseph Peacock, Sr.; George Rider; Isaac Johnson; O. P. Vaughan; W. A. Vaughan; Fred Brandes and M. C. Kincannon, a group of old Wauzeka area soldiers, attended a veterans reunion in Madison. |
| Kessler | Freddie | KC, p4c4, 4/5/1900 | "The following is a list of immigrants who left for McHenry, ND on Tuesday evening, April 3rd: Freddie Kessler, Almond Cooley, Ben Jones, Johnnie Harris, Robert Harris, Lee Dunbar, James Mason, Georgie Harris, Lou Folbrecht of Wauzeka; Hiram, Issac, and Milton Peterson, Daniel Phillips, John Nutter, Otto Chapman, Peter Pivot, Charles Scoville, William Myers, Miss Florence Myers, Miss Carrie Myers, Dennis Smith, Mr. and Mrs. Arthur Young, Burt Seely, Mrs. T Jones, Mr. B. Mrs. Clarence and Flora Bunnell, William Mercer, P.M. and M. J. Foley, Mrs. Mary and Miss Carrie Husher, Frank Myer, Silas Chadwick, Robert Standorf, C. J. Copan, William McDonald of Steuben; Walker and Edward McCord of Boscobel; John Porter of Seneca. We were displeased to see so many of our Crawford county people leaving for other climes, but we know full well that many will gladly return next fall, while others may find a more suitable location. All will be benefited by the experience." (This list incorrectly implies that many of the above were from Steuben.) |
| Kessler | Leo | KC, p8c3, 11/21/1901 | Married Anna Herold on Nov. 20, 1901. Bride daughter of George Herald of Prairie du Chien. Groom son of George Kessler of West Wauzeka. |
| Key | Alice | KC, p4c3, 4/1/1897 | Recently died from suicide at home in Patch Grove. Father committed suicide one and a half years ago. |
| Keyes | J. J. | KC, p1c5, 3/23/1899 | Blacksmith in Seneca. Invented a trip hammer. |
| Keyes | W. P. | KC, p5c1, 1/7/1897 | Resided in Wauzeka. Attended brother-in-law's funeral in Watertown. |
| Keyes | W. P., Mrs. | KC, p5c4, 6/17/1897 | Hosted sisters, Mrs. W. R. Owens of Randolph, WI and Mrs. Ashley of Spring Valley, at her home in Wauzeka. Mrs. Keyes' father, R. B. Thomas, planned to return to Randolph with Mrs. Owens. |
| Kidd | Allen Ramsey | KC, p8c4, 10/24/1901 | Married Gertrude Webster on October 15, 1901. Bride was from Prairie du Chien. Groom was from Lancaster. (They may have married in Rockville, MD.) |
| Kidd | Edward Isaac | KC, p8c4, 2/27/1902 | Died Tuesday in Prairie du Chien. Born May 10, 1844 in Millville, Grant Co. Had English ancestors. Served in Co. C, 25th WI Inf. Held many political offices. Portrait printed on p1c5. |
| Kielley | Archie | KC, p1c5, 11/11/1897 | Traveled from North Dakota to Steuben to visit family. Gone 5 years. Wife to spend winter with mother-in-law, Mrs. Kittie Kielley. |

Genealogical Gleanings From Early Newspapers for Residents In and Near
Crawford County, Wisconsin, 1897-1902

| LAST NAME | FIRST NAME | NEWSPAPER PAGE/COLUMN MONTH/DAY/YEAR | GENEALOGICAL DATA |
|---|---|---|---|
| Kielley | boy | KC, p8c3, 4/21/1898 | Son born April 12, 1898 to Archie Kielley of Steuben. |
| Kielley | Earl | KC, p1c3, 8/10/1899 | Mrs. Maggie Farris, Minnie Cantwell, Nellie Cantwell, Earl Kielley and G. W. Farris left Steuben for Countney, ND. "Courtney and vicinity now has a large number of Crawford County people among its inhabitants." |
| Kielley | girl | KC, p5c3, 5/9/1901 | Daughter born April 20, 1901 to W. W. Kielley of Steuben. |
| Kielley | Jack | KC, p5c2, 7/28/1898 | Jack Kielley, James Kielley and Walter Stevenson of Steuben went to Dakota this week. |
| Kielley | William | KC, p5c4, 8/29/1901 | Lived in Steuben. Went to Brodhead, WI to sell some valuable pearls. |
| Kielly | boy | KC, p4c6, 12/1/1898 | Wallace, infant son of Archie Kielly, died Nov. 22, 1898. |
| Kielly | W. W. | KC, p4c2, 8/26/1897 | Left Steuben for North Dakota. Took "a lot of nice sections of honey with him." |
| Kieser | Dora Fredericka, Mrs. | KC, p8c2, 9/21/1899 | Died Sept. 15, 1899 in Prairie du Chien. Nee Wildermuth. Born Sept. 20, 1836 at Bielinghausen, O____, Marbock, Wuertenberg, Germany. To America in 1853. Married Phillip Kieser in Prairie du Chien on Jan. 29, 1856. Husband died Dec. 4, 1895. Survived by children: George Emil, Otto Gustave and Minna (Mrs. Henry Turbil). |
| Kieser | Gustoph | KC, p8c4, 11/16/1899 | Married Martha J. Toepel at home of Mrs. John Borgendine, bride' sister, on Nov. 8 (or 15), 1899. Bride was daughter of Morris Toepel of Prairie du Chien. Bride from Buffalo, NY. Groom from Prairie du Chien. |
| Kieser | Mrs. | KC, p8c4, 9/12/1901 | Died Sept. 3, 1901 at Prairie du Chien. She was sister of Mrs. Burgeman of Buffalo and wife of Gus Kiezer. Funeral held at Lutheran Church. |
| Kieser | Murel | KC, p8c1, 10/7/1897 | Died Oct. 3, 1897 in Prairie du Chien. One year old. Daughter of George Kieser. |
| Kieser | Russell | KC, p8c4, 1/9/1902 | Died Jan. 7, 1902 in Prairie du Chien. Son of Gus Kieser |
| Kimbal | John | KC, p5c4, 5/17/1900 | Found a pearl worth $200 while clam fishing. |
| Kimball | Charlie | KC, p5c3, 2/20/1902 | Arrived from Woods Co., WI to visit family in Lynxville. |
| Kimble | Minnie | KC, p4c3, 7/22/1897 | Married Mr. Frasher on July 18, 1897. (Bride may be from Barnum.) |
| Kimble | Nancy | KC, Supp, 12/20/1900 | Crawford Co. Soldiers Relief Comm. approved aid to Nancy Kimble of Lynxville. |
| Kimmel | Berta D. | KC, p1c6, 1/27/1898 | Died Jan. 13, 1898 in Halcyon. Born in Haney on Dec. 1, 1881. Moved with parents in 1897 to Black River Falls, Jackson Co., WI. Buried in Bell Center Cemetery. |
| Kincaid | Forest | KC, Supp., 12/18/1902 | Crawford County Board of Supervisors allowed expenses in the Matter of Forest Kincaid, Writ of Habeas Corpus. |

Genealogical Gleanings From Early Newspapers for Residents In and Near
Crawford County, Wisconsin, 1897-1902

| LAST NAME | FIRST NAME | NEWSPAPER PAGE/COLUMN MONTH/DAY/YEAR | GENEALOGICAL DATA |
|---|---|---|---|
| Kincaid | Forest | KC, Supp., 12/18/1902 | Crawford County Board of Supervisors examined bills in the Justices and Constables' Account for State vs. Forest Kincaid. Charles Riley, James Tessar, Henry Reeter, Julius Feldman, William Cumberlidge and Dr. G. H. Perrin were witnesses. Undertaker expenses were allowed. |
| Kincaid | Forrest | KC, p1c5, 10/2/1902 | His body was found Sept. 27, 1902 in the Kickapoo River. Disappeared Sept. 18, 1902. Buried in Wauzeka Cemetery. Body was later transferred to Oshkosh, per p1c6. |
| Kincaid | I. L. | KC, p1c6, 10/2/1902 | Resided in Oshkosh. Had body of son, Forest Kincaid exhumed in Wauzeka and transferred to Oshkosh for final burial. |
| Kincannon | Ed | KC, p1c2, 6/14/1900 | Resided near Barnum. Sold 160-acre farm to M. Pelton of Edgerton, WI. |
| Kincannon | M. C. | KC, p1c6, 1/17/1901 | Wauzeka Village Marshall. Dr. Perrin removed a 21-foot tapeworm from Kincannon. |
| Kincannon | M. C. | KC, p1c5, 10/28/1897 | Traveled from Wauzeka to Glen Flora, Chippewa Co. to visit his oldest son. |
| Kincannon | M. C. | KC, p1c6, 4/7/1898 | Elected Marshall for the Village of Wauzeka. |
| Kincannon | M. C. | KC, p5c5, 4/5/1900 | Elected village marshall in Wauzeka. |
| Kincannon | M. C., Mrs. | KC, p1c3, 12/7/1899 | Mrs. M. C. Kincannon of Wauzeka and Mollie Copper traveled to Madison. Mollie was hired to work in a boarding house there that was operated by Mr. Mead, Mrs. Kincannon's brother. |
| Kincannon | Theo | KC, p1c3, 8/23/1900 | Departed Wauzeka for a visit with his sister in Seattle, WA and with Orlo Vaughan in Spokane. |
| Kincannon | Theo | KC, p1c5, 3/13/1902 | Left Wauzeka for a new home in Madison, SD. Family to follow. |
| Kincannon | Theo | KC, p1c2, 4/6/1899 | Planned to run the hotel formerly operated by William Hazelwood in Wauzeka. |
| Kincannon | Theodore | KC, p1c2, 11/24/1898 | Decided to move back to Wauzeka from Cayuga, MN. |
| Kincannon | Theodore, Mrs. | KC, p1c3, 5/1/1902 | Left Wauzeka to join husband in Madison, SD. He rented a 250-acre farm for the season. |
| Kinder | Bertha | KC, p5c3, 11/30/1899 | Left home in Boydtown to visit her brother in Viola. |
| Kinder | J. B. | KC, p5c5, 4/5/1900 | Elected supervisor in Marietta. |
| Kinder | Jerome | KC, p1c6, 4/7/1898 | Elected Supervisor for the Town of Marietta. |
| King | boy | KC, p5c2, 8/4/1898 | Son born last night to Ruby King of Mt. Sterling. |
| King | Grandpa | KC, p4c3, 1/13/1898 | From Bridgeport. Aged 95 years. Very feeble but still able to saw wood. |
| King | H. C. | KC, p8c7, 2/8/1900 | Merchant in Mt. Sterling. |
| King | H. C. | KC, p1c4, 9/26/1901 | Proprietor of a general merchandise store in Mt. Sterling. |

Genealogical Gleanings From Early Newspapers for Residents In and Near
Crawford County, Wisconsin, 1897-1902

| LAST NAME | FIRST NAME | NEWSPAPER PAGE/COLUMN MONTH/DAY/YEAR | GENEALOGICAL DATA |
|---|---|---|---|
| King | H. C. | KC, p1c2, 12/9/1897 | Advertised for "a competent girl to do housework. Small family, good wages." Lived in Mt. Sterling. |
| King | H. C. | KC, p1c4, 6/29/1899 | Published a card of thanks to the people of Mt. Sterling who helped clear away debris after a new store he was constructing blew down during a storm. The townspeople also helped put the store back on its foundation. |
| King | Lyman | KC, p1c4, 3/9/1899 | Died in autumn of 1898. Daughter, Mrs. Simpson, removed remains from Bridgeport and reinterred them with his wife who died 40 years ago in Westby, WI. Mentioned sons H. C. King of Mt. Sterling and S. O. King of Mobile, AL. |
| King | Mary | KC, p5c3, 6/13/1901 | Graduated from school in Mt. Sterling. |
| King | Robert | KC, p1c6, 5/12/1898 | Traveled from Alabama to visit in Gays Mills. |
| Kinion | Mr. | KC, p5c4, 3/29/1900 | Died last week at the county poor farm. He was a former resident of Prairie du Chien. (Pion?) |
| Kinney | Isaac | KC, p5c4, 2/6/1902 | Recently died in Cerlew, IA. He was uncle of Mrs. Alanson Taft, Jr. of the Town of Haney. |
| Kizer | Gladys | KC, p8c2, 3/2/1899 | Died Feb. 24, 1899 at age of 5 months and 3 days. Daughter of Amiel Kizer of Chicago. Buried in Lowertown Cemetery (Prairie du Chien.). |
| Klema | Frank | KC, p1c3, 12/22/1898 | Died Dec. 19, 1898 in Wauzeka. |
| Klema | Frank | KC, p1c7, 12/29/1898 | Died Dec. 18, 1898 in Wauzeka. Son of Joseph Klema of Wauzeka. Aged 25 years. |
| Klingenberg | James | KC, p1c5, 8/19/1897 | Returned to Norway (his homeland) from home in Soldiers Grove. Left a large estate by his father in Norway. Been in America for last 16 years. Planned to return. |
| Kloth | Arthur | KC, p8c4, 6/27/1901 | Married Louise Boucher on June 26, 1901 at St. Gabriel's Church in Prairie du Chien. |
| Kloth | Arthur and Bessie | KC, p5c3, 11/23/1899 | Arrived from Ohio to visit their aunt, Mrs. D. Twining of Gays Mills. They planned to move to Crawford Co. |
| Klotz | R. | KC, p5c3, 3/8/1900 | Teacher in Mt. Sterling. |
| Klotz | R. Q. | KC, p1c2, 8/24/1899 | Hired as principal of graded schools in the Mt. Sterling. |
| Klotz | Ralph Q. | KC, p1c5, 2/9/1899 | Taught school in Utica in 1899. E. E. Brindley, Crawford County Superintendent of Schools published a comprehensive list of all teachers in the county. |
| Kneeland | Catherine Ester | KC, p4c3, 12/13/1900 | Died Dec. 8, 1900. Aged 17 years, 11 months and 6 days. She was the oldest daughter of Bartley Kneeland. |
| Kneeland | girls | KC, p5c3, 4/24/1902 | Twin girls born April 17, 1902 to B. J. Kneeland of Seneca. |
| Kneeland | Katie | KC, p5c4, 10/4/1900 | Very ill. Resided in Seneca. Gave birth 2 weeks ago. Baby died. |
| Kneeland | Mr. | KC, p5c3, 11/7/1901 | Died Nov. 2, 1901 of blood poisoning. Funeral held at St. Patrick's Church. Father of Bartley Kneeland. |

Genealogical Gleanings From Early Newspapers for Residents In and Near
Crawford County, Wisconsin, 1897-1902

| LAST NAME | FIRST NAME | NEWSPAPER PAGE/COLUMN MONTH/DAY/YEAR | GENEALOGICAL DATA |
|---|---|---|---|
| Knoble | David | KC, p4c3, 7/18/1901 | Lived in Gays Mills. Father of twins (1 boy and 1 girl) born on July 8, 1901. He is also the father of 2-year old boy twins. |
| Knoble | twin boys | KC, p5c3, 5/18/1899 | Twin sons were born May 13, 1899 to David Knoble of Gays Mills. |
| Knoble | W. | KC, Supp., 12/18/1902 | Crawford County Soldiers Relief Committee provided funds to W. Knoble of Soldiers Grove. |
| Knott | Harry | KC, p8c3, 6/14/1900 | Married Barbara Biley on June 12, 1900. Bride and groom from Prairie du Chien. Planned to live in Winona, MN. |
| Knussman | Phillip | KC, p8c3, 12/12/1901 | Died Dec. 6, 1901 at Prairie du Chien. Aged over 70 years. |
| Knutson | C. J., Mrs. | KC, Supp., 12/18/1902 | Per Committee on County Poor, Crawford County received $24 from Mrs. C. J. Knutson as a refund for aid furnished. |
| Knutson | Carl | KC, p8c3, 3/28/1901 | Judge Curran found him to be sane at a hearing in January. Knutson judged insane in February. In March his brother applied to the court to have him reexamined before a jury. Declared sane. |
| Knutson | Carl F. | KC, p1c2, 10/3/1901 | Died Sept. 28, 1901 at home of brother in Mt. Sterling. |
| Knutson | George | KC, p1c5, 9/21/1901 | Died Sept. 8, 1901. He and George Halverson drowned. From Rush Creek. |
| Knutson | Gilbert, Mrs. | KC, p4c2, 4/14/1898 | Recently died. She was the sister-in-law of Mrs. Sam Halverson. |
| Knutson | Karl | KC, Supp., 12/12/1901 | Crawford Co. Board of Supervisors approved payments in the Matter of Karl Knutson, Insane. Witnesses were Dr. E. Steiger, Dr. J. C. Rowley, Mrs. J. Knutson, Mrs. Anderson, T. T. Sime, W. H. Davenport and Dr. Christenson. |
| Knutson | Martha | KC, p1c6, 2/3/1898 | Married Ever J. Nedredoe of Johnstown on Feb. 2, 1898 at the Utica Lutheran Church. Bride daughter of Erik Knutson of Mt. Sterling. |
| Knutson | Mr. | KC, p5c3, 11/2/1899 | Died Oct. 29, 1899 in Lynxville area. Aged over 90 years. He was father of George and Charles Knutson. |
| Knutson | C. J. | KC, Supp., 12/12/1901 | Crawford Co. Board of Supervisors approved payments in the case C. J. Knutson, Insane. |
| Koch | John | KC, p1c2, 4/5/1900 | Departed Wauzeka for Sedalia, CO to visit brother, David Koch. |
| Koch | John | KC, p1c4, 8/23/1900 | Returned to Wauzeka after visiting with relatives in Sedalia, CO. |
| Koch | John | KC, p1c5, 2/14/1901 | Worked as cashier at the Bank of Wauzeka. |
| Koch | John | KC, p1c3, 8/21/1902 | Lived in Wauzeka. Visited son, William Koch of Aberdeen, ND. (Should this be SD?) |
| Koch | John | KC, p1c2, 3/23/1899 | Planned to open a tailor shop in Wauzeka. Moved in with his daughter, Mrs. W. A. Vaughan. |
| Koep | J. George | KC, p5c3, 4/20/1899 | Worked as a harness maker in Eastman. |
| Koepp | George | KC, p5c5, 4/5/1900 | Elected clerk in Eastman. |

Genealogical Gleanings From Early Newspapers for Residents In and Near
Crawford County, Wisconsin, 1897-1902

| LAST NAME | FIRST NAME | NEWSPAPER PAGE/COLUMN MONTH/DAY/YEAR | GENEALOGICAL DATA |
|---|---|---|---|
| Kolar | William | KC, p4c2, 9/29/1898 | On furlough from base at Ft. Meade, PA. Went to Eastman. |
| Konecheck | Charles | KC, p8c3, 10/25/1900 | Married Mary Mara on Oct. 22, 1900. Bride and groom from Prairie du Chien. Bride daughter of Frank Mara. |
| Konklin | George E. | KC, p1c6, 5/19/1898 | Issue of Fact for Jury to be heard in the May term of the Crawford County Circuit Court. George E. Konklin vs. Peter O. Uttre (Yttri?) |
| Kopan | Alex | KC, p1c4, 5/9/1901 | Lived in Steuben area. Cared for his granddaughter, Gertrude Pollow, while his daughter, Mrs. Frances Pollow was getting medical treatment at Los Vegas, NM. |
| Kopan | Joe | KC, p8c1, 6/29/1899 | Married Queen Victoria Hobbs on June 28, 1899 at Trinity Episcopal Church (per KC, p1c5, 7/1/1899). Bride was daughter of Capt. Hobbs. Groom from Chicago. |
| Kopan | Lucy | KC, p1c4, 9/18/1902 | Native of Steuben. Taught school in Burnett Co., WI. Pay better wages there than in Crawford Co. |
| Kopan | Lucy | KC, Supp., 12/12/1901 | Attended a Teacher's Institute in Crawford County in 1901. Resided in Steuben. |
| Kopan | Mary | KC, p5c5, 1/18/1900 | Taught school in Crawford Co. |
| Kopan | Mary | KC, p1c3, 6/20/1901 | Returned home after spending the last year teaching in Seaforth, MN. |
| Kopan | Mary | KC, Supp., 12/12/1901 | Attended a Teacher's Institute in Crawford County in 1901. Resided in Steuben. |
| Kopan | McDowell | KC, p1c5, 2/9/1899 | Taught school in Marietta in 1899. E. E. Brindley, Crawford County Superintendent of Schools published a comprehensive list of all teachers in the county. |
| Kopats | Joseph | KC, p7c1, 10/13/1898 | Died Tuesday at Prairie du Chien. |
| Kosa | William | KC, p1c3, 8/11/1898 | Native of Wauzeka. Arrived from Chicago. Visited Uncle Frank Haddock of Crawford Co. |
| Kosharek | Emma | KC, p8c3, 3/17/1898 | Died Mar. 5, 1898 in Steuben. She was daughter of John Kosharek. Survived by parents and 4 brothers. |
| Kotera | Mr. | KC, p8c1, 9/21/1899 | An aged farmer who was "probably fatally injured" on Sept. 18, 1899 about 8 miles north of Prairie du Chien. |
| Kozelka | Joe | KC, p8c2, 11/13/1902 | Married Mary Cheaka on Nov. 11, 1902 at the Bohemian Catholic Church. |
| Krall | Stasia | KC, 1/21/1897 | Married Harry D. Fairbank of Cresco IA on Jan. 12, 1897 at the Dousman House. Bride from Calmar, IA. The Rev. G. W. Reichert officiated. |
| Kramer | Adeline | KC, p5c4, 6/20/1901 | Graduated from the Eastman graded schools. |
| Kramer | Ed, Mr. and Mrs. | KC, p4c4, 12/13/1900 | Departed Eastman for a new home in Austin, MN. |
| Kramer | Edward | KC, p8c3, 8/2/1900 | Married Etta Speck on August 1, 1900. Bride and groom from Town of Eastman. Bride daughter of C. Speck. |
| Kramer | Eli, Mrs. | KC, p5c3, 10/9/1902 | Lived in Eastman. Visited her sister in Vermillion, SD. |
| Kramer | J. | KC, p5c4, 8/16/1900 | Married May Larson on Aug. 8, 1900. Bride and groom from Town of Eastman. Planned to live in Austin, MN. |

Genealogical Gleanings From Early Newspapers for Residents In and Near
Crawford County, Wisconsin, 1897-1902

| LAST NAME | FIRST NAME | NEWSPAPER PAGE/COLUMN MONTH/DAY/YEAR | GENEALOGICAL DATA |
|---|---|---|---|
| Kramer | John, Mrs. | KC, p1c4, 3/29/1900 | Died Mar. 27, 1900 in Town of Eastman. Nee Oswald. |
| Kramer | Lawrence | KC, p5c3, 3/2/1899 | Returned to Eastman after attending dairy school in Madison for the last few months. |
| Kramer | Nellie, Mrs. | KC, p5c4, 5/22/1902 | She and her brother, Will Roach, called from Cloquet, MN to attend funeral of father, John Roach of Town of Eastman. |
| Kramer | Paul, Mr. and Mrs. | KC, p5c4, 6/27/1901 | Departed Eastman to visit their sons, "Ed and Jill", at Austin, MN. |
| Kramer | Ulysses | KC, p4c1, 3/31/1898 | Ulysses Krameer and Tommy Donahue left Eastman for jobs in Countney, ND. |
| Kramer | Ulysses | KC, p5c3, 11/16/1899 | Arrived from New Rockford, ND to visit parents in Eastman. |
| Kramer | Victor | KC, p5c3, 7/25/1901 | Married Nellie Roach on July 22, 1901. The Rev. Father Miller officiated. |
| Kramer | Victor | KC, p5c3, 4/12/1900 | Kramer and August Brady departed Eastman for summer work in North Dakota. |
| Kramer | William H. | KC, p1c2, 10/6/1898 | Married Rose Mathews on Sept. 22, 1898 at the M.E. parsonage in Boscobel. Daughter of John Mathews of Marietta. Groom from Lancaster. |
| Kratche | | KC, p1c4, 5/2/1901 | The infant child of John Kratche of Wauzeka died Tuesday. |
| Kraut | Mike | KC, p8c1, 4/21/1898 | Died about April 17, 1898 at a camp south of town. He was a Winnebago Indian. |
| Kremer | F. A. | KC, p5c6, 3/8/1900 | Organizes lodges for the M. W. W. |
| Kriz | Joseph | KC, p1c2, 3/14/1901 | Wagon maker in Steuben. |
| Kroker | Chris O. | KC, p5c3, 5/20/1897 | Issues of fact for court to be heard in the May term of the Crawford County Court. Joseph S. Olson vs. Chris O. Kroker. |
| Kronsage | George | KC, p1c5, 7/20/1899 | Recently died. Drowned near Boscobel. |
| Krouskup | A. H. | KC, p1c6, 5/19/1898 | Issue of Fact for Jury to be heard in the May term of the Crawford County Circuit Court. A. H. Krouskup vs. Urias Martin. |
| Kruckeberg | W., Mrs. | KC, p1c4, 8/30/1900 | Arrived from Los Angeles, CA (per KC, p1c2, 9/20/1900) to be with her ill sister, Mrs. T. Gink of Wauzeka. |
| Krukeberger | William | KC, p1c3, 11/1/1900 | Arrived from California. Called to Wauzeka due to illness of wife. Wife came here for illness and death of her sister, Mrs. Theodore Gink. |
| Kruschke | Bertha | KC, p1c2, 1/5/1899 | Married Robert P. Gugler Jan. 1, 1899 at Lutheran Church in Wauzeka. Bride from Wauzeka. Groom previously from Milwaukee, but now from Prairie du Chien. |
| Kruschke | Mrs. | KC, p1c2, 10/21/1897 | Celebrated 90th birthday on Oct. 17, 1897 at the Chris Kruschke residence. |
| Kuchenbecker | A. | KC, p1c6, 4/7/1898 | Elected Supervisor for the Town of Wauzeka. |

Genealogical Gleanings From Early Newspapers for Residents In and Near
Crawford County, Wisconsin, 1897-1902

| LAST NAME | FIRST NAME | NEWSPAPER PAGE/COLUMN MONTH/DAY/YEAR | GENEALOGICAL DATA |
|---|---|---|---|
| Kuchenbecker | Oscar | KC, p1c5, 1/20/1898 | Planned to hold an auction sale on his farm four miles west of Wauzeka. Entire stock of cattle, hogs, horses, grain and farm machinery to be sold. |
| Kuchenbecker | Rodolf | KC, p1c2, 12/1/1898 | Married Alice Schurtz on Nov. 24, 1898. Mrs. Louisa Kuchenbecker was the mother of the groom. Groom from Prairie du Chien. |
| Kuchenbecker | Rudolph | KC, p1c2, 8/26/1897 | Clothes became entangled in a thresher on Dutch Ridge. Nearly all clothing torn off. Almost died. |
| Kuchenbecker | William | KC, p1c3, 1/5/1899 | Returned from Walthan, MN to visit Wauzeka, his hometown. |
| Kuchenbecker | girl | KC, p1c2, 12/27/1900 | Daughter born Dec. 23, 1900 to Oscar Kuchenbecker (spelling?) of Wauzeka. |
| Kuchenbeeker | Otto | KC, p1c3, 1/18/1900 | Otto and brother, William, farm in Waltham, MN. Visited friends in Wauzeka. |
| Kunzman | John | KC, p8c3, 6/26/1902 | Died June 23, 1902 at Prairie du Chien. Father of Albert and 7 other children. Aged 79 years. |
| Kunzman | John | KC, p8c3, 6/26/1902 | Recently died. |
| Kussmaul | Albert | KC, p1c2, 6/20/1901 | Kussmaul and John Sprosty planned to run the Eastman hotel, hall and saloon as partners. |
| Kussmaul | Albert | KC, p1c4, 10/3/1901 | Lived in Eastman. Sold his hotel and saloon to M. Donahue for $3000. |
| Kussmaul | Otto | KC, p5c3, 2/6/1902 | Married Bertha Trautsch on Feb. 3, 1902. Bride daughter of Henry Trautsch. Bride and groom from Town of Eastman. |
| Kussmaul | William | KC, p5c5, 4/5/1900 | Elected assessor in Eastman. |
| Kvigne | J., Mrs. | KC, p5c4, 3/27/1902 | Buried Mar. 21, 1902 at Utica Lutheran Church. Resided in Mt. Sterling. |
| La Bonne | Mary | KC, p8c3, 7/4/1901 | Married Emery Valley on July 2, 1901 at St. Gabriel's Catholic Church in Prairie du Chien. |
| La Vake | Thomas A. | KC, p4c4, 11/10/1898 | Issues of Fact for Court heard in the November term of the Crawford County Circuit Court. Thomas A. La Vake vs. Francis M. Barker. |
| Laartz | Frederick | KC, p8c3, 6/8/1899 | Died May 26, 1899. Born Mar. 21, 1837 in Yredenfelde, Hecklenburg, Schwerin, Germany. Married Maria Krause in 1863. Moved to Middleton, Dane Co., WI in 1865. To Wauzeka in 1873. He was uncle of Mrs. Ernest Reichmann. Second wife was Pauline Pfeifer. Third wife was Mrs. Ernestine Walters (widow of Christian Walters), whom he married April 14, 1898. |
| Laartz | Fritze | KC, p5c4, 6/22/1899 | Notice of Hearing published for Probate Court, Crawford County. Ernest Reichmann applied to admit into probate the will of Fritze Laartz, late of the Town of Wauzeka. |
| LaBonne | Paul | KC, p4c1, 1/13/1898 | Married Annie du Chien on Jan. 10, 1898 at St. Gabriel Catholic Church. Bride and groom from Prairie du Chien. |
| Lacy | Emery B. | KC, p8c4, 11/16/1899 | Returned to Prairie du Chien after serving in the U. S. Volunteer Services in Manila. |

Genealogical Gleanings From Early Newspapers for Residents In and Near
Crawford County, Wisconsin, 1897-1902

| LAST NAME | FIRST NAME | NEWSPAPER PAGE/COLUMN MONTH/DAY/YEAR | GENEALOGICAL DATA |
|---|---|---|---|
| Lacy | Herbert, Mrs. | KC, p10c2, 10/13/1898 | Resided in St. Paul where she has gone insane. Also known as Hannah Oram of Prairie du Chien. |
| Lacy | J. C. | KC, p1c2, 3/25/1897 | Returned to Ora, IN after visiting relatives and friends in Prairie du Chien. |
| Lacy | Orlando | KC, p5c4, 5/22/1902 | Prairie du Chien High School class of 1902. |
| Lacy | Orlando | KC, p1c3, 3/11/1897 | Little Orlando Lacy of Prairie du Chien accidentally shot a finger off while handling a loaded revolver. |
| Lacy | T. W. | KC, p8c4, 10/30/1902 | Died Oct. 1902 in Prairie du Chien. Extensive obituary printed. Difficult to read. |
| Lagaman | Clara | KC, p1c3, 12/22/1898 | Married Rubert Meyer on Dec. 18, 1898. Bride and groom from Wauzeka. Bride daughter of John Lagaman. |
| Lagaman | Frank | KC, p1c3, 3/27/1902 | Planned to work as a fireman in Milwaukee. |
| Lagaman | Frank | KC, p1c3, 3/24/1898 | Adolph Sanger, Frank Lagaman and Willie Beier of Wauzeka departed for Grand Junction, CO to seek their fortune. |
| Lagaman | Grandma | KC, p1c2, 12/27/1900 | A surprise party was held last Thursday for her 79th birthday celebration. Resided in Wauzeka. |
| Lagaman | John | KC, p1c2, 4/26/1900 | Married Mrs. Anna Rhein on April 22, 1900 at home of bride in Boscobel. Groom was from Wauzeka. |
| Lagaman | John, Mrs. | KC, p1c3, 10/24/1901 | Departed Wauzeka for Janesville to visit her mother-in-law who was reported to be 82 years old and very feeble. |
| Lagaman | John, Mrs. | KC, p1c2, 4/14/1898 | Visited son in Janesville. Resided in Wauzeka. |
| Lagaman | Lena, Mrs. | KC, p4c4, 11/21/1901 | Born Dec. 22, 1820 in Germany. Died Nov. 9, 1901 at home of son, William Lagaman of Janesville. Married John Lagaman when she was 17 years old. Gave birth to 1 son who lived in Wauzeka. Remarried John's brother, Ludwig, a year after his death. Gave birth to 4 more children, of which 2 survive, William of Janesville and Henry of Buck Creek, WI. Had 21 grandchildren, 31 great grandchildren and 3 great great grandchildren. Mrs. Frank Wagner of Eastman and Mrs. Robert Meyer of Moose, MN were unable to attend the funeral. |
| Lagaman | Sophia, Mrs. | KC, p1c5, 9/29/1898 | Died Sept. 22, 1898 in Wauzeka. Aged 58 years. Wife of John Lagaman. Born in Thelkon, Maklainburg Province, Germany in 1840. Moved to Waukesha, WI when 25. Married husband there in 1867. Moved to Wauzeka in 1873. Survived by 7 of 10 children: Mrs. Emma McCurchy and Mrs. Minnie Brown of Janesville, Mrs. Frank Wagner and Miss Clara Lagaman of Wauzeka, John, Jr. of Janesville, George of Chicago and Frank of Alabama (in Army). Husband's mother and brothers live in Janesville. Funeral held at Evangelical Church. |

Genealogical Gleanings From Early Newspapers for Residents In and Near
Crawford County, Wisconsin, 1897-1902

| LAST NAME | FIRST NAME | NEWSPAPER PAGE/COLUMN MONTH/DAY/YEAR | GENEALOGICAL DATA |
|---|---|---|---|
| Lagan | Hugh | KC, p1c4, 12/5/1901 | Died Nov. 27, 1901 in Prairie du Chien. Born June 1856 in Dodge Co., WI to Patrick Lagan of Prairie du Chien. In 1856 he and parents and 3 older children moved to Mt. Sterling from Dodge Co. Married Maggie Burns in Spring 1879. She died in 1888. They had 4 children: Allie and Mamie of Minneapolis, Maggie of Town of Seneca and Edward of Prairie du Chien (who lives with Grandma Burns). Also survived by a brother, John, of Mt. Sterling and sisters, Mrs. P. Gilmartin and Lillie Lagan, of Prairie du Chien. Buried in Catholic Cemetery in Town of Seneca. Father and mother still alive. |
| Lagan | Mamie | KC, p1c5, 4/10/1902 | Married T. J. Crawford on April 9, 1902 at the Seneca Catholic Church. Bride daughter of John Lagan, a former teacher and resident of Mt. Sterling. Groom was proprietor of a general merchandise store in Petersburg. |
| Lagan | Mamie | KC, Supp., 12/12/1901 | Attended a Teacher's Institute in Crawford County in 1901. Resided in Mount Sterling |
| Lagan | Mamie A. | KC, p1c3, 3/27/1902 | T. J. Crawford of Petersburg and Mamie A. Lagan of Mt. Sterling planned to host a grand ball on April 9, 1902 at King's Hall in Mt. Sterling to celebrate their marriage (planned for April 9, 1902). |
| Lagan | Marie | KC, Supp., 12/12/1901 | Attended a Teacher's Institute in Crawford County in 1901. Resided in Prairie du Chien. |
| LaGeune | Andrew | KC, p8c3, 11/16/1899 | Plaintiff did not appear in the case Andrew LaGeune vs. Henry Buckmaster and P. W. Redfield. Plaintiff will have to pay costs to continue the same. Case heard at the November term of the Crawford County Circuit Court. |
| Laird | A. M. | KC, p5c3, 10/16/1902 | Lived in Lynxville. Received a barrel of Keiter pears from his parents in Indiana. |
| Laird | A. M., Rev. | KC, p5c3, 6/19/1902 | Preached in Lynxville and Seneca. |
| Laird | Max Allen | KC, p5c3 12/26/1901 | Married Sara O'Neil on Dec. 25, 1901. Bride and groom from Lynxville. |
| Lake | John R. | KC, p5c2, 2/3/1898 | Died Jan. 27, 1898 in Viroqua. |
| Lamoreau | William | KC, p1c3, 9/1/1898 | Worked as a miller at the Petersburg Roller Grist Mills. |
| Lamouthe | Emerence | KC, p5c3, 3/2/1899 | Emerence Lamouthe and Isabella Deroucher of Eastman visited relatives in Chippewa Falls. |
| Lance | George E. | KC, p5c2, 1/3/1901 | Married Ada Kast on Dec. 25, 1900 at home of bride's father in Petersburg. Bride, daughter of Ira Kast, taught school in Bell Center. Planned to continue the position until the school term ended in June. Groom from Platteville. Extensive guest list and gift list published. |
| Lance | J. T. | KC, p5c6, 3/8/1900 | Engaged in wood and bolt business in Belle Center. Intends to grow tobacco next year. |
| Lance | J. T. | KC, p5c5, 4/5/1900 | Elected supervisor in Town of Haney. |

Genealogical Gleanings From Early Newspapers for Residents In and Near
Crawford County, Wisconsin, 1897-1902

| LAST NAME | FIRST NAME | NEWSPAPER PAGE/COLUMN MONTH/DAY/YEAR | GENEALOGICAL DATA |
|---|---|---|---|
| Lance | George E. | KC, p5c2, 1/3/1901 | Married Ada Kast on Dec. 25, 1900. Bride was daughter of Ira Kast of Petersburg. Groom from Platteville. |
| Landis | Grace Adele | KC, p1c4, 4/25/1901 | Married Walter S. Mills on April 20, 1901. Bride from Valparaiso, IN. Groom from Marshalltown, IA. Son of Fergus Mills of Town of Seneca. |
| Lang | Eugene | KC, p5c3, 6/10/1897 | Arrested for attempting to rob Haggerty's Store in Gays Mills. |
| Lang | girl | KC, p4c2, 8/25/1898 | Daughter born August 19, 1898 to William Lang of Bell Center. |
| Lang | Lonie, Mrs. | KC, p8c4, 7/12/1900 | Died June 24,1900 at Bell Center. Born Aug. 19, 1881 at Bell Center. Daughter of Riley Rounds. Married William Lang of Iowa on July 4, 1897. After marriage lived in Bell Center and Gays Mills. Survived by husband, 1 child, parents, 2 sisters and 4 brothers. Buried in Gays Mills Cemetery. |
| Lang | Minnie | KC, p8c3, 1/9/1902 | Married H. G. Bailey on Jan. 1, 1902. Bride and groom from Prairie du Chien area. |
| Lang | Will | KC, p1c2, 7/26/1900 | Departed Gays Mills to visit daughter, mother and other relatives in Elkader, IA. |
| Lang | Will, Mrs. | KC, p1c5, 2/10/1898 | Resident of Petersburg. Visited brother, George Rounds of Barnum. |
| Lang | William | KC, p1c2, 7/24/1902 | Lived in Gays Mills. Went to Prairie du Chien to visit father who was "taking treatment at the Turkish Bath Institute." |
| Lang | William, Mrs. | KC, p5c3, 6/28/1900 | Died June 24, 1900. She was the daughter of Riley Rounds. (May be from Gays Mills area.) |
| Lang | William, Mrs. | KC, p5c5, 3/29/1900 | Resided in Gays Mills. Planned to go to her father's home to spend her remaining days. |
| Lang | Will | KC, p5c4, 8/15/1901 | Will Lang, Will Rhinehardt and Fred Miller prepared to leave Gays Mills for California. |
| Langdon | Jessie May | KC, p8c5, 3/29/1900 | Died Mar. 20, 1900 in Haney Valley. Wife of William H. Langdon. Daughter of Ambrose Thompson of Town of Seneca. Born Sept. 23, 1861 in Crawford Co. Married Dec. 25, 1882. Survived by 5 of 6 children. One girl, Sadie, dead. Youngest child is 1 week old. |
| Langdon | William | KC, p4c5, 12/20/1900 | Planned to leave the Haney Valley for California on Dec. 19th. |
| Langdon | William, Mrs. | KC, p1c2, 3/29/1900 | Funeral held Mar. 22, 1900 in Haney Valley. |
| Lange | Minnie | KC, p1c5, 7/12/1900 | Married Charles W. Miller on July 3, 1900. Bride from North McGregor, IA. |
| Langford | Ann Elizabeth | KC, Supp, 12/29/1898 | Crawford Co. Board of Supervisors approved Justices and Constables' expenses related to the case, State vs. Ann Elizabeth Langford. The witnesses were Sarah A. (Bodler or Bodier), Landon C. Osborn, George Bodler or Bodier?), Anne Elizabeth Langford, Burt Langford, Nettie Collins and J. W. Rice. |
| Lankford | Ellen | KC, Supp., 12/12/1901 | Attended a Teacher's Institute in Crawford County in 1901. Resided in Ferryville. |

Genealogical Gleanings From Early Newspapers for Residents In and Near
Crawford County, Wisconsin, 1897-1902

| LAST NAME | FIRST NAME | NEWSPAPER PAGE/COLUMN MONTH/DAY/YEAR | GENEALOGICAL DATA |
|---|---|---|---|
| Lankford | William | KC, p5c1, 6/2/1898 | Married Myrtle Warner on Mary 19, 1898 in De Soto. |
| Lankie | Mary | KC, p8c2, 1/6/1898 | Married Mr. Poladna on Jan. 3, 1898 at St. John Bohemian Catholic Church. Bride and groom from Prairie du Chien. |
| Lantry | M. C., Mrs. | KC, p1c4, 3/18/1897 | Recently died in Topeka, KS. Born in Prairie du Chien to Hon. John Lawler, Sr. Survived by husband, 2 children, mother, 2 sisters and 4 brothers. Buried in the Catholic Cemetery. |
| Larave | Joe | KC, Supp, 12/20/1900 | Crawford Co. Board of Supervisors approved payment of expenses in the matter of State vs. Joe Larave. George St. Clair and Hudson St. Clair were witnesses. |
| Laraviere | P. N. | KC, Supp., 12/12/1901 | State vs. P. N. Laraviere heard in Crawford Co. Court. Witnesses were Mrs. William G. Moshier, Willie Moshier, Louis Faroe, Tony Clark and Mrs. Laraviere. |
| LaRiviere |  | KC, p4c1, 5/27/1897 | LaRiviere brothers arrested in Lynxville for fighting and drunkenness. |
| Larocque | Joe | KC, Supp, 12/20/1900 | Crawford Co. Board of Supervisors approved payment of expenses in the matter of State vs. Joe Larocque. |
| Laroque | Joe | KC, Supp., 12/18/1902 | Crawford County Soldiers Relief Committee provided funds to Joe Laroque, Sr. of Prairie du Chien. |
| LaRoque | Joe, Mrs. | KC, Supp, 12/20/1900 | Crawford Co. Soldiers Relief Comm. approved aid to Mrs. Joe LaRoque |
| Larrabee | Hollace | KC, p5c3, 6/29/1899 | Resided in Colorado. Former resident of Eastman. Visited his mother, Mrs. Orpha Hazen, whom he had not seen for 22 years. |
| Larrivere | boy | KC, p8c3, 6/19/1902 | Died June 14, 1902 at 11 years of age. Son of Samuel Larrivere of Prairie du Chien. |
| Larrivere | Leonard | KC, p8c4, 11/27/1902 | Married Nov. 26, 1902 in Shermansville, IL. Bride's name not given. Groom brother of Sol Larrivere of Prairie du Chien. |
| Larsen | Baker | KC, p4c3, 12/13/1900 | Died Dec. 7, 1900 at home on Shanghi Ridge, Town of Eastman. Aged 84 years. Born in Norway and married there in 1844. Survived by wife and 7 children -- Melinda, Amos and John of Eastman; Louis of Lawler, IA; Mrs. Oscar Coates of Walworth Co., WI; Albert of Dakota and Mrs. Hank of Iowa. Buried in German Cemetery. |
| Larson | Andrew M. | KC, p4c4, 11/10/1898 | Issues of Default heard in the November term of the Crawford County Circuit Court. John A. Haggerty vs. Andrew M Larson. |
| Larson | Ike | KC, p5c3, 9/12/1901 | Returned to home in Eastman after visiting his brother, Aaron of Minneapolis. |
| Larson | Ike | KC, p1c4, 3/20/1902 | Resided at Hazens Corners. His 73 year old father, Peter Larson, had a paralytic stroke on Wednesday. |
| Larson | John S. | KC, p1c4, 3/17/1898 | Died last Thursday of consumption in California. Went there for his health. Lived in Viroqua. Served as district attorney of Vernon Co. |
| Larson | Kate | KC, p8c4, 11/15/1900 | Married Nov. 7, 1900 at West Superior. Former resident of Prairie du Chien. Husband's name not given. |

Genealogical Gleanings From Early Newspapers for Residents In and Near
Crawford County, Wisconsin, 1897-1902

| LAST NAME | FIRST NAME | NEWSPAPER PAGE/COLUMN MONTH/DAY/YEAR | GENEALOGICAL DATA |
|---|---|---|---|
| Larson | Lars | KC, p1c4, 4/26/1900 | He was a patient at the Vernon County Insane Asylum. Found on the farm of George Kesslar in Wauzeka area. |
| Larson | Louis | KC, p5c4, 6/19/1902 | Lived in Eastman. On vacation from school at the University of Wisconsin-Madison. |
| Larson | Louis | KC, p5c3, 10/9/1902 | Lived in Eastman. Visited sister in Austin, MN. |
| Larson | May | KC, p5c4, 8/16/1900 | Married J. Kramer on Aug. 8, 1900. Bride and groom from Town of Eastman. Planned to live in Austin, MN. |
| Larson | Miss | KC, p5c3, 12/21/1899 | Mr. Albert Johnson married Miss Larson last Saturday in Buck Creek, per the Mt. Sterling news column. |
| Larson | Peter | KC, p1c3, 3/23/1899 | Resided in Grand Grey. Received $835 from an insurance company to cover the loss of his home to fire. |
| Larson | T., Mrs. | KC, p1c3, 3/22/1900 | Died Mar. 8, 1900 in Mt. Sterling. An infant son died at the same time. Buried in Folsom Cemetery. Nee Crume. |
| Larson | Tom | KC, p8c3, 1/6/1898 | Married Sadie Crume on Dec. 29, 1897. Bride and groom from Towerville. |
| Lasche | Alfred, Mrs. | KC, p8c2, 2/16/1899 | Called from Milwaukee to the sick bed of sister, Miss Anna Oswald of Prairie du Chien. |
| Lathrop | B. F. | KC, p13c4, 12/12/1901 | Bought the Ray House (hotel) in Wauzeka. |
| Lathrop | boy | KC, p5c4, 3/20/1902 | Son born last Sunday to Fred Lathrop of West Wauzeka. |
| Lathrop | C. L. | KC, p1c5, 1/17/1901 | Spoke on the raising of strawberries at the Farmer's Institute held in Eastman. |
| Lathrop | Cyrus | KC, p1c2, 2/15/1900 | Appointed Town Chairman in Wauzeka. Fills the unexpired term of the late H. Anderson. |
| Lathrop | Elias | KC, p5c2, 6/10/1897 | Inventor of the Indiana road grader. Resided in Fort Wayne. Visited his cousins, Fred, Cyrus and Frank in Wauzeka area. |
| Lathrop | F. | KC, p5c5, 3/7/1901 | Published the following notice, "I desire to hereby notify merchants and others that I will not be responsible for goods purchased on credit by my wife as I desire to pay all accounts when made." |
| Lathrop | F. L., Mrs. | KC, p5c1, 1/7/1897 | Resided in Wauzeka. Spent Christmas with father, Sampson Turner of Towerville. |
| Lathrop | Fred, Mrs. | KC, p5c2, 1/13/1898 | Traveled from West Wauzeka to visit with parents, Mr. and Mrs. S. Turner of Towerville. |
| Lathrop | George | KC, p1c4, 11/20/1902 | Married Mrs. Harrington on Nov. 11, 1902 at Prairie du Chien. Bride from Muscoda. Groom from Gays Mills. Groom brother of C. L. and Fred Lathrop of Wauzeka. |
| Lathrop | girl | KC, p1c4, 1/3/1901 | Daughter born Dec. 27, 1900 to C. L. Lathrop of Wauzeka. |
| Lathrop | Lowell W. | KC, p1c6, 11/4/1897 | Issue of fact for court to be heard at the November term of the Circuit Court in Crawford County. Lowell Lathrop vs. William Allen Butler. |
| Lathrop | Lowell W. | KC, p1c6, 11/4/1897 | Issue of fact for court to be heard at the November term of the Circuit Court in Crawford County. Lowell W. Lathrop vs. R. J. Stevens. |

Genealogical Gleanings From Early Newspapers for Residents In and Near
Crawford County, Wisconsin, 1897-1902

| LAST NAME | FIRST NAME | NEWSPAPER PAGE/COLUMN MONTH/DAY/YEAR | GENEALOGICAL DATA |
|---|---|---|---|
| Lathrop | P. A. | KC, p5c3, 5/20/1897 | Issues of fact for jury to be heard in the May term of the Crawford County Court. Cream City Sash & Door Co. vs. P. A. Lathrop impleaded with H. J. Kast as co-partner, under name of P. A. Lathrop & Co. appellant. |
| Lathrop | Samantha | KC, p5c3, 8/13/1897 | Died Aug. 13, 1897 at home of son, Fred Lathrop. She was one of Wauzeka's oldest and earliest residents. Born May 25, 1825 in New York. Moved to Illinois when 14. At 18 moved to McGregor, IA and soon departed for Prairie du Chien. While there, married Levi Louis Lathrop and moved to Bridgeport and then Wauzeka. Gave birth to 5 sons and 4 daughters. Survived by sons and 1 daughter. |
| Lathrop | W. E. | KC, p1c5, 6/1/1899 | The May term of the Crawford County Circuit Court closed. The case W. E. Lathrop vs. J. W. Van Allen was continued. |
| Lathrop | W. E. | KC, p8c3, 11/16/1899 | In the case W. E. Lathrop vs. J. W. Van Allen, verdict for the defendant. The case was heard at the November term of the Crawford County Circuit Court. |
| Lathrop | William | KC, p1c3, 6/1/1899 | Worked as a land agent. Based in Fennimore. Took Felix Degnan and Eugene Smith to Dell Rapids, SD to show them property. While there, they visited Degnan's brother in Springfield, SD and Smith's brother-in-law and other relatives in Bridgewater, per KC, p1c4, 6/1/1899. |
| Lattimore | Isaac | KC, p4c1, 10/7/1897 | Celebrated 60th birthday on Oct. 2, 1897 in Ferryville. Over 100 guests were present. Many gifts were given. |
| Lawler | girl | KC, p1c5, 8/23/1900 | Daughter born August 16, 1900 to Richard Lawler of Lynxville. |
| Lawler | James | KC, p8c3, 11/30/1899 | Recently died. |
| Lawler | James | KC, p8c3, 12/7/1899 | Died Nov. 29, 1899 in Prairie du Chien. Born Mar. 25, 1843 in Goshen, Orange Co., NY. Moved to Wisconsin in 1861. Moved to Prairie du Chien in 1867. Married Sarah (Ca__os?) at Austin, MN in 1870. Survived by 6 children: Charles E. of Butte, MT; Eliza; James M. of Mason City, IA; Rev. Raymond (Will) of Somerset, OH; Mary Cantwell Lawler; and Irwin Irishman. |
| Lawler | Jerome | KC, p8c1, 1/19/1899 | Died Dec. 31, 1899 at Independence, IA. Former resident of Prairie du Chien. |
| Lawler | John | KC, p8c3, 1/7/1897 | Buried last Sunday at the Catholic Cem. From Lynxville. Formerly from Town of Seneca. Brother, M. Lawler, lived in Chicago. |
| Lawler | Mary | KC, p5c1, 3/10/1898 | Married Manford Sappington on Feb. 24, 1898 at Seneca. Father Keeley officiated. Lynxville news item. |
| Lawler | Nettie | KC, p1c6, 2/22/1900 | Married John J. Ingham on Feb. 14, 1900. Bride and groom from Town of Seneca. |
| Lawler | Patrick, Jr. | KC, p4c3, 1215/1898 | Died Dec. 3, 1898 in Seneca. Born Dec. 4, 1853 in Delaware Co., OH. He had 7 siblings. Mother died a few months ago. Funeral held at St. Patrick's Catholic Church in Seneca. |

Genealogical Gleanings From Early Newspapers for Residents In and Near
Crawford County, Wisconsin, 1897-1902

| LAST NAME | FIRST NAME | NEWSPAPER PAGE/COLUMN MONTH/DAY/YEAR | GENEALOGICAL DATA |
|---|---|---|---|
| Lawler | Patrick, Mrs. | KC, p5c2, 8/18/1898 | Died July 26, 1898 in Seneca at age 77. Born in Parish of Bally Heg, County Kerry, Ireland in 1821. Came to New York with husband and 1 child in 1848 where she lived for 2 years. Moved to Ohio. Moved to Mazomanie. Moved to Seneca. Survived by 4 of 8 children. |
| Lawler | Patsy, Mrs. | KC, p5c2, 8/4/1898 | Died July 26, 1898 at home in Lynxville. |
| Lawler | Richard E. | KC, 5/11/1899 | Recently married Richard E. Lawler at St. Patrick's Catholic Church in Seneca. Bride daughter of L. H. Noggle. |
| Lawless | Irene | KC, p8c3, 8/8/1901 | Married Charles O'Neil on August 1, 1901 at St. Gabriel's Church. Groom from Patch Grove. Planned to live in Patch Grove. |
| Lawless | Margaret | KC, Supp., 12/12/1901 | Margaret Lawless of Bridgeport attended the summer Teacher's Institute in Soldiers Grove. |
| Lawless | Margaret | KC, Supp., 12/12/1901 | Attended a Teacher's Institute in Crawford County in 1901. Resided in Bridgeport. |
| Lawrance | Edward | KC, Supp, 12/29/1898 | Crawford Co. Board of Supervisors approved Justices and Constables' expenses related to the case, State vs. Edward Lawrance |
| Lawrence | | KC, p4c5, 2/21/1901 | An infant child of Walter Lawrence died Wednesday of pneumonia. Buried in Boydtown Cemetery. |
| Lawrence | Adam, Mrs. | KC, p1c6, 3/13/1902 | Died Mar. 7, 1902 at home in Town of Scott. Aged 40 years. Survived by husband, 2 sons, 1 daughter, a number of brothers and 1 sister. She was the daughter of John Carlin of Georgetown Ridge. First married to John Kerrigan who died several years ago. He fathered 1 son. Married Adam Lawrence several years ago. They have 2 children. Buried at the Catholic Cemetery on Georgetown Ridge. |
| Lawrence | Albert | KC, Supp, 12/29/1898 | Received aid from the Crawford County Soldiers Relief Commission. Resided in Lynxville. |
| Lawrence | Bertha | KC, p1c3, 11/17/1898 | Married Lee Hein on Wednesday at Wm. Reeter residence. |
| Lawrence | Biddy | KC, p5c4, 3/20/1902 | Resolution of Respect published by Florence Nightingale Rebekah Lodge No. 85. Died Mar. 6, 1902. Signed by Maggie Stevenson, Ida Peck and Addie Coleman. |
| Lawrence | boy | KC, p1c4, 8/28/1902 | Son born August 25, 1902 to Ed Lawrence of La Farge. |
| Lawrence | Bridget | KC, p8c4, 4/3/1902 | Late of Town of Scott. Adam Lawrence petitioned the Crawford County courts to be named administrator of her estate. |
| Lawrence | D. R. | KC, p1c4, 9/8/1898 | Resided in Petersburg. Traded hotel property occupied by A. Taft to Mr. Chase of Prairie du Chien for the Chauncey Duncan farm near Hurlbut. |
| Lawrence | D. R. | KC, p1c6, 5/19/1898 | Issue of Law for Court to be heard in the May term of the Crawford County Circuit Court. D. R. Lawrence vs.. E. Stickler and Buckmaster et al. |

Genealogical Gleanings From Early Newspapers for Residents In and Near
Crawford County, Wisconsin, 1897-1902

| LAST NAME | FIRST NAME | NEWSPAPER PAGE/COLUMN MONTH/DAY/YEAR | GENEALOGICAL DATA |
|---|---|---|---|
| Lawrence | D. R. | KC, p5c4, 5/29/1902 | The case D. R. Lawrence vs. James Bannen was heard at the May term of the Crawford County Circuit Court. Continued. |
| Lawrence | D. R. | KC, p5c3, 5/20/1897 | Default case to be heard in the May term of the Crawford County Court. D. R. Lawrence vs. Elizabeth Stickler and E. Stickler, partners as E. Stickler & Co. |
| Lawrence | D. R. | KC, p1c6, 11/4/1897 | Issue of fact for court to be heard at the November term of the Circuit Court in Crawford County. D. R. Lawrence vs. E. Strickler et al. |
| Lawrence | D. R., Mrs. | KC, p4c1, 3/3/1898 | Died Feb. 24, 1898 at her home in Petersburg. Born Helen Caroline Thompson on April 19, 1844 in Huron Co., OH. Father died when she was 6. Came with mother (Mrs. Lucy Thompson) to Crawford Co. in 1856. Siblings were: Ambrose of Seneca; Mrs. John H. Lewis of Minneapolis; Mrs. Joseph Casewell of Alma, NB; Elias of Adrain, MN; William of Indianapolis; Mrs. E. D. Palmer of Yankton, SD and Jay and Merritt who were deceased. Married D. R. Lawrence in 1859. They lived in Crawford Co. and Boscobel, Grant Co. She was survived by husband and 4 of 7 children: Leslie D. of Denver, Nellie A. Thomson of Wauzeka, Daniel and Hazel. Norma, wife of A. H. Long (District Attorney of Crawford County), died April 17, 1894. |
| Lawrence | Daniel R. | KC, p1c2, 5/22/1902 | Resided in Petersburg. Recently married. "… this time the happy bride comes from Illinois." |
| Lawrence | Ed | KC, p5c4, 2/9/1899 | His home in Wauzeka destroyed by fire. House owned by Mr. Thiede. |
| Lawrence | Ed | KC, p1c4, 7/31/1902 | Lived in Wauzeka. Took a new job in La Farge as a railroad section foreman. |
| Lawrence | Frank | KC, p5c2, 7/28/1898 | Left Hurlbut for Iowa to spent balance of the season with his brother, Nelson. |
| Lawrence | G. D. | KC, p1c3, 9/14/1899 | Married Ollie Morse on Sept. 8, 1899 in Dubuque. Bride was daughter of Mrs. H. Hamilton of Steuben. Groom was youngest son of D. R. Lawrence of Petersburg. |
| Lawrence | G. D., Mrs. | KC, p5c4, 4/12/1900 | Visited with relatives in Steuben before departing for new home in North Dakota. |
| Lawrence | H. F. | KC, p1c2, 3/27/1902 | Employed as night watch and engine wiper at the roundhouse in Wauzeka. |
| Lawrence | H. F., Mrs. | KC, p1c5, 11/18/1897 | Installed as an officer at the International Order of Good Templars (I.O.G.T.) Lodge in Wauzeka. |
| Lawrence | Henry | KC, p1c2, 7/18/1901 | Left Wauzeka for Browersville, MN to get work on the railroad. |
| Lawrence | I. P. | KC, p1c2, 12/9/1897 | Lived in Petersburg. Took new position as a nursery stock salesman. |

Genealogical Gleanings From Early Newspapers for Residents In and Near
Crawford County, Wisconsin, 1897-1902

| LAST NAME | FIRST NAME | NEWSPAPER PAGE/COLUMN MONTH/DAY/YEAR | GENEALOGICAL DATA |
|---|---|---|---|
| Lawrence | Ira | KC, p2c2, 12/19/1901 | Ira Lawrence erected a frame hotel in 1854 at the site that became Petersburg. Many other settlers also located on what was known as Crow Creek which had a sawmill erected upon it by J. H. and C. Kast as early as 1853. T. J. Crawford, assisted by Nathan Garret, operate a general merchandise store in the village. Another general merchandise store is operated by Garner Bros. T. H. Ferrick runs a mattress factory. Charles Mitchell manages the hotel. Charles Welch has a large stock of lumber. William Jones ran the blacksmith shop. E. W. Hungerford is the manager of the Roller Mills that grinds feed and flour. D. R. Lawrence does a large stock business. A. H. Long provides legal services. Silas Garner is Justice of the Peace. (Notes on development of Petersburg, WI.) |
| Lawrence | L. D. | KC, p1c3, 2/10/1898 | Returned from Denver, CO to his former home in Petersburg. Summoned to bedside of his mother. Sister, Mrs. Rhode Lewis of Minneapolis, also summoned. Mrs. Lawrence's condition was slowly growing worse. |
| Lawrence | Lester | KC, p1c3, 6/26/1902 | Won his case against La Farge in circuit court. |
| Lawrence | Mr. | KC, p7c1, 7/8/1897 | Lived in Lynxville. Unable to find his daughter. She left West Salem for Stoddard to visit her brother-in-law, Peter Churchill (who was sick). She told hotel staff in West Salem she would be back. She did not return. |
| Lawrence | R. A. | KC, Supp., 12/12/1901 | Received money from the Crawford Co. Soldiers Relief Commission. Resided in Lynxville. |
| Lawrence | R. A. | KC, Supp, 12/29/1898 | Received aid from the Crawford County Soldiers Relief Commission. Resided in Lynxville. |
| Lawrence | Robert | KC, p5c3, 2/20/1902 | Served as Town Marshall in Lynxville. |
| Lawrence | Robert | KC, p5c4, 3/27/1902 | Left Lynxville for North Dakota with his grandchildren to live on his claim. |
| Lawrence | Robert, Mrs. | KC, p5c4, 8/7/1902 | Mrs. Lawrence and 2 children left Lynxville to join husband in North Dakota. He went west last spring. |
| Lawrence | Sarah Ann | KC, p1c6, 5/19/1898 | Issue of Fact for Jury to be heard in the May term of the Crawford County Circuit Court. Sarah Ann Lawrence vs. Daniel Vollmer. |
| Lawrence | Sarah Ann | KC, p1c6, 6/2/1898 | In Crawford County Circuit Court, Sarah Ann Lawrence vs. D. Vollmer and Emily Dunbar vs. D. Vollmer. Both cases were decided by one trial as practically the same testimony was to decide both cases. Verdict for defendant. |
| Lawrence | Thomas | KC, p4c3, 12/1/1898 | Married Ada Goodwin, daughter of A. D. Goodwin of Mazomanie, on Nov. 22, 1898. Planned to live in Tucson, AZ. Groom from De Soto. |
| Lawrence | Walter | KC, p1c2, 2/16/1899 | Married Rosa Jones on Feb. 12, 1899. Bride and groom from Boydtown. Joseph Peacock, J.P., officiated. |
| Lawrence | William, Mrs. | KC, p5c4, 7/25/1901 | Took train for Cleveland, OH to visit relatives for the next 3 months. From St. Phillips area of the Town of Clayton. |

Genealogical Gleanings From Early Newspapers for Residents In and Near
Crawford County, Wisconsin, 1897-1902

| LAST NAME | FIRST NAME | NEWSPAPER PAGE/COLUMN MONTH/DAY/YEAR | GENEALOGICAL DATA |
|---|---|---|---|
| Lawver | Thomas | KC, p5c3, 4/29/1897 | Rented the John Wagner place in Wauzeka. |
| Lawver | Thomas | KC, p1c2, 10/27/1898 | Resided in Wauzeka. Took daughter and went to northern Wisconsin to find a new home. |
| Lawver | Thomas, Mrs. | KC, p5c1, 6/23/1898 | Died June 17, 1898 in Wauzeka. Born Apr. 11, 1856 in Bell Center. Nee Nevada Whiteaker. First of 10 children in family to die. Married Thomas Lawver about 18 years ago. Had a 12-year-old daughter. Buried in Whiteaker Cemetery, Gays Mills. Survived by husband, daughter, 5 brothers, 4 sisters and a half brother. |
| Lawver | Thomas, Mrs. | KC, p1c4, 2/21/1898 | Resided in Wauzeka. Entertained her sister and brother-in-law, Mr. And Mrs. J. H. Thompson of Valley Junction, WI. Mr. Thompson was a former area resident who had been absent for several years. |
| Lawver | Tom | KC, p7c2, 7/8/1897 | Received .62 wages for working 1/2 day for Village of Wauzeka. |
| Layd | Hannah | KC, p10c3, 12/12/1901 | Resided at Knapps Creek. Taught school in Brady District. |
| Layd | Maggie | KC, p5c6, 2/8/1900 | Taught school in district 13 in Crawford Co. |
| Layd | Maggie | KC, p1c5, 2/9/1899 | Taught school in Haney in 1899. E. E. Brindley, Crawford County Superintendent of Schools published a comprehensive list of all teachers in the county. |
| Layd | Maggie | KC, Supp., 12/12/1901 | Attended a Teacher's Institute in Crawford County in 1901. Resided in Seneca. |
| Layton | L. D., Mrs. | KC, p5c4, 4/12/1900 | Resided in Mt. Sterling. S. P. Cogswell and wife of Steuben Co., NY visited as they traveled to Seattle, WA. Cogswell was Mrs. Layton's nephew. |
| Leahy | Girl | KC, p5c3, 3/8/1900 | Daughter born Feb. 22, 1900 to D. Leahy of Rising Sun. |
| Leary | Josie | KC, p1c5, 4/27/1899 | Recently married Michael Bernier at St. Patrick's Catholic Church in Seneca. |
| Leary | Lizzie | KC, p1c5, 10/10/1901 | Married Patrick C. Crowley on Oct. 7, 1901 at St. Patrick's in Seneca. Bride and groom from Seneca. Groom brother of Thomas Crowley. Bride sister of Maggie Leary. An extensive list of presents and guests given in a supplement to the Oct. 31, 1901 issue of this newspaper. |
| LeBaun | Peter, Mrs. | KC, p8c2, 2/2/1899 | Died Jan. 25, 1899 in Prairie du Chien. Survived by husband, 1 child, father (G. DuChane), 3 sisters and 1 brother. Buried in the Catholic Cemetery. |
| Lechner | George | KC, p8c1, 3/23/1899 | "Last Thursday G. L. Miller tried his shooting qualities upon a valuable dog belonging to George Lechner. George of course felt a little sore about it and swore out a warrant, charging him with carrying concealed weapons. The case came up before Justice Chase Tuesday. Mr. Miller plead guilty and was fined five dollars and costs." |
| Lechnir | George | KC, p8c3, 1/23/1902 | Married Anna Wher on Jan. 22, 1902. Recorded with Prairie du Chien news items. |

Genealogical Gleanings From Early Newspapers for Residents In and Near
Crawford County, Wisconsin, 1897-1902

| LAST NAME | FIRST NAME | NEWSPAPER PAGE/COLUMN MONTH/DAY/YEAR | GENEALOGICAL DATA |
|---|---|---|---|
| Lechnor | George | KC, p8c4, 4/11/1901 | Erected a button factory in Prairie du Chien. |
| Lee | Andrew | KC, p4c4, 5/2/1901 | Left Soldiers Grove for a trip to Norway, their native land. Andrew Lee, Peter Upholm, Elias Johnson and Christ Scoggen. |
| Lee | Andrew | KC, p1c2, 11/17/1898 | Resided in Pine Knob. Traveled to North Dakota to visit relatives. |
| Lee | Lena | KC, p5c3, 4/3/1902 | Lena Lee and Nettie Anderson opened a dressmaking shop in Gays Mills. |
| Lee | Lena | KC, p1c5, 2/9/1899 | Taught school in the Town of Clayton in 1899. E. E. Brindley, Crawford County Superintendent of Schools published a comprehensive list of all teachers in the county. |
| Lee | Lewis | KC, p5c3, 2/20/1902 | Busy hauling saw logs from his farm to the mill in Gays Mills. |
| Lee | Lewis | KC, p1c3, 5/22/1902 | Resided in Gays Mills. Received an insurance check for an accident in which he was kicked by a horse. |
| Lee | Malena | KC, Supp., 12/12/1901 | Attended a Teacher's Institute in Crawford County in 1901. Resided in Soldiers Grove. |
| Lee | Tob | KC, Supp, 12/29/1898 | Crawford Co. Board of Supervisors approved Justices and Constables' expenses related to the case, State vs. Tob Lee, Andrew Lee, Olaf Lee, Tobias Lee, Hiram Lee and Theodore Lee. The witnesses were William Devenport, Thos. Severson and Andrew Nash. Fred Copsey was the justice of the peace. |
| Lee | Tob | KC, Supp, 12/29/1898 | Crawford Co. Board of Supervisors approved Justices and Constables' expenses related to the case, State vs. Tob Lee and et al. |
| Lee | W. L. | KC, p5c3, 5/20/1897 | Issues of fact for jury to be heard in the May term of the Crawford County Court. Prairie City Electric Co. vs. W. L. Lee & Co. |
| Leefeldt | George | KC, p8c3, 8/16/1900 | Died Aug. 15, 1900 at Waukon, IA. Born Dec. 5, 1867 in Prairie du Chien. Married Celia Valley of Town of Eastman in 1892. Survived by wife and 3 brothers (William, Henry and Gustav). Buried in Lowertown Cemetery. |
| Leefeldt | Henry | KC, p1c4, 1/31/1901 | Leefeldt and wife of Waukon, IA visited Mrs. Leefeldt's parents, Mr. and Mrs. Frank Chapek of Wauzeka. |
| Leefeldt | Henry | KC, p1c3, 3/27/1902 | John Chapek and Henry Leefeldt left Wauzeka for their claims in Anamoose, ND. Took 2 carloads of goods, 10 horses, 3 cows, etc. |
| Leefelt | boy | KC, p5c4, 7/25/1901 | Son born Sunday to Henry Leefelt of the Wauzeka area. |
| Lefeldt | C., Mrs. | KC, p8c2, 4/6/1899 | Died April 5, 1899 in Prairie du Chien. |
| Leguene | Andrew | KC, p5c3, 10/27/1898 | Worked as a general blacksmith in Petersburg. |
| Leinfelder | P. H., Dr. | KC, p8c4, 6/21/1900 | Died June 19, 1900 in a La Crosse hospital. From Prairie du Chien. |

Genealogical Gleanings From Early Newspapers for Residents In and Near
Crawford County, Wisconsin, 1897-1902

| LAST NAME | FIRST NAME | NEWSPAPER PAGE/COLUMN MONTH/DAY/YEAR | GENEALOGICAL DATA |
|---|---|---|---|
| Leinfelder | P. H., Dr. | KC, p1c1, 1/18/1900 | Advertised medical services. Practice based in Prairie du Chien. |
| Leitner | Emma | KC, p8c2, 3/2/1899 | Married Milton Kellogg (Kellog) of Mason City, IA last Wednesday (Feb. 22, 1899?). Bride from Lynxville. Bride sister to Mrs. Fred Granzow and Otto Leitner. |
| Leitner | Will | KC, p5c3, 8/24/1899 | Will Leitner of Montana and Louis Leitner of Mason City, IA visited the Leitner residence of Poplar Ridge. |
| Lenehan | Kate and Mary | KC, p5c3, 2/1/1900 | Arrived from Minneapolis to visit parents in Pine Creek. |
| Lenehan | Patrick | KC, p5c3, 10/2/1902 | Resided in Eastman. Toe amputated. |
| Lennon | Mary, Mrs. | KC, p1c4, 2/6/1902 | Mrs. Mary Lennon of Colorado Springs, CO and Mrs. Peter Campbell of Bridgeport visited their brother, Joseph Tierney in Marietta. |
| Lenox | Wesley | KC, p5c2, 1/24/1901 | Recently died in Town of Clayton. Probate Hearing notice published. William Oscar Lenox applied to administer estate. |
| Lerche | William, MD | KC, p1c6, 3/8/1900 | Advertised his medical practice. Based in Soldiers Grove. |
| LeRoque | Joe | KC, p8c1, 4/13/1899 | Resided in Prairie du Chien where he worked on the pontoon bridge. He found 3 valuable pearls in clams left on the ice by clam diggers. Sold them for $150 and a gold watch. |
| LeRoque | Mary | KC, p8c3, 11/23/1899 | Died Nov. 17, 1899 in Chicago. Buried in Catholic Cemetery in Prairie du Chien. |
| Lesard | John | KC, p1c2, 1/7/1897 | Fined $10 in Prairie du Chien in an assault and battery case against George White. |
| Lessard | John | KC, Supp, 12/29/1898 | Received aid from the Crawford County Soldiers Relief Commission. Resided in Prairie du Chien. |
| Lester | Charles | KC, p5c4, 3/2/1899 | Died Dec. 26, 1898 at Hot Springs, SD. Aged 78 years. Born in Oswego Co., NY. Married Esther Keeney in Oswego Co. She died in 1860. Their children were Mary, wife of John E. Cooley of Marietta, and Clayton of Howard, SD. Moved to Mt. Hope, Grant Co., WI in 1855 and later moved to Wauzeka. To South Dakota in 1898. Survived by second wife, the former Mrs. Lucy Baker, and their children: William O. of Wyoming and Elmer of Minnesota. A daughter, Ester, is deceased. Served in Civil War. |
| Lester | John | KC, p8c2, 4/20/1899 | Married Olive C. Gaylord of Rochelle, IL on Tuesday (April 18, 1899?) in Prairie du Chien. Groom from Red Wing, MN. |
| Lester | John | KC, p1c5, 2/9/1899 | Taught school in Eastman in 1899. E. E. Brindley, Crawford County Superintendent of Schools published a comprehensive list of all teachers in the county. |
| Lester | John | KC, Supp., 12/12/1901 | Attended a Teacher's Institute in Crawford County in 1901. Resided in Gays Mill. |
| Lester | L. G. | KC, p5c3, 1/12/1899 | Elected to be an officer for the Modern Woodman Association (MWA) in Gays Mills. |

Genealogical Gleanings From Early Newspapers for Residents In and Near
Crawford County, Wisconsin, 1897-1902

| LAST NAME | FIRST NAME | NEWSPAPER PAGE/COLUMN MONTH/DAY/YEAR | GENEALOGICAL DATA |
|---|---|---|---|
| Lester | O. A., Miss | KC, p1c4, 5/15/1902 | Resided in Boydtown. Her leg was amputated. |
| Lester | Orin | KC, p5c3, 1/17/1901 | Town Treasurer in Mt. Sterling. Collected taxes. |
| Lester | Orrin | KC, p5c5, 4/5/1900 | Elected treasurer in Town of Utica. |
| Lewig | August, Mr. and Mrs. | KC, p1c4, 2/21/1898 | The Lewigs and Mrs. Anna Supke (nee Lewig), who reside in Iowa, attended last weeks' Williams-Lewig wedding. |
| Lewig | Bertha | KC, p1c5, 2/17/1898 | Married Henry Williams on Feb. 16, 1898 at the Lutheran Church in Wauzeka. Bride was daughter of John Lewig. |
| Lewig | Carl | KC, p1c3, 6/8/1899 | Lived near Boydtown. Large barn on his farm destroyed by high winds. |
| Lewig | John | KC, p1c4, 8/23/1900 | Sold his saloon in Wauzeka to William Stuckey. |
| Lewig | John | KC, p1c2, 8/30/1900 | Lewig and family departed in a surrey for Hawkeye, IA to visit Mrs. Lewig's parents. John planned to continue west for health benefits. |
| Lewig | John | KC, p5c2, 2/18/1897 | Left Wauzeka with family for new home in Iowa. |
| Lewig | John and wife | KC, p1c4, 5/24/1900 | Returned to Wauzeka after attending wedding of Mrs. Lewig's brother, William Hochberger, in Hawkeye, IA on May 17, 1900. |
| Lewig | William | KC, p1c4, 10/13/1898 | Married Ida Young of Prairie du Chien on Oct. 13, 1898. Groom from Wauzeka. |
| Lewis | Emma A. | KC, p1c3, 3/16/1899 | Osteopathic physician. Offered free examinations and consultations. |
| Lewis | F. W. | KC, p1c5, 2/28/1901 | Ex-County Treasurer. Purchased a half interest in the Flouring Mills at Gays Mills from J. A. Haggerty. R. M. McAuley, recent manager at the mill, gave up possession to return to a farm in De Soto, Vernon Co. R. L. Currie to remain as miller. |
| Lewis | F. W. | KC, Supp. 10/27/1898 | Nominated by the Crawford County Republican Party for the office of county treasurer. He had two years of experience in the position. Born in Bell Center on Dec. 25, 1860. Served as township treasurer from 1885 to 1895. He was also chairman of Town of Clayton for two terms. (Picture, short bio. and character sketch provided.) |
| Lewis | F. W. | KC, p1c2, 4/10/1902 | Sold his interest in the flouring mill in Gays Mills to J. A. Haggerty. |
| Lewis | F. W. and F. J. | KC, p1c3, 6/5/1902 | Attended the Masonic Lodge in Boscobel. From Gays Mills. |
| Lewis | Fred W. | KC, p5c4, 12/18/1902 | Left Gays Mills. Went into insurance business in Prairie du Chien. |
| Lewis | girl | KC, p5c3, 5/10/1900 | Daughter born May 6, 1900 to F. W. Lewis of Gays Mills. |
| Lewis | J. W. | KC, p5c6, 3/8/1900 | Operated a hoop business in Belle Center. |

Genealogical Gleanings From Early Newspapers for Residents In and Near
Crawford County, Wisconsin, 1897-1902

| LAST NAME | FIRST NAME | NEWSPAPER PAGE/COLUMN MONTH/DAY/YEAR | GENEALOGICAL DATA |
|---|---|---|---|
| Lewis | John | KC, p1c6, 11/4/1897 | Issue of fact for court to be heard at the November term of the Circuit Court in Crawford County. John Lewis vs. Ralph Copper. |
| Lewis | John, Mrs. | KC, p1c2, 11/6/1902 | Died Tuesday at home of son-in-law, Dietrick Vocht in Steuben area. Aged 77 years. Funeral held at Lutheran Church. |
| Lewis | Maude | KC, p5c1, 4/1/1897 | Maude Lewis of Bell Center married I. W. Schultz of Prairie du Chien on Mar. 25, 1897. (Announcement retracted KC, p5c2, 4/8/1897. Called a "joke.") |
| Lewis | Pognant | KC, Supp, 12/29/1898 | Crawford Co. Board of Supervisors approved Justices and Constables' expenses related to the case, State vs. Pognant Lewis. Roscoe Mitchell was the witness. |
| Lewison | L. O. | KC, p1c6, 4/7/1898 | Elected Chairman for the Town of Freeman. |
| Liddey | Timothy | KC, p8c1, 1/26/1899 | Died last Thursday (Jan. 19, 1899) while returning to his home in Waukon Junction, IA from Prairie du Chien. His team became unmanageable and he was thrown from his wagon. Found by his family, but died about three minutes after. He was married and had recently fallen heir to a large estate. |
| Lilly | Cyrus | KC, p5c4, 5/15/1902 | Resided in Mt. Sterling. Visited brother in Trempleau, WI. |
| Lilly | Cyrus | KC, p1c4, 10/28/1897 | Resided in Mt. Sterling. Received visit from brother, George of Iowa. They had not seen each other for 20 years. |
| Lilly | Foster | KC, p5c5, 11/28/1901 | Recently died. He was son of Cyrus Lilly |
| Lilly | Foster | KC, p5c3, 11/21/1901 | Died Monday at home in Mt. Sterling. Treated at St. Francis Hospital in La Crosse. Condition did not improve, so parents brought child home. |
| Linclemm | Lita | KC, p1c4, 5/1/1902 | Married Dexter M. Haskell on April 30, 1902. Bride from Wauzeka. Groom from (Fisktava?), IL. |
| Lindemann | Regina | KC, p8c1, 11/4/1897 | Wedding scheduled for Nov. 7, 1897. Planned to marry Dr. W. M. Trowbridge. Bride from Viroqua. |
| Linder | Ally | KC, p8c3, 9/8/1898 | Aged 15 years. Son of Marshall Charles Linder of Prairie du Chien. Ran away from home. He was 5' 5" tall, weighed 112 lbs., had a light complexion with light hair. Took his clothes, flute and money. This was unexpected. "He no doubt started out in the world to make his way, but his parents would be pleased to know his where-abouts." Per KC, p8c1, 9/22/1898, Linder returned home after visiting relatives in St. Paul. |
| Linder | Edward | KC, p8c4, 6/5/1902 | Married Mollie McCale on June 2, 1902 at St. Gabriel's Catholic Church in Prairie du Chien. |
| Linder | John | KC, p4c2, 4/29/1897 | Married Mary Clumfor on April 26, 1897. Bride and groom were from the Town of Eastman. |
| Lindig | Julius, Mrs. | KC, p1c3, 8/3/1899 | Arrived from home in Madison to visit mother, Mrs. F. Gink of Wauzeka. |
| Lindig | Martha, Mrs. | KC, p1c3, 8/23/1900 | Came from Madison to attend the funeral of her niece, Martha Reiger of Wauzeka. |

Genealogical Gleanings From Early Newspapers for Residents In and Near Crawford County, Wisconsin, 1897-1902

| LAST NAME | FIRST NAME | NEWSPAPER PAGE/COLUMN MONTH/DAY/YEAR | GENEALOGICAL DATA |
|---|---|---|---|
| Lindig | Mina | KC, p1c3, 2/18/1897 | Married Alpha Barrette on Feb. 17, 1897. Bride and groom from Prairie du Chien. |
| Lindmer | Cora | KC, p8c3, 11/14/1901 | Married Cliff Barr on Nov. 13, 1901. Bride may be from Prairie du Chien. The Rev. Arthur Pratt officiated. |
| Lindner | Charles | KC, p5c5, 4/5/1900 | Elected marshall in City of Prairie du Chien. |
| Lindstrom | boy | KC, p1c6, 3/4/1897 | Son of Mr. and Mrs. Lindstrom died Feb. 24, 1897 in Ferryville. Aged 3 months and 13 days. Buried in West Prairie Cem. |
| Lindstrom | girl | KC, p5c3, 12/14/1899 | Daughter recently born to T. G. Lindstrom of Mt. Sterling. |
| Linstrom | T. G. | KC, p1c3, 5/29/1902 | Died May 28, 1902 in Mt. Sterling. |
| Litze | Henry | KC, p1c1, 1/28/1897 | Died last Saturday in a blizzard north of Prairie du Chien. |
| Livingston | Arthur, Mr. and Mrs. | KC, p1c2, 2/2/1899 | Died Jan. 26, 1899 and Jan. 28, 1899 in Peoria, IL. Grandparents of Mrs. G. H. Perrin of Wauzeka. |
| Livingston | Minnie | KC, p1c2, 6/12/1902 | Resided in Wauzeka. Suffered with malaria. |
| Lock | Fletcher | KC, p5c3, 10/5/1899 | Married Mary Beaumont on Oct. 1, 1899. (Bride may be from Steuben.) |
| Lockart | Martha | KC, p8c2, 8/3/1899 | Recently buried in Prairie du Chien. |
| Lockart | Martha W. | KC, P8c2, 8/3/1899 | Recently died in Englewood, IL (suburban Chicago). Born 1855 in Prairie du Chien. Moved to Englewood with parents in 1889. Survived by brother, Dr. E. P. Lockart of Norway, MI, and sister, Mrs. B. F. Foy of Prairie du Chien. |
| Lockert | E. P., Mrs. | KC, p1c4, 4/1/1897 | Died a few days ago in Chicago. Former resident of Prairie du Chien. Buried in Lowertown Cemetery near her late husband. |
| Loftus | Martin | KC, Supp, 12/20/1900 | Represented De Soto on the Crawford Co. Board of Supervisors in 1900. |
| Logan | Charles | KC, Supp, 12/20/1900 | Crawford Co. Board of Supervisors approved payment of expenses in the matter of State vs. Charles Logan. |
| Logan | Edith | KC, p5c1, 4/8/1897 | Married Benjamin H. Bunnell on Mar. 27, 1897 at home of the groom. Bride and groom were from Marietta. J. P. McKinney, J. P. officiated. |
| Logan | Edith, Mrs. | KC, p5c1, 4/15/1897 | Married Benjamin H. Bunnell on Feb. 27. 1897. Bride and groom from Marietta. |
| Long | A. H. | KC, p4c4, 8/17/1899 | Married Pearl Dietrich on Aug. 17, 1899. Bride and groom from Prairie du Chien. |
| Long | Frank | KC, Supp, 12/20/1900 | Crawford Co. Board of Supervisors approved payment of expenses in the matter of State vs. Frank Long. |
| Long | John and wife | KC, p4c3, 6/24/1897 | Under care of son, Nick Long, have moved back to their farm in Ferryville area. |
| Long | John | KC, p4c1, 8/12/1897 | Resided in Ferryville. Suffered a stroke. Not expected to survive. |

Genealogical Gleanings From Early Newspapers for Residents In and Near
Crawford County, Wisconsin, 1897-1902

| LAST NAME | FIRST NAME | NEWSPAPER PAGE/COLUMN MONTH/DAY/YEAR | GENEALOGICAL DATA |
|---|---|---|---|
| Long | | KC, p1c6, 10/20/1898 | The Long and Lawrence sawmill at Petersburg destroyed by fire. Arson suspected. |
| Longstreth | Fay, Mrs. | KC, p5c3, 6/12/1902 | Resided in Ohio. Arrived in Bell Center to stay with her father, W. Shockley. Hoped to improve her health. |
| Longstreth | W. E., Dr. | KC, p1c5, 6/6/1901 | Married Fay Shockley on May 28, 1901. Bride daughter of Wilson Shockley of Bell Center and sister of Mrs. Neil Drake of same. Groom from Comley, OH. Planned to live in New York where groom will continue his medical training. |
| Loomis | A. A. | KC, p8c4, 9/30/1897 | At a conference of the Methodist Church held in Platteville, A. A. Loomis was assigned to Bloomington. |
| Loomis | D. | KC, p1c2, 11/2/1899 | Mr. D. Loomis and 2 little daughters traveled from South Dakota to Bell Center to visit relatives. |
| Loomis | Joe, Mrs. | KC, p8c3, 7/4/1901 | Died July 1, 1901 in Prairie du Chien. |
| Lortz | Fred | KC, p1c6, 4/21/1898 | Married Mrs. Waiters (Walters?) on Apr. 14, 1898. Bride and groom from Boscobel. |
| Lortz | Fred | KC, p1c3, 6/1/1899 | Died May 26, 1899 in Wauzeka. Age 62. |
| Louis | Pognant | KC, p4c4, 11/10/1898 | Criminal Issue to be heard in the November term of the Crawford County Circuit Court. State of Wisconsin vs. Pognant Louis. (See Lewis.) |
| Loveland | Mattie | KC, p8c3, 7/3/1902 | Recently married W. E. Burdick. Bride daughter of A. B. Loveland of Prairie du Chien. Groom from La Crosse. Planned to live in La Crosse. |
| Lowe | Annie Husted, Mrs. | KC, p1c5, 3/17/1898 | Died Feb. 18, 1898 in the Haney Valley. Born April 10, 1825 in Delaware Co., NY. Married John Lowe on Mar. 30, 1853. Moved to Wisconsin in 1865. Belonged to Methodist Church. Five of 6 children survive. One daughter deceased. |
| Lowe | Frank | KC, p8c3, 9/21/1899 | Died Sept. 7, 1899. Born May 8, 1896. Son of Frank and Annie Lowe of Gays Mills. |
| Lowe | Frank | KC, p5c3, 1/12/1899 | Elected to be an officer for the Modern Woodman Association (MWA) in Gays Mills. |
| Lowe | John | KC, p1c2, 4/17/1902 | Graduated from Haney Valley schools. |
| Lowe | John | KC, p4c4, 9/25/1902 | Lived in Petersburg. Advertised the sale of honey produced on his farm. |
| Lowe | Mrs. | KC, p5c2, 3/10/1898 | Funeral recently held at Barnum. |
| Lowe | W. H. | KC, p1c6, 4/7/1898 | Elected Supervisor for the Town of Haney. |
| Lowe | W. H., Mrs. | KC, p1c2, 6/9/1898 | Traveled from Haney Valley to Wauzeka to visit her sick sister, Mrs. Thomas Lawver. |
| Lowe | Willard | KC, p1c2, 4/17/1902 | Graduated from Haney Valley schools. |
| Lowe | Willie | KC, p1c5, 10/17/1901 | He was the youngest son of William H. Lowe of Petersburg. He was 15 years old and weighed 202 pounds. |

Genealogical Gleanings From Early Newspapers for Residents In and Near
Crawford County, Wisconsin, 1897-1902

| LAST NAME | FIRST NAME | NEWSPAPER PAGE/COLUMN MONTH/DAY/YEAR | GENEALOGICAL DATA |
|---|---|---|---|
| Lowe | | KC, p1c3, 9/14/1899 | Recently died in Gays Mills. He was 3 year old son of Frank Lowe. |
| Lubke | Dwarthy | KC, p5c4, 10/23/1902 | Probate Notice published. Late of Freeman. |
| Lubke | Dwarthy | KC, p5c4, 10/30/1902 | Notice to Creditors published by Probate Court in Crawford Co. for Dwarthy Lubke of the Town of Freeman. |
| Lubke | Henry, Mrs. | KC, p8c4, 2/20/1902 | Died Feb. 15, 1902 at home of daughter, Mrs. J. S. Steiner. Aged 76 years. Resided in Prairie du Chien. Funeral held at Lutheran Church. |
| Lucas | Mary | KC, p8c1, 11/18/1897 | Married Charles Nickel of Eastman on Nov. 15, 1897 at St. John's Bohemian Church. Bride from Prairie du Chien. Party held at Benish Hall |
| Lucy | boy | KC, p1c2, 7/13/1899 | Son born June 18, 1899 to William Lucy of Mt. Sterling. |
| Lucy | girl | KC, p1c5, 2/11/1897 | Daughter recently born to William Lucy of Seneca. |
| Lucy | P., Mr. and Mrs. | KC, p1c4, 8/2/1900 | Resided near Mt. Sterling. Entertained the family of their daughter, Mr. and Mrs. James Rogers of Chicago. Mr. Rogers was a ticket agent on the elevated railroad. |
| Ludden | S. D. | KC, p4c3, 12/19/1901 | Sold his general store in Boscobel to F. A. Chandler. Received Chandler's 310-acre farm, 4 and 1/2 miles NW of Steuben. Ludden may open a store in Eastman. |
| Ludewig | Anna, Mrs. | KC, p5c3, 3/8/1900 | Died Mar. 3, 1900 in Town of Eastman. She was wife of Albert Ludewig, a tinsmith. Aged 52 years. She was aunt of Mrs. George Volge. Buried in German Cemetery on Shanghi Ridge. |
| Ludoska | Frank | KC, p5c3, 3/2/1899 | Ludoska's house in Eastman destroyed by fire. |
| Ludwig | James | KC, p8c1, 5/25/1899 | Died May 23, 1899 in Prairie du Chien at age 14. |
| Ludwig | Josephine | KC, p1c4, 9/13/1900 | Married Dr. Harry Pier on Sept. 10, 1900. Bride daughter of Dr. and Mrs. Ludwig of Richland Co. Groom from Prairie du Chien. |
| Luetgert | | KC, p4c2, 11/4/1897 | "Mrs. Luetgert of Mt. Sterling may be getting revenge on her husband for his extremely courteous attentions to other ladies. Still no one wants Luetgert sentenced on circumstantial evidence." |
| Lumpkins | George W. | KC, p5c4, 6/8/1899 | Recently died. |
| Lurkins | William | KC, p8c4, 4/5/1900 | Died Mar. 30, 1900 in Wauzeka. Aged 70 years. Daughters lived in Richland Center. Buried in Milwaukee. |
| Lusky | Mrs. | KC, p4c1, 7/8/1897 | Traveled from Chicago to visit mother, Mrs. F. Zlabek of Eastman. |
| Lutz | Henry | KC, p1c2, 9/27/1900 | The court case, Henry Lutz vs. John Lutz was withdrawn and settled by arbitration. |
| Lynch | Abby | KC, Supp., 12/18/1902 | Crawford County Board of Supervisors allowed expenses in the Matter of Abby Lynch, Insane. |

Genealogical Gleanings From Early Newspapers for Residents In and Near
Crawford County, Wisconsin, 1897-1902

| LAST NAME | FIRST NAME | NEWSPAPER PAGE/COLUMN MONTH/DAY/YEAR | GENEALOGICAL DATA |
|---|---|---|---|
| Lynch | Catherine | KC, p5c3, 2/21/1901 | Married James F. Finley on Feb. 18, 1901. Bride was from Town of Seneca. Groom was from Boma. Bride was daughter of John Lynch and sister of Hannah Lynch. |
| Lynch | girl | KC, p5c3, 1/10/1901 | Daughter born Dec. 26, 1900 to John Lynch of Seneca. |
| Lynch | girl | KC, p5c3, 3/27/1902 | Daughter born Mar. 20, 1902 to John Lynch, Jr. of Seneca. |
| Lynch | John | KC, p5c4, 3/1/1900 | Married Agnes Bernier on Feb. 22, 1900. Bride and groom from Seneca. Bride's brother, Joe Bernier, runs a creamery in Iowa. |
| Lynch | Maggie | KC, p5c4, 2/15/1900 | Taught school in Seneca. |
| Lynch | Marguerite | KC, p5c4, 11/28/1901 | Taught at Halls Branch school. |
| Lynch | Marguerite | KC, Supp., 12/12/1901 | Attended a Teacher's Institute in Crawford County in 1901. Resided in Seneca. |
| Lynch | Thomas | KC, p5c5, 1/9/1902 | Died Jan. 1, 1902 at Sabula, IA. Lived many years in Seneca. Born in Ireland 73 years ago. Survived by children: John, Patrick, Richard Mrs. John Joy and Mrs. John Mahoney. |
| Lyness | Mrs. | KC, Supp., 6/6/1901 | Died in June 1901 in Prairie du Chien. Resided in Grant Co. She was sister of Mrs. Tiernay of Prairie du Chien. |
| Lyons | boy | KC, p1c2, 1/24/1901 | Son born Jan. 18, 1901 to D. Lyons of Wauzeka. Weighed 12 pounds. |
| Lyons | D. | KC, p1c2, 1/18/1900 | Advertised going out of business sale at his furniture store in Wauzeka. |
| Lyons | D. | KC, p1c5, 7/3/1902 | Marshall. Visited Darlington, WI, his boyhood home. |
| Lyons | D. | KC, p5c5, 4/5/1900 | Elected justice of the peace in Wauzeka. |
| Lyons | Daniel | KC, p1c4, 4/27/1899 | Recently married Hannah Ward of Glen Haven at Plymouth Congregational Church parsonage in Dodgeville. Groom from Wauzeka. Groom's parents lived in Darlington. |
| Lyons | Frank | KC, p5c3, 5/30/1901 | Departed with family from Lynxville for a new home in Manchester, MN. |
| Lyons | Frank | KC, p4c3, 6/16/1898 | Traveled from Stoddard to visit friends at Lynxville, his former home. |
| Lysne | Peter | KC, p5c5, 4/5/1900 | Elected assessor in Town of Freeman. |
| Lysue | Mrs. | KC, p5c3, 5/11/1899 | Died April 30, 1899. Resided on Copper Creek, Mt. Sterling. Aged 80 years. Survived by a daughter and 2 sons. Funeral held at the Lutheran Church. |
| Madden | M. H. | KC, p1c6, 3/10/1898 | Carried mail in Wheatville. |
| Maddox | F. M. | KC, p4c1, 1/7/1897 | Advertised sale of honey barrels. Resided in Barnum. |

Genealogical Gleanings From Early Newspapers for Residents In and Near
Crawford County, Wisconsin, 1897-1902

| LAST NAME | FIRST NAME | NEWSPAPER PAGE/COLUMN MONTH/DAY/YEAR | GENEALOGICAL DATA |
|---|---|---|---|
| Maddox | Warren | KC, Supp, 12/29/1898 | Crawford Co. Board of Supervisors approved Justices and Constables' expenses related to the case, State vs. Warren Maddox. The witnesses were Tom Welch, John Welch, Frank Welch, James Kelly, William Welch, Earl Rounds, W. J. Maddox and Cullon Kast. |
| Magee | J. N. | KC, Supp, 12/29/1898 | Received aid from the Crawford County Soldiers Relief Commission. Resided in Bridgeport. |
| Magie | J. M. | KC, Supp, 12/20/1900 | Crawford Co. Soldiers Relief Comm. approved aid to J. M. Magie of Bridgeport. |
| Maha | Frank | KC, p1c3, 12/2/1897 | Arrived from California to visit relatives and friends in Wauzeka. |
| Mahan | Jennie | KC, p1c5, 2/9/1899 | Taught school in Freeman in 1899. E. E. Brindley, Crawford County Superintendent of Schools published a comprehensive list of all teachers in the county. |
| Mahan | Margaret | KC, Supp., 12/12/1901 | Attended a Teacher's Institute in Crawford County in 1901. Resided in Rising Sun. |
| Mahan | William | KC, p1c3, 5/9/1901 | Married Mary Burns on May 6, 1901. Bride daughter of Mrs. M. A. Burns of Rising Sun and sister of Rose Burns of Wauzeka. Groom son of William Mahan deceased. |
| Maher | John | KC, p5c3, 5/20/1897 | Issues of fact for court to be heard in the May term of the Crawford County Court. John Maher, respondent vs. George E. Harrington, petitioner. |
| Maher | John | KC, p1c6, 11/4/1897 | Issue of fact for jury to be heard at the November term of the Circuit Court in Crawford County. John Maher vs. George E. Harrington. |
| Maher | John | KC, Supp, 12/20/1900 | Crawford Co. Board of Supervisors approved payment of expenses in the matter of State vs. John Maher. |
| Mahoney | Thomas | KC, Supp, 12/20/1900 | Crawford Co. Board of Supervisors approved payment of expenses in the matter of State vs. Thomas Mahoney. |
| Main | C. V. | KC, p1c4, 4/12/1900 | Kicked in the face by a horse at his home in Town of Marietta. Crushed his cheekbone. |
| Mallard | Frank | KC, Supp., 12/12/1901 | State vs. Frank Mallard heard in Crawford Co. Court. |
| Mallory | James | KC, Supp., 12/12/1901 | State vs. James Mallory heard in Crawford Co. Court. John Garrity made final returns. |
| Malone | James, Jr. | KC, p1c3, 10/5/1899 | Returned to Soldiers Grove after spending the last 6 months working in Spring Valley, MN. |
| Malone | John S. | KC, p1c6, 5/19/1898 | Issue of Fact for Jury to be heard in the May term of the Crawford County Circuit Court. Hammond V. Hayes, et al vs. John S. Malone. |
| Malone | M. | KC, p1c6, 4/7/1898 | Elected Treasurer for the Town of Clayton. |
| Malone | M. | KC, p5c5, 4/5/1900 | Elected treasurer in Town of Clayton. |
| Malone | M. | KC, p5c3, 2/15/1900 | Served as tax collector. |

Genealogical Gleanings From Early Newspapers for Residents In and Near
Crawford County, Wisconsin, 1897-1902

| LAST NAME | FIRST NAME | NEWSPAPER PAGE/COLUMN MONTH/DAY/YEAR | GENEALOGICAL DATA |
|---|---|---|---|
| Malone | M. | KC, p1c2, 10/23/1902 | Democratic candidate for sheriff in Crawford Co. Born at Monroe, Green Co., WI on May 23, 1857. Came to Town of Clayton with parents in 1858. Served on the Town Board of Supervisors 3 times. Lost John Stackland in 1894 when he ran for sheriff. Presently serves as Town Treasurer. Portrait published. |
| Malone | Manie | KC, p1c5, 2/9/1899 | Taught school in the Town of Clayton in 1899. E. E. Brindley, Crawford County Superintendent of Schools published a comprehensive list of all teachers in the county. |
| Malone | Mary | KC, p8c4, 3/7/1901 | Died Feb. 25, 1901 in Town of Clayton. Aged 26 years. Buried in St. Phillips Cemetery. |
| Malone | Mary J. | KC, p5c3, 5/4/1899 | Married Victor Fransche on April 25, 1899 at St. Phillip's Catholic Church. Bride and groom from Town of Scott. |
| Malone | Mary J. | KC, p8c3, 7/28/1898 | Arrived from Chicago to visit parents, Mr. and Mrs. M. Malone of Wheatville. |
| Maney | Ambrose | KC, p1c2, 3/1/1900 | Died Feb. 19, 1900. He was son of P. Maney of Town of Seneca. Aged 2 months and 12 days. |
| Maney | boy | KC, p5c3, 12/14/1899 | Son born Thursday to Pat Maney of Seneca. |
| Maney | Cornelius | KC, p4c5, 2/28/1901 | Died Feb. 25, 1901. Born Jan. 21, 1901 to P. Maney. |
| Maney | Cornelius | KC, p4c5, 2/28/1901 | Died Feb. 25, 1901 in Seneca. He was an infant son of P. Maney. |
| Maney | Deilia, Mrs. | KC, p5c3, 7/10/1902 | Mrs. Delia Maney and her nephews (Johnnie, Neal and Donald Kane) of Seneca visited Grandma Lewison in Eastman. |
| Maney | J. F. | KC, p4c2, 7/3/1902 | Bought J. A. Dworak's general store in Eastman. Maney was brother of P. T. Maney of Seneca and J. R. Maney of Lynxville. Worked for a streetcar company in Chicago for the last 16 years. Mr. Dworak planned to go into the wholesale grocery business in Chicago. |
| Maney | James | KC, p1c6, 3/4/1897 | Married Delia Flannagan on Mar. 1, 1897. Bride and groom may be from Town of Seneca. |
| Maney | James | KC, p8c4, 4/8/1897 | Took charge of the hotel in Lynxville. |
| Maney | James | KC, p1c2, 8/3/1899 | Resided in Lynxville. Operated on in La Crosse for an inflamed appendix. Recovering well. |
| Maney | Mary Ann | KC, p5c3, 1/16/1902 | Nee Meagher. Died Jan. 1, 1902 at home of son, Patrick. Born Feb. 2, 1838 in Parish of Lochmore, County Tipperary, Ireland. Moved with parents to Blackstone, Worchester Co., MA in 1850. Married Thomas Maney in 1860. Moved to Seneca, Crawford Co. in 1863. Husband died 1867. Survived by 3 sons, 1 sister (Mrs. M. Lenehan of Town of Eastman) and 3 brothers (James and William Meagher of Seneca and Thomas Meagher of Minneapolis). |
| Maney | Mary, Mrs. | KC, p5c3, 1/9/1902 | Died at home of son, P. J. Maney, on Jan. 1, 1902 in Town of (Seneca?). |
| Maney | P. J. | KC, p1c6, 4/7/1898 | Elected Assessor for the Town of Seneca. |

Genealogical Gleanings From Early Newspapers for Residents In and Near
Crawford County, Wisconsin, 1897-1902

| LAST NAME | FIRST NAME | NEWSPAPER PAGE/COLUMN MONTH/DAY/YEAR | GENEALOGICAL DATA |
|---|---|---|---|
| Maney | P. T. | KC, p5c5, 4/5/1900 | Elected assessor in Seneca. |
| Maney | twins | KC, p5c4, 1/24/1901 | Twins (1 boy and 1 girl) born on January 21, 1901 to Pat Maney of Seneca. |
| Manning | W. S. | KC, p1c2, 4/19/1900 | Went to Chippewa Co., WI to explore opportunities to invest in land. |
| Manning | Frank | KC, p1c5, 6/9/1898 | Mrs. M. C. Kincannon petitioned the Wauzeka Village Board to have Frank Manning put on the black list. |
| Manning | W. S. | KC, p5c4, 5/17/1900 | Applied for a charter to establish a national bank at Warner, Chippewa Co. (Warner was renamed Ladysmith.) |
| Manning | W. S. | KC, p1c2, 4/6/1899 | Appointed to be a land agent for the Northwestern Railway. |
| Manning | W. S. | KC, p1c6, 5/19/1898 | Issue of Law for Court to be heard in the May term of the Crawford County Circuit Court. W. S. Manning vs. A. B. Purrington. |
| Mansfield | Metta | KC, p8c3, 4/8/1897 | Married Guy Sampson of Gays Mills on April 4, 1897. Bride from Lynxville. J. L. Stowell, Justice of the Peace, officiated. |
| Mansfield | Jason | KC, Supp., 12/18/1902 | Crawford County Board of Supervisors allowed expenses in the Matter of Jason Mansfield, Blind. |
| Mansfield | Mrs. | KC, p1c6, 9/1/1898 | Resided in Lynxville. Visited daughter, Mrs. G. E. Sampson of Gays Mills. |
| Mansfield | Welhametta | KC, p5c3, 5/20/1897 | Issues of fact for jury to be heard in the May term of the Crawford County Court. Estella Vanderbilt and Welhametta Mansfield her guardian vs. G. Newton. |
| Mansfield | Emma, Miss | KC, p5c4, 12/29/1898 | Returned to home in Lynxville. Spent summer with sister, Mrs. G. D. Sampson of Gays Mills. |
| Mara | girl | KC, p1c5, 5/13/1897 | Four-year-old daughter of John Mara of Prairie du Chien recently died of typhoid fever. |
| Mara | Mary | KC, p8c3, 10/25/1900 | Married Charles Konecheck on Oct. 22, 1900. Bride and groom from Prairie du Chien. Bride daughter of Frank Mara. |
| Mara | Mike | KC, p1c5, 5/18/1899 | Wrote a letter from Woodhull, ND regarding conditions in North Dakota. It was published in the *Kickapoo Chief*. |
| Marfelius | Gus | KC, p1c4, 5/2/1901 | He held a large auction sale at his farm near Wauzeka. |
| Marfelius | Gus | KC, p1c4, 5/9/1901 | Planned to run a hotel in Boscobel. |
| Marfilius | Charles | KC, p1c3, 9/29/1898 | Marfilius and his son, William traveled from Farmersburg, IA to visit relatives in Wauzeka. |
| Marfilius | Grandma | KC, p1c5, 11/22/1900 | Returned to Wauzeka after a 6-month visit with her son, Charles of Farmersburg, IA. |
| Marfilius | Louis | KC, p1c5, 8/23/1900 | Resided in Wauzeka area. Published notice to dog owners that he will kill any dogs running at large on his property. Dogs have been killing his sheep. Six sheep lost last week. |
| Marfilius | | KC, p1c3, 10/7/1897 | Infant child of Gus Marfilius died Sept. 28, 1897 in Wauzeka. Funeral held at Evangelical Church. Buried in Wauzeka Cem. |

Genealogical Gleanings From Early Newspapers for Residents In and Near
Crawford County, Wisconsin, 1897-1902

| LAST NAME | FIRST NAME | NEWSPAPER PAGE/COLUMN MONTH/DAY/YEAR | GENEALOGICAL DATA |
|---|---|---|---|
| Marfillius | Lou | KC, p5c5, 4/5/1900 | Elected supervisor in Town of Wauzeka. |
| Marker | William | KC, p8c4, 2/8/1900 | Died Jan. 25, 1900 from a stabbing by Will McDonald that took place last September in Springville. |
| Markham | | KC, Supp., 12/19/1901 | Markham and Foster built the first steam sawmill in Wauzeka in 1858. |
| Marsten | Lotta | KC, p4c1, 9/29/1898 | Married Nathan Bourne of Freeman on Sept. 21, 1898. Bride from Gays Mills. Planned to live at West Prairie. |
| Marston | Archie | KC, p5c3, 5/10/1900 | Departed home in Gays Mills for a position with the Census Department in Washington, D. C. |
| Marston | Archie | KC, p1c5, 2/9/1899 | Taught school in the Town of Clayton in 1899. E. E. Brindley, Crawford County Superintendent of Schools published a comprehensive list of all teachers in the county. |
| Marston | girl | KC, p5c3, 2/23/1899 | Daughter recently born to W. R. Marston of Seneca. |
| Marston | Linda | KC, p5c3, 7/19/1900 | Hired to teach school in Gays Mills. From Gays Mills. |
| Marston | Percy, Mrs. | KC, p1c3 12/4/1902 | Resided in Gays Mills. Visited parents in Chicago. |
| Martel | Peter | KC, p8c5, 6/5/1902 | Recently died. Resided in Harpers Ferry. Drowned at age 13 years. He was son of Mrs. Martel and grandson of Charles Valley of Prairie du Chien. |
| Martell | Emma | KC, p8c3, 9/11/1902 | Married John Ducharme on Sept. 8, 1902 at St. Gabriel's Catholic Church in Prairie du Chien. Bride from Harper's Ferry, IA. Groom from Prairie du Chien. |
| Martilius | Mrs. | KC, p1c3, 9/23/1897 | Sold her property to the Evangelical Church in Wauzeka. She was allowed to remain in her home as long as she wished. |
| Martin | Arthur, Mrs. | KC, p5c3, 5/23/1901 | Arrived from Dakota to visit her mother, Mrs. Lewison of Eastman. |
| Martin | August, Mrs. | KC, p1c4, 2/4/1897 | Resided in pension. She will receive a pension. |
| Martin | boy | KC, p5c5, 1/10/1901 | Son born Jan. 4, 1901 to Will Martin of Eastman. |
| Martin | boy | KC, p4c1, 3/31/1898 | Son born Mar. 26, 1898 to Will Martin, a blacksmith in Eastman. |
| Martin | Eve | KC, p8c4, 11/16/1899 | Received marriage license in Crawford Co. to marry David Davenport. Bride and groom from Town of Clayton. |
| Martin | George | KC, p8c4, 11/13/1902 | In the November term of Crawford County Circuit Court, State vs. George Martin, case was discharged. |
| Martin | George | KC, Supp., 12/18/1902 | Crawford County Board of Supervisors examined bills in the Justices and Constables' Account for State vs. George Martin. Charles Garner, Atley Peterson, E. E. Rogers, John Lowery, Henry Buckmaster, Mr. Dodge and Delbert Martin were witnesses. |
| Martin | girl | KC, p5c2, 10/7/1897 | Daughter born Sept. 18, 1897 to Herman Martin of Steuben. |

Genealogical Gleanings From Early Newspapers for Residents In and Near
Crawford County, Wisconsin, 1897-1902

| LAST NAME | FIRST NAME | NEWSPAPER PAGE/COLUMN MONTH/DAY/YEAR | GENEALOGICAL DATA |
|---|---|---|---|
| Martin | Hannah | KC, p1c6, 3/23/1899 | Notice of Hearing published. Hannah Martin applied to be named guardian of the person and estate of Catherine Swatek, an incompetent person of the Town of Eastman. |
| Martin | Herman, Mrs. | KC, p1c4, 9/18/1902 | Funeral held Sept. 12, 1902. Lived near Patch Grove, Grant Co. She was the sister of Mrs. John Smethurst of Mt. Sterling and Mart and Dave Mullikin of Petersburg. |
| Martin | J. | KC, p1c4, 11/1/1900 | Arrived from Washington to visit sister, Mrs. G. Posey of Steuben. |
| Martin | J. C. | KC, p5c4, 8/9/1900 | Departed for home in Washington after visiting relatives and friends in Steuben. |
| Martin | James | KC, p8c3, 1/19/1899 | Died Jan. 9, 1899 at age 72 in Steuben. Born and raised in Virginia. Came to Wisconsin 43 years ago. Survived by wife and 5 children. Buried in Mt. Zion Cemetery near his brother, John, who died 4 years ago. |
| Martin | James | KC, p4c5, 11/22/1900 | Administrator's Sale notice published. Roxena Martin was the administratrix. |
| Martin | Roxena | KC, p5c4, 10/11/1900 | Applied to Probate Court in Crawford County to administer estate of James Martin, late of Marietta. |
| Martin | Roxena | KC, p4c3, 3/2/1899 | Probate Court in Crawford County published a Notice of Hearing. Roxena Martin applied to administer the estate of James Martin, late of the Town of Marietta. |
| Martin | Urias | KC, p5c3, 5/20/1897 | Criminal case to be heard in the May term of the Crawford County Court, State of Wisconsin vs. Urias Martin. |
| Martin | Urias | KC, p1c6, 11/4/1897 | Criminal issue to be heard at the November term of the Circuit Court in Crawford County. State of Wisconsin vs. Urias Martin, abusive language. |
| Martin | Urias | KC, Supp, 12/29/1898 | Crawford Co. Board of Supervisors approved Justices and Constables' expenses related to the case, State vs. Urias Martin. The witnesses were Richard Henthorn, Chester Clason and William Clason. |
| Martin | Urias | KC, p1c6, 5/19/1898 | Criminal case to be heard in the May term of the Crawford County Circuit Court. State of Wisconsin vs. Urias Martin. |
| Martin | Urias | KC, p1c6, 5/19/1898 | Issue of Fact for Jury to be heard in the May term of the Crawford County Circuit Court. A. H. Krouskup vs. Urias Martin. |
| Martin | William | KC, p4c2, 5/19/1898 | From Eastman. Visited very ill sister, Mrs. W. Thomas of Prairie du Chien. |
| Martner | Nettie W. | KC, p8c4, 6/21/1900 | Valedictorian at Wauzeka High School Class of 1900. |
| Martsalf | John, Mrs. | KC, p5c3, 8/9/1900 | Nee Fannie Sterling. Mrs. Martsalf and her daughter, Lenine, arrived from Missouri to visit relatives in Mt. Sterling. |
| Martsoff | Mrs. | KC, p5c3, 11/28/1901 | Moved into the Lindstrom resident in Mt. Sterling. Two daughters came from Joplin, MO to visit her. Planned to bring her father, William T. Sterling, to live with her there when permitted by health and weather. |
| Marush | Mrs. | KC, p5c3, 12/7/1899 | Recently died in Prairie du Chien. She was the mother of Mrs. A. Prochaska of Eastman. |

Genealogical Gleanings From Early Newspapers for Residents In and Near Crawford County, Wisconsin, 1897-1902

| LAST NAME | FIRST NAME | NEWSPAPER PAGE/COLUMN MONTH/DAY/YEAR | GENEALOGICAL DATA |
|---|---|---|---|
| Marvin | A., Mrs. | KC, p1c5, 7/15/1897 | Visited mother, Mrs. Benhardt of Eastman. |
| Marvin | Frank | KC, p1c2, 3/4/1897 | Arrived from Sioux Falls, SD to visit friends and relatives in Prairie du Chien. |
| Marvin | Gertrude | KC, p1c5, 2/9/1899 | Taught school in Prairie du Chien in 1899. E. E. Brindley, Crawford County Superintendent of Schools published a comprehensive list of all teachers in the county. |
| Marvin | Henry | KC, Supp., 10/6/1898 | Died of typhoid fever on Aug. 12, 1898 while serving in 5th U.S. Calvary at Tampa, FL. Remains may be brought back to Prairie du Chien. Mrs. Marvin wrote to Mrs. William McKinley, wife of the President, asking for body to be returned. Son of the late Henry Marvin. |
| Marvin | Henry E. | KC, p8c1, 8/25/1898 | Died Aug. 11, 1898 in West Tampa, FL from typhoid in a military camp. He was oldest son of Mrs. L. Marvin of Prairie du Chien. |
| Marvin | Katherine, Mrs. | KC, p8c2, 7/14/1898 | Died July 9, 1898 in Prairie du Chien at age of 83. Mother of John Marvin. Funeral held at St. John's Bohemian Catholic Church. |
| Marvin | Norman | KC, p5c3, 8/12/1897 | Resided in Union Center. Shot by Henry Wendel during a quarrel over cutting down a bee tree. Wendel had a wife and 7 children. In jail and waiting for a trial. |
| Mason | George | KC, Supp, 12/20/1900 | Crawford Co. Board of Supervisors approved payment of expenses in the matter of State vs. George Mason. |
| Mason | James | KC, p1c3, 3/10/1898 | Married Mrs. Delia Banta of Scott on Feb. 23, 1898. Groom from Steuben. The Rev. N. C. Bradley of Excelsior officiated. |
| Mason | James | KC, p5c1, 4/22/1897 | Now lives in Countney, ND. Former resident of Steuben. |
| Mason | James | KC, p1c3, 11/25/1897 | Returned to Steuben after spending the last year in North Dakota. |
| Mason | James | KC, p1c2, 12/8/1898 | Left home in Hurlbut to spend the winter at his former home in England. He was accompanied by a friend, Robert Walker of Courtney, ND. Walker was also a native of England. |
| Mason | Mr. | KC, p5c3, 3/2/1899 | Formerly from Steuben. Returned from a business trip to England. Stayed with Jehiel Day in Scott. |
| Masten | M. D. | KC, p5c6, 3/8/1900 | Operated a business in Belle Center where he had a fine stock of up-to-date goods. |
| Masten | M. D., Mrs. | KC, p5c3, 7/3/1902 | Mrs. Masten and her daughters, Lois, Mabel and Gladys (of Bell Center) went to North Dakota to spend the summer with Mrs. Masten's mother, Mrs. O. P. Rounds. |
| Masten | Mat | KC, p1c3, 6/5/1902 | Attended the Masonic Lodge in Boscobel. From Bell Center. |
| Mataka | Francis | KC, p8c3, 2/13/1902 | Married Allen Smith on Feb. 10, 1902 at Prairie du Chien. The Rev. Fr. Kiefner officiated. |
| Mataka | John | KC, p8c3, 11/2/1899 | Pulled out a 100-year-old flintlock rifle from the Wisconsin River while dragging for clams. It was 6 feet long and cocked to discharge. Per Prairie du Chien news items. |

Genealogical Gleanings From Early Newspapers for Residents In and Near
Crawford County, Wisconsin, 1897-1902

| LAST NAME | FIRST NAME | NEWSPAPER PAGE/COLUMN MONTH/DAY/YEAR | GENEALOGICAL DATA |
|---|---|---|---|
| Mather | P. S. | KC, p8c4, 9/30/1897 | At a conference of the Methodist Church held in Platteville, P. S. Mather was assigned to Monfort. |
| Mather | P. S. | KC, p1c4, 9/29/1898 | At a conference of the Methodist Church held in Eau Claire, P. S. Mather was assigned to the Dodgeville Circuit. |
| Mathews | C. A., Mrs. | KC, p1c4, 4/26/1900 | Proprietor of a general store in Bridgeport. |
| Mathews | Dick | KC, p8c4, 12/26/1901 | Resided in Prairie du Chien. Shot in the neck while fleeing arrest for being disorderly. Bullet removed. |
| Mathews | Ed | KC, p5c3, 2/21/1901 | Resided in Eastman. Sold a 500-acre farm near Steuben to Ed Crowley for $5000. |
| Mathews | Harry | KC, Supp., 12/18/1902 | Crawford County Board of Supervisors examined bills in the Justices and Constables' Account for State vs. Harry Mathews. |
| Mathews | J. E. | KC, p1c5, 8/4/1898 | Opened a saloon and poolroom in Steuben. |
| Mathews | James | KC, p5c3, 9/21/1899 | James Mathews and his son, Guy were badly injured in a horse runaway accident. Resided in Steuben. |
| Mathews | Blanch | KC, p5c2, 7/7/1898 | Recently died. (Part of obituary torn. Deceased may be from Lynxville.) |
| Mathews | Rose | KC, p1c2, 10/6/1898 | Married William H. Kramer of Lancaster on Sept. 22, 1898 at the M.E. parsonage in Boscobel. Daughter of John Mathews of Marietta. |
| Mattick | Rebecca | KC, Supp., 12/18/1902 | Crawford County Soldiers Relief Committee provided funds to Rebecca Mattick of Lynxville. |
| Mattie | S. E., Mrs. | KC, p5c3, 10/9/1902 | Lived in Eastman. Departed for Spokane, WA. Husband will join her as soon as stock and farm is sold. |
| Mattie | Emanuel | KC, p8c4, 1/14/1897 | Resided in Eastman. May go to California. |
| Mattie | Fred | KC, p5c3, 5/20/1897 | Issues of fact for jury to be heard in the May term of the Crawford County Court. J. F. Pier, respondent and plaintiff vs. Samuel Mattie and Fred Mattie, appellants and defendants. |
| Mattie | Samuel | KC, p5c3, 5/20/1897 | Issues of fact for jury to be heard in the May term of the Crawford County Court. J. F. Pier, respondent and plaintiff vs. Samuel Mattie and Fred Mattie, appellants and defendants. |
| Maxwell | Katie | KC, p1c3, 10/17/1901 | Recently married Thomas McCann at Devils Lake, ND. Bride, daughter of John Maxwell from Plum Creek. Groom son of James McCann, from Wauzeka. Planned to live in Velva, ND. |
| Maxwell | P. | KC, p1c3, 11/11/1897 | Married Lizzie Smith on Nov. 8, 1897 at Sacred Heart Church. |
| Mayhew | E. A. | KC, p1c5, 3/24/1898 | From Mt. Hope. Rented a farm near Boydtown for the coming year. |
| Maynard | Golda | KC, p4c2, 1/28/1897 | Married Sperry George on Jan 22, 1897. Bride and groom from Gays Mills. Justice Stowell officiated. |
| Maynard | Joe | KC, p5c4, 8/15/1901 | Harvested "one of the best tobacco crops in western Wisconsin" on his farm in Gays Mills. |

Genealogical Gleanings From Early Newspapers for Residents In and Near
Crawford County, Wisconsin, 1897-1902

| LAST NAME | FIRST NAME | NEWSPAPER PAGE/COLUMN MONTH/DAY/YEAR | GENEALOGICAL DATA |
|---|---|---|---|
| Mayock | Patrick, Mrs. | KC, p8c3, 3/6/1902 | Died Mar. 3, 1902 in St. Paul. Former resident of Prairie du Chien where she was buried. |
| Mazera | Mamie | KC, p8c3, 4/14/1898 | Married L. Dohse on Apr. 12, 1898 at St. John Bohemian Catholic Church. Bride and groom from Prairie du Chien. |
| McAuley | A. D. | KC, p1c5, 3/24/1898 | Resided in Mt. Sterling. Purchased the old homestead from other heirs. Planned to make it into a stock farm. |
| McAuley | Auley | KC, p5c5, 8/9/1900 | Advertised services as a real estate agent. Resided in Mt. Sterling. |
| McAuley | Jane, Mrs. | KC, p1c5, 8/16/1900 | Died Aug. 11, 1900. Born 1816 in Kentucky. Nee McGee. Married William McAuley, a native of Virginia, in 1832. Settled in Indiana for 3 years. Moved to Lancaster, WI in 1835. Moved to Mt. Sterling in 1854. Mother of Mrs. C. M. Butt of Viroqua, Mrs. M. J. Witcraft of Oklahoma, Mrs. J. A. Haggerty of Ferryville, Mrs. T. W. Tower of Mt Sterling, John of Mt. Sterling and A. D. of Mt. Sterling. Husband died in 1894. |
| McAuley | Jennie | KC, p5c3, 3/8/1900 | Teacher in Mt. Sterling. |
| McAuley | Jennie | KC, p1c5, 2/9/1899 | Taught school in Freeman in 1899. E. E. Brindley, Crawford County Superintendent of Schools published a comprehensive list of all teachers in the county. |
| McAuley | John | KC, p5c5, 10/25/1900 | Democratic candidate for Crawford County Sheriff. Born in 1848 in Lancaster, WI. Has Scotch Irish ancestry. Moved to Mt. Sterling in 1856. Farmed in Utica and Seneca. Moved to Mitchell, SD in 1882 and returned 8 years later to farm and keep hotel in Mt. Sterling. |
| McAuley | John | KC, p5c3, 11/22/1900 | Planned to sell his personal property at an auction in Mt. Sterling and then move to La Crosse. |
| McAuley | John, Mrs. | KC, p4c5, 1/10/1901 | Mrs. John McAuley and her mother, Mrs. L. D. Layton, and her daughter, Jennie, all of Mt. Sterling plan to take charge of the Davill Hotel in Lancaster. |
| McAuley | John, Mrs. | KC, p1c3, 8/3/1899 | From Gays Mills. Went to Mitchell, SD to visit relatives. |
| McAuley | Leona | KC, p1c3, 6/21/1900 | Taught (going to teach?) school in Beloit. (Recently?) Graduated from Milwaukee Normal School. Spending the summer with parents in Mt. Sterling. |
| McAuley | Lona | KC, p1c6, 4/8/1897 | Taught school in Soldiers Grove. From Mt. Sterling. |
| McAuley | Lona, Miss | KC, p1c3, 12/21/1899 | Taught school in Beloit. Returned to her home in Mt. Sterling for the holidays. |
| McAuley | May | KC, p5c5, 1/25/1900 | Married T. W. Swinson on Jan. 24, 1900. Bride daughter of R. D. McAuley, a miller. Bride and groom from Gays Mills. |
| McAuley | R. D. | KC, p5c3, 4/26/1900 | Miller in Gays Mills. Recently returned from a visit with friends and relatives in Arkansas and Nebraska. |
| McAuley | R. M. | KC, Supp, 12/20/1900 | Represented Gays Mills on the Crawford Co. Board of Supervisors in 1900. |

Genealogical Gleanings From Early Newspapers for Residents In and Near
Crawford County, Wisconsin, 1897-1902

| LAST NAME | FIRST NAME | NEWSPAPER PAGE/COLUMN MONTH/DAY/YEAR | GENEALOGICAL DATA |
|---|---|---|---|
| McAuley | Roy | KC, p1c5, 8/22/1901 | Visited his parents in De Soto and then left for North Dakota to be a foreman at an elevator for the Great Western Elevator Co. |
| McBurney | W., Mrs. | KC, p5c3, 2/15/1900 | Resided in Soldiers Grove. Visited sister, Mrs. John Smethurst of Mt. Sterling. |
| McCabe | Jennie, Mrs. | KC, p5c3, 2/15/1900 | Arrived from Tacoma, WA to visit relatives and friends in Town of Eastman and Prairie du Chien. |
| McCabe | Kate | KC, Supp., 12/18/1902 | Per Committee on County Poor, Crawford County received $47 from Kate McCabe for keeping her mother, Ann McCabe. |
| McCabe | Kate, Miss | KC, p5c3, 6/13/1901 | Arrived from Nebraska to visit friends in Lynxville. |
| McCabe | Terrance | KC, p5c6, 3/6/1902 | Probate Hearing notice published. Late of Town of Clayton. Patrick Kelly petitioned to be named administrator of estate. |
| McCabe | Terrance | KC, p5c6, 3/6/1902 | Patrick Kelly applied to the Crawford Count courts to administer the estate of Terrance McCabe late of the Town of Clayton. |
| McCabe | Terrence | KC, p1c2, 6/14/1900 | Died June 9, 1900 in the Gays Mills area. Aged about 45 years. |
| McCale | Mollie | KC, p8c4, 6/5/1902 | Married Edward Linder on June 2, 1902 at St. Gabriel's Catholic Church in Prairie du Chien. |
| McCann | boy | KC, p1c2, 12/29/1898 | Son born Dec. 22, 1898 to J. H. McCann of Wauzeka. Weighed 11 pounds. Died 9 days later (per KC, p1c4, 1/5/1899). |
| McCann | J. A. | KC, p1c4, 1/31/1901 | Visited parents in Wauzeka and returned to his home in Velva, ND. |
| McCann | James | KC, p1c4, 7/31/1902 | Lived in Wauzeka. Entertained daughters, Mrs. John Degnan of Clayton, IA and Mrs. A. G. Gebart of St. Paul, MN. |
| McCann | James, Jr. | KC, p1c3, 3/10/1898 | Arrived from Red Lake, MN to visit parents in Wauzeka. Later left with brother, Thomas, for Minot, ND. |
| McCann | James, Jr. | KC, p1c2, 3/2/1899 | Returned to Velva, ND after spending the last 2 months with parents in Wauzeka. |
| McCann | James, Mrs. | KC, p1c2, 5/23/1901 | Departed Wauzeka for Lismore, MN to visit her eldest son. |
| McCann | John | KC, p1c3, 3/2/1899 | Moved family to Milltown from Eastman. |
| McCann | Thomas | KC, p1c3, 10/17/1901 | Recently married Katie Maxwell at Devils Lake, ND. Bride, daughter of John Maxwell, from Plum Creek. Groom son of James McCann from Wauzeka. Planned to live in Velva, ND. |
| McCann | Thomas | KC, p5c3, 5/20/1897 | Issues of fact for court to be heard in the May term of the Crawford County Court. Barbara Dworak et. al. vs. McCann. |
| McCann | Thomas | KC, p5c3, 5/20/1897 | Issue of law for court to be heard in the May term of the Crawford County Court. Charles Weittenhiller vs. Thomas McCann. |

Genealogical Gleanings From Early Newspapers for Residents In and Near
Crawford County, Wisconsin, 1897-1902

| LAST NAME | FIRST NAME | NEWSPAPER PAGE/COLUMN MONTH/DAY/YEAR | GENEALOGICAL DATA |
|---|---|---|---|
| McCann | Thomas, Mrs. | KC, p1c5, 11/6/1902 | Lived in Velma, ND. Visited parents, Mr. and Mrs. John Maxwell of Wauzeka. |
| McCartney | boy | KC, Supp., 6/5/1902 | The 5-year-old son of Thomas McCartney of Lynxville badly crushed 3 fingers in a washing machine. Some were amputated. |
| McClerg | B. | KC, p5c1, 9/30/1897 | Died in Madison on Sept. 23, 1897. Buried in Retreat. |
| McCloskey | Frank | KC, p4c3, 11/8/1900 | Operated a barber shop in Eastman. |
| McCloskey | Mamie | KC, p8c3, 6/28/1900 | Married Peter Connely on June 27, 1900. Groom from Milwaukee. (Bride may be from Prairie du Chien.) |
| McClusky | F. J. | KC, p5c4, 3/8/1900 | Resided in Eastman. Advertised sale of tailor made gentlemen's clothing. |
| McClusky | Thomas | KC, p1c6, 5/19/1898 | Criminal case to be heard in the May term of the Crawford County Circuit Court. State of Wisconsin vs. George Quinn, Thomas McClusky and August Grapp, burglary. |
| McCone | Mr. and Mrs. | KC, p1c2, 3/23/1899 | Visited relatives on Harris Ridge (near Wauzeka) for the last 3 months and then returned to his home in Manitoba, Canada. |
| McConey | Thomas | KC, Supp, 12/20/1900 | Crawford Co. Board of Supervisors approved payment of expenses in the matter of State vs. Thomas McConey. Nancy McConey was the witness. |
| McConey | Thomas | KC, Supp, 12/20/1900 | Crawford Co. Board of Supervisors approved bills related to expenses of Thomas McConey, insane. |
| McCord | Walker | KC, p8c4, 4/4/1901 | Part of a group that left Steuben and Wauzeka for the West. Most of the group went to McHenry, North Dakota. |
| McCormack | Fred E., Jr. | KC, p1c3, 2/9/1899 | Arrested in Soldiers Grove. Former resident of Towerville. He had been out west since the first of July and came back to Crawford Co. a week ago. Failed to provide for his wife who lived in Ferryville during his absence. Wife swore out a warrant for his arrest. |
| McCormick | Allan | KC, p5c3, 5/12/1898 | Notice of Hearing published by Crawford County Probate Court. Allan McCormick petitioned to admit the will of Mary McCormick, late of Town of Clayton. |
| McCormick | Catherine, Mrs. | KC, p1c6, 3/24/1898 | Died Friday (Mar. 18, 1898?) in Town of Clayton. Aged nearly four score (aged about 70 years per p4c1). Settled in Crawford Co. in early 1860s. Survived by children: Peter, James Allen Mrs. William Horrigan and Mrs. William Ehorn. Husband, Michael McCormick died several years ago. Funeral held at St. Phillips Church in Clayton. |
| McCormick | Frank | KC, p5c3, 3/11/1897 | Left Wheatville for a new home in New Hampton, IA. |
| McCormick | Fred | KC, p4c1, 8/26/1897 | Married Lillian Howe of Ferryville on Aug. 25, 1897 at Town of Freeman. Groom from Towerville. |
| McCormick | John | KC, p1c2, 11/14/1901 | Died Nov. 17, 1901 while hunting in Wood Co. Resided near Excelsior. Foul play suspected. |

Genealogical Gleanings From Early Newspapers for Residents In and Near
Crawford County, Wisconsin, 1897-1902

| LAST NAME | FIRST NAME | NEWSPAPER PAGE/COLUMN MONTH/DAY/YEAR | GENEALOGICAL DATA |
|---|---|---|---|
| McCormick | Josephine | KC, p8c4, 11/20/1902 | In the November term of Crawford County Circuit Court, Josephine McCormick vs. John McCormick, verdict for plaintiff for divorce, $1200 alimony and $20 per month until the Mary term of court. |
| McCormick | Mary | KC, p8c4, 6/16/1898 | Crawford County Probate Court published a Notice to Creditors in regards to the estate of Mary McCormick. McCormick died June 8, 1898. |
| McCormick | Vernie | KC, p1c5, 2/9/1899 | Taught school in Utica in 1899. E. E. Brindley, Crawford County Superintendent of Schools published a comprehensive list of all teachers in the county. |
| McCormick | Vernie | KC, Supp., 12/12/1901 | Attended a Teacher's Institute in Crawford County in 1901. Resided in Towerville. |
| McCoy | Charles | KC, p1c4, 1/19/1899 | Moved from Long Prairie, MN to Wauzeka to operate the Wauzeka Meat Market. |
| McCrillis | Irving | KC, p1c4, 6/28/1900 | Former resident of Mt. Sterling. Now lives in Des Moines. Admitted to the State Bar in Iowa on June 10, 1900. |
| McCrillis | John | KC, p5c3, 3/2/1899 | Resided in Tomah. Visited friends in Mt. Sterling his former hometown. |
| McCullick | J. | KC, p5c5, 4/5/1900 | Elected supervisor in Town of Utica. |
| McCullick | J. W. | KC, p1c3, 1/5/1899 | Hosted family reunion in Mt. Sterling. Entire family, except 2 sisters, was there. Jonas McCullick, one of the brothers of Salinas, KS was home for the first time in 14 years. It was 28 years since he spent Christmas at homestead. |
| McCullick | J. W. | KC, p1c6, 4/7/1898 | Elected Chairman for the Town of Utica. |
| McCullick | J. W. | KC, p1c6, 6/2/1898 | Announced plans to run for Crawford County Sheriff. Resident of Utica. |
| McCullick | John | KC, p1c3, 8/9/1900 | Resided in Mt. Sterling. Running as the Republican candidate for Crawford County Sheriff. |
| McCullick | John | KC, p5c5, 1/30/1902 | Families of John McCullick and J. M. Dudley of Mt. Sterling attended the funeral of their sister, Mrs. J. Stevens near Ferryville last Sunday. |
| McCullick | John | KC, p5c4, 7/24/1902 | Hosted an ice cream social in Mt. Sterling to benefit Rev. Rowell. Proceeds were $10.00. |
| McCullick | John | KC, Supp, 12/20/1900 | Represented Utica on the Crawford Co. Board of Supervisors in 1900. |
| McCullick | Manda | KC, p5c4, 2/28/1901 | Resided in Mt. Sterling. Taught school in Petersburg. |
| McCullick | Sadie | KC, p8c3, 6/14/1900 | Marriage license issued to Sadie McCullick of Mt. Sterling and Fred Waddle of Lynxville. |
| McCullick | Sadie | KC, p5c4, 6/28/1900 | Married Fred Waddle of Lynxville on June 20, 1900. Bride from Mt. Sterling. |
| McCullick |  | KC, p5c3, 8/30/1900 | "The Old Lady McCullick is still very ill." Resided in Mt. Sterling area. |
| McCullock | girl | KC, p5c2, 3/3/1898 | Daughter recently born to John McCullock of Wheatville. |

Genealogical Gleanings From Early Newspapers for Residents In and Near
Crawford County, Wisconsin, 1897-1902

| LAST NAME | FIRST NAME | NEWSPAPER PAGE/COLUMN MONTH/DAY/YEAR | GENEALOGICAL DATA |
|---|---|---|---|
| McCullock | Grace | KC, p5c3 6/19/1902 | Married Tunis Nelson on June 15, 1902 at Mt. Sterling. Bride is sister of Mrs. Fred Waddle. |
| McCullock | J. W. | KC, p1c4, 3/15/1900 | Elected president of the newly formed Crawford County Farmers Mutual Insurance Co. Other officers were T. T. Sime, E. G. Briggs and J. A. Hays. |
| McCullock | J. W. | KC, p1c4, 5/22/1902 | Resided in Mt. Sterling. Republican candidate for sheriff in Crawford County. |
| McDaniel | Addie | KC, Supp., 12/15/1898 | Married Emmet Coleman on Dec. 8, 1898 in La Crosse. Bride and groom from Barnum. |
| McDaniel | Albert | KC, p1c4, 11/11/1897 | Announced public auction of stock and farm machinery at his farm 3 miles NE of Wauzeka. |
| McDaniel | Edward | KC, p1c4, 10/26/1899 | Died Oct. 23, 1899 in Town of Scott. Aged 37 years. Survived by wife and 5 children. Funeral held at Mt. Zion Church. |
| McDaniel | George | KC, p1c2, 3/27/1902 | Son of William McDaniel of McHenry, SD. Arrived from South Dakota to visit relatives in Wauzeka. |
| McDaniel | James | KC, Supp, 12/29/1898 | Crawford Co. Board of Supervisors approved Justices and Constables' expenses related to the case, State vs. James McDaniel. |
| McDaniel | John | KC, p4c3, 3/31/1898 | A large group left the Wauzeka train station for Courtney, ND. The group consisted of John, Albert and William McDaniel; Chester Pratt; John Harris; Frank Wayne and wife; Joseph Meyers and daughter; Sam Wayne; W. E. Mercer; Lee Dunbar; and James and Wallace Pratt. Another group left from Barnum. They were L. L. Lathrop, Abram Dowse, Robert Stantorf and Will Brock. |
| McDaniel | John | KC, p1c6, 4/7/1898 | Elected Supervisor for the Town of Clayton. |
| McDaniel | John and Albert | KC, p1c3, 8/24/1899 | John and Albert McDaniel, sons of Mr. McDaniel of Wauzeka area, lived in Glenfield, ND. |
| McDaniel | R. | KC, p1c3, 6/26/1902 | R. McDaniel and H. Dean ran hotels in Barnum. |
| McDaniel | Robert | KC, p5c1, 2/10/1898 | His store in Barnum was robbed. |
| McDaniel | | KC, p1c2, 7/14/1898 | The McDaniel case that was brought before Justice Peacock in Wauzeka dismissed for lack of evidence. |
| McDaniels | Mabel | KC,p5c4, 6/28/1900 | Recently graduated from the Barnum village school. |
| McDill | Ruth | KC, Supp., 12/12/1901 | Attended a Teacher's Institute in Crawford County in 1901. Resided in Prairie du Chien. |
| McDonald | Hattie | KC, p1c6, 8/19/1897 | Postmistress in Wauzeka. Returned from La Crosse after surgery to remove a tumor. |
| McDonald | Hattie, Mrs. | KC, p1c2, 4/5/1900 | Returned to Wauzeka after spending the winter with relatives in Basin, MT. |
| McDonald | J. H. | KC, p1c4, 5/1/1902 | J. H. McDonald and Benjamin J. Mindham were partners in a new livery business in Steuben. |
| McDonald | J. H. | KC, p1c5, 2/9/1899 | Taught school in Eastman in 1899. E. E. Brindley, Crawford County Superintendent of Schools published a comprehensive list of all teachers in the county. |

Genealogical Gleanings From Early Newspapers for Residents In and Near
Crawford County, Wisconsin, 1897-1902

| LAST NAME | FIRST NAME | NEWSPAPER PAGE/COLUMN MONTH/DAY/YEAR | GENEALOGICAL DATA |
|---|---|---|---|
| McDonald | Joe | KC, p5c5, 1/18/1900 | Taught school in Crawford Co. |
| McDonald | John F. | KC, p8c4, 6/21/1900 | Graduated at Wauzeka High School. Class of 1901. |
| McDonald | Mary | KC, p5c2, 3/3/1898 | Married William Morgan on Feb. 22, 1898 at St. Church. |
| McDonald | Mary | KC, p5c2, 3/3/1898 | Married William Moran on Feb. 22, 1898 at St. Phillip's Catholic Church, Town of Clayton. |
| McDonald | Mr. | KC, p4c3, 1/13/1898 | Recently died at age 111 in Dakota. He was well known in Lynxville. |
| McDonald | Paul | KC, p5c1, 11/18/1897 | Arrived from Dakota to visit his very ill aunt, Mrs. D. Heligas of Lynxville. |
| McDonnel | Hattie, Miss | KC, p1c2, 11/2/1899 | Traveled from Wauzeka to Besan, Montana to visit sister and other family members. |
| McDonnell | Herbert | KC, p1c6, 6/30/1898 | Herbert McDonnell, William Bauer, Henry Reeter and Frank Lagaman enlisted in the army at Boscobel in a company organized by Capt. Blanchard. This was Co. F of the 4th WI Regiment. They were transferred into Co. C. at a later date. From Wauzeka. |
| McDonnell | Herbert | KC, p1c5, 11/18/1897 | Installed as an officer at the International Order of Good Templars (I.O.G.T.) Lodge in Wauzeka. |
| McDonnell | James | KC, p1c2, 9/25/1902 | Lived in Wauzeka. Visited son, William of Brownstown, Green Co., WI and other relatives and friends at Cross Plains and Arena. He was the station agent and operator of the C. M. & St. Paul Railroad. |
| McDonnell | William, Mrs. | KC, p1c2, 12/1/1898 | Resided in Calamine. Visited husband's parents, Mr. and Mrs. James McDonnell of Wauzeka. |
| McDonough | Bernard J. | KC, Supp, 12/29/1898 | Crawford Co. Board of Supervisors approved Justices and Constables' expenses related to the case, State vs. Bernard J. McDonough. |
| McDougal | boy | KC, p5c2, 8/18/1898 | Son recently born to Darwin McDougal. |
| McDowell | A. J. | KC, p5c5, 4/5/1900 | Elected President of village board in Soldiers Grove. |
| McDowell | A. J., Dr. | KC, Supp, 12/29/1898 | In 1888, Dr. A. J. McDowell, former Crawford Co. Superintendent of Schools organized the first summer school to improve teacher skills. |
| McDowell | George | KC, p1c4, 3/22/1900 | Died Mar. 16, 1900 in Mt. Sterling. He was son of Dr. McDowell of Soldiers Grove. Buried in Hurlburt, WI. |
| McDowell | Ora | KC, p8c4, 8/2/1900 | Died July 25, 1900 at Town of Haney. Aged 22 years, 1 month and 9 days. Buried in Haney Cemetery. Survived by father, mother, 4 sisters and 3 brothers. One sister dead. |
| McDowell | Sophia | KC, p5c5, 1/18/1900 | Taught school in Crawford Co. |
| McDowell | Sophia E. | KC, p5c3, 6/20/1901 | Married Dwelly F. Haskins on June 12, 1901 at Harris Ridge. Rev. Harding Hogan officiated. Groom from Town of Haney. |
| McDowell | T. | KC, p5c5, 4/5/1900 | Elected assessor in Town of Haney. |

Genealogical Gleanings From Early Newspapers for Residents In and Near
Crawford County, Wisconsin, 1897-1902

| LAST NAME | FIRST NAME | NEWSPAPER PAGE/COLUMN MONTH/DAY/YEAR | GENEALOGICAL DATA |
|---|---|---|---|
| McEachern | boy | KC, p5c3, 9/27/1900 | Son recently born to John McEachern at Hurlbut, Town of Scott. |
| McElroy | Lulu | KC, p8c3, 9/11/1902 | Married John L. Fox on Aug. 21, 1902 at Joliet, IL. Bride from Sabula, IA. Groom from Prairie du Chien. |
| McEwen | Fannie, Mrs. | KC, p1c6, 9/16/1897 | Resided in Mt. Sterling. Taught a large music class in Soldiers Grove. |
| McEwen | Fannie, Mrs. | KC, p1c5, 10/21/1897 | Returned to her home in Sioux City after spending the summer with her parents, Mr. and Mrs. James Porter of Mt. Sterling. |
| McFarland | boy | KC, Supp., 12/15/1898 | Son recently born to John McFarland of East Gays Mills. |
| McFarland | J., Mrs. | KC, p5c2, 10/27/1898 | Resided in East Gays Mills. Entertained sister, Mrs. J. Ehorn of Chewelah, WA. |
| McFarland | Libbie, Miss | KC, p5c3, 1/26/1899 | Recently died in a Chicago hospital. From East Gays Mills. |
| McGarigle | Charles | KC, p5c3, 5/25/1899 | Admitted to a hospital in Idaho. Had small pox. He was the son of John McGarigle of East Gays Mills. |
| McGee | J. M. | KC, p1c2, 10/18/1900 | Resided in Bridgeport. Purchased Gays Mills property from his son, Charles. |
| McGinley | Charles | KC, Supp, 12/29/1898 | Crawford Co. Board of Supervisors approved Justices and Constables' expenses related to the case, State vs. Charles McGinley. |
| McGorvan | Cora | KC, p7c4, 1/25/1900 | Received marriage license in Crawford Co. Fred Worth was the prospective spouse. Bride and groom-to-be from Johnsonport, IA. |
| McGovern | Electa, Mrs. | KC, p5c3, 5/17/1900 | Arrived from Moorhead, MN to visit parents, Mr. and Mrs. W. P. Young of Eastman. |
| McGovern | William | KC, Supp., 10/3/1901 | Died Sept. 29, 1901 in Prairie du Chien. He was 9-month-old child of Mrs. Emma McGovern |
| McGowen | Agnes | KC, Supp, 12/29/1898 | Crawford Co. Board of Supervisors approved Justices and Constables' expenses related to the case, State vs. Agnes McGowen. |
| McGrath | Margurite | KC, p8c4, 5/17/1900 | Recently married J. V. Smith in Milwaukee. Bride was from New Richmond. Groom was a former resident of Wauzeka. |
| McGrath | Thomas | KC, p8c3, 10/17/1901 | Married Lucy Weniger on Oct. 15, 1901. The Rev. Fr. Joerres officiated. (Bride and/or groom may have been from Prairie du Chien.) |
| McGregor | I. C. | KC, p1c6, 5/19/1898 | Issue of Fact for Jury to be heard in the May term of the Crawford County Circuit Court. I. C. McGregor vs. Ernest Faber. |
| McHarg | John | KC, Supp., 12/19/1901 | Wauzeka was first settled by John McHarg in 1855, the year before the C. M. and St. Paul Railroad was built through the Wisconsin Valley. |
| McHarg | William | KC, p1c2, 10/27/1898 | Resided in Marion, IA. Formerly from Wauzeka. |

Genealogical Gleanings From Early Newspapers for Residents In and Near
Crawford County, Wisconsin, 1897-1902

| LAST NAME | FIRST NAME | NEWSPAPER PAGE/COLUMN MONTH/DAY/YEAR | GENEALOGICAL DATA |
|---|---|---|---|
| McKane | Dan | KC, Supp, 12/29/1898 | Crawford Co. of Supervisors approved Justices and Constables' expenses related to the case, State vs. Dan McKane and Geo. Sluk. The witnesses were A. Steinburg and D. St. Jaque. |
| McKay | Randolph | KC, p4c1, 10/7/1897 | Arrived from Calamine to visit sister, Mrs. L. P. Lawrence of Boydtown. |
| McKee | Almina | KC, p1c4, 4/8/1897 | Died Mar. 20, 1897 in (Wauzeka?). Born Feb. 12, 1809 in Delaware Co. NY. Joined Baptist Church. Moved to Belle Center, WI in 1869. Joined Methodist Episcopal Church in 1869. Married Isaiah Rounds in 1825 and had 10 children. Three children survive. Lived with son, Melville J. Rounds after husband died 18 years ago. (Unclear if she was born a McKee or if she remarried to a McKee.) |
| McKenney | Harry | KC, p5c3, 4/26/1900 | Departed Steuben for a new home in Minneapolis. |
| McKenney | Mr. | KC, p5c4, 2/7/1901 | Arrived from Idaho to visit brother in Steuben. |
| McKillip | child | KC, p1c2, 4/8/1897 | An 8-month-old child of Ed McKillip died Saturday in Prairie du Chien. |
| McKillip | Edward | KC, Supp., 12/18/1902 | Crawford County Board of Supervisors allowed expenses in the Matter of Edward McKillip, Incorrigible. |
| McKillip | Edward, Mrs. | KC, p8c3, 1/10/1901 | Died Jan. 7, 1901 in Prairie du Chien. |
| McKillip | James | KC, p8c3, 11/30/1899 | Died Nov. 28, 1899 in Prairie du Chien. Survived by wife and 2 children. |
| McKillip | Mike | KC, p8c3, 12/30/1897 | After visiting friends in Eastman, returned to his home in Maple Lake, MN. |
| McKillip | T. and family | KC, p4c1, 9/2/1897 | Old residents of Eastman. Moved to a new home in Maple Lake, MN. |
| McKillip | | KC, Supp., 4/24/1902 | Resided in Prairie du Chien. A young son of Ed McKillip sent to an orphans' home in La Crosse. |
| McKincannon | Mrs. | KC, p9c2, 7/1/1897 | Entertained her brother, Mr. Mead, at her home in Wauzeka. Mead was a railroad engineer. He lost an arm in a train wreck. Bravely stayed at his post and saved many lives. |
| McKinley | Barney | KC, p1c4, 7/14/1898 | Sold his farm in Town of Scott to John Jones. Planned to go east. |
| McKinley | Denis | KC, Supp, 12/29/1898 | Crawford Co. Board of Supervisors approved Justices and Constables' expenses related to the case, State vs. Denis McKinley. The witnesses were Herman Dunbar, J. F. McDaniel, Henry McDaniel, Willie Marshall, Lee Dunbar and Otto Chapman. |
| McKinley | George | KC, Supp., 12/18/1902 | Crawford County Board of Supervisors examined bills in the Justices and Constables' Account for State vs. George McKinley. |
| McKinley | Louis | KC, p1c2, 1/27/1898 | Defendant in court case, Wisconsin vs. Louis McKinley, in Wauzeka. William Dunbar was the complaining witness. McKinley settled the case without a trial. |

Genealogical Gleanings From Early Newspapers for Residents In and Near
Crawford County, Wisconsin, 1897-1902

| LAST NAME | FIRST NAME | NEWSPAPER PAGE/COLUMN MONTH/DAY/YEAR | GENEALOGICAL DATA |
|---|---|---|---|
| McKinley | William | KC, p4c1, 7/29/1897 | Died July 22, 1897 in Boydtown. Aged 35 years. |
| McKinney | Hester, Mrs. | KC, p1c2, 9/18/1902 | Died Sept. 5, 1902 at Minneapolis. Nee Ray. Survived by son, Harry, of Steuben and daughter of Minneapolis. She was the sister-in-law of Mrs. Ed Ray of Wauzeka and Mrs. Miles Ray of Steuben. |
| McKinney | J. P. | KC, p1c2, 12/5/1901 | Left Steuben with daughters, Mrs. Ed Ray of Wauzeka and Mrs. Miles Ray of Steuben for Sheboygan, WI to visit her son. |
| McKinney | J. P. | KC, Supp, 12/29/1898 | Received aid from the Crawford County Soldiers Relief Commission. Resided in Marietta. |
| McKinney | John, Mrs. | KC, p1c6, 9/26/1901 | Died Sept. 19, 1901 in Madison. Nee Maria Smith. Former resident of Wauzeka area. Survived by husband, 7 children, 5 brothers and 3 sisters. Her siblings were John and Frank of Milwaukee; Pat, Eugene and James of the west; Mrs. Felix Degnan and Mrs. Pat Maxwell of Crawford Co. and Mrs. McKinney of Madison. |
| McKnight | | KC, p5c3, 9/27/1900 | The youngest child of Ed McKnight of the Town of Scott died yesterday of catarrahal fever. Funeral was held at Maple Ridge Church. Buried at Christ Cemetery. |
| McKon | Mr. and Mrs. | KC, p5c4, 1/26/1899 | Arrived from Manitoba to visit James Turnbull of Harris Ridge. |
| McLaughlin | John | KC, p5c4, 10/4/1900 | John McLaughlin and T. and J. Dagnon planned to open a wagon making and repairing business in Seneca. |
| McLaughlin | John | KC, p1c4, 12/11/1902 | Blacksmith in Seneca. |
| McLaughlin | John L. | KC, p1c3, 9/28/1899 | Married Susan Garvey on Sept. 19, 1899 at St. Patrick's Catholic Church in Seneca. Bride sister of Julia V. Garvey. |
| McLaughlin | Minnie, Miss | KC, p5c3, 11/30/1899 | Resident of Seneca. Employed as a dressmaker at C. E. Thomson residence in Gays Mills. |
| McLenehan | Hulda | KC, p5c3, 4/10/1902 | Died April 1, 1902 at the County Poor Farm. |
| McManamy | P. J. | KC, p1c4, 7/21/1898 | Married Rosella Jamboi of Genoa on July 13, 1898. Groom from Liberty Pole. |
| McManus | boy | KC, p4c1, 7/22/1897 | Son recently born to William McManus of Rising Sun. |
| McManus | W., Mrs. | KC, p5c3, 3/9/1899 | Funeral recently held in Rising Sun. Attended by Mrs. T. Finley, sister of deceased, of Gays Mills. |
| McManus | William | KC, p8c3, 3/4/1897 | Married Mary Burns on Mar. 1, 1897. Bride and groom were from Rising Sun. |
| McManus | William | KC, p5c3, 2/9/1899 | Resolution of Respect for William McManus was published by the O. D. Chapman Post of the GAR in Gays Mills. Served in Co. H, 36th WI Inf. In the Civil War. Published by G. R. Rounds and R. S. DeLaMater. |
| McMasters | Ben | KC, p4c3, 6/17/1897 | Learning telegraphy from P. N. Smith, per Ferryville news items. |
| McMillin | Perley | KC, p4c1, 12/2/1897 | Died Saturday night in Sugar Grove. |

Genealogical Gleanings From Early Newspapers for Residents In and Near
Crawford County, Wisconsin, 1897-1902

| LAST NAME | FIRST NAME | NEWSPAPER PAGE/COLUMN MONTH/DAY/YEAR | GENEALOGICAL DATA |
|---|---|---|---|
| McMullen | Rose | KC, p8c4, 11/2/1899 | Married Simon Hess on Oct. 31, 1899 at the Catholic Church in Prairie du Chien. Bride from Eastman. Groom from Lowertown. |
| McNamara | Katie | KC, p5c3, 8/24/1899 | Hired to teach at Poplar Ridge school. |
| McNamara | Katie | KC, p1c5, 2/9/1899 | Taught school in the Wauzeka in 1899. E. E. Brindley, Crawford County Superintendent of Schools published a comprehensive list of all teachers in the county. |
| McNamara | Katie | KC, Supp., 12/12/1901 | Attended a Teacher's Institute in Crawford County in 1901. Resided in Seneca. |
| McNamara | Mary | KC, p1c4, 7/26/1900 | Married Frank Messling on July 17, 1900. Bride and groom from Town of Seneca. |
| McNamara | Mary | KC, p1c5, 11/18/1897 | Taught school in Leightner District. |
| McNamara | Mary | KC, p1c5, 2/9/1899 | Taught school in Seneca in 1899. E. E. Brindley, Crawford County Superintendent of Schools published a comprehensive list of all teachers in the county. |
| McPherson | L. D. | KC, p5c3, 8/30/1900 | The following Mt. Sterling residents attended the Buffalo Bill Wild West Show in Prairie du Chien: L. D. McPherson and family, Bert Bellows and wife, Mrs. D. Bell and children, Henry Mills, Thomas O'Neil, John Sherwood, Fred Freeman, Justin Thompson and sons, Charles McAuley, Ed Brockway and wife, Bessie Briggs and Mrs. John Smethurst. |
| McQuiggan | Peter | KC, p1c5, 2/3/1898 | Plead guilty to disturbing the peace in Wauzeka. Paid a $5.50 fine. |
| McReynolds | F. G., Dr. | KC, p5c3, 1/7/1898 | Married Josephine Muffley, daughter of Ald. L. Muffley, today. Bride from Boscobel. Groom former resident of Boscobel, from Tomah. |
| McWilliams | Thomas | KC, p1c5, 2/17/1898 | Married Anna Berry, daughter of John Berry of McGregor, IA on Feb. 7, 1898. Groom from Boscobel. Planned to live in Soldiers Grove. |
| Mead | O. M., Mrs. | KC, p1c3, 8/14/1902 | Lived in Mason City, IA. Visited parents, Mr. and Mrs. Edw. Crowley, Sr. of the Steuben area. |
| Mead | T., Mr. | KC, p1c2, 7/19/1900 | Worked as a contractor and builder in Madison. Arrived in Wauzeka to visit his sister, Mrs. M. C. Kincannon. |
| Meagher | James | KC, p5c3, 1/16/1902 | Returned from North Dakota, where he taught school, for funeral of brother, Will, in Seneca. |
| Meagher | Josie | KC, p5c3, 11/30/1899 | The Seneca news column reported she was at Thomas Garvey's making dresses. |
| Meagher | Maggie | KC, p5c3, 6/19/1902 | Installed as postmistress in Seneca. |
| Meagher | Maggie | KC, Supp., 12/12/1901 | Attended a Teacher's Institute in Crawford County in 1901 Resided in Seneca. |
| Meagher | Maggie | KC, p5c3, 3/21/1901 | Lived in Seneca. Took the teacher's examination in Gays Mills. |
| Meagher | Mary | KC, p5c4, 2/15/1900 | Former teacher in Crawford County. Departed for Chicago to take classes in painting and drawing. |

Genealogical Gleanings From Early Newspapers for Residents In and Near Crawford County, Wisconsin, 1897-1902

| LAST NAME | FIRST NAME | NEWSPAPER PAGE/COLUMN MONTH/DAY/YEAR | GENEALOGICAL DATA |
|---|---|---|---|
| Meagher | Mary | KC, Supp., 12/12/1901 | Attended a Teacher's Institute in Crawford County in 1901. Resided in Seneca. |
| Meagher | Will | KC, p5c3, 1/9/1902 | Resided in Seneca. Ill with lung fever. Under the care of Dr. Stanton. |
| Meagher | William | KC, p5c3, 1/16/1902 | Recently died in Seneca. Brother of James who taught school in North Dakota. |
| Meagher | William | KC, p5c3, 1/16/1902 | Died Jan. 9, 1902. Aged 26 years, 10 months and 23 days. Survived by father, mother, 4 sisters (Josie, Mary, Catherine and Margaret) and 3 brothers (James Richard and Dennis). Funeral held at St. Patrick's Catholic Church. |
| Megee | J. M. | KC, Supp., 12/12/1901 | Received funds from the Crawford Co. Soldiers Relief Commission. Resided in Gays Mills. |
| Meger | Marvin | KC, Supp., 12/18/1902 | Crawford County Soldiers Relief Committee provided funds to Marvin Meger of Gays Mills. |
| Mellin | Thomas | KC, p5c4, 7/29/1897 | Died about Thursday in Boydtown. Interred in Boydtown Cemetery. |
| Meltick | M. | KC, Supp, 12/29/1898 | Received aid from the Crawford County Soldiers Relief Commission. Resided in Utica. |
| Melvin | Ellen | KC, p5c3, 5/20/1897 | Issues of fact for jury to be heard in the May term of the Crawford County Court. Patrick Piesley vs. Bridget Piesley and Ellen Melvin et al. |
| Melvin | Joseph | KC, p5c3, 6/22/1899 | Married Sarah M. Peasley on June 19, 1899 at St. James Catholic Church at Rising Sun. |
| Melvin | Mary | KC, Supp., 12/12/1901 | Attended a Teacher's Institute in Crawford County in 1901. Resided in Rising Sun. |
| Menges | Helen Emma | KC, p8c3, 5/15/1902 | Planned to marry Eugene Amann on May 14, 1902. Bride from Prairie du Chien. Groom from La Crosse. |
| Menges | Helen Emma | KC, Supp., 5/15/1902 | Married Eugene Charles Amann on May 14, 1902. Bride daughter of Hon. and Mrs. M. Menges of Prairie du Chien. Groom son of Mrs. Charles Amann of La Crosse. Married at St. Gabriel's Catholic Church in Prairie du Chien. Many relatives and guests listed. |
| Menges | M. | KC, p1c5, 5/18/1899 | A Blank Button Factory was established in the Dousman block in Prairie du Chien. The incorporators were M. Menges, (B. E.?) Fay, H. Otto, E. I. Kidd, and S. Bisbee. |
| Menges | M. | KC, Supp, 12/20/1900 | Represented 2nd Ward of Prairie du Chien on the Crawford Co. Board of Supervisors in 1900. |
| Menges | Michael | KC, p8c2, 2/17/1898 | Celebrated 65th birthday anniversary on Feb. 13, 1898 in Prairie du Chien. |
| Mercer | boy | KC, p1c2, 7/3/1902 | Son born Tuesday to Frank Mercer of Wauzeka. |
| Mercer | Frank | KC, p1c4, 10/13/1898 | Married Mary Noe of Wauzeka on Oct. 2, 1898 at the David Staib residence in Barnum. Groom from Barnum. |
| Mercer | girl | KC, p1c5, 7/26/1900 | Daughter born July 20, 1900 to Frank Mercer of Wauzeka. |
| Mercer | Will | KC, p1c2, 11/23/1899 | Will Mercer and Albert Onstine returned to Wauzeka from McHenry, ND where they purchased farms. Planned to move next spring. |

Genealogical Gleanings From Early Newspapers for Residents In and Near
Crawford County, Wisconsin, 1897-1902

| LAST NAME | FIRST NAME | NEWSPAPER PAGE/COLUMN MONTH/DAY/YEAR | GENEALOGICAL DATA |
|---|---|---|---|
| Mercer | William | KC, p1c5, 1/10/1901 | Married Maggie Day on Jan. 3, 1901. Bride and groom from Wauzeka. |
| Merrell | John D. | KC, p5c4, 5/29/1902 | The case John D. Merrell vs. Mary F. Merrill was heard at the May term of the Crawford County Circuit Court. Continued on application of plaintiff. |
| Merrifield | George | KC, p8c4, 9/30/1897 | At a conference of the Methodist Church held in Platteville, George Merrifield was assigned to Darlington. |
| Merrifield | George | KC, p1c4, 9/29/1898 | At a conference of the Methodist Church held in Eau Claire, George Merrifield was assigned to Mineral Point. |
| Merrill | John D. | KC, p5c4, 5/29/1902 | The case John D. Merrill et al vs. William D. Merrill, et al. was heard at the May term of the Crawford County Circuit Court. Continued. |
| Merrill | John D. | KC, p8c4, 11/13/1902 | In the November term of Crawford County Circuit Court, John D. Merrill vs. Mary F. Merrill, case was settled. |
| Merrill | Victor A. W. | KC, p1c3, 11/8/1900 | Died Oct. 25, 1900 in Prairie du Chien at age 82. Father of William D. Merrill of Prairie du Chien. |
| Merville | Mrs. | KC, p1c5, 9/30/1897 | After visiting relatives in Wauzeka, returned to home in Milwaukee. Daughter of Henry Trautsch, Sr. of Wauzeka. |
| Messiling | L., Mrs. | KC, p5c4, 3/29/1900 | Recently died in Lynxville. |
| Messiling | Minnie, Mrs. | KC, p1c4, 4/5/1900 | Died Mar. 28, 1900 in Lynxville. Wife of Louis Messling. Aged 58 years and 5 days. Survived by husband, 1 son and 1 daughter. |
| Messling | Carl | KC, p5c4, 1/30/1902 | Messing and Will Benhart planned to move to Pocahontas, IA. |
| Messling | Carl | KC, p5c4, 3/20/1902 | Departed Lynxville for a new home in Iowa. |
| Messling | Carl | KC, p5c4, 7/31/1902 | Returned from Iowa to live in the Lynxville area. |
| Messling | Frank | KC, p1c4, 7/26/1900 | Married Mary McNamara on July 17, 1900. Bride and groom from Town of Seneca. |
| Messling | girl | KC, p5c4, 4/17/1902 | Daughter born last week to Paul Messling of Lynxville. |
| Mettic | M. | KC, Supp., 12/12/1901 | Received funds from the Crawford County Soldiers Relief Commission. Resided in Utica. |
| Mettic | Mathias | KC, p8c4, 4/11/1901 | Died Feb. 17, 1901. Born June 23, 1823 in Tuscarogo Co. (probably Tuscarawas Co.), OH. Married Becka Buckmaster on Mar. 30, 1848. Moved to Wisconsin in 1856. Served in Co. H, 36th Regiment, WI Vol. Inf. during Civil War. |
| Mettick | Frank, Mrs. | KC, p5c4, 2/2/1899 | Resided in Woodstock, MN. Visited sister, Mrs. H. C. George of Gays Mills. |
| Mettick | Mathias | KC, p4c5, 2/21/1901 | Died Feb. 17, 1901 at an advanced age. Resided between Mt. Sterling and Gays Mills. |
| Mettsick | M. | KC, Supp, 12/20/1900 | Crawford Co. Soldiers Relief Comm. approved aid to M. Mettsick of Utica. |
| Meyer | Bruno | KC, p1c2, 6/23/1898 | Helping to construct the new college buildings at Prairie du Chien. Resided in Wauzeka. |

Genealogical Gleanings From Early Newspapers for Residents In and Near
Crawford County, Wisconsin, 1897-1902

| LAST NAME | FIRST NAME | NEWSPAPER PAGE/COLUMN MONTH/DAY/YEAR | GENEALOGICAL DATA |
|---|---|---|---|
| Meyer | Fred A. | KC, p1c4, 9/15/1898 | Married Nellie E. Pengilly on Sept. 8, 1898 in Boscobel. |
| Meyer | girl | KC, p5c4, 7/25/1901 | Daughter born Saturday evening to Rubert Meyer of Moose, MN. |
| Meyer | girl | KC, p1c4, 4/13/1899 | Daughter born April 4, 1899 to Robert Meyer of Wauzeka. |
| Meyer | John | KC, Supp., 12/20/1900 | Crawford Co. Board of Supervisors approved payment of expenses in the matter of State vs. John Meyer. |
| Meyer | Katherine | KC, p8c1, 6/8/1899 | Married Charles F. New of Springbrook, IA on June 16, 1899 at St. Gabriel's Church. Bride from Prairie du Chien. Planned to live at Bellevue, IA. |
| Meyer | Paul | KC, p1c4, 4/11/1901 | Died April 8, 1901. He was an attorney in Boscobel. Shot self in the head. Funeral was held in Boscobel. |
| Meyer | Rubert | KC, p1c3, 12/22/1898 | Married Clara Lagaman on Dec. 18, 1898. Bride and groom from Wauzeka. Bride daughter of John Lagaman. |
| Meyers | Flora | KC, p1c4, 1/2/1902 | Married Norman Onstine on Dec. 26, 1901 at Carrington, ND. Bride formerly of Wauzeka. |
| Meyers | Flora | KC, p1c5, 2/9/1899 | Taught school in Wauzeka in 1899. E. E. Brindley, Crawford County Superintendent of Schools published a comprehensive list of all teachers in the county. |
| Meyers | Fred | KC, p8c4, 4/4/1901 | Part of a group that left Steuben and Wauzeka for the West. Most of the group went to McHenry, North Dakota. |
| Meyers | Fred A. | KC, p1c3, 10/6/1899 | Married Gertie M. Hughbanks of Marietta on Sept. 22, 1898. Groom from Lancaster. Rev. Webster of Boscobel officiated. |
| Meyers | Jack | KC, p1c5, 10/3/1901 | He was "an old time resident who has been out West for many years." Visited with friends in Lynxville area. |
| Meyers | John | KC, p1c5, 8/12/1897 | Died Aug. 9, 1897 while in Prairie du Chien jail. Aged 60 years. Came from Dubuque. Brothers lived in Milwaukee. |
| Meyers | Joseph | KC, p8c4, 4/4/1901 | Part of a group that left Steuben and Wauzeka for the West. Most of the group went to McHenry, North Dakota. |
| Meyers | Mary, Mrs. | KC, p1c4, 11/15/1900 | Died Nov. 13, 1900 in Wauzeka at 93 years and 26 days. Lived with son-in-law and daughter, Mr. and Mrs. Chris Kruschka. |
| Mezera | Anna | KC, Supp., 10/27/1898 | Married Frank Nocz on Oct. 24, 1898 at the Catholic Church in Eastman. |
| Mezera | Frank | KC, p7c1, 12/12/1901 | Crawford Co. District Attorney instructed to file suit against Frank Mezera to get financial support for his daughter, Rose Mezera. |
| Mezera | Rosa | KC, Supp., 12/20/1900 | Crawford Co. Board of Supervisors approved bills related to expenses of Rosa Mezera, insane. |
| Mezera | Rose | KC, Supp., 12/12/1901 | Crawford County filed suit against Frank Mezera, father of Rose Mezera, to recover costs for care provided his daughter at the State Hospital for the Insane. |
| Mezra | Thomas | KC, p8c3, 6/19/1902 | Died June 17, 1902 in Prairie du Chien. Struck by a train. |
| Michael | Kilean | KC, Supp., 12/12/1901 | State vs. Kilean Michael heard in Crawford Co. Court. |

Genealogical Gleanings From Early Newspapers for Residents In and Near
Crawford County, Wisconsin, 1897-1902

| LAST NAME | FIRST NAME | NEWSPAPER PAGE/COLUMN MONTH/DAY/YEAR | GENEALOGICAL DATA |
|---|---|---|---|
| Michael | Mary | KC, p8c3, 8/16/1900 | Marriage license issued to Mary Michael and Richard West. Both from Town of Eastman. |
| Michelson | Christina | KC, p8c3, 4/15/1897 | Recently married Bennie Johnson. (Bride may have been from Boma area.) |
| Michle | | KC, p4c2, 9/8/1898 | Infant child of Charles Michle died last week in the Town of Eastman. |
| Mickel | Joseph | KC, p4c3, 10/26/1899 | Received marriage license to marry Lillie Stram. Bride from Eastman. Groom probably from Eastman. |
| Mickleson | girl | KC, p8c4, 4/22/1897 | Daughter born April 12, 1897 to A. Mickleson of Mt. Sterling. |
| Miller | | KC, p5c4, 2/21/1901 | The infant daughter of William Miller recently died near Boydtown. Funeral was conducted by Mr. Hogan at the Wayne Schoolhouse. |
| Miller | | KC, p5c3, 12/21/1899 | The daughter of E. Miller died yesterday of inflammation of the bowels, per Mt. Sterling news. |
| Miller | A. and Orson | KC, p5c5, 4/12/1900 | Plan to leave Bell Center soon. Going to Minnesota. |
| Miller | Abigail, Mrs. | KC, p1c4, 12/8/1898 | Died Dec. 2, 1898 in Chicago. Born Abigail Genesee on Dec. 21, 1817 in New York. Married Stephen Miller in 1866. Husband died in 1873. Moved to Chicago in 1892. Survived by 3 of 8 children. |
| Miller | Albert | KC, p1c5, 2/3/1898 | Died Friday, Jan. 28, 1898 in Baraboo, WI. |
| Miller | Andrew | KC, p1c4, 4/8/1897 | Died Mar. 31, 1897. Born Feb. 8, 1827 in Genesee Co., NY. Moved to Ohio as a child. Married Clarinda Courtright in 1848. Survived by wife; son, J. H. Miller; daughter, Mrs. William Atchison and an adopted son living in Dakota. Funeral held at the Evangelical Church in (Wauzeka?). |
| Miller | C. | KC, Supp., 12/29/1898 | Received aid from the Crawford County Soldiers Relief Commission. Resided in Haney. |
| Miller | C., Mrs. | KC, p1c4, 7/26/1900 | Died July 25, 1900 at Bell Center from a rattlesnake bite. Aged 60 years. |
| Miller | Charles | KC, p1c4, 9/12/1901 | "The fat boy" and wife departed for Grantsburg, Burnette Co., WI where Charles accepted a position as editor and foreman of a newspaper. |
| Miller | Charles | KC, p1c3, 5/22/1902 | Formerly of Wauzeka. Arrived from Dell Rapids, SD to visit brother, J. Miller of Wauzeka. Charles worked for the Kenefick Land Agency in Dell Rapids. Been in the west for about 20 years. |
| Miller | Charles A. | KC, Supp., 12/20/1900 | Crawford Co. Soldiers Relief Comm. approved aid to Charles A. Miller of Haney. |
| Miller | Charles W. | KC, p1c5, 6/1/1899 | The May term of the Crawford County Circuit Court closed. In the case, Charles W. Miller vs. Crawford County, judgement for plaintiff. |
| Miller | Charles W. | KC, p1c5, 7/12/1900 | Married Minnie Lange on July 3, 1900. Bride from North McGregor, IA. |
| Miller | F. C. | KC, Supp., 12/12/1901 | Received funds from the Crawford Co. Soldiers Relief Commission. Resided in Soldiers Grove. |

Genealogical Gleanings From Early Newspapers for Residents In and Near
Crawford County, Wisconsin, 1897-1902

| LAST NAME | FIRST NAME | NEWSPAPER PAGE/COLUMN MONTH/DAY/YEAR | GENEALOGICAL DATA |
|---|---|---|---|
| Miller | Francis | KC, Supp., 12/12/1901 | Received funds from the Crawford Co. Soldiers Relief Commission. Resided in Town of Clayton. |
| Miller | Francisco | KC, Supp., 12/20/1900 | Crawford Co. Soldiers Relief Comm. approved aid to Francisco Miller of Clayton. |
| Miller | George L. | KC, Supp., 12/18/1902 | Crawford County Board of Supervisors examined bills in the Justices and Constables' Account for State vs. George L. Miller. R. E. McDaniel was a witness. |
| Miller | G. L. | KC, p1c3, 4/3/1902 | Sold the *Soldiers Grove Advance* (newspaper) to Attorney Cryderman and Roland McDaniel of Soldiers Grove. |
| Miller | G. L. | KC, p1c4, 3/25/1897 | Nominated for county judge in Crawford County. Lived in Prairie du Chien. Married Nancy J. McDill in 1875. She was daughter of Hugh McDill and niece of Hon. Alexander McDill, a former congressman from Wisconsin. He had 2 sons and 1 daughter. Practiced law and published a newspaper in Prairie du Chien. A detailed biography was published. |
| Miller | G. L. | KC, p5c4, 5/29/1902 | The case Wisconsin vs. G. L. Miller for libel was heard at the May term of the Crawford County Circuit Court. Continued. |
| Miller | G. L. | KC, p8c4, 11/13/1902 | In the November term of Crawford County Circuit Court, State vs. G. L. Miller, Nolle prosique entered by Dist. Atty. |
| Miller | G. L. | KC, p5c3, 5/20/1897 | Issues of fact for jury to be heard in the May term of the Crawford County Court. First State Bank of LeSeuer, MN vs. G. L. Miller. |
| Miller | G. L. | KC, p5c3, 5/20/1897 | Issues of fact for jury to be heard in the May term of the Crawford County Court. G. L. Miller vs. A. J. Tainter and Marie Tainter his wife. |
| Miller | G. L. | KC, p1c6, 11/4/1897 | Issue of fact for jury to be heard at the November term of the Circuit Court in Crawford County. First State Bank of LeSeuer, MN vs. G. L. Miller. |
| Miller | G. L. | KC, p1c5, 6/1/1899 | The May term of the Crawford County Circuit Court closed. In the case, G. L. Miller vs. Crawford County, judgement for plaintiff. |
| Miller | G. L., Mr. | KC, p8c2, 3/31/1898 | Celebrated 50th birthday on Saturday evening (Mar. 26, 1898?) in Prairie du Chien. |
| Miller | Henry, Mrs. | KC, p1c4, 5/27/1897 | Lived in Prairie du Chien. Very sick with malaria. |
| Miller | J. H. | KC, p1c2, 3/31/1898 | Married Jennie Atchison, daughter of James Atchison of Eastman, on Mar. 23, 1898. Groom from Wauzeka. |
| Miller | Jay | KC, p1c6, 4/7/1898 | Elected Councilman for the Village of Wauzeka. |
| Miller | Miss | KC, p1c2, 6/27/1901 | Married J. H. Benner on Mar. 29, 1901. Groom brother of Mrs. Lou Rider of Wauzeka. Bride from Milpitas, CA. Planned to live in Milpitas. |
| Miller | Nina | KC, p8c2, 12/30/1897 | Married Frank Gaylor of South Dakota on Dec. 26, 1897. Bride from Prairie du Chien. |
| Miller | Orris J. | KC, Supp., 12/20/1900 | Crawford Co. Board of Supervisors approved bills related to expenses of Orris J. Miller (Mider?), insane. |

Genealogical Gleanings From Early Newspapers for Residents In and Near
Crawford County, Wisconsin, 1897-1902

| LAST NAME | FIRST NAME | NEWSPAPER PAGE/COLUMN MONTH/DAY/YEAR | GENEALOGICAL DATA |
|---|---|---|---|
| Miller | Phillip, Mrs. | KC, p1c5, 5/26/1898 | Died May 24, 1898 in Esterville, IA. Former resident of Wauzeka. |
| Miller | Stella | KC, p1c2, 6/6/1901 | Graduated from Wauzeka graded schools. |
| Miller | Stella | KC, p1c5, 1/16/1902 | Resided in Wauzeka area. Hired to teach in Spring Green for $30 a month. |
| Miller | Stella | KC, Supp., 12/12/1901 | Attended a Teacher's Institute in Crawford County in 1901. Resided in Wauzeka. |
| Miller | W. W. | KC, p10c1, 10/13/1898 | Returned to Prairie du Chien from California. Not as pleased with area as he expected. |
| Milliner | Jay | KC, p1c2, 7/13/1899 | Resided in Viola. Former resident of Wauzeka. |
| Mills | A. E. | KC, p1c5, 2/9/1899 | Taught school in Haney in 1899. E. E. Brindley, Crawford County Superintendent of Schools published a comprehensive list of all teachers in the county. |
| Mills | A. E., Jr. | KC, p1c3, 10/12/1899 | Resided in Mt. Sterling. Visited relatives in Cracow, Shawano Co., WI. |
| Mills | A. E., Mrs. | KC, p1c2, 11/25/1897 | Mrs. A. E. Mills of Mt. Sterling and sister, Mrs. Goodnoe of Belleville, WI were guests at W. H. Thomson residence in Wauzeka. |
| Mills | Allie | KC, p5c4, 8/17/1899 | Visited his parents in Mt. Sterling after taking photography lessons in La Farge. |
| Mills | Clyde | KC, p1c4, 9/5/1901 | Died Aug. 26, 1901. Aged 13 years. Son of Fergus Mills of Town of Seneca. |
| Mills | Della | KC, p5c3, 3/8/1900 | Teacher in Mt. Sterling. |
| Mills | Della | KC, p5c3, 11/20/1902 | Left Mt. Sterling to see brother in Minneapolis. |
| Mills | Emma | KC, p1c5, 12/6/1900 | Married Joe Graves on Nov. 28, 1900 in Mt. Sterling. Bride was daughter of Mr. and Mrs. F. Mills of Town of Seneca. Groom from Town of Haney. |
| Mills | Emma | KC, p1c5, 2/9/1899 | Taught school in Seneca in 1899. E. E. Brindley, Crawford County Superintendent of Schools published a comprehensive list of all teachers in the county. |
| Mills | George | KC, p5c3, 3/8/1900 | Arrived from South Dakota to visit father, A. E. Mills of Mt. Sterling. |
| Mills | Henry | KC, p1c3, 6/6/1901 | Departed Mt. Sterling for a job at a barber shop in Elkhorn, WI. (Returned 2 weeks later, KC, p1c5, 6/13/1901.) |
| Mills | Mrs. | KC, p5c3, 4/26/1900 | Died April 14, 1900 in Town of Seneca. Aged 90 years. |
| Mills | R. | KC, p5c2, 7/28/1898 | Arrived from Nebraska to visit old friends in Steuben. Native of Crawford Co. |
| Mills | Ray | KC, Supp., 12/18/1902 | Crawford County Board of Supervisors allowed expenses in the Criminal Case, State vs. Ray Mills. |
| Mills | Susie | KC, p8c2, 10/12/1899 | Marriage license issued in Crawford Co. to Susie Mills and Enos Grate. Both parties from Seneca. |
| Mills | W. A. | KC, p4c4, 8/3/1899 | Married Nora Carpenter of Viola on Aug. 1, 1899 in Soldiers Grove. Groom from Wauzeka. |

Genealogical Gleanings From Early Newspapers for Residents In and Near
Crawford County, Wisconsin, 1897-1902

| LAST NAME | FIRST NAME | NEWSPAPER PAGE/COLUMN MONTH/DAY/YEAR | GENEALOGICAL DATA |
|---|---|---|---|
| Mills | W. S. | KC, p1c5, 2/17/1898 | Native of Crawford Co. Attended school in Valpariso, IN. Hired to teach in Solitude, IN. |
| Mills | Walter | KC, p5c3, 3/8/1900 | Arrived from Valparaiso, IN to visit relatives in Seneca and Mt. Sterling. |
| Mills | Walter S. | KC, p1c4, 4/25/1901 | Married Grace Adele Landis on April 20, 1901. Bride from Valparaiso, IN. Groom from Marshalltown, IA. Son of Fergus Mills of Town of Seneca. |
| Mills | Will, Mrs. | KC, p5c3, 8/17/1899 | Visited former home in Viola. Gays Mills news item. |
| Mills | Wilson | KC, p5c3, 12/29/1898 | Returned to Gays Mills. Spent last 2 years in Minnesota. Brought Mrs. Mettick with him. She will spend the winter with relatives in the area. |
| Millspaugh | Samuel, Mrs. | KC, p8c3, 3/16/1899 | Died Mar. 12, 1899 in Prairie du Chien. Aged 77 years. (Mother of Mrs. J. H. Peacock per Apr. 27, 1899, p1c2.) |
| Milner | Jay | KC, p1c4, 2/10/1898 | Traveled from Gays Mills to a state beekeepers meeting. |
| Milspaugh | Addie | KC, p1c5, 10/21/1897 | Married John H. Peacock on Oct. 20, 1897. Bride, daughter of S. Millspaugh, from Prairie du Chien. Groom from Wauzeka. |
| Mindham | Benjamin J. | KC, p1c4, 5/1/1902 | J. H. McDonald and Benjamin J. Mindham were partners in a new livery business in Steuben. |
| Mindham | Mrs. | KC, p1c3, 8/14/1902 | Took her 6-year-old son to North Dakota a month ago. At Mrs. Mindham's request, Undersheriff F. W. Lewis of Crawford County brought the boy to the home of Robert Mindham of Steuben. "The little fellow had taken quite a shine to Fred and had begun to call him papa." |
| Mindham | Rebecca | KC, Supp., 12/29/1898 | Received aid from the Crawford County Soldiers Relief Commission. Resided in Scott. |
| Mindham | Robert | KC, p5c4, 4/17/1902 | Took possession of a hotel in Steuben. |
| Mindham | Walter | KC, p5c4, 2/6/1902 | Resided in Haney. Getting the materials together to build a new house. |
| Minshall | Sheriff | KC, p1c3, 6/5/1902 | From Vernon Co. Making inquiries on Mayme Fish "who is becoming notorious for recent strange acts in Vernon as well as Crawford County." |
| Mitchell | Anna | KC, p4c1, 11/21/1901 | In the case Anna Mitchell (plaintiff) vs. J. D. Stuart and M. R. Barnum (defendants), plaintiff awarded $60.00 in Crawford County Circuit Court. |
| Mitchell | Anna | KC, Supp., 12/12/1901 | Attended a Teacher's Institute in Crawford County in 1901. Resided in Gays Mill. |
| Mitchell | Blanche | KC, Supp., 12/12/1901 | Attended a Teacher's Institute in Crawford County in 1901. Resided in Gays Mill. |
| Mitchell | Charles | KC, p5c1, 2/18/1897 | Elected an officer in Utica Farmers' Mutual Insurance Co. Resided in Town of Scott. |
| Mitchell | Charles | KC, Supp. 10/27/1898 | Nominated by the Crawford County Republican Party for the office of county clerk. Resident of the Town of Scott. Farmer. Served Scott on the county board for several terms. (Picture, short bio. and character sketch provided.) |

Genealogical Gleanings From Early Newspapers for Residents In and Near
Crawford County, Wisconsin, 1897-1902

| LAST NAME | FIRST NAME | NEWSPAPER PAGE/COLUMN MONTH/DAY/YEAR | GENEALOGICAL DATA |
|---|---|---|---|
| Mitchell | Edna | KC, p5c4, 5/22/1902 | Prairie du Chien High School class of 1902. |
| Mitchell | Edna | KC, p4c2, 12/30/1897 | Edna Mitchell, Florence Mitchell, Cora Dilly, May Hanby, John Lindsay, Vertice Mitchell, Millard Dilly, Jack Shaw and Charles Craig attended the Teachers Institute. They were from the Town of Scott. |
| Mitchell | Edna | KC, p4c1, 3/24/1898 | Hired to teach this summer at the Welch School on Knapps Creek. |
| Mitchell | Edna | KC, Supp., 12/12/1901 | Attended a Teacher's Institute in Crawford County in 1901. Resided in Prairie du Chien. |
| Mitchell | Florence | KC, p8c3, 9/5/1901 | Recently married Francis Umback. Bride daughter of Charles Mitchell of Prairie du Chien. |
| Mitchell | Florence | KC, p5c2, 10/14/1897 | From Town of Scott. Taught school in Marietta. |
| Mitchell | Florence | KC, Supp., 12/12/1901 | Attended a Teacher's Institute in Crawford County in 1901. Resided in Gays Mill. |
| Mitchell | George | KC, p5c5, 4/5/1900 | Elected assessor in Town of Utica. |
| Mitchell | George B. | KC, p1c2, 1/25/1900 | Resided in Gays Mills. Delivered a tobacco crop to Madison. |
| Mitchell | George, Mrs. | KC, p1c3, 6/14/1900 | Died June 9, 1900 in Soldiers Grove area. Survived by husband and 4 children. |
| Mitchell | girl | KC, p1c4, 11/21/1901 | Daughter born Monday to Mr. And Mrs. Vertice Mitchell of Wheatville. |
| Mitchell | Grandma | KC, p5c3, 3/22/1900 | Died Mar. 19, 1900 in Gays Mills. |
| Mitchell | Howard | KC, p1c3, 1/19/1899 | Moved to Bear, AR last spring where he is now engaged in the mercantile and lumber business. Former resident of Crawford Co. Visited friends in Prairie du Chien and Mt. Sterling (per KC, p5c3, 1/26/1899). |
| Mitchell | John | KC, p1c5, 1/19/1899 | Died Friday from pneumonia. Aged 39 years. Funeral held at Gays Mills Congregational Church. Survived by wife, 3 daughters, mother, 2 sisters and 2 brothers. |
| Mitchell | John F. | KC, p1c5, 1/19/1899 | Died Friday (Jan. 13, 1899?) in Gays Mills. Aged 39 years. Survived by wife, 3 daughters, mother, 2 sisters and 6 brothers. Funeral held at the Congregational Church. |
| Mitchell | John P. | KC, p1c5, 7/19/1900 | His barn in Johnstown burned to the ground. |
| Mitchell | Julia | KC, p1c3, 12/19/1901 | Married Ole Fortney on Dec. 18, 1901 at Johnstown, WI. |
| Mitchell | Maria, Aunt | KC, p5c5, 3/29/1900 | Recently died in Town of Utica. She was one of the oldest settlers in the area. |
| Mitchell | Marie, Mrs. | KC, p4c2, 7/1/1897 | Traveled from Johnstown to Gays Mills to visit daughter, Mrs. R. W. Abby. |
| Mitchell | Melvin | KC, p1c2, 11/16/1899 | Former resident of Soldiers Grove. Managed a large implement house in Madison. |

Genealogical Gleanings From Early Newspapers for Residents In and Near
Crawford County, Wisconsin, 1897-1902

| LAST NAME | FIRST NAME | NEWSPAPER PAGE/COLUMN MONTH/DAY/YEAR | GENEALOGICAL DATA |
|---|---|---|---|
| Mitchell | Orlo | KC, p8c2, 11/13/1902 | Died Nov. 9, 1902 at Soldiers Grove. Aged 78 years and 6 months. Moved to Town of Scott, Crawford Co. in 1855. Moved to Soldiers Grove in 1892. Survived by wife and 6 children, including Charles of Prairie du Chien, George of Soldiers Grove and Melvin of Madison. Buried in Pleasant Hill Cemetery, Town of Scott. The mother of Mrs. Charles Mitchell died near Madison on Nov. 9, 1902, too. |
| Mitchell | Rayme (Mayme?) | KC, Supp., 12/12/1901 | Attended a Teacher's Institute in Crawford County in 1901. Resided in Prairie du Chien. |
| Mitchell | Roscoe S. | KC, p5c5, 2/21/1901 | Died Feb. 15, 1901 in Mt. Sterling. Aged 33 years. Unmarried. Eldest son of Mr. and Mrs. Mahion Mitchell. Brother of H. P. Mitchell. |
| Mitchell | W. H. | KC, p1c2, 6/23/1898 | "Mitchell's Concert Band, consisting of Prof. W. H. Mitchell and his six daughters, from three to sixteen years old, gave a concert at Chapek's hall Monday night, which was very good. The solos on the slide trombone and alto were very well executed and the family is indeed one of talent." |
| Mizera | Mary | KC, p8c4, 1/16/1902 | Died Jan. 4, 1902 at home near Eastman. Eldest daughter of Joseph Mizera. Survived by parents, two brothers and 6 sisters. Sister of Mrs. Allie Zander of Arizona. |
| Mizera | Thomas | KC, p5c3, 1/24/1901 | Married Lizzie Sauk on Jan. 22, 1901. Bride Town of Seneca. Groom from Town of Eastman. Many wedding guests mentioned in an article published Jan. 31, 1901, p5c4. |
| Moch | Anton, Mrs. | KC, p5c2, 11/17/1898 | Died last week while visiting in Chicago. She was the mother of Anton Lustig of Eastman. |
| Mock | Mr. | KC, p8c3, 2/18/1897 | Died Feb. 15, 1897 in the Town of Eastman. Buried in the Catholic Cemetery. |
| Moe | Christina | KC, p5c1, 12/9/1897 | Married John Olson on Nov. 24, 1897. Bride and groom were from Sterling. |
| Moe | Mattie | KC, p5c4, 5/29/1902 | Recently divorced. Spouse was Sever O. Moe. |
| Moe | Mattie | KC, p5c4, 5/29/1902 | The case Mattie Moe vs. Sever O. Moe for divorce was heard at the May term of the Crawford County Circuit Court. Decree of divorce and judgement signed. |
| Moeller | George | KC, p8c1, 1/27/1898 | Married Lizzie Geisler on Jan. 20, 1898 at Evangelical Lutheran Church in Prairie du Chien. Bride and groom were from Wauzeka. |
| Mohr | Albert | KC, p1c5, 1/9/1902 | Arrived from Granger, MN to visit brothers, Hillmer, Ed and Ameil of West Wauzeka. |
| Moldren | Andrew | KC, p1c5, 2/9/1899 | Taught school in Freeman in 1899. E. E. Brindley, Crawford County Superintendent of Schools published a comprehensive list of all teachers in the county. |
| Moline | Dan | KC, Supp., 12/18/1902 | Crawford County Board of Supervisors examined bills in the Justices and Constables' Account for State vs. Dan Moline. |
| Molstad | Nels O. | KC, Supp., 12/12/1901 | Crawford Co. Board of Supervisors approved payments in the Matter of Nels O. Molstad, Insane. |

Genealogical Gleanings From Early Newspapers for Residents In and Near Crawford County, Wisconsin, 1897-1902

| LAST NAME | FIRST NAME | NEWSPAPER PAGE/COLUMN MONTH/DAY/YEAR | GENEALOGICAL DATA |
|---|---|---|---|
| Monehan | John | KC, p1c6, 3/10/1898 | Arrived from Charles City, IA to visit parents, Mr. and Mrs. William Monehan of Wheatville. |
| Monehan | John | KC, Supp., 12/20/1900 | A Committee of the Crawford Co. Board of Supervisors reported that John Monehan, insane, was not a resident of Crawford Co. and should not be supported by said county. |
| Monehan | John C. | KC, Supp., 12/12/1901 | Listed as an insane person whose support was charged to Crawford Co. |
| Monohan | Michael | KC, Supp., 12/18/1902 | Crawford County Board of Supervisors examined bills in the Justices and Constables' Account for State vs. Michael Monohan. Frank Fortcamp and James W. Quinn were witnesses. |
| Monson | Anna, Mrs. | KC, p4c1, 10/21/1897 | Died Oct. 14, 1897 in Ferryville. Aged 21 years, 9 months and 14 days. Buried in Lutheran Cemetery. Survived by husband, son, 2 sisters and 2 brothers. |
| Monson | Helma | KC, p8c4, 7/24/1902 | Lived in La Crosse. Visited parents in Ferryville. |
| Monson | Martin | KC, Supp., 12/29/1898 | Crawford Co. Board of Supervisors approved Justices and Constables' expenses related to the case, State vs. Martin Monson and Chris Hymn. |
| Montgomery | George | KC, p1c4, 11/15/1900 | Died Nov. 11, 1900 (in Wauzeka?). Born Oct. 9, 1870 at Gravesville, Calumet Co., WI. Parents moved to Lima, WI when he was 14 years old. Buried in Lima. |
| Montgomery | George | KC, p1c4, 11/8/1900 | Critically ill with typhoid fever in Wauzeka. Attended by sister from Clinton Junction, WI and 2 aunts, Doctress Montgomery of Clinton Junction and Mrs. Holbrook of Lyma. |
| Montgomery | Orlan | KC, p1c5, 2/9/1899 | Taught school in the Town of Clayton in 1899. E. E. Brindley, Crawford County Superintendent of Schools published a comprehensive list of all teachers in the county. |
| Montgomery | Orland | KC, Supp., 12/12/1901 | Attended a Teacher's Institute in Crawford County in 1901. Resided in Soldiers Grove. |
| Moon | A. E. | KC, p4c3, 4/25/1901 | Planned to move from Gays Mills to Bruce, Chippewa Co., WI, near the residence of R. W. Abby, Jr. (former Crawford Co. resident). |
| Moon | A. H. | KC, p1c2, 4/19/1900 | Departed Gays Mills for Chippewa Co., WI to explore opportunities to invest in land. |
| Moon | Charles | KC, p5c1, 7/14/1898 | Charles Moon, Nelson Randall, Sperry George, Fred Rhinehart and Claude Rounds of Gays Mills left for North Dakota to help with the harvest. |
| Moon | Eliza A. | KC, p5c1, 10/28/1897 | Recently died (presumably in the Gays Mills area). Born May 10, 1813 in Schenectady, NY. Nee Teal. Married King Moon on Jan. 20, 1831 at Whitehall, NY. Moved to Waukesha, WI in 1855. Later moved to Petersburg, WI. In 1870 moved to near Gays Mills. Husband died in the 1870s. She was the mother of 5 sons and 4 daughters. Survived by 4 children. Two sons, Chancey and King, froze to death at Battle Creek, NB. Another son, Nelson, died at Hazelton, IA. |

Genealogical Gleanings From Early Newspapers for Residents In and Near
Crawford County, Wisconsin, 1897-1902

| LAST NAME | FIRST NAME | NEWSPAPER PAGE/COLUMN MONTH/DAY/YEAR | GENEALOGICAL DATA |
|---|---|---|---|
| Moon | Eliza Ann, Mrs. | KC, p1c4, 10/7/1897 | Died Oct. 2, 1897 at age 84 in Gays Mills. Had a son named A. E. Moon. Funeral conducted by Rev. Crouch of Boscobel. |
| Moon | W. H. | KC, p1c6, 4/7/1898 | Elected Assessor for the Village of Soldiers Grove. |
| Moon | W. H. | KC, Supp., 12/20/1900 | Crawford Co. Soldiers Relief Comm. approved aid to W. H. Moon of Clayton. |
| Mooney | Robert | KC, p1c6, 10/21/1897 | Died Tuesday in Soldiers Grove. Committed suicide. Had relatives in Brodhead, WI, where he was later buried. |
| Moore | Charles | KC, p8c4, 10/26/1899 | Married Lizzie Portwein on Oct. 25, 1899. Bride from Eastman. Groom from Prairie du Chien. |
| Moore | James | KC, p5c4, 5/22/1902 | Formerly from Petersburg and Steuben. Returned from Webster, SD after selling his 1/2 interest in a 1000-acre tract for $9000. Bought it from Hugh Hamilton for $6000 a year ago. Sold to James Hamilton, eldest son of Henry Hamilton. Other 1/2 interest owned by Lot Hamilton. (Hamiltons were from Crawford Co., WI.) Sold out because water was bad and his wife's health suffered. |
| Moran | girl | KC, p4c3, 5/27/1898 | Daughter born May 7, 1898 to William Moran of Wheatville. |
| Moran | M. J. | KC, p1c5, 12/12/1901 | Former resident of the Town of Clayton. Lives in Chicago and works near the Union Stock Yards. |
| Moran | Martin | KC, p4c3, 5/27/1898 | Traveled to Wheatville from Chicago to visit parents. |
| Moran | William | KC, p5c2, 3/3/1898 | Married Mary McDonald on Feb. 22, 1898 at St. Phillip's Catholic Church, Town of Clayton. |
| Morehead | boy | KC, p5c4, 11/7/1901 | Son born Oct. 28, 1901 to B. Morehead of Lynxville. |
| Moreland | Will | KC, p5c4, 3/13/1902 | Resided in Lynxville. He was deaf and dumb. Completed construction of a 20-foot boat for clam fishing. |
| Moreland | | KC, p5c4, 11/27/1902 | The twin babies of Ben Moreland died Friday in Lynxville. He buried one child 4 weeks ago and another child less than a year ago. |
| Morgan | William | KC, p5c2, 3/3/1898 | Married Mary McDonald on Feb. 22, 1898 at St. Phillips Church. |
| Morgans | J. R. | KC, p1c4, 9/29/1898 | At a conference of the Methodist Church held in Eau Claire, J. R. Morgans was assigned to Lancaster. |
| Morkri | Chris | KC, p1c4, 4/7/1898 | Married Anna Severson on Mar. 17, 1898. Bride and groom from Folsom. |
| Morris | Joseph | KC, p1c6, 4/7/1898 | Elected Clerk for the Town of Eastman. |
| Morris | Maggie | KC, p5c3, 4/27/1899 | Recently married Nicholas Smith. Bride and groom from Seneca. |
| Morris | Stanley | KC, p4c4, 11/15/1900 | Left Gays Mills for a job at the new tobacco warehouse in Readstown. |
| Morrison | Henry | KC, p1c3, 12/22/1898 | Married Maude Peck on Dec. 13, 1898. Bride formerly from Seneca. Daughter of Clayton Peck. Groom from Eau Claire, WI. |

Genealogical Gleanings From Early Newspapers for Residents In and Near
Crawford County, Wisconsin, 1897-1902

| LAST NAME | FIRST NAME | NEWSPAPER PAGE/COLUMN MONTH/DAY/YEAR | GENEALOGICAL DATA |
|---|---|---|---|
| Morrissey | J. | KC, p8c3, 10/28/1897 | Married Katie Nolan of Prairie du Chien on Oct. 27, 1897. Groom from Sioux City, IA. |
| Morse | girl | KC, p5c3, 9/27/1900 | Daughter recently born to Park Morse of Mt. Sterling. |
| Morse | Hattie | KC, p1c4, 10/21/1897 | Married Harlow C. Musselman of Steuben on Oct. 20, 1897. Bride was the daughter of Mrs. Henry Hamilton. |
| Morse | James | KC, p1c4, 4/18/1901 | Departed from the Steuben railroad depot for a new home in Webster, SD. |
| Morse | Julia | KC, p1c5, 3/24/1898 | Married Thomas Shields on Mar. 17, 1898 in Boscobel. Bride and groom from Steuben. Bride daughter of Mrs. Henry Hamilton. The Rev. W. J. Bond officiated. |
| Morse | Julia | KC, p1c3, 12/1/1898 | E. W. Crowley married Julia Morse at Seneca on Nov. 24, 1898. The Rev. J. M. Kelley officiated. Groom was a junior partner in the firm of Crowley Bros., a general merchandise store in Steuben. Bride was daughter of Mrs. Henry Hamilton. |
| Morse | Mary | KC, p1c5, 7/6/1899 | Married Fred E. Seekatz on July 4, 1899 in Steuben. Bride and groom from Steuben. Bride was daughter of Mrs. H.. Hamilton. (See p5c3 for more details.) |
| Morse | Miss | KC, Supp., 11/24/1898 | Married Edward Crowley on Nov. 24, 1898. Bride from Steuben. |
| Morse | Ollie | KC, p1c3, 9/14/1899 | Married G. D. Lawrence of Petersburg on Sept. 8, 1899 in Dubuque. Bride was daughter of Mrs. H. Hamilton of Steuben. Groom was youngest son of D. R. Lawrence of Petersburg. |
| Morse | Park | KC, p1c4, 9/14/1899 | Recently married Bessie George of Mt. Sterling. Groom from Steuben. |
| Morten | John | KC, p8c3, 6/12/1902 | Recently died by suicide. Drowned. Buried in Lowertown Cemetery. Resided in Bridgeport. |
| Morton | Belle | KC, p1c2, 10/14/1897 | Returned to Gays Mills in greatly improved health from Montana. Gone for 3 months. |
| Morton | Belle | KC, p4c1, 6/2/1898 | From Gays Mills. Planned to spend the summer at Yellow Stone Park. |
| Morton | John | KC, Supp., 12/18/1902 | Crawford County Board of Supervisors examined bills in the Justices and Constables' Account for the case, State -- Inquisition of body of John Morton. H. B. Rittenhouse, Wallace Martner, William Jackson and Herman Stuckey were witnesses. Dr. Cole was the examining surgeon. |
| Morton | Belle | KC, p1c6, 7/8/1897 | Traveled to Montana from Gays Mills to visit sister. |
| Moses | Goldie | KC, Supp., 12/12/1901 | Attended a Teacher's Institute in Crawford County in 1901. Resided in Sugar Grove. |
| Moses | Julia A. | KC, Supp., 12/18/1902 | Crawford County Board of Supervisors allowed expenses in the Matter of Julia A. Moses, Insane. |
| Mosgrove | Edward | KC, Supp., 12/18/1902 | Crawford County Board of Supervisors examined bills in the Justices and Constables' Account for State vs. Edward Mosgrove. |
| Mosgrove | Frank | KC, p1c2, 10/28/1897 | Married Jessie Walters on Oct. 24, 1897. Bride and groom from La Farge. Justice Halsted of Wauzeka officiated. |

Genealogical Gleanings From Early Newspapers for Residents In and Near
Crawford County, Wisconsin, 1897-1902

| LAST NAME | FIRST NAME | NEWSPAPER PAGE/COLUMN MONTH/DAY/YEAR | GENEALOGICAL DATA |
|---|---|---|---|
| Mosgrove | Frank H. | KC, p5c4, 1/16/1902 | Wrote letter to parents, Mr. and Mrs. Edward H. Mosgrove of Prairie du Chien, from Barbados, West Indies that described his adventures at sea. First of a series of letters published in the newspaper. |
| Moshier | William G. | KC, p8c3, 9/2/1897 | Died Aug. 26, 1897 in Prairie du Chien. Born July 30, 1819 at Penn Yan, Yates Co., NY. Worked as a miller in earlier years. Moved to Ion, IA. To Prairie du Chien in 1863. Survived by wife, the former Mrs. Annie Stram, and their son. Also survived by a son and daughter from his first wife who died several years ago in Prairie du Chien. |
| Muck | Charles | KC, p4c3, 10/28/1897 | Probate hearing published. Mother, Mary Muck, petitioned to be named administratrix of estate. He resided in Town of Clayton. |
| Mueller | Mrs. | KC, p1c3, 10/24/1901 | Lived near Wausau in Marathon Co., WI. Visited brother, George Beier, and sister, Mrs. F. Gink, in Wauzeka. |
| Muffley | Charles | KC, p1c3, 11/15/1900 | Came from Boscobel to Wauzeka to embalm the body of George Montgomery. |
| Muffley | John, Mrs. | KC, p1c5, 3/14/1901 | Died Mar. 4, 1901 in Boscobel. Mother of Mrs. Eliza Wells of Fairbault, MN; Mrs. Hattie Hackney of Kansas City, MO; William of Chicago and Charley and John, Jr. of Boscobel. |
| Muffley | Josephine | KC, p5c3, 1/7/1897 | Married Dr. F. G. McReynolds of Tomah today. Bride, daughter of Ald. L. Muffley, from Boscobel. Groom former resident of Boscobel. |
| Mulaney | P. F. | KC, p5c4, 7/20/1899 | Opened a furniture and undertaking store in Seneca. |
| Mulchrone | Patrick | KC, p1c5, 9/14/1899 | About 70 years old. Found dead in his cottage, 3 miles west of Liberty Pole, Vernon Co. Dead about 9 days. Last seen August 25th by brother, Toney Mulchrone. Found by Perry Vance and Ed Pettygrove. Murder suspected. |
| Mullaney | Anna | KC, p1c5, 2/9/1899 | Taught school in Eastman in 1899. E. E. Brindley, Crawford County Superintendent of Schools published a comprehensive list of all teachers in the county. |
| Mullaney | girl | KC, p5c2, 11/8/1900 | Daughter born Oct. 29, 1900 to P. Mullaney of Seneca. |
| Mullaney | J. J. | KC, p5c3, 9/27/1900 | Departed Petersburg to teach school in Buffalo, North Dakota. |
| Mullaney | J. J. | KC, p5c5, 7/11/1901 | A letter written by Mullaney of Velva, ND to T. J. Crawford of Petersburg was printed. |
| Mullaney | J. J. | KC, p1c5, 2/9/1899 | Taught school in Freeman in 1899. E. E. Brindley, Crawford County Superintendent of Schools published a comprehensive list of all teachers in the county. |
| Mullaney | James, Jr., Mrs. | KC, p1c5, 2/1/1900 | Died Jan. 18, 1900. Aged 32 years. Survived by husband and 4 small children in (Wauzeka?). Funeral held at St. Patrick's of Seneca. |
| Mullaney | Lizzie | KC, p8c4, 5/24/1900 | Died May 17, 1900 in Seneca. She was the sister of Mrs. William White. |
| Mullaney | P. | KC, p1c4, 9/7/1899 | Married Clara Garvey, daughter of T. Garvey, on Sept. 6, 1899. |

Genealogical Gleanings From Early Newspapers for Residents In and Near
Crawford County, Wisconsin, 1897-1902

| LAST NAME | FIRST NAME | NEWSPAPER PAGE/COLUMN MONTH/DAY/YEAR | GENEALOGICAL DATA |
|---|---|---|---|
| Mullaney | Pat | KC, p5c4, 9/14/1899 | Married Clara Garvey of Seneca on Sept. 6, 1899. Extensive guest and gift list published. |
| Mullanley | Anna | KC, p5c3, 5/24/1900 | Taught school in Eastman. Called to Seneca for the burial of her sister. |
| Mulligan | Phil | KC, p8c4, 8/1/1901 | Died July 26, 1901 in Prairie du Chien. He was an "old pioneer resident." |
| Mulligan | Phillip | KC, p8c4, 8/8/1901 | Died July 26, 1901. Aged 78 years. Buried in Lowertown Cemetery. |
| Mulliken | boy | KC, p8c3, 4/1/1897 | Son born Mar. 6, 1897 to Thomas Mulliken of Haney. |
| Mullikin | Amanda, Mrs. | KC, p5c3, 4/26/1900 | Died April 16, 1900 at home of brother, Melvin Peck of Johnstown. Wife of Dave Mullikin of Town of Utica. |
| Mullikin | D. R. | KC, p1c2, 9/1/1898 | From Soldiers Grove. Brought mother to Boydtown to visit her brother, O. P. Peck. |
| Mullikin | David R., Sr. | KC, p1c3, 11/13/1902 | Lived in Soldiers Grove. Went to Muscoda to be examined by the pension department. |
| Mullikin | E. D. | KC, p5c5, 4/5/1900 | Elected supervisor in Town of Clayton. |
| Mullin | John | KC, p8c3, 11/10/1898 | Resided in Prairie du Chien. Lost part of a finger in a railroad accident. |
| Mumford | Henry | KC, p1c2, 9/13/1900 | Arrived from Osborne, KS to visit friends in Wauzeka. |
| Mumford | J. E. | KC, p1c4, 3/13/1902 | Lived in Olympia, WA. Bought a subscription to *Kickapoo Chief*. |
| Mun | Mrs. | KC, Supp., 5/15/1902 | Funeral held May 11, 1902 in Fennimore. Mother of Mr. Mun of Wauzeka. |
| Munson | Ed | KC, p5c4, 6/28/1900 | Recently died in Seneca. Buried in the Utica Cemetery. |
| Munson | Edd. | KC, p8c4, 8/2/1900 | Died June 21, 1900. Born March 11, 1878 in Seneca. Son of Michael Munson. Married in 1898 to Anna Nelson of Seneca. Father of 1 child. |
| Munson | Henry | KC, p5c1, 9/30/1897 | Died Sept. 26, 1897 at Poor Farm. Buried in West Prairie Lutheran Cemetery. |
| Munson | Julia | KC, p5c3, 3/27/1902 | Married Julia Munson last Thursday at the Norwegian Church in Utica. |
| Munson | Martin | KC, Supp., 12/29/1898 | Crawford Co. Board of Supervisors approved Justices and Constables' expenses related to the case, State vs. Martin Munson. The witnesses were Christina Strand, Ole Strand and Frank Hacket. |
| Munson | Mary | KC, p4c2, 4/8/1897 | From Ferryville. Left for Wilbur, MN. |
| Munson | Mathias | KC, Supp., 12/12/1901 | Attended a Teacher's Institute in Crawford County in 1901. Resided in Rising Sun. |
| Murley | Ethal | KC, p5c3, 9/7/1899 | Resident of Boscobel. Hired to teach school in Gays Mills. |
| Murley | Ethel L. | KC, p5c4, 6/21/1900 | Married O. B. Porter on June 13, 1900. Bride from Boscobel. Groom from Wauzeka. |
| Murley | T. | KC, p1c3, 7/5/1900 | Auctioneer at a horse auction in Steuben. |

Genealogical Gleanings From Early Newspapers for Residents In and Near
Crawford County, Wisconsin, 1897-1902

| LAST NAME | FIRST NAME | NEWSPAPER PAGE/COLUMN MONTH/DAY/YEAR | GENEALOGICAL DATA |
|---|---|---|---|
| Murphy | James | KC, p5c3, 4/4/1901 | Returned to Knapp's Creek after visiting a brother, Mike, in Eau Claire, WI. |
| Murphy | James | KC, p4c2, 8/3/1899 | Filed a notice of intent to make final proof for his claim to property in Steuben. His witnesses were J. Ed Mathews, Mike Clarke, Mike Crowley and Patrick Crowley, all of Steuben. |
| Murphy | John | KC, p5c4, 11/29/1900 | Died Nov. 20, 1900 in the Town of Clayton. Member of St. Phillips Parish. Born in County Carlow, Ireland in 1826. Moved to New York in 1846 and later to Milwaukee. Moved to Crawford Co. in 1859. |
| Murphy | Joseph | KC, Supp., 12/18/1902 | The Crawford County Board of Supervisors allowed expenses in the Matter of Joseph Murphy, Insane. |
| Murphy | Katie | KC, p1c5, 2/9/1899 | Taught school in Scott in 1899. E. E. Brindley, Crawford County Superintendent of Schools published a comprehensive list of all teachers in the county. |
| Murphy | Katie | KC, Supp., 12/12/1901 | Katie Murphy of Brady attended the summer Teacher's Institute in Soldiers Grove. |
| Murphy | Katie | KC, Supp., 12/12/1901 | Attended a Teacher's Institute in Crawford County in 1901. Resided in Brady. |
| Murphy | Laurence | KC, p4c3, 3/28/1901 | Recently died in Omaha, NB. Former resident of Knapp's Creek neighborhood, Town of Clayton. |
| Murphy | Maggie | KC, p1c5, 2/9/1899 | Taught school in the Town of Clayton in 1899. E. E. Brindley, Crawford County Superintendent of Schools published a comprehensive list of all teachers in the county. |
| Murphy | P. J. | KC, Supp., 12/18/1902 | Crawford County Board of Supervisors examined bills in the Justices and Constables' Account for State vs. P. J. Murphy. |
| Murray | Frank | KC, Supp., 12/20/1900 | Crawford Co. Board of Supervisors approved payment of expenses in the matter of State vs. Frank Murray. |
| Murry | John | KC, p1c5, 7/15/1897 | New blacksmith in Steuben. |
| Musselman | boy | KC, p5c3, 11/27/1902 | Son born Sunday morning to H. C. Musselman in Steuben. |
| Musselman | H. | KC, p4c1, 10/14/1897 | From Steuben. Tried out his new sorrels Sunday by giving some of the girls a buggy ride. |
| Musselman | H. C. | KC, p6c1, 11/15/1900 | Proprietor of a hardware store in Steuben. |
| Musselman | H. C. | KC, Supp., 12/19/1901 | Conducted a hardware business in Steuben. He succeeded B. F. Hancock of Chicago. Hancock succeeded John Widmann, Jr. in the business. |
| Musselman | Harley C. | KC, p4c4, 5/9/1901 | Killed 12 rattlesnakes in dens on the hillsides west of the village of Steuben. |
| Musselman | Harlow C. | KC, p1c4, 10/21/1897 | Married Hattie Morse, daughter of Mrs. Henry Hamilton, on Oct. 20, 1897. Groom was from Steuben. |
| Musselman | Roy | KC, p5c3, 2/15/1900 | Resided in Jefferson. Visited brother, Harley of Steuben. |

Genealogical Gleanings From Early Newspapers for Residents In and Near
Crawford County, Wisconsin, 1897-1902

| LAST NAME | FIRST NAME | NEWSPAPER PAGE/COLUMN MONTH/DAY/YEAR | GENEALOGICAL DATA |
|---|---|---|---|
| Musselman | | KC, Supp., 12/29/1898 | Crawford Co. Board of Supervisors approved Justices and Constables' expenses related to the case, State vs. Musselman. The witnesses were Lee Wanamaker, James Campbell, Forest Haines, William Steavenson, James Smith, William Ray, Charles S. Hayes, E(nos?) Gill, Henry Hamilton, Walter Steavenson, John Gisler, Hattie Musselman, Mary Morse, Ed Crowley, John Steavenson, David Steavenson and James McKinney. |
| Musser | Frances E. | KC, p1c4, 6/16/1898 | Died May 5, 1898 in Phoenix, AZ. She was the niece of A. M. Beach of Prairie du Chien. |
| Mutchmann | Rev. | KC, p1c3, 4/12/1900 | The following class received confirmation in the German Lutheran church last Sunday, Rev. Mutchmann officiating: Minnie and Johnnie Stukey, Mary Yonke, Mrs. William Lewig, Johnnie Lewig, John and Julius Feldmann, Alvina Thiede, Bena Sanger, Mary Boarth, Willie Foucht, Emma Kruschke, Louise Schoenknecht and Tillie Hamen. A number of friends of the young people attended. Those from Boscobel were Mrs. J. Gross, Phillip Gross, Anna Rhein, Miss Cora Sanger, Emma and Otto Obeleiter and Mrs. Mutchmann. Those from Woodman were Mr. and Mrs. Martin and daughter, Mr. and Mrs. Monson, and Adam Fritz. |
| Myers | Hattie, Mrs. | KC, p4c1, 9/2/1897 | Traveled from California to visit relatives in Crawford Co., per Scott news items. |
| Myers | Martha | KC, p5c3, 5/20/1897 | Issues of fact for jury to be heard in the May term of the Crawford County Court. Martha Myers vs. Town of Marietta. |
| Naes | O., Rev. | KC, p9c2, 7/1/1897 | Died June 17, 1897 at 63 years of age. Pastor of the Norwegian Lutheran Church in Boscobel the last 25 years. Sent by Swedish government as a missionary to Lapland and later transferred to America. Survived by a son and daughter. Wife died a year ago. |
| Nash | Christena | KC, Supp., 12/12/1901 | Attended a Teacher's Institute in Crawford County in 1901. Resided in Rising Sun. |
| Nash | Olena | KC, p1c5, 1/13/1898 | Died Dec. 29, 1897. Daughter of Mrs. O. T. Nash of Freeman. |
| Nash | Oliver | KC, p1c5, 6/1/1899 | The May term of the Crawford County Circuit Court closed. The case Oliver Nash vs. Henry Henderson was settled. |
| Nash | Oliver O. | KC, p4c4, 11/10/1898 | Issues of Fact for Jury heard in the November term of the Crawford County Circuit Court. Oliver O. Nash vs. Henry Henderson. |
| Nash | Rudolph | KC, p4c2, 10/13/1898 | Married Bertha Johnson (of Gays Mills area?) on Oct. 5, 1898 at the Utica Church. Groom from Decorah, IA. |
| Natwick | Hans | KC, p5c4, 7/18/1901 | Died July 16, 1901 at Soldiers Grove. Aged 83 years. Father of Peter and Henry Natwick of Soldiers Grove. Resided in America for the last 40 years. |
| Naurt | John H. | KC, p1c4, 11/22/1900 | Married Alice Rider on Nov. 21, 1900 at Woodman. Bride from Wauzeka. Groom from (Boscobel?). |

Genealogical Gleanings From Early Newspapers for Residents In and Near
Crawford County, Wisconsin, 1897-1902

| LAST NAME | FIRST NAME | NEWSPAPER PAGE/COLUMN MONTH/DAY/YEAR | GENEALOGICAL DATA |
|---|---|---|---|
| Nedredoe | Ever J. | KC, p1c6, 2/3/1898 | Married Martha Knutson on Feb. 2, 1898 at the Utica Lutheran Church. Bride daughter of Erik Knutson of Mt. Sterling. Groom from Johnstown. |
| Nedreloe | Ole J. | KC, p1c6, 4/7/1898 | Elected Assessor for the Town of Utica. |
| Neidig | Alverta | KC, p5c3, 3/27/1902 | Married William Baker on Mar. 19, 1902. Bride and groom from Town of Seneca. |
| Neilson | C. | KC, p1c3, 10/27/1898 | Jeweler. Stole watch from Abe Rosencrans and a ring from J. W. Becwar. |
| Nelson | Andrew | KC, p8c3, 10/25/1900 | Died Oct. 20, 1900 in Prairie du Chien. |
| Nelson | Andrew | KC, Supp., 11/15/1900 | Recently died. Member of Knights of Pythias. |
| Nelson | Anna | KC, p8c3, 6/15/1899 | Married Albert Week on May 31, 1899 at the Utica Lutheran Church. Bride and groom from Utica. Bride was sister of Susie and Mary. |
| Nelson | Anne | KC, p5c3, 6/8/1899 | Recently married A. Weeks. Bride was daughter of Knute Nelson (of Mt. Sterling?). |
| Nelson | Delia, Mrs. | KC, p4c2, 7/21/1898 | Traveled to Eastman from Tomahawk, WI to visit relatives. |
| Nelson | Ella | KC, p1c2, 7/17/1902 | Married James Smith on July 16, 1902 in Boscobel. Bride daughter of Thomas Nelson of Steuben. Groom from Steuben. |
| Nelson | George | KC, p4c3, 1/6/1898 | Married Jennie Austin on Dec. 23, 1897. (Bride and groom may be from Readstown area.) |
| Nelson | John W. | KC, p1c6, 11/4/1897 | Issue of fact for jury to be heard at the November term of the Circuit Court in Crawford County. I. C. McGregor Guy vs. John W. Nelson. |
| Nelson | Knute | KC, p5c4 12/4/1902 | Returned to the Boma area to attend the funeral of his grandchild, the Albert Weeks baby. |
| Nelson | Minnie | KC, p1c2, 10/4/1900 | Daughter of Thomas Nelson of Haney Valley. Departed for Platteville to work at the American Glove Publishing Co. |
| Nelson | Minnie | KC, p5c5, 1/18/1900 | Taught school in Crawford Co. |
| Nelson | Nels | KC, p4c4, 3/17/1898 | He was the new landlord of the Central House in Soldiers Grove. |
| Nelson | Peter | KC, Supp., 12/12/1901 | State vs. Peter Nelson heard in Crawford Co. Court. Christina May was the witness. |
| Nelson | Peter | KC, Supp., 12/18/1902 | Crawford County Board of Supervisors allowed expenses in the Criminal Case, State vs. Peter Nelson. |
| Nelson | Sidney | KC, p5c1, 5/20/1897 | Came down from Soldiers Grove on the K. V. & N. Railway on his way to Stoughton, WI where he will visit friends and relatives. |
| Nelson | Susan | KC, Supp., 12/12/1901 | Attended a Teacher's Institute in Crawford County in 1901. Resided in Mount Sterling. |

Genealogical Gleanings From Early Newspapers for Residents In and Near
Crawford County, Wisconsin, 1897-1902

| LAST NAME | FIRST NAME | NEWSPAPER PAGE/COLUMN MONTH/DAY/YEAR | GENEALOGICAL DATA |
|---|---|---|---|
| Nelson | Thomas | KC, p5c5, 10/25/1900 | Democratic candidate for Crawford County Register of Deeds. Born July 23, 1853 in Norway. When 4 years old, moved to Dane Co. and lived there 3 years. Moved to Seneca in 1860. In 1888 purchased a farm in Citron Valley, Town of Haney. Portrait printed in newspaper. |
| Nelson | Tunis | KC, p5c3 6/19/1902 | Married Grace McCullock on June 15, 1902 at Mt. Sterling. Bride is sister of Mrs. Fred Waddle. |
| Nelson | Tunis | KC, p1c3, 8/14/1902 | Buttermaker in Steuben. Went to Baraboo to visit parents. H. C. Musselman was left in charge of buttermaking operation. |
| Nett | Benjamin | KC, p8c4, 9/30/1897 | At a conference of the Methodist Church held in Platteville, Benjamin Nett was assigned to Hazel Green, WI. |
| Netz | Alfred Frederick | KC, p4c3, 12/1/1898 | Died last Thursday (Nov. 24, 1898?) in Prairie du Chien. Born Apr. 6, 1886 to Henry Netz. |
| Netz | Fred | KC, p8c3 7/24/1902 | Fred Netz and Mrs. Martin Netz of Patterson, NJ arrived in Prairie du Chien to visit with Mr. and Mrs. Henry Netz. Henry and Fred celebrated their birthdays on July 1. They were born 2 years apart. |
| Netz | Henry | KC, Supp., 12/12/1901 | State vs. Henry Netz heard in Crawford Co. Court. Witnesses were F. Bittner, E. W. Martner, Paul Stephan, G. L. Miller, George Gronert and Thomas Stackland. |
| New | Charles F. | KC, p8c1, 6/8/1899 | Married Katherine Meyer of Prairie du Chien on June 16, 1899 at St. Gabriel's Church. Groom from Springbrook, IA. The planned to live at Bellevue, IA. |
| Newcomb | | KC, Supp., 12/20/1900 | Crawford Co. Board of Supervisors approved payment of expenses in the matter of State vs. Newcomb. The witnesses were William Wayne, Eugene Wayne, Ralph Wayne, W. L. Wayne, John Dougherty, William Buckmaster and Mary R. Wayne. Claims were disallowed for James Newcomb, Norman Newcomb, George Newcomb, Lee Newcomb, Walter Newcomb, Lee Hinds and James McDaniels. |
| Newton | A. A. | KC, p5c3, 10/30/1902 | Building a butter factory on his premises in Ferryville. |
| Newton | A., Mrs. | KC, p1c4, 1/28/1897 | Returned to Ferryville after caring for her daughter, Mrs. J. Honnaker of Liberty Pole. |
| Newton | Al | KC, p1c3, 6/9/1898 | After a 17-year absence, traveled from Duluth, MN to visit his parents, Mr. and Mrs. John Newton of Wauzeka area. |
| Newton | E. W. | KC, p5c4, 3/18/1897 | Applied to Crawford County Courts to administer the estate of Frank Stemmeiler, late of Wauzeka. |
| Newton | E. W. | KC, p1c4, 8/26/1897 | E. W. Newton and Henry Evans of Wauzeka were inventors of an egg case. Patent received. |
| Newton | G. | KC, p5c3, 5/20/1897 | Issues of fact for jury to be heard in the May term of the Crawford County Court. Estella Vanderbilt and Welhametta Mansfield her guardian vs. G. Newton. |
| Newton | George, Mrs. | KC, p5c3, 8/11/1898 | From Lynxville. Entertained her sisters, Mrs. Turk of Bell Center, Mrs. Dikeman of Soldiers Grove and Mrs. West of Chicago. |

Genealogical Gleanings From Early Newspapers for Residents In and Near
Crawford County, Wisconsin, 1897-1902

| LAST NAME | FIRST NAME | NEWSPAPER PAGE/COLUMN MONTH/DAY/YEAR | GENEALOGICAL DATA |
|---|---|---|---|
| Newton | John and Ed | KC, p1c3, 3/10/1898 | Completed a bridge over the Kickapoo River for W. A. Chatterton. |
| Nice | Lucy, Mrs. | KC, p5c2, 11/18/1897 | Married James Trehey of Bell Center on Nov. 11, 1897 at Petersburg. Bride from Boydtown. |
| Nice | Lucy, Mrs. | KC, p4c1, 8/5/1897 | Traveled from Bell Center to Boydtown to visit parents, Mr. and Mrs. I. P. (or L. P.) Lawrence. |
| Nice | Walter | KC, p1c2, 9/1/1898 | Child. Fell from a horse and broke his arm. Lived with grandfather, I. P. Lawrence of Boydtown. |
| Nickel | Charles | KC, p8c1, 11/18/1897 | Married Mary Lucas of Prairie du Chien on Nov. 15, 1897 at St. John's Bohemian Church. Groom from Town of Eastman. Party held at Benish Hall. |
| Nickelson | J. | KC, p1c6, 5/5/1898 | Married Stella Whiteaker on April 24, 1898. Bride and groom may have been from Bell Center. |
| Nickerson | M. A. | KC, p5c4, 1/9/1902 | Resided in Seneca. Daughter, Mrs. L. Baker and Mrs. T. McMann, both of Lancaster, Grant Co. visited in the area. |
| Niland | M. | KC, p1c2, 11/28/1901 | Resided in Seneca. Visited daughter in Murray, MN. |
| Niland | Nellie | KC, p4c3, 2/25/1897 | Married Tom Foley on Feb. 22, 1897. Bride and groom were from Wauzeka. |
| Niland | Thomas | KC, p8c2, 10/12/1899 | Marriage license issued in Crawford Co. to Thomas Niland and Tessie Pivot. Both parties from Marietta. |
| Nocz | Frank | KC, Supp., 10/27/1898 | Married Anna Mezera on Oct. 24, 1898 at the Catholic Church in Eastman. |
| Noe | Arley | KC, p5c5, 3/21/1901 | Died Mar. 17, 1901. Son of Jake and Ollie Noe of Barnum. Aged 2 months and 15 days. |
| Noe | Fred | KC, p5c3, 3/4/1897 | Married Bridget Dunne on Mar. 1, 1897 at Wabasha, MN. Bride and groom may have been from Wauzeka. |
| Noe | Jake | KC, p5c3, 2/7/1901 | Lived in Barnum. Recently became a father. |
| Noe | Mary | KC, p1c4, 10/13/1898 | Married Frank Mercer of Barnum on Oct. 2, 1898 at the David Staib residence in Barnum. Bride from Wauzeka. |
| Noggle | Clyde | KC, p4c1, 4/28/1898 | Volunteered to fight in Spanish American War. From Lynxville. |
| Noggle | P. N., Mrs. | KC, p5c4, 7/24/1902 | Lived in Excelsior. Visited parents, Mr. and Mrs. Lloyd Kelley of Bell Center. |
| Noggle | Pearl | KC, p4c2, 1/19/1899 | Resided in Lynxville. Received sheet music from brother, Guy, who was working with a surveying party in Montana. |
| Noggle | Pearle | KC, p5c2, 9/9/1897 | From Lynxville. Organized a music class in Eastman. |
| Noggle | Pearle Gay | KC, 5/11/1899 | Recently married Richard E. Lawler at St. Patrick's Catholic Church in Seneca. Bride daughter of L. H. Noggle. |
| Noggle | Sybile | KC, p5c4, 4/10/1902 | New teacher in Lynxville. |
| Noggle | Clyde | KC, Supp., 12/12/1901 | State vs. Clyde Noggle heard in Crawford Co. Court. |
| Nolan | Katie | KC, p8c3, 10/28/1897 | Married J. Morrissey of Sioux City, IA on Oct. 27, 1897. Bride from Prairie du Chien. |

Genealogical Gleanings From Early Newspapers for Residents In and Near
Crawford County, Wisconsin, 1897-1902

| LAST NAME | FIRST NAME | NEWSPAPER PAGE/COLUMN MONTH/DAY/YEAR | GENEALOGICAL DATA |
|---|---|---|---|
| Nolan | Martin, Mrs. | KC, Supp., 12/20/1900 | Crawford Co. Board approved payment of expenses in the matter of State vs. Mrs. Martin Nolan. The witnesses were Mrs. Maud St. Clair, Helen St. Clair, John McCabe, Frank Mosgrove and Ed Mosgrove. |
| Noney | Joseph | KC, p4c4, 11/10/1898 | Issues of Default heard in the November term of the Crawford County Circuit Court. Frank H. Poehler vs. Joseph Noney et al. |
| Noon | Patrick | KC, Supp., 12/29/1898 | Crawford Co. Board of Supervisors approved payment of expenses in the matter of Patrick Noon, insane. |
| Noon | W. H. | KC, Supp., 12/20/1900 | Crawford Co. Soldiers Relief Comm. approved aid to W. H. Noon of Soldiers Grove. |
| Norris | James | KC, p8c4, 2/14/1901 | Married Agnew Burrel on Feb. 6, 1901 at St. Gabriel's Church. Bride and groom from Bridgeport. Planned to live at Wright's Ferry. |
| North | Stanley | KC, p1c3, 11/2/1899 | Died Oct. 26, 1899 in Spring Green. Aged about 60 years. |
| Nottingham | Willis | KC, p1c4, 12/11/1902 | Lived in Soldier Grove. Directed the Quaker Cornet Band in Gays Mills. Taught music. |
| Novak | Hannah | KC, p8c3, 11/10/1898 | Married Charles Kadoch on Nov. 4, 1898 at St. John's Bohemian Church. (Bride and groom may have been from Prairie du Chien area.) |
| Novey | J. and Mary | KC, Supp., 12/12/1901 | State vs. J. and Mary Novey heard in Crawford Co. Court. |
| Novey | Joseph | KC, Supp., 12/20/1900 | Crawford Co. Board of Supervisors approved payment of expenses in the matter of State vs. Joseph Novey. The witnesses were C. Tessar, J. Katuman, Norman Campbell and W. W. Miller. |
| Nugent | Barney | KC, p1c3, 5/22/1902 | Suffered heavy losses from a flood in the Pine Creek district, Town of Seneca. Barn, horses, 20 hogs and all his hay were swept away. (also p5c3 and p8c3) |
| Nugent | Bernadetta | KC, p1c2, 9/18/1902 | Died Sept. 17, 1902. She was the 6-year-old daughter of Bernard Nugent of Pine Creek. Buried in Catholic Cemetery of Seneca. |
| Nugent | Carrie | KC, Supp., 12/12/1901 | Attended a Teacher's Institute in Crawford County in 1901. Resided in Prairie du Chien. |
| Nugent | Chris. | KC, Supp., 12/20/1900 | Represented 4th Ward of Prairie du Chien on the Crawford Co. Board of Supervisors in 1900. |
| Nugent | Mamie | KC, Supp., 12/12/1901 | Attended a Teacher's Institute in Crawford County in 1901. Resided in Prairie du Chien. |
| Nugent | Thomas | KC, p8c1, 2/16/1899 | Married Mrs. Anna Fairfield on Feb. 14, 1899. Bride and groom from Prairie du Chien. |
| Nutter | Susie | KC, p5c3, 4/26/1900 | Left Steuben for North Dakota. |
| Oakes | Bessie | KC, p1c4, 12/15/1898 | Married Clinton Arms on Dec. 14, 1898 at the Methodist parsonage. Groom from Scott. Bride from Marietta. Rev. Webster officiated. |
| Oben | Mary, Mrs. | KC, p8c3, 11/1/1900 | Died Oct. 29, 1900 in Prairie du Chien at age 73. |

Genealogical Gleanings From Early Newspapers for Residents In and Near
Crawford County, Wisconsin, 1897-1902

| LAST NAME | FIRST NAME | NEWSPAPER PAGE/COLUMN MONTH/DAY/YEAR | GENEALOGICAL DATA |
|---|---|---|---|
| O'Brien | M. D. | KC, p1c3, 10/5/1899 | Blacksmith in Steuben. Visited relatives in Grant County. |
| O'Brien | | KC, Supp., 12/19/1901 | O'Brien & Kriz operated a blacksmithing and wagonmaking shop in Steuben. |
| Ochlschager | Peter | KC, p8c2, 8/18/1898 | Died Aug. 15, 1898 at 87 years of age. Immigrated to Prairie du Chien in 1857. Survived by wife, 1 son and 3 daughters. Funeral held at the Lutheran Church and buried at Lutheran Cemetery. Surname may be spelled Oehischiager. |
| Ochnasek | Frank | KC, p5c3, 5/25/1899 | Resided in Eastman. Broke his hip when a log stable barn he was taking down fell on him. |
| O'Connell | Patrick | KC, p1c5, 10/24/1901 | New blacksmith in George Sanger's Wauzeka shop. Hails from Indiana. Worked last summer in Prairie du Chien. |
| O'Day | Pat | KC, Supp., 12/20/1900 | Crawford Co. Board of Supervisors approved payment of expenses for burial of Pat O'Day. |
| O'Dea | E. J., Mrs. | KC, p4c2, 5/23/1901 | In the court case Mrs. E. J. O'Dea vs. City of Prairie du Chien. Mrs. O'Dea won $100 and court costs for damages suffered in last summer's Buffalo Bill riot. |
| O'Dea | Edward James | KC, p8c4, 12/14/1899 | Died Dec. 12, 1899 at Prairie du Chien. Born June 29, 1862 at Bowling Green, KY. Moved to Harpers Ferry, IA with parents in 1879. Later moved to Prairie du Chien. Married Mollie Sage in 1892. Survived by wife, 2 children, mother, sister and 2 brothers. Funeral held at Catholic Church. |
| O'Dea | Mr. | KC, p8c4, 2/1/1900 | Recently died in Lowertown. He was an old man. |
| Odenwald | Adam | KC, Supp., 12/12/1901 | Listed as an insane person whose support was charged to Crawford Co. |
| Odenwald | Adam | KC, Supp., 12/20/1900 | A Committee of the Crawford Co. Board of Supervisors reported that Adam Odenwald, insane, was not a resident of Crawford Co. and should not be supported by said county. |
| Oehlochlager | Henry | KC, p8c1, 1/20/1898 | Died Jan. 13, 1898 in Minneapolis. He was the son of John Oehlochlager of Prairie du Chien. |
| Oestrander | boy | KC, p5c1, 12/2/1897 | Son born Nov. 16, 1897 to J. E. Oestrander of Eastman. |
| Oestreich | August and John | KC, p1c5, 6/1/1899 | August Oestreich and his brother, John, did good and rapid work shearing sheep in the Wauzeka vicinity. |
| Oestreick | Otto | KC, Supp., 12/12/1901 | State vs. Otto Oestreick heard in Crawford Co. Court. Witnesses were C. E. Cole, Tom Stackland, Sylvester Larabee, Will Roach, Albert Picha, Frank McCloskey and John Oestreick. |
| O'Kane | Anna | KC, p1c2, 11/10/1898 | Married Thomas Ferrick on Nov. 9, 1898 at St. Patrick's Catholic Church in Town of Scott. |
| O'Keefe | Mattie | KC, p1c5, 2/9/1899 | Taught school in Wauzeka in 1899. E. E. Brindley, Crawford County Superintendent of Schools published a comprehensive list of all teachers in the county. |
| O'Keefe | Mattie | KC, Supp., 12/12/1901 | Attended a Teacher's Institute in Crawford County in 1901. Resided in Wauzeka. |
| O'Keif | M., Mrs. | KC, p1c2, 3/13/1902 | Resided in Wauzeka. Attended teachers meeting in Steuben. |

Genealogical Gleanings From Early Newspapers for Residents In and Near
Crawford County, Wisconsin, 1897-1902

| LAST NAME | FIRST NAME | NEWSPAPER PAGE/COLUMN MONTH/DAY/YEAR | GENEALOGICAL DATA |
|---|---|---|---|
| Oland | Robert | KC, p4c1, 5/12/1898 | Oland and wife left home in Sugar Creek area. Moved to Norway per Ferryville news items. |
| O'Leary | Will | KC, p4c2, 12/9/1897 | Married Cora Pettygrove on Nov. 20, 1897. (Bride and groom may be from Readstown area.) |
| Oleson | John | KC, Supp., 12/18/1902 | Crawford County Board of Supervisors examined bills in the Justices and Constables' Account for State vs. John Oleson. |
| Oleson | Mary | KC, p1c2, 3/3/1898 | Married Albert H. Erickson in Excelsior on Feb. 21, 1898. Bride and groom from Soldiers Grove. |
| Olsen | Ida | KC, p4c1, 4/15/1897 | Left Ferryville to join her father and brothers in Charles City, IA. |
| Olson | A. S. | KC, Supp., 12/29/1898 | Crawford Co. Board of Supervisors approved Justices and Constables' expenses related to the case, State vs. A. S. Olson. The witnesses were W. T. Robinson, Frank Hackett, Wm. H. Devenport, Fred Copsey, Nick Davis, John H. Finley, Peter Barklow, John Lynch, John Dolan, Lex Richardson, John C. Oleson, Jessee Adams and L. T. Thompson. |
| Olson | Barney | KC, p4c1, 11/21/1901 | In the case Barney Olson (plaintiff) vs. Joseph Morrow (defendant), the plaintiff was awarded $222.27 in Crawford County Circuit Court. |
| Olson | Bessie | KC, p5c3, 7/21/1898 | Married P. N. Smith on July 3, 1898 at Viroqua. Bride and groom from Ferryville. |
| Olson | boy | KC, p5c3, 4/26/1900 | Son recently born to Peter P. Olson of Mt. Sterling. |
| Olson | boy | KC, p4c1, 8/26/1897 | Son born August 9, 1897 to A. S. Olson of Ferryville. |
| Olson | Charles | KC, p1c2, 3/30/1899 | Partner in Olson Bros. Of Elkader, IA. Visited friends in Wauzeka, his former home. |
| Olson | Clara | KC, p4c4, 6/15/1899 | Died June 14, 1899 in Mt. Sterling at age 4. |
| Olson | Clare | KC, p5c4, 7/13/1899 | Died June 14, 1899 at Mt. Sterling. Aged 4 years. Daughter of Peter and Cora Olson. |
| Olson | Dale | KC, p5c4, 7/24/1902 | Lived in Viola. Visited his grandparents, Mr. and Mrs. A. E. Mills of Mt. Sterling. |
| Olson | girl | KC, p1c4, 4/28/1898 | Daughter born April 11, 1898 to Ole P. Oleson of Towerville. |
| Olson | John | KC, p5c1, 12/9/1897 | Married Christina Moe on Nov. 24, 1897. Bride and groom were from Sterling. |
| Olson | John S. | KC, p8c3, 1/14/1897 | Broke collarbone when thrown from a horse. Resided in Ferryville. |
| Olson | Joseph S. | KC, p5c3, 5/20/1897 | Issues of fact for court to be heard in the May term of the Crawford County Court. Joseph S. Olson vs. Chris O. Kroker. |
| Olson | Louis | KC, p1c6, 4/7/1898 | Elected Supervisor for the Town of Utica. |
| Olson | Mons | KC, p1c3, 6/6/1901 | Returned to Freeman from La Crosse where he received treatment for lung trouble. |

Genealogical Gleanings From Early Newspapers for Residents In and Near
Crawford County, Wisconsin, 1897-1902

| LAST NAME | FIRST NAME | NEWSPAPER PAGE/COLUMN MONTH/DAY/YEAR | GENEALOGICAL DATA |
|---|---|---|---|
| Olson | Mrs. | KC, p1c3, 1/5/1899 | Resided in Merrimac, WI. Spent holidays with mother, Mrs. M. C. Kincannon of Wauzeka. |
| Olson | Ole P. | KC, p1c6, 4/7/1898 | Elected Treasurer for the Town of Utica. |
| Olson | Ole P. | KC, p5c4, 5/29/1902 | The case Sutter Bros. vs. Ole P. Olson was heard at the May term of the Crawford County Circuit Court. Judgement for plaintiff. |
| Olson | P. P. | KC, p5c3, 3/9/1899 | From Mt. Sterling. Badly wrenched a foot while jumping from a train in Lynxville. |
| Olson | Sever | KC, p1c2, 5/17/1900 | Funeral held May 12, 1900 in Soldiers Grove. He was brother-in-law of P. Figum of Wauzeka. |
| O'Mailey | Catherine | KC, p1c1, 1/28/1897 | Married Otto H. Runkel of Monona on Jan. 26, 1897 in Prairie du Chien. Bride, daughter of Mrs. James O'Mailey, from Prairie du Chien. |
| O'Malley | Catherine, Miss | KC, p8c1, 5/19/1898 | Died about May 12, 1898 in Prairie du Chien. Widow. Grandmother of Pat Burke. Funeral held at St. Gabriel Catholic Church. |
| O'Malley | Peter | KC, p8c1, 2/3/1898 | Died Jan. 28, 1898 in Prairie du Chien. He was an old time resident. Survived by wife. |
| O'Mally | Mary | KC, p8c4, 11/13/1902 | In the November term of Crawford County Circuit Court, Mary O'Mally vs. C. M. & St. P. Ry., case dismissed by plaintiff. |
| O'Mally | P., Mrs. | KC, Supp., 12/29/1898 | Crawford Co. Board of Supervisors approved Justices and Constables' expenses related to the Mrs. P. O'Mally Inquest. |
| O'Neil | Andrew | KC, p5c4, 5/29/1902 | Lived in Rutland, ND. Subscribed to *Kickapoo Chief*. Son born May 12, 1902. Sold 160 acres of land for $1950 that he bought a year ago for $700. Planned to sell homestead and invest in Western Canada. |
| O'Neil | Anna | KC, p1c5, 11/3/1898 | Anna O'Neil, teacher at the Gays Mills primary school, reported the following pupils were not absent in September: Bertha Gilder; Curtis Gander; Mary Stowell; Frank, Elsie and Blanch Kennison; Henry George; Clarence Gander; Cecil Coalburn; Daisy Pierce; David and Herman Rounds; and Dave and Ica Lester. Those not absent in October were Hazel Reagles; Clarence Gander; Herman Rounds; Gladys Hays and Grace Kast. |
| O'Neil | Anna | KC, p1c5, 2/9/1899 | Taught school in the Town of Clayton in 1899. E. E. Brindley, Crawford County Superintendent of Schools published a comprehensive list of all teachers in the county. |
| O'Neil | B., Sr. | KC, p1c2, 6/22/1899 | Recently died in Easton, MN. Former resident of Rising Sun. Moved to Minnesota last spring. |
| O'Neil | Bernard (Ben) | KC, p1c6, 8/7/1902 | Married Alma Herrling on July 30, 1902 at Mazomanie. Bride from Cross Plains. Groom from Black Earth. |
| O'Neil | boy | KC, p5c3, 10/19/1899 | Son born Oct. 12, 1899 to J. O'Neil of Gays Mills. |
| O'Neil | Charles | KC, p8c3, 8/8/1901 | Married Irene Lawless on August 1, 1901 at St. Gabriel's Church. Groom from Patch Grove. Planned to live in Patch Grove. |

Genealogical Gleanings From Early Newspapers for Residents In and Near
Crawford County, Wisconsin, 1897-1902

| LAST NAME | FIRST NAME | NEWSPAPER PAGE/COLUMN MONTH/DAY/YEAR | GENEALOGICAL DATA |
|---|---|---|---|
| O'Neil | D. | KC, p6c2, 7/15/1897 | Remains brought from South Dakota to St. Patrick's Cemetery in Seneca. Interred July 5, 1897. |
| O'Neil | Dan | KC, p1c5, 10/26/1899 | Married Maria Connelly on Oct. 23, 1899 at the Catholic Church in Rising Sun. Bride was daughter of Jeremiah Connelly of Bray Ridge. Groom from Gays Mills. |
| O'Neil | girl | KC, p1c4, 8/30/1900 | Daughter born Saturday to Dan O'Neil of Gays Mills area. |
| O'Neil | J., Mrs. | KC, p1c3, 2/1/1900 | Resided in Wauzeka. Visited mother, Mrs. A. D. Bellows of Mt. Sterling and sister, Mrs. J. A. Hayes, and niece, Naomi, of Gays Mills. |
| O'Neil | Jeremiah | KC, p5c3, 1/26/1899 | Married Edna Bellows on Jan. 18, 1899. (Bride and groom may be from Mt. Sterling area.) |
| O'Neil | Jerry | KC, p4c1, 9/29/1898 | Studied law with A. H. Long for the last 2 years. Planned to open a law office in Gays Mills. |
| O'Neil | Jerry | KC, p1c5, 1/5/1899 | H. L. Sherwood and Jerry O'Neil acquired the *Kickapoo Chief* newspaper from Riley Thompson and J. A. Bellows. Published in Wauzeka. |
| O'Neil | Jerry | KC, Supp., 12/12/1901 | State vs. Jerry O'Neil heard in Crawford Co. Court. John Bigley and Charles Hazelwood were witnesses in the case. |
| O'Neil | Jerry, Sr. | KC, Supp., 12/12/1901 | Crawford County filed suit against Peter and Jerry O'Neil, sons of Jerry O'Neil, Sr., to recover costs for care provided their father at the State Hospital for the Insane. |
| O'Neil | Jerry, Sr. | KC, Supp., 12/18/1902 | Per Report of Special Committee on Insane, Crawford County, a guardian was appointed for person and property of Jerry O'Neil, Sr. to see that his property be devoted to payment of sums expended by county for his many years in the asylum. |
| O'Neil | John | KC, p1c3, 4/5/1900 | Departed Wheatville for North Dakota. |
| O'Neil | John | KC, p1c4, 7/5/1900 | Former resident of Wheatville. Recently lost his crop to drought in Rutland, ND. |
| O'Neil | Katie | KC, p9c1, 7/1/1897 | From Rising Sun. Taught school in Yankeetown. |
| O'Neil | Mary | KC, p5c3, 6/19/1902 | Graduated from school in Mt. Sterling. Her sister, Mrs. A. M. Laird of Lynxville, attended the commencement services. |
| O'Neil | Peter | KC, p1c6, 11/4/1897 | Issue of law for court to be heard at the November term of the Circuit Court in Crawford County. Charles Witenhiller vs. Peter O'Neil. |
| O'Neil | Peter | KC, p1c6, 5/19/1898 | Issue of Law for Court to be heard in the May term of the Crawford County Circuit Court. Charles Wittenheiler vs. Peter O'Neil. |
| O'Neil | Peter | KC, p4c4, 11/10/1898 | Issues of Fact for Court heard in the November term of the Crawford County Circuit Court. Charles Whittenheller (Whittenheiller?) vs. Peter O'Neil. |
| O'Neil | Peter | KC, p5c5, 4/5/1900 | Elected supervisor in Town of Utica. |

Genealogical Gleanings From Early Newspapers for Residents In and Near
Crawford County, Wisconsin, 1897-1902

| LAST NAME | FIRST NAME | NEWSPAPER PAGE/COLUMN MONTH/DAY/YEAR | GENEALOGICAL DATA |
|---|---|---|---|
| O'Neil | Peter and Jerry | KC, p7c1, 12/12/1901 | Crawford Co. District Attorney instructed to file suit against Peter and Jerry O'Neil to get financial support for their father, Jerry O'Neil, Sr.. |
| O'Neil | Sara | KC, p5c3 12/26/1901 | Married Max Allen Laird on Dec. 25, 1901. Bride and groom from Lynxville. |
| O'Neil | Sara | KC, p1c5, 10/23/1902 | Died of burns on Oct. 21, 1902. Aged 17 years 7 months. Daughter of Mrs. Peter O'Neil. Buried in St. Phillip's Cemetery. (May have lived in Rolling Ground area.) She was brother of Peter O'Neil, Jr. (KC, p1c3, Oct. 30, 1902) |
| O'Neil | Sarah | KC, p1c5, 2/9/1899 | Taught school in Seneca in 1899. E. E. Brindley, Crawford County Superintendent of Schools published a comprehensive list of all teachers in the county. |
| O'Neil | Sarah A. | KC, p5c2, 12/2/1897 | Sarah A. O'Neil, teacher for the Seneca Primary Department, reported the following pupils were not absent in November: Rubie Collins; France Halpin; Ray Chapman; Mary Twining; Ray Collins; Thecia Garvey; Edith Stewart; Leo Bowe; Earl Scoville; Lizzie Kane; Earl Bigelow; Leota Marston; (Eitz?) Smith; Leslie Collins; France Garvey; Dannie Kane and Aggie Garvey. |
| O'Neil | Thomas and Anna | KC, p1c2, 6/5/1902 | Returned to Mt. Sterling after teaching school in Dayton, MN. |
| O'Neil Bros. | | KC, p4c5, 1/18/1900 | Advertised robes and blankets for sale in Gays Mills. |
| Only | Frank | KC, p1c5, 10/21/1897 | Frank Only of Viola and his sister, Mrs. DeLorimer of Gays Mills, traveled to Clayton Co., IA, Mrs. DeLorimer's old home. |
| Onstine | boy | KC, p1c2, 3/24/1898 | Son born Mar. 16, 1898 to Abe Onstine of Wauzeka. Weighed 12 pounds. |
| Onstine | D., Mrs. | KC, p5c4, 6/6/1901 | Returned to Steuben after visiting her parents in Boscobel. |
| Onstine | Douglas | KC, p8c4, 4/4/1901 | Married Bessie Smith on April 3, 1901. Bride from Boscobel. Groom, son of Sam Onstine, from Steuben. |
| Onstine | F. A. | KC, p5c4, 3/14/1901 | Manned a sawmill in Bell Center. |
| Onstine | Frank | KC, p4c4, 8/3/1899 | Married Alice Heligas of Lynxville on July 30, 1899. Groom from Bell Center. |
| Onstine | John | KC, p1c2, 10/3/1901 | Arrived from Spokane, WA to visit his brother, Sam of Wauzeka. |
| Onstine | Norman | KC, p1c4, 1/2/1902 | Married Flora Meyers on Dec. 26, 1901 at Carrington, ND. Bride formerly of Wauzeka. |
| Onstine | Norman | KC, p8c4, 4/4/1901 | Part of a group that left Steuben and Wauzeka for the West. Most of the group went to McHenry, North Dakota. |
| Onstine | Norman | KC, p1c5, 8/4/1898 | Went to Courtney, ND to help with the harvest. |
| Onstine | Albert | KC, p1c2, 11/23/1899 | Will Mercer and Albert Onstine returned to Wauzeka from McHenry, ND where they purchased farms. Planned to move next spring. |
| Opprecht | B. | KC, p1c4, 5/31/1900 | Lived in Petersburg/Hall's Branch area. Seven nephews from Monticello, Green Co., WI came to visit him. |

Genealogical Gleanings From Early Newspapers for Residents In and Near
Crawford County, Wisconsin, 1897-1902

| LAST NAME | FIRST NAME | NEWSPAPER PAGE/COLUMN MONTH/DAY/YEAR | GENEALOGICAL DATA |
|---|---|---|---|
| Opprecht | Fred | KC, p5c3, 11/29/1900 | Married Anna Smith on Nov. 27, 1900. Groom from (Town of Seneca?). Bride taught school in Crawford County. |
| Opprecht | Jacob | KC, p5c2, 11/8/1900 | Died day after the funeral of his brother, Balthaser. Lived in Minwaukee (Milwaukee?). One surviving sibling, a brother, lived in Germany. |
| Oppreicht | B. | KC, p5c3, 11/30/1899 | Suffered from Bright's disease and dropsy, per Gays Mills news. He was the father of Joe and Willie. |
| Oppreicht | Balthasar | KC, Supp., 11/8/1900 | Died Oct. 26, 1900 in Town of Seneca. Born in town of Dorn House, Switzerland on June 28, 1830. Moved to New Glarus, Green Co., WI in 1853. Married there on April 29, 1858 to Regula Stussi. Moved to Crawford Co. Oct. 26, 1858. Survived by his wife, 6 children and a brother, Jacob of Milwaukee (who died a day after Balthasar's funeral). |
| Oppreicht | girl | KC, p5c3, 5/1/1902 | Daughter born April 22, 1902 to Fred Oppreicht of Seneca. |
| Oppreicht | Regula, Mrs. | KC, p1c4, 6/12/1902 | Died June 8, 1902 in Town of Haney. Born June 20, 1840 at Haslen, Glarus Co., Switzerland. Moved to America in 1857 with parents. Married Balthasar Oppreicht on April 29, 1858 at New Glarus, WI and soon moved to Crawford Co. Husband died 1 year and 7 months ago. Survived by 4 sons and 3 daughters. Funeral held at Congregational Church of Mt. Sterling. Buried in Willett's Cemetery/Mt. Sterling Cemetery. |
| Oriloff | William | KC, p1c6, 2/10/1898 | Held up by a tramp in Wauzeka. Escaped. |
| Ortlaff | Albert | KC, p5c2, 5/20/1897 | Had a narrow escape from drowning in the Kickapoo River while playing with two other boys. A large snake climbed into the boat. Jumped into the river to escape. His companions rescued him. |
| Ortlaff | Carl, Sr. | KC, p1c2, 8/8/1901 | Departed Wauzeka to visit daughter, Mrs. Sherman Johnson of Prairie du Chien. |
| Osbacher | boy | KC, p8c2, 1/26/1899 | Son born Jan. 22, 1899 to George Osbacher of Prairie du Chien. |
| Osborne | Landon | KC, p5c3, 2/9/1899 | Osborne and his mother left East Gays Mills for a new home in Quincy, IL. |
| O'Shaughessy | J. | KC, p1c5, 3/4/1897 | Married May Scoville on Feb. 22, 1897. The Rev. J. Keeley officiated. Bride and groom may have been from Town of Seneca. |
| O'Shaughnessy | J. | KC, p8c4, 4/8/1897 | Lived in Town of Seneca. Rumored that he planned to move to Washington State. |
| O'Shaughnessy | Mattie | KC, p1c5, 2/9/1899 | Taught school in Wauzeka in 1899. E. E. Brindley, Crawford County Superintendent of Schools published a comprehensive list of all teachers in the county. |
| O'Shaughnessy | Mr. | KC, p1c4, 4/1/1897 | Died Mar. 23, 1897 at home near Boydtown. |
| O'Shaughnessy | William | KC, p4c3, 4/8/1897 | Probate notice published. Peter J. O'Shaughnessy petitioned to be the administrator. |

Genealogical Gleanings From Early Newspapers for Residents In and Near
Crawford County, Wisconsin, 1897-1902

| LAST NAME | FIRST NAME | NEWSPAPER PAGE/COLUMN MONTH/DAY/YEAR | GENEALOGICAL DATA |
|---|---|---|---|
| O'Shaunessy | John, Mr. and Mrs. | KC, p1c5, 3/23/1899 | Recently moved into town (Seneca). Planned to move to Washington in the spring. |
| O'Shaunessy | Mattie | KC, p1c2, 1/2/1902 | Planned to marry P. A. Smith soon. |
| O'Shaunessy | Mattie | KC, p1c5, 1/9/1902 | Married P. A. Smith on Jan. 6, 1902. Bride was a teacher. Groom from Town of Eastman. |
| Oss | Peter | KC, p5c3, 3/20/1902 | Moved family from Gays Mills to Boscobel. |
| Ostrander | Jessie | KC, p5c4, 6/20/1901 | Graduated from the Eastman graded schools. |
| Ostrander | John | KC, p5c4, 2/8/1900 | Hand badly injured while working at his sawmill in Eastman. |
| Oswald | Anna Philomena | KC, p8c4, 1/24/1901 | Married Paul Herold on Jan. 22, 1901 at St. Gabriel Church. Bride daughter of George Oswald of Prairie du Chien. Groom son of John Herold of Prairie du Chien. |
| Oswald | boy | KC, p1c4, 4/20/1899 | Son born April 14, 1899 to Otto Oswald of Bridgeport. |
| Oswald | C. | KC, p1c3, 4/26/1900 | Died April 25, 1900 in Grand Grae. Wife died April 23, 1900. |
| Oswald | C., Mrs. | KC, p1c3, 4/26/1900 | Died April 23, 1900 in Grand Grae. Husband died April 25, 1900. Wife was mother of Henry Geitz of Wauzeka. |
| Oswald | Charles | KC, p1c4, 5/3/1900 | Died April 25, 1900. Born Feb. 11, 1814 in Germany. Married Julia Schally in March 1863. (This must be a newspaper typo. Maybe date is 1836.) Fathered 10 children. Seven died young. Family emigrated to Prairie du Chien in 1853. Later moved to Grand Grae. Married a second time to Mrs. Margaret Geitz. |
| Oswald | Charles | KC, p1c3, 2/15/1900 | Charles Oswald of Dakota and Louis Oswald of Elgin, IA visited their brother, Leo of the Wauzeka area. Planned to visit another brother, Otto, in Bridgeport and a sister in Grant Co. |
| Oswald | George | KC, p5c5, 4/5/1900 | Elected assessor in City of Prairie du Chien. |
| Oswald | Herman | KC, p1c4, 3/31/1898 | Left Wauzeka for new home in Garey, Dual Co., SD. |
| Oswald | Herman | KC, p5c3, 4/13/1899 | Departed West Wauzeka for South Dakota. |
| Oswald | Margaret | KC, p1c4, 5/3/1900 | Died April 23, 1900. Born May 23, 1819 in Bavaria, Germany. Came to U.S. when 15 years old. Married Leonard Geitz in 1840. Seven of 9 children died young. Married Charles Oswald in 1856 and had 5 children. One has died. Resided in Grand Grae. |
| Oswald | O. J. | KC, Supp., 12/20/1900 | Crawford Co. Board of Supervisors approved payment of expenses in the matter of State vs. O. J. Oswald. The witnesses were James Lawler, Sr.; James Lawler, Jr.; Henry Smith and C. Kuchenbecker. |
| Oswald | Otto | KC, p1c4, 4/26/1900 | Proprietor of the Bridgeport Hotel and the stage line to Bloomington. |

Genealogical Gleanings From Early Newspapers for Residents In and Near
Crawford County, Wisconsin, 1897-1902

| LAST NAME | FIRST NAME | NEWSPAPER PAGE/COLUMN MONTH/DAY/YEAR | GENEALOGICAL DATA |
|---|---|---|---|
| Otchenosock | Rosa | KC, p5c3, 10/5/1899 | Married Wallace Gossel last Monday (Oct. 2, 1899?). |
| Otman | Will | KC, p4c1, 11/11/1897 | Married Blanche Vanderbilt of Lynxville on Nov. 6, 1897 at Prairie du Chien. Groom from Town of Eastman. |
| O'Toole | Patrick | KC, p8c3, 6/12/1902 | Recently died in Prairie du Chien. Father of Rev. Fr. O'Toole of Mondovi, WI. |
| Ottman | Edna | KC, p8c3, 4/15/1897 | Married Walter West last Monday. Bride and groom from Town of Eastman. |
| Ottman | girl | KC, p5c3, 9/5/1901 | Infant daughter of William Ottman died last Wednesday in Lynxville. Funeral held at the Congregational Church. |
| Ottman | girl | KC, p5c3, 6/19/1902 | Daughter born Saturday to Will Ottman of Lynxville. |
| Otto | Emma | KC, p8c1, 10/20/1898 | Married Joseph Tesar, son of V. Tesar, on Oct. 19, 1898. Bride was daughter of the late Henry Otto, Jr. Bride and groom from Prairie du Chien. |
| Oustrich | Otto | KC, Supp., 12/12/1901 | State vs. Otto Oustrich heard in Crawford Co. Court. |
| Owens | James | KC, p1c4, 12/9/1897 | From Mazomanie. Struck in the back by a sharp axe that fell from the wall at the Keogh Excelsior Mfg. Co. in Petersburg. Taken to his home. |
| Page | C. E., Mrs. | KC, p1c5, 5/19/1898 | Widow. Lived near Ross. Lost her only cow. A friend, Dr. C. V. Porter, replaced it. |
| Pahrnum | Oscar | KC, Supp., 12/20/1900 | Crawford Co. Board of Supervisors approved payment of expenses in the matter of State vs. Oscar Pahrnum. Frank Brady, Herb Beach and Joe Palderson were witnesses. |
| Paine | Mr. | KC, p5c2, 8/7/1902 | Remodeled a building in Gays Mills to open a restaurant. Previously occupied by D. Green. |
| Pally | Rev. | KC, p5c3, 8/8/1901 | He was a "colored gentleman." Preached at the Christian Church in Lynxville. |
| Palmer | Ben | KC, p1c3, 11/3/1898 | Buggy ruined when horse broke lose from hitching post in front of Becwar's saloon in Wauzeka. Ran down Main Street. |
| Palmer | girl | KC, p8c4, 4/15/1897 | Daughter born April 8, 1897 to B. C. Palmer of Boydtown. |
| Palmer | Mary, Mrs. | KC, p12c3, 12/29/1898 | Died Dec. 21, 1898 in Bell Center. Born in 1850 in England. Moved to Galena, IL as a child. Lived there until 1867. Married Mars Schawtka and gave birth to 5 children. Husband died Oct. 19, 1880. Moved to Dubuque and lived there until 1891. Married R. H. Palmer in 1891 and moved to Bell Center. Buried in Bell Center Cemetery. |
| Palmer | Mr. | KC, p4c3, 6/2/1898 | From Belle Center. At age 82, has gone blind. |
| Palmer | W. G. | KC, p1c1, 1/18/1900 | Advertised legal services. Attorney based in Boscobel. |
| Palmer | | KC, p4c4, 11/15/1900 | The 4-year-old daughter of Ben Palmer of Boydtown died last Sunday while playing in a fishing tent that caught fire. |
| Pane | Joe | KC, p5c3, 3/14/1901 | Lived in Boydtown. Lost a horse while crossing the Wisconsin River with a load of railroad ties. (Payne or Paine?) |

Genealogical Gleanings From Early Newspapers for Residents In and Near
Crawford County, Wisconsin, 1897-1902

| LAST NAME | FIRST NAME | NEWSPAPER PAGE/COLUMN MONTH/DAY/YEAR | GENEALOGICAL DATA |
|---|---|---|---|
| Parfrey | E. H. | KC, p4c3, 5/13/1897 | Managed Keogh Excelsior Manufacturing Co. in Petersburg. |
| Parker | W. A. | KC, p1c3, 6/2/1898 | From Wauzeka. Worked as a civil engineer on the K. N. and N. Railway. Left for Joplin, MO to mine for zinc and lead. |
| Parsons | F. P., Mrs. | KC, p1c4, 4/28/1898 | Recently died at Faribault, MN. She was the former Genevieve R. Shipley. Previously lived in Prairie du Chien. Sister-in-law of Mrs. W. A. Chatterton. |
| Parsons | John M. | KC, p1c2, 4/21/1898 | Arrived from Faribuit, MN. Called to bedside of mother. Visited uncle, W. A. Chatterton. |
| Paskeivitz | boy | KC, p5c2, 3/10/1898 | Son born Feb. 26, 1898 to George Paskeivitz of Gays Mills. Weighed 13 pounds. |
| Paskewitz | George | KC, p4c3, 3/24/1898 | Moved family from Gays Mills to Echo, MN. |
| Patalaff | Charles | KC, p8c3, 6/14/1900 | Married Flora Bump on June 5, 1900. Bride from Cripple Creek, CO. Groom was mayor of Prairie du Chien. |
| Patch | Ralph E. | KC, p1c3, 3/16/1899 | Married Edna F. Hicklin of Patch Grove on Mar. 4, 1899 at Prairie du Chien. Bride was niece of Henry Evans of Wauzeka. Plan to move to Poplar, MT. |
| Patten | David | KC, p1c6, 4/7/1898 | Elected Treasurer for the Town of Marietta. |
| Patten | David | KC, p5c5, 4/5/1900 | Elected treasurer in Marietta. |
| Patten | David, Mrs. | KC, p5c2, 11/11/1897 | Visited mother, Mrs. Hazzart, per Christ Corners news. |
| Patten | Eva B. | KC, p1c6, 5/19/1898 | Issue of Default to be heard in the May term of the Crawford County Circuit Court. Sam E. Patten vs. Eva B. Patten. |
| Patten | James P. | KC, p4c3, 11/9/1899 | Died Nov. 3, 1899 in Town of Marietta. Aged 64 years. Survived by wife and 8 grown children. |
| Patten | James, Mrs. | KC, p5c4, 2/13/1902 | Recently died on Maple Ridge, Town of Haney. |
| Patten | Mae | KC, p1c5, 2/9/1899 | Taught school in Marietta in 1899. E. E. Brindley, Crawford County Superintendent of Schools published a comprehensive list of all teachers in the county. |
| Patten | Sam E. | KC, p1c6, 5/19/1898 | Issue of Default to be heard in the May term of the Crawford County Circuit Court. Sam E. Patten vs. Eva B. Patten. |
| Patten | Samuel E. | KC, p1c2, 8/22/1901 | Died Aug. 18, 1901at Columbus, WI. He was son of Mrs. James Patten of Town of Marietta. Married Lillian Spencer of Millett, WI several years ago. Buried at Maple Ridge Cemetery. |
| Patterson | Robert | KC, p5c1, 11/8/1900 | Returned to Gays Mills to visit. Has lived in Minneapolis for the last 2 years. |
| Patterson | Robert | KC, p1c6, 5/12/1898 | Planned to volunteer for Spanish American War. From Gays Mills area. |

Genealogical Gleanings From Early Newspapers for Residents In and Near
Crawford County, Wisconsin, 1897-1902

| LAST NAME | FIRST NAME | NEWSPAPER PAGE/COLUMN MONTH/DAY/YEAR | GENEALOGICAL DATA |
|---|---|---|---|
| Patton | James | KC, p4c1, 8/5/1897 | James Patton, Miles Campbell and Mr. Ayres were struck by lightning while riding in a wagon in Patton's field near Steuben. Nearly killed Ayres. Didn't recover his senses for nearly an hour. |
| Patton | Lee | KC, p8c2, 1/12/1899 | Home on furlough in Town of Scott from 4th Regt. WI Vol. |
| Patton | Mae, Miss | KC, p5c3, 8/3/1899 | Taught in Reynolds School. Visited her hometown, Calumet, IA. |
| Patzlaff | Carl | KC, p5c5, 4/5/1900 | Elected Mayor in City of Prairie du Chien. |
| Paulsen | Clara | KC, p5c3, 11/6/1902 | Married T. O. Hovey on Oct. 2, 1902 at Clear Lake, IA. Bride from Mason City. Groom from Prairie du Chien. |
| Paulson | Miss | KC, p5c3, 3/23/1899 | Miss Paulson of Minnesota visited her sister, Mrs. William Harris of Harris Ridge. |
| Payne | Joe | KC, p1c5, 2/11/1897 | Hired to operate the James Mason farm in Steuben this season while the latter is in Dakota. |
| Payne | Malinda, Mrs. | KC, p5c2, 11/8/1900 | Visited her grandson, P. L. Purrington of Bell Center. |
| Payne | W. | KC, p5c3, 10/16/1902 | Lived in Boscobel. Visited friends in Bell Center. |
| Payor | Joseph | KC, Supp., 12/18/1902 | Crawford County Board of Supervisors examined bills in the Justices and Constables' Account for State vs. Joseph Payor. |
| Peacha | Anthony | KC, Supp., 12/29/1898 | Crawford County Board of Supervisors approved Justices and Constables' expenses related to the case, State vs. Anthony Peacha. The witnesses were Robt. Fisher, Andrew Merrell, James Smrz, Hiram Walker, William White, Victor Jennings, William Curran, James Roach and Hubert Finney. |
| Peacock | boy | KC, p1c3, 5/31/1900 | Son recently born to J. H. Peacock of Wauzeka. |
| Peacock | boy | KC, p7c1, 7/15/1897 | Son born last Thursday to Joseph Peacock, Jr. of Wauzeka. Peacock owned a restaurant. |
| Peacock | girl | KC, p1c2, 10/6/1898 | Daughter born Oct. 3, 1898 to J. H. Peacock of Wauzeka. |
| Peacock | J. H., Mrs. | KC, p1c2, 3/16/1899 | Mother of Mrs. J. H. Peacock died last week. Funeral held Tuesday (Mar. 14, 1899?) in Prairie du Chien (Name given elsewhere in newspaper - Mrs. Samuel Millspaugh.) |
| Peacock | J. T. | KC, p1c2, 7/14/1898 | Planned to move from Wauzeka to Montfort and open a restaurant. |
| Peacock | James, Sr. | KC, p1c4, 4/12/1900 | Peacock and his son-in-law, Art Reeter, prospected for lead on the C. L. Lathrop farm in West Wauzeka. |
| Peacock | John | KC, p1c3, 9/6/1900 | Delegate to the Republican convention in Gays Mills. |
| Peacock | John | KC, p1c5, 10/21/1897 | Son of Joseph Peacock, Sr. of Wauzeka. Recently married in Prairie du Chien. Wife was a Milsbaugh, per KC, p1c2, 11/4/1897. |
| Peacock | John H. | KC, p1c5, 10/21/1897 | Married Addie Milspaugh, daughter of S. Millspaugh, on Oct. 20, 1897. Bride from Prairie du Chien. Groom from Wauzeka. |

Genealogical Gleanings From Early Newspapers for Residents In and Near
Crawford County, Wisconsin, 1897-1902

| LAST NAME | FIRST NAME | NEWSPAPER PAGE/COLUMN MONTH/DAY/YEAR | GENEALOGICAL DATA |
|---|---|---|---|
| Peacock | Joseph | KC, p4c3, 1/23/1902 | Charged in Madison with extorting more than regular fees as a pension attorney. Summoned to testify from the area were Mrs. Dworak (John Dworak's mother), Mrs. Phillip Steinbach and Marsha D. Lyons. |
| Peacock | Joseph | KC, p1c4, 4/17/1902 | Resided in Wauzeka. Arraigned in Federal Court. Charged with collecting more than legal fee for procuring pension for Barbara Dworak, an aged widow. Peacock very weak with consumption. |
| Peacock | Joseph | KC, p1c2, 3/9/1899 | Resident of Wauzeka. Rapidly improving after suffering a paralytic stroke while on legal business in Eastern Wisconsin. |
| Peacock | Joseph, Sr. | KC, p5c2, 1/18/1900 | Justice of the Peace. Advertised service helping with real estate transactions, pension claims and insurance. Resided in Wauzeka. |
| Peacock | Joseph, Sr. | KC, p1c3, 10/14/1897 | From Wauzeka. Scheduled to preach at Evangelical Church in Wauzeka. "He is an old preacher, although he has not been in the pulpit for several years." |
| Peacock | Joseph, Sr. | KC, p1c2, 4/7/1898 | Served as administrator of an estate in Darlington, WI. |
| Peacock | Joseph, Sr. | KC, p1c6, 4/7/1898 | Elected Justice of the Peace for the Village of Wauzeka. |
| Peacock | Mary | KC, p1c4, 1/18/1900 | Married Arthur Reiter on Jan. 17, 1900. Bride from Wauzeka. |
| Peacock | Mary | KC, p1c5, 11/18/1897 | Installed as an officer at the International Order of Good Templars (I.O.G.T.) Lodge in Wauzeka. |
| Peacock | William | KC, p7c2, 7/15/1897 | Funeral held last Friday in Benton, WI. Nephew, Joseph Peacock, Sr., from (Wauzeka?). |
| Peacock | Willie | KC, p1c2, 10/28/1897 | Moved to Elk Grove for a job. |
| Pease | George | KC, p4c2, 3/24/1898 | Charles Allen and George Pease of Lynxville were in Seattle on their way to the Klondike. Mrs. Pease visited her mother-in-law in Chicago. |
| Pease | George | KC, p5c4, 9/21/1899 | Returned to Lynxville from Klondike. |
| Pease | George | KC, p1c6, 11/4/1897 | Issue of fact for jury to be heard at the November term of the Circuit Court in Crawford County. George Pease vs. Chicago, Burlington & Northern Railroad Co. |
| Pease | Paul | KC, p5c3, 7/24/1902 | Visited parents in Lynxville. Preparing for the ministry in Epworth, IA. |
| Pease | Paul | KC, p5c2, 7/71898 | Paul Pease, Mike Lawler, Milo Wolcott and Len Newton of Lynxville enlisted in the army. Newton had a wife and a little daughter. |
| Peasley | Sarah | KC, p1c5, 2/9/1899 | Taught school in Utica in 1899. E. E. Brindley, Crawford County Superintendent of Schools published a comprehensive list of all teachers in the county. |
| Peasley | Sarah M. | KC, p5c3, 6/22/1899 | Married Joseph Melvin on June 19, 1899 at St. James Catholic Church at Rising Sun. |

Genealogical Gleanings From Early Newspapers for Residents In and Near
Crawford County, Wisconsin, 1897-1902

| LAST NAME | FIRST NAME | NEWSPAPER PAGE/COLUMN MONTH/DAY/YEAR | GENEALOGICAL DATA |
|---|---|---|---|
| Peck | Calvin | KC, p5c1, 5/27/1897 | Died May 17, 1897 in Viroqua. Born in Pennsylvania. Moved to Crawford Co. 44 years ago. Moved to Viroqua 3 years ago. Survived by wife and 2 sons. Buried in family burying ground in Towersville. |
| Peck | George | KC, p1c4, 6/9/1898 | Native of Crawford Co. Purchased *Cashton Record* (a newspaper). Was a foreman of the *Vernon Censor*. |
| Peck | Maude | KC, p1c3, 12/22/1898 | Married Henry Morrison of Eau Claire, WI on Dec. 13, 1898. Bride formerly from Seneca. Daughter of Clayton Peck. |
| Peck | O. P. | KC, p1c3, 4/5/1900 | Elected constable in Boydtown. |
| Peck | P. M. | KC, p1c2, 3/21/1901 | Lived in Towerville. Proprietor of the buckwheat and feed mill in Steuben. Visited relatives in Steuben. |
| Peck | P. M. | KC, p1c2, 12/2/1897 | Ran a buckwheat mill in Johnstown Valley. |
| Peck | Walter | KC, Supp., 12/12/1901 | State vs. Walter Peck heard in Crawford Co. Court. Witnesses were Ole Gunderson, Ole Davidson, Anna Wood, Dave Wood, Bridget Dunne, Fred J. McCormick, Bert Crume and Elmer Tainter. |
| Peck | Walter | KC, Supp., 12/12/1901 | State vs. Walter Peck and Arthur Finley heard in Crawford Co. Court. Witnesses were R. L. Smith, Bertha Smith, Mert. Munion, Alvin Dinsdale and Mary Dinsdale. |
| Pecor | Charles | KC, p5c2, 3/4/1897 | Married Kate Schwatka on Feb. 28, 1897 in Bell Center. The bridesmaid was Mrs. Lucy Nice. Groomsman was James Trehey. |
| Pecor | Charles | KC, p4c3, 4/21/1898 | Resided in Bell Center. Rented the H. Whiteaker farm. |
| Pecor | Charles, Mr. and Mrs. | KC, p5c5, 4/12/1900 | Recently departed Bell Center for the west. |
| Pecor | H. | KC, p5c6, 3/8/1900 | Did a lively blacksmith trade in Belle Center. |
| Pecor | Louis Alden | KC, p5c1, 10/6/1898 | Recently died. Son of Charles Pecor. Born Dec. 16, 1897 in Bell Center. |
| Peer | E. M. | KC, p4c3, 4/21/1898 | Guest of Mrs. William Whiteaker of Wheatville. Resided in Tacoma, WA. |
| Peerson | N. O. | KC, p1c6, 5/19/1898 | Issue of Fact for Court to be heard in the May term of the Crawford County Circuit Court. La Crosse Steel Roofing and Corrugation Co. vs. N. O. Peerson et al. |
| Peese | William | KC, p5c4, 4/17/1902 | Resided in Lynxville. Built a boat for clam fishing. |
| Pellock | Mike | KC, Supp., 12/18/1902 | Crawford County Board of Supervisors examined bills in the Justices and Constables' Account for State vs. Mike Pellock. |
| Pelock | James | KC, p8c1, 10/19/1899 | Married Annie Touble at St. John's Bohemian Church on Wednesday (Oct. 18, 1899?). |
| Pelok | Mike | KC, p8c3, 11/22/1900 | Married Mrs. T. Vauek on Nov. 19, 1900. Bride and groom from Prairie du Chien. |
| Pengilly | Nellie E. | KC, p1c4, 9/15/1898 | Married Fred Meyer on Sept. 8, 1898 in Boscobel. |

Genealogical Gleanings From Early Newspapers for Residents In and Near
Crawford County, Wisconsin, 1897-1902

| LAST NAME | FIRST NAME | NEWSPAPER PAGE/COLUMN MONTH/DAY/YEAR | GENEALOGICAL DATA |
|---|---|---|---|
| Pengilly | Richard | KC, p8c4, 9/30/1897 | At a conference of the Methodist Church held in Platteville, Richard Pengilly was assigned to Fennimore. |
| Pengilly | Richard | KC, p1c4, 9/29/1898 | At a conference of the Methodist Church held in Eau Claire, Richard Pengilly was assigned to Fennimore. |
| Perham | Helen | KC, p4c1, 6/10/1897 | Lived in Readstown. Planned to work for brother as a waitress at his restaurant in Sparta. |
| Perrin | boy | KC, p1c2, 7/21/1898 | Son born Monday to Dr. G. H. Perrin of Wauzeka. |
| Perrin | F. G. | KC, p5c5, 4/5/1900 | Elected village clerk in Wauzeka. |
| Perrin | F. J. | KC, p1c4, 7/3/1902 | Married Mollie Copper on June 26, 1902 in Prairie du Chien at the City Hotel. Bride, the youngest daughter of O. B. Copper, Sr., was from Ferryville. Groom, youngest brother of Dr. Perrin, was from Wauzeka. |
| Perrin | F. J. | KC, p1c2, 1/31/1901 | Village Clerk in Wauzeka. Purchased an artificial leg. |
| Perrin | F. J. | KC, p4c4, 1/7/1897 | Advertised services as a crayon portrait artist. Resided in Wauzeka. |
| Perrin | F. J. | KC, p1c2, 11/3/1898 | Installed as an officer at the International Order of Good Templars (I.O.G.T.) Lodge in Wauzeka. |
| Perrin | G. D., Dr. | KC, p1c1, 1/18/1900 | Advertised medical services. Practice based in Wauzeka. |
| Perrin | G. H. | KC, p5c5, 4/5/1900 | Elected village trustee in Wauzeka. |
| Perrin | G. H., Dr. | KC, p1c3, 1/25/1900 | Featured in an article on Wauzeka's business concerns. Practice was based in Wauzeka. Graduated from Keokuk Medical College of Iowa in 1892. |
| Perrin | G. H., MD | KC, p5c1, 1/7/1897 | Advertised medical services. Office based in Wauzeka. |
| Perrin | H. H. | KC, p1c1, 1/18/1900 | Advertised services as Justice of the Peace and notary. Resided in Wauzeka. |
| Perrin | H. Henry | KC, p5c5, 1/10/1901 | Died Jan. 5, 1901 in Wauzeka. Born in Cassville, Grant Co. on Nov. 15, 1873. Moved to Wauzeka in 1897. Brother of Dr. Perrin. |
| Perrin | Winnifred Louise | KC, p8c2, 6/10/1897 | Died June 8, 1897. Aged 6 months and 19 days. Daughter of Dr. and Mrs. G. H. Perrin. |
| Peterson | Alice | KC, p4c3, 5/12/1898 | Married James Shields on May 1, 1898 in Boscobel. Bride and groom from Steuben. |
| Peterson | Atley | KC, p1c2, 2/6/1902 | Officers of the Agricultural and Driving Park Association at Gays Mills: Atley Peterson, W. H. Thomsom, N. Jurgenson. Directors: J. A. Hayes, A. Peterson, J. W. McCullick, W. H. Thomson and M. Barham. |
| Peterson | Atley | KC, p1c6, 4/7/1898 | Elected Trustee for the Village of Soldiers Grove. |
| Peterson | Atley | KC, p1c6, 5/19/1898 | Issue of Fact for Court to be heard in the May term of the Crawford County Circuit Court. John Gerhardt vs. Betsey F. Peterson, Atley Peterson and others. |

Genealogical Gleanings From Early Newspapers for Residents In and Near
Crawford County, Wisconsin, 1897-1902

| LAST NAME | FIRST NAME | NEWSPAPER PAGE/COLUMN MONTH/DAY/YEAR | GENEALOGICAL DATA |
|---|---|---|---|
| Peterson | Betsey F. | KC, p1c6, 5/19/1898 | Issue of Fact for Court to be heard in the May term of the Crawford County Circuit Court. John Gerhardt vs. Betsey F. Peterson, Atley Peterson and others. |
| Peterson | Charley | KC, p1c5, 2/9/1899 | Taught school in Seneca in 1899. E. E. Brindley, Crawford County Superintendent of Schools published a comprehensive list of all teachers in the county. |
| Peterson | Christina | KC, p8c3, 9/25/1902 | Age 16. Stole a horse near Ferryville from M. Barbam and headed for Viroqua. Employed as a domestic in Ferryville. Took satchel, clothes and saddle of employer. Captured by Sheriff Bennett. Sentenced to the Industrial School in Milwaukee. |
| Peterson | Christina | KC, Supp., 12/18/1902 | Crawford County Board of Supervisors allowed expenses in the case against Christina Peterson for larceny. |
| Peterson | Fred | KC, p1c3, 8/31/1899 | Recently married. Lived in Milwaukee. Departed for new home in Salt Lake City. Son of Atley Peterson. |
| Peterson | Fred | KC, p4c4, 5/2/1901 | Graduated from Milwaukee Medical College. He was the son of Atley Peterson of Soldiers Grove. |
| Peterson | H. | KC, p8c4, 4/4/1901 | Part of a group that left Steuben and Wauzeka for the West. Most of the group went to McHenry, North Dakota. |
| Peterson | H. | KC, p4c2, 1/14/1897 | Family resided in Steuben. They were quarantined for 43 days with diphtheria. |
| Peterson | H. | KC, Supp., 12/12/1901 | Received funds from the Crawford Co. Soldiers Relief Commission. Resided in Steuben. |
| Peterson | H. | KC, Supp., 12/19/1901 | Resided in Steuben. Worked as a mason. |
| Peterson | H. | KC, Supp., 12/18/1902 | Crawford County Soldiers Relief Committee provided funds to H. Peterson of Steuben. |
| Peterson | Hiram | KC, p5c4, 8/10/1899 | Wrote a letter from Courtney, ND describing the area for publication in the *Kickapoo Chief*. " . . . greatest share of people in Stuttsman County are from Crawford County." |
| Peterson | Isaac | KC, p4c1, 6/3/1897 | Married Jane Tim on May 24, 1897 in Steuben. Justice J. P. McKinney officiated. (Bride and groom may be from Steuben.) |
| Peterson | Jennie | KC, p5c3, 7/6/1899 | Married J. J. Hurlburt on July 4, 1899. Bride and groom from Steuben. |
| Peterson | Jennie | KC, p4c3, 1/14/1897 | Jennie Peterson and Mandy Tim of Steuben planned to go to Dakota. |
| Peterson | Mary | KC, p1c5, 2/9/1899 | Taught school in Utica in 1899. E. E. Brindley, Crawford County Superintendent of Schools published a comprehensive list of all teachers in the county. |
| Peterson | N. O. and Betsey F. and Martin | KC, p1c6, 5/19/1898 | Issue of Law for Court to be heard in the May term of the Crawford County Circuit Court. Voluntary assignment of Soldiers Grove Hardware Co. and N. O. Peterson, Betsey F. Peterson and Martin Peterson, application to sell land. |
| Peterson | P. N. | KC, p5c5, 3/15/1900 | Addressed the Farmers Institute in Mt. Sterling on tobacco culture. Speech published. |
| Peterson | P. N. | KC, p5c4, 5/29/1902 | The case Sutter Bros. vs. P. N. Peterson was heard at the May term of the Crawford County Circuit Court. Judgement for the plaintiff. |

Genealogical Gleanings From Early Newspapers for Residents In and Near
Crawford County, Wisconsin, 1897-1902

| LAST NAME | FIRST NAME | NEWSPAPER PAGE/COLUMN MONTH/DAY/YEAR | GENEALOGICAL DATA |
|---|---|---|---|
| Peterson | P. N., Jr. | KC, p1c4, 9/12/1901 | Native of Soldiers Grove. Now lived at Ballard, Washington. |
| Peterson | Peter N. | KC, p1c3, 10/30/1902 | Democratic candidate for Crawford County Treasurer. Born Sept. 21, 1862 in Norway. Came to America with parents when he was 10 years old. In spring of 1855 the family settled in Crawford County. (Birthdate may be a newspaper typo.) Occupies a 400-acre farm in Utica. Served with Co. K in the Kickapoo Rangers 12th Inf. Reg. Wisconsin Volunteers in Civil War. Entered Oct. 2, 1861 and discharged August 11, 1865. "Mr. Peterson has held office and has been in public service in some capacity each and every year since he was enlisted ... in 1861 and he is the present town chairman of his town." |
| Peterson | Nels | KC, p1c5, 3/18/1897 | Resided at Pine Knob. Broke his leg near hip while cutting a hole in ice. Recovery doubtful. Aged 78 years. |
| Pettygrove | Cora | KC, p4c2, 12/9/1897 | Married Will O'Leary on Nov. 20, 1897. (Bride and groom may be from Readstown area.) |
| Pfahler | Albert | KC, p4c4, 11/10/1898 | Issues of Fact for Court heard in the November term of the Crawford County Circuit Court. Albert Pfahler vs. T. Savage and wife. |
| Pfahler | F. | KC, Supp., 12/18/1902 | Crawford County Board of Supervisors examined bills in the Justices and Constables' Account for State vs. F. Pfahler and R. Lawler, partners. F. Vanderbilt, George Hurd, John Heligas and J. W. Shoemaker were witnesses. |
| Pfhaler | Albert | KC, p8c1, 3/16/1899 | Albert Pfhaler of Madison and John Pfhaler of Mason City met their brother John (possibly from Prairie du Chien). They were orphaned 42 years ago and had not seen each other since. Each assumed the other was dead. Reunited in Prairie du Chien. Albert was a conductor on the Milwaukee railroad. |
| Phalen | Michael, Mrs. | KC, p8c3, 1/7/1897 | Died Dec 26, 1896. Resided in Rising Sun. Aged about 70 years. Leaves husband, 3 sons and 2 daughters. Granddaughters, Nellie and Rosa Burns, live in La Crosse. |
| Phalen | Peter | KC, p8c3, 3/4/1897 | Married Jane Rogers of Rising Sun. on Feb. 15, 1897 in the Catholic Church. Groom from Dakota. |
| Phalen | Peter | KC, p8c3, 1/7/1897 | Arrived from Dakota to spend winter with friends in Rising Sun. |
| Phaler | Fred | KC, p8c2, 3/23/1899 | "John and George Slater of Hawkeye, IA, Al Phaler of Madison and Fred Phaler of Lynxville meet for the first time in forty-two years in this city (Prairie du Chien) last Thursday. In honor of the event, John Ivers disengaged himself from his duties in the store and helped the boys celebrate. They were gathered at the home of the latter in the evening where an elegant time was had. The boys departed for their respective homes Friday morning." (See Pfhaler citations, too.) |
| Phalin | Frank | KC, p1c3, 4/11/1901 | Left Rising Sun for a new home in Soldiers Grove where he planned to open a barber shop. Just returned from Minneapolis where he went for training. |

Genealogical Gleanings From Early Newspapers for Residents In and Near
Crawford County, Wisconsin, 1897-1902

| LAST NAME | FIRST NAME | NEWSPAPER PAGE/COLUMN MONTH/DAY/YEAR | GENEALOGICAL DATA |
|---|---|---|---|
| Phalin | Maggie | KC, Supp., 12/12/1901 | Attended a Teacher's Institute in Crawford County in 1901. Resided in Rising Sun. |
| Philamolee | Lizzie, Mrs. | KC, p8c3, 1/28/1897 | Resided in Iowa. Visited parents, Mr. and Mrs. J. T. Farris of Steuben. |
| Philips | Dan | KC, p1c2, 11/9/1899 | Resided in Mt. Sterling. Planned to open a barber shop in Steuben. |
| Phillamale | Lizzie, Mrs. | KC, p4c2, 12/16/1897 | Traveled from Bailey, IA to visit parents, Mr. and Mrs. John Farris of Steuben. |
| Phillamalee | James, Mrs. | KC, p4c3, 6/9/1898 | Traveled from Bailey, IA to visit parents, Mr. and Mrs. John Farris of Steuben. |
| Phillips | A. D. | KC, p8c4, 7/25/1901 | Died July 21, 1901 at Richland Center. Buried at Lowertown Cemetery, Prairie du Chien. |
| Phillips | Atta | KC, Supp., 12/12/1901 | Attended a Teacher's Institute in Crawford County in 1901. Resided in Hurlbut. |
| Phillips | boy | KC, p1c4, 4/5/1900 | Three-year-old son of Lou Phillips died of lung fever on April 3, 1900. |
| Phillips | boy | KC, p5c1, 12/9/1897 | Son recently born to Sylvester Phillips of Mt. Sterling. |
| Phillips | Cora, Miss | KC, p5c3, 8/4/1898 | From Mt. Sterling. Employed at the hotel in Gays Mills. |
| Phillips | D. | KC, p5c4, 1/18/1900 | Resided in Steuben. Visited parents in Mt. Sterling. |
| Phillips | Dan | KC, p1c5, 8/22/1901 | Married Mabel Hurlbut on August 14, 1901. Bride from Readstown. Groom from Mt. Sterling. Planned to move to North Dakota. |
| Phillips | Dan | KC, p5c4, 3/29/1900 | Barber in Steuben. Planned to move to North Dakota in the spring. |
| Phillips | Dan | KC, P5c2, 1/6/1898 | Gone for last 14 months. Returned from Minneapolis with his uncle, Dave Phillips, to visit in Mt. Sterling. |
| Phillips | Jay | KC, p5c3, 3/2/1899 | Former resident of Monroe Co., WI. Recently returned to Crawford County to live. Included in Town of Scott news items. |
| Phillips | L. M. | KC, p7c4, 1/25/1900 | Received marriage license in Crawford Co. Miss L. E. Carron was the prospective spouse. Bride and groom-to-be from Howard Co., IA. |
| Phillips | Louis | KC, p1c3, 7/25/1901 | Funeral held Tuesday in Prairie du Chien. Worked as a station agent at Richland Center. |
| Phillips | Mastia H. | KC, p8c3, 11/24/1898 | Married A. L. Greeley on Nov. 20, 1898. Bride and groom from Arlington, IA. |
| Phillips | Mr. | KC, p5c1, 8/26/1897 | Departed Town of Scott for a new home in Monroe County, WI. |
| Phillips | Netta | KC, p8c1, 1/5/1899 | Married William Curley on Jan. 1, 1899 at the Congregational Church. (Bride and groom may be from Gays Mills.) |
| Phillips | Peter | KC, p8c2, 3/2/1899 | Died Feb. 28, 1899 in Chicago at age of 58. Former resident of Prairie du Chien. |
| Phillips | William W. | KC, p1c3, 6/2/1898 | Lived in Readstown. Government increased his pension from $6 to $8 a month. |

Genealogical Gleanings From Early Newspapers for Residents In and Near Crawford County, Wisconsin, 1897-1902

| LAST NAME | FIRST NAME | NEWSPAPER PAGE/COLUMN MONTH/DAY/YEAR | GENEALOGICAL DATA |
|---|---|---|---|
| Picha | girl | KC, p1c4, 1/17/1901 | Daughter born last week to Albert Picha of Eastman. |
| Picha | Mary | KC, p1c5, 10/10/1901 | Married Anthony Schwartz on Oct. 8, 1901. Bride was from the Town of Eastman. Groom was from Dutch Ridge. |
| Pickett | Nellie | KC, p5c4, 11/24/1898 | Married Emmet Haggerty on Nov. 20, 1898 in Boscobel. Bride and groom from Scott. |
| Pickett | Pearl | KC, p1c6, 1/28/1897 | Attended a teacher meeting in Haney. |
| Pickett | Pearl | KC, Supp., 12/12/1901 | Attended a Teacher's Institute in Crawford County in 1901. Resided in Hurlbut. |
| Pier | E. M. | KC, p4c3, 5/27/1898 | Traveled from Portland, OR to visit Eliza A. Whiteaker of Wheatville. |
| Pier | H. E., Dr. | KC, p10c3, 12/12/1901 | Dentist in Eastman. Planned to move to Milwaukee. |
| Pier | Harry, Dr. | KC, p1c4, 9/13/1900 | Married Josephine Ludwig on Sept. 10, 1900. Bride daughter of Dr. and Mrs. Ludwig of Richland Co. Groom from Prairie du Chien. |
| Pier | J. F. | KC, p1c3, 6/30/1898 | Named the new postmaster at Eastman. Succeeded H. M. Seekatz. |
| Pier | J. F. | KC, p5c3, 5/20/1897 | Issues of fact for jury to be heard in the May term of the Crawford County Court. J. F. Pier, respondent and plaintiff vs. Samuel Mattie and Fred Mattie, appellants and defendants. |
| Pier | Millard | KC, Supp., 12/29/1898 | Received aid from the Crawford County Soldiers Relief Commission. Resided in Haney. |
| Pier | Mr. | KC, p4c3, 3/20/1902 | Resided in Eastman. Summoned to Prairie du Chien on account of father's death. |
| Pierce | girl | KC, p5c4, 4/19/1900 | Daughter born Apr. 11, 1900 to Frank Pierce of Gays Mills. |
| Pierce | Myrtie and Howard | KC, p1c2, 10/9/1902 | Myrtie Pierce and brother, Howard, arrived from Custer Co., NB to visit relatives in Wauzeka. Mrs. Samuel Pierce, their mother, is a sister of the Lathrop brothers of Wauzeka. |
| Pierce | Samuel | KC, p1c2, 9/28/1899 | Former resident of Wauzeka. Now lives in Custer Co., NB. |
| Piesley | Bridget | KC, p5c3, 5/20/1897 | Issues of fact for jury to be heard in the May term of the Crawford County Court. Patrick Piesley vs. Bridget Piesley and Ellen Melvin et al. |
| Piesley | Patrick | KC, p5c3, 5/20/1897 | Issues of fact for jury to be heard in the May term of the Crawford County Court. Patrick Piesley vs. Bridget Piesley and Ellen Melvin et al. |
| Pion | John | KC, p1c2, 6/10/1897 | Found not guilty of larceny committed last winter. "The verdict was very unsatisfactory considering the evidence." |
| Pion | Louis | KC, Supp., 10/6/1898 | Resided in Rockford, IA. Visited relatives in Eastman. |
| Pitcka | Josephine | KC, p8c1, 2/3/1898 | Died Jan. 27, 1898 in Grand Grea. |
| Pitsenberger | Effie, Mrs. | KC, p1c5, 5/19/1898 | From Gays Mills. Had a cancer removed from left breast. Entire breast removed. |

Genealogical Gleanings From Early Newspapers for Residents In and Near
Crawford County, Wisconsin, 1897-1902

| LAST NAME | FIRST NAME | NEWSPAPER PAGE/COLUMN MONTH/DAY/YEAR | GENEALOGICAL DATA |
|---|---|---|---|
| Pitsenberger | Park | KC, p1c2, 1/27/1898 | Visited relatives in Wauzeka and then left for new home in Iowa. |
| Pitsenberger | Park | KC, p4c1, 2/10/1898 | "Park Pitsenberger (of Gays Mills) is again at his old stand on the section after a few days visit with friends in Iowa." |
| Pitsenberger | Park | KC, p1c6, 5/12/1898 | Planned to volunteer for Spanish American War. From Gays Mills area. |
| Pitsenberger | Sarah | KC, p1c4, 9/29/1898 | Recently married Lewis Clark. Bride and groom were former residents of Wauzeka area. Bride 66 years old. Groom 77 years old. |
| Pitsengerger | Ben | KC, p1c5, 11/18/1897 | Installed as an officer at the International Order of Good Templars (I.O.G.T.) Lodge in Wauzeka. |
| Pittsenberger | Eph., Mrs. | KC, p1c2, 4/10/1902 | Resided in Gays Mills. Visited her parents, Mr. and Mrs. W. P. Young of Eastman. |
| Pittsley | E. | KC, p5c5, 4/5/1900 | Elected treasurer in Town of Scott. |
| Pittzenberger | Ben | KC, p1c5, 6/21/1900 | Dell Brown and Ben Pittzenberger raked a Revolutionary War musket from the Mississippi River while clam fishing near the mouth of the Wisconsin River. |
| Pitzenberger | Ben | KC, p1c4, 5/29/1902 | Broke his collarbone while coupling railroad cars. |
| Pitzer | John | KC, p8c3, 12/6/1900 | Married Rosie Busch on Dec. 4, 1900. Bride from Prairie du Chien. Groom from Grant Co. |
| Pivot | Andrew, Mrs. | KC, p1c6, 7/21/1898 | Died July 18, 1898 at her home near Steuben/Wauzeka. Buried at Catholic Cemetery in Wauzeka. |
| Pivot | Peter | KC, p4c6, 12/1/1898 | Married Rosa Reynolds on Nov. 24, 1898 in Boscobel. Bride and groom from Marietta. |
| Pivot | Peter | KC, p5c4, 10/10/1901 | Married Anastacia Chitik at the Catholic Church in Wauzeka on Oct. 7, 1901. Bride from Ft. Atkinson, IA. Groom had a brother, Frank, and a sister, Kate. Planned to live in Marietta. |
| Pivot | Peter | KC, p5c3, 3/23/1899 | Peter Pivot and Zach Posey left Steuben for North Dakota. |
| Pivot | Tessie | KC, p8c2, 10/12/1899 | Marriage license issued in Crawford Co. to her and Thomas Niland. Both parties from Marietta. |
| Plimpton | Cora, Miss | KC, p1c4, 9/29/1898 | Traveled from Ann Arbor, MI to visit mother, Mrs. H. V. Rosencrans of Wauzeka. |
| Plimpton | Cora, Mrs. | KC, p1c3, 5/27/1898 | Left Wauzeka for new home in Benton Harbor, MI. |
| Plimpton | Harry | KC, p1c4, 11/17/1898 | Planned to open a furniture business in La Farge. Previously worked as a traveling salesman. |
| Plimpton | Harry C. | KC, p1c6, 4/21/1898 | Married Corrinne Rosencrans, daughter of Mrs. H. V. Rosencrans of Wauzeka, on April 15, 1898. Groom from Benton Harbor, MI. The Rev. F. A. Mundt officiated. |
| Plourd | boy | KC, p1c2, 12/25/1902 | Son born Dec. 21, 1902 to F. Plourd of Wauzeka. |
| Plourd | Delema | KC, p1c6, 9/25/1902 | Married Henry Schmidt on Sept. 22, 1902 at the Catholic Church. Bride and groom were from Wauzeka. |

Genealogical Gleanings From Early Newspapers for Residents In and Near
Crawford County, Wisconsin, 1897-1902

| LAST NAME | FIRST NAME | NEWSPAPER PAGE/COLUMN MONTH/DAY/YEAR | GENEALOGICAL DATA |
|---|---|---|---|
| Poehler | Frank H. | KC, p4c4, 11/10/1898 | Issues of Default heard in the November term of the Crawford County Circuit Court. Frank H. Poehler vs. Joseph Noney et al. |
| Poehler | H. C. | KC, Supp., 10/3/1901 | Died Sept. 29, 1901 in Prairie du Chien. He was an old resident. |
| Poehler | H. C., Mrs. | KC, p1c4, 10/31/1901 | Returned to Prairie du Chien after visiting daughter, Mrs. N. Jurgenson of Gays Mills. |
| Poehler | Harry | KC, p1c3, 1/21/1897 | Died Jan. 18, 1897 in Prairie du Chien. Born Nov. 11, 1891. Eldest son of Frank Poehler. |
| Poladna | | KC, p8c2, 1/6/1898 | Married Mary Lankie on Jan. 3, 1898 at St. John Bohemian Catholic Church. Bride and groom from Prairie du Chien. |
| Polda | John | KC, p8c4, 6/6/1901 | Married Mary Shemar (or Shener) on June 4, 1901 at St. John's Bohemian Church. Bride from Prairie du Chien. Groom from Bridgeport. |
| Pollen | Emerson | KC, p1c3, 10/25/1900 | Advertised an auction sale to be held at his home on Harris Ridge. |
| Pollow | Mr. | KC, p1c5, 7/20/1899 | Died July 8, 1899 in Chicago. He was the son-in-law of Alex Kopan of Steuben. The widow was the sister of Edward and Mary Kopan. |
| Polodna | Barbara | KC, Supp., 12/12/1901 | Crawford Co. Board of Supervisors approved payments to William Davenport, P. J. Sime and Edward O. Anderson in the Matter of Barbara Polodna, Insane. |
| Polodna | Barbara | KC, Supp., 12/20/1900 | Crawford Co. Board of Supervisors approved bills related to expenses of Barbara Polodna, insane. |
| Pomerening | Charles | KC, p1c4, 9/9/1897 | Charles Pomerening and Dell Brown of Wauzeka worked in Viola on the foundation for the new train depot. |
| Pomerening | Charles | KC, p1c2, 12/29/1898 | Planned to build a store with a second story for a hall and a large livery barn in Wauzeka. |
| Pomerening | Charles A. | KC, p1c6, 4/7/1898 | Elected Constable for the Village of Wauzeka. |
| Pomerning | C. A. | KC, p1c4, 4/11/1901 | Appointed Justice of the Peace in Wauzeka. D. Lyons resigned the position. |
| Pomeroy | Orin | KC, p1c4, 12/11/1902 | Pioneer tobacco grower in the area. 87 years old. Sold his 67th crop this year, the 50th crop in Wisconsin. Reported by Ole Rolfson. |
| Pond | H. M. | KC, p1c2, 9/20/1900 | The court case, H. M. Pond vs. Charles Hines, was withdrawn. |
| Pond | H. M. | KC, p1c3, 2/21/1901 | After resignation of Dave Syverson, appointed postmaster in Steuben. |
| Pond | H. M. | KC, p1c3, 10/17/1901 | Returned to Groton, SD to consider buying land. Lived in Steuben. |
| Pond | Holly M. | KC, p1c5, 2/17/1898 | Married Mertle Hurlburt on Feb. 16, 1898. Bride from Readstown, formerly from Wauzeka and Steuben. Bride daughter of W. S. Hurlburt. |
| Pond | John L. | KC, p4c2, 1/6/1898 | Died Dec. 24, 1897 in Readstown. Brother was Ellis Pond of Patch Grove (p4c3). |
| Pond | H. M. | KC, Supp., 12/19/1901 | Postmaster for Steuben. |

Genealogical Gleanings From Early Newspapers for Residents In and Near
Crawford County, Wisconsin, 1897-1902

| LAST NAME | FIRST NAME | NEWSPAPER PAGE/COLUMN MONTH/DAY/YEAR | GENEALOGICAL DATA |
|---|---|---|---|
| Popper | boy | KC, p1c2, 5/24/1900 | Son recently born to G. V. Popper of Wauzeka. |
| Popper | boy | KC, p1c4, 10/10/1901 | A son was born Oct. 7, 1901 to G. V. Popper of Wauzeka. |
| Popper | G. V. | KC, p4c4, 11/16/1899 | Mr. and Mrs. G. V. Popper arrived from Chicago. Hired to clerk for W. A. Vaughan in Wauzeka. |
| Porter | Archie | KC, p10c3, 12/12/1901 | Returned to Seneca after spending the summer in Dakota. |
| Porter | Archie W. | KC, p5c3, 6/14/1900 | Graduated from the graded school in Seneca. |
| Porter | C. V., Dr. | KC, p1c5, 6/23/1898 | Dr. C. V. Porter, "the best posted man on our local history", is working with the Pioneer Society of Vernon County to commemorate the anniversary of the Battle of the Bad Ax on August 1st and 2nd. A party will go over the trail as near as possible, beginning at Soldiers Grove and ending at Battle Island. |
| Porter | Charles | KC, p1c5, 10/14/1897 | Lived in Babcock, WI. Worked for Wisconsin Valley Railway. Visited parents in Boydtown. |
| Porter | Charles, Mr. and Mrs. | KC, p5c1, 10/14/1897 | From Boydtown. Traveled to Platteville to visit son, Fred. |
| Porter | Cora | KC, Supp., 12/20/1900 | Crawford Co. Board of Supervisors approved payment of expenses in the matter of State vs. Cora Porter. |
| Porter | Eva E. | KC, Supp., 12/20/1900 | Crawford Co. Board of Supervisors approved bills related to expenses of Eva E. Porter, dependent child. |
| Porter | George | KC, p5c3, 9/6/1900 | Resided in Barnum. New proprietor of the hotel in Petersburg. |
| Porter | George | KC, p1c4, 5/31/1900 | Proprietor of a blacksmith shop in Barnum. |
| Porter | Hannah, Mrs. | KC, p5c3, 7/24/1902 | Lived in Seneca. Visited brother, Orin White, who recently found 2 "good" pearls near Lynxville while clam fishing. |
| Porter | Hugh | KC, Supp. 10/27/1898 | Nominated by the Republican Party for Representative to the Wisconsin Assembly. As a boy he moved to Crawford County in 1855 with his parents. Owned a farm. Served in Assembly for two terms. (Picture, short bio. and character sketch provided.) |
| Porter | Hugh | KC, p5c5, 4/5/1900 | Elected supervisor in Seneca. |
| Porter | James A., Mr. and Mrs. | KC, p5c3, 1/18/1900 | Party was held to celebrate their 41st wedding anniversary on Jan. 11, 1900 at their home in Mt. Sterling. |
| Porter | Justin, Mrs. | KC, p5c3, 1/25/1900 | Arrived from Wood Co. to visit relatives in Seneca and Mt. Sterling. |
| Porter | Mrs. | KC, p5c4, 4/10/1902 | Died April 2, 1902 in Waukesha. She was the wife of the Rev. T. A. Porter of Lynxville. |
| Porter | O. B. | KC, p5c4, 6/21/1900 | Married Ethel L. Murley on June 13, 1900. Bride from Boscobel. Groom from Wauzeka. |
| Porter | O. B. | KC, p5c3, 9/7/1899 | Resident of Boydtown. Taught school in Gays Mills. |
| Porter | Obe | KC, p1c3, 9/7/1899 | Left the Wauzeka area to work as principal of schools in Gays Mills. |

Genealogical Gleanings From Early Newspapers for Residents In and Near
Crawford County, Wisconsin, 1897-1902

| LAST NAME | FIRST NAME | NEWSPAPER PAGE/COLUMN MONTH/DAY/YEAR | GENEALOGICAL DATA |
|---|---|---|---|
| Porter | Obie | KC, p1c5, 2/9/1899 | Taught school in Marietta in 1899. E. E. Brindley, Crawford County Superintendent of Schools published a comprehensive list of all teachers in the county. |
| Porter | T. A., Rev. | KC, Supp., 6/5/1902 | Preached a farewell sermon in Seneca. |
| Porter | T. A., Rev. | KC, p5c4, 6/12/1902 | Preached a farewell sermon in the Congregational Church in Lynxville. Planned to visit daughter, a dentist in Lone Rock, a son and daughter in northern Wisconsin and then engage in Evangelistic work. |
| Portwein | Lizzie | KC, p8c4, 10/26/1899 | Married Charles Moore on Oct. 25, 1899. Bride from Eastman. Groom from Prairie du Chien. |
| Portwine | Anna | KC, p8c3, 10/24/1901 | Died Oct. 20, 1901 at Town of Prairie du Chien. Funeral held at St. Gabriel's Catholic Church. |
| Portwine | Lizzie | KC, p8c4, 11/17/1898 | Married G. Traub on Nov. 15, 1898 at St. Gabriel Church in Prairie du Chien. |
| Posey | boy | KC, p8c3, 5/13/1897 | Son born May 8, 1897 to William Posey of Steuben. |
| Posey | boy | KC, p5c2, 7/28/1898 | Son born July 20, 1898 to Joe Posey of Steuben. |
| Posey | Clara, Mrs. | KC, p5c2, 12/2/1897 | From Steuben. Hosted a real "old-time quilting bee." |
| Posey | D. | KC, p5c3, 9/20/1900 | Residence 2 miles from Steuben was destroyed by fire. |
| Posey | D. C. | KC, p1c4, 10/17/1901 | Resided in Steuben. Received pension increase. |
| Posey | D. C. | KC, Supp., 12/12/1901 | Received funds from the Crawford Co. Soldiers Relief Commission. Resided in Steuben. |
| Posey | D. C. | KC, Supp., 12/18/1902 | Crawford County Soldiers Relief Committee provided funds to D. C. Posey of Steuben. |
| Posey | Dave | KC, p5c3, 10/5/1899 | Opened a butcher shop in Steuben. Otto Chapman was his assistant. |
| Posey | David C. | KC, p5c3, 6/14/1900 | Posey of Steuben and Frank Ward of Muscoda were comrades in the Mexican War. They were mustered into service in Galena, IL in 1847 and mustered out in Alton, IL in 1848. They both served in the Civil War. Posey was in Co. C, 43rd WI Regiment. Ward was a Lieut. from Co. H., 33rd WI Regiment. |
| Posey | Dennis | KC, p1c2, 3/16/1899 | Married Mattie Brock on Mar. 13, 1899 at the Boscobel Congregational Church. Bride from Haney. |
| Posey | Dennis | KC, p5c3, 9/27/1900 | Well-known well driller. Lost youngest child to "the summer complaint." Lost house and contents to a fire. |
| Posey | Dennis, Mr. and Mrs. | KC, p5c4, 2/13/1902 | Planned to leave Haney for Dakota in the spring. |
| Posey | G. D. | KC, Supp., 12/19/1901 | Operated a saloon in Steuben. |
| Posey | G. D., Mrs. | KC, p5c3, 8/2/1900 | Mrs. G. D. Posey of Steuben and her brother, James Martin of Seattle, WA, visited their mother and sister at Wyalusing, WI. |

Genealogical Gleanings From Early Newspapers for Residents In and Near
Crawford County, Wisconsin, 1897-1902

| LAST NAME | FIRST NAME | NEWSPAPER PAGE/COLUMN MONTH/DAY/YEAR | GENEALOGICAL DATA |
|---|---|---|---|
| Posey | Greg | KC, p5c4, 2/4/1897 | New proprietor of the Thiede saloon in Steuben. |
| Posey | I. F. (Ike) | KC, p1c5, 9/1/1898 | Struck by lightning at the farm of his brother, Dave Posey. Farm located 25 miles north of Jamestown, ND. He was unconscious for 4 hours. Recovered. Broke arm. Hearing was badly damaged. |
| Posey | I. F., Mrs. | KC, p1c4, 4/14/1898 | Native of Steuben. Forty-pound ovarian tumor removed from her at a Chicago hospital. |
| Posey | Isaac, Mrs. | KC, p4c1, 12/16/1897 | Lived in Steuben. Received treatment at a Chicago hospital. |
| Posey | James | KC, p4c2, 1/7/1897 | Died Dec. 29, 1896. Born Apr. 14, 1817 in TN. Married 1839 in IL. Worked in Galena, IL mines. Moved to a farm near Steuben, Crawford Co. in 1853. Wife died three years ago and then moved in with son, William. Survived by 7 of 10 children. |
| Posey | James | KC, p8c4, 4/1/1897 | Died Mar. 18, 1897 in Marietta. Aged 15 years and 7 months. Son of Mr. and Mrs. William Posey. Buried in James Posey Cemetery. |
| Posey | Joe | KC, p5c2, 7/22/1897 | Recently lost part of his right foot while working. Tried to cross a railroad track while train was moving. Happened at Haskin's sandpit below Soldiers Grove. From Petersburg. |
| Posey | John | KC, p4c3, 3/11/1897 | Former resident of Steuben. Now from North Dakota. Visited friends in hometown. |
| Posey | Joseph | KC, p1c4, 4/14/1898 | Toes crushed by a gravel train last summer. Lost rest of his foot on Friday. Amputation done by Dr. Trowbridge of Viroqua. |
| Posey | Mat | KC, p8c4, 4/4/1901 | Part of a group that left Steuben and Wauzeka for the West. Most of the group went to McHenry, North Dakota. |
| Posey | Nona | KC, p4c4, 4/20/1899 | Died Mar. 14, 1898 at Courtney, ND. Wife of James Posey, Jr. Former resident of Steuben. Aged 19 years. Daughter of George Cupps. Born in Marietta on Jan. 30, 1880. Moved with parents to North Dakota in August 1997. |
| Posey | Tom | KC, p1c5, 11/25/1897 | Arrived from North Dakota to visit relatives in Steuben. |
| Posey | Walter | KC, p8c4, 4/4/1901 | Part of a group that left Steuben and Wauzeka for the West. Most of the group went to McHenry, North Dakota. |
| Posey | William, Mrs. | KC, p5c4, 1/26/1899 | Recently died in Soldiers Grove area. |
| Posey | William, Mrs. | KC, p5c4, 2/9/1899 | Died Jan. 20, 1899 at son's home on Irish Ridge. Nee Mallissa Harned. Born April 9, 1840 in Crawford Co., PA. Married William Posey on Feb. 19, 1857 and then moved to Haney Township, Crawford Co, WI. Moved to Marietta in 1858. To Wauzeka in 1892. To Marietta in 1893. To Soldiers Grove in 1898. Survived by husband and 9 children: Mrs. Elvira Hamilton of SD, Mrs. Della Philamalee of Kansas, Jack and Dennis of Steuben, Ed of South Dakota, Abe of Irish Ridge, Mattie and James and Sarah of Soldiers Grove. Buried in Posey Cemetery. |

Genealogical Gleanings From Early Newspapers for Residents In and Near
Crawford County, Wisconsin, 1897-1902

| LAST NAME | FIRST NAME | NEWSPAPER PAGE/COLUMN MONTH/DAY/YEAR | GENEALOGICAL DATA |
|---|---|---|---|
| Postle & Schwingle | | KC, p1c4, 6/23/1898 | Owned a toll bridge over the Wisconsin River at Muscoda. Planned to sell bridge to the village. |
| Potter | Jennie O'Neil | KC, p4c4, 4/26/1900 | Died April 16, 1900 in New York. Buried in Patch Grove. |
| Potts | J. A. | KC, Supp., 12/18/1902 | Crawford County Soldiers Relief Committee provided funds to J. A. Potts of Soldiers Grove. |
| Potts | John | KC, Supp., 12/12/1901 | Received funds from the Crawford Co. Soldiers Relief Commission. Resided in Soldiers Grove. |
| Powell | Jasper N. | KC, Supp., 12/29/1898 | Received aid from the Crawford County Soldiers Relief Commission. Resided in De Soto. |
| Powell | Jasper, Mrs. | KC, Supp., 12/20/1900 | Crawford Co. Soldiers Relief Comm. approved aid to Mrs. Jasper Powell of De Soto. |
| Powell | Joseph, Mrs. | KC, Supp., 12/20/1900 | Crawford Co. Soldiers Relief Comm. approved aid to Mrs. Joseph Powell of De Soto. |
| Powell | Mr. | KC, p4c2, 11/25/1897 | Recently died in Town of Freeman. He was an early settler. |
| Powers | Alra, Mr. | KC, p5c3, 9/14/1899 | Left Haney Ridge to visit mother in New York. |
| Powers | Jason | KC, Supp., 12/29/1898 | Crawford Co. Board of Supervisors approved payment of expenses in the matter of Jason Powers, insane. |
| Powers | William | KC, p8c2, 12/30/1897 | Buried Wednesday (Dec. 22, 1897?). Lived in Patch Grove for the last 40 years. Buried in Catholic Cemetery. |
| Pratt | Ina, Miss | KC, p1c3, 8/9/1900 | Arrived from Tallapoosa, Georgia to attend her sick mother, Mrs. Pratt of Wauzeka. |
| Prechaska | Emanuel | KC, p8c4, 11/16/1899 | Received marriage license in Crawford Co. to marry Mary Fuke of Bridgeport. |
| Prentice | George | KC, p1c4, 4/20/1899 | Came from "abroad" to visit his sister, Mrs. J. W. MaGee of Bridgeport. |
| Prentice | John | KC, p8c1, 10/28/1897 | Married Lena Voth of Prairie du Chien on Oct. 22, 1897. Groom from Manistee, MI. |
| Prew | Henry | KC, p8c2, 7/27/1899 | Died July 22, 1899 in Prairie du Chien. Born July 13, 1831 in Canada. Married Oct. 5, 1856. Survived by wife, 4 daughters and 2 sons. Buried in Catholic Cemetery. |
| Prew | Henry | KC, p5c6, 3/6/1902 | Mary Nolan applied to the Crawford County courts to administer the estate of Henry Prew, late of Prairie du Chien. |
| Prey | Herman | KC, p1c2, 11/3/1898 | Managed the Campbell Coulee Farm outside Prairie du Chien. |
| Price | Lela | KC, p1c3, 12/22/1898 | Planned to marry Louis C. Widmann on Dec. 28, 1898. Bride, daughter of Daniel Price, from Lancaster. Groom, son of J. G. Widmann, originally from Wauzeka, but now from Church's Ferry, ND. |
| Prince | Grace | KC, p4c2, 9/2/1897 | Married Mr. Altizer of Mason City, IA on Aug. 23, 1897. (Bride probably from Lynxville.) Justice F. R. Pease officiated. |
| Prince | Henry | KC, p5c3, 8/11/1898 | Moved with parents to Irma, WI (northern WI) last fall. Henry decided to move back to Lynxville. |
| Prince | Mrs. | KC, p5c3, 2/2/1899 | Died last Friday (Jan. 27, 1899?) in northern Wisconsin. (Formerly from Lynxville?) |

Genealogical Gleanings From Early Newspapers for Residents In and Near
Crawford County, Wisconsin, 1897-1902

| LAST NAME | FIRST NAME | NEWSPAPER PAGE/COLUMN MONTH/DAY/YEAR | GENEALOGICAL DATA |
|---|---|---|---|
| Pritchett | John | KC, p1c4, 4/28/1898 | Died at Platteville, WI on Sunday, Apr. 24, 1898. He was son of P. S. Pritchett of Boydtown and brother of Hugh Pritchett of Platteville. Aged 23 years. |
| Pritts | Mrs. | KC, p1c5, 8/18/1898 | Lived in La Crosse. Visited parents, Mr. and Mrs. Denning of Rising Sun. |
| Puckett | C. B. | KC, p3c3, 10/31/1901 | Died Oct. 29, 1901 at home in Boydtown. Aged 42 years. Survived by wife and 5 children. |
| Pugh | Almira, Mrs. | KC, p5c4, 4/10/1902 | Funeral held April 3, 1902. She was a former resident of Readstown. Aunt of Mrs. Dr. Hopkins. |
| Pugh | boy | KC, p4c2, 10/6/1898 | Son recently born to W. Pugh of Gays Mills. |
| Pugmire | Joseph | KC, p8c3, 11/13/1902 | Died last Saturday. Aged 75 years. Served in Co. A, 31st WI Vol. during Civil War. Died on the street near the Bitterlee residence in Prairie du Chien. Resided in Prairie du Chien since end of the war. |
| Pullen | Nora | KC, p8c5, 4/19/1900 | Marriage license issued to Frank Reynolds of the Town of Scott and Nora Pullen of the Town of Marietta. |
| Purington | Phylander | KC, Supp., 12/29/1898 | Received aid from the Crawford County Soldiers Relief Commission. Resided in Haney. |
| Purrington | A. B. | KC, p1c6, 5/19/1898 | Issue of Law for Court to be heard in the May term of the Crawford County Circuit Court. W. S. Manning vs. A. B. Purrington. |
| Purrington | Abraham B., Dr. | KC, p8c4, 10/31/1901 | Died Oct. 25, 1901. Born Feb. 7, 1822 in Binghampton, Broom Co., NY. Moved to Bell Center in 1856. Served in Civil War. Survived by wife, brother (Philander of Bell Center), sister (Mrs. Lydia Wheeler of Iowa), 4 sons (E. B., William, Plummer and Elmer) and 2 daughters (Mrs. Kanouse and Mrs. Turk). |
| Purrington | George E. | KC, p7c4, 1/25/1900 | Received marriage license in Crawford Co. Kettie (Kittie?) Kelley was the prospective spouse. Bride and groom-to-be from Town of Clayton. |
| Purrington | P. L. | KC, p5c6, 3/8/1900 | Did a good trade in the barber business in Belle Center. |
| Purrington | Phillen | KC, Supp., 12/12/1901 | Received funds from the Crawford Co. Soldiers Relief Commission. Resided in Haney. |
| Purrington | Stella, Mrs. | KC, p1c2, 11/20/1902 | Brought 2 daughters with her from home in Binford, ND to spend the winter in Bell Center. |
| Purrington | William | KC, p5c5, 4/12/1900 | Purrington and children, Maude, Nettie and Eddie arrived from Iowa to visit father, Dr. A. B. Purrington of Bell Center. Dr. Purrington bought a gold watch for each child. |
| Purrington | A. B. | KC, p4c2, 11/21/1901 | Resolution of thanks passed by the Twilight Lodge No. 81, I. O. O. F., Bell Center for assistance provided by area lodges that helped in the burial of A. B. Purrington. |
| Purrington | E. B. | KC, p1c3, 3/3/1898 | Bought 6 thoroughbred Shropshire ewes, imported from Canada. |
| Purrington | Eliza | KC, Supp., 12/18/1902 | Crawford County Soldiers Relief Committee provided funds to Eliza Purrington of Bell Center. |
| Purrington | Isaac | KC, Supp., 12/12/1901 | Listed as an insane person whose support was charged to Crawford Co. |

Genealogical Gleanings From Early Newspapers for Residents In and Near
Crawford County, Wisconsin, 1897-1902

| LAST NAME | FIRST NAME | NEWSPAPER PAGE/COLUMN MONTH/DAY/YEAR | GENEALOGICAL DATA |
|---|---|---|---|
| Purrington | Philander | KC, Supp., 12/18/1902 | Crawford County Soldiers Relief Committee provided funds to Philander Purrington of Bell Center. |
| Putnam | Grace M. | KC, p1c4, 1/27/1898 | Married William H. Ransome on Jan. 19, 1898 at home of bride's parents. Bride from Haney. Groom from Elmira, NY. James Dowling, J.P. officiated at the ceremony. |
| Putnam | James, Mr. and Mrs. | KC, p5c1, 2/21/1898 | Returned to Haney after visiting a son in Iowa. |
| Putnam | Thadd | KC, p8c4, 2/18/1897 | Thadd Putnam of Iowa and Mrs. Flynn of Illinois visited their parents, Mr. and Mrs. James Putnam of the Town of Haney. |
| Pyer | Joe | KC, p8c1, 9/28/1899 | Arrested in Boscobel. Accused of stealing money and clothing from the Sheema residence in Prairie du Chien. |
| Pyer | Joseph | KC, p8c3, 11/16/1899 | In the criminal case, State vs. Joseph Pyer, the defendant was convicted. The case was heard at the November term of the Crawford County Circuit Court. |
| Qualiman | Olga | KC, p8c3, 8/13/1897 | Married Herman Gaulke on Aug. 17, 1897 at bride's home. Bride daughter of the late John Quallman of Grand Grey. Husband lived in La Crosse (formerly from Crawford Co.). |
| Qualman | John | KC, p8c4, 3/18/1897 | A letter written by O. B. Thomas was published regarding the legal handling of Qualman's estate. |
| Quame | Louis, Mrs. | KC, p8c2, 8/31/1899 | Died Saturday (Aug. 26, 1899?) in Prairie du Chien at age 26. She was a sister-in-law of Dora Quame of Elroy, WI. |
| Quillan | D. H. | KC, p1c5, 11/1/1900 | Democratic candidate for Crawford County Surveyor. |
| Quinian | Mrs. | KC, p1c4, 4/15/1897 | Died in Madison, WI a week ago. Resident of Prairie du Chien. She was the mother of Barney Lantry and Mrs. P. Donahue. |
| Quinn | Emma | KC, p8c3, 11/22/1900 | Married Louis Hunter on Nov. 21, 1900. Bride from Prairie du Chien. Groom from Ion, IA. |
| Quinn | George | KC, p1c6, 5/19/1898 | Criminal case to be heard in the May term of the Crawford County Circuit Court. State of Wisconsin vs. George Quinn, Thomas McClusky and August Grapp, burglary. |
| Quinn | George | KC, p4c4, 11/10/1898 | Criminal Issue to be heard in the November term of the Crawford County Circuit Court. State of Wisconsin vs. George Quinn, Thomas McClusky and August Grapp. |
| Quinn | Mary | KC, p4c4, 11/10/1898 | Issues of Default heard in the November term of the Crawford County Circuit Court. Maria Garvey vs. Mary Quinn. |
| Quinn | Thomas | KC, p8c2, 5/11/1899 | Recently died. He was the son of Ald. L. Quinn of Prairie du Chien. |
| Rabehl | boy | KC, p1c2, 7/18/1901 | Son born July 14, 1901 to Rev. and Mrs. Rabehl of Wauzeka. |
| Radka | Fred, Mr. and Mrs. | KC, p1c4, 1/27/1898 | Traveled from Rome, WI to visit Mrs. Radka's parents, Mr. and Mrs. Kruschke of Wauzeka. |
| Radka | girl | KC, p1c4, 2/13/1902 | Daughter born Jan. 29, 1902 to Fred Radka of the Wauzeka area. |
| Ragan | Arthur | KC, p8c2, 4/20/1899 | Died April 17, 1899 at Merrill, WI. Former resident of Prairie du Chien. Aged 41 years. Buried in Lowertown Cemetery (Prairie du Chien). |

Genealogical Gleanings From Early Newspapers for Residents In and Near
Crawford County, Wisconsin, 1897-1902

| LAST NAME | FIRST NAME | NEWSPAPER PAGE/COLUMN MONTH/DAY/YEAR | GENEALOGICAL DATA |
|---|---|---|---|
| Ragan | Lela | KC, p5c4, 5/22/1902 | Prairie du Chien High School class of 1902. |
| Ralph | John | KC, p4c2, 4/1/1897 | Spent part of the winter on Harris Ridge and then went to his home in Manitoba. |
| Randal | E. J. | KC, p5c5, 4/5/1900 | Elected assessor in Lynxville. |
| Randall | Anna | KC, Supp., 6/5/1902 | Married Fred Black on May 31, 1902. Included in section with news from Lynxville. |
| Randall | boy | KC, p5c3, 8/17/1899 | Son born August 11, 1899 to Nelson Randall of Gays Mills. |
| Randall | Earl | KC, p1c6, 5/12/1898 | Planned to volunteer for Spanish American War. From Gays Mills area. |
| Randall | Earl | KC, p5c3, 1/12/1899 | Elected to be an officer for the Modern Woodman Association (MWA) in Gays Mills. |
| Randall | Etta | KC, p5c5, 1/10/1901 | Taught school in Lynxville. |
| Randall | Etta | KC, p8c3, 5/6/1897 | Taught school in Howe District. |
| Randall | Etta | KC, p1c5, 2/9/1899 | Taught school in Utica in 1899. E. E. Brindley, Crawford County Superintendent of Schools published a comprehensive list of all teachers in the county. |
| Randall | Etta | KC, Supp., 12/12/1901 | Attended a Teacher's Institute in Crawford County in 1901. Resided in Lynxville. |
| Randall | girl | KC, p5c3, 10/2/1902 | Daughter born last week to Nelson Randall of Gays Mills. |
| Randall | I. M., Dr. | KC, p4c4, 11/15/1900 | Departed Gays Mills for a new home at Retreat, Wisconsin. |
| Randall | I. M., Dr. | KC, p5c4, 3/6/1902 | Moved back to Gays Mills. |
| Randall | Ida M., Dr. | KC, p1c1, 1/18/1900 | Advertised medical services. Practice based in Gays Mills. |
| Randall | John E. | KC, p4c1, 9/22/1898 | Married Mrs. Rose Randall on Sept. 11, 1898. (Bride and groom may have been from Lynxville.) |
| Randall | Leona | KC, Supp., 12/12/1901 | Attended a Teacher's Institute in Crawford County in 1901. Resided in Gays Mill. |
| Randall | Nelson | KC, p5c5, 3/29/1900 | Visited relatives in Gays Mills before departing for Sabula, IA where he had a job at an excelsior mill. |
| Randall | Nelson | KC, p5c4, 10/5/1899 | Planned to move from Gays Mills to Petersburg where he will work in the excelsior mills. |
| Randall | P. M. | KC, p1c6, 5/19/1898 | Issue of Fact for Jury to be heard in the May term of the Crawford County Circuit Court. Hammond V. Hayes, et al vs. P. M. Randall. |
| Randall | Rose, Mrs. | KC, p4c1, 9/22/1898 | Married John E. Randall on Sept. 11, 1898. (Bride and groom may have been from Lynxville.) |
| Randall | Rose, Mrs. | KC, p5c4, 11/7/1901 | Left home in Lynxville for Courtney, ND to care for her sister who had typhoid fever. |
| Ranek | Mr. | KC, p8c4, 2/13/1902 | Recently died in Racine. Father of Mrs. John Pokorney of Prairie du Chien. |

Genealogical Gleanings From Early Newspapers for Residents In and Near
Crawford County, Wisconsin, 1897-1902

| LAST NAME | FIRST NAME | NEWSPAPER PAGE/COLUMN MONTH/DAY/YEAR | GENEALOGICAL DATA |
|---|---|---|---|
| Ranney | G. W. | KC, p1c4, 9/30/1897 | Former proprietor of the Wauzeka House. Traveled from home in Waupaca Co. to visit nephew, W. A. Vaughan in Wauzeka. |
| Ranney | George W. | KC, p8c4, 8/9/1900 | Recently died. Resident of Little Wolf. Born Feb. 18, 1819 in New York. Married Fanny Coon on Feb.. 18, 1841. Moved to southern Wisconsin in the 1850s. Moved to Little Wolf in 1892 to be with daughter, Mrs. J. N. Booth. His son, George, lived in Wyoming. Wife died in 1894. Funeral by Rev. Herbert of Boyalton. |
| Ransom | W. H. | KC, p5c1, 2/21/1898 | Visited relatives in Haney and returned to his home in New York. |
| Ransome | William H. | KC, p1c4, 1/27/1898 | Married Grace M. Putnam on Jan. 19, 1898 at home of bride's parents. Bride from Haney. Groom from Elmira, NY. James Dowling, J.P. officiated at the ceremony. |
| Ratter | Dorsey, Mrs. | KC, p4c1, 12/9/1897 | Traveled from home in Freeman to visit her parents, Mr. and Mrs. Barham. |
| Rau | Adam | KC, p8c4, 6/21/1900 | Marriage license issued to Erne Steiner of Town of Eastman and Adam Rau of Prairie du Chien |
| Rau | John | KC, p5c3, 1/30/1902 | Gays Mills correspondent reported that Rau was rumored to have accidentally shot his brother in the neck. |
| Rau | John | KC, p1c6, 5/12/1898 | Planned to volunteer for Spanish American War. From Gays Mills area. |
| Rau | John, Jr. | KC, p5c5, 1/30/1902 | While wolf hunting with brother, John's gun accidentally discharged a few rods from his house, struck brother in chin, passed into neck. Taken to La Crosse. X-ray used to find bullet. From Mt. Sterling area. |
| Raukin | Tillie, Mrs. | KC, p1c5, 10/24/1901 | Mrs. Raukin, daughter of the late H. C. Poehler, arrived from Knoxville, TN to visit George Beier of Wauzeka. |
| Raw | Adam | KC, p8c3, 6/28/1900 | Married Ernestena Ziener on June 19, 1900. Bride from Town of Eastman. Groom from Prairie du Chien. |
| Ray | Edwin | KC, p1c5, 2/2/1899 | The nearly 9 month old son of Edwin and Lillian Ray died in Wauzeka on Jan. 21, 1899 from pneumonia. |
| Ray | Ernest | KC, p1c5, 2/2/1899 | Died Jan. 21, 1899 in Marietta. Aged nearly 9 months. Son of Edwin and Lilly Ray. |
| Ray | George | KC, p5c4, 4/8/1897 | Died April 5, 1897 at age 68. W. Ray of Wauzeka was his brother. Buried in Christ Cemetery. |
| Ray | George | KC, p8c3, 6/3/1897 | Died April 5, 1897. Born in Yorkshire, Catarangus Co., NY in 1830. To Ohio in 1832. To Platteville, WI in 1848. Married Miss Almira Taft of Crawford Co, PA in 1855. Moved to Marietta in 1873. Survived by wife, 4 sons, 2 brothers and 2 sisters. Joined Harris Ridge Congregational Church in June 1896. |
| Ray | Harry | KC, Supp., 4/20/1899 | Died April 6, 1899. Aged 9 years, 6 months and 18 days. Son of Miles A. and Almira I. Ray. |
| Ray | Mr. | KC, p1c3, 1/25/1900 | Featured in an article on Wauzeka's business concerns. Operated the Ray House. |
| Ray | W. | KC, p5c2, 1/18/1900 | Proprietor of the Wauzeka Hotel. |

Genealogical Gleanings From Early Newspapers for Residents In and Near
Crawford County, Wisconsin, 1897-1902

| LAST NAME | FIRST NAME | NEWSPAPER PAGE/COLUMN MONTH/DAY/YEAR | GENEALOGICAL DATA |
|---|---|---|---|
| Ray | W. A. | KC, p1c3, 12/5/1901 | Bought Wauzeka House from L. G. Armstrong. |
| Ray | W., Mrs. | KC, p1c3, 3/1/1900 | Mrs. W. Ray and her brother, Henry Brandes, departed Wauzeka to visit relatives in Fulton, IL. |
| Ray | William | KC, Supp., 12/12/1901 | State vs. William Ray heard in Crawford Co. Court. |
| Ray | William, Mrs. | KC, p1c2, 10/27/1898 | Resided in Wauzeka. Entertained father, Orin Lane of Platteville. |
| Raymond | Sarah, Mrs. | KC, p1c3, 8/30/1900 | Arrived from Minneapolis to visit with parents at Wheatville. |
| Rean | J., Mrs. | KC, p5c1, 11/3/1898 | Visited brother, J. McFarland, per East Gays Mills news items. |
| Redfield | P. W. | KC, p8c3, 11/16/1899 | Plaintiff did not appear in the case Andrew LaGeune vs. Henry Buckmaster and P. W. Redfield. Plaintiff will have to pay costs to continue the same. Case heard at the November term of the Crawford County Circuit Court. |
| Redmond | girl | KC, p1c4, 11/17/1898 | Daughter born Nov. 16, 1898 to Arthur Redmond of Marietta. |
| Reed | David | KC, p1c5, 8/26/1897 | Died a few days ago in Beetown. Aged 35 years. |
| Reed | Noma | KC, p5c3, 6/12/1902 | Recently died in Barnum. Daughter of Melvin J. and Laura Rounds of Bell Center. Funeral held at the Haney Church. Sister of Margie Rounds. |
| Reed | William | KC, p8c3, 11/16/1899 | Sold a pearl he found in a clam for $125. Resided in Prairie du Chien area. |
| Reed | Ziba | KC, p5c2, 8/7/1902 | Dept. of Interior published notice that Ziba E. Reed of Barnum, WI filed to make final proof in support of his claim for land at S.E. 1/4 , S.W.1/4 Sec. 23, T.9. N., R 4W. Named the following witnesses to prove continuous residence and cultivation of land: J. W. Lathrop, Thomas McDowell, Roswell Dowling and A. J. McDowell (all of Barnum). |
| Reed | Noma | KC, p5c4, 6/19/1902 | Resolution of Sympathy published by Twilight Lodge No. 81, I.O.O.F. and Peaceful Rebecca Lodge No. 17 of Bell Center for Melvin and Laura Rounds on the death of their daughter, Mrs. Noma Reed. Signed by George A. DiVall, J. H. Clark, Charles P. Jones, Eliza Purington, Emma DiVall and E. Coleman. |
| Rees | E. B. | KC, p5c4, 5/29/1902 | The case E. B. Rees vs. Harvey Wayne, Mary Wayne, Daniel Kramer and Catherine Kramer for foreclosure was heard at the May term of the Crawford County Circuit Court. Case was continued. |
| Rees | E. B., Mrs. | KC, p5c3, 4/4/1901 | Lived in Seneca. Visited father, Ed Garvey. |
| Rees | Earl Brooks | KC, p1c2, 11/1/1900 | Married Susanna E. Garvey at Dubuque, IA on Oct. 24, 1900. Bride daughter of Edward Garvey of Town of Seneca. Groom was a lawyer from Galena, IL. (also p5c3) |
| Reese | Earl B. | KC, p8c3, 10/25/1900 | Recently married Susie E. Garvey in Dubuque. Bride was from Town of Seneca. Groom was from Galena, IL. |

Genealogical Gleanings From Early Newspapers for Residents In and Near
Crawford County, Wisconsin, 1897-1902

| LAST NAME | FIRST NAME | NEWSPAPER PAGE/COLUMN MONTH/DAY/YEAR | GENEALOGICAL DATA |
|---|---|---|---|
| Reeter | H. | KC, p1c6, 4/7/1898 | Elected Councilman for the Village of Wauzeka. |
| Reeter | Henry | KC, p5c5, 4/5/1900 | Elected village assessor in Wauzeka. |
| Reeter | Henry, Sr. | KC, p1c3, 10/7/1897 | Resided in Wauzeka. Entertained his sisters, Mrs. Lamp of South Dakota and Mrs. Schiebel of Madison. |
| Reichman | Herman | KC, p1c3, 10/7/1897 | Plaintiff in a trespass suit against Louis Rider. |
| Reichmann | boy | KC, p1c2, 9/5/1901 | Son born Sept. 1, 1901 to Herman Reichmann of Wauzeka. |
| Reichmann | boy | KC, p1c2, 6/1/1899 | Son born Saturday to Herman Reichmann of Wauzeka. |
| Reichmann | Henry | KC, p1c2, 4/5/1900 | Moved to Maple Ridge to conduct a general store and farm. |
| Reichmann | Herman | KC, p1c3, 11/23/1899 | The court case of Herman Reichmann vs. Charles Brickner continued to Nov. 29th in Justice Peacock's court. |
| Reichmann | Herman | KC, p1c5, 11/30/1899 | In the trial of Reichmann vs. Brickner held in Wauzeka, the plaintiff won. The suit was over $60, the purchase price of a horse which Reichmann alleged he sold to Brickner. Brickner claimed he had the horse on trial for one week and that the horse died during that period. |
| Reichmann | Herman | KC, p1c6, 11/4/1897 | Issue of fact for court to be heard at the November term of the Circuit Court in Prairie du Chien, Crawford County. Egidius Schoeffer vs. Herman Reichmann. |
| Reichmann | Herman | KC, p1c6, 11/4/1897 | Issue of default to be heard at the November term of the Circuit Court in Crawford County. Bank of Prairie du Chien vs. Herman Reichmann, et al. |
| Reichmann | Jennie | KC, p1c5, 5/17/1900 | Died May 11, 1900. Born Jan. 6, 1883 in Wauzeka to Henry and Julia Reichmann. Member of St. Paul's Church of the Evangelical Association. |
| Reichmann | Laverne | KC, p1c5, 11/27/1902 | Died Nov. 20, 1902 with symptoms of strychnine poisoning. He was the 14-month-old son of Herman Reichmann. Children had been playing with sample pills. |
| Reichmann | Welhelmina Carolina | KC, p1c5, 7/14/1898 | Died July 7, 1898 in Wauzeka. Born Sept. 27, 1818 at Hackemeuhle, Germany. Married 1843 to Henry Reichmann, who died about 7 years ago. Family emigrated in 1852. Funeral held at Lutheran Church of Wauzeka. She was the mother of 5 sons and 3 daughters. Survived by Henry, Ernest and Herman of Wauzeka. All other children deceased. |
| Reiger | Earl | KC, p1c5, 10/18/1900 | Died Oct. 12, 1900 at Harris Ridge. Aged 3 years, 3 months and 17 days. Son of M. Reiger. |
| Reigh | M. | KC, p1c4, 9/27/1900 | Reigh's 2 youngest children suffering from malaria typhoid fever. Resided in Wauzeka. |
| Reik | Charles | KC, p6c3, 1/17/1901 | Married Anna Fuka on Jan. 9, 1901. Bride from Prairie du Chien. Groom from Chicago. They plan to live in Chicago. |

Genealogical Gleanings From Early Newspapers for Residents In and Near
Crawford County, Wisconsin, 1897-1902

| LAST NAME | FIRST NAME | NEWSPAPER PAGE/COLUMN MONTH/DAY/YEAR | GENEALOGICAL DATA |
|---|---|---|---|
| Reimer | A. H. | KC, p1c6, 11/4/1897 | Issue of law for court to be heard at the November term of the Circuit Court in Crawford County. A. H. Reimer & Co. vs. W. W. Tate and Mary B. Tate, partners as W. W. Tate & Co. |
| Reinhold | Catherine | KC, p8c1, 6/23/1898 | Married John Keago on June 16, 1898. Bride and groom from Prairie du Chien. |
| Reinow | Harry | KC, p1c2, 5/27/1897 | Died yesterday in Prairie du Chien. |
| Reinow | Henry, Mrs. | KC, p8c3, 5/16/1901 | Died May 12, 1901 in Prairie du Chien. |
| Reiser | Chris | KC, p8c3, 4/11/1901 | Died April 11, 1901 at Lake Charles, LA. He was the brother of John Reiser of (Prairie du Chien?). |
| Reiter | Arthur | KC, p1c4, 1/18/1900 | Married Mary Peacock on Jan. 17, 1900. Bride from Wauzeka. |
| Renak & Pokorny | | KC, p8c1, 1/7/1897 | Proprietors of a blacksmith shop in Lynxville. |
| Reynolds | Rosa | KC, p4c6, 12/1/1898 | Married Peter Pivot on Nov. 24, 1898 in Boscobel. Bride and groom from Marietta. |
| Reynolds | Bessie, Mrs. | KC, p5c2, 8/4/1898 | Traveled from Des Moines to be at the bedside of her grandmother Stolp last week. |
| Reynolds | Charles, Mr. and Mrs. | KC, p1c4, 10/21/1897 | Arrived from Des Moines to visit relatives in Gays Mills. |
| Reynolds | Eleanor | KC, Supp., 12/12/1901 | Received funds from the Crawford Co. Soldiers Relief Commission. Resided in Marietta. |
| Reynolds | Elmer | KC, P5c3, 3/20/1902 | Died Mar. 18, 1902 in Gays Mills. He was the son of Dan Reynolds. |
| Reynolds | Elmore | KC, Supp., 12/29/1898 | Received aid from the Crawford County Soldiers Relief Commission. Resided in Scott. |
| Reynolds | Frank | KC, p8c5, 4/19/1900 | Marriage license issued to Frank Reynolds of the Town of Scott and Nora Pullen of the Town of Marietta. |
| Reynolds | girl | KC, p1c2, 5/3/1900 | Daughter born April 21, 1900 to M. Reynolds of Steuben area. |
| Reynolds | girl | KC, p4c2, 2/10/1898 | Daughter born Jan. 30, 1898 to Sam Reynolds of Gays Mills. |
| Reynolds | girl | KC, p1c5, 1/19/1899 | Youngest daughter of S. P. Reynolds died Jan. 14, 1899. Aged 1 year. Per Gays Mills news. |
| Reynolds | J. | KC, p5c3, 1/18/1900 | Visited family in Gays Mills. Lives in Des Moines where he is learning the blacksmith trade. |
| Reynolds | Jane | KC, p4c4, 11/10/1898 | Issues of Fact for Jury heard in the November term of the Crawford County Circuit Court. A. H. Rounds vs. Jane Reynolds. |
| Reynolds | Jane | KC, p1c5, 6/1/1899 | The May term of the Crawford County Circuit Court closed. The case, A. H. Rounds, Rose B. Young and Mina DeLameter vs. Jane Reynolds, was referred to court. |
| Reynolds | Joseph | KC, Supp., 12/19/1901 | Joseph Reynolds established a boatyard in Wauzeka in the 1860s. He built the hulls for steamboats and barges that were used on the Wisconsin and Mississippi Rivers. |
| Reynolds | Laura | KC, p5c3, 9/27/1900 | Recently married Wilfred Snodgrass. (Bride and groom may be from Town of Scott.) |

Genealogical Gleanings From Early Newspapers for Residents In and Near
Crawford County, Wisconsin, 1897-1902

| LAST NAME | FIRST NAME | NEWSPAPER PAGE/COLUMN MONTH/DAY/YEAR | GENEALOGICAL DATA |
|---|---|---|---|
| Reynolds | Lev. | KC, p8c4, 4/4/1901 | He was part of a group that left Steuben and Wauzeka for the West. Most of this group went to McHenry, ND. |
| Reynolds | Seth | KC, p5c3, 6/15/1899 | J. T. Farris, A. Dowse, T. Kast and Seth Reynolds went to Iowa to do railway work. Resided in Steuben area. |
| Reynolds | Seth | KC, Supp., 12/19/1901 | Seth Reynolds operated a barber shop in Steuben. |
| Reynolds | Seth, Mrs. | KC, Supp., 12/29/1898 | Received aid from the Crawford County Soldiers Relief Commission. Resided in Scott. |
| Rheim | Herman | KC, p1c4, 3/13/1902 | Hired to be a clerk at the Wauzeka House. |
| Rhein | Anna, Mrs. | KC, p1c2, 4/26/1900 | Married Mrs. Anna Rhein on April 22, 1900 at home of bride in Boscobel. Groom was from Wauzeka. |
| Rhinehart | Fred | KC, p5c4, 4/19/1900 | Rhinehart, Z. Reynolds, and William Curley left homes in Gays Mills to go clam fishing for pearls in the Mississippi River. |
| Rhinehart | William | KC, p5c1, 3/1/1900 | Proprietor of a stage line that operated between Lynxville and Gays Mills. |
| Rholik | Wencil | KC, p1c2, 11/30/1899 | Resided in Wauzeka. Entertained his parents, Mr. and Mrs. John Rholik of Redwood Co., MN. |
| Rhyg | Mr. | KC, p5c3, 5/11/1899 | From Elgin, IL. Opened a jewelry store in Mt. Sterling. Sent for his family to join him. Had 30 years experience as a jeweler. |
| Rhynders | L. | KC, Supp., 12/12/1901 | State vs. L. Rhynders heard in Crawford Co. Court. |
| Rhyne | Michael | KC, p8c2, 9/2/1897 | Married Nellie Chase, daughter of C. C. Chase, on Sept. 1, 1897 at St. Gabriel's Catholic Church. Bride from Prairie du Chien. Groom from St. Paul Park. |
| Rice | Albert | KC, p5c4, 5/15/1902 | Married Allie Bright on Sunday. Bride from Lynxville. Groom from Boscobel. |
| Rice | Christian | KC, p1c5, 11/14/1901 | Horses became frightened while driving a team in Wauzeka. Threw the old gentleman to the ground. One wheel passed over him. |
| Rice | Gay | KC, p4c4, 3/16/1899 | Opened a barber shop in Village of Eastman. From McGregor, IA. |
| Rice | Gay | KC, p5c3, 4/20/1899 | Worked as a barber in Eastman. |
| Rice | George | KC, p1c5, 8/7/1902 | Proprietor of the Boydtown cheese factory. |
| Rice | George | KC, p1c3, 2/3/1898 | George Rice of St. Cloud, MN and sister, Mrs. Dr. Cole of Prairie du Chien, visited relatives in Wauzeka. Rice planned to leave for Klondike. |
| Rice | George E. | KC, p1c6, 3/17/1898 | Former resident of Wauzeka. Sent a letter from Klondike that was published in the newspaper. He advised people to not go to Alaska. |
| Rice | George E. | KC, p5c3, 7/14/1898 | Former resident of Wauzeka. Now from Menahga, MN. Letter written by Rice from Klondike was published. |
| Rice | John | KC, p1c3, 5/4/1899 | In failing health. Sold his Yankeetown farm to Ole Eggen of Edgerton. |

Genealogical Gleanings From Early Newspapers for Residents In and Near
Crawford County, Wisconsin, 1897-1902

| LAST NAME | FIRST NAME | NEWSPAPER PAGE/COLUMN MONTH/DAY/YEAR | GENEALOGICAL DATA |
|---|---|---|---|
| Rice | John | KC, Supp., 12/12/1901 | Received funds from the Crawford Co. Soldiers Relief Commission. Resided in Soldiers Grove. |
| Rice | John | KC, Supp., 12/18/1902 | Crawford County Soldiers Relief Committee provided funds to John Rice of Soldiers Grove. |
| Rice | John | KC, Supp., 12/20/1900 | Crawford Co. Soldiers Relief Comm. approved aid to John Rice of Clayton. |
| Rice | Mr. | KC, p5c3, 6/20/1901 | Lived in Mt. Sterling. Suffered from cancer on his face near his eye. |
| Rice | Mr. and Mrs. | KC, p1c4, 7/5/1900 | Arrived from Browerville, MN to visit parents, Mr. and Mrs. F. Gink of Wauzeka. |
| Rice | Will, Mrs. | KC, p1c2, 2/17/1898 | Traveled from Dalton, MN to visit parents, Mr. And Mrs. F. Gink of Wauzeka. |
| Rice | Albert, Rev. | KC, p5c5, 1/9/1902 | Spent holiday in Lynxville and then returned to Chicago Theological Seminary. |
| Rice | Andrew Jackson | KC, p1c6, 1/2/1902 | Died Dec. 19, 1901 at Mt. Sterling. Born Oct. 23, 1847 in McKean Co., PA. He was son of William and Betsey Elizabeth Rice. Moved to Crawford Co. 32 years ago. Married Melissa A. McDowell of Scott Township on July 31, 1881. They had two children, Manville, who died in infancy and Edith. (Long obituary.) |
| Rice | John | KC, Supp., 12/29/1898 | Received aid from the Crawford County Soldiers Relief Commission. Resided in Soldiers Grove. |
| Richard | Lizzie | KC, p8c1, 10/14/1897 | Married Peter Grenmore on Oct. 11, 1897 at St. Gabriel's Catholic Church. Bride and groom were from Prairie du Chien. |
| Richard | Mr. | KC, p8c3, 6/20/1901 | Recently died in Prairie du Chien. Aged 19 years. |
| Richards | Frank | KC, p8c4, 4/3/1902 | Died Mar. 27, 1902 in Prairie du Chien. Aged 18 years. Son of Mrs. A. Richards. |
| Richards | Mamie | KC, p8c1, 8/17/1899 | Married Will Gremore last week at Waukon, IA. |
| Richmond | girl | KC, p1c5, 12/22/1898 | Daughter of Mr. and Mrs. Richmond died Wednesday in Bell Center. |
| Richmond | N., Mrs. | KC, p1c3, 8/11/1898 | From Bell Center. Will hold a series of revival meetings in the Evangelical Church, Wauzeka. |
| Richmond | Susie, Miss | KC, p8c3, 12/29/1898 | Resided in Dubuque. Spent holidays with her mother in Bell Center. |
| Rickliffe | Fred | KC, p8c4, 8/7/1902 | Recently died in an accident in North La Crosse. Former resident of Grand Grae area. Aged 29 years. Buried in Dutch Ridge Cemetery. |
| Rider | Alice | KC, p1c4, 11/22/1900 | Married John H. Naurt on Nov. 21, 1900 at Woodman. Bride from Wauzeka. Groom from (Boscobel?). |
| Rider | boy | KC, p1c2, 5/24/1900 | Son born Wednesday to Lou Rider of Wauzeka. |
| Rider | Flora | KC, p1c5, 10/21/1897 | Died Oct. 13, 1897. Aged 11 years, 1 month and 15 days. She was the daughter of George and Esther Rider of (Wauzeka?). |
| Rider | Lou | KC, p1c3, 2/27/1902 | The George Benner family and Lou Rider family departed area for new homes in Rockford, WA. |

Genealogical Gleanings From Early Newspapers for Residents In and Near
Crawford County, Wisconsin, 1897-1902

| LAST NAME | FIRST NAME | NEWSPAPER PAGE/COLUMN MONTH/DAY/YEAR | GENEALOGICAL DATA |
|---|---|---|---|
| Rider | Lou | KC, p5c5, 4/5/1900 | Elected constable in Wauzeka. |
| Rider | Louis | KC, p5c1, 7/29/1897 | Married Emma Benner on June 30, 1897 in Madison. Bride and groom from Wauzeka. |
| Rider | Louis | KC, p1c3, 11/21/1901 | Returned to Wauzeka from the West where he ran a threshing machine during the harvest. |
| Rider | Louis | KC, p1c5, 5/23/1901 | While working with the Western Wisconsin Railroad bridge crew, the adz of Charles Gregerson accidentally cut off a finger from Rider's left hand. |
| Rieger | boy | KC, p9c1, 7/8/1897 | Son born June 27, 1897 to Mike Rieger of Wauzeka. |
| Rieger | Martha | KC, p1c5, 8/23/1900 | Died Aug. 16, 1900. Aged 17 years and 16 days. Buried in Wauzeka Cemetery. |
| Rieger | Martha | KC, p1c4, 6/22/1899 | Graduated from Harris Ridge School. |
| Rienow | Harry | KC, p1c4, 6/3/1897 | Died May 26, 1897 in Prairie du Chien. He was the youngest son of Henry Rienow. Born July 12, 1881 in North McGregor, IA. Buried in Lowertown Cemetery. |
| Rienow | Henry, Mr. and Mrs. | KC, p8c3, 8/11/1898 | Planned to leave Prairie du Chien for new home in Whitewater, WI to be near their son, Robert, a teacher in the public schools. |
| Rienow | Henry, Mr. and Mrs. | KC, p8c2, 8/25/1898 | Shipped their household goods from Prairie du Chien to Broadhead. Planned to make a home for their son, Robert, a professor in a school in Broadhead area. |
| Rienow | Mabel | KC, p8c2, 3/31/1898 | Married Fred Evans of McGregor, IA on Mar. 28, 1898. Bride was daughter of Henry Rienow of Prairie du Chien. Many relatives and guests mentioned. |
| Riley | C. S., Mrs. | KC, p1c2, 11/3/1898 | Installed as an officer at the International Order of Good Templars (I.O.G.T.) Lodge in Wauzeka. |
| Riley | Charles | KC, p1c3, 1/18/1900 | Riley, Charles Reeter, Ed Gregerson and A. Meyer employed as bridge carpenters. Put in a bridge at Petersburg and extended the sidetrack to the excelsior mill. |
| Riley | Charles | KC, p1c4, 11/8/1900 | Foreman of the bridge crew on the Western Wisconsin Railway. Leg mashed under the car wheels in Wauzeka. Leg amputated. |
| Riley | Charles | KC, p1c4, 4/7/1898 | Charles Riley, George Harris, Ed and Charley Gregerson, and A. B. Rounds built several bridges on Bear Creek and Gays Mills. They repaired a bridge at Barnum. |
| Riley | Charles, Mrs. | KC, p1c3, 8/1/1901 | Visited relatives in North Platte and other parts of Nebraska. |
| Riley | James | KC, Supp., 12/20/1900 | Crawford Co. Board of Supervisors approved payment of expenses in the matter of State vs. James Riley. |
| Riley | Julia | KC, p1c3, 12/1/1898 | Married John Fleeman on Nov. 22, 1898. Bride and groom from Seneca. Bride daughter of John Riley. |
| Riley | Nellie | KC, p1c4, 5/2/1901 | Taught school in the Taft District. |
| Riley | Nellie | KC, p1c2, 8/29/1901 | Hired to teach school at Mazomanie. |

Genealogical Gleanings From Early Newspapers for Residents In and Near
Crawford County, Wisconsin, 1897-1902

| LAST NAME | FIRST NAME | NEWSPAPER PAGE/COLUMN MONTH/DAY/YEAR | GENEALOGICAL DATA |
|---|---|---|---|
| Riley | Nellie | KC, p1c3, 7/31/1902 | Lived in Wauzeka. Hired as principal of the Steuben graded schools. |
| Riley | Nellie | KC, p1c3, 10/14/1897 | From Wauzeka. Taught school in Dutch Ridge District. |
| Riley | Nellie | KC, p1c3, 7/28/1898 | From Wauzeka. Hired to teach at Dutch Ridge school. |
| Riley | Nellie | KC, p1c5, 2/9/1899 | Taught school in Marietta in 1899. E. E. Brindley, Crawford County Superintendent of Schools published a comprehensive list of all teachers in the county. |
| Riley | Nellie | KC, Supp., 12/12/1901 | Attended a Teacher's Institute in Crawford County in 1901. Resided in Wauzeka. |
| Riley | Thompson | KC, p5c4, 2/8/1900 | Riley and family arrived from home in Bear, AR to spend the winter in Mt. Sterling area. |
| Rinehart | J. W. | KC, p8c4, 11/16/1899 | Received marriage license in Crawford Co. Bride, Sylvia Beebe, from Town of Clayton. Groom from Clayton. |
| Ringsack | boy | KC, p8c3, 6/10/1897 | Son recently born to Knute Ringsack of Halls Valley area. Weighted 10 lbs. |
| Rittenhouse | H. B. | KC, Supp., 12/18/1902 | Crawford County Soldiers Relief Committee provided funds to H. B. Rittenhouse of Prairie du Chien. |
| Rittenhouse | H. B. | KC, Supp., 12/29/1898 | Received aid from the Crawford County Soldiers Relief Commission. Resided in Prairie du Chien. |
| Rittenhouse | H. B. | KC, Supp., 12/20/1900 | Crawford Co. Soldiers Relief Comm. approved aid to H. B. Rittenhouse of Prairie du Chien. |
| Rittenhouse | H. R. | KC, Supp., 12/12/1901 | Received funds from the Crawford Co. Soldiers Relief Commission. Resided in Prairie du Chien. |
| Roach | John | KC, p5c4, 5/22/1902 | Died May 15, 1902 at Town of Eastman. Aged 55 years. Survived by wife, 4 sons, 5 daughters, 5 sisters and parents. James Roach of Veblin, SD and Mrs. Laura Kramer of Amenia, ND were unable to attend the funeral. His daughter, Mrs. Nellie Kramer, and son, Will Roach, came from Cloquet, MN. Funeral was held at the Catholic Church. |
| Roach | John | KC, p4c1, 3/31/1898 | John, Will and Nellie Roach of Eastman went to Armenia, ND to spend the summer. |
| Roach | John | KC, p5c4, 5/11/1899 | Hired to clerk in the store of H. M. Seekatz of Eastman. |
| Roach | Nellie | KC, p5c3, 7/25/1901 | Married Victor Kramer on July 22, 1901. The Rev. Father Miller officiated. |
| Roach | James | KC, p1c4, 6/10/1897 | Died June 3, 1897. Aged about 80 years. Born in Waterford, Ireland. Emigrated in 1850. Initially located to Illinois and later to a farm in Town of Haney, Crawford Co. Eight years ago, he and wife moved to Prairie du Chien to live with a daughter, Mrs. Jos. Sweiger. Funeral held at St. Gabriel Church. Wife died 3 years ago. |
| Robb | J. A. | KC, p1c5, 4/24/1902 | Returned to Gays Mills after spending the winter with daughter in Omaha. He also visited a daughter, Laura, in Minneapolis. |
| Robb | J. A. | KC, p5c3, 10/2/1902 | Arranged to have household goods in Gays Mills shipped to his new home in Omaha. |

Genealogical Gleanings From Early Newspapers for Residents In and Near
Crawford County, Wisconsin, 1897-1902

| LAST NAME | FIRST NAME | NEWSPAPER PAGE/COLUMN MONTH/DAY/YEAR | GENEALOGICAL DATA |
|---|---|---|---|
| Robb | J. G. | KC, p5c3, 7/26/1900 | Robb and E. Sherwood planned to leave Gays Mills and operate a mercantile in Viola. Mrs. Robb went to St. Paul to get household effects. |
| Robb | J. G. | KC, p1c3, 3/24/1898 | Returned to home in Gays Mills after an extended visit in the South. He especially liked Mississippi. |
| Robb | J. G. | KC, p4c1, 4/7/1898 | Wrote letter describing his trip to Mississippi. Published in newspaper. Purchased land in Madison, Mississippi. Planned to move there next year. |
| Robb | James, Mr. and Mrs. | KC, p1c3, 12/26/1901 | Left home in Gays Mills for Omaha where they planned to spend the winter with their daughter, Mrs. E. C. Ady. Planned to spend the summer in Colorado. |
| Robb | Lora | KC, p1c5, 6/24/1897 | Returned to Gays Mills for a vacation. Attended school at Northfield, MN. Accompanied by cousin, Laura Robb of St. Paul. |
| Robb | Lora | KC, p1c3, 3/31/1898 | Left Gays Mills for school at Carlton College in Northfield, MN. |
| Robb | Lora | KC, p1c2, 6/23/1898 | Graduated from Carlton College this spring. Daughter of J. A. Robb of Gays Mills. |
| Robb & Only | | KC, p8c1, 1/7/1897 | Proprietors of a flour mill in Gays Mills. |
| Robertson | boy | KC, p4c1, 8/26/1897 | Son born Aug. 23, 1897 to W. T. Robertson of Ferryville. Died Sept. 2, 1897 per KC, p5c1, 9/9/1897. |
| Robinson | James | KC, p1c6, 4/7/1898 | Elected Clerk for the Town of Freeman. |
| Robinson | Jane | KC, Supp., 12/12/1901 | Received funds from the Crawford Co. Soldiers Relief Commission. Resided in Prairie du Chien. |
| Robinson | Jane | KC, Supp., 12/18/1902 | Crawford County Soldiers Relief Committee provided funds to Mrs. Jane Robinson of Prairie du Chien. |
| Robinson | Jane, Mrs. | KC, Supp., 12/20/1900 | Crawford Co. Soldiers Relief Comm. approved aid to Mrs. Jane Robinson of Prairie du Chien. |
| Robinson | M. A. | KC, p1c5, 2/9/1899 | Taught school in Scott in 1899. E. E. Brindley, Crawford County Superintendent of Schools published a comprehensive list of all teachers in the county. |
| Robinson | M. J. | KC, p1c3, 12/9/1897 | Editor of the La Farge Enterprise. |
| Robinson | Martin | KC, Supp., 12/12/1901 | Attended a Teacher's Institute in Crawford County in 1901. Resided in Boscobel. |
| Robinson | Martin A. | KC, p1c6, 11/4/1897 | Issue of default to be heard at the November term of the Circuit Court in Crawford County. Celia Dawson vs. Martin A. Robinson. |
| Robinson | Thomas C. | KC, p8c3, 12/6/1900 | Married Bertha Root on Dec. 3, 1900. Groom from Clayton, IA. |

Genealogical Gleanings From Early Newspapers for Residents In and Near
Crawford County, Wisconsin, 1897-1902

| LAST NAME | FIRST NAME | NEWSPAPER PAGE/COLUMN MONTH/DAY/YEAR | GENEALOGICAL DATA |
|---|---|---|---|
| Rodgers | Ann | KC, p4c4, 4/26/1900 | Died April 21, 1900 in Prairie du Chien. Born in Ireland in 1838. Nee Rooney. Married Edward Rodgers on Aug. 13, 1858 in Chapel of St. Begas Catholic Church in Cleater (or Cieater), England. Husband came to U.S. in 1861. She moved here in 1862. Came to Prairie du Chien. Mother of Charles of Minneapolis; John of Williston, ND; Edward of Prairie du Chien; James of Skaguay, Alaska; George of Texas and William of Skaguay, Alaska. Buried in St. Gabriel Cemetery. |
| Rodgers | Jo. | KC, p4c2, 1/7/1897 | "Jo. Rodgers and Jane Wheeler were married together at the same time. Jo. and Jane still live together they moved to Boskobell." Town of Scott news item. |
| Rodgers | John | KC, p8c3, 11/30/1899 | He was bitten in the face by the pet dog of C. Nugent. "The dog, a valuable one, was drowned." John was the son of Mr. and Mrs. Edward Rodgers of Prairie du Chien. |
| Roe | John | KC, p4c2, 7/28/1898 | From Boma. Enlisted in army. |
| Rogers | A. E. | KC, p5c4, 5/29/1902 | The case A. E. Rogers, et al vs. Ole A. Gunderson, et al was heard at the May term of the Crawford County Circuit Court. Continued. |
| Rogers | Anna, Mrs. | KC, p1c2, 4/29/1897 | Widow of Ed Rogers, Sr. of Prairie du Chien. Advertised sale of her hotel due to her ill health. Mother of Charles and Edward Rogers of Minneapolis. |
| Rogers | Betsy, Mrs. | KC, p1c2, 3/10/1898 | Married Ole Gunderson on Feb. 23, 1898 in La Crosse. Bride and groom from Towerville. |
| Rogers | Charles A. | KC, p8c4, 8/8/1901 | Died Aug. 7, 1901 at Minneapolis. Born June 31, 1861 in England, but grew up in Prairie du Chien (There is no June 31st! Newspaper typo?) Survived by wife, 6 and 9 year old daughters and 4 brothers: J. P., William, J. F. and Edward. (William and James were from Skaquay per KC, p8c3, 8/15/1901.) |
| Rogers | J. P. | KC, p8c4, 11/20/1902 | Lived in Skagnay, Alaska. Served as Supt. of White Pass and Yukon Railroad. Visited brother, Edward Rogers of Prairie du Chien. |
| Rogers | Jane | KC, p8c3, 3/4/1897 | Married Peter Phalen of Dakota on Feb. 15, 1897 in the Catholic Church. Bride from Rising Sun. |
| Rogers | Mamie, Mrs. | KC, p5c4, 5/15/1902 | Came from Onalaska, WI to visit parents, Mr. and Mrs. Thomas Bright of Lynxville. |
| Rogers | Mercy, Mrs. | KC, p5c3, 8/8/1901 | Lived in Steuben. Badly hurt in a runaway accident. The daughters of Mr. and Mrs. Abe Douse were nearly killed. |
| Rogers | Oppie, Mrs. | KC, p5c3, 4/26/1900 | Resident of La Crosse. Visited parents in Lynxville. |
| Rogers | Thomas B. | KC, p4c3, 3/4/1897 | Resided in Sparta. Visited relatives in Towerville. |
| Rohlic | Wencil H. | KC, p1c4, 8/28/1902 | Lived in Wauzeka. Sold farm in exchange for a threshing outfit and planned to go west in the near future. (Went to Seaforth, MN and bought a 240 acre farm per KC, p1c4, 11/20/1902.) |

Genealogical Gleanings From Early Newspapers for Residents In and Near Crawford County, Wisconsin, 1897-1902

| LAST NAME | FIRST NAME | NEWSPAPER PAGE/COLUMN MONTH/DAY/YEAR | GENEALOGICAL DATA |
|---|---|---|---|
| Rohlik | Wencel | KC, p1c2, 9/4/1902 | Lived in Wauzeka. Returned from Battle Creek, MI where he selected a threshing machine. |
| Rohring | Henry, Mrs. | KC, p1c2, 6/12/1902 | Mrs. Henry Rohring of Stanley, IA visited her parents, Mr. and Mrs. Herman Schoenknecht of Wauzeka. |
| Root | Bertha | KC, p8c3, 12/6/1900 | Married Thomas C. Robinson on Dec. 3, 1900. Groom from Clayton, IA. |
| Rose | George | KC, p8c1, 4/7/1898 | Died Mar. 31, 1898 in Prairie du Chien. Aged 61 years. Funeral held at Lutheran Church. Buried in Lowertown Cemetery. |
| Rose | King and family | KC, p5c2, 10/14/1897 | Planned to return from North Dakota and live in Town of Scott their original home. |
| Rosencrans | Bernice | KC, p1c5, 11/20/1902 | Married O. Byron Copper on Nov. 20, 1902. Bride, daughter of A. Rosencrans, from Wauzeka and sister of Mrs. Henry Farris of Steuben (KC, p1c2, 11/27/1902). Groom from De Soto. |
| Rosencrans | Bernie | KC, p1c5, 11/18/1897 | Installed as an officer at the International Order of Good Templars (I.O.G.T.) Lodge in Wauzeka. |
| Rosencrans | Bernie | KC, Supp., 12/12/1901 | Attended a Teacher's Institute in Crawford County in 1901. Resided in Wauzeka. |
| Rosencrans | Bernie, Miss | KC, p1c3, 8/29/1901 | Hired to teach school at Petersburg. |
| Rosencrans | boy | KC, p1c4, 10/5/1899 | Son born last Saturday to Rob Rosencrans of Wauzeka. |
| Rosencrans | Corrinne | KC, p1c6, 4/21/1898 | Married Harry C. Plimpton of Benton Harbor, MI on April 15, 1898. Bride daughter of Mrs. H. V. Rosencrans of Wauzeka. The Rev. F. A. Mundt officiated. |
| Rosencrans | H. P. | KC, p1c2, 1/2/1902 | Planned to marry Mary Stukey. |
| Rosencrans | H. P. | KC, p1c6, 1/9/1902 | Married Mary Stuckey on Jan. 6, 1902. Bride was daughter of Fred Stuckey. Bride and groom from Wauzeka. |
| Rosencrans | H. V., Mrs. | KC, p4c2, 6/13/1901 | Mrs. Rosencrans and her daughter, Mrs. H. C. Plimpton of La Farge, returned home after spending several months traveling in Canada and the western states. |
| Rosencrans | H. V., Mrs. | KC, p1c3, 4/7/1898 | Entertained relatives, Mr. and Mrs. Napoleon Booth of Merrill, WI, at their home in Wauzeka. Mr. Booth was a native of Crawford Co. |
| Rosencrans | Howard | KC, p1c3, 11/22/1900 | Lived in Wauzeka. Replaced Roy McAuley of Gays Mills as brakeman on the Western Wisconsin Railroad. |
| Rosencrans | Rob, Mr. and Mrs. | KC, p5c1, 8/12/1897 | The Rosencrans and Miss Minnie Thiede left Wauzeka for new homes. Rob expected to settle in Courtney, ND. |
| Rosencrans | Robert | KC, p5c5, 4/5/1900 | Elected village trustee in Wauzeka. |
| Rosencrans | Sarah, Mrs. | KC, p1c2, 11/3/1898 | Installed as an officer at the International Order of Good Templars (I.O.G.T.) Lodge in Wauzeka. |
| Rotan | Stephan | KC, Supp., 12/12/1901 | State vs. Stephen Rotan et al. heard in Crawford Co. Court. Witnesses were William Montgomery, J. N. Campbell, James Nicholson, Clark Rounds, A. L. Funk. Ed Miller, E. M. Kast, W. Shockley and Elmer Turk. |

Genealogical Gleanings From Early Newspapers for Residents In and Near
Crawford County, Wisconsin, 1897-1902

| LAST NAME | FIRST NAME | NEWSPAPER PAGE/COLUMN MONTH/DAY/YEAR | GENEALOGICAL DATA |
|---|---|---|---|
| Roth | Anna | KC, Supp., 12/12/1901 | Attended a Teacher's Institute in Crawford County in 1901. Resided in Seneca. |
| Roth | Roman | KC, p8c2, 6/2/1898 | Died May 27, 1898 in Prairie du Chien. Funeral held at Evangelical Church. Buried in Lowertown Cemetery. |
| Round | John | KC, Supp., 12/20/1900 | Crawford Co. Soldiers Relief Comm. approved aid to John Round of Clayton. |
| Rounds | A. C., Mrs. | KC, p1c6, 5/12/1898 | Died May 6, 1898 in Gays Mills. Survived by husband, 3 sons, mother, 1 sister and 3 brothers. |
| Rounds | A. H. | KC, p4c4, 11/10/1898 | Issues of Fact for Jury heard in the November term of the Crawford County Circuit Court. A. H. Rounds vs. Jane Reynolds. |
| Rounds | A. H. | KC, p1c5, 6/1/1899 | The May term of the Crawford County Circuit Court closed. The case, A. H. Rounds, Rose B. Young and Mina DeLameter vs. Jane Reynolds, was referred to court. |
| Rounds | boy | KC, p1c5, 1/20/1898 | Son born Jan. 12, 1898 to A. H. Rounds of Gays Mills. |
| Rounds | Chan. | KC, p1c4, 3/14/1901 | Chan. Rounds and family, brother Melvin and family and their mother, Mrs. O. P. Rounds, departed Gays Mills for new homes in McHenry, ND. |
| Rounds | Charles | KC, p1c6, 5/19/1898 | Issue of Default to be heard in the May term of the Crawford County Circuit Court. Mary S. E. Rounds vs. Charles Rounds. |
| Rounds | Claude | KC, p5c4, 12/29/1898 | Married Bessie Gunderson on Dec. 25, 1898. Bride and groom from Gays Mills. |
| Rounds | Claude | KC, p5c3, 11/27/1902 | Bought a restaurant from Mr. Payne in Gays Mills. |
| Rounds | girl | KC, p5c3, 5/22/1902 | Daughter born May 13, 1902 to Claude Rounds of Gays Mills. |
| Rounds | James I. | KC, p5c3, 6/10/1897 | Traveled from Chicago to visit friends in Crawford Co. Native of Bell Center. Telegrapher. |
| Rounds | Margie | KC, Supp., 12/12/1901 | Attended a Teacher's Institute in Crawford County in 1901. Resided in Bell Center. |
| Rounds | Marianna | KC, p5c1, 6/9/1898 | Died May 27, 1898 in Gays Mills. Born Jan. 29, 1845 in Maine, Broome Co., NY. Moved to Grant Co., WI in 1854. To Crawford Co. in 1855. Married Charles R. Rounds on Feb. 24, 1861. Moved to Gays Mills in 1893. Nee Twining. Sister of D. M. Twining. Mother of Mrs. Almina DeLaMater, Arthur Rounds and Mrs. Rose Young. Funeral held at the Congregational Church. Known as Mary Rounds. |
| Rounds | Marjorie | KC, p5c4, 7/17/1902 | Died July 5, 1902. Aged 7 weeks. Daughter of Claude Rounds. Funeral held at Congregational Church. News from Gays Mills column. |
| Rounds | Mary S. E. | KC, p1c6, 5/19/1898 | Issue of Default to be heard in the May term of the Crawford County Circuit Court. Mary S. E. Rounds vs. Charles Rounds. |

Genealogical Gleanings From Early Newspapers for Residents In and Near
Crawford County, Wisconsin, 1897-1902

| LAST NAME | FIRST NAME | NEWSPAPER PAGE/COLUMN MONTH/DAY/YEAR | GENEALOGICAL DATA |
|---|---|---|---|
| Rounds | Mary, Mrs. | KC, p5c5, 4/4/1901 | Recently died. Resolution of Respect published by O. D. Chapman Corps, No. 23, Dept. of WI, WRC Auxiliary to the GAR Gay Mills. Signed by Lulu Hayes, Mae Twining and Mary Moon. |
| Rounds | Riley | KC, p1c4, 1/27/1898 | Left Bell Center for Edgewood, IA to take charge of a saw mill. |
| Rounds | W. E. | KC, p1c2, 3/24/1898 | From Bell Center. Operated the sawmill in Wauzeka. He is "one of the best sawyers in the country." |
| Rounds | William | KC, p5c4, 2/14/1901 | Operated a sawmill in Gays Mills. |
| Rounds | | KC, p1c2, 12/12/1901 | Youngest child of A. H. Rounds of Gays Mills died Sunday from diphtheria. |
| Rounds | | KC, p5c4, 7/10/1902 | The infant child of Claude Rounds of Gays Mills died July 5, 1902. |
| Rounds | A. H. | KC, p1c2, 4/19/1900 | Departed Gays Mills for Chippewa Co., WI to explore opportunities to invest in land. |
| Rounds | A. H. | KC, p4c2, 8/11/1898 | House in Gays Mills destroyed by fire. The nearby barns of J. A Hayes were rescued. |
| Rounds | Earl | KC, p5c5, 4/12/1900 | Recently departed Bell Center for the west. |
| Rounds | girl | KC, p5c4, 4/19/1900 | Daughter born April 5, 1900 to Claude Rounds of Gays Mills. |
| Rounds | Margie | KC, p5c3, 6/14/1900 | Graduated from Bell Center school. |
| Rounds | Marianna | KC, p8c4, 6/16/1898 | Crawford County Probate Court published a Notice of Hearing. D. W. Twining petitioned court to administer the estate of Marianna Rounds. |
| Rounds | William | KC, p1c4, 4/12/1900 | Resided in Gays Mills. Employed as a sawyer at the Wauzeka Lumber Co. |
| Rowan | Martin | KC, p5c2, 8/18/1898 | Sold his farm in Town of Scott. Called an "old resident." Intended to leave the area. |
| Rowan | Martin W. | KC, p1c5, 10/18/1900 | Died Oct. 12, 1900 of stomach cancer at home of William Shipley, his son-in-law, in the Town of Scott. Aged nearly 59 years. Civil War veteran. Buried in St. Phillips Cemetery. Probate notice published Nov. 22, 1900 on p4c5. |
| Rowan | Mary | KC, p4c5, 11/15/1900 | Applied to Crawford County Court to admit the will of Martin W. Rowan, late of Town of Scott. |
| Rowan | Mrs. | KC, p8c3, 2/4/1897 | Resided in Town of Clayton. Visited daughter, Mrs. W. H. Shipley of Seneca. |
| Rowe | girl | KC, p5c4, 6/1/1899 | Daughter born May 28, 1899 to Ed Rowe of East Gays Mills. |
| Rowe | Maggie, Mrs. | KC, p1c3, 12/22/1898 | Died Thursday (Dec. 15, 1898?) in Clayton Township. Wife of John Rowe, who died while serving as county sheriff. |
| Rowe | Mat | KC, p1c6, 4/7/1898 | Elected Chairman for the Town of Clayton. |
| Rowe | Mat | KC, p5c5, 4/5/1900 | Elected supervisor in Town of Clayton. |

Genealogical Gleanings From Early Newspapers for Residents In and Near
Crawford County, Wisconsin, 1897-1902

| LAST NAME | FIRST NAME | NEWSPAPER PAGE/COLUMN MONTH/DAY/YEAR | GENEALOGICAL DATA |
|---|---|---|---|
| Rowe | Matt | KC, Supp., 12/20/1900 | Represented Clayton on the Crawford Co. Board of Supervisors in 1900. |
| Rowe | William | KC, p1c4, 9/29/1898 | At a conference of the Methodist Church held in Eau Claire, William Rowe was assigned to Shullsburg. |
| Rowe | | KC, p1c2, 10/17/1901 | Died Oct. 9, 1901. Five month old twin child of Mat Rowe of Soldiers Grove. |
| Rowe | Matt, Mrs. | KC, p1c2, 11/27/1902 | Left Soldiers Grove for Waubasha, MN to visit parents and sister (Mrs. Fox). |
| Rowley | J. C., Dr. | KC, p7c5, 7/8/1897 | Medical Director for the Remedial Institute of Prairie du Chien. J. W. Rathbun, Proprietor. Provided medicated, Turkish, Russian, thermo-electric, sea salt and mineral water baths. |
| Rowley | J. C., Dr. | KC, p1c1, 1/18/1900 | Advertised medical services. Practice based in Prairie du Chien. |
| Royer | F. | KC, Supp., 12/12/1901 | Received funds from the Crawford Co. Soldiers Relief Commission. Resided in Prairie du Chien. |
| Royer | Frank | KC, p8c4, 2/20/1902 | Died Feb. 18, 1902. Born Dec. 1810 in France. Moved to Prairie du Chien 25 years ago. Married 3 times. Three girls and 1 son born to last union. |
| Royer | Frank | KC, Supp., 12/20/1900 | Crawford Co. Soldiers Relief Comm. approved aid to Frank Royer of Prairie du Chien. |
| Rublin | James, Mrs. | KC, p4c4, 1/31/1901 | Departed Mt. Sterling to visit her sister, Mrs. Wardell of Pradyville, Columbia Co., WI. |
| Rudd | Mrs. | KC, p4c2, 11/25/1897 | Died Nov. 19, 1897 at P. J. Simes home. Buried in La Crosse. |
| Rudd | John | KC, Supp., 12/20/1900 | Crawford Co. Board of Supervisors approved payment of expenses in the matter of State vs. John Rudd. |
| Ruiter | M., Mrs. | KC, p4c2, 7/11/1901 | Died June 23, 1901 in Luddington. Aged 16 years, 8 months and 3 days. Daughter of Ben Updike of Town of Haney. Born in Grant Co., WI on Oct. 10, 18__. Married William Ruiter and in 1901 moved to Eau Claire Co. Survived by husband and child. |
| Runice | Andrew | KC, p1c6, 4/7/1898 | Elected Supervisor for the Town of Freeman. |
| Runice | J. J. | KC, p5c5, 4/5/1900 | Elected supervisor in Town of Freeman. |
| Runkel | Otto H. | KC, p1c1, 1/28/1897 | Married Catherine O'Mailey, daughter of Mrs. James O'Mailey, of Prairie du Chien on Jan. 26, 1897 in Prairie du Chien. Groom from Monona. |
| Rupp | Anthone | KC, Supp., 12/29/1898 | Crawford Co. Board of Supervisors approved Justices and Constables' expenses related to the Inquest of the body of Anione (or Antone) Rupp. |
| Rupp | Anthony | KC, p8c1, 4/28/1898 | Died April 22, 1898 from suicide at home of Louis Raya (Caya?), his brother-in-law, in Prairie du Chien Township. Aged 35 years. Buried in Frenchtown Catholic Cemetery. |
| Russell | Ed, Mrs. | KC, p5c3, 4/4/1901 | Recently died in Lynxville. She was the daughter of M. D. Smith of Seneca. |
| Russell | Ed, Mrs. | KC, p5c4, 2/20/1902 | Lived near Lynxville. A jury found her death to be caused by suicide. |

Genealogical Gleanings From Early Newspapers for Residents In and Near
Crawford County, Wisconsin, 1897-1902

| LAST NAME | FIRST NAME | NEWSPAPER PAGE/COLUMN MONTH/DAY/YEAR | GENEALOGICAL DATA |
|---|---|---|---|
| Russell | Ed., Mrs. | KC, Supp., 12/18/1902 | Crawford County Board of Supervisors examined bills in the Justices and Constables' Account for State vs. Mrs. Ed. Russell, inquest. Byron Sutton, Mrs. Martha Mansfield, Mrs. Mary Hubbard, Mrs. Allen McCartny, James Haggerty and Edwin Russell were witnesses. |
| Russell | Edwin Perry | KC, p5c3, 6/6/1901 | Married Mary Sutton on June 3, 1901. Bride and groom were from Town of Seneca. |
| Russell | Mary | KC, p8c4, 2/6/1902 | Died Jan. 28, 1902 at her home near Lynxville. Wife of Edward Russell. |
| Russell | Mary, Mrs. | KC, p1c4, 2/27/1902 | Recently died from suicide in Lynxville. Suicide letter published in newspaper in 2 installments. Planned to use laudanum. Asked her husband, Ed Russell, to give her pearls to her Pa and Byron. Dora was to have her dresses. Wanted Kate to lay her out and comb her hair. Looked forward to seeing Emogene, Hannah, mother, grandpas and grandmother after she died. Left her love to husband, father, Byron and Ida. Letter made available by the Rev. A. M. Laird. |
| Russell | Mr. | KC, p5c4, 3/27/1902 | Died Mar. 25, 1902 at Lynxville. Aged 77 years. Married wife over 53 years ago. Grandfather of George Russell of Viroqua. |
| Rust | Louisa | KC, p4c2, 12/2/1897 | Taught school in Sugar Creek District, Town of Freeman |
| Rust | Louise | KC, p1c5, 2/9/1899 | Taught school in Freeman in 1899. E. E. Brindley, Crawford County Superintendent of Schools published a comprehensive list of all teachers in the county. |
| Rutter | Belle | KC, p5c4, 5/29/1902 | Belle Rutter and Pearl Rutter of Freeman attended a teacher institute in Crawford County. |
| Rutter | boy | KC, p4c2, 3/3/1898 | Son born Feb. 10, 1898 to Vern Rutter of Steuben. |
| Rutter | Henry | KC, p4c3, 6/17/1897 | Henry Rutter and family of Oak Ridge (near Ferryville) were struck by lightning. All okay. |
| Rutter | John | KC, p4c2, 11/25/1897 | Recently died in Town of Freeman. He was an early settler. |
| Rutter | Pearl | KC, Supp., 12/12/1901 | Pearl Rutter of Freeman attended the summer Teacher's Institute in Soldiers Grove. |
| Rutter | Pearl | KC, Supp., 12/12/1901 | Attended a Teacher's Institute in Crawford County in 1901. Resided in Freeman. |
| Rutter | William | KC, p5c4, 5/29/1902 | The case Henry Henderson vs. William Rutter impleaded with M. Barham, demurrer. Demurrer withdrawn and answer died. Case was heard at the May term of the Crawford County Circuit Court. |
| Ryan | J. M. | KC, p1c2, 1/2/1902 | Resided at Knapps Creek. Departed for Aberdeen, ND where he purchased land sight unseen. P. H. Doran of Knapps Creek went with him to see the country. |
| Ryan | Mathew | KC, p1c4, 3/20/1902 | Died Mar. 9, 1902. Resided in Town of Clayton. Born Aug. 22, 1819. Portrait printed. |

Genealogical Gleanings From Early Newspapers for Residents In and Near
Crawford County, Wisconsin, 1897-1902

| LAST NAME | FIRST NAME | NEWSPAPER PAGE/COLUMN MONTH/DAY/YEAR | GENEALOGICAL DATA |
|---|---|---|---|
| Ryan | Mathew | KC, p1c5, 11/1/1900 | Democratic candidate for Crawford County Coroner. Born Aug. 22, 1819 in Ireland. Moved to New York in 1846. Moved to Beloit, WI in 1848 where he worked as a mason and builder and freight handler. Moved to Town of Clayton in 1857. Served on Town Board of Supervisors and District School Board. Served as Assessor and Town Treasurer and County Coroner. |
| Ryan | Pat | KC, p1c5, 8/28/1902 | Jailed in Black River Falls for horse stealing. He was once sent to Waupon from La Crosse Co. and twice sent to Waupon from Crawford Co. |
| Ryan | Rosella | KC, Supp., 12/12/1901 | Attended a Teacher's Institute in Crawford County in 1901. Resided in Soldiers Grove. |
| Ryan | Dan | KC, p1c3, 8/8/1901 | Resided in Soldiers Grove. He was a salesman for the Northern Nursery Co. of St. Paul. |
| Ryne | Tom | KC, Supp., 12/18/1902 | Crawford County Board of Supervisors examined bills in the Justices and Constables' Account for State vs. Tom Ryne. |
| Sable | William | KC, p5c4, 11/27/1902 | Married Minnie Schultz last Tuesday. Bride from Town of Eastman. |
| Sage | Mat. | KC, Supp., 12/18/1902 | Crawford County Board of Supervisors examined bills in the Justices and Constables' Account for State vs. Mat. Sage. |
| Sage | Russell | KC, p8c3, 11/22/1900 | Married Nellie Stackland on Nov. 21, 1900. Bride daughter of John Stackland of Prairie du Chien. Groom from Tennessee. |
| Sage | W. F. | KC, p1c3, 9/4/1902 | Treasurer of the Pension Department at the Soldiers Home in Milwaukee. Went to Mt. Sterling to visit friends. |
| Salmon | Culter | KC, Supp., 12/18/1902 | Crawford Co. Soldiers Relief Committee provided funds to Culter Salmon of Soldiers Grove. |
| Salmon | Cutter | KC, Supp., 12/12/1901 | Received funds from the Crawford Co. Soldiers Relief Commission. Resided in Soldiers Grove. |
| Salsbury | J. J. | KC, Supp., 12/18/1902 | Crawford County Soldiers Relief Committee provided funds to J. J. Salsbury of Soldiers Grove. |
| Sampson | boy | KC, p5c3, 8/4/1898 | Son born Aug. 1, 1898 to G. E. Sampson of Gays Mills. |
| Sampson | G. | KC, p1c2, 12/19/1901 | Family quarantined with scarlet fever at their home in Wauzeka. |
| Sampson | G. E. | KC, p5c4, 2/2/1899 | Planned to move away from Gays Mills. Hired by T. W. Lucey & Son of St. Paul. |
| Sampson | G. E. | KC, p5c3, 1/12/1899 | Elected to be an officer for the Modern Woodman Association (MWA) in Gays Mills |
| Sampson | G. E. | KC, p1c2, 8/21/1902 | Moved from Wauzeka to La Crosse. |
| Sampson | George | KC, Supp., 12/12/1901 | Attended a Teacher's Institute in Crawford County in 1901. Resided in Millett. |
| Sampson | Guy | KC, 4/8/1898 | Married Metta Mansfield of Lynxville on April 4, 1897. Groom from Gays Mills. J. L. Stowell officiated. |

Genealogical Gleanings From Early Newspapers for Residents In and Near
Crawford County, Wisconsin, 1897-1902

| LAST NAME | FIRST NAME | NEWSPAPER PAGE/COLUMN MONTH/DAY/YEAR | GENEALOGICAL DATA |
|---|---|---|---|
| Sampson | Guy | KC, p5c4, 12/25/1902 | Worked for the railroad on a run between La Crosse and Portage. Lived in La Crosse. Wrote a letter that described his job and activities that was published in the newspaper. |
| Sampson | Guy | KC, p1c6, 5/12/1898 | Planned to volunteer for Spanish American War. From Gays Mills area. |
| Sampson | Guy | KC, p5c4, 12/1/1898 | Resided in Gays Mills. Nearly died when clothing caught in "one of the wheels." |
| Sampson | Herman | KC, p1c4, 12/19/1901 | Died Dec. 18, 1901 in Soldiers Grove. Son of O. P. Sampson. Aged 19 years. |
| Sampson | Herman Wilson | KC, p5c6, 1/2/1902 | Died Dec. 18, 1901. Born Mar. 2, 1883 in Gays Mills. He was youngest son of O. P. and Alice Sampson. Aged 18 years, 9 months and 16 days. Lived in Soldiers Grove for the last 4 years. Buried in North Clayton Cemetery. |
| Sampson | Mary | KC, Supp., 12/12/1901 | State vs. Mary Sampson heard in Crawford Co. Court. Case No. 54. |
| Sampson | Mary | KC, Supp., 12/12/1901 | State vs. Mary Sampson heard in Crawford Co. Court. Case No. 40. |
| Sampson | O. P. | KC, p1c4, 6/19/1902 | Traveled in Wauzeka, Gays Mills and Soldiers Grove in the interests of the La Crosse Roofing Company. |
| Sampson | O. P. | KC, p4c5, 1/7/1897 | Ran a meat market in Gays Mills. |
| Sampson | T. W. | KC, p8c4, 5/10/1900 | Received license to marry Mary Watson. Bride from Town of Scott. Groom from Soldiers Grove. |
| Sampson | T. W. | KC, p5c4, 5/17/1900 | Resided in Crawford Co. Married last week. Bride's name not given. |
| Sampson | T. W., Mrs. | KC, p5c1, 2/24/1898 | Died Feb. 22, 1898 at her home in Gays Mills. Buried in Elroy, WI, her former home. |
| Sampson | T. W., Mrs. | KC, p5c2, 3/3/1898 | Died Feb. 22, 1898 in Gays Mills. Born Aug. 18, 1853 as Aurilia Brintwell in Lake Mills, WI. Moved to Elroy, WI when very young where she married T. W. Sampson on Oct. 20, 1868. At different times lived in Elroy, Chicago, and Gays Mills. Survived by husband and 4 children: J. C. and C. T. Sampson of Oak Park, IL; Mrs. A. W. Bloom of St. Paul and George Sampson of Gays Mills. Four of her 11 siblings survive (named in obituary). Interred in Elroy. |
| Sampson | Theodore | KC, p5c2, 3/10/1898 | Sold his property in Gays Mills and moved to Chicago to make a home with his sons. |
| Sandusky | John | KC, Supp., 12/12/1901 | Listed as an insane person whose support was charged to Crawford Co. (Last name may be spelled Sinsky.) |
| Sandusky | John | KC, Supp., 12/20/1900 | A Committee of the Crawford Co. Board of Supervisors reported that John Sandusky, insane, was not a resident of Crawford Co. and should not be supported by said county. |

Genealogical Gleanings From Early Newspapers for Residents In and Near
Crawford County, Wisconsin, 1897-1902

| LAST NAME | FIRST NAME | NEWSPAPER PAGE/COLUMN MONTH/DAY/YEAR | GENEALOGICAL DATA |
|---|---|---|---|
| Sanger | Adolph and Edna | KC, p5c2, 8/12/1897 | A number of Good Templars from the lodge in Wauzeka attended the installation at the Steuben lodge last Saturday. Among the members were Adolph and Edna Sanger, Eva and Bernie Brandees, Mr. and Mrs. Ed Lawrence, Alma, Winnie and Mrs. Hoisington, Fred and Henry Perrin, Clara and Frank Lagaman, Ben Pitsenberger, Will Schueler, John Bauer, Zelma Beier, Grace Vaughan, Mrs. Henry Lawrence, Lucy Nice, Henry Reiter, Bernie Rosencranz, Himmie Harris, Rube Myer, Ida Henning, Mrs. Fred Batchelder and M. E. Hoover. |
| Sanger | Edna | KC, p1c5, 11/18/1897 | Installed as an officer at the International Order of Good Templars (I.O.G.T.) Lodge in Wauzeka. |
| Sanger | Emma | KC, p1c4, 2/28/1901 | Married A. Willis on Feb. 27, 1901. Bride daughter of John Sanger of Wauzeka. Groom from La Farge. |
| Sanger | George | KC, p1c6, 4/7/1898 | Elected Councilman for the Village of Wauzeka. |
| Sanger | George | KC, p5c5, 4/5/1900 | Elected President of village board in Wauzeka. |
| Sanger | Lillie | KC, p1c4, 11/20/1902 | Accepted a position as clerk in Steuben Post Office. |
| Sanger | Adolph | KC, p1c3, 3/24/1898 | Adolph Sanger, Frank Lagaman and Willie Beier of Wauzeka departed for Grand Junction, CO to seek their fortune. |
| Sanger | | KC, p1c3, 1/25/1900 | Featured in an article on Wauzeka's business concerns. Sanger Bros operated a blacksmith shop. |
| Sanger Bros | | KC, p5c1, 1/18/1900 | Advertised wagonmaking services. Based in Wauzeka. |
| Sankford | Lidia | KC, Supp., 12/12/1901 | Inquest on Body of Lidia Sankford heard in Crawford Co. Court. |
| Sappington | boy | KC, p4c2, 6/16/1898 | Son born June 6, 1898 to Dan Sappington of Lynxville. |
| Sappington | E., Mrs. | KC, p5c3, 4/19/1900 | Lived with her daughter, Mrs. Ray Copsey of Lynxville. |
| Sappington | Manford | KC, p5c1, 3/10/1898 | Married Mary Lawler on Feb. 24, 1898 at Seneca. Father Keeley officiated. Lynxville news item. |
| Sauk | Lizzie | KC, p5c3, 1/24/1901 | Married Thomas Mizera (or Mezera) on Jan. 22, 1901. Bride Town of Seneca. Groom from Town of Eastman. Many wedding guests mentioned in an article published Jan. 31, 1901, p5c4. |
| Sauk (or Zoch) | Joe | KC, p5c3, 1/24/1901 | Married Mary Stluka on Jan. 22, 1901. Bride from Town of Eastman. Groom from Town of Seneca. Many wedding guests mentioned in an article published Jan. 31, 1901, p5c4. |
| Savage | T. and wife | KC, p4c4, 11/10/1898 | Issues of Fact for Court heard in the November term of the Crawford County Circuit Court. Albert Pfahler vs. T. Savage and wife. |
| Savage | Thomas | KC, p8c3, 11/1/1900 | Died Oct. 30, 1900 in Prairie du Chien. |

Genealogical Gleanings From Early Newspapers for Residents In and Near
Crawford County, Wisconsin, 1897-1902

| LAST NAME | FIRST NAME | NEWSPAPER PAGE/COLUMN MONTH/DAY/YEAR | GENEALOGICAL DATA |
|---|---|---|---|
| Savage | Thomas | KC, p8c3, 11/15/1900 | Recently died. (Former resident of Prairie du Chien. who recently lived in Minneapolis?) |
| Scanlon | John | KC, p5c3, 2/21/1898 | Traveled from Oregon, WI to visit brother in Mt. Sterling. |
| Scanlon | Michael | KC, p1c2, 2/27/1902 | Died Feb. 24, 1902 in Mt. Sterling at an advanced age. He was father of John, of the homestead; James, teacher in Dakota; William, physician in Page, ND; Daniel, physician in Volga, SD and Katie, of North Dakota. |
| Scanlon | William, Dr. | KC, p1c2, 12/5/1901 | He and son arrived from Page, ND to visit the homestead near Mt. Sterling. Later traveled to St. Paul for the wedding of brother, D. L. Scanlon. Dr. D. L. Scanlon lived in Vienna, SD. |
| Schaufenbuhl | Julia | KC, p8c1, 10/14/1897 | Pending wedding to Alfred Cornford announced. Bride and groom from Prairie du Chien. |
| Schaufenbuhl | Julia | KC, p8c3, 10/28/1897 | Married Alfred Cornford on Oct. 26, 1897. Bride and groom were from Prairie du Chien. |
| Scheinpilug | F. | KC, Supp., 12/20/1900 | Crawford Co. Board of Supervisors approved payment of funeral expenses for F. Scheinpilug. |
| Schlager | Christian | KC, p1c2, 3/4/1897 | Died Feb. 21, 1897 in Prairie du Chien. Born Sept. 24, 1823 in Switzerland. Survived by wife, the former Mrs. Scherlin, 1 son, 1 daughter, 2 stepsons, 1 stepdaughter and 2 sisters. Buried in Lowertown Cemetery. |
| Schmidt | Henry | KC, p1c6, 9/25/1902 | Married Delema Plourd on Sept. 22, 1902 at the Catholic Church. Bride and groom were from Wauzeka. |
| Schmidt | John | KC, p1c6, 1/30/1902 | Married Emma Widmann on Jan. 26, 1902 at the German Lutheran Church. Bride daughter of J. G. Widmann of Wauzeka. Groom son of John Schmidt, Sr. of Eastern Wauzeka, and brother of Henry and Charles Schmidt. |
| Schmidt | John | KC, p1c2, 8/29/1901 | The case John Schmidt vs. William Dunbar was settled out of court in Wauzeka. It was a trespass and damages suit. |
| Schockley | Ben | KC, p6c1, 3/18/1897 | Married Edith Comerine last week. Bride and groom may have been from the Town of Marietta. |
| Schoeffer | Egidius | KC, p1c6, 11/4/1897 | Issue of fact for court to be heard at the November term of the Circuit Court in Prairie du Chien, Crawford County. Egidius Schoeffer vs. Herman Reichmann. |
| Schoeffer | George | KC, p1c2, 10/21/1897 | Married Anna Doll, daughter of Joseph Doll, on Oct. 18, 1897. Bride and groom from Wauzeka. |
| Schoeffer | Lena | KC, p1c4, 1/20/1897 | Married Joseph Doll, Jr. on Monday (Jan. 17, 1898?) at Prairie du Chien. Bride and groom from Wauzeka. Bride daughter of E. Schoeffer of Prairie du Chien. |
| Schoenberger | L. C. | KC, p1c3, 2/6/1902 | Officers of the Utica Farmers Mutual Insurance Co. of 1902 were L. C. Schoenberger, Pres., of Viroqua; Charles Mitchell, VP, of Prairie du Chien; O. H. Larson, Secry., of Manning; Joseph H. McLess, Treas., of Viroqua. |
| Schoenknecht | Herman | KC, p1c2, 12/26/1901 | Ordered the newspaper for his daughter, Mrs. Henry Rohrig of Stanley, IA. His son, Gustav, who is single, has land in the west, but is spending the winter with his parents. |

Genealogical Gleanings From Early Newspapers for Residents In and Near
Crawford County, Wisconsin, 1897-1902

| LAST NAME | FIRST NAME | NEWSPAPER PAGE/COLUMN MONTH/DAY/YEAR | GENEALOGICAL DATA |
|---|---|---|---|
| Schoenknecht | | KC, p1c3, 6/27/1901 | The 10-year-old son of Herman Schoenknecht of Wauzeka fell from a wagon after a horse was frightened. Horse ran over him. Doing well. |
| Schofield | Mrs. | KC, Supp., 12/20/1900 | Crawford Co. Soldiers Relief Comm. approved aid to Mrs. Schofield of Prairie du Chien. |
| Schrader | Lizzie | KC, p8c1, 9/23/1897 | Pending wedding (Sept. 23, 1897) to John Schwartz of Bridgeport announced. Bride from Prairie du Chien. |
| Schrader | M. | KC, p1c2, 7/29/1897 | Daughter born July 25, 1897 to M. Schrader of Bridgeport. |
| Schueler | girl | KC, p1c2, 5/18/1899 | Daughter born May 11, 1899 to William Schueler of Dubuque, IA, formerly of Wauzeka. |
| Schueler | William | KC, p1c2, 11/3/1898 | Installed as an officer at the International Order of Good Templars (I.O.G.T.) Lodge in Wauzeka. |
| Schueler | William F. | KC, p1c2, 6/16/1898 | Married Hattie Hazelwood on June 7, 1898 at Boscobel. Bride and groom may be from Wauzeka. The Rev. Crouch officiated. |
| Schueler | William, Mrs. | KC, p8c4, 12/7/1899 | Died Dec. 3, 1899 in Dubuque. Born 19 years ago in Wauzeka. Married a little more than a year ago. Survived by husband, mother and 3 brothers. Buried in St. Mary's Cemetery. |
| Schulenberg | Herman | KC, p5c3, 6/24/1897 | Traveled to his former home in Cross Plains from South Dakota. Relative of Ernest Reichman family of Wauzeka. |
| Schuler | William | KC, p1c3, 8/10/1899 | Worked at Dubuque Telegraph Office. Mr. and Mrs. William Schuler visited friends in Wauzeka. |
| Schulka | A. | KC, Supp., 12/20/1900 | Crawford Co. Soldiers Relief Comm. approved aid to A. Schulka of Prairie du Chien. |
| Schultz | Ferdinand | KC, p1c5, 11/1/1900 | Democratic candidate for Crawford County Treasurer. Born May 16, 1855 in Germany. Lived in Milwaukee when first came to America. Moved to Prairie du Chien in 1884. Established the Fort Crawford Mineral Water Co. Former mayor of Prairie du Chien. Portrait published. |
| Schultz | Johanna, Mrs. | KC, p8c3, 12/25/1902 | Died at home of V. Steiner on Dec. 19, 1902. Aged 80 years. Resided in Prairie du Chien. |
| Schultz | John | KC, p8c3, 4/10/1902 | Died April 4, 1902 in Prairie du Chien. Aged 80 years. Father of Henry Schultz. Survived by wife of 56 years. Funeral held at Evangelical Church. |
| Schultz | Minnie | KC, p5c4, 11/27/1902 | Married William Sable last Tuesday. Bride from Town of Eastman. |
| Schurada | Mike | KC, Supp., 12/12/1901 | State vs. Mike Schurada heard in Crawford Co. Court. Witnesses were Peter Campbell, Clark Chase, Peter Flannigan, John Zeman, Charles Speck, Dan McKey, Mark Hamley, F. M. Phillips, Frank Voth, William West, Elizabeth West, Joseph Lanka, John Shurada, Herman Koch, Joe Steiner, Mike Suhrada, Anna Suhrada and Charles Tesar. |
| Schurtz | Alice | KC, p1c2, 12/1/1898 | Married Rodolf Kuchenbecker of Prairie du Chien on Nov. 24, 1898. Mrs. Louisa Kuchenbecker was the mother of the groom. |

Genealogical Gleanings From Early Newspapers for Residents In and Near
Crawford County, Wisconsin, 1897-1902

| LAST NAME | FIRST NAME | NEWSPAPER PAGE/COLUMN MONTH/DAY/YEAR | GENEALOGICAL DATA |
|---|---|---|---|
| Schurtz | John | KC, p5c5, 4/5/1900 | Elected assessor in Town of Wauzeka. |
| Schurtz | Wallace | KC, p1c3, 6/5/1902 | Married Anna Herold on June 9, 1902. Bride and groom from Wauzeka. |
| Schwartz | Anthony | KC, p1c5, 10/10/1901 | Married Mary Picha on Oct. 8, 1901. Bride was from the Town of Eastman. Groom was from Dutch Ridge. |
| Schwartz | Anton, Mrs. | KC, p1c2, 10/12/1899 | Died Oct. 7, 1899 near Wauzeka. Aged 68 years. Survived by husband, 3 sons and 4 daughters. Buried in Catholic Cemetery. |
| Schwartz | child | KC, p5c2, 4/7/1898 | Died April 14, 1898 in Wauzeka. |
| Schwartz | Clara | KC, p1c5, 10/26/1899 | Married Louis Geitz of Gran Grae on Oct. 25, 1899. Groom was brother of Mrs. H. J. Wagner, whose residence the wedding was held. Bride, of Wauzeka, was daughter of Anthony Swartz. |
| Schwartz | Frank | KC, p1c5, 10/26/1899 | Married Edith Cooley, daughter of John Cooley of Marietta, on Oct. 25, 1899. Groom was from Wauzeka. |
| Schwartz | Joe | KC, p5c5, 4/5/1900 | Elected treasurer in Town of Wauzeka. |
| Schwartz | John | KC, p8c1, 9/23/1897 | Pending wedding (Sept. 23, 1897) to Lizzie Schrader of Prairie du Chien announced. Groom from Bridgeport. |
| Schwartz | John, Mrs. | KC, p1c3, 3/11/1897 | Died Mar. 5, 1897. Funeral held at Lutheran Church in Prairie du Chien. Aged 32 years, 4 months and 7 days. She was the daughter of Mr. and Mrs. Fred Trautsch. Survived by husband and 2 children. |
| Schwartz | Jos. | KC, p1c6, 4/7/1898 | Elected Treasurer for the Town of Wauzeka. |
| Schwartz | Joseph | KC, p1c2, 4/28/1898 | Defendant in court case against Oscar Kuchenbecker. Newspaper called it a "sham lawsuit" regarding a dog held at Rider School House. Verdict for defendant. Schwartz represented by James Tesar and C. L. Lathrop. |
| Schwartz | Otto, Mrs. | KC, p8c4, 7/18/1901 | Died July 12, 1901 in Milwaukee. She was daughter of Fred Karnopp of Prairie du Chien. Funeral held at Lutheran Church. Buried in Lowertown Cemetery. |
| Schwatka | Kate | KC, p5c2, 3/4/1897 | Married Charles Pecor on Feb. 28, 1897 in Bell Center. The bridesmaid was Mrs. Lucy Nice. Groomsman was James Trehey. |
| Schweiger | Willie | KC, p1c3, 10/24/1901 | Eldest son of George Schweiger of Steuben. Accidently shot a rifle into the calf of his leg. Bullet came out his ankle. His condition was improving. |
| Schweiger | girl | KC, p5c1, 2/10/1898 | Daughter born Feb. 6, 1898 to George Schweiger of Steuben. Weighed 14 pounds. |
| Schwert | Andrew | KC, p5c3, 7/25/1901 | Resided on Dutch Ridge. His large new barn burned to ground. |
| Schwert | Dora | KC, p1c2, 12/19/1901 | Recently died in Patch Grove. Aged 15 years. Daughter of John Schwert. |
| Schwert | John | KC, p1c6, 4/7/1898 | Elected Assessor for the Town of Wauzeka. |

Genealogical Gleanings From Early Newspapers for Residents In and Near
Crawford County, Wisconsin, 1897-1902

| LAST NAME | FIRST NAME | NEWSPAPER PAGE/COLUMN MONTH/DAY/YEAR | GENEALOGICAL DATA |
|---|---|---|---|
| Schwert | Mrs. | KC, p1c3, 2/7/1901 | Died Feb. 1, 1901 at home of son, Andrew Schwert of Dutch Ridge. Aged 87 years. |
| Scofield | John | KC, p5c3, 10/16/1902 | Married Lottie Gardner on Oct. 13, 1902. Bride from Lynxville. Groom from Boscobel. |
| Scoggen | Christ | KC, p4c4, 5/2/1901 | Left Soldiers Grove for a trip to Norway, their native land. Andrew Lee, Peter Upholm, Elias Johnson and Christ Scoggen. |
| Scott | Frank | KC, p6c3, 11/15/1900 | Married Minnie Keilley on Nov. 10, 1900. Included in Steuben news column. |
| Scott | Trelle | KC, Supp., 12/18/1902 | Crawford County Board of Supervisors allowed expenses in the Matter of Trelle Scott, Insane. |
| Scott | Winfield | KC, p5c5, 4/5/1900 | Elected supervisor in Marietta. |
| Scoville | A. N. | KC, p1c3, 3/29/1900 | Resident of Seneca. He was Supt. of the Crawford Co. Poor Farm. Bought a prize horse in Lansing. |
| Scoville | Charles | KC, p5c4, 3/29/1900 | Planned to leave Pine Creek for Dakota on April 3, 1900. |
| Scoville | Charles | KC, p5c3, 7/11/1901 | Lived in Steuben. Eye removed when injured by barbed wire. |
| Scoville | May | KC, p1c5, 3/4/1897 | Married J. O'Shaughessy on Feb. 22, 1897. The Rev. J. Keeley officiated. Bride and groom may have been from Town of Seneca. |
| Scoville | N., Mrs. | KC, p5c3, 10/24/1901 | Resided in Seneca. Visited mother, Mrs. Barnum of Barnum. |
| Scroggum | Jac. | KC, p8c4, 11/13/1902 | In the November term of Crawford County Circuit Court, State vs. Jac. Scroggum and M. Monahan, case was continued. |
| Scroggum | Jacob | KC, Supp., 12/18/1902 | Crawford County Board of Supervisors examined bills in the Justices and Constables' Account for State vs. Jacob Scroggum and Michael Monohan. A. E. Stoors, G. L. Miller, Joseph Pryor and F. T. Hobbs were witnesses. |
| Searle | A. N. | KC, p5c3, 5/20/1897 | Issues of fact for jury to be heard in the May term of the Crawford County Court. A. N. Searle vs. J. J. Crowley, Dan Garvey and Frank White. |
| Searle | A. N. | KC, p1c6, 11/4/1897 | Issue of fact for jury to be heard at the November term of the Circuit Court in Crawford County. A. N. Searle vs. J. J. Crowley, Dan Garvey and Frank White. |
| Searle | A. N. | KC, p1c6, 11/4/1897 | Issue of law for court to be heard at the November term of the Circuit Court in Crawford County. A. N. Searle vs. Thomas H. Joy et al. |
| Searle | Allie | KC, p5c5, 1/10/1901 | Taught school in Lynxville. |
| Searle | Allie | KC, p1c5, 2/9/1899 | Taught school in Wauzeka in 1899. E. E. Brindley, Crawford County Superintendent of Schools published a comprehensive list of all teachers in the county. |
| Searle | Allie | KC, Supp., 12/12/1901 | Attended a Teacher's Institute in Crawford County in 1901. Resided in Lynxville. |
| Searles | A., Miss | KC, p5c3, 4/19/1900 | Postmistress in Lynxville. |

Genealogical Gleanings From Early Newspapers for Residents In and Near
Crawford County, Wisconsin, 1897-1902

| LAST NAME | FIRST NAME | NEWSPAPER PAGE/COLUMN MONTH/DAY/YEAR | GENEALOGICAL DATA |
|---|---|---|---|
| Searles | Raleigh | KC, p5c3, 12/18/1902 | Taught school on DuCharme Ridge. |
| Sebastian | Anna Bitterlee, Mrs. | KC, p5c1, 9/29/1898 | Died Sept. 24, 1898 in Prairie du Chien. Daughter of Laurence Bitterlee of Prairie du Chien. Born July 15, 1860. Married William Sebastian on Nov. 13, 1882. Survived by husband, 3 sons and 2 daughters, parents, and 3 brothers. Funeral held at St. Gabriel Catholic Church. |
| Sebastian | John | KC, p8c2, 2/16/1899 | Died Feb. 14, 1899 in Town of Prairie du Chien. Aged 82 years. Born in Rhine Province. Came to America in 1891. Survived by 3 sons and a daughter (Mrs. L. Cornelius of Prairie du Chien). |
| Seehuus | O. M. | KC, p1c2, 10/26/1899 | Advertised his services as a physician and surgeon. Resided in Mt. Sterling. |
| Seehuus | O. M., Dr. | KC, p5c2, 1/18/1900 | Advertised medical services. Practice based in Mt. Sterling. |
| Seekatz | Fred E. | KC, p1c5, 7/6/1899 | Married Mary Morse on July 4, 1899 in Steuben. Bride and groom from Steuben. Bride was daughter of Mrs. H. Hamilton. (See p5c3 for more details.) |
| Seekatz | girl | KC, p5c3, 6/7/1900 | Daughter recently born to Fred Seekatz of Eastman. |
| Seekatz | H. M. | KC, p5c5, 2/22/1900 | Treasurer for Town of Eastman. |
| Seekatz | H. M. | KC, p4c2, 6/20/1901 | Sold his general merchandise business in Eastman to J. A. Dvorak of Waubena. |
| Seekatz | Henry M. | KC, p5c4, 5/24/1900 | Married Julia A. Brady on May 21, 1900. Bride and groom from Town of Eastman. Bride daughter of Frank Brady. |
| Seekatz | J. A. | KC, p5c3, 6/7/1900 | Former resident of Eastman. He was a graduate optician of Hoopeston, IL. Visited his uncle, John Seekatz. |
| Seeley | Ernest | KC, p1c3, 11/18/1897 | Injured by a bear while hunting for deer in the northern woods. Brought home to heal. He was son of Charles Seeley, lumber dealer in La Farge. |
| Seely | Mary, Mrs. | KC, Supp., 6/8/1899 | Died May 28, 1899. Born Jan 24, 1831 in Ogdenburg, NY. Nee Lampman. Moved to Ohio in 1839 with parents. Moved to Crawford Co. WI in 1852. Married D. F. Seely in 1853. Gave birth to 3 boys and 3 girls (2 now dead). Funeral held at German Evangelical Church in Wauzeka. |
| Seeman | Knute | KC, Supp., 12/20/1900 | Crawford Co. Board of Supervisors approved payment of expenses in the matter of State vs. Knute Seeman. The witnesses were (E.?) C. Kincannon; A. Taft; Art Stearns; D. Holliday, Jr.; D. Staib; Ezra Jenkins; William Stevenson; John Hahn; Jno. Stevenson, Jr.; Charles White; Walker Stevenson, Henry Scott, Dike Haskins, D. Holliday, Sr. and L. W. Lathrop. In a second trial George Porter, Henry Scott, S. Thompson and Ed Rhone also served as witnesses. |
| Seidal | Carl | KC, p1c6, 1/20/1898 | Died last week at home on Shanghai Ridge. Buried in Milwaukee. |
| Sekatz | Fred | KC, p1c2, 1/18/1900 | Mr. And Mrs. Fred Sekatz and sister, Elsa, of Steuben visited their sister, Mrs. Otto Drezel of Decorah, IA. |

Genealogical Gleanings From Early Newspapers for Residents In and Near
Crawford County, Wisconsin, 1897-1902

| LAST NAME | FIRST NAME | NEWSPAPER PAGE/COLUMN MONTH/DAY/YEAR | GENEALOGICAL DATA |
|---|---|---|---|
| Sekatz | Henry M. | KC, p1c3, 8/1/1901 | Departed Eastman for new home in Wadena, MN. William Brady of Wauzeka was his brother-in-law. |
| Selzman | John | KC, p1c2, 4/21/1898 | Planned to move from Richland Center to Soldiers Grove to open a meat market. |
| Severson | Anna | KC, p1c4, 4/7/1898 | Married Chris Morkri on Mar. 17, 1898. Bride and groom from Folsom. |
| Severson | Anna | KC, Supp., 12/12/1901 | Attended a Teacher's Institute in Crawford County in 1901. Resided in Rising Sun. |
| Severson | Betsey | KC, p5c3, 4/3/1902 | Married Thomas Aspenson last Wednesday at the Norwegian Church in Utica. Bride was from Seneca. |
| Severson | Betsy | KC, Supp., 12/12/1901 | Attended a Teacher's Institute in Crawford County in 1901. Resided in Seneca. |
| Seward | M. B. | KC, p5c3, 5/20/1897 | Issues of fact for court to be heard in the May term of the Crawford County Court. William Cater vs. M. B. Seward and William Barney. |
| Seymour | girl | KC, p1c5, 11/17/1898 | Daughter born Nov. 12, 1898 to Thomas Seymour of Marietta. |
| Seymour | Thomas | KC, p4c1, 11/25/1897 | Married Bertha Curtis of Scott on Nov. 17, 1897. Groom from Marietta. Many relatives mentioned. |
| Seymour | Tom, Mr. and Mrs. | KC, p4c2, 9/22/1898 | Guests of their parents, Mr. and Mrs. Dan Curtis. Per Hurlbut news items. |
| Shabshab | Milhiem | KC, p5c3, 5/20/1897 | Issues of fact for jury to be heard in the May term of the Crawford County Court. William Abraham vs. Milhiem Shabshab. |
| Shaw | boy | KC, p4c2, 7/22/1897 | Son born July 16, 1897 to Ernest Shaw of Barnum. |
| Shaw | J. W. | KC, Supp., 12/12/1901 | Attended a Teacher's Institute in Crawford County in 1901. Resided in Excelsior. |
| Shaw | Jack | KC, p5c3, 8/22/1901 | Lived in Knapps Creek area. Hired to teach in Millet. |
| Shaw | William | KC, p1c2, 10/30/1902 | His house on Harris Ridge was destroyed by fire. Insurance policy had expired. |
| Sheats | William F. | KC, Supp., 12/12/1901 | Received funds from the Crawford Co. Soldiers Relief Commission. Resided in De Soto. |
| Shemar or Shener | Mary | KC, p8c4, 6/6/1901 | Married John Polda on June 4, 1901 at St. John's Bohemian Church. Bride from Prairie du Chien. Groom from Bridgeport. |
| Shepard | William | KC, p8c4, 9/30/1897 | At a conference of the Methodist Church held in Platteville, William Shepard was assigned to Mt. Hope, WI. |
| Shephard | William | KC, p1c4, 9/29/1898 | At a conference of the Methodist Church held in Eau Claire, William Shephard was assigned to Benton. |
| Sherhon | Vaclav | KC, Supp., 12/12/1901 | Inquest on body of Vaclav Sherhon heard in Crawford Co. Court. |
| Sherhunt | Mary | KC, p4c2, 12/2/1897 | Married Frank Woodnal at St. John parsonage. (Reported in Bridgeport column.) |
| Sherick | David | KC, Supp., 12/18/1902 | Crawford County Soldiers Relief Committee provided funds to David Sherick of Soldiers Grove. |

Genealogical Gleanings From Early Newspapers for Residents In and Near
Crawford County, Wisconsin, 1897-1902

| LAST NAME | FIRST NAME | NEWSPAPER PAGE/COLUMN MONTH/DAY/YEAR | GENEALOGICAL DATA |
|---|---|---|---|
| Sheridan | Mary | KC, p1c5, 10/28/1897 | Died Oct. 20, 1897 at her father's home near Soldiers Grove. She was the oldest daughter. Mother deceased. Funeral held at St. Phillip's Catholic Church. |
| Sherlin | Fred | KC, p7c4, 1/25/1900 | Received marriage license in Crawford Co. Nettie Steiner was prospective spouse. Bride and groom-to-be from Prairie du Chien. |
| Sherman | Marguerite | KC, p4c5, 12/20/1900 | Married Joe Collins on Wednesday in Cassville, at the home of the bride's parents. Planned to live in Minneapolis. |
| Sherman | Marguerite, Miss | KC, p1c5, 3/23/1899 | Postmistress of Seneca. |
| Sherry | Edward P. | KC, p8c3, 1/23/1902 | Married Laura Case on Jan. 22, 1902. Bride daughter of Lawrence Case of Prairie du Chien and sister of Mrs. Carrie Gilchrist. Groom from Milwaukee. Planned to live in Milwaukee. |
| Sherwood | A. M. | KC, p5c3, 1/2/1902 | Sold his Mt. Sterling farm and home to Henry Quamme and Albert Anderson for $7000. Planned to go west in April. |
| Sherwood | A. M., Mrs. | KC, p5c1, 10/6/1898 | Arrived from Colorado to make Mt. Sterling their home. |
| Sherwood | Bert | KC, p4c1, 3/24/1898 | Rented his Mt. Sterling farm to Herb Sherwood. Planned to move to Colorado. |
| Sherwood | E. E. | KC, p5c3, 9/13/1900 | Moved from Mt. Sterling to Viola. |
| Sherwood | Ella, Mrs. | KC, p4c2, 11/4/1897 | Resided in Mt. Sterling. Took her daughter to Colorado for the winter in hopes of improving daughter's health. |
| Sherwood | H. A. | KC, p1c2, 9/11/1902 | Recently died. Father of O. A. Sherwood of Rockford, IL. |
| Sherwood | H. A., Mrs. | KC, p1c2, 10/3/1901 | Lived in Mt. Sterling. Visited her sister, Mrs. N. Wells of Bellville, KS. |
| Sherwood | H. L. | KC, p5c1, 5/27/1898 | Wrote an article on poultry that was published in newspaper. From Mt. Sterling. |
| Sherwood | H. L. | KC, p1c5, 1/5/1899 | H. L. Sherwood and Jerry O'Neil acquired the *Kickapoo Chief* newspaper from Riley Thompson and J. A. Bellows. Published in Wauzeka. |
| Sherwood | H. L., Mrs. | KC, p4c2, 1/21/1897 | Lived in Mt. Sterling. Suffered with a felon. Finger was amputated. |
| Sherwood | Harvey Alexander | KC, p1c4, 9/11/1902 | Died Sept. 5, 1902. Born July 5, 1834 in Saratoga Springs, NY. He was eldest son of Isaac Sherwood. In 1835 he and family moved to Milwaukee Co. and then Walworth Co. In 1854 moved to Mt. Sterling. Father of Frank A., Orrin A., Edward E. and Herbert L., all of Mt. Sterling. |
| Sherwood | Mary | KC, p1c4, 2/28/1901 | Married Norman Coulson on Feb. 14, 1901 in Boulder, CO. Bride was daughter of Mr. and Mrs. Sherwood of Mt. Sterling. Groom was from Boulder, CO. |
| Sherwood | William A. | KC, p5c4, 6/26/1902 | Died June 22, 1902 at Mt. Sterling. Funeral held at Utica Church. |
| Shields | girl | KC, p5c3, 7/11/1901 | Daughter recently born to T. Shields in Steuben. |
| Shields | James | KC, p4c3, 5/12/1898 | Married Alice Peterson on May 1, 1898 in Boscobel. Bride and groom from Steuben. |

Genealogical Gleanings From Early Newspapers for Residents In and Near Crawford County, Wisconsin, 1897-1902

| LAST NAME | FIRST NAME | NEWSPAPER PAGE/COLUMN MONTH/DAY/YEAR | GENEALOGICAL DATA |
|---|---|---|---|
| Shields | Thomas | KC, p1c5, 3/24/1898 | Married Julia Morse on Mar. 17, 1898 in Boscobel. Bride and groom from Steuben. Bride daughter of Mrs. Henry Hamilton. The Rev. W. J. Bond officiated. |
| Shields | Thomas J. | KC, p1c4, 3/31/1898 | Lived in Steuben. Recently married. Went on a wedding trip to Milwaukee and Chicago. |
| Shimmer | Charles | KC, p5c3, 10/24/1901 | Married Fern Taft on Oct. 16, 1901. Bride from Taft Ridge. Planned to live in Bell Center. |
| Shimmins | Charles | KC, p5c4, 7/24/1902 | Lived in Bell Center. Lost 23 hogs to a lightning strike. |
| Shimmins | girl | KC, p10c4, 12/12/1901 | Daughter recently born to George Shimmins of Bell Center. |
| Shinka | Joseph | KC, p5c2, 11/17/1898 | Barn and granary destroyed by fire on Swatek Ridge, Eastman. |
| Shinka | Mr. | KC, p5c3, 8/28/1902 | Died Aug. 18, 1902 in Town of Eastman. He was an aged Bohemian man. |
| Shipley | Albert, Mrs. | KC, p1c3, 8/8/1901 | Departed Wauzeka to visit parents in Arkansas City, KS. |
| Shipley | Bert | KC, p1c3, 3/14/1901 | Married Stella Guernsey on Mar. 12, 1901. Groom was from Boscobel. They planned to live in Wauzeka. |
| Shipley | Bert | KC, p8c4, 3/21/1901 | Married Stella Guernsey on Mar. 12, 1901 at the residence of A. J. Guernsey of Boscobel. The Rev. Thomas Crouch officiated. |
| Shipley | Bert | KC, p1c4, 3/28/1901 | Advertised the purchase of a barbershop in Wauzeka from J. H. Peacock. |
| Shipley | boy | KC, p1c2, 3/6/1902 | Son born Wednesday to Bert Shipley of Wauzeka. Weighed 10 pounds. |
| Shipley | George | KC, p1c2, 11/21/1901 | Resided in Boscobel. Did carpentry work for Mr. Divail of Bell Center. |
| Shipley | W. H. | KC, p1c5, 2/9/1899 | Taught school in Seneca in 1899. E. E. Brindley, Crawford County Superintendent of Schools published a comprehensive list of all teachers in the county. |
| Shipton | Mrs. | KC, p1c2, 4/12/1900 | Recently died in Wapello, IA. Buried in Platteville. Niece of Mr. and Mrs. Ray of Wauzeka. |
| Shirlin | Fred C. | KC, p8c4, 1/25/1900 | Married Nettie Steiner on Jan. 23, 1900. Bride and groom from Prairie du Chien. Bride daughter of John Steiner. |
| Shockey | Laura | KC, p4c2, 1/14/1897 | Resided in Bell Center. Visited sister, Mrs. F. M. Hayes of Steuben. |
| Shockley | Fay | KC, p1c5, 6/6/1901 | Married Dr. W. E. Longstreth on May 28, 1901. Bride daughter of Wilson Shockley of Bell Center and sister of Mrs. Neil Drake of same. Groom from Comley, OH. Planned to live in New York where groom will continue his medical training. |
| Shockley | John | KC, p5c5, 4/12/1900 | Recently departed Bell Center for the west. |
| Shockley | S. C. | KC, p1c2, 1/2/1902 | Arrived from Courtney, ND to visit parents in Bell Center. His brother will go to Courtney to take charge of S. C.'s claim. S. C. was in the machinery and implement business. |
| Shockley | Sam | KC, p1c6, 5/5/1898 | Officer in Good Templars Lodge in Bell Center. |

Genealogical Gleanings From Early Newspapers for Residents In and Near Crawford County, Wisconsin, 1897-1902

| LAST NAME | FIRST NAME | NEWSPAPER PAGE/COLUMN MONTH/DAY/YEAR | GENEALOGICAL DATA |
|---|---|---|---|
| Shoemaker | boy | KC, p5c3, 12/18/1902 | Son recently born to Sam Shoemaker of Lynxville. |
| Shoemaker | girl | KC, p5c3, 3/21/1901 | Daughter recently born to W. Shoemaker of Lynxville. |
| Shuka | Anton | KC, Supp., 12/29/1898 | Received aid from the Crawford County Soldiers Relief Commission. Resided in Prairie du Chien. |
| Shulka | A. | KC, Supp., 12/12/1901 | Received funds from the Crawford Co. Soldiers Relief Commission. Resided in Prairie du Chien. |
| Shulka | A. | KC, Supp., 12/18/1902 | Crawford County Soldiers Relief Committee provided funds to A. Shulka of Prairie du Chien. |
| Shulka | Anton | KC, Supp., 12/29/1898 | Received aid from the Crawford County Soldiers Relief Commission. Resided in Prairie du Chien. |
| Shulka | Herman | KC, p5c4, 5/16/1901 | Lived in Eastman. Collected a bounty for killing 45 rattlesnakes. |
| Shulkey | Charles | KC, Supp., 12/12/1901 | State vs. Charles Shulkey heard in Crawford Co. Court. Daniel Carlin was the witness. |
| Shumaker | James | KC, p5c4, 3/27/1902 | Appointed marshall in Lynxville. Replaced Robert Lawrence. |
| Siefert | Henry | KC, p8c4, 1/2/1902 | Married Lydia E. Stark on Dec. 25, 1901. |
| Siegert | William | KC, p1c5, 12/19/1901 | Resided in Wauzeka. Taken to Judge Curran in Prairie du Chien and adjudged to be insane. Escaped. Captured and taken to Mendota. |
| Siegert | William | KC, p1c2, 9/4/1902 | Native of Wauzeka. Discharged from the State Hospital in Mendota. He is now in good mental and physical health. |
| Siegert | William | KC, Supp., 12/18/1902 | The Crawford County Board of Supervisors allowed expenses in the Matter of William Siegert, Insane. |
| Silbaugh | Jackson, Capt. | KC, p4c4, 10/30/1902 | Democratic nominee for Congress against J. W. Babcock in the Third District. Born Oct. 15, 1863 on a farm near Viroqua, Vernon County. Graduated from Viroqua High School in 1885 and in 1888 from the law department of Union University of Albany, NY. Served as Viroqua postmaster, journal clerk of the state senate and chairman of the Democratic county committee of Vernon County. He is an officer in the Mystic Workers lodge at Viroqua, a Knight Templar in Masonry, a member of the Woodman lodge and was grandmaster of the Grand Lodge of Odd Fellows. During Spanish-American War he raised a company in Viroqua and served as captain of Co. M., 4th Wisconsin. Practiced law with H. Henry Bennett. Married in September 1901 to Rosetta Bold (Boid?), who graduated from the state university in 189(?). She has taught in Chippewa Falls and Pueblo, CO. |
| Silbaugh | Jackson, Mrs. | KC, p5c4, 2/27/1902 | Resided in Viroqua. Scheduled to speak in Mt. Sterling on "Bits of Travel" and "Power of Habit." |
| Sillge | H. O. | KC, p1c2, 1/31/1901 | Married on Jan. 23, 1901 in Estherville, IA. Honeymooned at home of William Sillge in Wauzeka. Sillge was the proprietor of a harness shop. |

Genealogical Gleanings From Early Newspapers for Residents In and Near Crawford County, Wisconsin, 1897-1902

| LAST NAME | FIRST NAME | NEWSPAPER PAGE/COLUMN MONTH/DAY/YEAR | GENEALOGICAL DATA |
|---|---|---|---|
| Sillge | William | KC, p1c4, 8/24/1899 | Mr. and Mrs. William Sillge and their daughters, Winnie and Sadie, returned to Wauzeka after a visit with relatives in Estherville, IA. A brother was the editor and owner of the Estherville Democrat. Another brother worked as a harness maker in Esterville. |
| Sime | Anna | KC, Supp., 12/12/1901 | Attended a Teacher's Institute in Crawford County in 1901. Resided in Soldiers Grove. |
| Sime | boy | KC, p5c3, 12/14/1899 | Son recently born to Peter J. Sime of Freeman. |
| Sime | Dr. | KC, p1c2, 12/2/1897 | Recently died in Soldiers Grove. |
| Sime | J. | KC, p4c2, 11/25/1897 | Married Emma Torgerson on Nov. 18, 1897 at Utica Lutheran Church. |
| Sime | Mary | KC, p1c3, 10/10/1901 | Died Oct. 3, 1901 in Soldiers Grove. |
| Sime | N. A., Dr. | KC, p1c6, 12/2/1897 | Died Nov. 18, 1897 in Soldiers Grove. Aged 25 years and 1 day. Son of T. N. Sime. Married Louise Severson a year ago. |
| Sime | T. T. | KC, p1c4, 3/15/1900 | Elected vice president of the newly formed Crawford County Farmers Mutual Insurance Co. Other officers were J. W. McCullock, E. G. Briggs and J. A. Hays. |
| Sime | T. T. | KC, p1c6, 6/2/1898 | Expected to run for re-election as Crawford County Sheriff. |
| Sime | T. T. | KC, p5c5, 4/5/1900 | Elected supervisor in Town of Freeman. |
| Sime | T. T. | KC, Supp., 12/20/1900 | Represented Freeman on the Crawford Co. Board of Supervisors in 1900. |
| Sime | T. T., Mrs. | KC, p5c2, 6/24/1897 | Took care of her sick mother, Mrs. Uphome of near Pine Knob. |
| Sime | T. T., Sheriff | KC, p5c3, 1/7/1897 | P. S. Sime of Freeman, A. E. Spencer of Utica, Albert Aspenson of Seneca, William Barney of Clayton and J. M. Ferrell of Marietta were appointed deputy sheriffs by Sheriff T. T. Sime. |
| Simek | Mary | KC, p1c3, 11/11/1897 | Married Eugene Smith on Nov. 8, 1897 at St. Vaclev's Church in Eastman. |
| Simek | Mary | KC, p1c4, 2/11/1897 | Married George Davis on Feb. 3, 1897 in Prairie du Chien. Bride and groom from Clayton Co., IA. |
| Simrod | Charles | KC, Supp., 12/20/1900 | Crawford Co. Board of Supervisors approved payment of expenses in the matter of State vs. Charles Simrod. Frank Stark and C. W. Hufschmidt were the witnesses. |
| Sinclair | D. M. | KC, p8c4, 9/30/1897 | At a conference of the Methodist Church held in Platteville, D. M. Sinclair was assigned to Lancaster. |
| Sinclair | D. M. | KC, p1c4, 9/29/1898 | At a conference of the Methodist Church held in Eau Claire, D. M. Sinclair was assigned to Hazel Green. |
| Sincola | Charles | KC, p1c3, 6/17/1897 | Died June 10, 1897. Aged 14 years. Son of James Sincola of Prairie du Chien. Funeral held at St. John's Bohemian Catholic Church. |
| Singles | Charles | KC, Supp., 12/12/1901 | State vs. Charles Singles heard in Crawford Co. Court. |

Genealogical Gleanings From Early Newspapers for Residents In and Near
Crawford County, Wisconsin, 1897-1902

| LAST NAME | FIRST NAME | NEWSPAPER PAGE/COLUMN MONTH/DAY/YEAR | GENEALOGICAL DATA |
|---|---|---|---|
| Skinner | Charles E. | KC, p8c3, 7/4/1901 | Married Minnie Heilman on July 3, 1901 at Trinity Church. The Rev. Arthur Pratt officiated. |
| Slade | Odell | KC, p1c3, 6/19/1902 | Lived in Petersburg. Sold telephones and telephone supplies. |
| Slama | John | KC, p5c4, 6/8/1899 | The barns of John and Mike Slama were destroyed by a windstorm in Eastman. |
| Slama | Joseph | KC, p8c3, 12/22/1898 | Died last week in Chicago. Aged 21 years. Daughter of John Slama of Eastman. Buried in Eastman. |
| Slama | Mrs. | KC, p1c5, 1/12/1899 | Recently married William Hackheimer of Eastman. Bride from Prairie du Chien. |
| Slane | Irving | KC, p4c1, 6/23/1898 | Died June 17, 1898 in Iowa. Resident of Scott. |
| Slater | John | KC, p8c2, 3/23/1899 | "John and George Slater of Hawkeye, IA, Al Phaler of Madison and Fred Phaler of Lynxville meet for the first time in forty-two years in this city (Prairie du Chien) last Thursday. In honor of the event, John Ivers disengaged himself from his duties in the store and helped the boys celebrate. They were gathered at the home of the latter in the evening where an elegant time was had. The boys departed for their respective homes Friday morning." (See Pfhaler citations, too.) |
| Sleighback | Frank | KC, Supp., 12/29/1898 | Crawford Co. Board of Supervisors approved Justices and Constables' expenses related to the case, State vs. Frank Sleighback. |
| Slightam | Dave | KC, p5c4, 5/22/1902 | Prairie du Chien High School class of 1902. |
| Slightam | J. | KC, p1c6, 4/7/1898 | Elected Supervisor for the Village of Soldiers Grove. |
| Slightam | Sadie | KC, Supp., 12/12/1901 | Attended a Teacher's Institute in Crawford County in 1901. Resided in Soldiers Grove. |
| Slightam | W. H., Mrs. | KC, p4c4, 3/17/1898 | Left Soldiers Grove for Chicago/Evanston area to visit friends and relatives. |
| Slighter | V. and wife | KC, p5c4, 2/13/1902 | Resided in West Union, IA. Visited relatives in Lynxville. |
| Sloan | George | KC, p1c6, 12/30/1897 | Traveled from Bailey, IA to Steuben, his former home. Guest of Mr. and Mrs. John Farris. |
| Sloan | girl | KC, p8c3, 6/17/1897 | Daughter born June 13, 1897 to Frank Sloan of Steuben. |
| Sloan | Mae, Miss | KC, p8c1, 2/24/1898 | Funeral recently held at St. Gabriel Catholic Church of Prairie du Chien. Resided in North McGregor. |
| Sloane | Kittie | KC, p8c1, 4/13/1899 | Died Monday (April 10, 1899?) in North McGregor. Aged 18. Buried in Prairie du Chien. |
| Slocum | John, Mrs. | KC, p5c3, 2/15/1900 | Arrived from Soldiers Grove to visit sister, Mrs. Robert Currie of Gays Mills |
| Sluka | William | KC, p5c3, 2/2/1899 | Died Sunday (Jan. 29, 1899?) in Lynxville. |

Genealogical Gleanings From Early Newspapers for Residents In and Near
Crawford County, Wisconsin, 1897-1902

| LAST NAME | FIRST NAME | NEWSPAPER PAGE/COLUMN MONTH/DAY/YEAR | GENEALOGICAL DATA |
|---|---|---|---|
| Slunt | Henry, Sr. | KC, p1c3, 7/4/1901 | The remains of Henry Slunt, Sr., 2 children of F. Stuckey and 1 child of Mrs. Walters were removed from Chapeks Cemetery and moved to the Wauzeka Cemetery by John Lagaman. They were buried about 25 years ago. |
| Smethurst | Bert | KC, p5c3, 9/20/1900 | Arrived from O'Dell, NB to visit brother, John of Mt. Sterling, and sister, Mrs. Robert Campbell, of Steuben. |
| Smethurst | Charles | KC, p1c5, 12/9/1897 | Planned to move from Citron Valley to Grant Co. |
| Smethurst | Fred | KC, p8c4, 8/29/1901 | Married Catherine Finley on Aug. 26, 1901 at Catholic Church in Town of Seneca. Bride and groom were from Town of Seneca. |
| Smethurst | girl | KC, p5c3 12/4/1902 | Daughter recently born to Fred Smethurst of Seneca. |
| Smethurst | James, Mr. and Mrs. | KC, p5c4, 4/12/1900 | Arrived from Odell, NB to visit relatives in Steuben area. |
| Smethurst | James, Mr. and Mrs. | KC, p5c1, 11/18/1897 | Traveled from Odell, NB to visit daughter, Mrs. Robert Campbell of Steuben. |
| Smethurst | Joe | KC, p1c4, 4/5/1900 | Returned to Madison after visiting his ill mother-in-law, Mrs. Mills of Seneca. |
| Smethurst | John | KC, p1c2, 5/17/1900 | Worked as superintendent of the Crawford County Telephone Company. |
| Smethurst | Willie | KC, p5c5, 2/8/1900 | Arrived from Iowa to visit relatives in Town of Seneca. |
| Smircina | John | KC, p8c3, 8/3/1899 | John Smircina was arrested last week. Justice Harrington bound him over to the November term of the Circuit Court in Crawford County. |
| Smith | Allen | KC, p8c3, 2/13/1902 | Married Francis Mataka on Feb. 10, 1902 at Prairie du Chien. The Rev. Fr. Kiefner officiated. |
| Smith | Anna | KC, p5c3, 11/29/1900 | Married Fred Opprecht on Nov. 27, 1900. Groom from (Town of Seneca?). Bride taught school in Crawford County. |
| Smith | Anna | KC, p1c5, 2/9/1899 | Taught school in Haney in 1899. E. E. Brindley, Crawford County Superintendent of Schools published a comprehensive list of all teachers in the county. |
| Smith | Anne | KC, p5c5, 1/18/1900 | Taught school in Crawford Co. |
| Smith | Aubrey | KC, p5c3, 3/7/1901 | Family arrived from Mississippi to visit his mother in Seneca. |
| Smith | Bessie | KC, p8c4, 4/4/1901 | Married Douglas Onstine on April 3, 1901. Bride from Boscobel. Groom son of Sam Onstine, from Steuben. |
| Smith | boy | KC, p1c6, 9/30/1897 | Two year old son of Jonas Smith died of worm trouble at home in Seneca. |
| Smith | boy | KC, p1c4, 5/19/1898 | Son born May 15, 1898 to Fred Smith of Mt. Sterling. |
| Smith | Capt. | KC, p1c3, 6/10/1897 | Visited father in Mt. Sterling. Officer under Gen. Gomez in Cuba. |
| Smith | Charles | KC, p1c6, 11/4/1897 | Issue of fact for court to be heard at the November term of the Circuit Court in Crawford County. Flora Smith vs. Charles Smith. |

Genealogical Gleanings From Early Newspapers for Residents In and Near
Crawford County, Wisconsin, 1897-1902

| LAST NAME | FIRST NAME | NEWSPAPER PAGE/COLUMN MONTH/DAY/YEAR | GENEALOGICAL DATA |
|---|---|---|---|
| Smith | Charles | KC, Supp., 12/29/1898 | Crawford Co. Board of Supervisors approved payment of expenses in the matter of Charles Smith, incorrigible. |
| Smith | Charles E. | KC, p1c3, 9/22/1898 | Married Lillie May Updyke of Barnum on Sept. 11, 1898 in Seneca. (Groom may be from Seneca.) This was a double wedding with Rosa Farris and Marcus D. Smith. |
| Smith | Charles E. | KC, p5c3, 3/16/1899 | Died Feb. 22, 1899 in Seneca. Survived by wife, parents, brothers and sisters. Buried in Mt. Sterling Cemetery. |
| Smith | Clarence | KC, p5c3, 2/11/1897 | Died Sunday. Survived by wife and 4 children. Funeral held at Methodist Church in Springville. Reported in Viroqua Republican. |
| Smith | Elizabeth | KC, Supp., 12/20/1900 | Crawford Co. Soldiers Relief Comm. approved aid to Elizabeth Smith of Marietta. |
| Smith | Ella, Mrs. | KC, p1c3, 9/29/1898 | Planned to move to Wauzeka from Dodge Center, MN and offer dressmaking services. She was the sister of Mrs. J. W. Becwar. |
| Smith | Emma | KC, p4c3, 12/8/1898 | Married George Updike of Haney on Dec. 4, 1898. Bride from Seneca. John Lowe, J.P. officiated. |
| Smith | Eugene | KC, p1c3, 11/11/1897 | Married Mary Simek on Nov. 8, 1897 at St. Vaclev's Church in Eastman. |
| Smith | Eugene | KC, p4c1, 11/11/1897 | Married Mary Simek on Nov. 8, 1897. Groom from Wauzeka. |
| Smith | Eugene | KC, p1c4, 3/15/1900 | Departed Wauzeka for Dell Rapids, SD with 2 loads of stock. Pat Smith, brother of Eugene, rented out farm to William Maxwell. Planned to spend the season in South Dakota. |
| Smith | Flora | KC, p1c6, 11/4/1897 | Issue of fact for court to be heard at the November term of the Circuit Court in Crawford County. Flora Smith vs. Charles Smith. |
| Smith | Frances May | KC, p5c1, 10/28/1897 | Died Oct. 21, 1897 in Bell Center. Nee Turk. Born May 31, 1872 in Town of Clayton. Married Lucius Smith on April 8, 1894. Survived by husband, 1 son, mother, 4 brothers and 3 sisters. Buried in Coleman Cemetery. |
| Smith | Frank | KC, p5c2, 8/11/1898 | Returned from Soldiers Home for the summer. Planned to stay with daughter, Mrs. C. Buckmaster of Bell Center. |
| Smith | Frank | KC, p1c4, 9/8/1898 | Resided in Bagley. Killed last Wednesday while working on a steam thresher in the Town of Ida. |
| Smith | Frank | KC, p1c4, 9/8/1898 | Died Wednesday (Aug. 31, 1898?) in Bagley. |
| Smith | Fred | KC, p5c3, 5/3/1900 | Native of Mt. Sterling. Recently graduated from Chicago Homeopathic Medical School. |
| Smith | Fred | KC, p5c4, 12/29/1898 | Returned to Mt. Sterling from Chicago to spend Christmas with wife and parents. |
| Smith | Fred | KC, Supp., 12/12/1901 | Attended a Teacher's Institute in Crawford County in 1901. Resided in Soldiers Grove. |
| Smith | Fred, Mrs. | KC, p5c3, 8/8/1901 | Lived in Gays Mills. He father, Mr. Anderson, and aunt arrived from Kewaunee, IL for a visit. |
| Smith | George | KC, Supp., 12/29/1898 | Received aid from the Crawford County Soldiers Relief Commission. Resided in Prairie du Chien. |

Genealogical Gleanings From Early Newspapers for Residents In and Near
Crawford County, Wisconsin, 1897-1902

| LAST NAME | FIRST NAME | NEWSPAPER PAGE/COLUMN MONTH/DAY/YEAR | GENEALOGICAL DATA |
|---|---|---|---|
| Smith | George | KC, Supp., 12/20/1900 | Crawford Co. Board of Supervisors approved payment of expenses in the matter of State vs. George Smith. The witnesses were Henry Gilbert, Emma Gilbert, John Gilbert, John Clark, E. E. Hagerty, William Gilbert, Lillian Gobin and Liddie Gilbert. |
| Smith | George A. | KC, p1c5, 5/10/1900 | Died May 6, 1900 in Soldiers Grove at age 75 years. Survived by wife, 3 sons and 2 daughters. Son, Frank, lived in Grand Junction, CO and daughter, Mrs. Harriman, lived in Hampton, IA. (per 5/17/1900 issue). |
| Smith | George A. | KC, p5c5, 5/17/1900 | Died May 6, 1900 in Soldiers Grove. Born Union, Broome Co., NY on Mar. 23, 1825. Married in Union in 1847 to Jane Edson. Survived by wife and children: Helen M. Harriman of Hampton, IA; Frank W. of Grand Junction, CO; and Doane and Ross and Minnie E. (Willis) of Soldiers Grove. One child died in Galena, IL. Served in 17th WI Volunteers in Civil War. Also survived by sister, Mrs. Elizabeth Baker. |
| Smith | George W. | KC, Supp., 12/12/1901 | Received funds from the Crawford Co. Soldiers Relief Commission. Resided in Prairie du Chien. |
| Smith | George, Mrs. | KC, p8c2, 3/16/1899 | Died Feb. 21, 1899 in Monsfield (Mansfield?), TX. Aunt of Mrs. John Bundis of Lowertown. |
| Smith | girl | KC, p1c2, 8/11/1898 | Daughter born Friday to Eugene Smith of Wauzeka. |
| Smith | girl | KC, p5c3, 8/7/1902 | Daughter recently born to P. N. Smith of Ferryville. |
| Smith | girl | KC, p5c4, 8/7/1902 | Daughter born Wednesday to Dr. Fred Smith of the Gays Mills area. |
| Smith | Grace | KC, p10c4, 12/12/1901 | United Brethren evangelist. Held quarterly meetings in Bell Center. |
| Smith | H. D. | KC, p1c4, 12/26/1901 | Married Jennie Wardell on Dec. 25, 1901. Bride and groom from Excelsior. |
| Smith | Henry | KC, p4c4, 9/13/1900 | From Bridgeport. Democratic candidate for county sheriff. |
| Smith | Henry | KC, Supp., 12/18/1902 | Crawford County Board of Supervisors examined bills in the Justices and Constables' Account for State vs. Henry Smith. |
| Smith | J. C., Mrs. | KC, p8c3, 4/29/1897 | Died April 22, 1897 in a Milwaukee hospital. Funeral was held in Seneca. |
| Smith | J. V. | KC, p8c4, 5/17/1900 | Recently married Margurite McGrath in Milwaukee. Bride was from New Richmond. Groom was a former resident of Wauzeka. |
| Smith | James | KC, p8c3, 1/12/1899 | Died Dec. 31, 1898 in Seneca. Born Oct. 15, 1827 in Belmont Co., OH. Came to Seneca in 1856. Survived by wife and 9 children. Several children named. They were Mrs. T. T. Smethurst of Manilia, IA; O. M. Smith of Brandon, MS and Mrs. A. McDaniel of Courtney, ND. |
| Smith | James | KC, p1c2, 7/17/1902 | Married Ella Nelson on July 16, 1902 in Boscobel. Bride daughter of Thomas Nelson of Steuben. Groom from Steuben. |

Genealogical Gleanings From Early Newspapers for Residents In and Near
Crawford County, Wisconsin, 1897-1902

| LAST NAME | FIRST NAME | NEWSPAPER PAGE/COLUMN MONTH/DAY/YEAR | GENEALOGICAL DATA |
|---|---|---|---|
| Smith | James and Henry | KC, p4c3, 1/13/1898 | Entertained their brothers from Duluth at their homes in Bridgeport. |
| Smith | James, Mrs. | KC, p1c6, 3/10/1898 | Returned to Bridgeport after spending part of the winter with mother, Mrs. O'Malley of Prairie du Chien. |
| Smith | John | KC, p5c4, 5/29/1902 | The case Wisconsin vs. John Smith, for larceny, was heard at the May term of the Crawford County Circuit Court. Convicted. Sentenced to one year in prison. |
| Smith | John | KC, Supp., 12/18/1902 | Crawford County Board of Supervisors allowed expenses in the Criminal Case, State vs. John Smith. |
| Smith | John | KC, p5c3, 3/20/1902 | Arrested for stealing a suit of clothes from Isaac Gaul of Seneca. |
| Smith | Lee | KC, Supp., 12/12/1901 | Attended a Teacher's Institute in Crawford County in 1901. Resided in Soldiers Grove. |
| Smith | Lilly | KC, p1c5, 9/16/1897 | Married Arthur Young of Boydtown on Sept. 1, 1897. Bride from Town of Steuben. Joseph Newcomb, J. P., officiated. |
| Smith | Lizzie | KC, p1c3, 11/11/1897 | Married P. Maxwell on Nov. 8, 1897 at Sacred Heart Church. |
| Smith | Lottie | KC, p1c4, 6/9/1898 | Married Albert Dyer of Marietta on May 26, 1898. Bride from Haney. M. A. Robinson, Justice of the Peace, officiated. |
| Smith | Louis | KC, p1c3, 12/7/1899 | Resident of Lowertown, Prairie du Chien. Taken to Soldiers Grove for trial by Wallace Bennett, deputy sheriff. "Mr. Wendt and Mr. Smith had some trouble about a line fence whereupon Smith used very harsh language and made violent threats against Wendt . . ." Nicolas Wendt and G. L. Miller of Prairie du Chien went to Soldiers Grove for the trial. "Nic says he will have justice." |
| Smith | Louis | KC, Supp., 12/20/1900 | Crawford Co. Board of Supervisors approved payment of expenses in the matter of State vs. Louis Smith. The witnesses were Nick Wendt, Michael Rubjecek, Thomas Dohse and William White. |
| Smith | Louis | KC, Supp., 12/20/1900 | Crawford Co. Board of Supervisors approved payment of expenses in the matter of State vs. Louis Smith. The witnesses were N. Wendt and Thomas Dosch. |
| Smith | Maggie | KC, p1c6, 2/3/1898 | Died Jan. 27, 1898 in Town of Eastman. Aged 31 years. Daughter of John Maxwell. Born in Prairie du Chien. Married John Smith 6 years ago. |
| Smith | Marcus D. | KC, p1c3, 9/22/1898 | Married Rosa Farris of Steuben on Sept. 11, 1898 in Seneca. (Groom may be from Seneca.) This was a double wedding with Lillie May Updyke and Charles E. Smith. |
| Smith | Nicholas | KC, p5c3, 4/27/1899 | Recently married Maggie Morris. Bride and groom from Seneca. |
| Smith | O. M. | KC, p5c1, 2/21/1898 | Departed Seneca for old home in Mississippi where he intends to remain. |
| Smith | Obey | KC, p8c3, 2/17/1898 | Moved his family from Seneca to the state of Mississippi. |
| Smith | Oliver | KC, p5c4, 5/29/1902 | Oliver Smith and J. W. Shaw of Excelsior attended a teacher institute in Crawford County. |

Genealogical Gleanings From Early Newspapers for Residents In and Near Crawford County, Wisconsin, 1897-1902

| LAST NAME | FIRST NAME | NEWSPAPER PAGE/COLUMN MONTH/DAY/YEAR | GENEALOGICAL DATA |
|---|---|---|---|
| Smith | P. A. | KC, p1c2, 1/2/1902 | Planned to marry Mattie O'Shaunessy soon. |
| Smith | P. A. | KC, p1c5, 1/9/1902 | Married Mattie O'Shaunessy on Jan. 6, 1902. Bride was a teacher. Groom was from the Town of Eastman. |
| Smith | P. N. | KC, p5c3, 7/21/1898 | Married Bessie Olson on July 3, 1898 at Viroqua. Bride and groom from Ferryville. |
| Smith | Ralph, Mrs. | KC, p1c3, 5/29/1902 | Formerly of Wauzeka. Arrived from Flandreau, ND to visit Wauzeka friends. |
| Smith | T. Preston | KC, p4c4, 5/11/1899 | Returned to Harris Ridge after serving as a cook in the late war. |
| Smith | W. D, Dr. | KC, p1c6, 1/18/1900 | Advertised medical services. Practice based in Mt. Sterling. |
| Smith | W. D., MD | KC, p5c1, 1/7/1897 | Advertised medical services. Office based in Mt. Sterling. |
| Smith | W. D., Mrs. | KC, p1c8, 3/11/1897 | Left home in Mt. Sterling to visit daughter, Mrs. Frank Cole of Chicago. |
| Smith | W. H. | KC, Supp., 12/20/1900 | Crawford Co. Soldiers Relief Comm. approved aid to W. H. Smith of Clayton. |
| Smith | William | KC, p5c2, 10/27/1898 | Resided in Bell Center. Applied for an increase in his pension. |
| Smith | William D., Maj. | KC, p1c5, 5/19/1898 | Reported to be captured and killed in Cuba. Previously practiced law in Soldiers Grove. Enlisted in the insurgent army a year ago. He was wounded and disgusted and returned to U.S. Later returned. Son of Dr. Smith of Mt. Sterling. Death report in error per KC, p4c2, 6/16/1898. |
| Smith | Willie, Mrs. | KC, p1c5, 11/18/1897 | Traveled from Spring Valley, MN to visit in Seneca, her former home. |
| Smrcina | Frank | KC, p5c5, 4/5/1900 | Elected treasurer in City of Prairie du Chien. |
| Smrcina | John | KC, p8c3, 9/12/1901 | Married Anna Isabel Donahue on Sept. 10, 1901 at St. Raphaels Catholic Church in Madison. Bride was daughter of J. J. Donahue of Madison. Groom was second son of F. Smrcina of Prairie du Chien. |
| Smrcina | John | KC, p8c4, 11/23/1899 | Found not guilty of murdering Lawrence Bitterlee at court in Prairie du Chien |
| Smrz | Frank | KC, p5c3, 3/27/1902 | Moved to Chicago from Eastman. |
| Smrz | Fred | KC, p5c3, 2/23/1899 | Planned to move family from Eastman to Chicago. |
| Smrz | James | KC, p5c4, 2/7/1901 | Sold his interested in Eastman Saw Mill to Robert Eigum of Eastman. |
| Snell | Michael | KC, p5c4, 9/21/1901 | Died Sept. 6, 1901 in Town of Seneca. Born 1823 in County Cork, Ireland. Came to America with parents in 1851. First lived in Freeport, IL. Married Ellen Casey in 1853 in Freeport and soon after moved to Town of Seneca. Survived by wife and 3 sons. |
| Snodgrass | Wilfred | KC, p5c3, 9/27/1900 | Recently married Laura Reynolds. (Bride and groom may be from Town of Scott.) |

Genealogical Gleanings From Early Newspapers for Residents In and Near
Crawford County, Wisconsin, 1897-1902

| LAST NAME | FIRST NAME | NEWSPAPER PAGE/COLUMN MONTH/DAY/YEAR | GENEALOGICAL DATA |
|---|---|---|---|
| Solan | Mike | KC, p8c4, 3/11/1897 | Mike Solan and William Devine of Ferryville drove cattle to Iowa. |
| Solom | Mathias | KC, p5c4, 3/27/1902 | Died Mar. 21, 1902 in Mt. Sterling. Funeral held at Utica Lutheran Church. |
| Solomon | Johnny | KC, p1c4, 4/17/1902 | Johnny Solomon, his parents and sister (Mrs. Tom Sloan) left their homes in Steuben for Wellington, ND. Mr. Sloan preceded them. |
| Somers | Joe | KC, Supp., 12/18/1902 | Crawford County Board of Supervisors examined bills in the Justices and Constables' Account for State vs. Joe Somers. |
| Sorenson | Erick | KC, p4c2, 3/31/1898 | Home in Readstown destroyed by fire. Also lost $300 worth of carpenter tools. |
| Sorenson | J. | KC, p1c6, 4/7/1898 | Elected Trustee for the Village of Soldiers Grove. |
| Sorrum | Anton | KC, p5c4, 5/27/1897 | Visited relatives in Boma. Lived in Dakota for the last 7 years. |
| Soucby | Mr. | KC, p4c1, 1/28/1897 | Barber in Lynxville. |
| Soucy | boy | KC, p1c5, 4/21/1898 | Son born Easter Sunday to Phil Soucy of Lynxville. |
| Soucy | Phil | KC, p4c1, 7/1/1897 | Married Alice Wing on June 19, 1897 per Lynxville news. F. R. Pease officiated. |
| Sousey | Phillip | KC, p5c3, 5/3/1900 | Departed Lynxville for new home in Dakota. |
| Southard | George | KC, p4c1, 11/9/1899 | Mr. and Mrs. George Southard of Richland City arrived in Wauzeka to honeymoon. |
| Speck | (Bessie?) | KC, p5c4, 11/7/1901 | Married Albert Belrichard on Oct. 28, 1901 at Methodist Episcopal Church in Hazen's Corners. Bride from (Town of Eastman?). Emma Cherrier was a cousin of bride. Henry Belrichard was a brother of groom. |
| Speck | B. F. | KC, p5c3, 10/23/1902 | Planned to move from Eastman to Prairie du Chien to be a clerk in H. Otto's store. |
| Speck | Ben | KC, Supp., 4/24/1902 | Succeeded John Roach as clerk in J. A. Dworak's store in Eastman. |
| Speck | Benjamin F. | KC, p5c3, 4/11/1901 | Married Lottie May Hazen on April 8, 1901. Bride and groom from Town of Eastman. |
| Speck | C. H. | KC, p5c4, 10/5/1899 | Leader of the Eastman Cornet Band. Furnished music for the Crawford Co. Agricultural Society meeting at Seneca. |
| Speck | C. H. | KC, p5c4, 4/13/1899 | Leader of the Eastman Brass Band. Other members were M. R. Sullivan, Ben Speck, Elra Hall, C. E. Campbell, Flora Harvat, Ed Iverson, James Smrz, C. E. Alder, Steve Allen, Seymour Allen, Robert Granzow and Zenas Wallin. |
| Speck | C. H., Mrs. | KC, p5c4, 1/18/1900 | Resided in Tacoma, WA. Visited relatives in Town of Eastman. |
| Speck | C. H., Mrs. | KC, p4c2, 9/29/1898 | Returned to Town of Eastman after attending to her critically ill father, Mark Ingle of Prairie du Chien. His death expected at any time. (p8c2) |

Genealogical Gleanings From Early Newspapers for Residents In and Near
Crawford County, Wisconsin, 1897-1902

| LAST NAME | FIRST NAME | NEWSPAPER PAGE/COLUMN MONTH/DAY/YEAR | GENEALOGICAL DATA |
|---|---|---|---|
| Speck | Charles | KC, p1c3, 12/9/1897 | Narrowly escaped injury. Horses frightened by a train. Although he only has one hand, he was able to bring horses back under control. |
| Speck | Etta | KC, p8c3, 8/2/1900 | Married Edward Kramer on August 1, 1900. Bride and groom from Town of Eastman. Bride daughter of C. Speck. |
| Speck | Fred | KC, p5c3, 3/6/1902 | Fred Speck and Arthur Wallin of Eastman departed for Tacoma, WA where they intended to stay for some time. |
| Speck | girl | KC, p1c6, 7/1/1897 | Daughter born June 25, 1897 to Charles Speck of Eastman. |
| Speck | C. H. | KC, p1c6, 4/7/1898 | Elected Assessor for the Town of Eastman. |
| Spencer | Dessa | KC, p5c3, 4/4/1901 | Sold millinery goods in Mt. Sterling. |
| Spencer | Georgianna | KC, Supp., 12/20/1900 | Crawford Co. Board of Supervisors approved payment of expenses in the matter of State vs. Georgianna Spencer. The witnesses were W. Mindham, Charles Culver, Etheh Culver, Evert Culver, Sarah Childs, M__ne Spencer, Genevie Pettit, Cari (or Carl?) Childs, Catharine Kramer and Ralph Childs. |
| Spencer | Lillian | KC, p1c5, 2/9/1899 | Taught school in the Town of Clayton in 1899. E. E. Brindley, Crawford County Superintendent of Schools published a comprehensive list of all teachers in the county. |
| Spencer | Stella | KC, p1c3, 12/25/1902 | Taught school in Rider District. Daughter of M. O. Spencer of Town of Scott. |
| Spencer | Stella | KC, Supp., 12/12/1901 | Attended a Teacher's Institute in Crawford County in 1901. Resided in Millett. |
| Spencer | Adessa | KC, p1c4, 4/26/1900 | Opened a millinery shop in Mt. Sterling. |
| Spencer | Dessa | KC, p5c1, 9/16/1897 | Ran a millinery shop in Mt. Sterling. |
| Spencer | girl | KC, p5c5, 4/12/1900 | Daughter born April 1, 1900 to James Spencer of Bell Center. |
| Sperbach | Albert B. | KC, p8c4, 6/21/1900 | Married Minnie H. Hobbs on June 20, 1900. Bride was from Prairie du Chien. Groom was from Marinette, WI. |
| Spero | Max | KC, p1c6, 5/19/1898 | Issue of Fact for Jury to be heard in the May term of the Crawford County Circuit Court. Max Spero vs. B. Anderson. |
| Spero | Max | KC, p1c6, 6/2/1898 | In Crawford County Circuit Court, Max Spero vs. B. Anderson; verdict for plaintiff; $15 and cost, amounting to $15 more, allowed. |
| Spicher | Albert | KC, Supp., 12/12/1901 | Crawford Co. Board of Supervisors approved payments in the Matter of Albert Spicher, Insane. |
| Spiker | A. | KC, Supp., 12/12/1901 | State vs. A. Spiker heard in Crawford Co. Court. |
| Spiker | Maggie | KC, p1c2, 7/24/1902 | Married H. J. Faust on July 19, 1902. Groom from Steuben. J. O. Hanks, J.P. officiated. |
| Spiker | Mr. | KC, p1c3, 3/27/1902 | Worked as a sawyer at the Wauzeka Lumber Co. |

Genealogical Gleanings From Early Newspapers for Residents In and Near
Crawford County, Wisconsin, 1897-1902

| LAST NAME | FIRST NAME | NEWSPAPER PAGE/COLUMN MONTH/DAY/YEAR | GENEALOGICAL DATA |
|---|---|---|---|
| Spiker | Randolph | KC, Supp., 12/29/1898 | Crawford Co. Board of Supervisors approved Justices and Constables' expenses related to the case, State vs. Randolph Spiker. The witnesses were Albert Picha, Otto Oswald, John Milheim, James Nolan and Dr. Lienfelder. |
| Spiker | Rudolph | KC, p1c6, 5/19/1898 | Criminal case to be heard in the May term of the Crawford County Circuit Court. State of Wisconsin vs. Rudolph Spiker. |
| Spiker | Rudolph | KC, p4c4, 11/10/1898 | Criminal Issue to be heard in the November term of the Crawford County Circuit Court. State of Wisconsin vs. Rudolph Spiker. |
| Sprosty | J. F., Mr. and Mrs. | KC, p5c3, 10/5/1899 | Arrived from Cleveland, OH to visit the Iverson family in Eastman. |
| Sprosty | John | KC, p1c2, 6/20/1901 | Albert Kussmaul and John Sprosty planned to run the Eastman hotel, hall and saloon as partners. |
| Sprosty | Joseph F. | KC, p1c4, 11/1/1900 | Democratic candidate for Clerk of Circuit Court in Crawford County. Born in Bohemia in 1850. Came to America in 1853. Moved to Prairie du Chien in 1856 and to Eastman in 1860. Has held several political offices. Portrait printed. |
| Sprosty | Julia | KC, p5c4, 2/28/1901 | Taught school at Shanghi Ridge. |
| Sprosty | Julia | KC, Supp., 12/12/1901 | Attended a Teacher's Institute in Crawford County in 1901. Resided in Eastman. |
| Sprosty | Regina | KC, p5c3, 5/29/1902 | Reinstalled as postmistress in Seneca. |
| Spuiker | John | KC, p8c4, 9/21/1901 | Married Sophia Walker on Sept. 17, 1901 at Lutheran Church. Bride and groom were from Prairie du Chien. |
| Squire | G. W. | KC, Supp., 12/12/1901 | Received funds from the Crawford Co. Soldiers Relief Commission. Resided in Scott. |
| Squire | George | KC, Supp., 12/29/1898 | Received aid from the Crawford County Soldiers Relief Commission. Resided in Scott. |
| Squire | G. W. | KC, Supp., 12/20/1900 | Crawford Co. Soldiers Relief Comm. approved aid to G. W. Squire of Scott. |
| Squires | G. W. | KC, Supp., 12/18/1902 | Crawford County Soldiers Relief Committee provided funds to G. W. Squires of Scott. |
| St. Clair | George | KC, Supp., 12/20/1900 | Crawford Co. Soldiers Relief Comm. approved aid to George St. Clair of Lynxville. |
| St. Clair | Robert and Hattie | KC, Supp., 12/20/1900 | Crawford Co. Board of Supervisors approved bills related to expenses of Robert and Hattie St. Clair, dependent children. |
| St. Claire | George H. | KC, Supp., 12/29/1898 | Received aid from the Crawford County Soldiers Relief Commission. Resided in Lynxville. |
| St. Jacque | Louis | KC, p5c1, 11/3/1898 | Louis St. Jacque and Louis DeSaire, both of Prairie du Chien and Jerry Day of Grant Co. did brickwork on the Catholic parsonage in Eastman. |
| St. Jacque | Miss | KC, Supp., 4/24/1902 | Married Felix Valley on April 23, 1902 at St. Gabriel's Catholic Church in Prairie du Chien. |
| St. Jacque | Miss | KC, Supp., 4/24/1902 | Married Felix Valley on Wednesday at St. Gabriel's Catholic Church in Prairie du Chien. |

Genealogical Gleanings From Early Newspapers for Residents In and Near
Crawford County, Wisconsin, 1897-1902

| LAST NAME | FIRST NAME | NEWSPAPER PAGE/COLUMN MONTH/DAY/YEAR | GENEALOGICAL DATA |
|---|---|---|---|
| St. Jocque | girl | KC, p1c5, 10/6/1898 | Daughter born Sept. 29, 1898 to Louis St. Jocque of Prairie du Chien. |
| St. Jocque | Louis | KC, Supp., 12/29/1898 | Hired by Crawford County to calcumin and cement the vault in the county Judge's office. |
| St. John | C. W. | KC, p5c3, 9/21/1899 | Resided in Steuben. Constructing a wagon shop in Gays Mills. |
| Staar | Tressa | KC, p5c4, 11/16/1899 | Married Lincoln Heisz on Nov. 13, 1899 at Seneca. Bride was daughter of Andrew Staar of Seneca. Groom was son of Michael Heisz of Steuben. The Rev. J. M. Keeley officiated. |
| Stabin | Elsie | KC, p8c3, 12/13/1900 | Died Dec. 12, 1900. Born June 21, 1887 to Charles Stabin of Prairie du Chien |
| Stackland | Dan | KC, Supp., 12/29/1898 | Crawford Co. Board of Supervisors approved Justices and Constables' expenses related to the case, State vs. Dan Stackland. The witnesses were August Steinburg, Ed Case and Albert Nelson. |
| Stackland | Nellie | KC, p8c3, 11/22/1900 | Married Russell Sage on Nov. 21, 1900. Bride daughter of John Stackland of Prairie du Chien. Groom from Tennessee. |
| Staib | D., Mrs. | KC, p1c4, 5/31/1900 | Proprietor of a millinery shop in Barnum |
| Staib | Dave | KC, p1c3, 6/6/1901 | Ran a hotel in Barnum. |
| Staib | Dave | KC, p1c4, 2/6/1902 | Resided in Barnum. Rented the Jap Davis farm near Petersburg. |
| Stamp | T. W. | KC, p8c4, 9/30/1897 | At a conference of the Methodist Church held in Platteville, T. W. Stamp was assigned to Soldiers Grove. |
| Stamp | Thomas | KC, p1c2, 11/4/1897 | Principal at Wauzeka school. Gave a good gospel talk at the Evangelical Church. |
| Standorf | Abraham | KC, Supp., 12/20/1900 | Crawford Co. Board of Supervisors approved payment of expenses in the matter of State vs. Abraham Standorf. Charles Stone, Nancy Stone and Willie Mabee were witnesses. |
| Standorf | Jennie | KC, p8c3, 11/27/1902 | Married August Herpel last week. Groom was brother of Julius Herpel of Richland Center and Mrs. Umpaugh. |
| Standorf | Robert | KC, p8c4, 4/4/1901 | Part of a group that left Steuben and Wauzeka for the West. Most of the group went to McHenry, North Dakota. |
| Standorf | Ruth | KC, p8c3, 11/22/1900 | Died Nov. 17, 1900 at Prairie du Chien. |
| Stantorf | Dellema, Miss | KC, p5c1, 2/24/1898 | Died Feb. 7, 1898 at her home in Town of Haney. |
| Stantorf | E. H. | KC, Supp., 12/20/1900 | Represented 1st Ward of Prairie du Chien on the Crawford Co. Board of Supervisors in 1900. |
| Stantorf | George, Mrs. | KC, p5c4, 1/17/1901 | Mrs. George Stantorf and her daughter, Ethel, left Petersburg to visit her parents, Mr. and Mrs. Williams in Barnum. |
| Stantorf | George, Mrs. | KC, p8c3, 6/16/1898 | Visited her parents, Mr. and Mrs. Williams of Barnum. |

Genealogical Gleanings From Early Newspapers for Residents In and Near
Crawford County, Wisconsin, 1897-1902

| LAST NAME | FIRST NAME | NEWSPAPER PAGE/COLUMN MONTH/DAY/YEAR | GENEALOGICAL DATA |
|---|---|---|---|
| Stantorf | girl | KC, p4c2, 5/27/1898 | Daughter born May 22, 1898 to George Stantorf of Barnum. |
| Stantorf | Lillian | KC, p5c5, 1/18/1900 | Taught school in Crawford Co. |
| Stantorf | W. A. | KC, p1c2, 5/23/1901 | Married Minnie Alderman on May 20, 1901. Bride and groom from Barnum. |
| Star | Anthony | KC, p1c5, 11/18/1897 | Traveled from California to visit in Seneca. |
| Stark | Lydia E. | KC, p8c4, 1/2/1902 | Married Henry Siefert on Dec. 25, 1901. |
| Stauer | | KC, p5c3, 5/20/1897 | Issues of fact for jury to be heard in the May term of the Crawford County Court. Stauer & Daubenberger vs. Lytle & Baker. |
| Stavos | John | KC, p4c4, 1/7/1897 | Advertised services. Merchant tailor in Prairie du Chien. |
| Stayer | Mr. | KC, p4c2, 1/13/1898 | Recently died at son's home in LaFayette Co. Formerly from Lowertown (Prairie du Chien) where he was a caretaker at the Lowertown Cemetery. |
| Stearns | Charley | KC, p1c3, 9/15/1898 | Caught a 140 lb. (when dressed) catfish in Lost Channel of the Mississippi River, below Victory. It was the biggest fish ever caught in this section of the country. |
| Stearns | Frank | KC, p1c4, 3/2/1899 | Married Jennie Jenkins of Barnum on Feb. 15, 1899 in Gays Mills. Groom from Barnum. |
| Stearns | Maud | KC, p5c4, 6/28/1900 | Recently graduated from the Barnum village school. |
| Steele | Frank | KC, Supp., 12/29/1898 | Crawford Co. Board of Supervisors approved Justices and Constables' expenses related to the case, State vs. Frank Steele. The witnesses were William Hysall, William Green and Lintner Green. |
| Steiben | Emma | KC, p8c3, 12/6/1900 | Married John Zirl on Nov. 29, 1900. Bride and groom from (Prairie du Chien?). |
| Steil | W. N. | KC, p1c3, 4/12/1900 | Principal of schools in Wauzeka. Parents lived in Platteville. |
| Stein | John | KC, Supp., 12/20/1900 | Crawford Co. Board of Supervisors approved payment of expenses in the matter of State vs. John Stein. |
| Steinbach | Charles | KC, p1c5, 1/3/1901 | Arrived from Galveston, TX to spend the holidays with his parents, Mr. and Mrs. John Steinbach of Wauzeka. (Steinback?) |
| Steinbach | Charles | KC, p1c2, 6/2/1898 | Carried mail between Bridgeport and Bloomington. Son of John Steinbach. |
| Steinbach | John | KC, p1c2, 3/27/1902 | Resided in Wauzeka. Ordered newspaper subscription for his son, Louis, of Coleman, SD. |
| Steinbach | John | KC, p1c3 12/4/1902 | Moved from Wauzeka to Petersburg to go into the mercantile business. |
| Steinbach | Louis | KC, p1c3, 6/5/1902 | Married Edith Herold on June 4, 1902. Bride daughter of George Herold of Wauzeka. Groom son of Mrs. Phillip Steinbach. |

Genealogical Gleanings From Early Newspapers for Residents In and Near
Crawford County, Wisconsin, 1897-1902

| LAST NAME | FIRST NAME | NEWSPAPER PAGE/COLUMN MONTH/DAY/YEAR | GENEALOGICAL DATA |
|---|---|---|---|
| Steinbach | Philip | KC, p5c1, 4/7/1898 | Died April 1, 1898 at Grand Gray Valley of Wauzeka. Born Nov. 19, 1815 in E_sas, Germany. Came to America when 17. Served in Mexican War. Married Margaret Herold in 1849. Fathered 7 sons and 3 daughters. Survived by 5 children. Belonged to Evangelical Church. Buried in Wauzeka Cemetery. |
| Steinbach | Phillip, Sr., Mrs. | KC, p1c4, 6/1/1899 | Federal government allowed her a pension of $8/month and back pay of $140. |
| Steinback | John | KC, p5c5, 4/5/1900 | Elected village trustee in Wauzeka. |
| Steinburg | Mete | KC, p8c3, 8/23/1900 | Died Aug. 21, 1900 in Prairie du Chien. Daughter of August Steinburg. |
| Steiner | Erne | KC, p8c4, 6/21/1900 | Marriage license issued to Erne Steiner of Town of Eastman and Adam Rau of Prairie du Chien. |
| Steiner | John W. | KC, Supp., 12/12/1901 | Crawford County Board of Supervisors approved payments in the Matter of John W. Steiner, Insane. |
| Steiner | Nettie | KC, p7c4, 1/25/1900 | Received marriage license in Crawford Co. Fred Sherlin was prospective spouse. Bride and groom-to-be from Prairie du Chien. |
| Steiner | Nettie | KC, p8c4, 1/25/1900 | Married Fred C. Shirlin on Jan. 23, 1900. Bride and groom from Prairie du Chien. Bride daughter of John Steiner. |
| Steiner | Adam | KC, p1c5, 6/20/1901 | Brought grist to Wauzeka to be milled. |
| Steinwand | Mary | KC, p8c4, 5/9/1901 | Married William Garriety on May 6, 1901. Bride and groom from Prairie du Chien. |
| Stell | William N. | KC, p1c5, 8/21/1902 | Married Florence C. Vaughan on Aug. 19, 1902 in Platteville. Bride and groom were teachers in Wauzeka schools. Bride, daughter of O. P. Vaughan of Wauzeka. Groom from Platteville. |
| Stemmeiler | Frank | KC, p5c4, 2/18/1897 | Late of Wauzeka. Notice for Administration of his estate published. |
| Stephenson | Seiger | KC, p5c1, 7/71898 | Seiger Stephenson, Walter Peck and Ed Tainter of Towerville enlisted in army. |
| Sterling | Clay | KC, p5c3, 12/11/1902 | Rented his Mt. Sterling farm to his son, Will, and moved into rooms over King's Store. |
| Sterling | girl | KC, p1c4, 8/10/1899 | Daughter recently born to W. A. Sterling of Mt. Sterling. |
| Sterling | John | KC, p1c5, 3/20/1902 | Sold farm in Mt. Sterling to Warren Easton and bought the Hugh Bonney farm in Eastman. |
| Sterling | John | KC, p1c6, 4/7/1898 | Elected Treasurer for the Town of Freeman. |

Genealogical Gleanings From Early Newspapers for Residents In and Near
Crawford County, Wisconsin, 1897-1902

| LAST NAME | FIRST NAME | NEWSPAPER PAGE/COLUMN MONTH/DAY/YEAR | GENEALOGICAL DATA |
|---|---|---|---|
| Sterling | William T. | KC, p5c4, 11/22/1900 | Extensive biography published in Nov. 22 and Nov. 29, 1900 issues. Born in Woodford Co., KY in 1808. Received scholarship when 16 to attend the university in Georgetown, KY. Organized a mining company in Galena, IL. Managed mines for 10 years throughout region. Received a clerkship in 1837 at the Wisconsin and Iowa legislature held in Belmont, Grant Co. in 1837. Appointed by Gov. Dodge to be Wisconsin's Territorial Librarian and Superintendent of Public Property. In 1840 he and three others ascended Kickapoo River and visited a Winnebago village at Haney Valley that was later burned by Edward V. Whiton. One of the party also burned a village above the forks of the Kickapoo. Sterling moved to what became Mt. Sterling in May 1842. Found copper there in 1843 and opened a mine. Elected representative to state legislature in 1848. Father was Henry Sterling who was born in 1774 in Hagerstown, MD and died in Retreat, WI in 1855 or 1856. (Continued) |
| Sterling | William T. | KC, p5c4, 11/22/1900 | (Part 2) Mother was a daughter of Jacob Harper, who came from Holland and settled at Harpers Ferry, VA. Sterling's mental health failed six years ago. His brother, Le Grant Sterling, came with his parents to Vernon Co. in 1846 and recently died near Retreat. Another brother, Lewis, was sheriff of Vernon Co. 30 years ago, while an older brother, Levi, was a member of the Territorial council from 1839-1840 and sheriff of Dane Co. many years ago. (Sterling descendants should get a photocopy of this sketch from the newspapers.) |
| Sterling | J. H., Mrs. | KC, p1c3, 3/30/1899 | Buried Sunday (Mar. 26, 1899?). Resided in Ferryville. |
| Sterling | Luna | KC, p1c2, 10/18/1900 | Married Leslie Tichenor on Oct. 10, 1900 at Gays Mills. Bride from Mt. Sterling. Groom from Town of Seneca. |
| Sterling | Will | KC, p5c3, 6/20/1901 | Will Sterling and Leslie Tichenor of Mt. Sterling dug into an Indian mound last week and exhumed a skeleton and some arrow heads and other Indian relics. All in fair condition. |
| Sterling | Will | KC, p8c3, 4/1/1897 | Married Lizzie Dudley on Mar. 23, 1897 at Gays Mills. Bride and groom from Mt. Sterling. |
| Sterner | J. | KC, Supp., 12/12/1901 | Inquest of J. Sterner heard in Crawford Co. Court. G. J. Harrington was the witness. |
| Sterner | Jake | KC, p8c4, 6/6/1901 | Recently died in Prairie du Chien. Survived by wife and 2 children. Buried in the Lowertown Cemetery. |
| Steven | Joe | KC, p5c5, 3/1/1900 | Arrived from Nebraska to visit parents in Town of Eastman. |
| Stevens | boy | KC, p11c1, 12/18/1902 | Recently died. Aged 12 years. Son of Anthony Stevens of Town of Eastman. |
| Stevens | boy | KC, p11c1, 12/18/1902 | Recently died. Aged 9 years. Son of Anthony Stevens of Town of Eastman. |
| Stevens | Elsa | KC, p5c3, 1/17/1901 | Resided in Retreat, WI. Doing dressmaking work in Mt. Sterling. |

Genealogical Gleanings From Early Newspapers for Residents In and Near
Crawford County, Wisconsin, 1897-1902

| LAST NAME | FIRST NAME | NEWSPAPER PAGE/COLUMN MONTH/DAY/YEAR | GENEALOGICAL DATA |
|---|---|---|---|
| Stevens | Lucy | KC, p1c5, 2/9/1899 | Taught school in Freeman in 1899. E. E. Brindley, Crawford County Superintendent of Schools published a comprehensive list of all teachers in the county. |
| Stevens | Mary | KC, p8c4, 11/16/1899 | Recently married Joseph Kavanda at the Bohemian Catholic Church in Prairie du Chien. |
| Stevens | Mr. | KC, p5c5, 1/9/1902 | Recently died at St. Cloud, MN. He was the brother of Myra Stevens of Lynxville. |
| Stevens | R. J. | KC, p1c6, 11/4/1897 | Issue of fact for court to be heard at the November term of the Circuit Court in Crawford County. Lowell W. Lathrop vs. R. J. Stevens. |
| Stevens | Thoma, Mrs. | KC, p4c4, 12/13/1900 | Died Nov. 28, 1900 in (Town of Eastman?). She was "an aged Bohemian lady." Survived by husband and 8 children. Buried in the Catholic Cemetery. |
| Stevenson | Catherine | KC, Supp., 12/12/1901 | Received funds from the Crawford County Soldiers Relief Commission. Resided in Haney. |
| Stevenson | Catherine | KC, Supp., 12/20/1900 | Crawford Co. Soldiers Relief Comm. approved aid to Catherine Stevenson of Haney. |
| Stevenson | John | KC, p5c2, 11/18/1897 | Returned to Steuben after working in South Dakota for the last 2 years. |
| Stevenson | John | KC, p1c3, 12/16/1897 | Left Barnum for Pennsylvania to be with his wife who is seriously ill. |
| Stevenson | Kate | KC, p5c3, 7/11/1901 | Married George S. Daugherty on July 6, 1901 in Boydtown. Bride from Barnum. Groom from Boydtown. |
| Stevenson | Nettie | KC, p8c3, 6/24/1897 | Buried June 20, 1897. She was the daughter of William Stevenson of Steuben. Aged 10 years, 7 months and 16 days. |
| Stevenson | William | KC, p1c3, 12/19/1901 | Resided in Barnum. Arrested after Enos Grate complained that Stevenson carried dangerous weapons and made vicious threats. Arrested by Marshall Charlie Lindner of Prairie du Chien. |
| Stevenson | Catherine | KC, Supp., 12/18/1902 | Crawford County Soldiers Relief Committee provided funds to Catherine Stevenson of Barnum. |
| Stevenson | Christian | KC, Supp., 12/18/1902 | Crawford County Board of Supervisors examined bills in the Justices and Constables' Account for State vs. Christian Stevenson. |
| Stevson | William | KC, Supp., 12/18/1902 | Crawford County Board of Supervisors examined bills in the Justices and Constables' Account for State vs. William Stevson. |
| Stewart | Gilbert, Mrs. | KC, Supp., 11/24/1898 | Resided in Los Angeles (Riverside, per KC, p8c6, 12/8/1898), CA. Visited relatives in Seneca. Her sister-in-law, Mrs. John Stuart, came with her from Riverside for the visit. |
| Stewart | Henry | KC, p1c4, 9/29/1898 | At a conference of the Methodist Church held in Eau Claire, Henry Stewart was assigned to Patch Grove. |
| Stickler | E. | KC, p1c6, 11/4/1897 | Issue of fact for court to be heard at the November term of the Circuit Court in Crawford County. D. R. Lawrence vs. E. Strickler et al. |

Genealogical Gleanings From Early Newspapers for Residents In and Near
Crawford County, Wisconsin, 1897-1902

| LAST NAME | FIRST NAME | NEWSPAPER PAGE/COLUMN MONTH/DAY/YEAR | GENEALOGICAL DATA |
|---|---|---|---|
| Stickler | E. | KC, p1c6, 5/19/1898 | Issue of Law for Court to be heard in the May term of the Crawford County Circuit Court. D. R. Lawrence vs. E. Stickler and Buckmaster et al. |
| Stickler | Jennie, Mrs. | KC, p1c3, 7/10/1902 | Lived in Galesville, WI. Visited her sister-in-law, Mrs. J. W. Bowers of Eastman. |
| Stickler | L. H. | KC, p4c1, 1/7/1897 | Proprietor of Petersburg Woolen Mills in Petersburg. |
| Stickler | L. H. | KC, p5c4, 7/29/1897 | Proprietor of Petersburg Woolen Mills and Knitting Works. |
| Still | Grace | KC, Supp., 12/18/1902 | Crawford County Soldiers Relief Committee provided funds to Grace Still of De Soto. |
| Still | Isaac | KC, Supp., 12/12/1901 | Received funds from the Crawford County Soldiers Relief Commission. Resided in De Soto. |
| Still | Isaac | KC, Supp., 12/18/1902 | Crawford County Soldiers Relief Committee provided funds to Isaac Still of De Soto. |
| Still | Isaac | KC, Supp., 12/29/1898 | Received aid from the Crawford County Soldiers Relief Commission. Resided in De Soto. |
| Still | Isaac | KC, Supp., 12/20/1900 | Crawford Co. Soldiers Relief Comm. approved aid to Isaac Still of De Soto. |
| Stluka | Mary | KC, p5c3, 1/24/1901 | Married Joe Zoch (or Sauk) on Jan. 22, 1901. Bride from Town of Eastman. Groom from Town of Seneca. Many wedding guests mentioned in an article published Jan. 31, 1901, p5c4. |
| Stluka | T. | KC, p4c2, 2/2/1899 | Died Sunday (Jan. 29, 1899?) in Eastman. Buried in the Catholic Cemetery. |
| Stluka | | KC, p5c4, 2/8/1900 | Twins (boy and girl) born to Mike Stluka of Eastman. Stluka also has five-year-old twins, a boy and girl. |
| Stluke | Joe | KC, p5c3, 11/16/1899 | Died Nov. 12, 1899. (May have lived in Eastman.) |
| Stocum (Slocum?) | Jack | KC, p1c4, 6/8/1899 | Married Georgie Jewett on June 4, 1899. Groom from Avalanche. |
| Stoehr | Joseph | KC, p5c3, 5/30/1901 | Graduated from school in Lynxville. Gave a speech on Abe Lincoln. |
| Stolp | boy | KC, p5c1, 10/7/1897 | Son recently born to Sydney Stolp of Mt. Sterling. Weighed 12 lbs. |
| Stolp | Jane, Mrs. | KC, p1c4, 8/4/1898 | Died July 27, 1898 at Mt. Sterling. Mother of Alfred of Iowa and Sidney B. of Mt. Sterling. Buried in Stuart Cemetery. Per p5c2, aged 76 years and resided in county 42 years. |
| Stolp | Jennie | KC, p1c3, 9/18/1902 | Married Scott Vanderport Sept. 2, 1902 at Bell Center. Bride from Mt. Sterling. Groom from Petersburg. |
| Stolp | S. | KC, p5c3, 3/1/1900 | Resided in Mt. Sterling. Sold 2 loads of tobacco in Ferryville. |
| Stone | boy | KC, p5c3, 8/4/1898 | Son born July 24, 1898 to John Stone of Gays Mills. |

Genealogical Gleanings From Early Newspapers for Residents In and Near
Crawford County, Wisconsin, 1897-1902

| LAST NAME | FIRST NAME | NEWSPAPER PAGE/COLUMN MONTH/DAY/YEAR | GENEALOGICAL DATA |
|---|---|---|---|
| Stone | J. K. | KC, p1c2, 8/25/1898 | Moved to Madison, MS from Gays Mills. Planned to move near the land purchased by J. G. Robb, formerly of Gays Mills, and George Moore, formerly of Seneca. Several others in the area, including Richard Miller and C. R. Barker, also planned to move south. |
| Stone | J. K. | KC, p1c4, 10/13/1898 | Returned to Gays Mills to live. Not pleased with Mississippi. |
| Stone | John | KC, p8c3, 4/8/1897 | John Stone and Melvin Rounds drove through from Gays Mills to new homes in North Dakota. |
| Stone | John | KC, p5c3, 3/23/1899 | Worked as a photographer in Steuben. |
| Stout | William | KC, p1c2, 1/24/1901 | Shot and killed in a Yuba saloon quarrel by the proprietor, Mr. Kolash. |
| Stove | Lena | KC, Supp., 12/12/1901 | Crawford County filed suit against Jens Stove, father of Lena A. Stove, to recover costs for care provided his daughter at the State Hospital for the Insane. |
| Stove | Lena | KC, Supp., 12/18/1902 | Per Report of Special Committee on Insane, Crawford County, a claim of the county to the State Board has been satisfactorily adjusted in the case of Lena Stove. |
| Stove | Nels | KC, p5c3, 3/27/1902 | Married Julia Munson last Thursday at the Norwegian Church in Utica. |
| Stowell | A. L. | KC, Supp., 12/29/1898 | From County Board Proceedings, A. L. Stowell mistakenly paid the 1895 taxes on a lot in Gays Mills that he did not own and the 1895 taxes for a nearby lot, which he did own, were returned. The land he owned was sold for taxes to E. I. Kidd for $5.08. Board ordered amount of tax sale certificate be returned to Mr. Kidd and the certificate be cancelled. |
| Stowell | A. L. | KC, Supp., 12/19/1901 | Operated a blacksmith shop in Gays Mills. |
| Stowell | boy | KC, p5c1, 7/28/1898 | Son born July 18, 1898 to A. L. Stowell of Gays Mills. |
| Stowell | J. L. | KC, p1c6, 4/7/1898 | Elected Clerk for the Town of Clayton. |
| Stowell | J. L. | KC, p5c5, 4/5/1900 | Elected clerk in Town of Clayton. |
| Stowell | John, Mrs. | KC, p5c4, 2/15/1900 | Recently died at home near Gays Mills. Funeral held at Congregational Church. Buried in Gays Mills Cemetery. She was sister of S. L. Brown of Prairie du Chien. |
| Stowell | W. A. | KC, Supp., 12/12/1901 | Attended a Teacher's Institute in Crawford County in 1901. Resided in Gays Mill. |
| Straka | Mr. | KC, p1c5, 8/1/1901 | Found a pearl while clam fishing in the Kickapoo River. Sold it for $500. Rented the Abe Onstine farm 4 miles north of Wauzeka. |
| Stram | A., Mrs. | KC, p8c2, 4/13/1899 | Died April 12, 1899 in Frenchtown (Prairie du Chien). Survived by husband, 4 sons and 3 daughters. |
| Stram | Lillie | KC, p4c3, 10/26/1899 | Received marriage license to marry Joseph Mickel. Bride from Eastman. Groom probably from Eastman. |

Genealogical Gleanings From Early Newspapers for Residents In and Near
Crawford County, Wisconsin, 1897-1902

| LAST NAME | FIRST NAME | NEWSPAPER PAGE/COLUMN MONTH/DAY/YEAR | GENEALOGICAL DATA |
|---|---|---|---|
| Stranskey | V., Mrs. | KC, p8c4, 2/20/1902 | Died Feb. 19, 1902 in Prairie du Chien. |
| Stransky | Frank | KC, p8c1, 5/5/1898 | Died Apr. 23, 1898 at home of parents in Prairie du Chien. Aged 15 years. Funeral held at St. John Bohemian Catholic Church. |
| Stransky | Stasia | KC, p8c4, 6/6/1901 | Died May 30, 1901. Only daughter of V. Stransky of Prairie du Chien. Buried in St. Gabriel's Church Cemetery. |
| Straub | Albert | KC, p1c2, 11/25/1897 | Married Mary Hendrick on Nov. 17, 1897 at St. Vaclav Catholic Church. Of Eastman. |
| Strayer | Jacob, Mrs. | KC, Supp., 11/24/1898 | Widow. Died about 2 weeks ago at home of daughter, Mrs. L. Mitchell. Per Town of Scott news items. |
| Strayer | John | KC, p1c4, 3/11/1897 | Died a few weeks ago in FL. Former resident of Lowertown. |
| Strecker | Ed | KC, p1c6, 4/7/1898 | Elected Clerk for the Town of Utica. |
| Streker | E. | KC, p5c5, 4/5/1900 | Elected clerk in Town of Utica. |
| Strong | Rachael | KC, p5c1, 4/7/1898 | Rachel McCullick Strong died Mar. 29, 1898 near Bell Center. Born Mar. 16, 1821 in Tyler Co., WV. When 16, moved with parents to Wells Co., IN. Married Levi Philips on Mar. 18, 1840. Moved to Crawford Co. in 1869. Husband died 1881. Survived by 6 of 11 children. Married J. R. Strong on Dec. 26, 18_6. Interred in Coleman Cemetery. |
| Strong | Rachael, Mrs. | KC, p1c2, 2/10/1898 | Government granted her a pension of $12/month. |
| Strouse | Henry | KC, p8c1, 10/21/1897 | Died Saturday evening in McGregor. Remains were taken to La Crosse where a brother resided. |
| Stuart | Gilbert | KC, p5c4, 3/29/1900 | Celebrated his 70th birthday last Sunday at his home on Pine Creek. |
| Stuart | girl | KC, p1c2, 4/8/1897 | Daughter born April 5, 1897 to Joseph Stuart of Prairie du Chien. |
| Stuart | Robert | KC, p5c5, 4/5/1900 | Elected supervisor in Seneca. |
| Stuart | Robert | KC, Supp., 12/20/1900 | Represented Seneca on the Crawford Co. Board of Supervisors in 1900. |
| Stuckey | Aug. | KC, p1c3, 7/25/1901 | Intense heat caused the death of horses owned by Aug. Stuckey, John Schmidt and Joe Noe of the Wauzeka area. |
| Stuckey | August | KC, p1c5, 6/1/1899 | The May term of the Crawford County Circuit Court closed. In the case, August Stuckey vs. Utica Farmers Fire and Lighting Insurance Co., judgement for plaintiff. |
| Stuckey | boy | KC, p1c2, 10/12/1899 | Son born Tuesday to Fred Stuckey of Marietta. Weighed 12 pounds. |
| Stuckey | Fritz | KC, p5c4, 9/18/1902 | Published a notice that his 17-year-old son, Johnnie, left home without his consent and would not be responsible for any bills contracted by the son. |
| Stuckey | Henry | KC, p8c2, 6/17/1897 | Henry Stuckey and sister, Mrs. N. Jurgenson, went to Wauzeka to meet relatives from St. Louis. |

Genealogical Gleanings From Early Newspapers for Residents In and Near
Crawford County, Wisconsin, 1897-1902

| LAST NAME | FIRST NAME | NEWSPAPER PAGE/COLUMN MONTH/DAY/YEAR | GENEALOGICAL DATA |
|---|---|---|---|
| Stuckey | Mary | KC, p1c6, 1/9/1902 | Married H. P. Rosencrans on Jan. 6, 1902. Bride was daughter of Fred Stuckey. Bride and groom from Wauzeka. |
| Stucky | Henry, Sr. | KC, p1c3, 5/16/1901 | The remains of Henry Stucky, Sr. and wife and son were removed from the Chapek farm and interred in the Wauzeka Cemetery. They were originally interred in 1880, 1875 and 1849 respectively. |
| Stukey | Edna | KC, p5c3, 11/28/1901 | Died Nov. 14, 1901. She was a twin daughter of Mr. and Mrs. Charles Stuckey of Town of Eastman. Aged 1 year, 9 months and 3 days. Buried in Hural Cemetery. |
| Stukey | Fred B. | KC, p1c5, 3/20/1902 | Finger amputated after it was caught in the gears of a windmill. Lived on Eastman road, 3 miles from Wauzeka. |
| Stukey | girl | KC, p1c3, 9/26/1901 | Daughter born Sept. 19, 1901 to Fritz Stukey of Wauzeka. |
| Stukey | Mary | KC, p1c2, 1/2/1902 | Planned to marry H. P. Rosencrans. |
| Stukey | William | KC, p1c5, 5/10/1900 | Married Louisa Chapek on May 6, 1900. Groom from Solon Springs. |
| Stukey | William | KC, p1c2, 2/15/1900 | Recently rented out his 160-acre farm in Dell Rapids, SD. Visited in Wauzeka. |
| Stukey | William | KC, p1c2, 3/1/1900 | Hotelkeeper in Senora Spring, WI. Visited relatives in Wauzeka area. |
| Stukey | William | KC, p1c3, 7/12/1900 | Formerly of Wauzeka. Recently worked on the railroad. Purchased a quarter section near Dell Rapids, SD. |
| Stunkard | boy | KC, p1c4, 9/8/1898 | Son born Aug. 23, 1898 to Clin. Stunkard of Towerville. |
| Sturnot | John | KC, p8c3, 1/30/1902 | Married Mary Kalina on Jan. 28, 1902 at St. John's Bohemian Catholic Church. Included in Prairie du Chien news items. |
| Stuss | girl | KC, p5c1, 3/3/1898 | Infant daughter of P. Stuss died Feb. 14, 1898 in Gays Mills. |
| Stussy | girl | KC, p8c4, 2/18/1897 | Daughter born Feb. 12, 1897 to Peter Stussy of Gays Mills. |
| Sullivan | boy | KC, p4c1, 9/22/1898 | Son born Sept. 4, 1898 to John Sullivan of Lynxville. He may be named Dewey. |
| Sullivan | girl | KC, p1c5, 8/23/1900 | Daughter born August 1, 1900 to John Sullivan of Lynxville. |
| Sullivan | girl | KC, p5c3, 9/18/1902 | Daughter born Sept. 13, 1902 to John Sullivan of Lynxville. This was his sixth child. |
| Sullivan | James | KC, p5c3, 3/13/1902 | Arrived from St. Charles, MO to visit mother and relatives in Seneca. |
| Sullivan | M. R. | KC, p5c3, 8/31/1899 | Resigned as creamery operator at Eastman. Planned to open a furniture store in Lone Rock. |
| Sullivan | Mrs. | KC, p5c3, 8/10/1899 | Lived in Richland City. Visited son, Rodell Sullivan, a butter maker in Eastman. |
| Sullivan | Robbie | KC, p4c3, 1/26/1899 | Died Sunday (Jan. 22, 1899?) in Seneca. Aged 2 years 4 months. Son of E. M. Sullivan. |
| Sullivan | Rodell | KC, p8c3, 6/28/1900 | Married Irene E. West on June 20, 1900 in Monroe, WI. Groom was a former resident of the Town of Eastman. |

Genealogical Gleanings From Early Newspapers for Residents In and Near
Crawford County, Wisconsin, 1897-1902

| LAST NAME | FIRST NAME | NEWSPAPER PAGE/COLUMN MONTH/DAY/YEAR | GENEALOGICAL DATA |
|---|---|---|---|
| Sullivan | William and R. | KC, p5c2, 11/17/1898 | Opened a furniture store in Eastman. |
| Surges | Minnie, Mrs. | KC, p1c3, 9/20/1900 | After visiting relatives in Wauzeka, departed for home in Gray, ND. |
| Surley | Rufus | KC, Supp., 12/18/1902 | Crawford County Board of Supervisors examined bills in the Justices and Constables' Account for State vs. Rufus Surley. |
| Sutherland | Alonzo | KC, Supp., 12/29/1898 | Crawford Co. Board of Supervisors approved Justices and Constables' expenses related to the case, State vs. Alonzo Sutherland. |
| Sutherland | Alphonso | KC, p1c2, 8/11/1898 | Alphonso Sutherland of Readstown and Eugene Clark of Victory were charged in court for fishing with a seine in the Mississippi River. Plead guilty. Fined $25 and costs. Sutherland refused to pay fine and spent 45 days in jail. |
| Sutton | Andrew | KC, Supp., 12/12/1901 | State vs. Andrew Sutton heard in Crawford Co. Court. |
| Sutton | George | KC, p5c3, 2/13/1902 | Resided in Seneca. Lost a horse when going through a large snowdrift. Horse fell and was crushed when sleigh turned over it. |
| Sutton | Ida | KC, Supp., 12/12/1901 | Crawford Co. Board of Supervisors approved payments in the Matter of Ida Sutton, Feeble Minded. Taken to Chippewa Falls. |
| Sutton | Lillian | KC, p8c4, 4/8/1897 | Married James Heal on April 4, 1897. Bride from Seneca. |
| Sutton | Lillian | KC, p1c6, 4/8/1897 | Married Jim Heal on Sunday. Bride from Lynxville. Groom from Mt. Sterling area. |
| Sutton | Mary | KC, p5c3, 6/6/1901 | Married Edwin Perry Russell on June 3, 1901. Bride and groom were from Town of Seneca. |
| Sutton | William | KC, p5c2, 8/4/1898 | Died July 26, 1898 at home in Lynxville. Buried in Dickson Cemetery. (Per KC, 8/25/1898, p1c3, William was father of Andrew and George.) |
| Swateak | Charles and Celia | KC, p4c3, 4/7/1898 | Traveled from Chicago to visit friends in Eastman. Brought with them the 3 sons and 2 daughters of B. Vavruska. |
| Swatek | Albert | KC, p8c4, 1/16/1902 | Died Jan. 13, 1902 in Town of Eastman. He was an "aged resident." |
| Swatek | Albert | KC, p5c4, 1/30/1902 | Died Jan. 13, 1902 in (or near) the Town of Eastman. Born April 25, 1825 in Bohemia. Came to America in 1878 and moved directly to Eastman. Survived by 10 children and 2 brothers, John of Eastman and Lawrence of Bohemia. Wife and youngest child died several years ago. He was father of Charles, Mrs. Stammer and Mrs. Yara of Chicago. |
| Swatek | Hannah | KC, p5c3, 5/17/1900 | Employed at the Maney Hotel in Lynxville. |
| Swatek | J. W. | KC, p1c3, 2/21/1901 | Arrived from Wagner, SD to visit relatives in Eastman. |
| Swatek | John | KC, p1c2, 7/5/1900 | Resided in Eastman. Bought a newspaper subscription for his son, J. W. Swatek of Wagner, SD. |
| Swedenskey | Albert | KC, p5c4, 2/22/1900 | Sold an 80-acre farm in Town of Eastman to Michael Lechnier for $1100. |

Genealogical Gleanings From Early Newspapers for Residents In and Near
Crawford County, Wisconsin, 1897-1902

| LAST NAME | FIRST NAME | NEWSPAPER PAGE/COLUMN MONTH/DAY/YEAR | GENEALOGICAL DATA |
|---|---|---|---|
| Sweeney | boy | KC, p8c3, 1/14/1897 | Son born Jan. 4, 1897 to John Sweeney of Ferryville. |
| Sweeney | Katharyn | KC, p5c4, 5/29/1902 | Katharyn Sweeney of McGregor, IA attended a teacher institute in Crawford County. |
| Sweeney | Katie | KC, p5c3, 3/20/1902 | Taught in Seneca's Citron Valley school. Spent summer at her home in McGregor. |
| Sweeney | Katie | KC, p1c5, 2/9/1899 | Taught school in Eastman in 1899. E. E. Brindley, Crawford County Superintendent of Schools published a comprehensive list of all teachers in the county. |
| Sweeney | Maggie | KC, p1c5, 2/9/1899 | Taught school in Prairie du Chien in 1899. E. E. Brindley, Crawford County Superintendent of Schools published a comprehensive list of all teachers in the county. |
| Sweeney | Mrs. | KC, p5c3, 12/6/1900 | Funeral recently held in Town of Seneca. |
| Sweeny | Katie | KC, Supp., 12/12/1901 | Attended a Teacher's Institute in Crawford County in 1901. Resided in McGregor. |
| Sweeny | Katie and Maggie | KC, Supp., 12/12/1901 | Katie and Maggie Sweeny of McGregor attended the summer Teacher's Institute in Soldiers Grove. |
| Sweeny | Maggie | KC, Supp., 12/12/1901 | Attended a Teacher's Institute in Crawford County in 1901. Resided in McGregor. |
| Sweiger | George | KC, p5c4, 11/30/1899 | Ready to take possession of his new dwelling in Gays Mills and open a restaurant in it. |
| Sweiger | girl | KC, p5c3, 1/12/1899 | Infant daughter of George Sweiger died Dec. 29, 1898 in Steuben. |
| Swinson | boy | KC, p4c4, 12/20/1900 | Son was born Dec. 13, 1900 to T. Swinson of Gays Mills. |
| Swinson | T. W. | KC, p5c5, 1/25/1900 | Married May McAuley on Jan. 24, 1900. Bride daughter of R. D. McAuley, a miller. Bride and groom from Gays Mills. |
| Swinson | T. W. | KC, p8c1, 1/18/1900 | Advertised his furniture store, caskets, undertaking services and funeral directing services. Store in Gays Mills. |
| Swinson | T. W. | KC, p1c2, 4/19/1900 | Departed Gays Mills for Chippewa Co., WI to explore opportunities to invest in land. |
| Swinson | T. W. | KC, p1c3, 7/28/1898 | Promoted to sergeant. |
| Swinson | Thomas | KC, p1c6, 5/12/1898 | Planned to volunteer for Spanish American War. From Gays Mills area. |
| Swinson | Thomas | KC, p5c3, 4/27/1899 | Planned to erect a furniture store in Gays Mills. |
| Sylvester | C. R. | KC, p5c3, 12/2/1897 | Plaintiff in a foreclosure sale in Crawford Co. Circuit Court against Isaac Harland and Florence Underwood and Garvial Harland. (Garvial Harland per KC, p5c3, 12/9/1897) |
| Syverson | boy | KC, p1c4, 5/20/1897 | Son recently born to Dan Syverson of Steuben. |
| Syverson | D. | KC, p5c2, 1/18/1900 | Proprietor of a hotel, The Steuben House, in Steuben, WI. |
| Syverson | David | KC, p1c4, 8/23/1900 | Married Cora Hoopman on Aug. 20, 1900 at Prairie du Chien. Bride and groom from Steuben. |

Genealogical Gleanings From Early Newspapers for Residents In and Near
Crawford County, Wisconsin, 1897-1902

| LAST NAME | FIRST NAME | NEWSPAPER PAGE/COLUMN MONTH/DAY/YEAR | GENEALOGICAL DATA |
|---|---|---|---|
| Syverson | Larson | KC, p5c3, 1/12/1899 | Larson Syverson, Sam Turner and George Cupps resided in North Dakota. Returned to Steuben to visit old friends. |
| Syverson | William | KC, p5c3, 8/1/1901 | Arrived from Courtney, SD to visit relatives in Steuben. His mother, brother Dave and wife and brother Dan plan to move to Courtney. Ike Posey left with the Syversons to help his son with the harvest but planned to return to Crawford Co. |
| Taft | A. | KC, p4c2, 3/16/1899 | Proprietor of the Petersburg Hotel. Advertisement published. |
| Taft | A., Mr. and Mrs. | KC, p10c4, 12/12/1901 | Lived on Viniger Ridge. Called on daughter, Mrs. Charles Shimmins. |
| Taft | Addie, Miss | KC, p1c6, 8/19/1897 | Died Aug. 15, 1897 in Town of Haney. Mrs. James Harris was a sister. |
| Taft | Alanson | KC, p1c6, 4/7/1898 | Elected Clerk for the Town of Haney. |
| Taft | Alma Adelaide | KC, p1c6, 8/26/1897 | Died Aug. 15, 1897. Born Nov. 15, 1862 in Haney Township. He was the youngest child of Alanson and Elizabeth Taft. Funeral held at Haney Ridge Church. |
| Taft | Fern | KC, p5c3, 10/24/1901 | Married Charles Shimmir on Oct. 16, 1901. Bride from Taft Ridge. Planned to live in Bell Center. |
| Taft | Gustave | KC, p1c3, 11/16/1899 | Arrived from home in Harris, IA to visit his brother, Oscar Taft of the Wauzeka area. |
| Taft | Lant | KC, p5c5, 4/5/1900 | Elected clerk in Town of Haney. |
| Taft | Myrtle | KC, Supp., 12/12/1901 | Attended a Teacher's Institute in Crawford County in 1901. Resided in Wauzeka. |
| Taft | Myrtle | KC, p1c2, 6/6/1901 | Graduated from Wauzeka graded schools. |
| Taft | Oliver R. | KC, p1c2, 9/1/1898 | Married Rose Coleman of Bell Center on Aug. 22, 1898 at the Congregational Church in Boscobel. Groom from Petersburg. |
| Taft | Oscar | KC, p1c2, 7/24/1902 | Lived in Wauzeka. Worked as a broom maker. |
| Taft | Reuel | KC, p1c6, 2/16/1899 | Notice of Final Proof published. Needed to establish continued residence on property in Town of Petersburg to finalize his land claim. |
| Taft | Reuel | KC, p4c3, 3/2/1899 | Reuel Taft of Petersburg filed a Notice of Final Proof with the Land Office in Eau Claire to support his claim for SW 1/4 of SW 1/4 Section 15 Town 9N Range 4 West. Witnesses to support the claim were Fred R. Smith, George H. Holden, Alanson Taft, all of Petersburg, and D. C. Bakeman of Barnum. |
| Taft | Serena | KC, p1c2, 6/6/1901 | Graduated from Wauzeka graded schools. |
| Taft | Serena | KC, p5c4, 12/19/1901 | Resided in Wauzeka. Taught in Woodman school. |
| Taft | Serena | KC, p1c2, 10/9/1902 | Taught school in the Taft District near Barnum. |

Genealogical Gleanings From Early Newspapers for Residents In and Near
Crawford County, Wisconsin, 1897-1902

| LAST NAME | FIRST NAME | NEWSPAPER PAGE/COLUMN MONTH/DAY/YEAR | GENEALOGICAL DATA |
|---|---|---|---|
| Taft | Serena | KC, Supp., 12/12/1901 | Attended a Teacher's Institute in Crawford County in 1901. Resided in Wauzeka. |
| Taho | girl | KC, p5c3, 4/19/1900 | Daughter recently born to J. Taho of Town of Seneca. |
| Tainter | A. J. and Marie | KC, p5c3, 5/20/1897 | Issues of fact for jury to be heard in the May term of the Crawford County Court. G. L. Miller vs. A. J. Tainter and Marie Tainter his wife. |
| Tainter | Ana. | KC, p1c2, 9/6/1900 | Resided in Gays Mills. He was the second pioneer in northern Crawford County. Arrived soon after William Sterling. Mr. Tainter was 77 and hale and hearty. He cultivated a good crop this year, including several acres of tobacco. His present wife was 23 years old. |
| Tainter | girl | KC, p1c3, 10/18/1900 | Daughter born Oct. 12, 1900 to A. G. Tainter of Towerville. |
| Tainter | girl | KC, p1c2, 3/27/1902 | Daughter born Mar. 19, 1902 to F. S. Tainter of the Wauzeka area. |
| Talcott | M. N. | KC, p4c4, 11/10/1898 | Issues of Fact for Jury heard in the November term of the Crawford County Circuit Court. Milo Freeman vs. M. N. Talcott. |
| Talcott | M. N. | KC, Supp., 12/18/1902 | Crawford County Soldiers Relief Committee provided funds to M. N. Talcott of Gays Mill. |
| Talcott | M. N. | KC, Supp., 12/29/1898 | Received aid from the Crawford County Soldiers Relief Commission. Resided in Soldiers Grove. |
| Talcott | M. W. and wife | KC, Supp., 12/18/1902 | Crawford County Board of Supervisors allowed expenses for taking M. W. Talcott and wife to Waupaca by Order of Court. |
| Talcott | Marvin | KC, Supp., 12/18/1902 | Crawford County Soldiers Relief Committee provided funds to Marvin Talcott of Grays Mill (should this be Gays Mill?). |
| Talcott | Percy, Byran, Julia and Newell | KC, Supp., 12/18/1902 | Crawford County Board of Supervisors allowed expenses in the Matter of Percy, Bryan, Julia and Newell Talcott, Dependent Children. |
| Talkot | William | KC, Supp., 12/18/1902 | Crawford County Board of Supervisors examined bills in the Justices and Constables' Account for State vs. William Talkot (Talcott?) et al. |
| Tallman | Clara S. | KC, p5c2, 11/15/1900 | Operated a millinery shop in Gays Mills. |
| Tallman | Clara, Miss | KC, Supp., 12/19/1901 | Operated a millinery shop in Gays Mills. |
| Tate | Mrs. | KC, p1c6, 5/5/1898 | Prepared to move to the Klondike from Bell Center. Received visits from the Frank Lewis family of Lynxville and the H. McWilliams family. |
| Tate | W. W. | KC, p5c2, 4/7/1898 | Planned to leave for the Klondike. Resided in Bell Center. |
| Tate | W. W. and Mary B. | KC, p1c6, 11/4/1897 | Issue of law for court to be heard at the November term of the Circuit Court in Crawford County. A. H. Reimer & Co. vs. W. W. Tate and Mary B. Tate, partners as W. W. Tate & Co. |

Genealogical Gleanings From Early Newspapers for Residents In and Near
Crawford County, Wisconsin, 1897-1902

| LAST NAME | FIRST NAME | NEWSPAPER PAGE/COLUMN MONTH/DAY/YEAR | GENEALOGICAL DATA |
|---|---|---|---|
| Taubleman | Agnes | KC, p8c4, 10/17/1901 | Recently burned to death. Oldest daughter in family. Lived in Town of Eastman area. Buried in Catholic Cemetery. |
| Taylor | Adam | KC, p1c5, 12/2/1897 | Married Nora Gay on Nov. 17, 1897. Bride daughter of Lot Gay of Seneca. |
| Taylor | girl | KC, p5c3, 4/17/1902 | Daughter born April 9, 1902 to Thomas Taylor of Seneca. |
| Taylor | Martha | KC, p1c3, 6/14/1900 | Married Enos Gill on June 15, 1900 in Dubuque, IA. Bride and groom were from Town of Seneca. |
| Taylor | Thomas | KC, p8c4, 11/21/1901 | Resided in Seneca. Chosen to be Supervisor of Assessor. |
| Taylor | Thomas | KC, p5c5, 4/5/1900 | Elected clerk in Seneca. |
| Taylor | Thomas | KC, p1c2, 10/23/1902 | Democratic candidate for member of Wisconsin Assembly. Resident of Seneca. Born on a farm. Spent about 5 years teaching in Crawford County schools and then became a farmer. Has served last 7 years on Town Board of Supervisors. Also served on County Board. Has carefully studied the taxation question. Portrait published. |
| Taylor | William | KC, p5c3, 3/14/1901 | Robbed of $62 by 2 young men who stopped at his home asking for supper. $60 was later returned. |
| Teacher Institute | | KC, Supp., 12/12/1901 | The following people from Millett attended the summer Teacher's Institute in Soldiers Grove: Lottie Childs, Etta Hughbanks, George Sampson, Harry Childs, Mamie Trumbull, Grace Calloway, Willie Infield and Stella Spencer. |
| Teacher Institute | | KC, Supp., 12/12/1901 | Julia Anderson and Helen Carter, both from Readstown, attended the summer Teacher's Institute in Soldiers Grove. |
| Teacher Institute | | KC, Supp., 12/12/1901 | The following people from Ferryville attended the summer Teacher's Institute in Soldiers Grove: Ellen Lankford, Frances Howe, Olive Hudson and James Devine. |
| Teacher Institute | | KC, Supp., 12/12/1901 | The following people from Rising Sun attended the summer Teacher's Institute in Soldiers Grove: Sophia Iverson, Anna Severson, Mary Melvin, Maggie Phalin, Mathias Munson, Christena Nash, Margaret Mahan and Winnie Dolan. |
| Teacher Institute | | KC, Supp., 12/12/1901 | The following people from Gays Mills attended the summer Teacher's Institute in Soldiers Grove: Florence Mitchell, W. A. Stowell, Blanche Mitchell, Anna Mitchell, John Lester, Lillian De Lamater and Leona Randall. |
| Teacher Institute | | KC, Supp., 12/12/1901 | The following people from Mt. Sterling attended the summer Teacher's Institute in Soldiers Grove: Susan Nelson, K. O. Johnson, Grace Caswell, Emma Bellows, Mae Briggs and Mamie Lagan. |
| Teacher Institute | | KC, Supp., 12/12/1901 | The following people from Sugar Grove attended the summer Teacher's Institute in Soldiers Grove: Stella Henthorn, Zora Haskins, Nina Williams, Goldie Moses and Elmer Williams. |

Genealogical Gleanings From Early Newspapers for Residents In and Near
Crawford County, Wisconsin, 1897-1902

| LAST NAME | FIRST NAME | NEWSPAPER PAGE/COLUMN MONTH/DAY/YEAR | GENEALOGICAL DATA |
|---|---|---|---|
| Teacher Institute | | KC, Supp., 12/12/1901 | The following people from Wauzeka attended the summer Teacher's Institute in Soldiers Grove: Myrtle Taft, Serena Taft, Bernie Rosencrans, Mattie O'Keefe, Ella Dunn, Edith Folbrecht, Alma Hoisington, Nellie Riley, Edith Herold and Stella Miller. |
| Teacher Institute | | KC, Supp., 12/12/1901 | The following people from Eastman attended the summer Teacher's Institute in Soldiers Grove: J. C. Ertel, Nellie Iverson, Hattie Iverson, Stella Wallin and Julia Sprosty. |
| Teacher Institute | | KC, Supp., 12/12/1901 | The following people from Steuben attended the summer Teacher's Institute in Soldiers Grove: Lucy Kopan, Mary Kopan, Alma Wannamaker and Herbert Campbell. |
| Teacher Institute | | KC, Supp., 12/12/1901 | The following people from Lynxville attended the summer Teacher's Institute in Soldiers Grove: Allie Bright, Anna Horal, Mary Davidson, Allie Searle and Etta Randall. |
| Teacher Institute | | KC, Supp., 12/12/1901 | The following people from Prairie du Chien attended the summer Teacher's Institute in Soldiers Grove: Rayme Mitchell, F. Umback, Mayme Doyle, Cecilia Welsh, Minnie Griesbach, Laura Cherrier, Emma Cherrier, Isabell Valley, Rose Curran, Mamie Nugent, Carrie Nugent, Ruth McDill, Marie Lagan and Edna Mitchell. |
| Teacher Institute | | KC, Supp., 12/12/1901 | The following people from Excelsior attended the summer Teacher's Institute in Soldiers Grove: Coosa Dilley, J. W. Shaw and Mary Wilt. |
| Teacher Institute | | KC, Supp., 12/12/1901 | The following people from Bell Center attended the summer Teacher's Institute in Soldiers Grove: Margie Rounds, Mae Brightman, Elma Heligas and Lucy Kast. |
| Teacher Institute | | KC, Supp., 12/12/1901 | The following people from Hurlbut attended the summer Teacher's Institute in Soldiers Grove: Pearl Pickett (Puckett?), Alta Phillips, Mabel Arms, Mary Bannen, Willie Bannen and M. R. Dilley. |
| Teacher Institute | | KC, Supp., 12/12/1901 | The following people from Soldiers Grove attended the summer Teacher's Institute in Soldiers Grove: Albert Davig, Tom Gander, Orland Montgomery, Dora Hoffland, Lee Smith, Fred Smith, Alvena Thiede, Anna Sime, Lizzie Hansen, Rosella Ryan, Sadie Slightam and Malena Lee. |
| Teacher Institute | | KC, Supp., 12/12/1901 | The following people from Seneca attended the summer Teacher's Institute in Soldiers Grove: Maggie Layd, Anna Roth, Mary Meagher, Maggie Meagher, Katie McNamara, Anna Boland, Regis Keeley, Marguerite Lynch, Betsy Severson, Hannah Joy and Abbie Joy. |
| Teacher Institute | | KC, p5c4, 5/29/1902 | The following people from Wauzeka attended a teacher institute in Crawford County: Serena Taft, Stella Miller, Bernice Rosencrans, Mrs. O'Keefe, Myrtle Taft, Mae Patton, Nellie Riley and Eda Folbrecht. |

Genealogical Gleanings From Early Newspapers for Residents In and Near
Crawford County, Wisconsin, 1897-1902

| LAST NAME | FIRST NAME | NEWSPAPER PAGE/COLUMN MONTH/DAY/YEAR | GENEALOGICAL DATA |
|---|---|---|---|
| Teacher Institute | | KC, p5c4, 5/29/1902 | The following people from Prairie du Chien attended a teacher institute in Crawford County: Mayme Mitchell, Edna Mitchell, Marie Griesbach, Emma Kasparek, Laura Cherrier, Nona Evans, Anna Garrity, Katharyn Doyle, Minnie Griesbach, Stasia Zeman, Ruth McDill, Emma Cherrier, Isabella Valley and Mayme Nugent. |
| Teacher Institute | | KC, p5c4, 5/29/1902 | The following people from Soldiers Grove attended a teacher institute in Crawford County: Tressa Welch, Alvina Thiede, Katie Murphy, Edith Burroughs, Eliza Welch, Alvina Dinsdale, Maggie Murphy and Alice Dodge. |
| Teacher Institute | | KC, p5c4, 5/29/1902 | The following people from Gays Mills attended a teacher institute in Crawford County: Emily Mitchell, John Leater, Blanche Mitchell, Florence Mitchell and Anna Mitchell. |
| Teacher Institute | | KC, p5c4, 5/29/1902 | The following people from Mt. Sterling attended a teacher institute in Crawford County: Mary King, Bessie Briggs, Frances Howe, Susan Nelson, Edith Rice, Mary Briggs, Knute Johnson, Mary O'Neil. |
| Teacher Institute | | KC, p5c4, 5/29/1902 | The following people from Seneca attended a teacher institute in Crawford County: Abbie Joy, Maggie Lagan, Mary Meagher, Maggie Layd, Mayme Joy, Anna Roth and Mande Layd. |
| Teacher Institute | | KC, p5c4, 5/29/1902 | The following people from Eastman attended a teacher institute in Crawford County: Olive Thomson, Mabel Iverson, Estella Wallin and Nellie Iverson. |
| Teacher Institute | | KC, p5c4, 5/29/1902 | The following Lynxville residents attended a teacher institute in Crawford County: Mayme L. Joy, Raleigh Searle, Joseph Stoehr, Allie Searle, A. M. Laird, Dwight Randall and Katie McNamara. |
| Teacher Institute | | KC, p5c4, 5/29/1902 | The following people from Steuben attended a teacher institute in Crawford County: Minnie Sanders, Lucy Kopan and Mary Kopan. |
| Teacher Institute | | KC, p5c4, 5/29/1902 | The following people from Rising Sun attended a teacher institute in Crawford County: Winifred Dolan, Sophia Iverson, Mathias Munson, Hannah Munson, Christena Nash and Mary Melvin. |
| Teacher Institute | | KC, p5c4, 5/29/1902 | The following people from Towerville attended a teacher institute in Crawford County: Effie Salmon, Dora Hoffland, Margaret Phalin, Goldie E. Davis and Verna McCormick. |
| Teacher Institute | | KC, p5c4, 5/29/1902 | The following people from Boscobel attended a teacher institute in Crawford County: Mary Wilt, Sadie Wright, Jessie Spencer, Ada Daugherty, Mary Bannen, W. E. Bannen, Marie Greene, Mae Scott, Mabel Arms, Pearl Pickett, Stella Spencer, Etta Phillips, Willie Infield, Mamie Trumble, Donnie Greene and Nettie Dennis. |

Genealogical Gleanings From Early Newspapers for Residents In and Near
Crawford County, Wisconsin, 1897-1902

| LAST NAME | FIRST NAME | NEWSPAPER PAGE/COLUMN MONTH/DAY/YEAR | GENEALOGICAL DATA |
|---|---|---|---|
| Teachers' Institute | | KC, p1c2, 3/4/1897 | A Teachers' Institute was held in Prairie du Chien last week. The attendees were: Lynxville -- J. H. McDonald, Clyde Noggle, Stacy Wolcott, Etta Randall, and Cecelia Walsh; Eastman -- Berdie Fisher, Bertha French, May Larson Carrie Finney and Bertha Finney; Wauzeka -- Floy Vaughan, W. R. Graves, C. J. Kopan, Nellie Riley, Zelma Beier and Mary Cushing; Rising Sun -- Jennie Mahan; Mt. Sterling -- Dana Duffy; Seneca -- Anna Roth; Boydtown -- Mattie O'Shaughnessy; Bridgeport -- Katie Doyle and Mabel McReynolds; McGregor, IA -- Prof. Williams, Katie Sweeney and Maggie Sweeney. |
| Terman | Knute | KC, Supp., 12/20/1900 | Crawford Co. Board of Supervisors approved payment of expenses in the matter of State vs. Knute Terman. |
| Tesar | Anna, Mrs. | KC, p5c1, 9/15/1898 | Died Sept. 1, 1898 at home in Wauzeka. Born 1835 in Bohemia. Married Joseph Tesar in Bohemia. Husband died less than a year ago. Moved to Chicago in 1866 and to Prairie du Chien in 1871. To Wauzeka in 1879. Survived by 1 of 7 children, James. |
| Tesar | James | KC, p1c3, 4/3/1902 | Owned the Opera House in Wauzeka. |
| Tesar | James | KC, p5c3, 4/13/1899 | Daughter born Mar. 30, 1899 to James Tesar of West Wauzeka. |
| Tesar | Joseph | KC, p4c2, 9/30/1897 | Died Sept. 28, 1897 in Wauzeka. Born July 10, 1827 in Bohemia. Immigrated in 1874 to Chicago. Five years later moved to Vineyard Coulee outside Prairie du Chien where he lived for 8 years. Moved to Wauzeka. One of 7 children survives, James of Wauzeka. |
| Tesar | Joseph | KC, p8c1, 10/20/1898 | Married Emma Otto, daughter of the late Henry Otto, Jr., on Oct. 19, 1898. Groom was son of V. Tesar. Bride and groom from Prairie du Chien. |
| Tesar | Joseph | KC, p5c4, 4/24/1902 | Probate Hearing notice published. Late of Town of Wauzeka. |
| Tesar | Joseph | KC, p5c1, 1/17/1901 | Notice to Creditors published by Crawford County Court regarding the estate of the late Joseph Tesar of the Town of Wauzeka. |
| Tesar | Joseph, Mrs. | KC, p1c2, 9/15/1898 | Funeral recently held. Sister of John Burenka of Chicago. |
| Tesar | V. | KC, p8c2, 9/30/1897 | Called to Wauzeka from his home in Prairie du Chien. Received dispatch announcing the approaching death of his brother. The brother died before Mr. Tesar arrived. |
| Tesar | Joseph | KC, p4c5, 11/22/1900 | Late of Wauzeka. Probate Hearing notice published. Vaclav (James) Tesar applied to administer estate. |
| Teynor | Joseph | KC, p1c5, 3/10/1898 | Former Wauzeka butcher. Worked at a meat market at Waukon, IA. |
| Teynor & Schoeffer | | KC, p4c1, 1/7/1897 | Proprietor of Wauzeka Palace Meat Market. |

Genealogical Gleanings From Early Newspapers for Residents In and Near
Crawford County, Wisconsin, 1897-1902

| LAST NAME | FIRST NAME | NEWSPAPER PAGE/COLUMN MONTH/DAY/YEAR | GENEALOGICAL DATA |
|---|---|---|---|
| Teynor & Schoeffer | | KC, p1c6, 2/10/1898 | Fire destroyed Teynor & Schoeffer's Meat Market in Wauzeka. Adjoining office of C. F. Rice also destroyed. Joseph and Peter Teynor saved some articles. Household furniture of Mr. and Mrs. George Schoeffer (recently married) lost. Loss valued at $2000. Insured for $1000. |
| Thayer | Mr. | KC, p4c1, 12/9/1897 | Moved his mercantile business to La Farge. |
| Thiede | Alvena | KC, Supp., 12/12/1901 | Attended a Teacher's Institute in Crawford County in 1901. Resided in Soldiers Grove. |
| Thiede | Alvina | KC, p1c2, 4/12/1900 | Resided in Soldiers Grove. Attended the German School in Wauzeka to prepare for confirmation in the Lutheran Church. |
| Thiede | Louise | KC, p1c2, 11/17/1898 | Traveled to Courtney, ND to visit siblings. |
| Thiede & Syverson | | KC, p4c4, 1/7/1897 | Ran a lumberyard in Steuben. |
| Thill | J. J. | KC, p1c6, 7/29/1897 | Resided in De Soto. Worked as a barber. "Made his weekly business call to Ferryville." |
| Thomas | Fred, Mrs. | KC, p1c3, 10/23/1902 | Went to La Crosse to have a skin cancer removed from her face. Husband operated a cheese and butter plant in village of Steuben. |
| Thomas | O. B. | KC, p1c6, 1/18/1900 | Advertised legal services. Attorney based in Prairie du Chien. |
| Thomas | O. B. | KC, Supp. 10/27/1898 | Nominated by the Crawford County Republican Party for the office of Representative to Congress (news item not clear which office he seeks!). Oldest member of the Bar in Crawford County. Practiced law here for 41 years. Born in Bennington, VT on Aug. 21, 1832. Moved to Prairie du Chien in 1836. Graduated from the National Law School of Poughkeepsie, NY in 1856 and started practicing in Crawford County in 1857. Served three terms as representative in Congress from this district. (Short bio. and character sketch provided.) |
| Thomas | Virginia, Miss | KC, p8c3, 5/26/1898 | Died May 18, 1898 in Prairie du Chien. Born Feb. 14, 1865 in Wheatling, MN. Married W. G. Thomas on April 28, 1890 in Eastman. Husband died 2 years ago in Prairie du Chien. Funeral held at St. Gabriel Catholic Church. |
| Thompson | Ambrose | KC, p5c4, 5/8/1902 | Married Mrs. Estella Vanderbilt on April 30, 1902. Bride from Lynxville. Groom from the Town of Seneca. |
| Thompson | Ambrose | KC, p5c4, 10/25/1900 | Democratic candidate for Wisconsin Assembly. Born July 10, 1835 in Huron Co., OH. Moved to Town of Clayton, Crawford Co. in 1855. Moved to Seneca in 1865. Helped organize the Crawford Co. Agricultural Society and became its first president. Elected to the Assembly in 1890. Portrait printed in newspaper. |
| Thompson | Bert | KC, p5c3, 5/1/1902 | Married Ethel Beach on April 30, 1902. Married at Christian Church in Lynxville. |
| Thompson | boy | KC, p5c2, 2/18/1897 | Son born Feb. 12, 1897 to Riley Thompson of Wauzeka. |

Genealogical Gleanings From Early Newspapers for Residents In and Near
Crawford County, Wisconsin, 1897-1902

| LAST NAME | FIRST NAME | NEWSPAPER PAGE/COLUMN MONTH/DAY/YEAR | GENEALOGICAL DATA |
|---|---|---|---|
| Thompson | Edwin | KC, p1c2, 11/18/1897 | Resided in Mt. Sterling. Visited son, Riley Thompson, editor of the Kickapoo Chief. |
| Thompson | Edwin E. | KC, p1c5, 7/20/1899 | Lived in Mt. Sterling. Entertained his daughters, Mrs. H. Drake and Mrs. E. Langdon of Nebraska. (also mentioned in KC, p5c3, 8/3/1899) |
| Thompson | George | KC, p8c3, 6/10/1897 | Left for Two Harbors, MN after visiting relatives in Halls Valley. |
| Thompson | George | KC, p4c1, 3/24/1898 | Traveled from Poplar Ridge to Viola to visit his brother, Emery, who recently had one of his legs amputated. |
| Thompson | George | KC, Supp., 12/18/1902 | Crawford County Board of Supervisors allowed expenses in the Matter of George Thompson, Incorrigible. |
| Thompson | Ica | KC, p1c5, 11/18/1897 | From Seneca. Taught school in Bell Center. |
| Thompson | Ica | KC, p1c5, 2/9/1899 | Taught school in the Town of Clayton in 1899. E. E. Brindley, Crawford County Superintendent of Schools published a comprehensive list of all teachers in the county. |
| Thompson | Ica (or Ida?) | KC, p1c3, 9/7/1899 | Married James Kane of Gays Mills on Sept. 5, 1899. Bride was a teacher. |
| Thompson | J. H. | KC, p1c6, 5/19/1898 | Issue of Fact for Court to be heard in the May term of the Crawford County Circuit Court. J. M. Dowling vs. J. L. Courtney and J. H. Thompson. |
| Thompson | James | KC, Supp., 12/20/1900 | Crawford Co. Board of Supervisors approved payment of expenses in the matter of State vs. James Thompson. |
| Thompson | James H. | KC, p1c6, 11/4/1897 | Issue of fact for jury to be heard at the November term of the Circuit Court in Crawford County. Albert Holverson vs. James H. Thompson. |
| Thompson | James H. | KC, p1c6, 6/2/1898 | In Crawford County Circuit Court, Albert Holverson vs. James H. Thompson; verdict for plaintiff; $35 allowed Holverson. |
| Thompson | James H. | KC, p1c5, 6/1/1899 | The May term of the Crawford County Circuit Court closed. In the case James H. Thompson vs. George W. Kast, judgement for plaintiffs. |
| Thompson | Martha, Mrs. | KC, p1c4, 12/22/1898 | Died Dec. 19, 1898 in Seneca. Wife of Ambrose Thompson. Survived by husband and children: George of Two Harbors, MN; Mrs. Jessie Langdon of Haney, Mrs. Lucy Pickett of Hurlburt, Mrs. Sadie Umbeck of Soldiers Grove and Charles of Seneca. |
| Thompson | Mary | KC, Supp., 12/12/1901 | Attended a Teacher's Institute in Crawford County in 1901. Resided in Ferryville. |
| Thompson | Miss | KC, p5c4, 7/27/1899 | Died June 8, 1899. Born Aug. 23, 1882 to Agrim Thompson. Buried in Utica Lutheran Church Cemetery. |
| Thompson | Ole | KC, p1c6, 4/7/1898 | Elected Supervisor for the Town of Utica. |
| Thompson | Ole | KC, p1c6, 4/7/1898 | Elected Clerk for the Village of Soldiers Grove. |
| Thompson | Riley | KC, p1c1, 1/7/1897 | Published the *Kickapoo Chief* in Wauzeka, WI. |
| Thompson | Soren S. | KC, Supp., 12/12/1901 | Crawford Co. Board of Supervisors approved payments in the Matter of Soren S. Thompson, Insane. |

Genealogical Gleanings From Early Newspapers for Residents In and Near
Crawford County, Wisconsin, 1897-1902

| LAST NAME | FIRST NAME | NEWSPAPER PAGE/COLUMN MONTH/DAY/YEAR | GENEALOGICAL DATA |
|---|---|---|---|
| Thompson | Sorren | KC, p1c4, 10/24/1901 | Resided in Soldiers Grove. Found insane and sent to a hospital in Mendota. |
| Thompson | T. T., Mr. & Mrs. | KC, p1c4, 4/22/1897 | Resided in Ferryville. Celebrated their crystal wedding anniversary last Saturday. |
| Thompson | W. H. | KC, p1c2, 3/1/1900 | Lived in Wauzeka. Purchased property in Viola, WI. |
| Thompson & Kane | | KC, p8c5, 1/18/1900 | Proprietors of the Gays Mills Livery. |
| Thomson | Ambrose | KC, p5c4, 9/5/1901 | Served as President at the Seneca Fair. |
| Thomson | Belle | KC, p1c2, 4/20/1899 | Lived in Prairie du Chien. Taught vocal music classes in Wauzeka. |
| Thomson | C. E. | KC, p5c4, 7/26/1900 | Thomson and James Kane of Gays Mills published notice of dissolution of partnership. |
| Thomson | Charles | KC, p1c2, 4/19/1900 | Departed Gays Mills for Chippewa Co., WI to explore opportunities to invest in land. |
| Thomson | Charles E. | KC, Supp., 12/19/1901 | Operated a livery and feed barn in Gays Mills. |
| Thomson | Charles, Mrs. | KC, p5c3, 5/22/1902 | Resided in Gays Mills. Visited her parents, Mr. and Mrs. V. Ertel of Seneca. |
| Thomson | Cynthia | KC, Supp., 11/8/1900 | Recently died. Daughter of Augrim Thomson of Gays Mills. |
| Thomson | Edwin | KC, p1c4, 8/18/1898 | Hosted a family reunion in Mt. Sterling. Attended by sisters: Mrs. N. Grant of Mason City, IA; Mrs. E. Donahue of Columbus, WI; Mrs. P. Cleary of North Bristol, WI and Mrs. Edwin Thomson. First time they had all been together in 16 years. |
| Thomson | girl | KC, p1c3, 11/10/1898 | Daughter born Nov. 6, 1898 to Riley Thomson of Wauzeka. |
| Thomson | Ica | KC, p5c2, 12/2/1897 | Ica Thomson, teacher for the Belle Center Primary Department, reported the following pupils were not absent in November: Willie Whiteaker, Roy Whitaker, Mart (or Mary?) Campbell, Clyde Copas, Latie Whiteaker, Henry Rounds, Ora Campbell, Lois Masten, Hallie Huffman Frankie Pecor, Jakey Courtney, Willie Young and Maude Purrington. |
| Thomson | Ica | KC, p1c5, 11/3/1898 | Ica Thomson, teacher for the Bell Center School, reported the following pupils were not absent in October: Maud Purrington, Lettie Turk, Emma Wensel, Mable Pecor, Roy Whiteaker, Luis Wunsch, Gladys Campbell, Maurice Lewis, Hazel Purrington, Ora Campbell and Theo Rounds. |
| Thomson | Icy | KC, P5c2, 1/6/1898 | From Seneca. Taught school in Bell Center. |
| Thomson | James A. | KC, p1c6, 5/19/1898 | Issue of Fact for Jury to be heard in the May term of the Crawford County Circuit Court. Albert Holverson vs. James A. Thomson. |
| Thomson | Julia | KC, p5c3, 6/28/1900 | Daughter of Anna Thomson of Gays Mills area. Recently went blind from the effects of measles. |

Genealogical Gleanings From Early Newspapers for Residents In and Near
Crawford County, Wisconsin, 1897-1902

| LAST NAME | FIRST NAME | NEWSPAPER PAGE/COLUMN MONTH/DAY/YEAR | GENEALOGICAL DATA |
|---|---|---|---|
| Thomson | Ole | KC, p5c5, 4/5/1900 | Elected supervisor in Town of Utica. |
| Thomson | Ole R. | KC, p8c3, 8/16/1900 | Marriage license issued to Hannah Hanson and Ole R. Thomson. Both from Town of Utica. |
| Thomson | Riley | KC, p5c3, 9/12/1901 | Moved from Mt. Sterling to Petersburg. |
| Thomson | Riley | KC, p4c2, 12/26/1901 | Published an estray notice. Found a calf on his Petersburg farm. |
| Thorpe | Bert | KC, p5c3, 11/23/1899 | Resided in Tavera. Hired to install a farmer's telephone line between Excelsior and Mt. Zion, Crawford Co. |
| Thorpe | J. C., Mrs. | KC, p1c3, 1/5/1899 | Died Dec. 56, 1898 (probably supposed to be Dec. 26, 1898) in Tavera. Richland Co. Formerly of eastern Clayton. Wife of S. C. Thorpe. |
| Thyle | C. G. | KC, p1c3, 5/6/1897 | Celebrated his twentieth wedding anniversary last Saturday in Prairie du Chien. |
| Tichenor | Art | KC, p1c2, 11/28/1901 | Resided in Seneca. Leader of an orchestra. Scheduled to play at a grand ball in Muscoda. |
| Tichenor | Leslie | KC, p1c2, 10/18/1900 | Married Luna Sterling on Oct. 10, 1900 at Gays Mills. Bride from Mt. Sterling. Groom from Town of Seneca. |
| Tichenor | Leslie | KC, p5c3, 6/14/1900 | Hired to take the Federal Census in Town of Seneca and Village of Lynxville. |
| Tichenor | Leslie | KC, p5c3, 6/20/1901 | Will Sterling and Leslie Tichenor of Mt. Sterling dug into an Indian mound last week and exhumed a skeleton and some arrow heads and other Indian relics. All in fair condition. |
| Tiechenor | Hooker | KC, p5c1, 3/10/1898 | Hooker's Lynxville home and contents destroyed by fire. Fire caused by a lamp that was knocked off a table. Lamp rolled under a bed, setting it on fire. |
| Tienenor | Art | KC, p1c3, 3/7/1901 | Resided in Seneca. He expects to entertain with his "talking machine" and violin. |
| Tierney | Joe | KC, p1c2, 4/17/1902 | Resided in Town of Scott. Visited brother-in-law, Sam Elton of Bloomington, who was seriously ill. |
| Tierney | Laura | KC, p1c5, 2/9/1899 | Taught school in Bridgeport in 1899. E. E. Brindley, Crawford County Superintendent of Schools published a comprehensive list of all teachers in the county. |
| Tierney | Lauretta | KC, p5c3, 3/30/1899 | Taught school in Bridgeport. |
| Tierney | Loretta | KC, p1c2, 7/11/1901 | Died July 3, 1901 in Prairie du Chien. Born at Little Grant, WI. Moved to Prairie du Chien several years ago. Buried in Patch Grove. |

Genealogical Gleanings From Early Newspapers for Residents In and Near
Crawford County, Wisconsin, 1897-1902

| LAST NAME | FIRST NAME | NEWSPAPER PAGE/COLUMN MONTH/DAY/YEAR | GENEALOGICAL DATA |
|---|---|---|---|
| Tierney | Loretta | KC, p1c5, 11/3/1898 | Loretta Tierney, teacher for the Bridgeport School, reported the following pupils were not absent in October: Ethel Magee, Rose Burrell, Susan Fritsche and Freddie Schwartz. The following students were not tardy: Lilly Carl, Nettie Carl, Oscar Carl, Grace Briggs, Leona Garrow, Cleora Garrow, Don Magee, Eddie Bremer, Louis Oswald, Alice Oswald, Otto Oswald, Nettie Oswald, Lydia Oswald, Ashby Thomson, Maud Higgins, Pearle Oswald, Bennie Burrel, Mary Davis, Bessie Davis, Cora Davis, Carrie Bean, Amanda Bean, Bessie Fagan, Anna Fagan and Regina Fagan. |
| Tim | Jane | KC, p4c1, 6/3/1897 | Married Isaac Peterson on May 24, 1897 in Steuben. Justice J. P. McKinney officiated. (Bride and groom may be from Steuben.) |
| Timan | K. and J. | KC, Supp., 12/12/1901 | State vs. K. and J. Timan heard in Crawford Co. Court. |
| Todd | H. A. | KC, Supp., 12/20/1900 | Crawford Co. Board of Supervisors approved payment of expenses in the matter of State vs. H. A. Todd. The witnesses were John Legroo, Sarah Legroo, (Clance?) Yosnes and Ole Thompson. |
| Toepel | Martha J. | KC, p8c4, 11/16/1899 | Married Gustoph Kieser at home of Mrs. John Borgendine, the bride's sister, on Nov. 8 (or 15), 1899. Bride was daughter of Morris Toepel of Prairie du Chien. Bride from Buffalo, NY. Groom from Prairie du Chien. |
| Tomsecek | Josephine and Katie | KC, p1c5, 6/1/1899 | The May term of the Crawford County Circuit Court closed. In the case, Josephine and Katie Tomsecek vs. Travelers Insurance Co., judgement for plaintiff. |
| Toney | C. M. | KC, p1c3, 11/22/1900 | Lived in Town of Clayton. Appointed by Crawford County Board to be Superintendent of the County Poor Farm. |
| Torger | T. O. | KC, p5c5, 4/5/1900 | Elected assessor in Soldiers Grove. |
| Torgerson | boy | KC, p5c3, 7/21/1898 | Son born July 3, 1898 to Peter Torgerson of Ferryville. Weighed 14 pounds. |
| Torgerson | Emma | KC, p4c2, 11/25/1897 | Married J. Sime on Nov. 18, 1897 at Utica Lutheran Church. |
| Touble | Annie | KC, p8c1, 10/19/1899 | Married James Pelock at St. John's Bohemian Church on Wednesday (Oct. 18, 1899?). |
| Tower | Fern | KC, p1c2, 1/30/1902 | Resided in Freeman. Worked as a sawyer and lumber contractor. |
| Tower | Fred | KC, p1c2, 12/25/1902 | Built several bridges in the Town of Freeman. |
| Tower | Hannah P. | KC, Supp., 12/20/1900 | Crawford Co. Board of Supervisors approved bills related to expenses of Hannah P. Tower, insane. |
| Tower | John | KC, p8c3, 2/14/1901 | Died Feb. 11, 1901 in Ferryville. He was "one of the oldest residents in county." |
| Tower | T. W. | KC, p5c3, 11/14/1901 | Quite Ill. His son, John Tower of Nebraska, and grandson, T. W. Swinson of De Soto, came for a visit. |
| Tower | W. H. | KC, Supp., 12/12/1901 | Inquest of W. H. Tower heard in Crawford Co. Court. F. G. Andrews, physician. |

Genealogical Gleanings From Early Newspapers for Residents In and Near
Crawford County, Wisconsin, 1897-1902

| LAST NAME | FIRST NAME | NEWSPAPER PAGE/COLUMN MONTH/DAY/YEAR | GENEALOGICAL DATA |
|---|---|---|---|
| Tower | W. H. | KC, Supp., 12/20/1900 | Crawford Co. Board of Supervisors approved payment of expenses in the matter of State vs. W. H. Tower. |
| Tower | William | KC, p8c4, 10/18/1900 | Died Oct. 16, 1900 of suicide in the Town of Freeman. Aged 35 years. Wife is in an insane asylum. |
| Tower | C. P. | KC, p5c5, 4/5/1900 | Elected clerk in Town of Freeman. |
| Tower | T. W. | KC, p8c4, 12/12/1901 | Died Dec. 4, 1901 in Mt. Sterling. Aged 76 years. Survived by wife, 1 son and 3 daughters. |
| Tower | Thomas W. | KC, p1c5, 12/26/1901 | Died Dec. 4, 1901. Born April 21, 1824 in Underhill, Chittendon Co., VT. He was the son of Hon.. John H. and Phoebe Tower. Brought up in mercantile business. Studied law. Moved to Crawford Co. in 1854. Built a mill, platted village of Towerville and started a mercantile business. Married (1) ____ Maria Livingston of Vermont in 1846. She died in 1855, leaving Ida (Mrs. Ida Tooker of Sutton, NB), Eva (now dead) and DeWitt (now dead). Married (2) Anna Lester in 1856. She died in 1875, leaving Mrs. L. Tibbets and Mrs. Pearl E. Thomson of Sumner, IA and John of Sutton, NB. Married (3) Rosalie McAuley in 1879. Moved to Mt. Sterling in 1884. Served in Wisconsin Legislature in 1858. Buried in McAuley Cemetery. |
| Townsend | Grace | KC, p8c4, 8/15/1901 | Married H. W. Turner on Aug. 13, 1901. Bride from Waukon. Groom from Prairie du Chien. |
| Townsend | Theodosha, Miss | KC, p4c2, 4/7/1898 | Resided in Petersburg. (per KC, p4c2, 4/14/1898) Hired to work for Mrs. A. H. Rounds of Gays Mills. Visited relatives in Crows Hollow. |
| Trahae | Dan | KC, p1c3, 11/21/1901 | Resided in Petersburg. Bought a newspaper subscription for his sister, Mr. P. H. Maloney of Elkton, ND. |
| Trahae | Dan | KC, p1c2, 2/27/1902 | Resided in Petersburg. Sold his interest in family homestead to brother-in-law, Norm Mitchell. Planned to depart for Elkton, SD to visit sister, Mrs. P. H. Maloney. May move west. |
| Trahae | Dan | KC, p1c3, 5/8/1902 | Returned to Petersburg from Kenmore, ND, where he has made a land claim. Father very ill. |
| Trahae | Timothy | KC, p1c4, 6/5/1902 | Died May 31, 1902 in Petersburg. Aged over 80 years. Survived by wife, 3 sons and 2 daughters. Buried in Catholic Cemetery in Town of Seneca. Name also spelled Treahy. |
| Traub | G. | KC, p8c4, 11/17/1898 | Married Lizzie Portwine on Nov. 15, 1898 at St. Gabriel Church in Prairie du Chien. |
| Trautch | E. E. | KC, p1c5, 6/21/1900 | Trautch and his brother-in-law, J. L. Merville of Milwaukee, opened an Indian mound near Stuckey's Creek west of Wauzeka and found human bones. |
| Trautch | Emma, Miss | KC, p1c3, 10/19/1899 | Traveled from Milwaukee to visit father and brother (Edward) from Wauzeka and brother (Henry) of Eastman. |
| Trautch | girl | KC, p1c3, 12/21/1899 | Daughter born Saturday morning to Edward Trautch of Wauzeka. |

Genealogical Gleanings From Early Newspapers for Residents In and Near
Crawford County, Wisconsin, 1897-1902

| LAST NAME | FIRST NAME | NEWSPAPER PAGE/COLUMN MONTH/DAY/YEAR | GENEALOGICAL DATA |
|---|---|---|---|
| Trautch | Henry, Mrs. | KC, p1c4, 3/18/1897 | Died Mar. 12, 1897. Born in Damburg, Germany. Aged 63 years, 11 months and 8 days. Came to America in 1857. Resided on farm on Dutch Ridge. Survived by husband and 8 children. Buried in Dutch Ridge Cemetery. |
| Trautsch | Allie | KC, p1c2, 2/27/1902 | Died Feb. 20, 1902. Aged 3 days. One of the twin babies of E. E. Trautsch of Prairie du Chien. |
| Trautsch | Bertha | KC, p5c3, 2/6/1902 | Married Otto Kussmaul on Feb. 3, 1902. Bride daughter of Henry Trautsch. Bride and groom from Town of Eastman. |
| Trautsch | E. | KC, p1c6, 4/7/1898 | Elected Clerk for the Town of Wauzeka. |
| Trautsch | E. E. | KC, p1c2, 5/31/1900 | Resided in Wauzeka. Recently adopted an 11-year-old boy and a 6-year-old girl who were from Richland Center. |
| Trautsch | E. E. | KC, p5c5, 4/5/1900 | Elected clerk in Town of Wauzeka. |
| Trautsch | Ed, Mrs. | KC, p1c2, 9/9/1897 | Lived in Wauzeka. Entertained her brother, Lee Merril of Chicago. |
| Trautsch | Emma | KC, p1c2, 5/26/1898 | Died May 20, 1898 at Grand Grey. Sister of Mrs. Henry Reeter of Wauzeka. Buried in Dutch Ridge Cemetery. |
| Trautsch | Frederick | KC, p1c4, 12/9/1897 | Died Dec. 5, 1897 at Dutch Ridge. Aged 76 years. Brother of Henry Trautsch, Sr. and Mrs. Walters. Father of Mrs. Henry Reeter. Interred in Dutch Ridge Cemetery. |
| Trautsch | Henry | KC, p1c2, 10/4/1900 | Children came to visit him in Wauzeka for a family reunion. They were Emma Trautsch and Mrs. Theo Mahr of Milwaukee, E. E. Trautsch of Wauzeka and Mrs. Ed Weiderandres of Oelwein, Iowa. |
| Trautsch | Henry | KC, p5c4, 7/18/1901 | Lived in Wauzeka. Received a letter from his granddaughter, Bertha Wiederanders, saying that her father had been injured in a car shop accident in (Octwein?), IA. The injury was expected to be fatal. |
| Trautsch | Henry, Jr. | KC, p4c2, 9/29/1898 | Planned to sell his farm in Eastman at auction and go into business. |
| Trautsch | twin girls | KC, p1c3, 2/20/1902 | Twin daughters born Feb. 17, 1902 to E. E. Trautsch of Wauzeka. |
| Traversy | Emma | KC, p5c5, 1/18/1900 | Taught school in Crawford Co. |
| Traversy | Emma | KC, p5c4, 2/8/1900 | Taught school in Lower Shanghi Ridge District. |
| Traversy | Emma | KC, p1c5, 2/9/1899 | Taught school in Seneca in 1899. E. E. Brindley, Crawford County Superintendent of Schools published a comprehensive list of all teachers in the county. |
| Trehey | James | KC, p5c2, 11/18/1897 | Married Mrs. Lucy Nice of Boydtown on Nov. 11, 1897 at Petersburg. Groom from Bell Center. |
| Tresidder | Rev. | KC, p1c1, 1/7/1897 | Presiding elder for the Methodist Church in "this district." |
| Tressider | John | KC, p8c4, 9/30/1897 | Assignments were made at the Platteville conference of the Methodist Church. John Tresidder, presiding elder. |
| Trousdale | S. W. | KC, p8c4, 9/30/1897 | At a conference of the Methodist Church held in Platteville, S. W. Trousdale was assigned to Mineral Point. |

Genealogical Gleanings From Early Newspapers for Residents In and Near
Crawford County, Wisconsin, 1897-1902

| LAST NAME | FIRST NAME | NEWSPAPER PAGE/COLUMN MONTH/DAY/YEAR | GENEALOGICAL DATA |
|---|---|---|---|
| Trousdale | W. | KC, p1c4, 9/29/1898 | The Eau Claire conference of the Methodist Church appointed W. Trousdale, president elder, Platteville. |
| Trowbridge | W. M., Dr. | KC, p8c1, 11/4/1897 | Wedding scheduled for Nov. 7, 1897. Planned to marry Regina Lindemann. Bride from Viroqua. |
| Troy | H. W. | KC, p8c4, 9/30/1897 | At a conference of the Methodist Church held in Platteville, H. W. Troy was assigned to Platteville. |
| Troy | H. W. | KC, p1c4, 9/29/1898 | At a conference of the Methodist Church held in Eau Claire, H. W. Troy was assigned to Platteville. |
| Truesdale | Earl | KC, p1c4, 1/5/1899 | Married Bertha Gander on Jan. 1, 1899. Bride daughter of G. J. Gander of near Soldiers Grove. Groom from Viola. |
| Trum | Josephene | KC, Supp., 12/29/1898 | Crawford Co. Board of Supervisors approved Justices and Constables' expenses related to the case, State vs. Josephene Trum and Virginia Lessare. The witnesses were George Oben, Louis Lessare, C. Lessare, F. T. Hobbs, Sarah West, A. G. McKight, Geo. Coorough, D. St. Jaque, A. Steinburg, C. Delosmier and Anna Hobbs. |
| Trumbell | E. | KC, p4c3, 3/11/1897 | Resided in Bell Center. Opened a barbershop in Steuben. |
| Trumbell | Elsworth | KC, p1c2, 8/30/1900 | Married Eva Harrington in Prairie du Chien on August 26, 1900. Bride from Prairie du Chien. Groom from Boscobel. |
| Trumbell | Elsworth | KC, Supp., 12/20/1900 | Crawford Co. Board of Supervisors approved payment of expenses in the matter of State vs. Elsworth Trumbell. The witnesses were Lauretta Mathews, Dr. A. E. Dillman, A. C. Kast, J. J. Hurlbut, Fred Walker, H. Peterson, Zeb Faust and J. E. Mathews. |
| Trumble | Mr. | KC, p4c1, 10/14/1897 | Barber in Steuben. Building a new home. |
| Trumbull | Mamie | KC, Supp., 12/12/1901 | Attended a Teacher's Institute in Crawford County in 1901. Resided in Millett. |
| Tucker | boy | KC, p5c3, 10/18/1900 | Son recently born to Tom Tucker of Steuben. |
| Tucker | Hannah | KC, p5c5, 2/21/1901 | Died Feb. 16, 1901. Born in 1810 in County Cork, Ireland. She and husband, Thomas Tucker, emigrated in 1850 to Massachusetts. Moved to Town of Eastman, Crawford Co., Wisconsin in 1855. Mother of Thomas, John, James, Mary and Kate. Husband died in 1865. Thomas and James served in Civil War. Since 1892 lived with son, Thomas, in Steuben. Buried in Catholic Cemetery in Town of Seneca. |
| Tulcot | | KC, Supp., 12/18/1902 | Per Committee on County Poor, Crawford County spent $59 to remove Tulcot (Talcot?) family from Grant Co. |
| Tulley | John | KC, p8c4, 6/20/1901 | Married Kate Geider on June 19, 1901 in Lansing, Iowa. |
| Tulley | Michael J. | KC, Supp., 12/20/1900 | Crawford Co. Board of Supervisors approved payment of expenses in the matter of State vs. Michael J. Tulley. |
| Tulley | Michael, Mrs. | KC, p5c3, 8/22/1901 | Died Aug. 20, 1901 in Mt. Sterling area home. |
| Tulley | Mike | KC, p1c5, 2/9/1899 | Taught school in Utica in 1899. E. E. Brindley, Crawford County Superintendent of Schools published a comprehensive list of all teachers in the county. |

Genealogical Gleanings From Early Newspapers for Residents In and Near
Crawford County, Wisconsin, 1897-1902

| LAST NAME | FIRST NAME | NEWSPAPER PAGE/COLUMN MONTH/DAY/YEAR | GENEALOGICAL DATA |
|---|---|---|---|
| Tulley | Minnie | KC, p4c1, 5/5/1898 | Resident of Boma. Taught her 13th term of school at Towerville. |
| Turk | A. E. | KC, p1c3, 3/27/1902 | Former resident of Bell Center. Has now lived in McHenry, ND for last 4 years. Owns a half section. Plummer Purrington visited him in McHenry. Plans to move there. |
| Turk | Albert | KC, Supp., 12/29/1898 | Crawford Co. Board of Supervisors approved Justices and Constables' expenses related to the case, State vs. Albert Turk. |
| Turk | Jackson | KC, p8c2, 1/12/1899 | Received contract to carry mail between Wheatville and Boscobel. |
| Turk | Jackson, Mrs. | KC, p1c5, 1/31/1901 | Died Jan. 29, 1901 in Town of Scott. |
| Turk | Jackson, Mrs. | KC, p1c4, 1/31/1901 | Funeral held for her on Thursday in the Town of Scott. William T. Smith and wife of Prairie du Chien attended. |
| Turk | James | KC, p1c4, 4/5/1900 | Served as Town Chairman for Scott. |
| Turk | James M. | KC, p1c3, 10/30/1902 | Democratic candidate for Crawford County Register of Deeds. Born in Mercer Co., PA in 1853 and came with parents to Grant Co., WI in 1856. In November of 1856 the family settled in Town of Scott, Crawford Co. Served as Sladesburg, Town of Scott, postmaster from Aug. 24, 1880 until it was discontinued in 1887. Served on town board for 8 years. Also served on school board and county board. Portrait published. |
| Turk | Minnie | KC, p1c6, 5/5/1898 | Officer in Good Templars Lodge in Bell Center. |
| Turk | Minnie, Miss | KC, p4c3, 4/21/1898 | Baptized by Rev. Casper of the Methodist Church according to Bell Center news. |
| Turk | Rose | KC, p1c5, 1/20/1898 | Married Ernest Haynes of Gays Mills last Sunday (Jan. 16, 1898?). Bride from Bell Center. |
| Turk | S. M. | KC, Supp., 12/29/1898 | Received aid from the Crawford County Soldiers Relief Commission. Resided in Haney. |
| Turk | S. M. | KC, Supp., 12/20/1900 | Crawford Co. Soldiers Relief Comm. approved aid to S. M. Turk of Haney. |
| Turk | S., Mrs. | KC, p5c3, 3/1/1900 | Arrived from Gays Mills to visit sister, Mrs. Sylvester Phillips of Mt. Sterling. |
| Turk | Sam | KC, Supp., 12/18/1902 | Crawford County Soldiers Relief Committee provided funds to Sam Turk of Bell Center. |
| Turk | Sarah A. | KC, Supp., 12/29/1898 | Received aid from the Crawford County Soldiers Relief Commission. Resided in Haney. |
| Turk | Sarah Jane, Mrs. | KC, p1c3, 1/23/1902 | Returned to Bell Center after visiting relatives in Indiana |
| Turk | Sherman | KC, p5c2, 1/18/1900 | Proprietor of the Gays Mills Hotel. |
| Turnbull | David | KC, p1c3, 10/31/1901 | Funeral held Oct. 28, 1901 at Prairie du Chien. He was uncle of James Harris and wife of Prairie du Chien. |

Genealogical Gleanings From Early Newspapers for Residents In and Near
Crawford County, Wisconsin, 1897-1902

| LAST NAME | FIRST NAME | NEWSPAPER PAGE/COLUMN MONTH/DAY/YEAR | GENEALOGICAL DATA |
|---|---|---|---|
| Turnbull | David | KC, p3c2, 10/31/1901 | Died October 26, 1901. Born in February 1828 in Springfield, Perthshire, Scotland. Died at home in Marietta. Married Anne Balharre on Sept. 28, 1858. They left Scotland for Liverpool, England. Wife died there Feb. 1, 1883. In 1887 he and family moved to U.S. and settled on Harris Ridge in Town of Marietta. He was the father of Belle (Mrs. T. Day) and Nellie (Mrs. G. W. Douse). He was the brother of James Turnbull and Mrs. A. G. Campbell. |
| Turner | H. W. | KC, p8c4, 8/15/1901 | Married Grace Townsend on Aug. 13, 1901. Bride from Waukon. Groom from Prairie du Chien. |
| Turner | Sampson | KC, p5c1, 6/17/1897 | Arrived from Towerville to visit daughter, Mrs. Fred Lathrop of Wauzeka. |
| Turner | George | KC, p8c1, 8/17/1899 | Ed Hawthorne and George Turner were jailed for stealing from Morrison's store in Prairie du Chien. They picked the jail lock and escaped. It was believed they swam the river into Iowa. |
| Twining | B. H. | KC, p4c5, 1/18/1900 | Successor to Riley Thompson. Advertised real estate, insurance and loan services in Gays Mills. |
| Twining | B. H. | KC, p4c5, 12/14/1899 | Advertised that he was the successor to Riley Thompson's business. He had money to loan on real estate at 6 percent. |
| Twining | B. H. | KC, p5c3, 1/12/1899 | Elected to be an officer for the Modern Woodman Association (MWA) in Gays Mills. |
| Twining | B. H., Mrs. | KC, p5c2, 1/28/1897 | Resided in Gays Mills. Visited the "old home" in Wyalusing. |
| Twining | Ben | KC, p5c1, 11/8/1900 | Lived in Gays Mills. Went north on a hunting trip. Planned to visit R. W. Abby, Jr. at his home near Bruce, Chippewa Co. |
| Twining | Cora | KC, p4c1, 6/2/1898 | Cora Twining, Maggie Lynch, Mae Bowe, Arthur Finley, Bessie Cron, Otto Moore, Willie Garvey and Maggie Layd graduated from the Seneca schools. |
| Twining | D. M. | KC, p1c2, 10/5/1899 | D. M. Twining & Son of Gays Mills advertised the sale of shingles. |
| Twining | girl | KC, p4c3, 3/24/1898 | Daughter born Mar. 22, 1898 to B. H. Twining of Gays Mills. |
| Twining | Katie | KC, p5c3, 8/9/1900 | Infant daughter of Robert Twining, Jr. of Gays Mills. Died Monday. |
| Twining | Mae, Mrs. | KC, p1c2, 12/26/1901 | Arrived from Great Falls, MT to visit relatives in Gays Mills and parents in Wyalusing. |
| Twining | R. H. | KC, p1c2, 4/19/1900 | Departed Gays Mills for Chippewa Co., WI to explore opportunities to invest in land. |
| Tyron | Cyrus | KC, p8c3, 10/28/1897 | Died last week in Owatoona, MN. Formerly from Prairie du Chien. |
| Tystad | Joseph O. | KC, Supp., 12/12/1901 | State vs. Joseph O. Tystad heard in Crawford Co. Court. W. Davenport, Justice. C. P. Tower Justice. Witnesses were Thomas W. Elch, _. T. Sime, Ed Kenefic, Henry Henderson, _ Ames, _ance Knutson, Peter Knutson, Joseph Bates, George Davenport. W. H. Davenport, books and papers. |

Genealogical Gleanings From Early Newspapers for Residents In and Near
Crawford County, Wisconsin, 1897-1902

| LAST NAME | FIRST NAME | NEWSPAPER PAGE/COLUMN MONTH/DAY/YEAR | GENEALOGICAL DATA |
|---|---|---|---|
| Udelhofen | Matt | KC, p5c3, 7/22/1897 | Age 17. Struck by lightning and instantly killed on July 9, 1897 at his home in Town of Waterloo, Grant Co. He and a brother went into a log barn that was entirely destroyed by fire. |
| Uher | Frank | KC, Supp., 12/18/1902 | Crawford County Board of Supervisors allowed expenses in the Matter of Frank Uher, Insane. |
| Umbach | Francis | KC, p1c5, 2/9/1899 | Taught school in Scott in 1899. E. E. Brindley, Crawford County Superintendent of Schools published a comprehensive list of all teachers in the county. |
| Umback | F. | KC, Supp., 12/12/1901 | Attended a Teacher's Institute in Crawford County in 1901. Resided in Prairie du Chien. |
| Umback | Francis | KC, p8c3, 9/5/1901 | Recently married Florence Mitchell. Bride daughter of Charles Mitchell of Prairie du Chien. |
| Umbeck | Francis | KC, p1c4, 12/15/1898 | Taught school at Lawrence District per Scott news items. |
| Umbrora | Mrs. | KC, p4c3, 4/28/1898 | Died last Tuesday in Town of Eastman. Survived by husband and 2 sons. Youngest son was 5 years old. |
| Updike | Aimison | KC, Supp., 12/12/1901 | Received funds from the Crawford Co. Soldiers Relief Commission. Resided in Haney. |
| Updike | Charles | KC, p1c3, 10/25/1900 | Advertised an auction sale to be held at his home in Wauzeka. |
| Updike | George | KC, p4c3, 12/8/1898 | Married Emma Smith of Seneca on Dec. 4, 1898. Groom from Haney. John Lowe, J.P. officiated. |
| Updyke | Charles | KC, p5c4, 1/25/1900 | Lived in Grant Co. Received a contract to haul mail between Wauzeka and Gays Mills. |
| Updyke | Charles | KC, p5c3, 4/3/1902 | Resided in Wauzeka. Younger brother recently died in Barnum. |
| Updyke | Lillie May | KC, p1c3, 9/22/1898 | Married Charles E. Smith of (Seneca?) on Sept. 11, 1898 in Seneca. Bride from Barnum. This was a double wedding with Rosa Farris and Marcus D. Smith. |
| Upholm | Peter | KC, p4c4, 5/2/1901 | Left Soldiers Grove for a trip to Norway, their native land. Andrew Lee, Peter Upholm, Elias Johnson and Christ Scoggen. |
| Uphome | Herman, Mrs. | KC, p5c3, 10/4/1900 | Died last week at home in Pine Knob. |
| Uttre (Yttri) | Peter O. | KC, p1c6, 5/19/1898 | Issue of Fact for Jury to be heard in the May term of the Crawford County Circuit Court. George E. Konklin vs. Peter O. Uttre (Yttri?). |
| Vainhouse | Mr. | KC, p5c3, 9/25/1902 | Recently died at Hot Springs. Buried at the Lutheran Cemetery in Ferryville. |
| Valacity | Joe | KC, p8c4, 9/12/1901 | Married Stasia Chabela at St. Johns Church on Monday (Sept. 7, 1901?) and left for Chicago. |
| Valley | Dan | KC, p8c4, 11/10/1898 | Returned to Prairie du Chien from the Klondike. Left his outfit with companion, Mike McDermott. |
| Valley | Emery | KC, p8c3, 7/4/1901 | Married Mary La Bonne on July 2, 1901 at St. Gabriel's Catholic Church in Prairie du Chien. |
| Valley | Felix | KC, Supp., 4/24/1902 | Married Miss St. Jacque on April 23, 1902 at St. Gabriel's Catholic Church in Prairie du Chien. |

Genealogical Gleanings From Early Newspapers for Residents In and Near Crawford County, Wisconsin, 1897-1902

| LAST NAME | FIRST NAME | NEWSPAPER PAGE/COLUMN MONTH/DAY/YEAR | GENEALOGICAL DATA |
|---|---|---|---|
| Valley | Felix | KC, Supp., 4/24/1902 | Married Miss St. Jacque on Wednesday at St. Gabriel's Catholic Church in Prairie du Chien. |
| Valley | Felix, Mrs. | KC, p8c2, 12/22/1898 | Died Dec. 15, 1898 at age 44 in Frenchtown (Prairie du Chien. Survived by husband, 6 sons and 2 daughters. |
| Valley | girl | KC, p5c4, 12/14/1899 | Daughter recently born to Eugene Valley of Lynxville. |
| Valley | Isabelle | KC, Supp., 12/12/1901 | Attended a Teacher's Institute in Crawford County in 1901. Resided in Prairie du Chien. |
| Valley | twin girls | KC, p5c2, 11/3/1898 | Twin daughters recently born to Albert Valley of Lowertown (Prairie du Chien. |
| Van Allen | Charles, Mrs. | KC, p5c3, 8/16/1900 | Arrived from Helena, MT to visit relatives in Steuben. |
| Van Allen | J. W. | KC, p4c1, 2/4/1897 | Gave a speech on beekeeping to the Farmer's Institute at Bell Center. Speech was published. |
| Van Allen | J. W. | KC, p1c2, 11/24/1898 | Sold his farm in Haney to Fred Hammerly. Will probably move to a town and manufacture his "Automatic Honey Extractor." |
| Van Allen | J. W. | KC, p1c5, 6/1/1899 | The May term of the Crawford County Circuit Court closed. The case W. E. Lathrop vs. J. W. Van Allen was continued. |
| Van Allen | J. W. | KC, p8c3, 11/16/1899 | In the case W. E. Lathrop vs. J. W. Van Allen, verdict for the defendant. The case was heard at the November term of the Crawford County Circuit Court. |
| Van Horn | Cora | KC, p5c4, 6/28/1900 | Recently graduated from the Barnum village school. |
| Van Horn | Cora | KC, Supp., 12/12/1901 | Attended a Teacher's Institute in Crawford County in 1901. Resided in Barnum. |
| Van Horn | W. E. | KC, p1c4, 5/31/1900 | Resided in Barnum. Postmaster and proprietor of a general store. |
| Van Horn | W. E. | KC, p5c2, 7/28/1898 | Served as the Barnum postmaster. |
| Van Natta | girl | KC, p1c3, 2/16/1899 | Daughter born Feb. 13, 1899 to Harvey Van Natta in Boydtown. |
| Vance | Anna | KC, Supp., 12/12/1901 | Anna Vance of Tavera attended the summer Teacher's Institute in Soldiers Grove. |
| Vance | Anna | KC, Supp., 12/12/1901 | Attended a Teacher's Institute in Crawford County in 1901. Resided in Tavera. |
| Vance | Perry | KC, Supp., 12/20/1900 | Crawford Co. Board of Supervisors approved payment of expenses in the matter of State vs. Perry Vance. |
| Vanderbilt | (Wilford?) | KC, Supp., 12/29/1898 | Crawford Co. Board of Supervisors approved Justices and Constables' expenses related to the case, State vs. (Wilford?) Vanderbilt. |
| Vanderbilt | Blanche | KC, p4c1, 11/11/1897 | Married Will Otman of Eastman on Nov. 6, 1897 at Prairie du Chien. Bride from Lynxville. |
| Vanderbilt | child | KC, p5c3, 4/12/1900 | Youngest child of Claud Vanderbilt died Friday in Lynxville. |
| Vanderbilt | E., Mrs. | KC, p4c1, 5/20/1897 | Rented the hotel property of Mr. Huard in Lynxville. |

Genealogical Gleanings From Early Newspapers for Residents In and Near
Crawford County, Wisconsin, 1897-1902

| LAST NAME | FIRST NAME | NEWSPAPER PAGE/COLUMN MONTH/DAY/YEAR | GENEALOGICAL DATA |
|---|---|---|---|
| Vanderbilt | Estella | KC, p5c3, 5/20/1897 | Issues of fact for jury to be heard in the May term of the Crawford County Court. Estella Vanderbilt and Welhametta Mansfield, her guardian vs. G. Newton. |
| Vanderbilt | Estella, Mrs. | KC, p5c4, 5/8/1902 | Married Ambrose Thompson on April 30, 1902. Bride from Lynxville. Groom from the Town of Seneca. |
| Vanderbilt | Estella, Mrs. | KC, p5c3, 3/8/1900 | Home in Lynxville destroyed by fire. |
| Vanderbilt | J., Mrs. | KC, p5c3, 2/14/1901 | Died Feb. 7, 1901 in Lynxville. Nee Prince. Survived by husband; daughters Mrs. T. Bright and Mrs. H. Gifford; brother, C. Prince and sister, Mrs. D. Haskell. |
| Vanderbilt | John | KC, p1c5, 4/13/1899 | Fire destroyed the John Vanderbilt & Co. Building, Davidson's livery barn and T. C. Bright's home and store in Lynxville. The fire later reached the A. E. Wolcott and W. A. Allen home, the William Huard home, the R. E. Hazen home and saloon, the T. C. Bright warehouse and the Schumann & Menges ice house. |
| Vanderbilt | John | KC, Supp., 12/12/1901 | Appeared before a Committee of the Crawford County Board and reimbursed the County for care provided to an insane person. |
| Vanderbilt | Wilford | KC, Supp., 12/29/1898 | Crawford Co. Board of Supervisors approved Justices and Constables' expenses related to the case, State vs. Wilford Vanderbilt. |
| Vanderbilt | Wilfred | KC, p1c6, 5/19/1898 | Criminal case to be heard in the May term of the Crawford County Circuit Court. State of Wisconsin vs. Wilfred Vanderbilt, adultery. |
| Vanderbilt | | KC, p5c4, 3/1/1900 | Family lived in Lynxville. Received a legacy from a sister of John Vanderbilt. Mrs. A. E. Wolcott, niece of deceased, will also receive a share. |
| Vanderbilt and Sappington | Madams | KC, p8c4, 1/14/1897 | Hotel firm partnership in Lynxville. Dissolved. Mrs. Vanderbilt planned to continue the business. |
| Vanderport | Scott | KC, p1c3, 9/18/1902 | Married Jennie Stolp Sept. 2, 1902 at Bell Center. Bride from Mt. Sterling. Groom from Petersburg. |
| Vanwormer | Ester, Mrs. | KC, p5c4, 4/10/1902 | Died April 4, 1902 at home of daughter, Mrs. Walter Cooper. Aged 72 years. Moved to Lynxville in 1853. Funeral held at Lynxville Christian Church. |
| Vanworner | E. J. | KC, Supp., 12/29/1898 | Received aid from the Crawford County Soldiers Relief Commission. Resided in Lynxville. |
| Varo | Louis | KC, p8c1, 4/21/1898 | Married Anna Kaiser on April 12, 1898. Bride was daughter of Louis Kaiser of Prairie du Chien. Groom from Eastman. |
| Varrell | John | KC, p5c3, 5/20/1897 | Issues of fact for jury to be heard in the May term of the Crawford County Court. Elisha Hughbanks vs. John Varrell. |
| Vauek | T., Mrs. | KC, p8c3, 11/22/1900 | Married Mike Pelok on Nov. 19, 1900. Bride and groom from Prairie du Chien. |
| Vaughan | boy | KC, p1c2, 1/2/1902 | Son born Dec. 26, 1902 to Mrs. Orlo P. Vaughan at Forman, ND. |

Genealogical Gleanings From Early Newspapers for Residents In and Near
Crawford County, Wisconsin, 1897-1902

| LAST NAME | FIRST NAME | NEWSPAPER PAGE/COLUMN MONTH/DAY/YEAR | GENEALOGICAL DATA |
|---|---|---|---|
| Vaughan | Florence C. | KC, p1c5, 8/21/1902 | Married William N. Stell on Aug. 19, 1902 in Platteville. Bride and groom were teachers in Wauzeka schools. Bride, daughter of O. P. Vaughan of Wauzeka. Groom from Platteville. |
| Vaughan | Floy | KC, p1c2, 3/13/1902 | Resided in Wauzeka. Attended teachers meeting in Steuben. |
| Vaughan | Floy | KC, p1c3, 7/28/1898 | From Wauzeka. Hired to teach at the school in Barnum. |
| Vaughan | girl | KC, p1c2, 7/3/1902 | Daughter born last Thursday to Roy Vaughan of Wauzeka. |
| Vaughan | Harry | KC, p1c4, 1/16/1902 | Son of L. Vaughan of Jasper, MN. Visited relatives in Wauzeka. |
| Vaughan | Lulu | KC, p1c4, 11/20/1902 | Taught school at the Milwaukee Industrial School. Has suffered with typhoid fever for the last 2 months. Returned to Wauzeka with her nurse. Very emaciated. |
| Vaughan | Lulu | KC, p1c5, 11/18/1897 | Installed as an officer at the International Order of Good Templars (I.O.G.T.) Lodge in Wauzeka. |
| Vaughan | Lulu and Gracie | KC, p1c3, 4/5/1900 | Returned to Wauzeka from Platteville Normal School. |
| Vaughan | O. P. | KC, p1c2, 9/15/1898 | Celebrated 50th birthday on Sept. 11, 1898 at home in Wauzeka. |
| Vaughan | O. P. | KC, p8c5, 1/18/1900 | Manager of the Wauzeka Lumber Co. |
| Vaughan | O. P. | KC, p1c6, 4/7/1898 | Elected Supervisor for the Village of Wauzeka. |
| Vaughan | O. P. | KC, p1c3, 1/25/1900 | Featured in an article on Wauzeka's business concerns. Manager of the Wauzeka Lumber Co. Manufactures hardwood and pine lumber. Sells Cooper wagons, buggies and carriages. |
| Vaughan | O. P. | KC, p5c5, 4/5/1900 | Elected village supervisor in Wauzeka. |
| Vaughan | O. P. | KC, Supp., 12/20/1900 | Represented Village of Wauzeka on the Crawford Co. Board of Supervisors in 1900. |
| Vaughan | Orla | KC, p1c4, 5/12/1898 | Son of O. P. Vaughan of Wauzeka. Enlisted in Washington State Militia in Tacoma. Expected to be shipped to the Philippines. |
| Vaughan | Orlando Phineas | KC, p1c4, 7/4/1901 | Died June 23, 1901 in Wardner, ID. Born June 26, 1874 in Wauzeka. Married March 28, 1901 to Lydia Styenhke of Cayuga, ND at Spokane, WA. Died in a mine accident. Survived by wife, father, mother, 5 sisters and 2 brothers. |
| Vaughan | Orlo | KC, p1c5, 6/27/1901 | Recently died in a mine accident in Wardner, ID. He was son of O. P. Vaughan. Married Mar. 26, 1901 in Cayuga, ND. He was the nephew of Mrs. Charles French and cousin of Mrs. E. Wayne (daughter of Mrs. French). |
| Vaughan | Ray | KC, p8c2, 9/28/1899 | Married May Beaumeister of Boscobel on Sept. 28, 1899 in Boscobel. Groom son of O. P. Vaughan of Wauzeka (per 10/5/1899 issue, p1c3). |

Genealogical Gleanings From Early Newspapers for Residents In and Near
Crawford County, Wisconsin, 1897-1902

| LAST NAME | FIRST NAME | NEWSPAPER PAGE/COLUMN MONTH/DAY/YEAR | GENEALOGICAL DATA |
|---|---|---|---|
| Vaughan | Sadie | KC, p4c2, 11/7/1901 | Resided in Wauzeka. Wrote an essay on Abraham Lincoln. Printed in newspaper. Took first place at the Gays Mills Fair (KC, p1c2, 11/14/1901). |
| Vaughan | W. A. | KC, p1c2, 12/7/1900 | Celebrated 25th wedding anniversary on Thanksgiving (Nov. 30, 1899?). |
| Vaughan | W. A. | KC, p5c5, 1/18/1900 | Advertised his clothing store in Wauzeka. |
| Vaughan | W. A. | KC, p1c2, 8/16/1900 | Resided in Wauzeka. Listed as a victim of malaria. |
| Vaughan | W. A. | KC, p1c3, 2/10/1898 | W. A. Vaughan and P. J. Bush were involved in a garnishment suit in Wauzeka before Justice Peacock. |
| Vaughan | W. A. | KC, p1c3, 1/25/1900 | Featured in an article on Wauzeka's business concerns. Operated a general merchandise store. Article described his character. |
| Vaughan | W. A. | KC, p5c5, 4/5/1900 | Elected village trustee in Wauzeka. |
| Vaughan | W. I. | KC, p1c2, 12/22/1898 | A.K.A. "Cappie." Replaced D. R. Lawrence as station agent at Petersburg. Lawrence resigned. |
| Vaughan | girl | KC, p1c4, 2/7/1901 | Daughter was recently born to Roy Vaughan of Wauzeka. |
| Vaughan | Grace | KC, p1c3, 4/11/1901 | Student at Platteville Normal School. Native of Wauzeka. |
| Vaughan | O. P. | KC, p4c2, 6/13/1901 | Received a letter from his son, Orlo, who was working in the Idaho silver mines. Son paid $2.50 a day. Willie Beier and Adolph Sanger, who had gone west with him, recently quit the mines and now work in the timber. |
| Vaughan | Walter | KC, p1c4, 1/24/1901 | Operated a clothing store in La Farge for the last 2 years. Shipped all his goods to Ladysmith to open a store in that location. |
| Vaughn | A. C. | KC, p8c4, 9/30/1897 | At a conference of the Methodist Church held in Platteville, A. C. Vaughn was assigned to Rewey, Wisconsin. |
| Vaughn | A. C. | KC, p1c4, 9/29/1898 | At a conference of the Methodist Church held in Eau Claire, A. C. Vaughn was assigned to Argyle, Wisconsin. |
| Vaughn | W. A. | KC, p1c6, 4/7/1898 | Elected President for the Village of Wauzeka. |
| Vavra | Tom | KC, Supp., 12/20/1900 | Crawford Co. Board of Supervisors approved payment of expenses in the matter of State vs. Tom Vavra. |
| Vavruska | Christena | KC, p4c2, 6/17/1897 | Arrived from Chicago to spend summer with parents in Town of Eastman. |
| Veglahn | Herman | KC, p5c1, 7/22/1897 | Died last Friday after being thrown from a wagon. Lived about 6 miles south of Genoa. |
| Velt | Mary | KC, p5c3, 5/20/1897 | Issues of fact for jury to be heard in the May term of the Crawford County Court. Mary Velt vs. James Fischeretal. |
| Vero | Cora | KC, p8c4, 1/30/1902 | Married Fred Campbell on Jan. 29, 1902. Bride sister of Eda Vero. Groom brother of Rob Campbell. Included in Prairie du Chien news items. |

Genealogical Gleanings From Early Newspapers for Residents In and Near
Crawford County, Wisconsin, 1897-1902

| LAST NAME | FIRST NAME | NEWSPAPER PAGE/COLUMN MONTH/DAY/YEAR | GENEALOGICAL DATA |
|---|---|---|---|
| Viele | L. F. S., Major | KC, p8c4, 2/15/1900 | Died Feb. 10, 1900 in Prairie du Chien. Born in Seneca Falls, NY about 71 years ago. He was the son of Stephen A. Viele and Caroline Mary Lum. Moved to Boscobel in 1862 and later that year moved to Prairie du Chien. He was a lawyer. |
| Viele | L. F. S. | KC, p1c1, 1/18/1900 | Advertised legal services. Attorney based in Prairie du Chien. |
| Viet | Mary | KC, p1c6, 11/4/1897 | Issue of fact for court to be heard at the November term of the Circuit Court in Crawford County. Mary Viet vs. James Fisher. |
| Viktora | M. J. | KC, p5c4, 5/29/1902 | The case M. J. Viktora vs. Olive T. Weldy et al was heard at the May term of the Crawford County Circuit Court. Case Continued. |
| Vilieman | George | KC, Supp., 12/20/1900 | Crawford Co. Soldiers Relief Comm. approved aid to George Vilieman of Prairie du Chien. |
| Vodicka | Frank | KC, p5c3, 10/4/1900 | Purchased hotel in Eastman owned by S. Hazen, Jr. for $2300. |
| Voght | Dietrich, Mrs. | KC, p1c5, 7/3/1902 | Died July 1, 1902 at Steuben. She was sister of John Lewig of Wauzeka and niece of Carl Lewig, Sr. Survived by husband and 2 children. Funeral held at Lutheran Church. |
| Vollmer | D. | KC, p4c5, 1/7/1897 | Ran a hardware store in Wauzeka. |
| Vollmer | D. | KC, p1c3, 3/17/1898 | Planned to relocate family to Grand Junction, CO. Mrs. Vollmer visited friends at her former home in Bridgeport before leaving for new home, per KC, p1c2, 3/31/1898. |
| Vollmer | D. | KC, p1c6, 6/2/1898 | In Crawford County Circuit Court, Sarah Ann Lawrence vs. D. Vollmer and Emily Dunbar vs. D. Vollmer. Both cases were decided by one trial as practically the same testimony was to decide both cases. Verdict for defendant. |
| Vollmer | Daniel | KC, p1c6, 5/19/1898 | Issue of Fact for Jury to be heard in the May term of the Crawford County Circuit Court. Sarah Ann Lawrence vs. Daniel Vollmer. |
| Vollmer | Daniel | KC, p1c6, 5/19/1898 | Issue of Fact for Jury to be heard in the May term of the Crawford County Circuit Court. Emily Dunbar vs. Daniel Vollmer. |
| Vollmer | John | KC, p5c3, 5/4/1899 | Died April 29, 1899 in Soldiers Grove. Civil War veteran. |
| Volmer | D., Mrs. | KC, p1c3, 7/5/1900 | Arrived from Grand Junction, CO to visit friends in Wauzeka. |
| Volmer | Joseph | KC, Supp., 12/29/1898 | Crawford Co. Board of Supervisors approved Justices and Constables' expenses related to the case, State vs. Joseph Volmer. The witnesses were Emma Volmer, Albert Volmer, Mrs. Dora Pugh, Mrs. Hattie Sands, Mrs. Amenda Hobbs, Mrs. Rebbeca Hill, Miss Jane Hill, Mrs. Adeline Freeman, James Dinsdale and J. F. Brown. |
| Volmer | N. | KC, Supp., 12/12/1901 | Received money from the Crawford Co. Soldiers Relief Commission. Resided in Soldiers Grove. |
| Volmer | Nora | KC, Supp., 12/20/1900 | Crawford Co. Soldiers Relief Comm. approved aid to Nora Volmer of Soldiers Grove. |

Genealogical Gleanings From Early Newspapers for Residents In and Near
Crawford County, Wisconsin, 1897-1902

| LAST NAME | FIRST NAME | NEWSPAPER PAGE/COLUMN MONTH/DAY/YEAR | GENEALOGICAL DATA |
|---|---|---|---|
| Von Bernauer | Julius, Dr. | KC, p4c1, 1/18/1900 | Advertised medical services. Practice based in Prairie du Chien. |
| Vondrak | Albert | KC, p8c1, 9/6/1900 | Married Mrs. Barbara Bauer on Sept. 2, 1900. Bride from Chicago. Groom from Prairie du Chien. |
| Voth | Fred | KC, p8c4, 11/23/1899 | Resided in Prairie du Chien area. Invented a clam-digging machine. |
| Voth | Lena | KC, p8c1, 10/28/1897 | Married John Prentice of Manistee, MI on Oct. 22, 1897. Bride from Prairie du Chien. |
| Voth | Miss | KC, p8c4, 7/4/1901 | Recently died. Aged 13 years. Daughter of Frank Voth of Prairie du Chien. |
| Wacher | Henry | KC, p8c3, 4/12/1900 | Died April 6, 1900 at Mill Coulee. Per KC, 4/26/1900 the widow and son, Casper, were going to live in Pennsylvania. |
| Wachter | Casper | KC, Supp., 10/3/1901 | Married Carrie Greisback on Sept. 25, 1901. Bride from Prairie du Chien. |
| Wachuta | Albert | KC, p1c2, 6/2/1898 | He owned the "fine Percheron stallion, Hugenot, a beautiful six year old black weighing 1850 pounds." |
| Wachuta | Joseph | KC, p8c1, 8/17/1899 | Planned to open a grocery store in Prairie du Chien. |
| Wachute | Josephine, Mrs. | KC, p1c3, 2/18/1897 | Died Feb. 16, 1897 in Prairie du Chien. Aged about 70 years. Funeral held at St. John's Bohemian Catholic Church. |
| Waddle | Fred | KC, p8c3, 6/14/1900 | Marriage license issued to Sadie McCullick of Mt. Sterling and Fred Waddle of Lynxville. |
| Waddle | Fred | KC, p5c4, 6/28/1900 | Married Sadie McCullick of Mt. Sterling on June 20, 1900. Groom from Lynxville. |
| Waddle | Fred | KC, p5c4, 3/1/1900 | Resided in Lynxville. Refused an offer of $1000 for a pearl he found in the river. |
| Waddle | Fred | KC, p5c3, 9/20/1900 | Purchased the James Dickson home in Lynxville. |
| Waddle | Fred | KC, p5c3, 8/28/1902 | Fred Black, Fred Waddle and Arthur Hopkins left Lynxville for North Dakota to take up land. |
| Waddle | Fred, Mrs. | KC, p5c4, 8/2/1900 | Planned to move into a home owned by W. Benhart in Lynxville as soon as J. Dagett family moves out. |
| Waddle | Fred, Mrs. | KC, p5c3, 6/19/1902 | Lived in Lynxville. Attended the wedding of her sister, Grace McCullock, to Tunis Nelson at Mt. Sterling last Sunday. |
| Wade | John | KC, p1c5, 6/1/1899 | The May term of the Crawford County Circuit Court closed. In the case, State of Wisconsin vs. John Wade, guilty. |
| Wagner | Albert | KC, p1c4, 4/11/1901 | Painted the Geitz home in Wauzeka. |
| Wagner | Albert | KC, p1c3, 4/25/1901 | Appointed section foreman for the Western Wisconsin Railroad at Barnum. |
| Wagner | Albert H. | KC, p1c4, 6/6/1901 | Married Louisa M. Geitz on June 4, 1901. Bride was daughter of Henry Geitz of Wauzeka. Groom from Steuben. |
| Wagner | C. F., Mrs. | KC, p1c2, 9/30/1897 | Visited the farm she grew up on. Located in Grant Co., about 4 miles below Wauzeka. Had not seen the farm for 20 years. Nee Laura Slunt. |

Genealogical Gleanings From Early Newspapers for Residents In and Near
Crawford County, Wisconsin, 1897-1902

| LAST NAME | FIRST NAME | NEWSPAPER PAGE/COLUMN MONTH/DAY/YEAR | GENEALOGICAL DATA |
|---|---|---|---|
| Wagner | Carl F. | KC, p1c4, 6/13/1901 | Died June 11, 1901 at home of son, C. G. Wagner, in Little Gran Grae. Born in Germany in 1826. Immigrated to New York in 1860 with wife and family. After 6 months, moved to Baltimore. After another 6 months he moved to Dane Co., WI. To Wauzeka in 1865. Father of C. F., J. C., H. M., Mrs. H. Mohr, Mrs. Ed. Mohr, Mrs. H. H. Walters and Mrs. Wm. Graul. Mrs. Walters died years ago. All other children survive. Wife died 13 years ago. Buried in Dutch Ridge Cemetery. |
| Wagner | Carl L. | KC, p1c2, 7/17/1902 | Died July 13, 1902 in Wauzeka. Aged 67 years. Brother of Mrs. Loomis of Prairie du Chien. |
| Wagner | Frank | KC, p5c5, 10/18/1900 | Lost house and contents to flooding of the Kickapoo River. |
| Wagner | G. A. | KC, p7c2, 7/15/1897 | Rented the Petersburg Roller Mills. |
| Wagner | girl | KC, p1c2, 6/15/1899 | Daughter recently born to Albert Wagner of Wauzeka. |
| Wagner | H. | KC, p1c3, 9/6/1900 | Delegate to the Republican convention in Gays Mills. |
| Wagner | Ivey | KC, p1c4, 6/26/1902 | Married Henry Bellrichard on June 18, 1902 in La Crosse. Bride daughter of Frank Wagner of Wauzeka. Groom brother of Albert Bellrichard of Town of Eastman. |
| Wagner | J. | KC, p1c6, 4/7/1898 | Elected Assessor for the Village of Wauzeka. |
| Wagner | John C. | KC, p1c5, 12/19/1901 | Died Dec. 14, 1901. Born at Priemen, near Berlin, Germany on Sept. 13, 1855. Moved with father to Baltimore, MD in 1860. Soon after, moved to Westport, Dane Co., WI where he stayed until Nov. 25, 1865 at which time he moved to Wauzeka. Married Matilda Geitz in April 1890. Moved to Soldiers Grove in 1891 or 1892 and back to Wauzeka in 1894 or 1895. He was survived by wife, 2 sons (10 years old and 6 years old), 2 brothers (C. F. and H. M.) and 3 sisters (Mrs. William Graul, Mrs. Hilmor Mohr and Mrs. Ed Mohr). |
| Wagner | Nellie M. | KC, p8c4, 5/31/1900 | Married Dr. W. E. Butt on May 28, 1900 at the W. H. Thompson residence. Bride from Hillsboro. Groom from La Farge. He was son of Col. C. M. Butt of Viroqua. |
| Wagner | William, Mrs. | KC, p4c4, 11/10/1898 | Mrs. William Wagner and daughters, Mary and Louise, all of Boscobel, in jail and charged with murder of a 6 day old girl born on Oct. 10th to Louise. Detailed story printed. |
| Wagner | boy | KC, p5c3, 8/17/1899 | The little son of Herman Wagner was bitten by a rattlesnake. Medical aid summoned. Recovery is hopeful. Eastman news item. |
| Wainscott | F., Mrs. | KC, p1c4, 12/27/1900 | Arrived from Muscatine, IA to visit her mother and brother in Wauzeka. Nee Popper. |
| Wainscott | Frank, Mrs. | KC, p1c3, 10/10/1901 | Lived in Winona, MN. Husband managed a button factory in Arkansas. Family was considering a permanent relocation to Arkansas. Mrs. Wainscott was a sister of G. V. Popper of Wauzeka. |

Genealogical Gleanings From Early Newspapers for Residents In and Near
Crawford County, Wisconsin, 1897-1902

| LAST NAME | FIRST NAME | NEWSPAPER PAGE/COLUMN MONTH/DAY/YEAR | GENEALOGICAL DATA |
|---|---|---|---|
| Waiters | Mrs. | KC, p1c6, 4/21/1898 | Married Fred Lortz on Apr. 14, 1898. Bride and groom from Boscobel. (Is this Walters?) |
| Walcott | Stacey | KC, p4c2, 9/2/1897 | Lynxville delegates to an International Order of Good Templars Convention in Wauzeka: Stacey Walcott, Etta Randall, Allie Searles, Emma Traversey, Mary Davidson, Perry Copsey, Harry Sutton, Mrs. N. C. Haskell and Mamie Bright. |
| Waldin | Clara | KC, Supp., 12/12/1901 | Clara Waldin of De Soto attended the summer Teacher's Institute in Soldiers Grove. |
| Waldin | Clara | KC, Supp., 12/12/1901 | Attended a Teacher's Institute in Crawford County in 1901. Resided in De Soto. |
| Waldorth | boy | KC, p8c1, 2/9/1899 | Son born last Tuesday to Louis Waldorth of Prairie du Chien. |
| Walker | Frank | KC, p1c6, 2/25/1897 | Married Emma Haddock on Feb. 17, 1897. Rev. Reichert officiated. Bride and groom were from the Town of Eastman. |
| Walker | H. Mrs. | KC, p5c3, 10/25/1900 | Entertained her aunt, Mrs. O'Hara of Nebraska. |
| Walker | Hamilton | KC, p5c4, 9/27/1900 | Mrs. F. A. Porter of Mt. Sterling and Hamilton Walker of Seneca traveled to Philadelphia to attend the funeral of their brother, Harvey Walker. (also KC, p5c3, 10/4/1900) |
| Walker | Joseph, Mrs. | KC, p1c3, 3/14/1901 | Nee Martha Syverson. Arrived from Countney, ND to visit relatives in Steuben. |
| Walker | Mary | KC, p1c3, 4/8/1897 | Died Apr. 1, 1897. Resided in Prairie du Chien. Funeral held at the Lutheran Church. Born Nov. 25, 1869. |
| Walker | Mr. | KC, p5c4, 9/27/1900 | Recently died in Philadelphia. He was the brother of H. Walker of Seneca and Mrs. F. Porter of Mt. Sterling |
| Walker | Mr. and Mrs. | KC, p5c1, 8/18/1898 | Returned to Philadelphia after a visit with a son in Seneca. |
| Walker | N. | KC, p1c5, 5/22/1902 | Resided in Boscobel. Completed a farmers telephone line from Boscobel to Wauzeka. |
| Walker | Sophia | KC, p8c4, 9/21/1901 | Married John Spuiker on Sept. 17, 1901 at Lutheran Church. Bride and groom were from Prairie du Chien. |
| Walker | John, Mrs. | KC, p1c6, 9/16/1897 | Resided in Wauzeka. Visited parents, Mr. and Mrs. E. Fisher of Eastman. |
| Wall | Frank | KC, p1c6, 4/7/1898 | Elected Chairman for the Town of Eastman. |
| Wall | Fred | KC, p5c3, 4/11/1901 | Purchased the "little Catholic Church" used many years ago in Seneca. |
| Wall | Kitty, Miss | KC, p5c4, 8/9/1900 | Departed from Eastman to visit aunt, Mrs. Gerton of La Crosse. |
| Wallace | Catharine | KC, Supp., 12/12/1901 | Crawford Co. Board of Supervisors approved payments in the Matter of Catherine Wallice, Insane. |
| Wallace | C., Mrs. | KC, Supp., 12/18/1902 | The Crawford County Board of Supervisors allowed expenses in the Matter of Mrs. C. Wallace, Insane. |
| Wallace | W. J. | KC, p5c2, 2/4/1897 | Purchased an interest in the E. W. Newton furniture store. Wauzeka news item. |
| Wallin | Arthur | KC, p5c3, 3/6/1902 | Fred Speck and Arthur Wallin of Eastman departed for Tacoma, WA where they intended to stay for some time. |

Genealogical Gleanings From Early Newspapers for Residents In and Near
Crawford County, Wisconsin, 1897-1902

| LAST NAME | FIRST NAME | NEWSPAPER PAGE/COLUMN MONTH/DAY/YEAR | GENEALOGICAL DATA |
|---|---|---|---|
| Wallin | Ed | KC, p1c5, 6/1/1899 | The May term of the Crawford County Circuit Court closed. In the case, Cornelius Cane vs. Ed Wallin and J. N. Kast, judgement against Wallin for $1. |
| Wallin | Ellen, Mrs. | KC, p5c3, 11/9/1899 | After spending the summer in Washington, returned to Eastman. |
| Wallin | Estella | KC, p5c4, 4/11/1901 | Taught school in the Hunter District School on Shanghi Ridge. |
| Wallin | Fred | KC, p1c4, 5/3/1900 | Recently died in Town of Seneca. Aged 20 years. |
| Wallin | Hattie | KC, p5c4, 6/19/1902 | Daughter of James Wallin of Eastman. Took train for Chicago to get training as a nurse. |
| Wallin | J. W. | KC, p1c5, 1/17/1901 | Spoke on the sheep industry at the Farmer's Institute held in Eastman. |
| Wallin | Oscar | KC, p5c4, 5/22/1902 | Prairie du Chien High School class of 1902. |
| Wallin | Richard | KC, p4c1, 3/31/1898 | Died Mar. 24, 1898 at 20 years, 2 months and 21 days of age. He was son of James and Elvira Wallin of Eastman. Buried in Crandall Cemetery. |
| Wallin | Richard, Mr. and Mrs. | KC, p5c3, 8/2/1900 | Both aged 81 years. Resided in Prairie du Chien. Emigrated to Eastman in 1857. Located on a farm on head of Pine Creek. Left farm 12 years ago. Mr. Wallin is a staunch Republican. Visited their son, James, of Eastman. |
| Wallin | Stella | KC, Supp., 12/12/1901 | Attended a Teacher's Institute in Crawford County in 1901. Resided in Eastman. |
| Wallin | Z. B. | KC, p5c6, 2/8/1900 | Taught school in district 11, Town of Eastman. |
| Wallin | Zena | KC, p1c5, 2/9/1899 | Taught school in Eastman in 1899. E. E. Brindley, Crawford County Superintendent of Schools published a comprehensive list of all teachers in the county. |
| Wallin | Zenas | KC, p5c4, 1/2/1902 | Resided in Eastman. Attended Normal School in Platteville. |
| Wallin | Zenas | KC, p1c3, 6/26/1902 | Returned from Platteville Normal School. Son of James Wallin of Eastman. |
| Wallin | Zenas B. | KC, p4c3, 4/25/1901 | Native of Eastman. Won First Place in the Declamatory Contest of the Freshman class at Platteville Normal School. His subject was "Each to Interpret the Law for Himself." |
| Walters | Bertha, Miss | KC, p1c3, 9/26/1901 | Native of Wauzeka. Moved to Barnesville, MN for work in mercantile business for George Montgomery, an uncle of the late George Montgomery. |
| Walters | boy | KC, p1c2, 1/9/1902 | Son born Jan. 1, 1902 to Louis Walters of Wauzeka. |
| Walters | Dora Sophia | KC, p9c4, 7/1/1897 | Nee Wagner. Died June 25, 1897. Wife of Herman Walters. Born Jan. 26, 1869 in Wauzeka. Married Nov. 6, 1869. (Birth or marriage year printed in error in newspaper.) Survived by sons Alvin and Eddie. Funeral held at Evangelical Church. |
| Walters | H. | KC, p5c2, 1/18/1900 | Proprietor of the City Dray Line in Wauzeka. |

Genealogical Gleanings From Early Newspapers for Residents In and Near
Crawford County, Wisconsin, 1897-1902

| LAST NAME | FIRST NAME | NEWSPAPER PAGE/COLUMN MONTH/DAY/YEAR | GENEALOGICAL DATA |
|---|---|---|---|
| Walters | Herman | KC, p1c2, 6/27/1901 | Set up a livery business in Wauzeka. |
| Walters | James | KC, p7c4, 1/25/1900 | Received marriage license in Crawford Co. Mary Heiden was prospective spouse. Bride-to-be from Elkander and groom-to-be from Waukon Junction. |
| Walters | Jessie | KC, p1c2, 10/28/1897 | Married Frank Mosgrove on Oct. 24, 1897. Bride and groom from La Farge. Justice Halsted of Wauzeka officiated. |
| Walters | John | KC, p5c3, 4/11/1901 | Married Margaret Welsh on April 9, 1901. Bride from (Seneca?). Groom from Minnesota. Plan to live on the Walters farm in Minnesota. |
| Walton | Andrew, Sr. | KC, p5c2, 3/31/1898 | Recently died in Marietta at home of son, Andrew, Jr. Born Feb. 21, 1808 in Providence, R.I. Survived by wife and 3 sons: Henry and Charles of Dakota and Andrew of Marietta. Belonged to United Brethren faith. Buried in Boscobel. |
| Walton | Joseph E. | KC, p4c4, 8/3/1899 | Married Emma White of Millett last Wednesday (July 26, 1899?). Groom from Town of Scott. |
| Walton | William B. | KC, p1c6, 9/23/1897 | Funeral held Sept. 17, 1897. Born in Birmingham, England in 1826. Married Sarah J. Butler at Worchestershire, England in 1851. Moved to Madison, WI in 1856. Moved to Town of Scott in 1859. Survived by 6 of 7 children. One son, William, died in 1882 in Wisconsin. |
| Waltz | Josie | KC, p5c4, 2/8/1900 | Lived in Seneca. Employed by T. Finley as a dressmaker. |
| Waltz and Dagnon | | KC, p5c4, 2/15/1900 | Operated a sawmill in Town of Seneca. |
| Wanamaker | Alma | KC, Supp., 12/12/1901 | Attended a Teacher's Institute in Crawford County in 1901. Resided in Steuben. |
| Wanamaker | baby | KC, p8c3, 6/17/1897 | Baby born June 12, 1897 to Lee Wanamaker of Steuben. |
| Wanamaker | E. L. | KC, p1c3, 11/20/1902 | E. L. Wanamaker (and son, Charlie) of Marietta spent a few days in Wauzeka working for brother, L. E. Wanamaker, on the new school building. |
| Wanamaker | Grace | KC, Supp., 12/12/1901 | Attended a Teacher's Institute in Crawford County in 1901. Resided in Boscobel. |
| Wannaker | Lee | KC, p1c4, 4/17/1902 | Resided in Steuben. Worked for the Austin Road Grader Man'fg. Co. |
| Wannamaker | boy | KC, p5c2, 4/7/1898 | Infant son of Lee Wannamaker died Mar. 25, 1898. Aged 7 months and 20 days. |
| Wannamaker | Charles E. | KC, p1c6, 4/20/1899 | Probate Court Notice published. Deceased from Marietta. Mary Wannamaker applied to administer estate. |
| Wannamaker | Charles E. | KC, p1c5, 6/8/1899 | Edgar L. Wannamaker was granted letters of administration for the estate of Charles E. Wannamaker. |
| Wannamaker | Edgar L. | KC, p5c5, 2/15/1900 | Petitioned Crawford County Probate Court to administer estate of Charles E. Wannamaker, late of Marietta. |
| Wannamaker | Lee, Mrs. | KC, p5c3, 2/1/1900 | Resided in Steuben. Visited brother, W. G. Campbell, of Soldiers Grove. |

Genealogical Gleanings From Early Newspapers for Residents In and Near
Crawford County, Wisconsin, 1897-1902

| LAST NAME | FIRST NAME | NEWSPAPER PAGE/COLUMN MONTH/DAY/YEAR | GENEALOGICAL DATA |
|---|---|---|---|
| Wannemaker | Alma | KC, p5c3, 6/20/1901 | Graduated from Steuben schools. |
| Wannemaker | Jay | KC, p1c4, 7/24/1902 | Son of Lee Wannemaker of Steuben. Broke leg while mowing. Team became unmanageable and refused to make a turn. Jay crushed by a horse. Treated by Dr. L. G. Armstrong of Boscobel. |
| Wannemaker | Lee | KC, Supp., 12/20/1900 | Represented Steuben on the Crawford Co. Board of Supervisors in 1900. |
| Ward | Alonzo | KC, p5c4, 5/29/1902 | The case James Dinsdale vs. Alonzo Ward was heard at the May term of the Crawford County Circuit Court. Judgement for defendant. |
| Ward | Frank | KC, p5c3, 6/14/1900 | Ward of Muscoda and David C. Posey of Steuben were comrades in the Mexican War. They were mustered into service in Galena, IL in 1847 and mustered out in Alton, IL in 1848. They both served in the Civil War. Posey was in Co. C, 43rd WI Regiment. Ward was a Lieut. in Co. H., 33rd WI Regiment. |
| Ward | George | KC, p1c2, 7/22/1897 | Traveled from Minneapolis to visit friends in Prairie du Chien. Previously lived in Bridgeport. |
| Ward | Hannah | KC, p1c4, 4/27/1899 | Recently married Daniel Lyons of Wauzeka at Plymouth Congregational Church parsonage in Dodgeville. Bride from Glen Haven. Groom's parents lived in Darlington. |
| Ward | Herbert | KC, p5c2, 3/3/1898 | Married Mabel Curtis last Wednesday (Feb. 23, 1898?). (Bride may be from Steuben.) Groom from Boscobel. |
| Ward | Herbert | KC, p1c4, 3/10/1898 | Married Mabel Curtis on Feb. 223, 1898. Bride from Steuben. Groom from Boscobel. The Rev. Thomas Crouch officiated. |
| Ward | Jonathan | KC, p5c1, 2/21/1898 | Resided in Boydtown. Suffered from an eye infection and swollen jaw caused by ulcerated teeth. |
| Ward | M. M. | KC, p1c3, 1/24/1901 | Announced that he was expanding the Hotel Ward in La Farge. |
| Ward | Mrs. | KC, p1c5, 2/11/1897 | Died Monday in Soldiers Grove. Survived by husband and 7 children. |
| Ward | N. M. | KC, Supp., 12/12/1901 | Received money from the Crawford Co. Soldiers Relief Commission. Resided in Soldiers Grove. |
| Ward | N. W. | KC, Supp., 12/29/1898 | Received aid from the Crawford County Soldiers Relief Commission. Resided in Soldiers Grove. |
| Ward | Tom | KC, p1c4, 12/7/1899 | Wrote a letter from the Philippines to his brothers, Mike (of ?) and John (of La Farge) Ward. It was published in the newspaper. |
| Wardell | Jennie | KC, p1c4, 12/26/1901 | Married H. D. Smith on Dec. 25, 1901. Bride and groom from Excelsior. |
| Wardell | Mrs. | KC, p5c2, 8/4/1898 | Arrived from Milwaukee to visit her sisters, Mrs. C. Lilly and Mrs. Reublin of Mt. Sterling. |
| Warner | Myrtle | KC, p5c1, 6/2/1898 | Married William Lankford on Mary 19, 1898 in De Soto. |
| Watrous | H. L. | KC, p4c2, 3/6/1902 | Sent letter from his home in Lindsey, Wood Co., WI that described the area. Published in paper. Former Crawford Co. resident. |

Genealogical Gleanings From Early Newspapers for Residents In and Near Crawford County, Wisconsin, 1897-1902

| LAST NAME | FIRST NAME | NEWSPAPER PAGE/COLUMN MONTH/DAY/YEAR | GENEALOGICAL DATA |
|---|---|---|---|
| Watrous | H. L., MD | KC, p5c5, 12/19/1901 | Published a notice asking all persons indebted to him to pay by Jan.1, 1902 or be sued. |
| Watrous | H. L., MD | KC, p5c1, 1/7/1897 | Advertised medical services. Office based in Seneca. |
| Watson | Ann | KC, Supp., 12/20/1900 | Crawford Co. Soldiers Relief Comm. approved aid to Ann Watson of Lynxville. |
| Watson | girl | KC, p5c3, 2/8/1900 | Daughter born Jan. 27, 1900 to J. Watson of Lynxville area. |
| Watson | J. | KC, p4c1, 9/2/1897 | Resided in Town of Scott. Sick with typhoid fever. |
| Watson | John | KC, p5c3, 1/24/1901 | Lived in Eastman. Worked as a mail carrier. Recently lost a horse. |
| Watson | John | KC, p4c2, 1/7/1897 | Resided in Town of Scott. Purchased a new steam saw mill. |
| Watson | John | KC, Supp., 12/20/1900 | Crawford Co. Board of Supervisors approved payment of expenses in the matter of State vs. John Watson. The witnesses were George Maney, J. W. Brockway, J. S. Davidson and G. W. Pease. |
| Watson | Julia | KC, p5c4, 3/6/1902 | Served as postmistress of Seneca. |
| Watson | Mary | KC, p8c4, 5/10/1900 | Received license to marry T. W. Sampson. Bride from Town of Scott. Groom from Soldiers Grove. |
| Watson | Ann, Mrs. | KC, Supp., 12/12/1901 | Received funds from the Crawford Co. Soldiers Relief Commission. Resided in Lynxville. |
| Watson | Jonathan | KC, p1c2, 9/9/1897 | Died Sept. 1, 1897 in Marietta of typhoid fever. |
| Watson Bros | | KC, p5c3, 9/27/1900 | Resided in Town of Scott. Traded their sawmill to James Childs for a farm. |
| Way | William | KC, Supp., 12/29/1898 | Crawford Co. Board of Supervisors approved Justices and Constables' expenses related to the case, State vs. William Way. |
| Wayne | Arthur | KC, p1c3, 4/6/1899 | "We regret to say that a number of Crawford's enterprising citizens departed for Courtney, ND Tuesday and Wednesday. Among the number were the following: Arthur Wayne and family, Lewis Wayne, Eugene Wayne, Etta and Flora Meyers, Bert Seeley, Willie Mercer, Emmett Coleman and wife, Lee Dunbar, John Harris, George Turnbull, Joe Noe, Dan Smith, John Pratt, Ezra Jenkins and wife, Frank Stearns and wife, Arthur Stearns and Will Coleman. Three freight cars were employed of the St. Paul Co. for the transportation of their horses, grain and provisions. Though we wish them success, we almost hope to see a number of them return to old Crawford before long and partake of our prosperity here. Courtney contains a large number of Crawford County people and judging from the number immigrating there it must be a very good locality." |
| Wayne | Cynthia, Mrs. | KC, p4c1, 10/7/1897 | Traveled from Boydtown to South Dakota to visit son, Frank Wayne. |

Genealogical Gleanings From Early Newspapers for Residents In and Near
Crawford County, Wisconsin, 1897-1902

| LAST NAME | FIRST NAME | NEWSPAPER PAGE/COLUMN MONTH/DAY/YEAR | GENEALOGICAL DATA |
|---|---|---|---|
| Wayne | Frank | KC, p1c2, 1/12/1899 | Resided in Boydtown. Bought a store in Wauzeka from his brother, Will. |
| Wayne | Frank | KC, p5c4, 12/14/1899 | He was building a blacksmith shop in Boydtown. |
| Wayne | Frank and wife | KC, p5c2, 11/18/1897 | Traveled from Brookings, SD to visit his parents in Boydtown. |
| Wayne | Harvey | KC, p8c4, 4/22/1897 | Son recently born to Harvey Wayne of the Barnum area. |
| Wayne | Harvey | KC, p5c4, 5/29/1902 | The case E. B. Rees vs. Harvey Wayne, Mary Wayne, Daniel Kramer and Catherine Kramer for foreclosure was heard at the May term of the Crawford County Circuit Court. Case was continued. |
| Wayne | James | KC, p6c1, 3/18/1897 | Married Julia Bacon last week. Bride and groom may have been from Town of Marietta. |
| Wayne | W. A. | KC, p1c3, 7/11/1901 | Sold Boydtown farm. Planned to travel north and west to find a new home. |
| Wayne | W. A. | KC, p1c5, 8/22/1901 | Lived in Boydtown. Bought 200 acres in Clark Co., Wisconsin. |
| Wayne | W. A. | KC, p1c2, 10/3/1901 | Lived in Boydtown. Moved to Bailey, IA to open a mercantile business. |
| Webster | Gertrude | KC, p8c4, 10/24/1901 | Married Allen Ramsey Kidd on October 15, 1901. Bride was from Prairie du Chien. Groom was from Lancaster. (They may have married in Rockville, MD.) |
| Webster | J. E. | KC, p8c4, 9/30/1897 | At a conference of the Methodist Church held in Platteville, J. E. Webster was assigned to Boscobel, WI. |
| Webster | J. E. | KC, p1c4, 9/29/1898 | At a conference of the Methodist Church held in Eau Claire, J. E. Webster was assigned to Boscobel. |
| Webster | Rev. | KC, p5c4, 7/22/1897 | Rev. Webster, from Boscobel, and Rev. Maes, of Lancaster, entertained the audience at a soldiers' reunion held in Steuben. They were Civil War veterans. Officers for the ensuing year were: J. B. Rittenhouse, Pres.; N. S. Bull, Vice Pres.; A. C. Wallin, Sec'y.; Ed Whaley, Treas.,; G. C. Wurster, Q. M.; and C. C. Chase, Commissary. |
| Week | Albert | KC, p5c3, 7/12/1900 | Parents and 2 sisters from Norway arrived to visit. Week had not seen them for 9 years. |
| Week | Albert | KC, p1c4, 9/18/1902 | Rented out his farm in Utica. Planned to move to Baldwin, St. Croix Co. to teach Norwegian. |
| Weeks | A. | KC, p5c3, 6/8/1899 | Recently married Anne Nelson. Bride was daughter of Knute Nelson (of Mt. Sterling?). |
| Weeks | boy | KC, p1c4 12/4/1902 | The 8-month-old son of Albert Weeks of Utica recently died. |
| Weeks | girl | KC, p5c4, 4/19/1900 | Daughter recently born to Albert Weeks of Mt. Sterling. |

Genealogical Gleanings From Early Newspapers for Residents In and Near
Crawford County, Wisconsin, 1897-1902

| LAST NAME | FIRST NAME | NEWSPAPER PAGE/COLUMN MONTH/DAY/YEAR | GENEALOGICAL DATA |
|---|---|---|---|
| Weighner | Adam | KC, p4c4, 7/24/1902 | Died July 16, 1902 in Wauzeka. Born April 1823 in Germany. Married in Germany. He and family moved to Wauzeka in 1860. Fathered 6 sons (2 died young) and 2 daughters. Survived by wife and the following children: Philip of Prairie du Chien; Herman of Postville, IA; Ameal of Wauzeka; Charles of Prairie du Chien; Mrs. Robert Proeter of Detroit, MI. Other daughter not mentioned. Buried in Dutch Ridge Cemetery. |
| Weigner | Fred | KC, Supp., 12/5/1901 | Left Eastman for Gays Mills to do missionary work. |
| Weigner | Mrs. | KC, p8c3, 12/29/1898 | Resided in Dubuque. Attended Thursday's funeral for her mother, Mrs. Mary Palmer, per Bell Center news items. |
| Weisenberger | Jennie | KC, p5c4, 5/22/1902 | Prairie du Chien High School class of 1902. |
| Weittenhiller | Charles | KC, p5c3, 5/20/1897 | Issue of law for court to be heard in the May term of the Crawford County Court. Charles Weittenhiller vs. Thomas McCann. |
| Welch | boy | KC, p1c3, 8/8/1901 | Son recently born to Thomas Welch of Rolling Ground. |
| Welch | Cecelia M. | KC, p1c5, 2/15/1900 | Taught school in Town of Seneca. |
| Welch | Cecilia M. | KC, p5c2, 12/2/1897 | Cecilia M. Welch, teacher for the Eastman Primary Department, reported the following pupils were not absent in November: Anthony Prochaska; Edna Ellis; Daniel Martan; Genevieve Martan; Eddie Horal; Emma Koepp; Rudolph Koepp; Louis Speck; Rosa, Mamie and Frank Vedicka; May Hazen; Willie Horal; Frank Speck; Michael Jambura; Anastatia Betscha; and Wencil and Daniel Brady. |
| Welch | Cecilia M. | KC, p1c5, 2/9/1899 | Taught school in Eastman in 1899. E. E. Brindley, Crawford County Superintendent of Schools published a comprehensive list of all teachers in the county. |
| Welch | Charles | KC, p1c3, 11/15/1900 | Operated a lumberyard in Petersburg. |
| Welch | Charles | KC, p1c5, 1/17/1901 | Spoke on the "boy and girl on the farm" (farm best place for development of good character) at the Farmer's Institute held in Eastman. |
| Welch | Eliza | KC, p5c1, 2/17/1898 | Taught school at Sand Creek in Wheatville. |
| Welch | Eliza | KC, p1c5, 2/9/1899 | Taught school in Marietta in 1899. E. E. Brindley, Crawford County Superintendent of Schools published a comprehensive list of all teachers in the county. |
| Welch | Eliza | KC, Supp., 12/12/1901 | Attended a Teacher's Institute in Crawford County in 1901. Resided in Wheatville. |
| Welch | Hazel | KC, p8c3, 9/21/1899 | Died Sept. 8, 1899. Aged 7 weeks. Daughter of F. Welch of Hurlburt, Town of Scott, WI. |

Genealogical Gleanings From Early Newspapers for Residents In and Near
Crawford County, Wisconsin, 1897-1902

| LAST NAME | FIRST NAME | NEWSPAPER PAGE/COLUMN MONTH/DAY/YEAR | GENEALOGICAL DATA |
|---|---|---|---|
| Welch | Ida J. | KC, p4c4, 7/27/1899 | Died July 6, 1899. Born Aug. 27, 1861 near Racine, WI. Moved to Crawford Co. in 1869. Married J. W. Van Allen on July 18, 1882. Six of 8 children are still alive. The oldest child was 16 and youngest was 4. Buried in Haney Cemetery. |
| Welch | John | KC, p1c2, 11/3/1898 | Ten dollars worth of stock stolen from his saloon in Petersburg. |
| Welch | Kate, Mrs. | KC, p1c6, 11/4/1897 | Resided in Wheatville. Completely recovered after being seriously ill for the last year. |
| Welch | Martin | KC, p8c3, 7/28/1898 | Planned to leave Wheatville for Courtney, ND. |
| Welch | Samuel | KC, p1c6, 6/9/1898 | Died from poisoning on June 3, 1898 at Steuben at 48 years of age. He and Ray Curtis mistook hemlock root for artichoke. |
| Welch | Samuel B. | KC, Supp., 12/29/1898 | Crawford Co. Board of Supervisors approved Justices and Constables' expenses related to the Samuel B. Welch and Ray Curtis Inquest. |
| Welch | Tessa and Eliza | KC, p1c3, 4/11/1901 | Left Wheatville for new homes in Denver, CO. (May have gone their to teach school.) |
| Welch | Thomas | KC, p8c3, 5/26/1898 | Died May 18, 1898. Aged 70 years. Survived by 4 children: Mrs. Maggie Lucas, Sadie Welch, J. Welch of Minneapolis and another son. |
| Welch | Thomas | KC, p1c2, 6/7/1900 | Arrived from Minneapolis to visit relatives in his former home of Soldiers Grove. |
| Welch | Tressa | KC, Supp., 12/12/1901 | Attended a Teacher's Institute in Crawford County in 1901. Resided in Wheatville. |
| Welch | Tressa and Eliza | KC, Supp., 12/12/1901 | Tressa and Eliza Welch of Wheatville attended the summer Teacher's Institute in Soldiers Grove. |
| Wells | George | KC, p8c3, 7/11/1901 | Married Maggie Kern on July 8, 1901. |
| Welsch | Tressie | KC, p1c5, 2/9/1899 | Taught school in Seneca in 1899. E. E. Brindley, Crawford County Superintendent of Schools published a comprehensive list of all teachers in the county. |
| Welsh | Cecelia | KC, p5c1, 9/9/1897 | Hired to teach in Eastman. From Lynxville. |
| Welsh | Cecilia | KC, Supp., 12/12/1901 | Attended a Teacher's Institute in Crawford County in 1901. Resided in Prairie du Chien. |
| Welsh | Cecilia M. | KC, p1c5, 11/3/1898 | Cecilia M. Welch, teacher for the Eastman school, reported the following pupils were not absent in October: Beatris Young, Etta Speck, Edna Ellis, Daniel Martan, Genevieve Martin, George Horal, Anna Horal, Rudolph Koepp, Louie Speck, Frank Speck, Frank Vodicka, Mamie Vodicka, Mike Jambura, Mamie Ostrander and Joe Vodicka. |
| Welsh | Jack | KC, p1c6, 11/4/1897 | Criminal issue to be heard at the November term of the Circuit Court in Crawford County. State of Wisconsin vs. Jack Welsh, burglary. |
| Welsh | Margaret | KC, p5c3, 4/11/1901 | Married John Walters on April 9, 1901. Bride from (Seneca?). Groom from Minnesota. Plan to live on the Walters farm in Minnesota. |

Genealogical Gleanings From Early Newspapers for Residents In and Near
Crawford County, Wisconsin, 1897-1902

| LAST NAME | FIRST NAME | NEWSPAPER PAGE/COLUMN MONTH/DAY/YEAR | GENEALOGICAL DATA |
|---|---|---|---|
| Welsh | Mary | KC, p1c2, 2/17/1898 | Married Valentine Ertel of Lynxville on Feb. 7, 1898. Bride from Glen Haven Township. Andrew Welsh was a cousin of bride. Maggie Welsh was bride's sister. |
| Wendt | Nicholas | KC, p1c2, 5/27/1897 | Left Prairie du Chien for a visit in Germany. Joined by a brother living in Cleveland, OH. |
| Wendt | Otto | KC, p8c4, 5/10/1900 | Pending wedding to Virginia Ducharme was announced. Bride and groom were from Prairie du Chien. |
| Wendt | Otto | KC, p8c4, 5/24/1900 | Married Virginia DuCharme on May 23, 1900. Bride and groom from Prairie du Chien. |
| Weneger | girl | KC, p1c3, 11/15/1900 | Daughter born Friday to Fred Weneger of Wauzeka. |
| Weniger | baby | KC, p5c3, 9/21/1901 | Fred Weniger's baby died Sunday in Lynxville. |
| Weniger | Dan | KC, p1c2, 6/20/1901 | Traveled from Wauzeka to Flandreau, Moody Co., ND to visit his nephew, Robert Weniger. |
| Weniger | Daniel | KC, p1c2, 8/17/1899 | Purchased a residence from his son-in-law, John Woodnal of Wauzeka, and will retire from farming. |
| Weniger | Lucy | KC, p8c3, 10/17/1901 | Married Thomas McGrath on Oct. 15, 1901. The Rev. Fr. Joerres officiated. (Bride and/or groom may have been from Prairie du Chien.) |
| Weniger | Mr. | KC, p5c4, 3/2/1899 | Resident of Mt. Sterling. Left for South America to work as a missionary. |
| Wertzel | William | KC, p8c1, 6/30/1898 | Recently died. Murdered by son-in-law in Tomah. Buried in Lowertown Cemetery. |
| West | Asa | KC, p1c2, 4/7/1898 | Estate recently settled. Mrs. B. F. Lathrop of Wauzeka and her brother, Orval West of Mondovi, Buffalo Co., WI were heirs. |
| West | Asa F. | KC, p5c3, 2/21/1898 | Crawford Co. Probate Court published announcement for a final hearing in the case of Asa F. West lately deceased. Henry Trautsch administered the estate. |
| West | H. | KC, p5c3, 4/11/1901 | Sold his 160-acre farm in Eastman to E. Thomas for $1500. |
| West | Herman | KC, p5c4, 5/9/1901 | Died May 4, 1901 at age 24 years, 2 months and 25 days. Born in Town of Eastman. Survived by father, 2 brothers and 3 sisters. He was the brother of Mrs. George Bonner of Chicago and Charles West of Chicago. Buried in Crandall Cemetery. |
| West | Irene E. | KC, p8c3, 6/28/1900 | Married Rodell Sullivan on June 20, 1900 in Monroe, WI. Groom was a former resident of the Town of Eastman. |
| West | J. O. | KC, Supp., 12/20/1900 | Crawford Co. Board of Supervisors approved payment of expenses in the matter of State vs. J. O. West. |
| West | James Orville | KC, p1c6, 11/4/1897 | Issue of fact for court to be heard at the November term of the Circuit Court in Crawford County. William F. West vs. James Orville West. |
| West | Mrs. | KC, p5c1, 8/11/1898 | Traveled from Chicago to visit sister, Mrs. Sam Turk of Bell Center. |
| West | Orpha, Miss | KC, p1c2, 7/71898 | Traveled from South Dakota to Wauzeka to visit old friends after an absence of 12 years. |

Genealogical Gleanings From Early Newspapers for Residents In and Near
Crawford County, Wisconsin, 1897-1902

| LAST NAME | FIRST NAME | NEWSPAPER PAGE/COLUMN MONTH/DAY/YEAR | GENEALOGICAL DATA |
|---|---|---|---|
| West | Richard | KC, p8c3, 8/16/1900 | Marriage license issued to Mary Michael and Richard West. Both from Town of Eastman. |
| West | Richard, Mrs. | KC, p5c3, 1/24/1901 | Died Jan. 11, 1901 in the Town of Eastman. She was a "bride of but a few days." Buried in Catholic Cemetery in Prairie du Chien. |
| West | T., Mrs. | KC, p5c2, 7/21/1898 | Arrived from Chicago to visit mother, Mrs. Watson of Lynxville, and sister, Mrs. Susie Digtman of Soldiers Grove. |
| West | Walter | KC, p8c3, 4/15/1897 | Married Edna Ottman last Monday. Bride and groom from Town of Eastman. |
| West | William F. | KC, p1c6, 11/4/1897 | Issue of fact for court to be heard at the November term of the Circuit Court in Crawford County. William F. West vs. James Orville West. |
| Westphal | Mrs. | KC, p4c1, 8/19/1897 | Died last Thursday at home of daughter, Mrs. Mahnert of Town of Eastman. Interred in Dutch Cemetery. |
| Wetzel | Amelia | KC, p5c4, 5/29/1902 | The case Amelia Wetzel, et al. vs. Lena Rose, et al. was heard at the May term of the Crawford County Circuit Court. Judgement for sale of premises by stipulation. |
| Wetzel | John | KC, p8c2, 5/18/1899 | Married Elizabeth I. Ewell on May 17, 1899 in Prairie du Chien. Bride and groom from Charles City, IA. |
| Whaley | Ada | KC, p8c3, 6/27/1901 | Married Gardner Briggs at Tomahawk, WI last Monday evening. Bride and groom from Prairie du Chien. |
| Whaley | Edward H. | KC, p8c2, 2/3/1898 | Died Jan. 27, 1898 in Prairie du Chien. Born July 12, 1837 in Athens, OH. Served as Major in the Civil War. Appointed postmaster. Married Adela Ryan of Harper's Ferrry, IA on Oct. 30, 1865. She died, leaving son, William, who survives. Married Anda Spraque on June 30, 1872. A daughter, Miss Anda M. Whaley, survives this marriage. Extensive military history given. |
| Whaley | William | KC, p8c1, 8/24/1899 | Served in 1st Regt. SD Vol., Co. H. Departed Manila for a hospital in San Francisco. He was the Assistant Postmaster in Prairie du Chien for many years. |
| Wheeler | Clara | KC, Supp., 10/31/1901 | Married Ed Heise on Oct. 30, 1901. Bride from Bell Center. Groom, son of M. Heisz, from Steuben. (also KC, p8c5, 10/31/1901) |
| Wheeler | Jane | KC, p4c2, 1/7/1897 | "Jo. Rodgers and Jane Wheeler were married together at the same time. Jo. and Jane still live together they moved to Boskobell." Town of Scott news item. |
| Wher | Anna | KC, p8c3, 1/23/1902 | Married George Lechnir on Jan. 22, 1902. Recorded with Prairie du Chien news items. |
| Wher | Frank | KC, p8c3, 9/18/1902 | Judged insane in Prairie du Chien after an unsuccessful suicide attempt. Taken to the hospital in Mendota. |
| Wher | Mary | KC, p8c3, 11/7/1901 | Married John Fuka on Nov. 4, 1901. Bride and groom from Prairie du Chien. |
| Whistler | Florence, Mrs. | KC, p5c3, 7/25/1901 | Arrived from Albany, IA to visit her sister, Mrs. Phil Sousy of Lynxville. |
| White | A. M., Mr. | KC, p5c3, 7/10/1902 | Visited sister, Mrs. Emma Walton of Rolling Ground. |

Genealogical Gleanings From Early Newspapers for Residents In and Near
Crawford County, Wisconsin, 1897-1902

| LAST NAME | FIRST NAME | NEWSPAPER PAGE/COLUMN MONTH/DAY/YEAR | GENEALOGICAL DATA |
|---|---|---|---|
| White | A. W., Mrs. | KC, p5c3, 6/19/1902 | Resided in Bell Center. Visited parents, Mr. and Mrs. Lightfoot of Knapps Creek. |
| White | boy | KC, p1c5, 6/1/1899 | Son born June 1, 1899 to Abraham White of Wauzeka. |
| White | Emma | KC, p1c5, 2/9/1899 | Taught school in Marietta in 1899. E. E. Brindley, Crawford County Superintendent of Schools published a comprehensive list of all teachers in the county. |
| White | Emma | KC, p4c4, 8/3/1899 | Married Joseph E. Walton of Scott last Wednesday (July 26, 1899?). Bride from Millett. |
| White | Frank | KC, p5c3, 5/20/1897 | Issues of fact for jury to be heard in the May term of the Crawford County Court. A. N. Searle vs. J. J. Crowley, Dan Garvey and Frank White. |
| White | girl | KC, p1c6, 7/8/1897 | Daughter recently born to Monroe White of Barnum. |
| White | Lena | KC, p1c3, 12/15/1898 | Died Dec. 11, 1898 at age 28 (or 20?). Resident of Pine Creek in Town of Eastman. |
| White | M. | KC, p5c3, 7/25/1901 | Entertained his 75-year-old grandmother who arrived from Boston. Grandmother also visited relatives in Emmettsburg, IA. |
| White | Maggie, Mrs. | KC, p1c5, 2/9/1899 | Taught school in Seneca in 1899. E. E. Brindley, Crawford County Superintendent of Schools published a comprehensive list of all teachers in the county. |
| White | Mike | KC, Supp., 12/18/1902 | Crawford County Board of Supervisors examined bills in the Justices and Constables' Account for State vs. Mike White. |
| White | Mr. | KC, p5c4, 5/18/1899 | Died May 11, 1899 in Steuben area. Wife died May 8, 1899. |
| White | Mrs. | KC, p5c4, 5/11/1899 | Died May 8, 1899 in Steuben area. Survived by husband (84 years old), 4 sons and 4 daughters. |
| White | Orrin | KC, p5c3, 3/2/1899 | He was the new blacksmith at Watson's Mill in Scott. |
| White | William | KC, p5c3, 5/20/1897 | Criminal case to be heard in the May term of the Crawford County Court, State of Wisconsin vs. William White. |
| White Cloud | Mike | KC, Supp., 12/29/1898 | Crawford Co. Board of Supervisors approved Justices and Constables' expenses related to the Mike White Cloud Inquest. |
| Whiteaker | Alvin | KC, p5c2, 10/27/1898 | Resided in Mapleville. Returned home after spending summer in Courtney, ND (per Wheatville news items). |
| Whiteaker | Dan, Mrs. | KC, p1c3, 6/9/1898 | Lived in Bell Center. Went to Wauzeka to care for her sick sister-in-law, Mrs. Thomas Lawver. |
| Whiteaker | Edith | KC, p5c3, 6/14/1900 | Graduated from Bell Center school. |
| Whiteaker | girl | KC, p1c6, 3/10/1898 | Daughter recently born to Wilson Whiteaker of Wheatville. |
| Whiteaker | H. C. | KC, p5c6, 3/8/1900 | Recently sold his establishment in Belle Center to Huffman and is now employed in insurance work for the Mystic Workers. |
| Whiteaker | Ike | KC, p5c4, 3/6/1902 | Recently married. Resided in Bell Center. |

Genealogical Gleanings From Early Newspapers for Residents In and Near
Crawford County, Wisconsin, 1897-1902

| LAST NAME | FIRST NAME | NEWSPAPER PAGE/COLUMN MONTH/DAY/YEAR | GENEALOGICAL DATA |
|---|---|---|---|
| Whiteaker | Ike | KC, p5c4, 3/6/1902 | Whiteaker and his wife went to Bell Center on a wedding tour. (Recently married?) |
| Whiteaker | Isaac | KC, p5c2, 4/8/1897 | Resided in Bell Center. Visited his sister, Mrs. Thomas Lawver. Mrs. Lawver was very sick with lung fever. |
| Whiteaker | Jacob | KC, p5c2, 3/3/1898 | Visited parents in Wheatville. Spent last year working in Richland Co. |
| Whiteaker | Latie | KC, p1c4, 2/6/1902 | Died Jan. 27, 1902 at Bell Center. Aged 13 years, 9 months and 12 days. She was daughter of H. C. Whiteaker. Funeral was held at Methodist Episcopal Church. Buried in the Whiteaker Cemetery. |
| Whiteaker | Stella | KC, p1c6, 5/5/1898 | Married J. Nickelson on April 24, 1898. Bride and groom may have been from Bell Center. |
| Whiteaker | Wilson | KC, p5c1, 2/17/1898 | Worked as a blacksmith in Wheatville. |
| Whiteaker & Johnson | | KC, p4c4, 7/6/1899 | Notice of Dissolution published by H. C. Whiteaker and William Johnson. They dissolved their mercantile business in Bell Center. |
| Whitemore | Fred | KC, p1c4, 4/26/1900 | Operated a stockyard in Bridgeport. |
| Whitemore | Georgie E. | KC, p5c4, 5/25/1899 | Married William Fisher of Fennimore on May 17, 1899. (Bride may have been from Gays Mills area.) |
| Whiting | D. J. | KC, p8c4, 9/30/1897 | At a conference of the Methodist Church held in Platteville, D. J. Whiting was assigned to the Dodgeville circuit. |
| Whitman | Platt | KC, p1c1, 1/18/1900 | Advertised legal services. Attorney based in Boscobel. |
| Whitteker | Latie | KC, p1c2, 1/30/1902 | Died Jan. 26, 1902 in Bell Center. |
| Whittenheller | Charles | KC, p4c4, 11/10/1898 | Issues of Fact for Court heard in the November term of the Crawford County Circuit Court. Charles Whittenheller (Whittenheiller?) vs. Peter O'Neil. |
| Widman | John, Jr. | KC, p1c3, 5/3/1900 | Resident of Wauzeka. Clerking in a Milwaukee drug store and studying pharmacy. |
| Widman | son | KC, p1c4, 11/16/1899 | The son of Louis Widman was buried in Lancaster, WI. Died of the cold. Louis operated the depot building in Barlett, IA. Grandparents were Mr. and Mrs. J. G. Widman of Wauzeka. |
| Widmann | Emma | KC, p4c5, 1/24/1901 | Daughter of J. G. Widmann of Wauzeka. Professional nurse. Spent last 3 years in Massachusetts and Pennsylvania. Planned to the winter with her parents. |
| Widmann | Emma | KC, p1c2, 3/2/1899 | Professional nurse in Atlantic City, NJ. She was the daughter of J. G. Widmann of Wauzeka. |
| Widmann | Emma | KC, p1c6, 1/30/1902 | Married John Schmidt on Jan. 26, 1902 at the German Lutheran Church. Bride daughter of J. G. Widmann of Wauzeka. Groom son of John Schmidt, Sr. of Eastern Wauzeka, and brother of Henry and Charles Schmidt. |
| Widmann | J. D. | KC, p1c5, 8/7/1902 | Wrote a letter for the newspaper called "A Farewell Word" which discussed his plans to leave Wauzeka. |
| Widmann | J. G. | KC, p1c3, 7/24/1902 | Resigned as Wauzeka Village treasurer. Planned to move to Worthington, MN. Replaced by Leo Kessler. |

Genealogical Gleanings From Early Newspapers for Residents In and Near
Crawford County, Wisconsin, 1897-1902

| LAST NAME | FIRST NAME | NEWSPAPER PAGE/COLUMN MONTH/DAY/YEAR | GENEALOGICAL DATA |
|---|---|---|---|
| Widmann | J. G. | KC, p1c3, 9/8/1898 | Planned to open a branch of his hardware store in Steuben. |
| Widmann | J. G. | KC, p1c6, 4/7/1898 | Elected Treasurer for the Village of Wauzeka. |
| Widmann | J. G. | KC, p1c3, 1/25/1900 | Featured in an article on Wauzeka's business concerns. Operated a hardware store. |
| Widmann | J. G. | KC, p5c5, 4/5/1900 | Elected village treasurer in Wauzeka. |
| Widmann | L. C., Mr. and Mrs. | KC, p1c3, 1/5/1899 | Married last Thursday in Lancaster. John Widmann, Jr. was present for ceremony. Spent day with his parents in Wauzeka before departing for new home in Church's Ferry, ND. (per KC, p1c2, 1/12/1899) |
| Widmann | Louis, Mrs. | KC, p1c2, 10/16/1902 | Funeral held Oct. 12, 1902 in Lancaster. She was sister of John Schmidt, Jr. and wife of Wauzeka. |
| Widmann | Louis, Mrs. | KC, p1c4, 10/16/1902 | Died Oct. 9, 1902. Recently lived in Fosston, MN. Survived by husband and a 2-year-old son. Native of Lancaster. |
| Widmann | Louise C. | KC, p1c3, 12/22/1898 | Planned to marry Lela Price on Dec. 28, 1898. Bride, daughter of Daniel Price, from Lancaster. Groom son of J. G. Widmann, originally from Wauzeka, but now from Church's Ferry, ND. |
| Widmann | Sophia | KC, p1c2, 3/1/1900 | Died Feb. 23, 1900 in Wauzeka at 76 years of age. Mother of Henry who lived in Dakota. |
| Widmann | Sophia | KC, p1c5, 3/8/1900 | Recently died in Wauzeka. She was mother of J. G. Widmann. Born at Mintzheim, Wurtenberg, Germany on Sept. 20, 1824 where she married John C. Widmann in 1848. Two of her 10 children, John and Henry, survived to adulthood. Emigrated in 1851. Landed in New York. Later moved to Milwaukee, Watertown, Madison and Wauzeka. Husband died in 1886. Funeral held at German Lutheran Church. |
| Wiegand | J. B. | KC, p5c3, 3/4/1897 | Received a patent for an improved way to adjust cameras. |
| Wightacan | Nellie | KC, p5c3, 6/8/1899 | Recently married D. Williams at St. Luke's Church in Mazomanie. (Spelling of bride's name is unclear.) |
| Wikins | T. E. | KC, p5c4, 9/21/1899 | Resided in Bridgeport. Purchased a farm in Allemakee Co., IA. |
| Wilbur | Theron R. | KC, p5c1, 4/7/1898 | Died April 1, 1898 in Gays Mills. Born Dec. 27, 1845 in Rising Sun, IN. Moved to Utica Township when 11. To Gays Mills in 1865. To Towerville in 1867. To Johnstown in 1876. Married Alice Rounds on Oct. 27, 1890. She died in 1894. Survived by 1 son. |
| Wilharber | Emanuel | KC, p8c3, 5/1/1902 | Died April 29, 1902 in Prairie du Chien. He was a Civil War veteran. |

Genealogical Gleanings From Early Newspapers for Residents In and Near
Crawford County, Wisconsin, 1897-1902

| LAST NAME | FIRST NAME | NEWSPAPER PAGE/COLUMN MONTH/DAY/YEAR | GENEALOGICAL DATA |
|---|---|---|---|
| Wilharber | Emanuel | KC, Supp., 5/8/1902 | Died April 29, 1902. Born Mar. 5, 1839 in St. Gallen, Switzerland. He was the youngest of 7 children. Moved with parents to Illinois in 1843. To Grant Co., WI in 1845. Father died in 1846 and soon moved to Prairie du Chien. Married Rosalie Cherrier in 1860. Eight of 10 children survive. Served in Civil War. Moved to Wauzeka in 1893. |
| Wilharber | Joe | KC, p8c3, 2/6/1902 | Died Jan. 30, 1902 in St. Paul. He was a former resident of Prairie du Chien. Born in 1836 in St. Gallen, Switzerland. Moved to America in 1844. Survived by wife, 5 sons, 2 daughters and a brother, Emmanuel Wilharber (or Wilhaber?) of Prairie du Chien. |
| Wilharber | Violet | KC, Supp., 4/24/1902 | Arrived from Webster, SD to care for her father, Emanuel Wilharber, who suffered from heart trouble. |
| Wilharber | Violet | KC, p1c5, 2/9/1899 | Taught school in Bridgeport in 1899. E. E. Brindley, Crawford County Superintendent of Schools published a comprehensive list of all teachers in the county. |
| Wilkins | Ted | KC, p8c1, 4/13/1899 | Recently married Laura Kaiser of Prairie du Chien. Groom from Bridgeport. |
| Willetts | Arthur, Mrs. | KC, p1c6, 4/28/1898 | Died near Barnum on April 12, 1898. Nee Pearl Curtis. Born Jan. 6, 1877 in Iowa. Reared in Haney Valley by mother, Mrs. Elsie Curtis. Married Arthur Willetts on Nov. 10, 1897. Methodist. Buried in Haney Valley Cemetery. |
| Willey | J. A. | KC, p8c4, 9/30/1897 | At a conference of the Methodist Church held in Platteville, J. A. Willey was assigned to Shullsburg. |
| William | Elmer | KC, p1c5, 2/9/1899 | Taught school in the Town of Clayton in 1899. E. E. Brindley, Crawford County Superintendent of Schools published a comprehensive list of all teachers in the county. |
| Williams | boy | KC, p1c4, 3/7/1901 | Son born Mar. 4, 1901 to Henry Williams of Wauzeka. |
| Williams | Clyde and Jennie | KC, p1c2, 12/9/1897 | Joined Good Templar Lodge in Wauzeka. |
| Williams | D. | KC, p5c3, 6/8/1899 | Recently married Nellie Wightacan at St. Luke's Church in Mazomanie. Spelling of bride's name is unclear. |
| Williams | Edna | KC, p1c3, 12/11/1902 | Married Robert Harris on Nov. 28, 1902 at Madison, WI. Bride from Barnum. Groom from Maple Ridge, Crawford Co. |
| Williams | Edna | KC, Supp., 12/12/1901 | Edna Williams and Cora Van Horn of Barnum attended the summer Teacher's Institute in Soldiers Grove. |
| Williams | Edna | KC, Supp., 12/12/1901 | Attended a Teacher's Institute in Crawford County in 1901. Resided in Barnum. |
| Williams | Elmer | KC, Supp., 12/12/1901 | Attended a Teacher's Institute in Crawford County in 1901. Resided in Sugar Grove. |
| Williams | George | KC, p8c3, 6/16/1898 | Little Georgie Williams of Barnum went to a Chicago hospital to have a large tumor removed from his neck. |
| Williams | George O. | KC, p1c5, 7/13/1899 | Died June 15, 1899 at age 12 years and 20 days. He was only son and youngest child of Horace and Emma Williams. Funeral was held at the Haney Church. |
| Williams | Grant | KC, p5c1, 9/30/1897 | Married Minnie Gluss on Sept. 16, 1897. Bride and groom from Readstown. The Rev. Nuzum of Viroqua officiated. |

Genealogical Gleanings From Early Newspapers for Residents In and Near
Crawford County, Wisconsin, 1897-1902

| LAST NAME | FIRST NAME | NEWSPAPER PAGE/COLUMN MONTH/DAY/YEAR | GENEALOGICAL DATA |
|---|---|---|---|
| Williams | Henry | KC, p1c5, 2/17/1898 | Married Bertha Lewig, daughter of John Lewig, on Feb. 16, 1898 at the Lutheran Church in Wauzeka. |
| Williams | Henry | KC, p5c4, 6/12/1902 | Resided in Lynxville. Found a pearl valued at $500 and another pearl valued at $300. |
| Williams | Nina | KC, Supp., 12/12/1901 | Attended a Teacher's Institute in Crawford County in 1901. Resided in Sugar Grove. |
| Williams | W. | KC, p8c3, 11/16/1899 | The case Birdsall Mfg. Co. vs. W. Williams, was settled. The case was heard at the November term of the Crawford County Circuit Court. |
| Williams | Wayne | KC, p1c3, 1/25/1900 | Featured in an article on Wauzeka's business concerns. Leading stock dealer in the region. |
| Williams | William | KC, Supp., 12/18/1902 | Crawford County Board of Supervisors examined bills in the Justices and Constables' Account for State vs. William Williams and J. M. Ellis and Robert Pidd. G. L. Miller was a witness. |
| Willis | A. | KC, p1c4, 2/28/1901 | Married Emma Sanger is on Feb. 27, 1901. Bride daughter of John Sanger of Wauzeka. Groom from La Farge. |
| Willis | girl | KC, p1c4, 1/30/1902 | Daughter born Monday to Art Willis of La Farge. |
| Willis | Henry, Mr. and Mrs. | KC, p1c3, 6/9/1898 | Traveled from North Webster, IN to visit friends in Crawford Co. Formerly in milling business in Gays Mills and other points on Kickapoo River. |
| Willis | William | KC, p1c3, 8/30/1900 | Willis and Mrs. George A. Smith of Soldiers Grove departed for Indiana to visit Willis' parents. |
| Willits | Arthur | KC, p1c2, 1/17/1901 | Brought grist to the Wauzeka mills from his home in Eastman. |
| Willits | Ed | KC, p8c3, 3/4/1897 | Recently died in Melbourne, IA. Former resident of Mt. Sterling. |
| Willits | Hazel | KC, p5c3, 8/29/1901 | Died Aug. 17, 1901 in Amenia, ND. She was the granddaughter of Charles Iverson of the Town of Eastman. |
| Willits | Hazel Alice | KC, p5c3, 8/29/1901 | Died of cholera on Aug. 17, 1901 at Amenia, ND. She was granddaughter of Charles Iverson of Eastman. |
| Willits | M., Mrs. | KC, p5c4, 5/16/1901 | She and daughter, Haidee, departed Eastman for a new home at Amenia, ND. |
| Wilson | Fred | KC, p1c4, 5/27/1897 | Chicken thieves raided his hen house in Prairie du Chien. |
| Wilson | J. D. | KC, p5c4, 3/25/1897 | Died Sunday in Boscobel. Aged 44 years. Worked as an attorney. Born in New Hampshire. Had Scotch heritage. Came to LaFayette Co, WI in 1866 and to Boscobel in 1875. |
| Wilson | John | KC, p5c3, 12/19/1901 | "The blind musician" left Eastman to visit relatives in Grant Co. |
| Wilt | Bolser | KC, p5c2, 7/28/1898 | Left Hurlbut for Dakota. |
| Wilt | Mary | KC, Supp., 12/12/1901 | Attended a Teacher's Institute in Crawford County in 1901. Resided in Excelsior. |
| Wilt | William | KC, p5c5, 4/5/1900 | Elected assessor in Town of Scott. |

Genealogical Gleanings From Early Newspapers for Residents In and Near Crawford County, Wisconsin, 1897-1902

| LAST NAME | FIRST NAME | NEWSPAPER PAGE/COLUMN MONTH/DAY/YEAR | GENEALOGICAL DATA |
|---|---|---|---|
| Windham | Robert | KC, Supp., 12/29/1898 | Crawford Co. Board of Supervisors approved Justices and Constables' expenses related to the case, State vs. Robert Windham (or Mindham?). The witnesses were Bert Wilson, M. D. Crow and M. J. Grauk. |
| Windsor | Mae | KC, Supp., 12/18/1902 | Crawford County Board of Supervisors allowed expenses in the Matter of Mae Windsor, Incorrigible. |
| Winegar | Jane | KC, Supp., 12/12/1901 | Crawford County Board appealed a decision by State regarding the financial responsibility for Jane Winegar, an insane woman. |
| Winegar | Jane | KC, Supp., 12/20/1900 | A Committee of the Crawford Co. Board of Supervisors reported that Jane Winegar, insane, was not a resident of Crawford Co. and should not be supported by said county. |
| Winegar | John | KC, Supp., 12/18/1902 | Per Report of Special Committee on Insane, Crawford County, John Winegar, a non-resident of the State, was a charge of the county by the State Board for services at the asylum. |
| Wines | John E. | KC, Supp., 12/18/1902 | Crawford County Soldiers Relief Committee provided funds to John E. Wines of Soldiers Grove. |
| Wing | Alice | KC, p4c1, 7/1/1897 | Married Phil Soucy on June 19, 1897 per Lynxville news. F. R. Pease officiated. |
| Wing | boy | KC, p1c5, 11/25/1897 | Son born Nov. 14, 1897 to John Wing of Lynxville. |
| Wing | George, Mrs. | KC, p5c3, 8/17/1899 | Resided in Lynxville area. Sold a very valuable pearl last week. |
| Wing | Isaac | KC, p8c1, 9/21/1899 | Found a pearl in a Mississippi River clam and sold to George W. Thruman of Albany for $375. Ten days later, Thruman sold the pearl in Madison for $3500 to a Chicago firm. |
| Wing | Isaac | KC, p1c6, 5/19/1898 | Issue of Fact for Jury to be heard in the May term of the Crawford County Circuit Court. Isaac Wing vs. Crawford County. |
| Wing | Isaac | KC, p1c5, 6/1/1899 | The May term of the Crawford County Circuit Court closed. In the case, Isaac Wing vs. Crawford County, judgement for plaintiff. |
| Winn | A. D., Mrs. | KC, p5c4, 5/16/1901 | Died May 9, 1901. Moved to Harris, IA 4 weeks ago from Town of Eastman. She was the wife of Dr. Winn. |
| Winn | A., Dr. | KC, p1c4, 11/10/1898 | Resided in Glen Ellyn, IL. Planned to move to Eastman. |
| Winn | Erle | KC, Supp., 12/12/1901 | Attended a Teacher's Institute in Crawford County in 1901. Resided in Soldiers Grove. |
| Winn | Freda Alice | KC, p8c4, 12/13/1900 | Died Dec. 28, 1900. Aged 2 days. Daughter of H. O. Winn. |
| Winn | George | KC, p5c3, 7/27/1899 | Died July 23, 1899 in Denver, CO. Son of L. D. Winn of Soldiers Grove. |
| Winn | L. D. | KC, p1c6, 4/7/1898 | Elected Justice of the Peace for the Village of Soldiers Grove. |
| Winn | Mrs. | KC, p5c3, 8/30/1900 | Resided in Eastman. Entertained her sister, Mrs. L. Winn of New Hampshire. |

Genealogical Gleanings From Early Newspapers for Residents In and Near
Crawford County, Wisconsin, 1897-1902

| LAST NAME | FIRST NAME | NEWSPAPER PAGE/COLUMN MONTH/DAY/YEAR | GENEALOGICAL DATA |
|---|---|---|---|
| Winnegar | Jane | KC, Supp., 12/12/1901 | Listed as an insane person whose support was charged to Crawford Co. |
| Wiser | William | KC, Supp., 12/29/1898 | Crawford Co. Board of Supervisors approved Justices and Constables' expenses related to the case, State vs. William Wiser. The witnesses were Meloina Montgomery, Henry Smith and J. R. Smith. |
| Witenhiller | Charles | KC, p1c6, 11/4/1897 | Issue of law for court to be heard at the November term of the Circuit Court in Crawford County. Charles Witenhiller vs. Peter O'Neil. |
| Withee | A. B. | KC, p1c6, 4/7/1898 | Elected Clerk for the Town of Seneca. |
| Withee | A. C. | KC, p5c3, 3/13/1902 | Died Mar. 4, 1902 in Town of Seneca. Aged 74 years. Father of Orris, George, Andrew and Mrs. Frank Griffin. Buried in Campbell Cemetery. |
| Withee | Andrew B. | KC, p5c3, 3/13/1902 | Died Mar. 4, 1902. Aged 73 years, 10 months and 22 days. Born in Industry, ME. Married Margaret Hayden in 1853. Moved to Wisconsin in 1854. Moved to Seneca in 1863. Fathered 6 children, 2 daughters dead. |
| Withee | Daniel M. | KC, p1c2, 9/7/1899 | Married Ida M. Chilson on Aug. 20, 1899 at residence of A. B. Withee. Bride and groom from Seneca. |
| Withee | G. | KC, p1c5, 11/14/1901 | A farewell party was held for Madams G. Withee and Daggett in Seneca. Planned to leave for the Pacific Coast. |
| Withee | Sadie | KC, p1c3, 7/12/1900 | Died July 6, 1900. Aged 17 years. Daughter of A. C. Withee of near Seneca. |
| Withey | girl | KC, p5c4, 6/12/1902 | Daughter born Monday to Ansel Withey of Lynxville. This was the fourth child. |
| Wittenheiler | Charles | KC, p1c6, 5/19/1898 | Issue of Law for Court to be heard in the May term of the Crawford County Circuit Court. Charles Wittenheiler vs. Peter O'Neil. |
| Wolcott | A. E. | KC, p1c5, 9/8/1898 | Appointed postmaster in Lynxville. |
| Wolcott | A. E. | KC, p1c5, 4/13/1899 | Fire destroyed the John Vanderbilt & Co. Building, Davidson's livery barn and T. C. Bright's home and store in Lynxville. The fire later reached the A. E. Wolcott and W. A. Allen home, the William Huard home, the R. E. Hazen home and saloon, the T. C. Bright warehouse and the Schumann & Menges ice house. |
| Wolcott | Milo | KC, p4c1, 4/28/1898 | Volunteered to fight in Spanish American War. From Lynxville. |
| Wolcott | Milo | KC, p4c2, 6/30/1898 | From Lynxville. Enlisted in army at Boscobel. Failed the examination. |
| Wolcott | Milo | KC, p1c3, 7/28/1898 | Promoted to sergeant. |
| Wolcott | Stacey | KC, p4c1, 7/1/1897 | Taught school in Lynxville. |
| Wolcott | Stacey | KC, p5c1, 9/9/1897 | Hired to teach in Eastman. From Lynxville. |
| Wolcott | Stacy | KC, p5c3, 3/1/1900 | Departed Lynxville for Oshkosh where he went to learn telegraphy. |

Genealogical Gleanings From Early Newspapers for Residents In and Near Crawford County, Wisconsin, 1897-1902

| LAST NAME | FIRST NAME | NEWSPAPER PAGE/COLUMN MONTH/DAY/YEAR | GENEALOGICAL DATA |
|---|---|---|---|
| Wolcutt | A. E. | KC, p5c3, 6/21/1900 | Resided in Lynxville area. Sister and niece of Sutton, NB planned to visit Wolcutt. |
| Wolf | A. | KC, p5c3, 5/23/1901 | Departed Mt. Sterling for Viroqua to work as a barber. |
| Wolf | Anna, Mrs. | KC, p8c5, 5/10/1900 | Died May 7, 1900 in Town of Eastman. Aged 87 years. |
| Wolfe | E. V. | KC, p5c3, 7/11/1901 | Sold his Mt. Sterling area residence to Hamilton Walker of Seneca. Planned to move to Viroqua. |
| Womberg | Henry | KC, p5c3, 4/8/1897 | Planned to build a hotel near the railroad depot in Readstown. |
| Wondrak | Albert, Mrs. | KC, p8c2, 2/2/1899 | Died Jan. 29, 1899 in Prairie du Chien at 38 years of age. |
| Wood | Bert | KC, Supp., 12/29/1898 | Crawford Co. Board of Supervisors approved Justices and Constables' expenses related to the case, State vs. Bert Wood and Hugh (James or Amos?). |
| Wood | Elva | KC, p1c6, 3/31/1898 | Thirteen year old daughter of Mrs. Densmore Ewers. Died from a dynamite explosion at home in Readstown. Father placed dynamite sticks in oven to warm it to make rock quarrying easier and forgot about them. Mother also badly hurt. |
| Wood | John T. | KC, p4c4, 3/9/1899 | Resided in Twin Bluffs, WI where he operated a tree nursery. Through the newspaper he warned residents that S. A. Freeborn has made false claims. Freeborn owned Pioneer Nursery. |
| Wood | L. N., Dr. | KC, p5c1, 7/22/1897 | Moved to Gays Mills from Rockford, IL. |
| Wood | L. N., Dr. | KC, p4c1, 7/29/1897 | Purchased a home in Readstown. From Rockford. |
| Wood | Lester | KC, p1c5, 4/18/1901 | Returned to La Farge after serving as a soldier in the Philippines. |
| Wood | Julia Bakes | KC, p5c4, 5/30/1901 | Died May 22, 1901 at Belle Center. Born July 29, 1832 in Somerset Co., ME. Moved to Van Buren Co. IA in 1851. She was the youngest of 12 children. Married George E. Wood in Nov. 1852. Mother of 6 children. Moved to Belle Center in 1855. Has lived in Belle Center and Petersburg areas since move to Crawford Co. Husband died August 1886. Two children live in Belle Center. One son lives in Cresco, IA. Had daughters living in Nebraska and Kansas. She was Methodist. |
| Woodnal | Frank | KC, p4c2, 12/2/1897 | Married Mary Sherhunt at St. John's parsonage. (Reported in Bridgeport column.) |
| Woodnal | | KC, p1c4, 7/19/1900 | Infant of John Woodnal of Wauzeka died Monday. |
| Woods | Guy | KC, p4c1, 6/20/1901 | Guy Woods and Ben Roberts of La Farge arrested for nearly causing a train wreck in Potosi, IA. |
| Worth | Fred | KC, p7c4, 1/25/1900 | Received marriage license in Crawford Co. Cora McGorvan was the prospective spouse. Bride and groom-to-be from Johnsonport, IA. |

Genealogical Gleanings From Early Newspapers for Residents In and Near
Crawford County, Wisconsin, 1897-1902

| LAST NAME | FIRST NAME | NEWSPAPER PAGE/COLUMN MONTH/DAY/YEAR | GENEALOGICAL DATA |
|---|---|---|---|
| Wrecht | Mrs. | KC, p8c3, 1/9/1902 | Died Jan. 1, 1902. She was mother of Mrs. Aug. Steinberg. |
| Wright | George | KC, p8c3, 7/13/1899 | Died July 12, 1899 in Prairie du Chien. |
| Wright | George | KC, p8c3, 7/27/1899 | Died July 12, 1899 in Prairie du Chien. Born Aug. 11, 1844 at Clayton, St. Lawrence Co., NY. Came west as a young man. Married first wife in Wauzeka. She died June 17, 18__. (Newspaper typo says she died 1899.) They had 2 sons, Laverne of Milwaukee and Clinton of Minneapolis. Moved to Prairie du Chien in 1867. Married Mary Mosgrove on Jan. 31, 1877. Six of 9 children survive from this union. Funeral was held at Methodist Church. He was buried in the Lowertown Cemetery. |
| Wright | Mabel | KC, p1c5, 2/9/1899 | Taught school in Bridgeport in 1899. E. E. Brindley, Crawford County Superintendent of Schools published a comprehensive list of all teachers in the county. |
| Wright | Mertie | KC, p1c4, 6/3/1897 | Died May 29, 1897 in Prairie du Chien. She was the twin daughter of E. M. Wright. Sister died 4 weeks ago. |
| Wright | Nettie, Miss | KC, p1c2, 5/6/1897 | Died May 4, 1897. Aged 23 years, 11 months and 4 days. She was a twin daughter of Edward Wright of Prairie du Chien. |
| Wright | Nettie, Miss | KC, p4c2, 5/13/1897 | Died May 4, 1897 of typhoid fever. Born May 24, 1873. Daughter of L. M. Wright of Prairie du Chien. Extensive obituary. |
| Wunch | J. L. | KC, p1c2, 2/8/1900 | Resided in Seneca. Named the new butter maker for the Wauzeka Creamery. |
| Wurster | Agnes | KC, p8c4, 7/14/1898 | Died July 10, 1898 in Prairie du Chien. |
| Wurster | G. C. | KC, Supp., 12/12/1901 | Received funds from the Crawford Co. Soldiers Relief Commission. Resided in Prairie du Chien. |
| Wurster | Gotleib | KC, p8c3, 12/14/1899 | Died Dec. 1, 1899 in Prairie du Chien. |
| Wuster | Fred | KC, p8c3, 11/24/1898 | Died Nov. 17, 1898 in Prairie du Chien. He was the 11-year-old son of G. C. Wuster. |
| Yahn or Yann | Peter | KC, p5c4, 2/22/1900 | Died in spring of 1899 in Lynxville. His house and goods were sold and proceeds were sent to relatives in Scotland. |
| Yara | Anthony, Mr. and Mrs. | KC, p5c3, 8/14/1923 | Lived in Chicago. Visited relatives in Town of Eastman. |
| Yeadon | Mrs. | KC, p5c3, 11/30/1899 | Resident of Boydtown. Had a rainy day for her bee. |
| Yetter | Peter O. | KC, p1c6, 11/4/1897 | Issue of fact for jury to be heard at the November term of the Circuit Court in Crawford County. George E. Conklin et al vs. Peter O. Yetter. |
| Yonke | Ida | KC, p1c4, 10/13/1898 | Married William Lewig of Wauzeka on Oct. 13, 1898. Bride from Prairie du Chien. |
| Yonke | J. F. | KC, p5c4, 11/21/1901 | Published a notice that he had sold hunting rights to his land to Walter Hazelwood and Henry Gregerson. |
| Yonke | John | KC, p1c2, 1/30/1902 | Expects to bring 800 logs into the Wauzeka Lumber Co. |

Genealogical Gleanings From Early Newspapers for Residents In and Near
Crawford County, Wisconsin, 1897-1902

| LAST NAME | FIRST NAME | NEWSPAPER PAGE/COLUMN MONTH/DAY/YEAR | GENEALOGICAL DATA |
|---|---|---|---|
| York | Mr. | KC, p5c1, 4/22/1897 | Left Wauzeka to visit daughter in Jasper, MN. May move there. |
| Young | C. O. | KC, p1c3, 8/9/1900 | Died Aug. 5, 1900 at Bell Center. Aged 76 years. He was a Civil War veteran. Buried in the Bell Center Cemetery. |
| Young | Arthur | KC, p1c5, 9/16/1897 | Married Lilly Smith of Town of Steuben on Sept. 1, 1897. Groom from Boydtown. Joseph Newcomb, J. P., officiated. |
| Young | boy | KC, 10/25/1900 | Infant son of Frank Young died Monday in Seneca. He was 1 month old. |
| Young | boy | KC, p5c3, 4/24/1902 | Son born April 19, 1902 to Frank Young of Seneca. |
| Young | boy | KC, p4c2, 9/15/1898 | Son recently born to Charles Young of Steuben. |
| Young | C. R., Mrs. | KC, Supp., 12/12/1901 | Received funds from the Crawford County Soldiers Relief Commission. Resided in Haney. |
| Young | Caroline | KC, p5c5, 3/14/1901 | Died Mar. 4, 1901. Born 37 years ago in Lansing, IA. Married John Young of Town of Eastman on Oct. 29, 1897. Mother and brother live in Ft. Atkinson, IA. Buried in Lansing, IA. |
| Young | Caroline | KC, p5c3, 10/9/1902 | Died Sept. 29, 1902 in Eastman. Nee Eredenberg. She was wife of William Porter Young. Born in Rochester, NY on Feb. 13, 1841. Married in 1858 in Illinois. Moved to Eastman in 1861. Survived by 11 of 11 children. Funeral held at German Church and buried in church graveyard. |
| Young | E. M. | KC, Supp., 12/12/1901 | Received funds from the Crawford Co. Soldiers Relief Commission. Resided in Bell Center. |
| Young | E. M. | KC, Supp., 12/18/1902 | Crawford County Soldiers Relief Committee provided funds to E. M. Young of Bell Center. |
| Young | Elizabeth, Mrs. | KC, p1c2, 8/15/1901 | Lived in Bell Center. Granted a special widow's pension of $12 per month. |
| Young | Frank | KC, Supp., 12/18/1902 | Crawford County Board of Supervisors allowed expenses in the Criminal Case, State vs. Frank Young, George Young and Ben Willard. |
| Young | Frank | KC, Supp., 12/18/1902 | Crawford County Board of Supervisors examined bills in the Justices and Constables' Account for State vs. Frank Young, Ben Willard and Aug. Young. Joe Drew, Louis Karnopp, John Crawford and Sylvester Michel were witnesses. |
| Young | J. E. | KC, p5c3, 7/31/1902 | Lived in Hammond, LA (or IA?). Visited sick mother in the Town of Eastman. |
| Young | J. E. | KC, p8c3, 12/30/1897 | From Eastman. Recently married in Ft. Atchison, IA. |
| Young | James | KC, p1c4, 7/15/1897 | Married Josie Adams on July 3, 1897. Bride and groom from Town of Marietta. |
| Young | Maud | KC, p5c3, 3/2/1899 | From Scott. Recently became Mrs. Johnson. |
| Young | Mrs. | KC, p5c3, 10/23/1902 | Recently died in Eastman. Mother of John and Alonzo Young. |

Genealogical Gleanings From Early Newspapers for Residents In and Near
Crawford County, Wisconsin, 1897-1902

| LAST NAME | FIRST NAME | NEWSPAPER PAGE/COLUMN MONTH/DAY/YEAR | GENEALOGICAL DATA |
|---|---|---|---|
| Young | Peter | KC, p4c3, 3/30/1899 | Died Mar. 20, 1899 in Lynxville. Born in Dunbar, Haddingtonshire, Scotland on Mar. 31, 1824. Came to America in 1840. Mined in Pennsylvania and later moved to Crawford Co., WI. Brother of Mrs. William Dickson of (Lynxville?). |
| Young | Rosa A. | KC, p4c4, 8/3/1899 | Married Lot Hamilton of Steuben last Wednesday (July 26, 1899?). Bride from Town of Scott. |
| Young | Rose | KC, p1c5, 2/9/1899 | Taught school in Scott in 1899. E. E. Brindley, Crawford County Superintendent of Schools published a comprehensive list of all teachers in the county. |
| Young | Rose B. | KC, p1c5, 6/1/1899 | The May term of the Crawford County Circuit Court closed. The case, A. H. Rounds, Rose B. Young and Mina DeLameter vs. Jane Reynolds, was referred to court. |
| Young | T. | KC, p1c4, 8/14/1902 | Bound over for trial. Justice Case found probable cause to bind for assault to do great bodily harm. |
| Young | Thurlow | KC, p5c3, 3/25/1897 | Planned to move to the West from Wauzeka. |
| Young | Truman | KC, Supp., 12/18/1902 | Crawford County Board of Supervisors examined bills in the Justices and Constables' Account for State vs. Truman Young. Andres Brown, Effie Brown, Frank Cooley and Dr. D. H. Perrin were witnesses. |
| Young | Will | KC, p4c1, 11/11/1897 | Returned from a 3 year absence in Minnesota to visit parents in Eastman. His brother, Thurlow, had gone west for the season and came back, too. |
| Young | William | KC, Supp., 12/5/1901 | Married Miss Fredenberg on Nov. 28, 1901. Groom former resident of Eastman. Now from Moose Lake, MN. Bride from Moose Lake, MN. |
| Young | William | KC, p5c4, 5/11/1899 | Departed Eastman for a new home in Minnesota. |
| Young | Willis | KC, Supp., 12/12/1901 | State vs. Willis Young heard in Crawford Co. Court. Witnesses were Mike Conley, Israel Johnson, _. S. Courtney, Matt Courtney, E. M. Kast, Ambrose Thompson, _. Opreicht, _. H. McCullick and _ N. Campbell. Dan Whiteaker, constable. |
| Young | | KC, Supp., 12/19/1901 | Young & Ward operated a meat market in Steuben. |
| Yumbara | John | KC, p5c3, 12/14/1899 | George Becwar and John Yumbara of Eastman left for the pineries. |
| Zabel | Fred | KC, p1c5, 6/1/1899 | The May term of the Crawford County Circuit Court closed. In the case, Fred Zabel vs. H. W. H. Zabel, judgement for plaintiff. |
| Zabel | H. W. H. | KC, p1c5, 6/1/1899 | The May term of the Crawford County Circuit Court closed. In the case, Fred Zabel vs. H. W. H. Zabel, judgement for plaintiff. |
| Zander | Allie D. | KC, p4c2, 3/17/1898 | Former resident of Eastman. Left home in Sheridan, WY for the Klondike. |
| Zeber | Julius | KC, Supp., 12/20/1900 | Crawford Co. Board of Supervisors approved payment of expenses in the matter of State vs. Julius Zeber. Will Zeber was the witness. |

Genealogical Gleanings From Early Newspapers for Residents In and Near
Crawford County, Wisconsin, 1897-1902

| LAST NAME | FIRST NAME | NEWSPAPER PAGE/COLUMN MONTH/DAY/YEAR | GENEALOGICAL DATA |
|---|---|---|---|
| Zech | William | KC, Supp., 12/29/1898 | Crawford Co. Board of Supervisors approved Justices and Constables' expenses related to the case, State vs. William Zech. |
| Zeeh | Josephine, Mrs. | KC, p5c3, 7/24/1902 | Lived in Dakota. Visited sister, Mrs. A. Allen and brother, Frank Brady, in the Town of Eastman. |
| Zeeh | William | KC, Supp., 12/18/1902 | Crawford County Board of Supervisors allowed expenses in the Matter of William Zeeh, Insane. |
| Zeman | F. V. | KC, p5c4, 5/29/1902 | The case Klauer M'n'f'g. Co. vs. F. V. Zeman was heard at the May term of the Crawford County Circuit Court. Taken under advisement. |
| Zeman | John | KC, Supp., 12/20/1900 | Crawford Co. Board of Supervisors approved payment of expenses in the matter of State vs. John Zeman. |
| Zeman | Rose | KC, p8c2, 9/22/1898 | Died Sept. 15, 1898 at age of 11. Daughter of James Zeman of Prairie du Chien. |
| Zeman | Stasia | KC, p1c3, 1/7/1897 | Resigned as teacher in Frenchtown (Prairie du Chien. Kate Foshag was appointed to take her place. |
| Ziebert | Julius | KC, Supp., 12/12/1901 | State vs. Julius Ziebert heard in Crawford Co. Court. |
| Ziel | Edward | KC, p8c3, 7/11/1901 | Married Caroline Burkhard on July 8, 1901. |
| Ziel | Emma | KC, p7c3, 1/25/1900 | Married Louis Cherrier on Jan. 20, 1900 at the Catholic Parsonage. Bride and groom from Prairie du Chien. |
| Ziel | George and Emma | KC, Supp., 12/29/1898 | Crawford Co. Board of Supervisors approved Justices and Constables' expenses related to the case, State vs. George Ziel and Emma Ziel. The witnesses were Bridget White, Mike White and Joseph Stuart. |
| Ziener | Ernestena | KC, p8c3, 6/28/1900 | Married Adam Raw on June 19, 1900. Bride from Town of Eastman. Groom from Prairie du Chien |
| Zillmer | Mrs. | KC, p5c4, 7/24/1902 | Lived in Boydtown. Visited parents, Mr. and Mrs. N. E. Birchard of Bell Center. |
| Zilmer | Charles | KC, p5c1, 12/11/1902 | Proprietor of a general store in Steuben. |
| Zimmerman | Ed | KC, p5c3, 8/31/1899 | Native of Mt. Hope, Grant Co. Visited relatives in Eastman and then returned to Portland, ND, where he had been principal for the last 3 years. |
| Zirl | John | KC, p8c3, 12/6/190 | Married Emma Steiben on Nov. 29, 1900. Bride and groom from (Prairie du Chien). |

Genealogical Gleanings From Early Newspapers for Residents In and Near Crawford County, Wisconsin, 1897-1902

# APPENDIX

Genealogical Gleanings From Early Newspapers for Residents In and Near Crawford County, Wisconsin, 1897-1902

Genealogical Gleanings From Early Newspapers for Residents In and Near
Crawford County, Wisconsin, 1897-1902

## Appendix 1

## MAPS

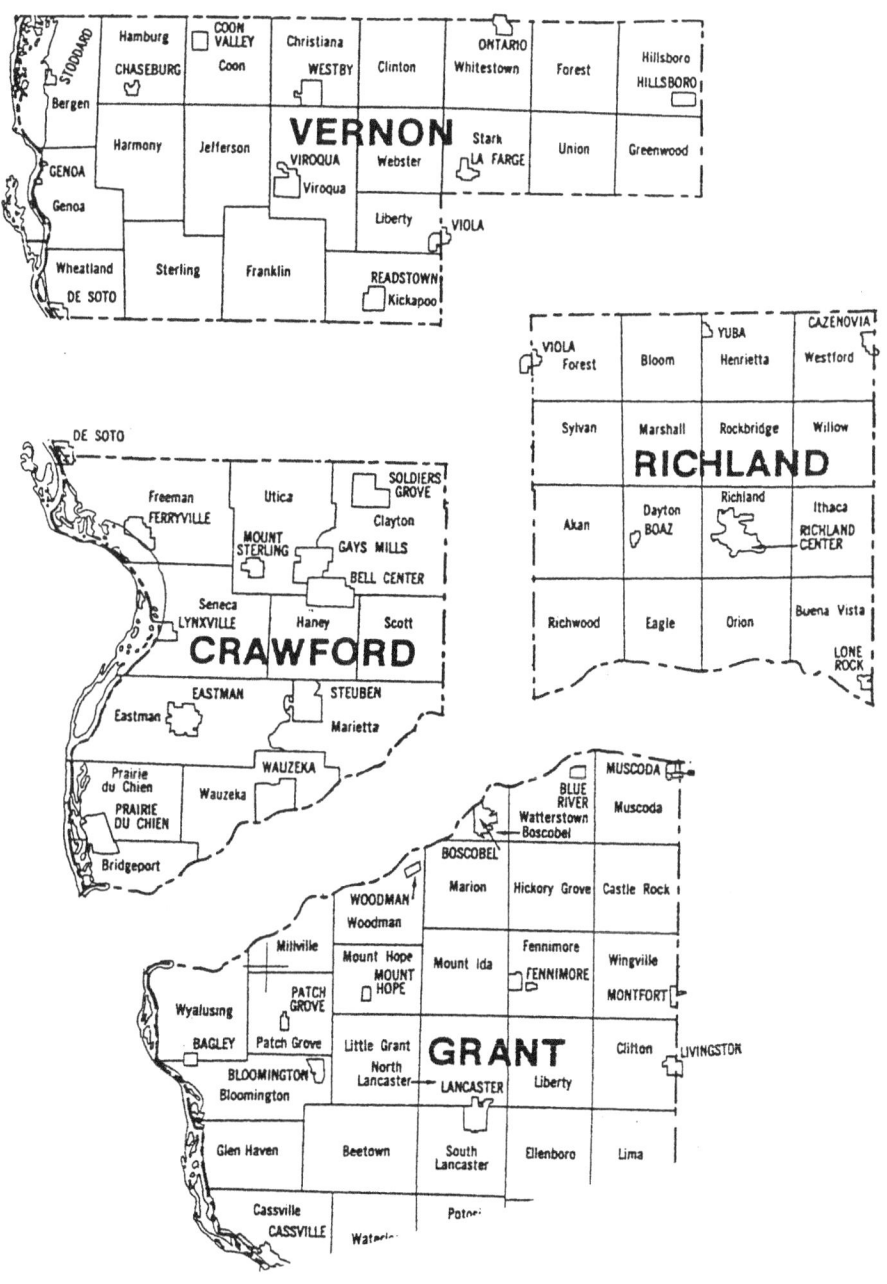

**Townships in Crawford, Vernon, Richland and Grant Counties**

Genealogical Gleanings From Early Newspapers for Residents In and Near Crawford County, Wisconsin, 1897-1902

**Southwestern Wisconsin**

Genealogical Gleanings From Early Newspapers for Residents In and Near
Crawford County, Wisconsin, 1897 - 1902

## Appendix 2

### GAZETTEER

| | |
|---|---|
| Adney | Post office in the eastern part of the Town of Clayton, Crawford County. |
| Akan | Township in Richland County. Sometimes spelled Aiken. |
| Ash Ridge | Village in Town of Bloom, Richland County. |
| Avalanche | Village on West Branch of Kickapoo River in Town of Webster, Vernon County. |
| Barnum | Village in Town of Haney, Crawford County. |
| Bear Creek | Creek in Town of Clayton, Crawford County. |
| Belle Center | Village in Town of Clayton, Crawford County. Sometimes spelled Bell Center. |
| Bloom | Township in Richland County. |
| Bloom City | Village in Town of Bloom, Richland County. |
| Boma | Neighborhood in Town of Utica, Crawford County. |
| Boscobel | Village in Town of Boscobel, Grant County. |
| Brady | Post office in western part of the Town of Akan, Richland County. |
| Bridgeport | Township in Crawford County. |
| Cadott | Village in Chippwa County. Center of lumber industry in late 19th century and early 20th century. |
| Chippewa Falls | City in Chippewa County. Center of lumber industry in late 19th century and early 20th century. |
| Citron Valley | Valley in Town of Haney, Crawford County. |
| Clayton | Township in Crawford County. |
| Crawford | County in southwest Wisconsin. Bounded by Vernon County to the north, Richland County to east, Grant County to the south and the Mississippi River to the west. |
| DeSoto | Village in town of Wheatland, Vernon County and Town of Freeman, Crawford County. |
| Eagle | Township in Richland County. |
| Eagle Corners | Village in Town of Eagle, Richland County. |
| Eastman | Township in Crawford County. Village in Town of Eastman, Crawford County. |
| English Ridge | Ridge in eastern part of the Town of Clayton, Crawford County. |
| English Run | Tributary of Knapps Creek in the eastern part of the Town of Clayton, Crawford County. |
| Excelsior | Village in Town of Richwood, Richland County. |
| Fennimore | Township in Grant County. Village in Town of Fennimore, Grant County. |
| Ferryville | Village in Town of Freeman, Crawford County. |
| Five Points | Village in Town of Akan, Richland County. |
| Folsom | Village in Town of Franklin, Vernon County. |
| Forest | Township in Richland County. |
| Franklin | Township in Vernon County. |

343

Genealogical Gleanings From Early Newspapers for Residents In and Near
Crawford County, Wisconsin, 1897 - 1902

| | |
|---|---|
| Freeman | Township in Crawford County. |
| French Town | A section of Prairie du Chien, Crawford County. |
| Gays Mill | Village on Kickapoo River in Town of Clayton, Crawford County. Also called Gays Mills. |
| Georgetown | Village in Town of Smelser, Grant County. |
| Georgetown | Neighborhood in Town of Scott, Crawford County. |
| Grant County | County in southwest Wisconsin. Bounded by Crawford County to the north, Iowa and Lafayette Counties to the west, Illinois to the south and the Mississippi River to the west. |
| Halls Valley | Valley in Town of Seneca, Crawford County. |
| Haney | Township in Crawford County. |
| Henrietta | Township in Richland County. |
| Highland | Township in Iowa County. |
| Hurlbuts | Village in Town of Scott, Crawford County. |
| Hustler Ridge | Neighborhood near Sugar Grove, Vernon County. |
| Irish Ridge | Neighborhood in Town of Scott, Crawford County. Neighborhood in Town of Prairie du Chien, Crawford County. |
| Jimtown | Neighborhood in the western part of the Town of Akan, Richland County. |
| Johnstown | Neighborhood on Tainter's Creek in Section 9 of the Town of Utica, Crawford County. |
| Kickapoo | Township in Vernon County. |
| Kickapoo Center | Village on Kickapoo River in Town of Kickapoo, Vernon County. |
| Kickapoo River | River which flows through eastern Vernon County and eastern Crawford County before it discharges into the Wisconsin River. |
| Knapps Creek | Creek which drains eastern Crawford County and western Richland County before it discharges into the Wisconsin River. |
| LaFarge | Village on Kickapoo River in Town of Stark, Vernon County. |
| Lancaster | City in Grant County. |
| Liberty Pole | Village in Town of Franklin, Vernon County. |
| Lower Town | A section of Prairie du Chien, Crawford County. |
| Lynxville | Village in Town of Seneca, Crawford County. |
| Manning | Village in Town of Kickapoo, Vernon County. |
| Marietta | Township in Crawford County. |
| Mt. Sterling | Village in Town of Utica, Crawford County. |
| Mt. Zion | Village in Town of Scott, Crawford County. |
| North Clayton | Village in northern Town of Clayton, Crawford County. |
| Petersburg | Village on Kickapoo River in Town of Haney, Crawford County. |
| Pine Grove | Early name for Soldiers Grove, Crawford County. |
| Pine Knob | Village in Town of Utica, Crawford County. |
| Poplar Ridge | A neighborhood between Lynxville and Eastman in Crawford County. |
| Prairie du Chien | County seat of Crawford County. Located on Mississippi River in Town of Prairie du Chien. |
| Purdy | Village in southwest Vernon County. |
| Readstown | Village on Kickapoo River in town of Kickapoo, Vernon County. |
| Retreat | Village in Town of Sterling, Vernon County. |

Genealogical Gleanings From Early Newspapers for Residents In and Near
Crawford County, Wisconsin, 1897 - 1902

| | |
|---|---|
| Richland | County in southwest Wisconsin. Bounded by Vernon County to the north, Crawford County to the west, Grant County and Iowa County to the south and Sauk County to the east. |
| Richland Center | County seat of Richland County. Located in Town of Richland. |
| Richwood | Township in Richland County. |
| Rising Sun | Village in Town of Freeman, Crawford County. |
| Rolling Ground | Neighborhood in southern Town of Clayton, Crawford County. |
| Rush Creek | Village in Town of Freeman, Crawford County and creek in Town of Freeman which empties into the Mississippi River. |
| Sabin | Village in Town of Sylvan, Richland County. |
| Scott | Township in Crawford County. |
| Seneca | Township in Crawford County. Village in Town of Seneca, Crawford County. |
| Soldiers Grove | Village on Kickapoo River in Town of Clayton, Crawford County. |
| St. Philips | Neighborhood around St. Philips Catholic Church in southern Town of Clayton, Crawford County. |
| Sterling | Township in Vernon County. |
| Steuben | Village on Kickapoo River in Town of Marietta, Crawford County. |
| Sugar Grove | Village in Town of Kickapoo, Vernon County. |
| Sylvan | Township in Richland County. |
| Tainter Creek | Creek which flows through the Town of Franklin, Vernon County and the Town of Utica, Crawford County. |
| Tavera | Village in Town of Richwood, Richland County. |
| Towerville | Village in Town of Utica, Crawford County. |
| Trout Creek | Creek east of Soldiers Grove in Town of Clayton, Crawford County. |
| Utica | Township in Crawford County. |
| Vernon County | County in southwest Wisconsin. Bounded by La Crosse County and Monroe County to the north, Richland County to the east, Crawford County to the south and the Mississippi River to the west. |
| Victory | Village on the Mississippi River in Vernon County. |
| Viola | Village in Town of Forest, Richland County and Town of Liberty, Vernon County. |
| Viroqua | County seat of Vernon County in Town of Viroqua. |
| Wauzeka | Village in Town of Wauzeka, Crawford County. |
| Webster | Township in Richland County. |
| West Prairie | Village in Town of Sterling, Vernon County. |
| Wheatland | Township in Vernon County. |
| Wheatville | Post office in the northern part (Section 5) of the Town of Scott, Crawford County. |
| Wooster | Village on Kickapoo River in Town of Clayton, Crawford County. |
| Yankeetown | Neighborhood west of Soldiers Grove in Town of Clayton, Crawford County. |

Genealogical Gleanings From Early Newspapers for Residents In and Near
Crawford County, Wisconsin, 1897-1902

## Appendix 3

### NEWSPAPERS RESEARCHED FOR THIS PROJECT

| Newspaper/Where Published | Code | Years | Call Numbers |
|---|---|---|---|
| *Kickapoo Chief*/ Wauzeka, WI | KC | 1897 – 1899 | P76-5667 |
| *Kickapoo Chief*/ Wauzeka, WI | KC | 1900 – 1902 | P76-5668 |

The State Historical Society of Wisconsin Library in Madison, Wisconsin has an outstanding collection of microfilmed newspapers. I have provided the call numbers used at the State Historical Society of Wisconsin for researchers who wish to consult the original sources for the citations contained in this book. The Lower Wisconsin River Genealogical and Historical Research Center also has copies of early Wauzeka, Wisconsin newspapers (*Kickapoo Chief, Kickapoo Papoose, Wauzeka Chief* and *Wauzeka Kickapoo Chief*). This genealogical society can be contacted at P.O. Box 202, Wauzeka, WI 53826.

Genealogical Gleanings From Early Newspapers for Residents In and Near
Crawford County, Wisconsin, 1897-1902

## Appendix 4

## Crawford County Census

We give below a table showing the actual figures for Crawford County as taken from the official count of the returns of the Twelfth census, taken as of June 1, 1900.

|  |  | 1900 | 1890 |
|---|---|---|---|
| CRAWFORD COUNTY |  | 17,286 | 15,877 |
| Bridgeport town |  | 357 | 410 |
| Clayton town |  | 2080 | 2050 |
| DeSoto village (part of) |  | 87 | 79 |
| Eastman town |  | 1471 | 1436 |
| Freeman town |  | 1533 | 1417 |
| Haney town |  | 868 | 738 |
| Lynxville village |  | 322 | 243 |
| Marietta town |  | 1262 | 1300 |
| Prairie du Chien city |  | 3232 | 3131 |
| Ward 1 | 626 |  |  |
| Ward 2 | 1049 |  |  |
| Ward 3 | 1211 |  |  |
| Ward 4 | 346 |  |  |
| Prairie du Chien town |  | 595 | 602 |
| Scott town |  | 1004 | 1079 |
| Seneca town |  | 1200 | 1197 |
| Soldiers Grove village |  | 680 | .... |
| Utica town |  | 1548 | 1389 |
| Wauzeka town |  | 576 | 916 |
| Wauzeka village |  | 471 | .... |

From the above it will be seen that every town and village in the county except the towns of Prairie du Chien, Marietta, Scott and Bridgeport have increased in population in the last ten years. It will also be seen that the largest gain in any town in the county was made by the town of Clayton and the village of Soldiers Grove, of which fact we are justly proud. In 1890 the population of our town and village together was 2,050. Since that time the village has become independent of the town with 680 people, and notwithstanding that loss the town still shows a gain of 30, giving a combined population to the town and village of 2,760, a gain of 710, or over 34 ½ percent. The next largest gain in the county was made by the town of Utica which increased by 159 souls or 11 ½ percent. The town of Haney, however, had a larger percent gain than Utica, gaining 130 over its population of 738, or about 18 percent.

Genealogical Gleanings From Early Newspapers for Residents In and Near
Crawford County, Wisconsin, 1897-1902

Our neighbor, Readstown, for which has been claimed such unprecedented growth, has a population of 403. It was not returned separately from the town of Kickapoo, (Vernon Co.) in 1890, the two then having 1185. The combined population of both now is 1277, or a gain of less than 8 percent.

Neighbor Viola, organized since 1890 from the towns of Forest in Richland County, and liberty in Vernon County, shows a combined population with those towns now of 1804 as against 1814 in 1890.

La Farge, the best town on the Wisconsin Western, (nit) has 488 and includes all the adjacent territory that can be claimed.

The city of Prairie du Chien shows a gain or 101 or about 3 percent.

Boscobel gained 67 over 1570 or a gain of 4 ½ per cent.

Taken from the *Crawford County Advance*; Soldiers Grove, WI; March 22, 1901; Page 1, Column 3.

Genealogical Gleanings From Early Newspapers for Residents In and Near Crawford County, Wisconsin, 1897-1902

**INDEX**

-A-

Aaland, 1
Abbey, 1, 107
Abby, 1, 127, 206, 208, 308
Abel, 43
Abraham, 1, 268
Ackerly, 1
Adams, 1, 2, 133, 152, 220, 336
Adlington, 2
Adney, 2
Ady, 2, 253
Ahrens, 7, 136
Aikens, 2
Aikins, 2
Akerman, 2
Aland, 2
Alder, 2, 3, 40, 74, 279
Alderman, 3, 120, 136, 283
Alex, 3
Alexander, 3, 203
Alien, 3, 74
Alington, 27
Alland, 3, 84
Allen, 4, 5, 9, 30, 61, 74, 84, 85, 117, 125, 129, 140, 229, 279, 311, 333, 338
Allington, 5
Altenberg, 5
Altizer, 241
Amann, 5, 199
Ambler, 5, 145
Ames, 5, 37, 57, 308
Anderson, 5, 6, 7, 18, 52, 64, 73, 77, 78, 96, 121, 134, 160, 168, 174, 237, 269, 275, 280, 295
Andrew, 7, 78
Andrews, 7, 303
Antony, 116
Appleby, 7
Arden, 7
Arius, 7
Arms, 7, 108, 148, 296, 297
Armstrong, 2, 7, 246, 320
Ashbacher, 7
Ashley, 156
Aspenson, 7, 21, 268, 272
Ataya, 71
Atchison, 7, 8, 124, 202, 203
Atherton, 8, 9, 83
Athey, 9
Atkinson, 9, 236
Atwood, 9, 118
Ault, 9, 10
Austin, 10, 215, 319
Avery, 10
Ayres, 228

-B-

Babcock, 10, 271
Bachna, 8
Bacon, 10, 52, 86, 107, 322
Bailey, 10, 122, 166
Bakeman, 10, 293
Baker, 10, 11, 29, 40, 50, 175, 215, 217, 276, 283
Balch, 11
Balderston, 11
Balharre, 308
Bandier, 11
Bandler, 11
Bangs, 11
Banks, 11
Banmeister, 41
Bannen, 11, 151, 171, 296, 297
Bannon, 12
Banta, 12, 187
Barette, 12
Barfell, 12
Barham, 12, 131, 151, 231, 245, 259
Barker, 12, 33, 84, 163, 288
Barklow, 220
Barlow, 12, 85
Barnes, 12, 43
Barnett, 12
Barney, 12, 43, 65, 153, 268, 272
Barnum, 9, 13, 47, 151, 205, 266
Barr, 13, 178
Barrett, 13
Barrette, 13, 28, 106, 178
Barton, 13, 14, 37, 80
Bartos, 14
Batchelder, 14, 109, 114, 144, 262
Bateman, 38, 126
Bates, 14, 308
Bauer, 1, 14, 194, 262, 315
Baugherty, 14
Bazal, 46
Beach, 15, 144, 214, 226, 299
Bean, 15, 303
Bear, 15
Beaumaster, 15
Beaumeister, 15, 312
Beaumont, 15, 178
Beck, 15
Beckendorf, 15, 28
Beckwith, 15, 107
Becor, 15
Becwar, 16, 27, 45, 84, 215, 226, 275, 337
Becwith, 16
Beebe, 16, 55, 252
Beer, 16, 136
Beers, 16
Beeseckee, 83
Beesecker, 15, 16
Begley, 16
Behnken, 16
Beier, 16, 17, 164, 211, 262, 298, 313
Beir, 17
Bell, 18, 20, 50, 51, 79, 123, 198, 257, 270
Bellows, 18, 19, 83, 198, 222, 269, 295
Bellrichard, 19, 26, 316
Belrichard, 19, 279

Genealogical Gleanings From Early Newspapers for Residents In and Near
Crawford County, Wisconsin, 1897-1902

Bender, 19
Benhardt, 187
Benhart, 19, 20, 200, 315
Benish, 20, 180, 217
Bennart, 20
Benner, 20, 251
Bennett, 13, 20, 21, 61, 84, 107, 118, 232, 271, 277
Berg, 21, 137
Bernann, 21
Bernier, 21, 173, 181
Berry, 21, 198
Bertbeck, 21
Besaw, 21
Betscha, 323
Biddy, 21
Biederman, 21, 65
Biehloh, 22, 102
Biehn, 22
Bieloh, 16, 22, 85, 102, 144
Biely, 22
Bier, 22, 114
Bigelow, 22, 25, 56, 223
Bigley, 22, 222
Biitner, 22
Biley, 22, 160
Biller, 22
Birch, 22
Birchard, 22, 32, 338
Bisbee, 47, 199
Bishop, 84
Bitterlee, 22, 242, 267
Bitterly, 3, 23
Bittner, 22, 216
Bjornsen, 5
Bjornson, 5
Black, 23, 138, 244, 315
Blackburn, 23
Blaha, 23
Blahna, 23
Blakesly, 23
Blanchard, 23, 194
Blancher, 9
Blasek, 23
Blazek, 23, 46
Bliss, 23, 24
Blojeck, 24
Blondell, 24, 132
Bloom, 24, 261
Blosser, 24
Bluet, 24
Boarth, 214
Bock, 16, 24
Bodier, 166
Bodler, 166
Bogar, 29
Boid, 271
Boisvert, 24
Boland, 24, 25, 296
Bold, 271
Bolstad, 25
Bolstead, 25
Bolsted, 25
Bomaster, 25

Bond, 25, 210, 270
Bonner, 325
Bonney, 2, 26, 27, 41, 284
Booman, 26, 29
Booth, 245, 255
Borgendine, 26, 111, 157, 303
Bosch, 26
Boucher, 26, 78, 94, 104, 159
Bourne, 26, 185
Bourque, 84
Bowe, 25, 26, 27, 223, 308
Bower, 27
Bowers, 27, 287
Boyd, 27
Bradley, 12, 27, 187
Brady, 4, 22, 27, 28, 58, 61, 64, 162, 173, 213, 226, 267, 268, 323, 338
Brainard, 28
Brainerd, 28, 41
Brandees, 262
Brandes, 12, 13, 15, 28, 29, 108, 156, 246
Brandt, 29
Breedlove, 85
Breinard, 29, 124
Bremer, 303
Brennan, 29
Brenner, 29
Brertsprcher, 26, 29
Brew, 29, 85
Bricker, 29
Brickner, 29, 247
Briggs, 12, 24, 29, 30, 67, 85, 128, 193, 198, 272, 295, 297, 303, 326
Bright, 4, 30, 123, 129, 140, 249, 254, 296, 311, 317, 333
Brightman, 30, 31, 101, 120, 296
Brimer, 31
Brindley, 3, 11, 17, 19, 21, 25, 31, 47, 51, 53, 58, 59, 63, 64, 75, 76, 77, 78, 80, 86, 91, 92, 93, 95, 101, 102, 103, 106, 115, 118, 123, 126, 131, 134, 135, 139, 140, 144, 147, 149, 153, 159, 161, 173, 174, 175, 182, 183, 185, 187, 189, 192, 193, 198, 201, 204, 207, 208, 211, 213, 219, 221, 223, 224, 227, 229, 232, 239, 244, 252, 253, 259, 266, 270, 274, 280, 286, 292, 300, 302, 305, 306, 309, 318, 323, 324, 327, 330, 335, 337
Bringe, 25
Bringes, 25
Brintwell, 261
Brisbois, 31, 148
Brittner, 31
Brock, 31, 32, 113, 193
Brockway, 19, 32, 68, 106, 198, 321
Brodt, 32
Bromley, 144
Bronson, 32
Brookins, 22, 32, 128
Brooks, 32, 246
Brose, 32
Brown, 6, 12, 23, 32, 33, 34, 45, 52, 54, 73, 84, 91, 99, 112, 114, 119, 128, 152, 164, 236, 237, 288, 314, 337
Brownly, 148
Brudes, 34
Brudos, 34
Brumfield, 35

Brunson, 35
Bryan, 35
Bryant, 1, 35, 64
Buchanan, 35
Buckmaster, 6, 35, 36, 62, 86, 165, 170, 185, 200, 216, 246, 275, 287
Bull, 36, 322
Bump, 36, 227
Bundis, 276
Bunnel, 36
Bunnell, 36, 86, 156, 178
Burdick, 36, 179
Burgeman, 157
Burgess, 16, 37, 133
Burk, 37, 84
Burke, 14, 37, 80, 221
Burkhard, 37, 338
Burns, 37, 38, 108, 165, 182, 197, 233
Burrel, 38, 218, 303
Burrell, 38, 303
Burris, 38
Burroughs, 297
Burrows, 38
Burt, 38, 166
Burton, 38, 62, 94
Busch, 38, 236
Busche, 39, 114
Bush, 39, 313
Bushey, 39
Buske, 99
Butler, 39, 168, 319
Butt, 39, 189, 316
Byer, 2
Byers, 39

-C-

Cahill, 39
Calahan, 25, 39, 99
Calkins, 39
Callaway, 11, 39, 40
Callinan, 40
Calloway, 40, 295
Cameron, 12, 25, 30, 40
Campbell, 3, 18, 26, 27, 28, 40, 41, 59, 74, 84, 99, 149, 150, 151, 175, 214, 218, 228, 241, 255, 264, 274, 279, 296, 301, 308, 313, 319, 333, 337
Cane, 41, 318
Canfield, 41, 42
Cannon, 42
Cantwell, 42, 90, 157, 169
Card, 42
Cardin, 42
Cardine, 42
Carey, 42, 72
Carl, 42, 303
Carlin, 152, 170, 271
Carmack, 42
Carney, 25
Carpenter, 42, 204
Carr, 78, 83
Carrell, 42
Carrol, 43

Carron, 43, 234
Carson, 43
Carter, 2, 43, 295
Case, 43, 269, 282, 337
Casewell, 171
Casey, 103
Caskey, 12, 43
Casper, 43, 53, 111, 307
Caswell, 43, 295
Cater, 12, 43, 268
Cavanaugh, 43, 44
Caya, 44, 67, 70, 109, 133, 258
Cecka, 44
Chabela, 44, 309
Chadwick, 45, 86, 156
Chamberlain, 45, 96
Chambers, 45, 104
Chandler, 45, 180
Chapek, 16, 45, 46, 114, 144, 174, 207, 290
Chapman, 46, 134, 154, 156, 196, 197, 223, 239, 257
Chase, 10, 46, 47, 111, 133, 170, 173, 249, 264, 322
Chatman, 47
Chatterton, 47, 217, 227
Cheaka, 47, 161
Check, 47
Cheney, 25
Cherrier, 19, 24, 47, 48, 84, 279, 296, 297, 330, 338
Cherwak, 48
Chierrier, 48
Childs, 48, 76, 280, 295, 321
Chilson, 48, 333
Chitik, 48, 236
Christ, 5, 17, 48, 146
Christenson, 151, 160
Christianson, 48, 69
Christie, 48, 54, 85
Chunot, 48, 122
Churchhill, 48
Churchill, 49, 119, 172
Chynoweth, 49
Clack, 49
Clancy, 49, 152
Clark, 2, 25, 49, 50, 102, 136, 167, 246, 276, 291
Clarke, 50, 213
Clason, 186
Cleary, 31, 50, 103, 301
Clement, 50, 151
Clemons, 11, 50
Clinton, 50
Clumfor, 50, 177
Coalburn, 11, 18, 50, 51, 221
Coates, 106, 167
Coats, 51, 93
Cobb, 51, 85
Coburn, 51, 70
Colburn, 51
Cole, 31, 51, 137, 210, 219, 249, 278
Coleman, 6, 10, 35, 51, 52, 53, 67, 79, 84, 155, 170, 193, 246, 275, 289, 293, 321
Collins, 11, 25, 53, 166, 223, 269
Coltard, 53
Comb, 53
Comerine, 53, 263

Genealogical Gleanings From Early Newspapers for Residents In and Near
Crawford County, Wisconsin, 1897-1902

Compa, 53
Comstock, 53, 99, 121
Coney, 53, 54
Conklin, 54, 335
Conley, 54, 337
Connell, 48, 54, 219
Connelly, 54, 151, 222
Connely, 54, 191
Conopa, 54
Conopy, 54, 98
Contel, 54
Cook, 25, 40, 54, 55
Cooley, 55, 86, 156, 175, 265, 337
Coon, 245
Coope, 55
Cooper, 46, 55, 64, 311, 312
Coorough, 55, 115, 306
Copan, 156
Copas, 6, 55, 56, 67, 85, 101, 301
Copper, 56, 57, 61, 138, 143, 151, 158, 177, 231, 255
Copsey, 57, 58, 85, 113, 139, 174, 220, 262, 317
Copus, 58
Corbett, 58
Corcoran, 58, 59
Cornell, 59
Cornford, 59, 83, 115, 263
Coryer, 133
Cotter, 59
Cotton, 39, 59
Cottrell, 122
Couey, 59
Coughlin, 59
Coulson, 40, 59, 60, 269
Courtney, 60, 78, 86, 96, 300, 301, 337
Courtright, 202
Coville, 60
Cowder, 60
Cowdery, 60
Cowdrey, 60
Cox, 31, 60, 123
Coyer, 60
Coyne, 60
Cradwell, 60, 61
Craig, 60, 65, 206
Craigo, 60, 147
Crandall, 2, 60, 318, 325
Crasper, 60
Crawford, 60, 61, 103, 165, 211, 336
Crehan, 61
Croft, 61
Cron, 57, 61, 308
Cronsage, 61
Croome, 61
Crouch, 66, 116, 128, 209, 264, 270, 320
Crow, 62, 116, 332
Crowley, 62, 63, 67, 83, 95, 103, 137, 173, 188, 198, 210, 213, 214, 266, 327
Crume, 63, 64, 121, 168, 230
Crusan, 64
Cryderman, 85, 203
Cuban, 64
Cullen, 64
Culver, 64, 280

Cumberlidge, 158
Cumerine, 64
Cummings, 27, 64, 126
Cummins, 18, 60, 64, 65
Cupps, 65, 240, 293
Curley, 21, 65, 84, 234, 249
Curran, 52, 59, 65, 127, 160, 228, 271, 296
Currie, 66, 99, 146, 176, 273
Curry, 66
Curtis, 2, 66, 145, 268, 320, 324, 330
Curtiss, 66
Cushing, 66, 298
Custer, 66, 67

-D-

Dab, 25
Dagett, 315
Daggert, 67
Daggett, 67, 333
Dagnon, 25, 67, 197, 319
Dahigg, 118
Dahlmer, 67
Daily, 40
Damm, 67
Daniels, 67
Darrow, 67
Dase, 67
Daubenberger, 13
Daugherty, 67, 148, 286, 297
Davenport, 5, 67, 68, 76, 77, 160, 185, 237, 308
Davey, 46, 68, 86
David, 38, 68, 118
Davidson, 4, 24, 30, 68, 69, 70, 129, 140, 230, 296, 311, 317, 321, 333
Davig, 69, 296
Davis, 69, 116, 220, 272, 282, 297, 303
Davit, 69
Davitt, 69, 70
Davy, 70
Daw, 67
Dawse, 70
Dawson, 70, 253
Day, 23, 44, 47, 70, 187, 200, 219, 281, 308
De Lacy, 70, 85
De Lamater, 71, 295
De Larimier, 71
Dean, 71, 193
Dearman, 2, 71
Deary, 71
DeChamp, 71
Deering, 71
Deerman, 71
Deggon, 71
Degnan, 71, 72, 81, 91, 129, 169, 190, 197
Deidlehof, 72
Deidrick, 54
Delamater, 72, 107
DeLaMater, 102, 197, 256
DeLameter, 72, 248, 256, 337
Delano, 72
Delap, 72, 109
DeLap, 42, 65, 72

Delarimere, 71
DeLorimer, 223
Delosmier, 306
Delury, 72
Demock, 139
Denio, 72
Denneman, 72
Denning, 72, 90, 133, 242
Dennis, 33, 34, 73, 83, 297
Derouche, 73
Deroucher, 165
Derry, 73
Desch, 73
DesChamps, 73
Desmond, 73
Devenport, 74, 174, 220
Devine, 74, 279, 295
Dewane, 74
Dewey, 74, 290
Dexter, 74
Dick, 37
Dicks, 74
Dickson, 3, 48, 70, 74, 131, 291, 315, 337
Dieter, 74, 118
Dietrich, 3, 10, 74, 79, 178
Dietrick, 115
Dietzman, 52, 74
Digtman, 326
Dikeman, 74, 216
Dilley, 11, 75, 296
Dillman, 75, 83, 120, 306
Dilly, 75, 206
Dimock, 75
Dinsdale, 61, 75, 84, 230, 297, 314, 320
Dittman, 75
Divers, 75, 88
Dixon, 4, 76
Dobson, 76
Dodd, 76
Dodge, 285, 297
Doge, 76
Dogg, 76
Dohse, 3, 76, 189, 277
Dolan, 68, 76, 77, 151, 220, 295, 297
Dolejs, 77
Doll, 61, 77, 83, 263
Dolphin, 77
Donahue, 54, 63, 77, 108, 155, 162, 163, 243, 278, 301
Doner, 77
Donner, 77, 96
Donovan, 78
Doran, 26, 78, 259
Dosch, 277
Dougherty, 78, 216
Douse, 254, 308
Dousman, 89, 154, 161, 199
Dowie, 34
Dowling, 34, 60, 78, 81, 98, 141, 243, 245, 246, 300
Dowse, 78, 90, 154, 193, 249
Doyle, 78, 296, 297, 298
Drake, 6, 7, 58, 78, 121, 179, 270, 300
Drew, 74, 78, 79, 336
Drexel, 79

Drezel, 267
Drinkhorn, 121
Drudik, 79
Drummel, 42
du Chien, 79, 163
DuChane, 173
Ducharme, 27, 79, 185, 325
DuCharme, 54, 65, 79, 267, 325
Dudley, 23, 79, 80, 89, 192, 285
Duffy, 27, 64, 80, 84, 298
Duha, 80
Duke, 101
Dull, 80, 85, 155
Dunbar, 35, 80, 81, 86, 156, 172, 193, 196, 263, 314, 321
Duncan, 47, 81, 122, 141, 170
Dunham, 81
Dunn, 71, 81, 296
Dunne, 78, 81, 84, 217, 230
Dupee, 102
Duquette, 71, 73
Durham, 81, 82
Durocher, 44
Duselaf, 82
Dvorak, 82, 267
Dworak, 82, 183, 190, 229, 279
Dwork, 82
Dyer, 82, 128, 148, 277

-E-

Easton, 82, 83, 284
Eckenberger, 83
Edlebach, 59, 83
Edson, 276
Edwards, 83, 254
Egan, 83, 117
Ehorn, 83, 191, 195
Eigum, 278
Eitsert, 83
Elch, 308
Eldridge, 83
Election Returns, 83, 84, 85
Eley, 85, 104
Elgar, 85
Ellefson, 85
Elliot, 36, 85
Ellis, 8, 36, 85, 86, 124, 155, 323, 324, 331
Ellithorpe, 86
Ellithrope, 86
Ellston, 86
Ellsworth, 86
Elsworth, 125
Elton, 86, 302
Elvin, 86
Emerson, 86
Emery, 86
Emigrant train, 86
Emshoff, 86, 119
Enerson, 87, 146
England, 87
English, 87
Enke, 87
Enright, 87, 118

Eredenberg, 336
Erickson, 87, 146, 220
Ertel, 87, 102, 296, 301, 325
Espenet, 100
Eukey, 84
Evans, 5, 6, 12, 16, 44, 65, 83, 84, 87, 88, 96, 99, 103, 133, 139, 155, 216, 227, 251, 297
Evert, 61, 75, 88
Everts, 88
Ewell, 88, 326
Ewers, 2, 88, 334
Eyers, 88

### -F-

Faber, 89, 117, 195
Fach, 89
Fagan, 89, 303
Fagen, 89
Fairbank, 89, 161
Fairfield, 89, 218
Falkner, 89
Fannon, 89
Farley, 89
Farmer, 89
Faroe, 167
Farr, 80, 89
Farrington, 89
Farris, 42, 45, 56, 78, 86, 89, 90, 108, 154, 157, 234, 249, 255, 273, 275, 277, 309
Fauke, 64, 121
Faulkner, 90
Faust, 90, 95, 96, 280, 306
Favor, 72, 90
Favre, 90, 98
Fay, 2, 199
Felde, 90, 91
Feldman, 91, 113, 158
Feldmann, 71, 91, 214
Ferguson, 91
Fernett, 91
Fernette, 91
Ferrel, 91
Ferrell, 84, 91, 272
Ferrick, 91, 152, 172, 219
Ferris, 137
Figum, 91, 92, 221
Fillmore, 92
Filmore, 92
Finke, 67
Finley, 92, 93, 149, 151, 181, 197, 220, 230, 274, 308, 319
Finn, 93
Finnette, 93
Finney, 8, 27, 41, 51, 93, 228, 298
Fischeretal, 93, 313
Fish, 2, 93, 205
Fisher, 8, 26, 93, 94, 102, 145, 228, 298, 314, 317, 328
Fisk, 34
Fitch, 94
Fitzgibbon, 84, 94
Fitzgibbons, 21, 94
Fitzsimmons, 94
Fiuke, 94

Flaherty, 21, 95
Flanagan, 88, 95
Flannagan, 95, 133, 183
Flannigan, 264
Fleeman, 95, 251
Fleming, 95
Flemming, 102
Flett, 25
Flucke, 35, 54
Flueke, 37
Fluke, 95
Flynn, 95, 243
Fogarty, 62, 63, 95
Fogel, 38
Fogh, 95
Folbrecht, 14, 59, 95, 123, 156, 296
Foley, 65, 77, 83, 95, 96, 120, 128, 143, 156, 217
Foran, 61, 84, 85, 96
Forde, 5, 96
Forst, 96
Forsythe, 11
Fortcamp, 208
Fortney, 96, 97, 101, 130, 206
Fortun, 97
Foshag, 338
Fosnow, 11
Foss, 97
Foucht, 214
Fountain, 97
Foust, 46, 83, 97
Fox, 6, 16, 44, 54, 90, 98, 137, 195, 258
Foy, 178
Foye, 98
Fralick, 98
Frame, 40
France, 98
Francis, 97
Fransburg, 78, 98
Fransche, 98, 183
Frasher, 98, 157
Frasier, 98
Frazier, 98
Fredenberg, 98, 337
Freeborn, 334
Freeman, 98, 99, 145, 198, 294, 314
French, 66, 99, 136, 298, 312
Fresche, 99
Friar, 99
Fritche, 99
Fritsche, 99, 303
Fritz, 214
Frost, 96
Fry, 100
Fryseth, 100
Fuhrman, 114
Fuka, 3, 100, 247, 326
Fuke, 100, 241
Fuller, 100
Funk, 100, 108, 255
Furgurson, 100
Furman, 100
Fusbi, 100

Genealogical Gleanings From Early Newspapers for Residents In and Near Crawford County, Wisconsin, 1897-1902

## -G-

Gable, 57
Gaffney, 100
Gage, 100
Gald, 100, 119
Gambel, 100
Gamble, 100
Gander, 84, 96, 100, 101, 113, 221, 296, 306
Ganyer, 101
Gardipe, 101
Gardner, 101, 266
Garner, 35, 84, 101, 102, 172, 185
Garrett, 102, 152
Garriety, 284
Garrison, 102
Garrity, 50, 67, 87, 102, 127, 155, 182, 297
Garrow, 102, 119, 303
Garvey, 25, 31, 44, 45, 50, 63, 84, 88, 102, 103, 104, 151, 197, 198, 211, 212, 223, 243, 246, 266, 308, 327
Gasligh, 104
Gauche, 104
Gaul, 277
Gaulke, 104, 243
Gaunsor, 104
Gay, 85, 86, 104, 217, 295
Gaylor, 105, 203
Gaylord, 105, 175
Gebart, 190
Geider, 105, 306
Geisler, 105, 207
Geitz, 83, 105, 225, 265, 315, 316
Geld (Gald?), 105
Gentil, 105
George, 32, 105, 106, 188, 208, 210, 221
Gerhardt, 106, 231, 232
Gerhart, 106
Gerton, 317
Gibbs, 76, 106
Giddings, 106
Giegel, 106
Gierhart, 106
Gifford, 106, 139, 311
Gilbert, 276
Gilchrist, 43, 269
Gilder, 1, 106, 107, 221
Gill, 107, 108, 214, 295
Gilligan, 84, 108, 127, 128
Gillis, 108, 148
Gilman, 108
Gilmartin, 40, 165
Gimmel, 108
Gink, 17, 108, 162, 177, 211, 250
Girdler, 108, 152
Gisler, 214
Gleason, 77, 105, 108, 109
Glenn, 109
Glover, 109
Glovke, 109
Gluss, 109, 330
Glynn, 109
Gobin, 276
Going, 109, 202
Gokey, 72, 109, 115
Goldfinger, 109
Goldsmith, 109
Gommell, 109
Gonier, 109
Goodnoe, 204
Goodwin, 21, 109, 110, 172
Gordon, 94, 110
Gorman, 110, 117
Gossel, 14, 110, 112, 143
Gossell, 83, 110
Grant, 301
Granzow, 27, 111, 155, 175, 279
Grap, 111
Grapp, 26, 111, 191, 243
Grate, 111, 204, 286
Gratton, 43, 111
Grauk, 332
Graul, 111, 316
Gravel, 133
Graves, 37, 111, 112, 204, 298
Gray, 99, 112, 284
Greele, 84
Greeley, 112, 234
Greemore, 112
Green, 31, 58, 96, 101, 112, 113, 226, 283
Greene, 113, 297
Gregerson, 91, 113, 114, 251, 335
Gregeson, 114
Gregorsen, 114
Gregorson, 114, 128
Greisbach, 114
Greisback, 114, 315
Grell, 114
Grelle, 39, 44, 54, 114
Gremore, 19, 115, 133, 250
Grenmore, 115, 250
Grey, 115
Gribble, 115
Griesbach, 115, 296, 297
Griffin, 116, 333
Griffith, 116
Gronert, 64, 116, 216
Groom, 116, 172, 278
Gross, 214
Grow, 116
Guernsey, 116, 270
Gugler, 116, 162
Guilder, 6, 107
Guist, 11, 116
Gunderson, 116, 117, 151, 230, 254, 256
Gurman, 117
Gurnsey, 117
Gurtson, 117
Gutherie, 83, 117
Guthrie, 41
Gutknecht, 117
Guy, 89, 117, 215
Gwindle, 117

## -H-

Haas, 117

Genealogical Gleanings From Early Newspapers for Residents In and Near
Crawford County, Wisconsin, 1897-1902

Hacket, 212
Hackett, 220
Hackheimer, 117, 273
Hadden, 117
Haddock, 4, 117, 123, 161, 317
Hadick, 8
Haffa, 118
Hagerty, 276
Haggarty, 118
Haggerty, 9, 36, 37, 38, 74, 77, 104, 118, 166, 167, 176, 189, 235, 259
Hagie, 25
Hagne, 118
Hahn, 119, 132, 267
Hail, 119
Haines, 49, 86, 119, 214
Hains, 119
Hall, 33, 88, 119, 279
Halpin, 25, 27, 223
Halsey, 119
Halsted, 114, 119, 210, 319
Halton, 11
Halverson, 87, 100, 107, 119, 120, 146, 147, 160
Halvorson, 25
Hamen, 214
Hamilton, 3, 36, 63, 65, 96, 120, 125, 171, 209, 210, 213, 214, 240, 267, 270, 334, 337
Hamley, 264
Hammerly, 61, 84, 85, 120, 121, 310
Hammond, 33
Hanby, 206
Hancock, 121, 213
Hand, 53, 121
Haney, 121
Hank, 167
Hankins, 64, 121
Hanks, 90, 121, 280
Hansen, 121, 296
Hanson, 6, 78, 121, 151, 302
Hanthack, 122
Harding, 96, 122, 126, 194
Harford, 122
Harkheimer, 122
Harkneimer, 10, 122
Harland, 292
Harned, 240
Harriman, 122, 276
Harrington, 84, 115, 122, 123, 168, 182, 274, 285, 306
Harris, 8, 61, 86, 108, 123, 124, 135, 154, 156, 191, 193, 194, 197, 228, 262, 278, 293, 307, 321, 330
Harrison, 79, 124
Hart, 29, 124, 125, 137
Hartford, 125
Hartley, 125
Hartnet, 29
Harvat, 125, 279
Harvey, 125
Hasart, 125
Haskel, 125
Haskell, 125, 177, 311, 317
Haskin, 240
Haskins, 13, 31, 62, 85, 125, 126, 136, 148, 153, 194, 267, 295

Hasselbach, 126
Hauge, 126
Haupt, 83, 127, 147
Hawthorne, 127, 308
Hayden, 127, 333
Hayes, 19, 84, 118, 127, 128, 151, 182, 214, 222, 231, 244, 257, 270
Hayman, 152
Haynes, 49, 108, 119, 127, 128, 307
Hays, 30, 34, 83, 107, 124, 128, 151, 193, 221, 272
Hayward, 128
Hazelbach, 128
Hazelwood, 128, 129, 158, 222, 264, 335
Hazen, 4, 8, 19, 27, 30, 46, 86, 100, 129, 140, 144, 154, 167, 279, 311, 314, 323, 333
Hazzart, 227
Heal, 65, 121, 129, 130, 291
Healy, 130
Heaman, 78
Heaton, 10, 130
Heide, 42, 54
Heiden, 130, 319
Heidenwald, 130
Heilman, 130, 273
Hein, 130, 170
Heirs, 57, 114, 137
Heise, 130, 326
Heisz, 130, 282, 326
Helgerson, 126, 130
Heligas, 130, 131, 194, 223, 233, 296
Helligas, 131
Helmont, 131
Helwig, 47
Henderson, 12, 131, 214, 259, 308
Hendrick, 131, 289
Hennesey, 131
Hennessy, 131
Henning, 6, 131, 262
Henry, 33
Henthorn, 131, 186, 295
Henthorne, 132
Herald, 24, 132
Herbert, 245
Herold, 39, 85, 127, 132, 156, 225, 265, 283, 284, 296
Herpel, 132, 282
Herrling, 132, 221
Hess, 132, 133, 198
Hesse, 133
Hickey, 133
Hicklin, 133, 227
Hiena, 133
Hiers, 37, 133
Higgins, 37, 133, 303
Hilfritch, 133
Hill, 5, 85, 133, 314
Hilldritsch, 133, 150
Hillfritch, 133
Hilliman, 133, 134
Hillman, 134
Hiltan, 134
Himley, 84, 134
Hinds, 216
Hines, 40, 89, 90, 134, 237

Genealogical Gleanings From Early Newspapers for Residents In and Near
Crawford County, Wisconsin, 1897-1902

Hired, 134
Hobble, 2
Hobbs, 7, 10, 134, 135, 141, 161, 266, 280, 306, 314
Hochberger, 176
Hodge, 135
Hoffland, 135, 296, 297
Hoffman, 27, 84, 135
Hogan, 135, 202
Hogenfrost, 135
Hoisington, 14, 135, 262, 296
Holbrook, 208
Holden, 3, 16, 135, 136, 293
Holiday, 136
Holiday?, 136
Holister, 136
Holliday, 136, 267
Hollister, 136
Holly, 136, 137
Holm, 137
Holman, 137
Holverson, 21, 137, 300, 301
Home, 137, 260, 275
Homewood, 137
Homuth, 137
Hon, 137
Honnaker, 216
Honsel, 137
Honslik, 84
Honzel, 137
Honzell, 44
Hoopman, 137, 292
Hoover, 27, 83, 262
Hopkins, 23, 138, 242, 315
Hopkin's, 137
Hopwood, 138
Horal, 80, 138, 296, 323, 324
Horan, 138
Horrigan, 138, 191
Horsfall, 10, 138
Host, 57, 138
Houga, 138
Hounsel, 139
Hounsell, 85
Houston, 139, 142, 143
Hover, 139
Hovey, 139, 228
Howard, 139
Howe, 22, 102, 130, 139, 191, 244, 295, 297
Howell, 139
Huard, 4, 30, 82, 85, 129, 139, 140, 310, 311, 333
Hubanks, 35
Hubbard, 259
Hubbel, 140
Hubert, 140
Hudson, 61, 84, 140, 167, 295
Huffman, 18, 101, 110, 140, 141, 301, 327
Huffman & Onstine, 18, 141
Huffsmidth, 141
Hufschmidt, 272
Hughbank, 141
Hughbanks, 81, 141, 201, 295, 311
Hughes, 141
Hughey, 141

Hughs, 141
Hungerford, 172
Hunt, 141
Hunter, 51, 59, 93, 141, 243, 318
Huntington, 142
Hural, 290
Hurd, 142, 233
Hurlburt, 142, 232, 237
Hurlbut, 17, 142, 234, 306
Husher, 139, 142, 148, 156
Hutchison, 143
Hutson, 143
Hutt, 110, 112, 143
Hyde, 143
Hymn, 208
Hysall, 283

-I-

Igles, 143
immigrants, 156
Immigrants, 143
Infield, 143, 295, 297
Ingham, 133, 143, 169
Ingle, 279
Ingles, 37, 143, 144
Inter City Concert Co., 144
Irishman, 169
Ishmael, 144
Ivers, 233, 273
Iverson, 83, 84, 144, 151, 279, 281, 295, 296, 297, 331

-J-

Jackson, 94, 144, 145, 210
Jacob, 145, 146
Jacobs, 5, 145
Jamboi, 145, 197
Jambura, 323, 324
James, 145, 157
Jarvis, 145, 148
Jeffries, 143, 145
Jenkins, 66, 99, 121, 145, 146, 267, 283, 321
Jennay, 146
Jennings, 128, 228
Jetter, 17, 146
Jewett, 146, 287
Joerres, 195, 325
Johnson, 7, 18, 22, 25, 60, 65, 77, 87, 120, 127, 137, 145, 146,
    147, 148, 156, 168, 174, 202, 214, 224, 266, 295, 297, 309,
    328, 336, 337
Jones, 26, 36, 61, 82, 83, 85, 90, 119, 142, 148, 149, 156, 172,
    196, 246
Joy, 38, 77, 92, 149, 152, 181, 266, 296, 297
Junker, 149
Jurgensen, 55, 84, 149, 150
Jurgenson, 150, 231, 237, 289

-K-

Kadoch, 150, 218
Kage, 150
Kahlar, 142

Genealogical Gleanings From Early Newspapers for Residents In and Near
Crawford County, Wisconsin, 1897-1902

Kahler, 23, 133, 150
Kahoun, 150
Kaiser, 150, 311, 330
Kaizer, 84
Kalina, 150, 290
Kalinn, 37
Kane, 41, 49, 76, 77, 91, 108, 150, 151, 152, 183, 219, 223, 300, 301
Kanouse, 242
Karnopp, 152, 265, 336
Karon, 152
Karr, 102, 152
Kasparek, 297
Kasperek, 12, 153
Kast, 41, 62, 78, 84, 85, 86, 90, 126, 136, 153, 154, 165, 166, 169, 172, 182, 221, 249, 255, 296, 300, 306, 318, 337
Katuman, 218
Kavanda, 154, 286
Kazda, 16, 41, 154
Keago, 154, 248
Keeley, 130, 154, 169, 224, 262, 266, 282, 296
Keely, 108, 127
Keenan, 130, 154
Keifer, 54, 154
Keilley, 154, 266
Keiser, 111
Keizer, 154
Kelana, 19
Kelina, 65
Kelley, 46, 63, 72, 83, 96, 154, 155, 210, 217, 242
Kellogg, 155, 175
Kelly, 52, 65, 90, 96, 102, 155, 182, 190
Kelts, 155
Kenefic, 308
Kennedy, 155
Kenneson, 155
Kennison, 221
Kenyon, 155
Keop, 155
Kepler, 80, 155
Kern, 155, 324
Kerrigan, 155, 156, 170
Kessler, 16, 132, 156, 328
Kettle, 84
Key, 156
Keyes, 34, 156
Keys, 73
Kidd, 156, 199, 288, 322
Kiefner, 96, 120, 187, 274
Kielley, 42, 45, 90, 97, 156, 157
Kielly, 157
Kieser, 44, 157, 303
Kimbal, 157
Kimball, 157
Kimble, 98, 157
Kimmel, 84, 153, 157
Kincaid, 157, 158
Kincannon, 8, 9, 112, 114, 133, 156, 158, 184, 198, 221, 267
Kinder, 54, 84, 85, 158
King, 49, 61, 94, 158, 159, 165, 284, 297
Kingsland, 125
Kinion, 159
Kinney, 159

Kivgne, 151
Kizer, 159
Klema, 159
Klingenberg, 159
Kloak, 50
Kloth, 26, 127, 159
Klotz, 159
Klucka, 37
Knapp, 116
Kneeland, 31, 84, 137, 159
Knoble, 160
Knops, 144
Knott, 22, 160
Knudson, 77
Knussman, 160
Knutson, 134, 160, 215, 308
Koch, 160, 264
Koep, 160
Koepp, 160, 323, 324
Kolar, 161
Kolash, 288
Konecheck, 161, 184
Konechek, 133
Konklin, 161, 309
Kopan, 135, 161, 237, 296, 297, 298
Kopats, 161
Kosa, 161
Kosharek, 161
Kotera, 161
Kozelka, 47, 161
Krall, 89, 161
Krameer, 162
Kramer, 96, 144, 161, 162, 168, 188, 246, 252, 280, 322
Kratche, 162
Krause, 163
Kraut, 162
Kremer, 162
Kries, 111
Kriz, 10, 122, 162, 219
Kroker, 162, 220
Kronsage, 162
Krouskup, 162, 186
Kruckeberg, 162
Krukeberger, 162
Kruscheke, 116
Kruschka, 201
Kruschke, 162, 214, 243
Kuchenbecker, 39, 99, 162, 163, 225, 264, 265
Kuchenbeeker, 163
Kuckenbecker, 85
Kunzman, 163
Kurtz, 104
Kussmaul, 94, 123, 163, 281, 305
Kvigne, 151, 163

-L-

La Baron, 145, 146
La Bonne, 163, 309
La Vake, 12, 163
Laartz, 163
Lable, 6
LaBon, 115

Genealogical Gleanings From Early Newspapers for Residents In and Near
Crawford County, Wisconsin, 1897-1902

LaBonne, 79, 163
Lacy, 163, 164
Lagaman, 1, 14, 17, 164, 194, 201, 262, 274
Lagamann, 34
Lagan, 61, 165, 295, 296, 297
Lageman, 139
LaGeune, 35, 165, 246
Laird, 44, 141, 165, 222, 223, 259, 297
Lake, 165
Lambrecht, 40
Lamoreau, 165
Lamouthe, 165
Lamp, 247
Lampman, 267
Lamson, 67
Lance, 152, 153, 165, 166
Landis, 166, 205
Lang, 10, 166
Langaman, 17
Langdon, 31, 166, 300
Lange, 32, 166, 202
Langford, 166
Lanka, 264
Lankford, 11, 143, 166, 167, 295, 320
Lankie, 167, 237
Lantry, 167, 243
Lapoint, 21
LaPointe, 71
Larabee, 129, 219
Larave, 167
Laraviere, 85, 167
LaRiviere, 167
LaRocke, 42
Larocque, 167
Laroque, 141, 167
LaRoque, 167
Larrabee, 167
Larrivere, 167
Larsen, 129, 167
Larson, 26, 64, 111, 118, 123, 146, 161, 167, 168, 263, 298
Lasche, 168
Lathrop, 7, 10, 36, 39, 76, 122, 126, 134, 153, 168, 169, 193,
   228, 235, 246, 265, 267, 286, 308, 310, 325
Latimore, 76
Lattimore, 77, 169
Lawler, 42, 143, 167, 169, 170, 217, 225, 229, 233, 262
Lawless, 85, 170, 221
Lawrance, 170
Lawrence, 14, 35, 49, 51, 81, 83, 86, 101, 109, 130, 148, 170,
   171, 172, 179, 196, 210, 217, 262, 271, 278, 286, 287, 309,
   313, 314
Lawver, 173, 179, 327, 328
Layd, 173, 296, 297, 308
Layton, 173, 189
Leahy, 173
Leary, 21, 62, 63, 137, 173, 220, 233
Leater, 297
LeBaun, 173
Lechher, 3
Lechner, 27, 173
Lechnir, 44, 84, 173, 326
Lechnor, 174
Lee, 57, 107, 146, 151, 174, 266, 309

Leefeldt, 46, 111, 174
Leefelt, 174
Lees, 57
Lefeldt, 174
Legroo, 303
Leguene, 174
Leinfelder, 174, 175
Leitner, 155, 175
Leivig, 139
Lemere, 8
Lenehan, 85, 155, 175, 183
Lennehan, 150
Lennon, 175
Lenox, 175
Lerche, 127, 138, 175
LeRoque, 175
Lesard, 175
Lescke, 25
Lessard, 37, 175
Lessare, 306
Lester, 83, 84, 105, 175, 176, 221, 295, 304
Lewig, 16, 154, 176, 214, 314, 331, 335
Lewis, 55, 57, 58, 84, 85, 104, 140, 171, 172, 176, 177, 179,
   205, 294, 301
Lewison, 140, 177, 183, 185
Liddey, 177
Lienfelder, 281
Lightfoot, 327
Lilly, 108, 177, 320
Linclemm, 125, 177
Lindemann, 177, 306
Linder, 50, 177, 190
Lindig, 13, 177, 178
Lindmer, 13, 178
Lindner, 37, 65, 84, 178, 286
Lindsay, 206
Lindstrom, 6, 59, 178, 186
Linstrom, 178
Littlejohn, 33
Litze, 178
Livingston, 178, 304
Lock, 15, 178
Lockart, 178
Lockert, 178
LoeBaron, 11
Loftus, 61, 178
Logan, 36, 178
Logerman, 114
Long, 74, 171, 172, 178, 179, 222, 250
Longstreth, 179, 270
Loomis, 152, 179, 316
Lortz, 179, 317
Louis, 179, 251, 289
Loveland, 36, 179
Lowe, 31, 46, 53, 84, 179, 180, 275, 309
Lubke, 180
Lucas, 180, 217, 324
Lucey, 260
Lucy, 21, 77, 180
Ludden, 180
Ludewig, 180
Ludoska, 180
Ludwig, 164, 180, 235

# Genealogical Gleanings From Early Newspapers for Residents In and Near Crawford County, Wisconsin, 1897-1902

Luetgert, 180
Lum, 314
Lumpkins, 180
Lurkins, 180
Lusky, 180
Lutz, 180
Lynch, 21, 84, 92, 180, 181, 220, 296, 308
Lyness, 181
Lynn, 56
Lyons, 67, 83, 181, 229, 237, 320
Lysne, 84, 181
Lysue, 181
Lytle, 283

## -M-

Mabee, 282
Madden, 181
Maddox, 181, 182
Magee, 182, 303
MaGee, 48, 241
Magie, 182
Maha, 182
Mahan, 38, 182, 295, 298
Maher, 122, 182
Mahnert, 326
Mahoney, 103, 181, 182
Mahr, 305
Main, 182
Mallard, 182
Mallory, 182
Malone, 85, 98, 110, 127, 182, 183
Maloney, 304
Maney, 4, 95, 151, 183, 184, 291, 321
Manning, 184, 242, 263
Mansfield, 49, 184, 216, 259, 260, 276, 311
Mara, 44, 161, 184
Marfelius, 83, 184
Marfilius, 184
Marfillius, 185
Marker, 185
Markham, 185
Marshall, 196
Marsten, 26, 185
Marston, 25, 125, 151, 185, 223
Martan, 323, 324
Martel, 185
Martell, 79, 185
Martilius, 185
Martin, 44, 67, 162, 185, 186, 214, 239, 324
Martner, 1, 54, 186, 216
Martsalf, 186
Martsoff, 186
Marush, 186
Marvin, 115, 187
Mason, 12, 86, 156, 187, 228
Masten, 52, 101, 187, 301
Mataka, 187, 274
Mather, 188
Mathew, 9
Mathews, 162, 188, 213, 306
Matthews, 5
Mattick, 188

Mattie, 188, 235, 278
Maxwell, 8, 188, 190, 191, 197, 275, 277
Mayhew, 188
Maynard, 106, 188
Mayo, 99
Mayock, 189
Mazera, 76, 189
McAuley, 61, 176, 189, 190, 198, 255, 292, 304
McBurney, 190
McCabe, 190, 218
McCale, 177, 190
McCann, 82, 138, 188, 190, 191, 323
McCartney, 191
McCartny, 259
McClerg, 191
McCloskey, 54, 191, 219
McCluskey, 84
McClusky, 111, 191, 243
McCoey, 71
McCone, 191
McConey, 191
McCord, 143, 156, 191
McCormack, 191
McCormick, 16, 59, 69, 116, 139, 151, 191, 192, 230, 297
McCouey, 71
McCoy, 192
McCrillis, 192
McCullick, 52, 56, 61, 83, 192, 231, 289, 315, 337
McCullock, 30, 128, 192, 193, 216, 272, 315
McCurchy, 164
McDaniel, 51, 65, 136, 193, 196, 203, 276
McDaniels, 193, 216
McDermott, 309
McDill, 193, 203, 296, 297
McDonald, 10, 156, 185, 193, 194, 205, 209, 298
McDonnel, 194
McDonnell, 1, 14, 194
McDonough, 194
McDougal, 194
McDowell, 36, 58, 84, 126, 138, 194, 246, 250
McEachern, 195
McElroy, 98, 195
McEwen, 195
McFarland, 195, 246
McGarigle, 195
McGaughey, 37
McGee, 189, 195
McGinley, 195
McGorvan, 195, 334
McGovern, 195
McGowen, 129, 195
McGrath, 78, 195, 276, 325
McGraw, 152
McGree, 85
McGregor, 195, 289
McGuiness, 55
McHarg, 195
McKane, 196
McKay, 196
McKee, 196
McKenney, 196
McKey, 264
McKight, 306

Genealogical Gleanings From Early Newspapers for Residents In and Near
Crawford County, Wisconsin, 1897-1902

McKillip, 196
McKillop, 6
McKincannon, 196
McKinley, 187, 196, 197
McKinney, 36, 178, 197, 214, 232, 303
McKnight, 197
McKon, 197
McLaughlin, 104, 197
McLenehan, 197
McLess, 263
McLusky, 49
McManamy, 145, 197
McMann, 217
McManus, 38, 197
McMasters, 197
McMillan, 83
McMillin, 197
McMullen, 133, 198
McNamara, 84, 198, 200, 296, 297
McPherson, 68, 198
McQuiggan, 198
McReynolds, 198, 211, 298
McWilliams, 21, 198, 294
Mead, 158, 196, 198
Meagher, 183, 198, 199, 296, 297
Megee, 199
Meger, 199
Meisenbek, 111
Mellin, 199
Meltick, 199
Melvin, 199, 229, 235, 295, 297
Menges, 4, 5, 30, 44, 61, 70, 84, 116, 129, 140, 199, 311, 333
Mercer, 70, 146, 156, 193, 199, 200, 217, 223, 321
Merrell, 137, 200, 228
Merrifield, 200
Merrill, 18, 65, 200
Merville, 200, 304
Messiling, 200
Messling, 19, 198, 200
Mettic, 200
Mettick, 200, 205
Mettsick, 200
Meyer, 86, 123, 125, 129, 164, 200, 201, 216, 230, 251
Meyers, 86, 141, 143, 193, 201, 223, 321
Mezera, 27, 201, 217, 262
Mezra, 201
Michael, 116, 201, 202, 326
Michelson, 146, 202
Michle, 202
Mickel, 202, 288
Mickleson, 202
Mider, 203
Miller, 6, 8, 20, 34, 42, 54, 62, 64, 66, 84, 86, 105, 115, 139,
    151, 162, 166, 173, 202, 203, 204, 216, 218, 252, 255, 266,
    277, 288, 294, 296, 331
Milliner, 204
Mills, 42, 64, 82, 83, 104, 111, 112, 166, 198, 204, 205, 220,
    274, 292
Millspaugh, 108, 205, 228
Milluce, 32
Milner, 205
Milspaugh, 205, 228
Mindham, 193, 205, 280

Minshall, 205
Mitchell, 13, 72, 83, 84, 97, 127, 172, 177, 205, 206, 207, 263,
    289, 295, 296, 297, 304, 309
Mizera, 207, 262
Moch, 207
Mock, 207
Moe, 207, 220
Moeller, 105, 207
Mohr, 207, 316
Moldren, 207
Moline, 207
Molstad, 207
Monahan, 35, 109, 266
Monehan, 208
Monohan, 109, 208, 266
Monson, 208, 214
Montgomery, 70, 208, 255, 296, 318, 333
Mook, 67, 139
Moon, 46, 67, 84, 122, 208, 209, 257
Mooney, 209
Moore, 4, 29, 34, 209, 239, 288, 308
Moran, 194, 209
Morehead, 209
Moreland, 209
Morgan, 194, 209
Morgans, 209
Morkri, 209, 268
Morley, 143
Morris, 84, 209, 277
Morrison, 88, 127, 209, 230, 308
Morrissey, 210, 217
Morrow, 220
Morse, 62, 63, 106, 171, 210, 213, 214, 267, 270
Morten, 210
Morton, 210
Moses, 12, 210, 295
Mosgrove, 210, 211, 218, 319, 335
Moshier, 167, 211
Muck, 211
Mueller, 211
Muffley, 198, 211
Mulaney, 211
Mulchrone, 211
Mulhiem, 93
Mullaney, 102, 103, 211, 212
Mullanley, 212
Mulligan, 212
Mulliken, 212
Mullikin, 36, 38, 85, 186, 212
Mullin, 212
Mumford, 212
Mun, 212
Mundt, 73, 110, 236, 255
Munion, 230
Muns, 20
Munson, 151, 212, 288, 295, 297
Murley, 212, 238
Murphy, 37, 47, 54, 85, 100, 213, 297
Murrane, 59
Murray, 213
Murry, 213
Musselman, 83, 210, 213, 214, 216
Musser, 214

Mustum, 18
Mutchmann, 214
Myer, 262
Myers, 156, 214

## -N-

Naes, 214
Nash, 25, 131, 146, 151, 174, 214, 295, 297
Natwick, 84, 214
Naurt, 214, 250
Neable, 47
Nedredoe, 160, 215
Nedreloe, 215
Neidig, 11, 215
Neilson, 215
Nelson, 10, 41, 117, 118, 193, 212, 215, 216, 276, 282, 295, 297, 315, 322
Nett, 37, 216, 270, 286
Netz, 216
New, 201, 202, 216
Newcomb, 36, 86, 216, 277, 336
Newman, 11
Newton, 77, 86, 88, 184, 216, 217, 229, 311, 317
Nice, 217, 230, 262, 265, 305
Nicholson, 136, 255
Nickel, 180, 217
Nickelson, 217, 328
Nickerson, 84, 87, 217
Nightingale, 170
Niland, 96, 217, 236
Nocz, 201, 217
Noe, 81, 199, 217, 289, 321
Noggle, 141, 170, 217, 298
Nolan, 44, 78, 115, 210, 217, 218, 241, 281
Noney, 218, 237
Noon, 152, 218
Norris, 38, 80, 218
North, 89, 218
Nottingham, 218
Novak, 150, 218
Novey, 218
Nugent, 61, 84, 89, 124, 151, 218, 254, 296, 297
Nurphy, 54
Nutter, 6, 218
Nuzum, 21, 33, 57, 72, 90, 109, 119, 137, 330

## -O-

Oakes, 7, 218
Obeleiter, 214
Oben, 6, 218, 306
O'Brien, 10, 96, 122, 219
Ochlschager, 219
Ochnasek, 219
O'Dea, 96, 219
Odenwald, 219
Oehlochlager, 219
Oehring, 104
Oestrander, 219
Oestreich, 219
Oestreick, 219
O'Keefe, 219, 296

Oland, 220
Oleson, 25, 87, 220
Olsen, 145, 220
Olson, 25, 84, 130, 151, 162, 207, 220, 221, 278
O'Mailey, 221, 258
O'Malley, 221
O'Mally, 221
O'Neil, 19, 26, 54, 83, 93, 132, 133, 134, 165, 170, 198, 221, 222, 223, 241, 269, 297, 328, 333
Only, 223, 253
Onstine, 18, 27, 72, 86, 130, 143, 199, 201, 223, 274, 288
Opprecht, 223, 224, 274
Oppreicht, 92, 224
Opreicht, 337
Oriloff, 224
Ortlaff, 224
Osbacher, 224
Osborn, 166
Osborne, 224
O'Shaughessy, 224, 266
O'Shaughnessy, 298
O'Shaunessy, 278
Oss, 225
Ostrander, 85, 225, 324
Oswald, 29, 84, 132, 162, 168, 225, 281, 303
Otchenosock, 110, 226
Otman, 44, 226, 310
O'Toole, 226
Ottman, 226, 326
Otto, 65, 79, 85, 199, 225, 226, 279, 298
Oustrich, 226
Overton, 113, 114
Owens, 156, 226

## -P-

Page, 226
Pahrnum, 226
Paine, 226
Palderson, 226
Pally, 226
Palmer, 6, 171, 226, 323
Pane, 226
Panka, 27
Parfrey, 227
Parker, 227
Parsons, 47, 227
Paskeivitz, 227
Paskewitz, 227
Patalaff, 36, 227
Patch, 133, 227
Patten, 84, 125, 227
Patterson, 227
Patton, 228, 296
Patzlaff, 44, 228
Paulsen, 139, 228
Paulson, 228
Payman, 11
Payne, 226, 228, 256
Payor, 228
Peacha, 8, 228
Peacock, 17, 53, 85, 99, 104, 114, 148, 156, 172, 193, 205, 228, 229, 247, 248, 270, 313

Pease, 4, 229, 241, 279, 321, 332
Peasley, 199, 229
Peck, 35, 36, 51, 75, 83, 170, 209, 212, 230, 284
Pecor, 6, 230, 265, 301
Peer, 230
Peerson, 230
Peese, 230
Pellock, 230
Pelock, 230, 303
Pelok, 230, 311
Pelton, 10, 158
Pengilly, 201, 230, 231
Perham, 231
Perrin, 56, 81, 83, 94, 114, 158, 178, 231, 262, 337
Peterson, 25, 34, 84, 85, 86, 97, 106, 142, 143, 156, 185, 231, 232, 233, 269, 303, 306
Pettit, 280
Pettygrove, 211, 220, 233
Pfahler, 18, 233, 262
Pfeifer, 163
Pfhaler, 233, 273
Phalen, 233, 254
Phaler, 20, 233, 273
Phalin, 83, 233, 234, 295, 297
Phelan, 80
Philamalee, 240
Philamolee, 234
Philips, 234, 289
Phillamale, 234
Phillamalee, 234
Phillips, 43, 64, 65, 112, 142, 156, 234, 264, 296, 297, 307
Picha, 219, 235, 265, 281
Pickett, 118, 235, 296, 297, 300
Pidd, 331
Pier, 45, 180, 188, 235
Pierce, 55, 221, 235
Piesley, 199, 235
Pinkham, 67
Pion, 159, 235
Pitcka, 235
Pitsenberger, 50, 235, 236, 262
Pitsengerger, 236
Pittsenberger, 236
Pittsley, 84, 113, 236
Pittzenberger, 33, 236
Pitzenberger, 236
Pitzer, 38, 236
Pivot, 48, 81, 156, 217, 236, 248
Pleuard, 114
Plimpton, 236, 255
Plourd, 236, 263
Poehler, 218, 237, 245
Pokorny, 248
Poladna, 167, 237
Polda, 237, 268
Pollen, 237
Pollow, 161, 237
Polodna, 237
Pomeraning, 139
Pomerening, 237
Pomerning, 237
Pomeroy, 237
Pond, 83, 140, 142, 237

Popper, 60, 238, 316
Portcamp, 35
Porter, 25, 35, 44, 55, 83, 136, 156, 195, 212, 226, 238, 239, 317
Portwein, 209, 239
Portwine, 239, 304
Posey, 32, 65, 86, 90, 96, 108, 143, 186, 236, 239, 240, 293, 320
Postle, 241
Potter, 241
Potts, 241
Poupe, 27
Powell, 241
Powers, 126, 241
Pratt, 13, 79, 130, 178, 193, 241, 273, 321
Prechaska, 100, 241
Prentice, 241, 315
Prew, 115, 241
Prey, 241
Price, 241, 329
Prince, 241, 311
Pritchett, 242
Pritts, 242
Prochaska, 84, 93, 186, 323
Proeter, 323
Pryor, 266
Puckett, 242, 296
Pugh, 242, 314
Pugmire, 242
Pullen, 242, 248
Purington, 242, 246
Purrington, 6, 57, 86, 154, 184, 228, 242, 243, 301, 307
Putnam, 40, 243, 245
Pyer, 243

-Q-

Qualiman, 104, 243
Quallman, 104, 243
Qualman, 243
Quame, 243
Quamme, 269
Quillan, 243
Quinian, 243
Quinn, 35, 59, 84, 103, 111, 118, 141, 208, 243

-R-

Rabehl, 243
Racey, 38
Radka, 243
Raffauf, 127, 139
Ragan, 243, 244
Ralph, 244
Ran, 245, 284
Randal, 244
Randall, 23, 58, 127, 208, 244, 295, 296, 297, 298, 317
Ranek, 244
Ranney, 245
Ransom, 245
Ransome, 243, 245
Rathbun, 258
Rathburn, 37, 123

Genealogical Gleanings From Early Newspapers for Residents In and Near
Crawford County, Wisconsin, 1897-1902

Ratter, 245
Rau, 1, 245
Raukin, 245
Raw, 245, 338
Ray, 27, 55, 82, 112, 118, 168, 197, 214, 245, 246, 270
Raymond, 246
Reagles, 221
Rean, 246
Redfield, 35, 165, 246
Redmond, 246
Reed, 107, 246
Reeder, 114
Rees, 104, 246, 322
Reese, 104, 246
Reeter, 1, 83, 130, 158, 170, 194, 228, 247, 251, 305
Reichert, 75, 88, 89, 117, 134, 161, 317
Reichman, 247, 264
Reichmann, 48, 61, 163, 247, 263
Reiger, 177, 247
Reigh, 247
Reik, 100, 247
Reimer, 248, 294
Reinhart, 118
Reinhold, 154, 248
Reinow, 248
Reiser, 248
Reitemeyr, 133
Reiter, 229, 248, 262
Renak, 248
Reublin, 320
Revelix, 21
Reynolds, 38, 72, 78, 90, 108, 125, 126, 143, 148, 154, 228, 236, 242, 248, 249, 256, 278, 337
Rheim, 249
Rhein, 37, 164, 214, 249
Rhienhart, 84
Rhinehart, 36, 46, 107, 208, 249
Rholik, 249
Rhone, 267
Rhyg, 249
Rhynders, 249
Rhyne, 47, 249
Rice, 30, 51, 166, 249, 250, 297, 299
Richard, 96, 115, 250
Richards, 37, 115, 250
Richardson, 42, 90, 220
Richmond, 3, 250
Rickliffe, 250
Rider, 20, 83, 134, 156, 203, 214, 247, 250, 251, 265, 280
Ridgeman, 18
Ridgman, 67
Rieger, 251
Rienow, 87, 251
Riley, 2, 14, 62, 95, 158, 222, 251, 252, 296, 298
Rinehart, 16, 252
Ringsack, 252
Rinter, 136
Rittenhouse, 36, 210, 252, 322
Roach, 3, 8, 65, 84, 92, 139, 140, 162, 219, 228, 252, 279
Robb, 2, 104, 127, 252, 253, 288
Roberts, 334
Robertson, 77, 253
Robinson, 37, 70, 82, 84, 107, 152, 220, 253, 255, 277

Rod, 137
Rodgers, 254, 326
Roe, 254
Rogers, 27, 77, 84, 116, 117, 118, 180, 185, 233, 254
Rohlic, 254
Rohlik, 255
Rohrig, 263
Rohring, 255
Rolfson, 237
Root, 253, 255
Rose, 83, 133, 255, 326
Rosencrans, 56, 215, 236, 255, 290, 296
Rosencranz, 262
Rotan, 86, 101, 255
Roth, 10, 256, 296, 297, 298
Round, 256
Rounds, 46, 57, 60, 72, 75, 84, 86, 101, 107, 116, 166, 182, 187, 196, 197, 208, 221, 246, 248, 251, 255, 256, 257, 288, 296, 301, 304, 329, 337
Rowan, 257
Rowe, 16, 55, 61, 102, 257, 258
Rowell, 192
Rowley, 36, 37, 80, 160, 258
Royer, 258
Rubecheck, 137
Rubjecek, 277
Rublin, 258
Rudd, 258
Ruiter, 258
Runice, 84, 258
Runkel, 221, 258
Rupp, 258
Russell, 148, 258, 259, 291
Rust, 259
Rutter, 5, 259
Ryan, 47, 110, 259, 260, 296, 326
Ryne, 260

-S-

Sable, 260, 264
Sage, 133, 137, 219, 260, 282
Salmon, 260, 297
Salsbury, 260
Sampson, 24, 76, 184, 260, 261, 295, 308, 321
Sands, 314
Sandusky, 261
Sandy, 25
Sanger, 14, 17, 51, 83, 164, 214, 219, 262, 313, 331
Sankford, 262
Sappington, 50, 169, 262, 311
Sauk, 207, 262, 287
Sauk (or Zoch), 262
Savage, 49, 114, 233, 262, 263
Scanlon, 263
Schaer, 118
Schally, 225
Schaufenbuhl, 59, 263
Schawtka, 226
Scheinpilug, 263
Scherlin, 263
Schiebel, 247
Schlager, 263

Genealogical Gleanings From Early Newspapers for Residents In and Near
Crawford County, Wisconsin, 1897-1902

Schmidt, 81, 117, 236, 263, 289, 328, 329
Schockley, 53, 263
Schoeffer, 77, 247, 263, 298, 299
Schoenberger, 263
Schoenknecht, 214, 255, 263, 264
Schofield, 152, 264
Schrader, 264, 265
Schreader, 44
Schueler, 14, 113, 128, 262, 264
Schulenberg, 264
Schuler, 264
Schulka, 264
Schultz, 24, 177, 260, 264
Schumann, 4, 30, 129, 140, 311, 333
Schurada, 264
Schurtz, 132, 163, 264, 265
Schwartz, 55, 85, 105, 235, 264, 265, 303
Schwatka, 230, 265
Schweiger, 90, 128, 265
Schwert, 83, 123, 265, 266
Schwingle, 241
Scoffeld, 15
Scofield, 101, 266
Scoggen, 146, 174, 266, 309
Scott, 84, 134, 154, 266, 267, 297
Scoville, 13, 38, 151, 156, 223, 224, 266
Scrivens, 97
Scroggum, 266
Searle, 63, 103, 149, 266, 296, 297, 327
Searles, 266, 267, 317
Searls, 71
Sebastian, 118, 267
Seehuus, 267
Seekatz, 27, 28, 79, 84, 210, 235, 252, 267
Seeley, 267, 321
Seely, 156, 267
Seeman, 267
Seidal, 267
Sekatz, 79, 267, 268
Sells, 134
Selzman, 268
Serabda, 24
Severson, 7, 174, 209, 268, 272, 295, 296
Seward, 12, 43, 268
Seymour, 66, 268
Shabshab, 1, 268
Shaw, 34, 136, 206, 268, 277, 296
Shcor, 2
Sheats, 268
Shemar or Shener, 268
Shepard, 268
Shephard, 268
Shepherd, 34
Sherhon, 268
Sherhunt, 268, 334
Sherick, 268
Sheridan, 269
Sherlin, 269, 284
Sherman, 53, 269
Sherry, 43, 269
Sherwood, 18, 60, 198, 222, 253, 269
Shields, 1, 2, 152, 210, 231, 269, 270
Shimmer, 270

Shimmins, 270, 293
Shinka, 270
Shipley, 58, 116, 131, 227, 257, 270
Shipton, 270
Shirlin, 270, 284
Shockey, 52, 270
Shockley, 52, 101, 128, 152, 179, 255, 270
Shoemaker, 233, 271
Shuka, 271
Shulka, 271
Shulkey, 271
Shultz, 18, 44, 59
Shumaker, 271
Shurada, 264
Siefert, 271, 283
Siegert, 271
Silbaugh, 64, 271
Sillge, 271, 272
Sime, 2, 30, 61, 84, 128, 160, 193, 237, 272, 296, 303, 308
Simek, 69, 272, 275
Simes, 258
Simons, 29, 98
Simpson, 159
Simrod, 272
Sinclair, 272
Sincola, 272
Singles, 272
Sinko, 27
Sinsky, 261
Skinner, 130, 273
Slade, 273
Slama, 46, 117, 273
Slane, 273
Slater, 233, 273
Sleighback, 273
Slightam, 273, 296
Slighter, 273
Sloan, 65, 273, 279
Sloane, 86, 273
Slocum, 146, 273
Sluk, 196
Sluka, 273
Slunt, 274, 315
Smethurst, 41, 92, 186, 190, 198, 274, 276
Smircina, 44, 274
Smith, 1, 2, 6, 8, 11, 36, 37, 49, 51, 56, 82, 84, 90, 118, 122,
    124, 136, 153, 156, 169, 187, 188, 195, 197, 209, 214, 215,
    220, 223, 224, 225, 230, 258, 272, 274, 275, 276, 277, 278,
    293, 296, 307, 309, 320, 321, 331, 333, 336
Smrcina, 3, 47, 77, 84, 278
Smrz, 8, 228, 278, 279
Snell, 133, 278
Snodgrass, 248, 278
Solan, 279
Solboda, 46
Solom, 279
Solomon, 279
Somers, 279
Sorena, 130
Sorenson, 84, 279
Sorrum, 279
Soucby, 279
Soucy, 85, 279, 332

Sousey, 279
Sousy, 326
Southard, 279
Speck, 19, 50, 87, 102, 110, 125, 129, 143, 144, 149, 161, 264, 279, 280, 317, 323, 324
Spencer, 10, 21, 83, 86, 227, 272, 280, 295, 297
Sperbach, 134, 280
Spero, 5, 6, 280
Spicher, 280
Spiker, 44, 90, 280, 281
Spraque, 326
Sprosty, 84, 163, 281, 296
Spuiker, 281, 317
Squire, 281
Squires, 125, 281
St. Clair, 167, 218, 281
St. Claire, 281
St. Germain, 29
St. Jacque, 281, 309, 310
St. Jaque, 196, 306
St. Jocque, 282
St. John, 55, 107, 282
St. Joque, 21
Staar, 130, 282
Stabin, 282
Stackland, 37, 54, 141, 183, 216, 219, 260, 282
Staib, 199, 217, 267, 282
Stammer, 291
Stamp, 14, 282
Standorf, 61, 132, 143, 156, 282
Stanton, 199
Stantorf, 3, 31, 136, 193, 282, 283
Star, 283
Stark, 271, 272, 283
Stauer, 13, 283
Stavos, 283
Stayer, 283
Stearns, 146, 267, 283, 321
Steavenson, 214
Steele, 1, 2, 35, 152, 283
Steiben, 283, 338
Steiger, 160
Steil, 283
Stein, 283
Steinbach, 132, 229, 283, 284
Steinback, 283, 284
Steinburg, 8, 196, 282, 284, 306
Steiner, 6, 115, 180, 264, 269, 270, 284
Steinwand, 102, 284
Steisel, 27, 33
Stell, 284, 312
Stemmeiler, 216, 284
Stemmiller, 143
Stephenson, 94, 284
Sterling, 77, 84, 158, 186, 284, 285, 294, 302
Sterner, 285
Steven, 285
Stevens, 33, 101, 154, 168, 192, 285, 286
Stevenson, 67, 136, 145, 157, 170, 267, 286
Stevson, 286
Stewart, 114, 223, 286
Stiab, 136
Stickler, 35, 170, 171, 286, 287

Still, 287
Stluka, 262, 287
Stluke, 287
Stocum, 146
Stocum (Slocum?), 287
Stoehr, 287, 297
Stolp, 248, 287, 311
Stone, 210, 282, 287, 288
Stoors, 266
Stout, 288
Stove, 288
Stowell, 1, 12, 32, 33, 55, 84, 86, 106, 107, 184, 188, 221, 260, 288, 295
Straka, 288
Stram, 202, 211, 288
Strand, 212
Stranskey, 289
Stransky, 289
Straub, 131, 289
Strayer, 289
Strecker, 83, 151, 289
Streeter, 83
Streker, 289
Strong, 289
Strouse, 289
Stuart, 25, 31, 61, 84, 94, 113, 205, 286, 287, 289, 338
Stuckey, 24, 84, 93, 114, 119, 176, 210, 255, 274, 289, 290, 304
Stucky, 290
Stukey, 46, 85, 151, 214, 255, 290
Stulka, 38
Stunkard, 290
Sturnot, 150, 290
Stuss, 290
Stussy, 290
Styenhke, 312
Suhrada, 264
Sullivan, 279, 290, 291, 325
Surges, 291
Surley, 291
Sutherland, 2, 291
Sutton, 129, 130, 259, 291, 317
Swartz, 105, 265
Swateak, 291
Swatek, 63, 186, 270, 291
Swedenskey, 291
Sweeney, 80, 292, 298
Sweeny, 292
Sweiger, 252, 292
Swingle, 54
Swinson, 1, 189, 292, 303
Sylvester, 292
Syverson, 45, 93, 112, 137, 237, 292, 293, 299, 317

-T-

Taff, 136
Taft, 36, 43, 52, 53, 84, 100, 159, 170, 245, 251, 267, 270, 293, 294, 296
Taho, 294
Tainter, 83, 203, 230, 284, 294
Talcot, 306
Talcott, 99, 294

Talkot, 294
Tallman, 46, 101, 104, 294
Tate, 18, 31, 248, 294
Taubleman, 295
Taylor, 24, 84, 104, 107, 133, 295
Teacher Institute, 295, 296, 297
Teal, 208
Terman, 298
Tesar, 45, 83, 84, 122, 226, 264, 265, 298
Tessar, 158, 218
Teynor, 298, 299
Thayer, 299
Thiede, 171, 214, 240, 255, 296, 297, 299
Thill, 299
Thomas, 41, 136, 156, 243, 277, 299, 325
Thompson, 15, 39, 41, 60, 78, 83, 87, 136, 137, 152, 153, 166, 171, 173, 198, 220, 222, 267, 269, 299, 300, 301, 303, 308, 311, 316, 337
Thomsom, 231
Thomson, 10, 34, 84, 87, 121, 137, 151, 171, 197, 204, 231, 297, 301, 302, 303, 304
Thorpe, 302
Thruman, 332
Thyle, 302
Thythamer, 151
Tibbets, 304
Tichenor, 285, 302
Tiechenor, 302
Tienenor, 302
Tiernay, 181
Tierney, 152, 175, 302, 303
Tiffin, 25
Tim, 232, 303
Timan, 303
Todd, 303
Toepel, 157, 303
Tomsecek, 303
Toney, 55, 303
Tooker, 304
Torger, 303
Torgerson, 56, 57, 272, 303
Torgeson, 57
Touble, 230, 303
Tower, 84, 155, 189, 303, 304, 308
Townsend, 11, 304, 308
Trahae, 304
Trant, 45, 104
Traub, 239, 304
Trautch, 304, 305
Trautsch, 83, 163, 200, 265, 305, 325
Traversey, 317
Traversy, 305
Trehey, 217, 230, 265, 305
Tresidder, 305
Tressider, 305
Trousdale, 305, 306
Trowbridge, 177, 240, 306
Troy, 306
Truesdale, 100, 306
Trum, 306
Trumbell, 306
Trumble, 297, 306
Trumbull, 84, 122, 152, 295, 306

Tucker, 306
Tulcot, 306
Tulley, 105, 306, 307
Turbil, 157
Turgenson, 151
Turk, 46, 56, 84, 85, 86, 127, 216, 242, 255, 275, 301, 307, 325
Turnbull, 124, 197, 307, 308, 321
Turner, 127, 168, 293, 304, 308
Twining, 46, 84, 107, 118, 151, 159, 223, 256, 257, 308
Tyron, 308
Tystad, 308

-U-

Udelhofen, 309
Uher, 44, 309
Umbach, 309
Umback, 206, 296, 309
Umbeck, 300, 309
Umbrora, 309
Umpaugh, 132, 282
Underburger, 44
Underwood, 292
Updike, 258, 275, 309
Updyke, 90, 275, 277, 309
Upholm, 146, 174, 266, 309
Uphome, 272, 309
Uttre, 161, 309

-V-

Vainhouse, 309
Valacity, 44, 309
Valentine, 57
Valley, 163, 174, 185, 296, 297, 309, 310
Van Allen, 169, 310, 324
Van Clees, 78
Van Horn, 310, 330
Van Natta, 310
Vance, 211, 310
Vanderbilt, 4, 30, 44, 129, 140, 184, 216, 226, 233, 299, 310, 311, 333
Vanderport, 35, 36, 287, 311
Vanhorn, 136
Vanwormer, 311
Vanworner, 311
Varo, 150, 311
Varrell, 141, 311
Vauek, 230, 311
Vaughan, 14, 15, 20, 61, 82, 83, 85, 94, 147, 154, 155, 156, 158, 160, 238, 245, 262, 284, 298, 311, 312, 313
Vaughn, 313
Vavra, 313
Vavruska, 27, 291, 313
Vedicka, 323
Veglahn, 313
Velt, 93, 313
Venish, 37
Vernon, 132
Vero, 313
Viele, 13, 314
Viet, 94, 314

Viktora, 314
Vilieman, 314
Vodicka, 314, 324
Voght, 314
Volge, 180
Vollmer, 81, 172, 314
Volmer, 314
Von Bernauer, 315
Vondrak, 14, 315
Voth, 241, 264, 315
Votruba, 138

## -W-

Wacher, 315
Wachter, 114, 315
Wachuta, 8, 315
Wachute, 315
Waddle, 23, 44, 138, 192, 193, 216, 315
Wade, 315
Wagner, 19, 83, 105, 124, 164, 173, 265, 315, 316, 318
Wainscott, 316
Waite, 68
Waiters, 179, 317
Walcott, 317
Waldin, 317
Waldorth, 317
Walker, 8, 47, 60, 117, 187, 228, 281, 306, 317
Wall, 150, 317
Wallace, 317
Wallice, 317
Wallin, 41, 153, 279, 280, 296, 297, 317, 318, 322
Walters, 130, 163, 179, 210, 274, 305, 316, 317, 318, 319, 324
Walton, 319, 326, 327
Waltz, 319
Wanamaker, 214, 319
Wannaker, 319
Wannamaker, 113, 296, 319
Wannemaker, 41, 61, 83, 320
Ward, 10, 36, 66, 85, 97, 181, 199, 239, 320, 337
Wardell, 258, 276, 320
Warner, 9, 167, 184, 320
Warren, 123
Wasco, 104
Watrous, 112, 320, 321
Watson, 125, 143, 261, 321, 326, 327
Way, 321
Wayne, 10, 17, 79, 86, 141, 152, 193, 216, 246, 312, 321, 322
Webb, 47
Webster, 7, 13, 141, 156, 201, 218, 322
Week, 215, 322
Weeks, 215, 322
Weiderandres, 305
Weighner, 323
Weigner, 323
Weisenberger, 14, 323
Weittenhiller, 190, 323
Welch, 6, 35, 37, 66, 172, 182, 206, 297, 323, 324
Weldon, 34
Weldy, 314
Wells, 35, 211, 269, 324
Welsch, 324
Welsh, 87, 296, 319, 324, 325

Wendel, 187
Wendt, 65, 79, 144, 277, 325
Weneger, 325
Weniger, 83, 195, 325
Wensel, 301
Wertzel, 325
West, 202, 216, 226, 264, 290, 306, 325, 326
Westphal, 326
Wetzel, 88, 89, 326
Whaley, 30, 322, 326
Whalley, 99
Wheeler, 36, 130, 242, 254, 326
Wher, 100, 173, 326
Whistler, 326
White, 8, 29, 63, 68, 70, 103, 211, 228, 238, 254, 266, 267, 277, 319, 326, 327, 338
White Cloud, 327
Whiteaker, 10, 12, 52, 84, 89, 101, 173, 217, 230, 235, 301, 327, 328, 337
Whitemore, 94, 328
Whitewater, 33
Whiting, 328
Whitman, 328
Whiton, 285
Whitteker, 328
Whittenheller, 222, 328
Widman, 328
Widmann, 83, 91, 213, 241, 263, 328, 329
Wiederanders, 305
Wiegand, 329
Wightacan, 329, 330
Wikins, 329
Wilbur, 104, 329
Wilder, 57
Wilharber, 329, 330
Wilkins, 121, 150, 330
Willard, 336
Willetts, 330
Willey, 330
William, 1, 4, 30, 82, 114, 277, 330
Williams, 2, 51, 57, 109, 114, 124, 139, 176, 282, 295, 298, 329, 330, 331
Williamson, 10
Willis, 57, 119, 262, 276, 331
Willits, 331
Willitts, 58
Wilson, 32, 327, 331, 332
Wilt, 84, 296, 297, 331
Wilwarth, 68
Winden, 52
Windham, 332
Windsor, 332
Winegar, 332
Wines, 332
Wing, 279, 332
Winn, 332
Winnegar, 333
Winsworth, 138
Wiser, 333
Witcraft, 189
Witenhiller, 222, 333
Withee, 48, 84, 333
Withey, 333

Wittenheiler, 222, 333
Wolcott, 4, 30, 85, 129, 140, 229, 298, 311, 333
Wolcutt, 334
Wolf, 334
Wolfe, 334
Womberg, 334
Wondrak, 334
Wood, 84, 153, 230, 334
Woodnal, 268, 325, 334
Woods, 334
Worth, 195, 334
Wrecht, 335
Wright, 119, 297, 335
Wunch, 335
Wunsch, 301
Wurster, 322, 335
Wuster, 335

-Y-

Yahn, 335
Yann, 335
Yara, 291, 335
Yeadon, 335
Yetter, 54, 335
Yonke, 214, 335
York, 124, 336

Yosnes, 303
Young, 1, 32, 64, 72, 83, 84, 86, 98, 120, 156, 176, 195, 236, 248, 256, 277, 301, 324, 336, 337
Yttri, 161, 309
Yumbara, 16, 337

-Z-

Zabel, 337
Zable, 73, 84
Zack, 96
Zander, 15, 207, 337
Zeber, 337
Zech, 338
Zeeh, 338
Zeil, 54
Zeman, 137, 144, 264, 297, 338
Ziebert, 338
Ziel, 37, 44, 48, 338
Ziener, 245, 338
Zillmer, 338
Zilmer, 338
Zimmerman, 338
Zirl, 283, 338
Zlabek, 180
Zoch, 287

www.ingramcontent.com/pod-product-compliance
Lightning Source LLC
Chambersburg PA
CBHW080724300426
44114CB00019B/2479